Outstanding International Press Reporting

Volume 2: 1946–1962

Outstanding International Press Reporting

Pulitzer Prize Winning Articles
in Foreign Correspondence

Editor: Heinz-Dietrich Fischer

Volume 2: 1946–1962

From the End of World War II
to the Various Stations of the Cold War

Walter de Gruyter · Berlin · New York 1985

Dr. Heinz-Dietrich Fischer

Professor of International Journalism and Communication
at the Ruhr-Universität Bochum, FRG

Library of Congress Cataloging in Publication Data

> Outstanding international press reporting.
>
> Includes bibliographies and index.
> Contents: v. 1. 1928-1945, from the consequences of World War I to the end of the World War II – v. 2. 1946-1962, from the end fo World War II to the various stations of the Cold War.
>
> 1. World politics-20th century-Addresses, essays, lectures. 2. Pulitzer prizes-Addresses, essays, lectures. 3. Journalists-United States-Addresses, essays, lectures. 4. Foreign news-Unites States-Addresses, essays, lectures. I. Fischer, Heinz
> Dietrich, 1937- .
> D445.088 1984   909.82   83-18962
> ISBN 3-11008918-1 (v. 1)

CIP-Kurztitelaufnahme der Deutschen Bibliothek

> **Outstanding international press reporting** : Pulitzer price winning articles in foreign correspondance / ed.: Heinz-Dietrich Fischer. – Berlin ; New York : de Gruyter
>
> NE: Fischer, Heinz-Dietrich [Hrsg.]
>
> Vol. 2. 1946 – 1962 : from the end of World War II to the various stations of the Cold War. – 1985.
>   ISBN 3-11-009824-5

Copyright © 1985 by Walter de Gruyter & Co., Berlin 30.
All rights reserved, including those of translation into foreign languages. No part this book may reproduced in any form – by photoprint, microfilm or any other means nor transmitted nor translated into a machine language without written permission from the publisher. – Typesetting and printing: Wagner GmbH, Nördlingen. – Binding: Dieter Mikolai, Berlin. – Cover design: Lothar Hildebrand, Berlin. Printed in Germany.

PREFACE

About one year after publication of the first volume of this edition the second volume is now at hand. As in the case of its predecessor, much time had to be spent on documentation and research work for the realization of this tome. This was completed partly by extensive correspondence. Again it has to be gratefully mentioned that the sources of the Pulitzer Prize Collection at Columbia University, New York, had been made available as well as the confidential Jury Reports. These were most valuable for the classification and evaluation of the individual prize-winners and of their articles. Moreover, several archives and libraries had to be consulted in order to provide missing materials or to decide on contradictory source information.

While the period of documentation could be easily defined for the first volume – the end of World War II formed a distinct incision –, it proved somewhat difficult to define a final point for the book at hand. Finally, a pragmatic solution was decided upon. The entire post-war period up to the Cuban Crisis, which usually is regarded as the climax and the conclusion of the Cold War, have been chosen for documentation. The following years, which will be featured in the third volume, are essentially marked by the period before the Vietnam War, its course, and its lasting impact on world policies.

As far as the selection and presentation of the prize-winning press materials are concerned, the same principles were applied in this volume as in the first volume of this edition. In order to make transparent these selective and editorial criteria also for those readers who have not at hand the preceding volume, the "Editorial Remarks" are reprinted in the present book. As most of the reprinted articles did not contain any context material for a further explanation of the issues involved this volume again contains various maps, diagrams, and other survey materials to supplement the on-the-spot reports and other contributions of the prize-winners. Thus, an element of diversity is added to the texts.

Again it is due to the encouragement and support with materials and information by members of Columbia University (New York, N. Y.) that this volume could be completed. Here, I am especially indebted to Dean Osborn Elliot (Graduate School of Journalism), Mr. Robert C. Christopher (Administrator of the Pulitzer Prizes), Mrs. Robin Kuzen (Assistant Administrator of the Pulitzer Prizes), Mr. Wade A. Doares (Head of the Arthur Hays Sulzberger Library at the Graduate School of Journalism), Mr. Manny Warman † (Photo Department of the Graduate School of Journalism) as well as several employees of the Butler Library and various department libraries on the Columbia campus.

For the granting of copyrights and for the provision of information and/or important documents I am grateful to the following members of American media organizations: Mrs. Kathleen A. Allison (*The Christian Science Monitor*, Boston), Mr. Richard F. Bauer (*The Milwaukee Journal*), Mr. Charles M. McClatchy (*The Sacramento Bee*), Mr. William

E. Chilton III. (*The Charleston Gazette*), Mr. Donald J. Clifford (*The Standard-Times*, New Bedford, Mass.), Mr. William H. Cowles III. (*The Spokesman-Review*, Spokane, Wash.), Mr. Richard Hancock (*Roanoke Times & World News*), Mr. Larry E. Heinzerling (*The Associated Press*, New York), Mrs. Barbara Hespe (*The Associated Press*, Frankfurt/Main), Mr. John T. Hough (*Falmouth Enterprise*, Falmouth, Mass.), Mr. David Kraslow (*The Miami News*), Mrs. Barbara Langenberger (*The New York Times*), Mrs. Natalie Layzell (*International Herald-Tribune*, New York), Mr. Richard H. Leonard (*The Milwaukee Journal*), Mr. James Maloney (*St. Louis Post-Dispatch*), Mr. John H. Metcalfe (*Daily News*, New York), Mr. John J. O'Connell (*Hearst Newspapers*, New York), Mr. Donald H. Patterson (*The Sun*, Baltimore, Md.), Mr. C. Vaughn Porter (*Roanoke Times & World News*), Mr. John S. Prescott (*International Herald-Tribune*, New York), Mrs. Cheryl Preston (*Los Angeles Times*), Mr. Earl H. Richert (*Scripps-Howard Newspapers*, Washington, D. C.), Mr. Foster L. Spencer (*Buffalo Evening News*), Mr. H. L. Stevenson (*United Press International*, New York), Mr. Ronald E. Thompson (*The Associated Press*, New York), and Mr. Toni Wells (*The Sun*, Baltimore, Md.).

The final research for this volume in American archives and libraries has been supported with a grant by Mr. Dietrich Oppenberg, publisher and editor of the 'NRZ – Neue Rhein/Ruhr Zeitung' (Essen). Professor Elie Abel (Stanford University) readily contributed information on his person. Mr. Frank J. Carroll (The Library of Congress, Washington, D. C.), Mrs. Brigitte Keller-Hüschemenger (Library, U. S. Embassy, Bonn), Mr. Martin F. McGann (John F. Kennedy Library, Boston, Mass.), Mr. John Muirhead (John F. Kennedy Institute for North American Studies, Free University, Berlin) and Dr. Hans-Joachim Pretsch (Political Archives of the Foreign Office, Bonn) repeatedly made available important sources. Mr. David Klein (The American Council on Germany, New York) established several important contacts.

At the Ruhr University, Bochum, Dr. Dietrich Roessler (Main Library) and Mr. Johannes Dedek (Library, Department of Education and Communication) assisted in providing source materials, while Mr. Benno Wagner contributed to the editorial make-up of the manuscript. Again it was Mrs. Ingrid Dickhut who helped in the final draft of the manuscript, which also was contributed to by Mr. Frank Frewer and Mr. Aichard Hoffmann who did some bibliographical research work. Erika J. Fischer was, again, particularly involved in the final edition of the manuscript and the preceding provision of various materials and information. I wish to acknowledge my gratitude to all these persons for their contributions in time and labor to this volume.

Heinz-Dietrich Fischer
Spring, 1985

CONTENTS

Preface   v

Contents of Past Volume   xiii
Contents of Future Volumes   xvii

Introduction: The Pulitzer Prizes for International Reporting in the
    Second Phase of Their Development, 1946–1962
    by *Heinz-Dietrich Fischer*   xxi

Editorial Remarks   lxv

Chapter 19 REPORTS ABOUT THE SOVIET UNION IN 1946

The Post-War Situation and Some Typical Characteristics of the Country
by *J. Brooks Atkinson (The New York Times)*   3

    Introductory Notes   4
    19.1 The Byrnes Plan and How Moscow Views It   5
    19.2 America's Aims and Structure in the Soviet Press   6
    19.3 A System of Permanent Distrust and Its Purpose   8
    19.4 The Socialist Landscape and Its Climate   12
    19.5 Russo-American Relations and Their Future Outlook   17
    Related Readings   20

Chapter 20 REPORTS ABOUT THE SOVIET UNION IN 1947

The Cultural Situation and How It Is Formed by the Party
by *Paul W. Ward (The Sun*, Baltimore)   21

    Introductory Notes   22
    20.1 The Russian Sense of Humor and Some of Its Products   23
    20.2 The Idea of an Ethnic Plurality and Its Reality   25
    20.3 Religion in Soviet Russia and the Various Churches   29
    20.4 A 'Purge' in Arts and Its Consequences   33

20.5 'Socialist' Art and How It Is Produced	36
Related Readings	40

Chapter 21 REPORTS ABOUT INDIA IN 1948

The Country's Way to Sovereignty and the Cultural Impediments
by *Price Day (The Sun*, Baltimore) — 41

Introductory Notes	42
21.1 Britain's Influence on India and Its Remainders	43
21.2 Nehru as a Leader of Gentleness and Impatience	47
21.3 Pakistan's Situation and Her Future Outlook	50
21.4 The Cow and the Caste as Bars for Development	54
21.5 Undernourishment and Overpopulation as Main Problems	57
Related Readings	60

Chapter 22 REPORTS ABOUT THE SOVIET UNION IN 1949

The Structure of the Government and the Way It Acts on the People
by *Edmund W. Stevens*
(The Christian Science Monitor, Boston) — 61

Introductory Notes	62
22.1 The Supreme Soviet and What It Symbolizes	63
22.2 Stalin's Secret Police and a Bitter Paradox	66
22.3 The Order of Ascendency and the Favoured Candidates	68
22.4 Bureaucracy and the Reversal of an Idea	70
22.5 Trade Unions and Their Effects on Production	73
Related Readings	75

Chapter 23 REPORTS ABOUT KOREA IN 1950

America's Fight Against Communism and the Conquest of Seoul
by *Marguerite Higgins (New York Herald-Tribune)* — 77

Introductory Notes	78
23.1 Korean Resistance and the American Way of Breaking It	79
23.2 Vignettes of Terror and the Liberation of Seoul	80
23.3 Crowds Cheer and Liberators Inspect Conquered Area	83
23.4 Works of Reconstruction and the Communist Practise	85
23.5 The Victor's Ceremony and Further Casualties	86
Related Readings	88

Contents ix

Chapter 24 REPORTS ABOUT KOREA IN 1951

The Final Stage of the War and the Conditions for Peace
by *John M. Hightower (The Associated Press)*   91

Introductory Notes	92
24.1 America's Educational Aim and Her Main Apprehension	93
24.2 MacArthur's Policy and the Consequences at Home	95
24.3 Plans for an Armistice and America's Precautions	97
24.4 Negotiations for Peace and Communist Hospitality	98
24.5 Early Negotiations for Peace and Their Main Issues	101
Related Readings	102

Chapter 25 REPORTS ABOUT CANADA IN 1952

The Country's Great Fortunes and How They are Exploited
by *Austin C. Wehrwein (The Milwaukee Journal)*   103

Introductory Notes	104
25.1 Raw Materials Grow and Industry Expands	105
25.2 The Canadian Stock Market and the Problem of Fraud	107
25.3 Canada Starts on Seaway and America Missed the Boat	111
25.4 Population Problems and How They Might be Solved	114
25.5 A Province of Superlatives and Its Riches	118
Related Readings	122

Chapter 26 REPORTS ABOUT KOREA IN 1953

The Front and How the Soldiers Face It
by *Jim G. Lucas (Scripps-Howard Newspapers)*   125

Introductory Notes	126
26.1 'Our Town' and Its Social Order	127
26.2 A Basic Rule of War and Changes It Brings Along	128
26.3 Nights of Terror and No End to be Seen	131
26.4 Replacements Face Strange Country and 'Fear Future'	132
26.5 Death-Bringing Planes and a Special Sort of a Bomb	135
Related Readings	136

Chapter 27 REPORTS ABOUT THE SOVIET UNION IN 1954

The Post-Stalin Era and Important Events Connected With His Death
by *Harrison E. Salisbury (The New York Times)*   137

Introductory Notes — 138
27.1 A New Regime and Tactical Political Changes — 139
27.2 The Death of Stalin and an Avoided Disaster — 146
27.3 Beria's Coup and Why It Brought Along His End — 152
27.4 Numerous Intrigues and a Toast to Justice — 158
27.5 The New Junta and How It Works Together — 163
Related Readings — 169

Chapter 28 REPORTS ABOUT THE SOVIET UNION IN 1955

Changes in the Leadership and Several Important Statements by Its Members
by *J. Kingsbury Smith (International News Service)* — 171

Introductory Notes — 172
28.1 Molotow Judges Chinese Conflict and Charges the U. S. — 173
28.2 Russia's View on Peace and Coexistence With America — 177
28.3 The Fall of Malenkov and Communist Democracy — 182
28.4 How Stalin Used to Relax and the Fall of His Brother — 185
28.5 Soviet Policy and the Role of the Journalists — 186
Related Readings — 192

Chapter 29 REPORTS ABOUT HUNGARY IN 1956

The Civil War and the Exposition of Communism
by *Russell Jones (United Press)* — 193

Introductory Notes — 194
29.1 The Ten-Day Revolution and Its Violent End — 195
29.2 A Ship named 'Liberty' and Her Harbour — 197
29.3 Hope For Western Aid and Widespread Disappointment — 198
29.4 Masses Fight Fearlessly and Russia Now Sends Planes — 201
29.5 Hungarian 'Capitalism' and Why It Cannot be Extinguished — 203
Related Readings — 204

Chapter 30 REPORTS ABOUT YUGOSLAVIA IN 1957

Tito's Brand of Communism and Quarrels With Moscow
by *Elie Abel (The New York Times)* — 207

Introductory Notes — 208
30.1 Yugoslavia's Illusion and How It Is Destroyed — 209
30.2 A Promised Credit and Its Political Implications — 211
30.3 Tito's Refusal to Changes and Rumors About a Meeting — 213

Contents xi

30.4 Soviet Fulfills Promise and Opens a New Phase	214
30.5 A Secret Meeting and Its Impact on the Future	215
Related Readings	217

Chapter 31 REPORTS ABOUT CUBA IN 1958

The Batista Rule and Rumors About Revolution
by *Joseph G. Martin/Philip J. Santora (Daily News,* New York) 219

Introductory Notes	220
31.1 Batista's Reign of Terror and the Fight for Freedom	221
31.2 Official Sadism and Its Various Exponents	225
31.3 The Batista Coup and the Fruits of Temptation	228
31.4 Cuba's Captive Press and How It Is Run	232
31.5 The Dictator and His Counterpart Castro	235
Related Readings	238

Chapter 32 REPORTS ABOUT POLAND IN 1959

The Gomulka Government and the Structure of the Warsaw Pact
by *Abraham M. Rosenthal (The New York Times)* 239

Introductory Notes	240
32.1 Gomulka's Move to Russia and the Polish Communism	241
32.2 A Historic Event and Its Interpretation	243
32.3 Poland's New Territory and How It Develops	245
32.4 A Warsaw Pact Discussion and Its Premises	247
32.5 Communist Diplomacy and Its Tactical Function	250
Related Readings	251

Chapter 33 REPORTS ABOUT THE CONGO IN 1960

A Period of Unrest and Lumumba's Struggle for Unity
by *Lynn L. Heinzerling (The Associated Press)* 253

Introductory Notes	254
33.1 Lumumba's Aims and a Change of Direction	255
33.2 Secessionist Movements and The Role of the U. N.	256
33.3 Lumumba's Fight for Unity and Pressures From Without	258
33.4 A Two-Hour Coup and Its Reported Details	260
33.5 The Premier's Comeback and Several New Plans	264
Related Readings	265

Chapter 34 REPORTS ABOUT THE SOVIET UNION IN 1961

Some Important Political Questions and How They Are Viewed in Communism
by *Walter Lippmann (New York Herald-Tribune)*   267

Introductory Notes	268
34.1 Khrushchev Views Disarmament and Denies Neutrality	269
34.2 The Inevitable Run of History and Its Social Changes	271
34.3 The German Question and Three Ways of Answering It	273
34.4 Communist Philosophy and the Only Real Alternative	277
34.5 Two Important Talks and a New Political Philosophy	279
Related Readings	281

Chapter 35 REPORTS ABOUT CUBA IN 1962

The Escalation of a Global Crisis and How It Was Managed in Washington
by *Harold V. Hendrix (The Miami News)*   283

Introductory Notes	284
35.1 Soviet Bases in Cuba and America's First Reactions	285
35.2 The Cuban Challenge and Reactions in America	287
35.3 Russia's Installment Effort and Her Technical Problems	289
35.4 An Exhibition of Power and Reasons for an Invasion	290
35.5 Early Intelligence and How It Was Handled	294
Related Readings	296

Index   299

CONTENTS OF PAST VOLUME

Volume I Covering the Period from 1928–1945

Chapter 0 REPORTS ABOUT GERMANY IN 1916
    The Situation and Several Upcoming Problems of the Country in the Third Year of the War
    by *Herbert B. Swope (The World*, New York)

Chapter 1 REPORTS ABOUT SWITZERLAND IN 1928
    Negotiations About a New Peace Concept and the Various Points of Dissent
    by *Paul S. Mowrer (The Chicago Daily News)*

Chapter 2 REPORTS ABOUT FRANCE IN 1929
    The Reparations Problem and the Struggle for Its Solution
    by *Leland Stowe (New York Herald-Tribune)*

Chapter 3 REPORTS ABOUT THE SOVIET UNION IN 1930
    The Russian Economic System and the Situation of the Population
    by *Hubert R. Knickerbocker (New York Evening Post)*

Chapter 4 REPORTS ABOUT THE SOVIET UNION IN 1931
    The Soviet Policy and the Personal Impact of Stalin
    by *Walter Duranty (The New York Times)*

Chapter 5 REPORTS ABOUT GERMANY IN 1932
    Germany Between Radicalism and the Hope for a Better Future
    by *Edgar A. Mowrer (The Chicago Daily News)*

Chapter 6 REPORTS ABOUT GERMANY IN 1933
    The Germans Under Fascist Rule and the Heralds of Destruction
    by *Frederick T. Birchall (The New York Times)*

Chapter 7 REPORTS ABOUT THE UNITED STATES IN 1934
    Centers of International Crises and the Ways They Might Develop
    by *Artur Krock (The New York Times)*

Chapter 8 REPORTS ABOUT ETHIOPIA IN 1935
An Underdeveloped Country as It Faces the Menace of Imperialism
by *William C. Barber (Chicago Daily Tribune)*

Chapter 9 REPORTS ABOUT ITALY IN 1936
Italy Under the Mussolini Rule and the Reasons for Her Turn to Militarism
by *Anne O'Hare McCormick (The New York Times)*

Chapter 10 REPORTS ABOUT THE UNITED STATES IN 1937
Problems Facing the President and Discussions About Their Solutions
by *Arthur Krock (The New York Times)*

Chapter 11 REPORTS ABOUT GERMANY IN 1938
Hitler's Sudetenland Campaign and Europe's Attempts to Avoid War
by *Louis P. Lochner (The Associated Press)*

Chapter 12 REPORTS ABOUT GERMANY IN 1939
The German Situation in the First Weeks of World War II and the Nazi's Interior Policy
by *Otto D. Tolischus (The New York Times)*

Chapter 13 REPORTS ABOUT FRANCE IN 1940
The Situation of France Under Nazi Occupation and the Mistakes Made by the Vichy Rule
by *Percy J. Philip (The New York Times)*

Chapter 14 REPORTS ABOUT CHINA IN 1941
The Political Situation in Far East and the Special Importance of Free China
by *Carlos P. Romulo (The Philippines Herald)*

Chapter 15 REPORTS ABOUT THE SOLOMONS IN 1942
The Pacific War Theatre and the American Plans and Operations
by *Hanson W. Baldwin (The New York Times)*

Chapter 16 REPORTS ABOUT YUGOSLAVIA IN 1943
The Partisan Organization in Yugoslavia and Its Strikes Against the Germans
by *Daniel de Luce (The Associated Press)*

Chapter 17 REPORTS ABOUT ENGLAND IN 1944
The Allies' Invasion Into France and the Important Contributions of Her Various Formations
by *Mark S. Watson (The Evening Sun, Baltimore)*

Chapter 18 REPORTS ABOUT JAPAN IN 1945
America's Fight Against Japan and the Consequent Way of Finishing It
by *Homer W. Bigart (New York Herald-Tribune)*

Index

CONTENTS OF FUTURE VOLUMES

Volume 3 Covering the Period from 1963–1977

Chapter 36 REPORTS ABOUT VIETNAM IN 1963
    International Quarrels and Their Impact on the Fratricical War
    by *David Halberstam (The New York Times)*

Chapter 37 REPORTS ABOUT EAST EUROPE IN 1964
    The Turn Toward the West and Its Economic Reasons
    by *Joseph A. Livingston (Philadelphia Bulletin)*

Chapter 38 REPORTS ABOUT VIETNAM IN 1965
    The War and Some of Its Typical Stories
    by *Peter G. Arnett (The Associated Press)*

Chapter 39 REPORTS ABOUT INDONESIA IN 1966
    The Change of Government and How It Was Performed
    by *R. John Hughes (The Christian Science Monitor)*

Chapter 40 REPORTS ABOUT THE MIDDLE EAST IN 1967
    The Six-Day War and Its World-Political Consequences
    by *Alfred Friendly (The Washington Post)*

Chapter 41 REPORTS ABOUT VIETNAM IN 1968
    The Fourth Year of the War and a Case of Atrocity
    by *William K. Tuohy (Los Angeles Times)*

Chapter 42 REPORTS ABOUT THE UNITED STATES IN 1969
    The My Lai Massacre and the Futile Search For Its Reasons
    by *Seymour M. Hersh (Dispatch News Service)*

Chapter 43 REPORTS ABOUT SOUTH AFRICA IN 1970
    The Apartheid System and the Misery of the Black People
    by *Jimmie L. Hoagland (The Washington Post)*

Chapter 44 REPORTS ABOUT PAKISTAN IN 1971
      The Fratricical War and the Problems Left After Its Settlement
by *Peter R. Kann (The Wall Street Journal)*

Chapter 45 REPORTS ABOUT RED CHINA IN 1972
      The Unexpected Nixon Visit and Its Most Important Stations
by *Max Frankel (The New York Times)*

Chapter 46 REPORTS ABOUT THE SOVIET UNION IN 1973
      Some Characteristic Traits of the Country and the Mentality of the People
by *Hedrick L. Smith (The New York Times)*

Chapter 47 REPORTS ABOUT NORTH AFRICA IN 1974
      The Famine Areas and Their Technical and Cultural Problems
by *Ovie Carter/William C. Mullen (Chicago Tribune)*

Chapter 48 REPORTS ABOUT CAMBODIA IN 1975
      The Communists' Take-Over and Some Accompanying Circumstances
by *Sydney H. Schanberg (The New York Times)*

Chapter 49 REPORTS ABOUT GREAT BRITAIN IN 1976
      The Struggle of National Minorities and the Country's Economic Problems
by *George F. Will (The Washington Post)*

Chapter 50 REPORTS ABOUT THAILAND IN 1977
      The Boat People and the Trouble They Are Causing the Western World
by *Henry Kamm (The New York Times)*

Volume 4 Covering the Period from 1978 on

Chapter 51 REPORTS ABOUT THE MIDDLE EAST IN 1978
      Some Centers of Crisis and How Life Goes on There
by *Richard B. Cramer (The Philadelphia Inquirer)*

Chapter 52 REPORTS ABOUT CAMBODIA IN 1979
      The Refugee Problem and Some of Its Most Shocking Aspects
by *Joe Brinkley/Jay Mather (Courier-Journal*, Louisville)

Chapter 53 REPORTS ABOUT EL SALVADOR IN 1980
      The Brutal Civil War and Its World Political Background
by *Shirley Christian (The Miami Herald)*

Contents of Future Volumes

Chapter 54 REPORTS ABOUT POLAND IN 1981
The Worker Resistance and the Establishment of Material Law
by *John Darnton (The New York Times)*

Chapter 55 REPORTS ABOUT LEBANON IN 1982
The Massacre of Palestinians and Reactions in Two Refugee Camps
by *Loren Jenkins (The Washington Post)*

Chapter 56 REPORTS ABOUT JORDAN IN 1983
The Crisis in Middle East and the Involvement of King Hussein
by *Karen E. House (The Wall Street Journal)*

(will be continued)

INTRODUCTION

THE PULITZER PRIZES FOR INTERNATIONAL REPORTING IN THE SECOND PHASE OF THEIR DEVELOPMENT, 1946–1962

Heinz-Dietrich Fischer

"All in all", George N. Gordon summarizes in his History of the Mass Media in the United States, "1,646 people were accredited as news correspondents by the Army and Navy during World War II, representing all of the media – press, radio, and film. In addition to the news services, 12 magazines and 30 newspapers sent their own exclusive correspondents into the fray. History had never before seen such an inundation of journalists into any war. If we add the thousands of 'public information' officers and enlisted men whose service jobs were largely journalistic, it almost seems that one of the major activities of World War II was, for the first time in history, linking the various combat areas with the world's networks of mass communication. On an international basis this task was, of course, monumental... World War II was the first 'mass communications' war, in that much self-consciousness and a sense of 'history-in-the-making' impelled the military forces of all the billigerent nations and most especially those of the U.S.A., to go to great pains to record for posterity as much of it as accurately as possible."[1]

Shortly before the end of the war a book by the later Pulitzer Prize-winner Jim G. Lucas dealt with the problems of a war correspondent.[2] After the combat activities had ceased the memoirs of a former Pulitzer Prize-winner and leading war correspondent, Ernest Taylor Pyle, who got killed at the Japanese front in April 1945, were published; both books reflected the assumption that the exceptional[3] version of the foreign correspondent, the war correspondent, had ended for good. The book of another former Pulitzer Prize-winner, likewise published in the first year after the war, turned out to be more far-sighted and more pessimistic in its basic estimation of the future international political and communicative constellations; the author was Leland Stowe, one of the first laureates in the category of internationally oriented awards. Stowe, too, regarded in his publication the end of World War II as an essential historical caesura, but his reflections went beyond this date and were directed to

---

[1] George N. Gordon: The Communications Revolution – A History of Mass Media in the United States. New York: Hastings House, Publishers, 1977, pp. 225 f.
[2] Cf. Jim Lucas: Combat Correspondence, New York: Raynal & Hitchcock, 1944.
[3] Cf. Ernie Pyle: Last Chapter, New York: Henry Holt & Co., 1946, p. 143.

the future. He criticized American policy with respect to the atom bomb and discussed the need and outlook for world government along with education for peace, one of the most important future functions of the international press.[4]

Nearly simultaneously the American Commission on Freedom of the Press tried to take stock of the international media system. "Discrimination and censorship," a study of the commission ran, "are the two broad headings that cover those evils of which foreign correspondents (and natives, too, for that matter) most often complain . . . The defeat of Germany brought an end to Goebbels; but correspondents may face precisely the same type of discrimination, in varying degree, for a long time to come" in several regions of the world.[5] "The new world journalism which must develop on the basis of technical progress in the field of transmission," another outlook on the international post-war press states, "can combine some of the traditions of European newspaper work and the fresh approach of journalistic pioneers in the United States . . . There is a lot of surface reporting going on in the columns of many American newspapers and during much of the wire time of American news agencies. The reason for this can be found in the background and training of many news writers and correspondents. It is a rare foreign correspondent . . . who can write with full competence about the events and trends of most of the European continent and the Middle East. Men who have made names for themselves frequently are more or less specialized . . . No reporter can be better than his sources and his knowledge of the things he writes about. No cable editor can function in a way best suited to the needs of a responsible agency without both a substantial background in the international field and a high degree of personal integrity. The frontiers of world journalism, therefore, cannot be exploited through scoops for the sake of scoops."[6]

With regard to the educational goals of the schools and departments of journalism in the U.S.A., as far as foreign correspondents were concerned the following aims should be pursued according to the conception of the then head of the Department of Journalism at Boston University: "Journalism students need much more understanding of international law and diplomacy; of the structure and function of the United Nations; of general and contemporary European history. These courses – for journalism students interested in foreign correspondence – are practically vocational . . . As the world gets smaller, news beats become more diversified; so do public attention and interest. Schools of journalism should be mindful of the future."[7] These reflections were formulated just at the time when the Pulitzer Prize juries were concerned with the selection candidates for prizes in the International Reporting categories and with the presentation of their proposals. Nearly simultaneously, another report of the Commission on Freedom of the Press under the direction of the chancellor of the University of Chicago, published in the spring of 1947, attempted to take stock of the

---

[4] Cf. Leland Stowe: While Time Remains, New York: Alfred A. Knopf, 1947, pp. 3–9; see also Robert W. Desmond: Tides of War. World News Reporting 1931–1945, Iowa City, Iowa: University of Iowa Press, 1984.

[5] Llewellyn White/Robert D. Leigh: Peoples speaking to Peoples. A Report on International Mass Communication from The Commission on Freedom of the Press, Chicago: The University of Chicago Press, 1946, p. 65.

[6] Martin Ebon: New World Journalism Demands Background and Responsibility, in: *Journalism Quarterly* (Emory/Georgia), Vol. 23/No. 1, March 1946, pp. 9 f.

[7] Max R. Grossman: Some Contemporary Problems of Foreign Correspondence, in: *Journalism Quarterly* (Emory/Georgia), Vol. 24/No. 1, March 1947, p. 42.

A new procedure for studying material submitted for Pulitzer Prizes in Journalism was introduced in the academic year under review. Through the cooperation of the American Society of Newspaper Editors, sixteen editors were appointed to the following Journalism Juries:

"Disinterested and meritorious public service"
A. H. Kirchhofer, Managing Editor, *Buffalo Evening News*
Donald J. Sterling, Managing Editor, *Oregon Journal*

"Distinguished editorial writing"
Henry J. Haskell, Editor, *Kansas City Star*
Hamilton Owens, Editor, *Baltimore Sun*

"Distinguished correspondence"
Stephen C. Noland, Editor, *The Indianapolis News*
Marvin H. Creager, Editorial Adviser, *The Milwaukee Journal*

"Distinguished example of a cartoonist's work"
Walker Stone, Editor, Scripps-Howard Newspaper Alliance
Basil L. Walters, Executive Editor, Knight Newspapers

"Outstanding example of news photography"
N. R. Howard, Editor, *Cleveland News*
E. Z. Dimituan, Executive Editor, *The Chicago Sun*

"Distinguished example of telegraphic reporting on national affairs"
Dwight S. Perrin, Managing Editor, *The Evening Bulletin* (Philadelphia)
Laurence L. Winship, Managing Editor, *The Globe* (Boston)

"Distinguished example of telegraphic reporting of international affairs"
Erwin D. Canham, Editor, *Christian Science Monitor*
Carroll Binder, Editorial Editor, *The Tribune* (Minneapolis)

"Distinguished example of a reporter's work"
George A. Cornish, Managing Editor, *New York Herald Tribune*
W. S. Gilmore, Editor, *The Detroit News*

They met in New York, March 9–11, 1947, and submitted their recommendations to the Advisory Board. The record of the awards has been published by the University in *Plan for the Award of the Pulitzer Prizes and Scholarships Established in Columbia University by the Will of the Late Joseph Pulitzer*, revised as of May, 1947. This revision also recorded the changes in the terms of the Pulitzer Prizes. The new formula for the Prizes reads as follows:

1. For the most disinterested and meritorious public service rendered by an American newspaper during the year, a gold medal costing Five hundred dollars ($500).

2. For a distinguished example of local reporting during the year, the test being accuracy and terseness, the preference being given to news stories published in a daily newspaper prepared under the pressure of edition time, Five hundred dollars ($500).

3. For a distinguished example of reporting on national affairs, published in a daily newspaper in the United States, Five hundred dollars ($500).

4. For a distinguished example of reporting of international affairs, published in a daily newspaper in the United States, Five hundred dollars ($500).

5. For distinguished editorial writing during the year, the test of excellence being clearness of style, moral purpose, sound reasoning, and power to influence public opinion in what the writer conceives to be the right direction, due account being taken of the whole volume of the editorial writer's work during the year, Five hundred dollars ($500).

6. For a distinguished example of a cartoonist's work published in an American newspaper during the year, the determining qualities being that the cartoon shall embody an idea made clearly apparent, shall show good drawing and striking pictorial effect, and shall be intended to be helpful to some commendable cause of public importance, due account being taken of the whole volume of the artist's work during the year, Five hundred dollars ($500).

7. For an outstanding example of news photography as exemplified by a news photograph published in a daily newspaper, Five hundred dollars ($500). (This prize is open to amateurs as well as to photographers regularly employed by newspapers, press associations, or syndicates.)

Respectfully submitted,

CARL W. ACKERMAN
Dean

December 31, 1947

Revisions of the Pulitzer Prize Procedure

[*Source:* Carl W. Ackerman: One Million for the Advancement of Journalism – A Report by the Dean of the Graduate School of Journalism for the Academic Year ending June 30, 1947, New York: Columbia University, 1947, pp. 12–14.]

tasks and functioning of the American post-war press and, where necessary, to present proposals for reforms.[8]

This report of the Hutchins Commission, which was received rather critically, charged with being written by gentlemen far removed from the practice of journalism or even unacquainted with it,[9] dealt, among other things, with the educational situation and conditions of schools or departments of journalism at American universities. Especially this point of the report caused the co-publisher of a leading American special periodical for journalism to write an editorial containing the following passage: "In referring to the contribution of schools of journalism on the critical level, the members of the Commission apparently never have heard of the encouragement given, on a constructive note, by those schools and their personnel to the best in journalism. Perhaps they conceive criticism to be exclusively negative and fault-finding. Nor do they make any reference to such extra-curricular contributions as the numerous press institutes and 'short courses' conducted for years by some schools for the benefit of practicing journalists and others. They ignore the incentives to better journalism implicit in the Pulitzer Prize awards, the University of Missouri Journalism Week and medal awards, the Sigma Delta Chi activities and awards, and others in that spirit."[10] These formulations, pointing out in general the exemplary character of prize-winning journalistic products, appeared at a time when the Pulitzer Prizes were still afflicted with the relics of the category system developed during the war.

For it was in 1947 when Pulitzer Prizes were awarded in the two internationally oriented categories for the last time. While in the traditional Correspondence category, existing since 1929, the honor was bestowed on Brooks Atkinson of the *New York Times* "for distinguished correspondence during 1946, as exemplified by his series of articles on Russia," the prize in the International Telegraphic Reporting category, created in 1942, was awarded to Eddy Gilmore of the *Associated Press* "for his correspondence from Moscow in 1946."[11] Thus in both cases awards were given for reporting about the Soviet Union. "It is one of the oddities of journalism," Hohenberg remarks about the backgrounds of the prize given to Atkinson, "that the articles about the Soviet Union . . . were written by a drama critic on wartime leave from his aisle seat and not a foreign affairs specialist. The reason the pieces created a stir when they were published . . . was that Atkinson gave his views of the American-Soviet post-war relationship in blunt language. 'Although we are not enemies, we are not friends,' Atkinson wrote, 'and the most we can hope for is an armed peace for the next few years. Where our interests lie, we have to apply equal power in the opposite direction. It is a pity, perhaps it will be a tragedy, that as a nation we have to live with the Russian nation in an atmosphere of bitterness and tension. But we have to. There is no other way.' *Pravda* angrily attacked Atkinson and the *Times* when the articles were published. *Life,* duly impressed,

---

[8] Cf. The Commission on Freedom of the Press. A Free and Responsible Press. A General Report on Mass Communication, Chicago: The University of Chicago Press, 1947, pp. 90 ff.

[9] Cf. the respective critical remarks of the journalism professor of Columbia University and the temporary Pulitzer Prize juror, William O. Trapp, in: *Journalism Quarterly* (Emory/Georgia), Vol. 24/No. 2, June 1947, pp. 160 f.

[10] Robert W. Desmond: Of a Free and Responsible Press, in: *Journalism Quarterly* (Emory/Georgia), Vol. 24/No. 2, June, 1947, p. 191.

[11] Advisory Board on the Pulitzer Prizes (Ed.): The Pulitzer Prizes, 1917–1977, New York: Columbia University, 1977, pp. 23, 27.

reprinted them. And, without even a struggle, they won for their author the last Pulitzer Prize for Correspondence ... A quarter-century thereafter ... the now-retired critic recalled that it took an order from the acting publisher ... to get the series printed in the *Times*. He added: 'The Prize legitimized those articles about the 'paranoid' Russian government. I was grateful and still am. But there is something ironic about the fact that I received a Prize in a field in which, owing to the exigencies of the war, I was a temporary intruder.'"[12]

The problems of the juries to differentiate the Correspondence award from the International Telegraphic Reporting award, which had been existing for years, in 1948 finally led to a fusion of these two Pulitzer Prizes which had been awarded simultaneously since 1942.[13] The first prize-winner in the new International Reporting category was Paul W. Ward of the newspaper *The Sun*, Baltimore, Maryland, "for his series of articles published in 1947 on 'Life in the Soviet Union.'" In 1949, the prize was awarded to a journalist from the same newspaper, namely to Price Day, "for his series of articles entitled 'Experiment in Freedom – India and Its First Year of Independence,'" while in 1950 Edmund Stevens of the *Christian Science Monitor* was honored "for his series of 43 articles written over a three-year residence in Moscow entitled 'This is Russia – Uncensored.'"[14] "The cold war abroad and its effect on civil liberties at home," Hohenberg writes in analyzing the obvious concentration of most of the international prizes on one main subject, "became another major source of concern for the American press in the post-World War II period. No fewer than four prizes were awarded between 1947 and 1950 for correspondence from the Soviet Union ... In 1951, C. L. Sulzberger won a special award for interviewing Archbishop Stepinac. There was, in addition, a prize for Frederick Woltman of the *New York World-Telegram* in 1947 for his investigation of Communism in the United States ... The impact of the cold war on the American public also was registered picturesquely in the work of the Pulitzer Prize cartoonists.[15] There was," Hohenberg writes "in 1946, Bruce Russells's drawing in the *Los Angeles Times* of a deepening chasm that separated the American eagle and Russian bear, surmounted by the caption: 'Time to Bridge That Gulch.' There followed, in 1948, Rube Goldberg's New York *Sun* cartoon entitled 'Peace Today,' showing the atomic bomb balanced between world peace and world destruction."[16]

Although the principle, applied since the mid-thirties, to admit to the juries only faculty members of the Graduate School of Journalism, Columbia University, was abandoned in 1947 and representatives of the American press being allowed to function from then on as jury members, too,[17] there still was a latent uneasiness about the modus of making the award

---

[12] John Hohenberg: The Pulitzer Prizes. A History of the Awards in Books, Drama, Music, and Journalism, based on the private files over six decades, New York–London: Columbia University Press, 1974, p. 190.

[13] Cf. Advisory Board on the Pulitzer Prizes (Ed.): The Pulitzer Prizes, 1917–1977, op. cit., p. 13.

[14] Ibid., p. 27.

[15] Cf. Dick Spencer, III.: Pulitzer Prize Cartoons. The Men and their Masterpieces, 2. ed., Ames/Iowa: The Iowa State College Press, 1955, pp. 98 ff.

[16] John Hohenberg: The Pulitzer Prizes, op. cit., p. 190; cf. also George E. Simmons: The "Cold War" in Large-City Dailies of the United States, in: *Journalism Quarterly* (Emory/Georgia), Vol. 25/No. 4, December 1948, pp. 354 ff.

[17] Cf. the listing "Pulitzer Prize Jurors," typewritten manuscript, for the years 1947 ff., Pulitzer Prize Office (PPO).

MORNING   EVENING   SUNDAY

THE SUN

THE A.S. ABELL COMPANY, PUBLISHERS
BALTIMORE-3, MD.

January 30, 1948

Dean Carl W. Ackerman
Secretary, Advisory Board
Pulitzer Prizes in Journalism
Columbia University
New York 27, New York

Dear Dean Ackerman:

      This letter brings you the formal nomination of Paul W. Ward, now a member of the Washington bureau staff of the Baltimore Sun, for the 1947 Pulitzer Prize in journalism for distinguished reporting of international affairs.

      The nomination is based specifically upon a series of 19 articles on LIFE IN THE SOVIET UNION written by Mr. Ward and published in the Baltimore Sun between April 30 and May 18, 1947. However, it is requested that so far as it is possible, the series of articles upon which specifically the nomination is made shall be considered by the Advisory Board in connection with the whole body of Mr. Ward's work in 1947, and against the background of his work over a period of ten years -- a period which particularly prepared him to produce his report on LIFE IN THE SOVIET UNION.

      The nomination is made in the belief that Mr. Ward's work, as a whole and specifically in the series of nineteen articles, constitutes a truly distinguished example of reporting of international affairs. It represented a long period of preparation, and was the fruition of a decade of specializing in reporting of international affairs.

      His series of articles on LIFE IN THE SOVIET UNION was objective, was remarkably well and clearly written and was done on his own initiative, over and above the call of duty on his specific assignment to Moscow. Because the series dealt with the human aspects of life in the Soviet Union, it is believed that it constitutes one of the best and most revealing pieces of reporting ever done in that field.

      The series of articles attracted so much attention that they were collected after publication in The Sun and published in a pamphlet.

      I am forwarding to you by registered mail an exhibit marked Paul W. Ward - 1, consisting of the series of articles as it appeared in The Sun; an exhibit marked Paul W. Ward - 2, which is the pamphlet in which the series was republished; an exhibit marked Paul W. Ward - 3, consisting of his dispatches to The Sun during the time he was in Russia, from March 9 to April 24, 1947; and an exhibit marked Paul W. Ward - 4-a and 4-b, consisting of the whole body of his work in the year 1947.

Accompanying Letter for

We hope that the nomination of Mr. Ward for the 1947 Pulitzer Prize for distinguished reporting of international affairs will be favorably considered not only because of the outstanding excellence of the specific series or of the general excellence of his work in international affairs during 1947, but also because both the series and the body of his work are an outstanding example of the way in which the best interests of American journalism and the American public may be served by the happy combination of a newspaper man who works intensively to prepare himself to take advantage of opportunities and a newspaper which constantly seeks to make such opportunities available.

Mr. Ward came to The Sun in 1930. After three years on the staff in Baltimore, he was transferred to the Washington bureau to give him an opportunity for diversified experience in the coverage of congressional and departmental affairs and to lay a broad foundation for his development as a correspondent. Mr. Ward took advantage of this opportunity, preparing himself so thoroughly that in the spring of 1937 he became chief of The Sun's London Bureau. In that capacity he covered the Nine-Power Conference at Brussels in the fall of 1937; Hitler's seizure of Austria in 1938; the Munich crisis in September, 1938; Hitler's seizure of Czechoslovakia in March 1939; and Mussolini's seizure of Albania in April of that year.

In May, 1939, Mr. Ward was assigned to Moscow with instructions to tour and report on, en route, the other areas then threatened by Hitler. He worked in Berlin, Vienna, Budapest and Warsaw until, despite assurances from the Soviet Embassy, it had become apparent that his visa for Russia would not be forthcoming. He was then assigned to Paris, shortly before the Hitler-Stalin pact of August, 1939; reported the beginning of World War II; and was one of a group of four correspondents who, without permission and at risk of official wrath, were the first reporters to cross the Maginot Line and visit the French front.

In February of 1940, Mr. Ward returned to The Sun's Washington bureau, covered the Conference of American Foreign Ministers that summer and thereafter, during the war years, specialized in covering war legislation and our foreign relations from the Capitol. Beginning in the spring of 1945, Mr. Ward was assigned to concentrate exclusively on foreign affairs. He covered the Dumbarton Oaks conference at which the Big Four devised the initial draft of the United Nations Charter and, later that year, the United Nations Conference at San Francisco which perfected that charter.

In April, 1946, Mr. Ward was assigned to Paris to cover the meeting there of the Council of (Big Four) Foreign Ministers, an assignment which was prolonged to cover the Council's second session in Paris and the 21-power peace conference there that followed. Between conference and council sessions, he visited the British, French and American zones of Germany, plus Berlin, Vienna, Trieste and Rome.

I have set forth so fully the background of Mr. Ward's experience, which led up to his series on LIFE IN THE SOVIET UNION, because it seems to me not only to establish the competence and soundness which made possible his Russian series, but also because it affords a valuable example of the way in which better reporting of international affairs may be developed by American newspapers.

Sincerely yours,

Neil H. Swanson,
Executive Editor

a Nomination in 1948

in some cases. This feeling was clearly expressed in 1948, when Carroll Binder, editorial editor of the *Tribune,* Minneapolis, and member of the 1947 jury for Telegraphic Reporting (International), attacked the Advisory Board polemically: "Can those twelve newspapermen," Binder opened his charge against the Advisory Board, "completely detach themselves from the competitive interests of the newspaper or the press association which provides their living when they go to Morningside Hights to award Pulitzer Prizes? ... Most mentioned in this connection is Kent Cooper, executive director of the *Associated Press,* who has been a member of the adivsory board for eighteen years. While not all of the eleven Pulitzer Prizes boasted by the *Associated Press* were awarded during Cooper's service as a prize bestower, some of the most criticized awards to the Associated Press are associated with Cooper's presence on the board ... Perhaps these circumstances help to explain occasional contradictory actions on the board such as the 1947 prize ... to Eddy Gilmore of the *Asssociated Press* for dispatches filed through the Russian censorship. Gilmore is notorious for his sins of omission in his reports from Russia ... Gilmore cannot be blamed for pulling his punches in his dispatches. Besides, the *Associated Press* is probably more interested in maintaining representation in Russia than in telling the story of what really goes on ... But why give a Pulitzer Prize for the kind of reporting Gilmore does from Russia? Why give a prize to a man who once excused the Soviet censor as 'a necessary adjunct to a foreign correspondent to correct errors of fact in his copy'?"[18]

"The Board's response," Hohenberg found out, "was to express its confidence in the dean's impartiality. It also accepted as a matter of record, but not for publication, a statement by Cooper in which he listed all Scripps-Howard new organizations under the general heading of *United Press,* a rather large assumption, and showed that the representatives of this general grouping and of the Associated Press each had won six prizes between 1933 and 1947. The most that the Board did with this compilation was to ask informally that it be brought to Binder's attention. As for the UP boycott, it continued. There is also a recurring dissatisfaction with the dominance of what ciritics called 'the large Eastern and Elite newspapers' in the award for journalism. It was pointed out with considerable regularity that great newspapers, which were represented on the Advisory Board, also won numerous prizes ... In answering a critic, Arthur Krock once agreed that large and powerful newspapers in all parts of the land had won a 'notable and recurrent percentage of the journalism awards,' but argued that this was due mainly to their superior resources, facilities and wealth rather than to favoritism."[19] Moreover, it still was not intelligible for everybody – despite the respective regulations – why the jury decisions about the potential prize-winners could be changed or even completely ignored by the Advisory Board. A member of the 1949 Cartoon Jury, James Kerney, who had functioned already in the year before as juror in the International Reporting category,[20] presented, in the middle of March, a remarkable suggestion.

"The purpose of the Pulitzer Prizes," he wrote, "is to raise the quality of journalism by honoring its outstanding practitioners. Hewing to this end, the Pulitzer Prizes have become the most coveted awards among newspapermen. The American Society of Newspaper Editors joins in the selection of these prime winners by naming jurors to recommend prize

---

[18] Carroll Binder: The Press and the Pulitzer Prizes, in: *American Mercury* (New York, N. Y.), Vol. 66/No. 292, April 1948, pp. 463, 465, 469 f.
[19] John Hohenberg: The Pulitzer Prizes, op. cit., p. 174.
[20] Cf. the listing "Pulitzer Prize Jurors," op. cit., for the years 1948 and 1949.

Toward a new jury system....

ADVISORY BOARD TO DEVOTE ENTIRE ENERGY TO SELECTION OF PULITZER PRIZE WINNERS; WILL LEAVE SCHOOL PROBLEMS TO TRUSTEES

The Advisory Board of the Graduate School of Journalism of Columbia University has decided to devote its attention to the annual selection of winners of the Pulitzer Prizes-- the Nation's outstanding journalism, literary and music awards and to withdraw from any duties in connection with the administration of the School.

Its action, taken at the last session of the Board, actually legalizes what has been a de facto relationship with the School for many years. Since the first awards, endowed by Joseph Pulitzer, were made in 1917, the Advisory Board has left the management of the School to the Trustees of Columbia and the Faculty and concerned itself only with the yearly prizes.

The Advisory Board also adopted a resolution terminating the official jury relationship with the American Society of Newspaper Editors but expressed the hope that the friendly cooperation of the individual members would be continued. Furthermore, the Board declined to change its unbroken precedent of not making public any jury recommendations.

Word of this action by the group led to the almost immediate decision by the ASNE Board to discontinue appointing members of the society to serve as jurors. For several years ASNE juries had screened the material submitted and recommended nominees for each prize.

In a letter to Dean Ackerman, who is also Secretary of the Advisory Board, B. M. McKelway, Editor of THE EVENING STAR, [Washington, D. C.], and President of the ASNE, explained the Society's action.

"I think all of us understand the contradictions implicit in official participation by ASNE, as a society, in the Pulitzer awards and the fact that the Pulitzer Advisory Board has the indivisible responsibility for final decision. The Society's withdrawal from the practice of recent years reflects no hostility of any sort and merely affirms the opinion of many friendly and competent observers on and off the Pulitzer Board that the practice was not wholly feasible."

As a result of these moves by the Advisory Board and the ASNE a new committee of jurors, to be selected from the ASNE, but to act only as individuals, was decided upon.

Dean Ackerman announced that the following well-known newspapermen have accepted his invitation to serve on the 1951 juries:

§"Disinterested and meritorious public service"

Frank C. Clough, Editorial Director, Speidel Newspapers, Inc. [Palo Alto, California]

Lee Hills, Managing Editor, THE MIAMI [Florida] HERALD

§"Distinguished example of local reporting"

Stanley P. Barnett, Managing Editor, THE CLEVELAND [O.] PLAIN DEALER

Samuel L. Latimer, Jr., Editor and Publisher, THE STATE [Columbia, S.C.]

§"Distinguished example of reporting on national affairs"

Richard W. Clarke, Executive Editor, NEW YORK [N.Y.] DAILY NEWS

A. Y. Aronson, Managing Editor, THE LOUISVILLE [Ky.] TIMES

§"Distinguished example of reporting of international affairs"

W. C. Stoutfer, Managing Editor, ROANOKE [Va.] WORLD NEWS

Virginius Dabney, Editor, RICHMOND [Va.] TIMES DISPATCH

§"Distinguished editorial writing"

F. W. Brinkerhoff, Editor and Manager, THE PITTSBURG [Kansas] PUBLISHING COMPANY

Roger C. Williams, GUY GANNET PUBLISHING COMPANY, Portland, Maine

§"Distinguished example of a cartoonist's work"

Felix R. McKnight, Assistant Managing Editor, THE DALLAS [Texas] MORNING NEWS

Holger Doran Paulson, Editor, THE FARGO [N.D.] FORUM

§ Outstanding example of news photography"

Carl E. Lindstrom, Managing Editor, HARTFORD [Conn.] TIMES

W. R. Walton, Managing Editor, THE TRIBUNE [South Bend, Indiana]

Changes in the Administration of the Prizes

[*Source:* Allan Keller (Ed.): Gist – Annual Report of Dean Carl W. Ackerman to President Dwight D. Eisenhower, New York 1950, p. 7.]

winners. It is acknowledged, of course, that under the will of Joseph Pulitzer the final responsibility to determine the awards lies with the Advisory Board. It is the conviction of the undersigned jurors that interest in the Pulitzer Prizes would be increased in keeping with their purpose if the recommendations of the jurors were made public in conjunction with the awards of the prizes."[21] One does not know if this submission impressed the Board or the Trustees very much, but it is not likely. Nevertheless, in the following year the name of the Advisory Board was somewhat changed, at least optically. "In a resolution adopted at its meeting on April 18, 1950," Hohenberg describes the alteration, "the Board changed its name from the Advisory Board of the Graduate School of Journalism to the Advisory Board on the Pulitzer Prizes. Through this symbolic act, the Board confined its scope to 'the control of the annual selection of the winners of the Pulitzer Prizes and the jurors who screen the material, and of the form in which the public announcements are made.' The university's Trustees ratified the change on October 2, 1950."[22] This incident, however, was highly important in fact, as it made unequivocally clear to everybody that the Advisory Board exclusively was competent for the final determination of the Pulitzer Prize-winners.

But when in 1951 the award in the International Reporting category was being made, the Advisory Board on the Pulitzer Prizes did not, as one would have supposed in view of the newly confirmed self-confidence, appear souvereign at all in the finding of its final judgment. "By that time," Hohenberg explains, "six combat correspondents had been nominated for the Pulitzer Prize in International Reporting by a new type of journalism jury," consisting of two newspapermen from Virginia. "They had supplanted the one-member juries of the Journalism faculty along with editors in other categories who had accepted appointments offered by Dean Ackerman. Their recommendations" for prize-winners, "dated March 21, 1951, and based on work done in 1950, were as follows: Keyes Beech, *Chicago Daily News*, for his graphic, concise, well-written, informed dispatches from the Korean war front. His work shows background, courageous willingness to state unpleasant facts, and great resourcefulness under the most trying and hazardous conditions. – Homer Bigart, *New York Herald-Tribune*, for his outstanding reports from Korea. Rather than take the easy way by writing far behind the lines, he wrote his vivid reports from the front. He went to extraordinary risks in gathering his facts. – Marguerite Higgins, *New York Herald-Tribune*, for fine front line reporting showing enterprise and courage. She is entitled to special consideration by reason of being a woman, since she had to work under unusual dangers. – Relman Morin, *Associated Press*, for his on-the-spot articles from Korea, marked by good writing and excellent explanatory coverage. – Fred Sparks, *Chicago Daily News*, for his well-written dispatches, and espescially the fine job of bachgrounding. – Don Whitehead, *Associated Press*, for his superlative reporting, much under fire. He also scored major scoops."[23]

"It became the business of the Advisory Board," Hohenberg reconstructs the process of decision making for the internationally oriented prize of 1951, "to determine which of the six reporters, alphabetically listed in the report, should be given the prize. After considerable debate, however, the Board was unable to come to a decision and voted to give all six candidates individual Pulitzer Prizes – an unprecedent action in the history of the awards.

---

[21] N. N. (James Kerney): Resolution, attached to a note from Foster (Haley) to Dean Ackerman of March 15, 1949 (PPO).
[22] John Hohenberg: The Pulitzer Prizes, op. cit., p. 229.
[23] Ibid., pp. 193 f.

MARGUERITE HIGGINS — Herald Tribune Correspondent

When war broke out in Korea, a somewhat winsome, slight, blond correspondent moved swiftly from the Herald Tribune Tokyo bureau to the Korean battlefront, and began filing the first-eye-witness reports of American troops in action.

Her name is Marguerite Higgins, young war correspondent for the New York Herald Tribune - known to thousands of GI's as just plain Maggie.

Miss Higgins has already become a legend, both in Korea and the United States. In the war theatre she proved herself alarmingly brave and extraordinarily durable. In the Herald Tribune her dispatches have been exciting if not brilliant, and they have revealed, by modest implication, that Miss Higgins was customarily in the thick of battle.

Maggie was only in Korea for a few days when Army orders called for her return to Tokyo. Lt. General Walton Walker, head of American troops in Korea, felt "this is just not the type of war where women ought to be running around the front lines."

Perhaps the General was right - but he didn't know Maggie. Within 24 hours General Douglas MacArthur cabled the New York Herald Tribune: "Marguerite Higgins is held in highest esteem by everyone." Even while MacArthur was issuing orders permitting Miss Higgins to return to the front lines, Maggie had gone to General Walker's headquarters to convince him that "I'm here as a newspaper correspondent - not as a woman."

Press Release About the Korea Reports of Marguerite Higgins

When the university's Trustee ratified the Board's recommendation, that was the way it was announced."[24] Thus, the official reason for the prize ran accordingly, saying that Keyes Beech, Homer Bigart, Marguerite Higgins, Relman Morin, Fred Sparks, and Don Whitehead had been awarded the Pulitzer Prize "for their reporting of the Korean War."[25] After the presentation of this rather extraordinary award the then foreign editorial editor of McGraw-Hill Publishing Company regretted the alarming reduction of the number of American foreign correspondents since the end of World War II in a magazine article. "That the overseas press ranks should be thinned at the end of the war," he specified, "was only natural. But that the dilution should be so complete as to eliminate eight out of every nine foreign correspondents is another matter. What this means to the United States – in desperate need of eyes and ears in all parts of the globe – requires no dramatic explanation. The danger to this country is self-evident . . . Just as the press met the challenge in World War II and expanded the foreign news corps, and met it again more recently in Korea, there is no doubt that it will face its responsibility in any broadening military activity."[26]

As can be seen from the presentation of six individual Pulitzer Prizes for International Reporting in 1951, interest again focused on war correspondence since the outbreak of the war in Korea – for the first time after the end of World War II. "The old correspondents of World War II and some of the younger ones of more recent vintage came straight in," Hohenberg states and completes: "And so did the combat photographers. But the story they had to tell this time was disappointing and even tragic. For MacArthur's boastful predictions of victory were proved wrong, as was his assurance that the Chinese would not enter the war . . . (So) three other prizes were granted for outstanding correspondence connection with the Korean War and the long and difficult in peacemaking."[27] Thus, the international Pulitzer Prize of the following year was given to John M. Hightower of the *Associated Press* "for the sustained quality of his coverage of news of international affairs" during 1951.[28] Despite this rather general formulation in the case of Hightower it was also primarily his correspondence from Korea that yielded him the honor. "Hightower's prize was notable," Hohenberg explains in this connection, "because it gave recognition to one of the most trusted Washington correspondents, the confidant of a succession of Secretaries of State, and the most widely read writer on the diplomatic circuit. He was among the first to report the quarrel between President Truman and General MacArthur. He also made it clear that the basis of their dispute was MacArthur's continual challenges to Peking and President Truman's unwillingness to risk a war with China. And finally, three days before the President took his decisive action, Hightower wrote a piece predicting that the commander-in-chief would relieve the general of some or all of his powers. It was on the basis of this record that the correspondent won the International Reporting Prize in 1952."[29]

An outstanding general finding about this period is the decline of the number of U.S. foreign correspondents from about 2,700 in 1946 to less than 300 in 1951 – with the exception

---

[24] Ibid., p. 194.
[25] Advisory Board on the Pulitzer Prizes (Ed.): The Pulitzer Prizes, 1917–1977, op. cit., p. 27.
[26] Russell F. Anderson: News from Nowhere. Our Disappearing Foreign Correspondents, in: *The Saturday Review of Literature* (New York), Vol. 34, November 17, 1951, pp. 11, 81.
[27] John Hohenberg: The Pulitzer Prizes, op. cit., pp. 193 f.
[28] Advisory Board on the Pulitzer Prizes (Ed.): The Pulitzer Prizes, 1917–1977, op. cit., p. 27.
[29] John Hohenberg: The Pulitzer Prizes, op. cit., p. 194.

THE ASSOCIATED PRESS
GENERAL OFFICE
50 ROCKEFELLER PLAZA
NEW YORK 20, N. Y.

February 1, 1952

Dr. Carl W. Ackerman,
Secretary of the Advisory Board,
501 Journalism Building,
Columbia University,
New York 27, N. Y.

Dear Dean Ackerman:

      This is to nominate John Hightower for the Pulitzer Prize for National Reporting for 1951. We base the nomination on his spot news stories, interpretives and analytical stories on the MacArthur dismissal and related events.

      These stories are reproduced on pages 3-8, inclusive, of this presentation.

      Additionally, the caliber of Hightower's work is evidenced by his writings in two other categories:

1. Interpretives---many of them exclusive---that he wrote throughout the year on virtually every one of the confusing facets of U. S. foreign policy. Typical interpretives, all written within one 30-day period, are on pages 9-12, inclusive.

2. The Japanese peace conference in September. Representative stories are on pages 13-14.

      This presentation ends with a typical Hightower beat-- the exclusive forecast that Winston Churchill would visit President Truman in January of this year, including details on the groundwork conversations then under way.

      With best regards,

Sincerely yours,

OLIVER GRAMLING
ASSISTANT GENERAL MANAGER

Accompanying Letter for a Nomination in 1952

of war correspondents.[30] The greater part of American newspapers – as a 1953 study of the International Press Institute shows – received their foreign news and reports at that time mainly from the big agencies *(Associated Press, United Press, International News Service).*[31] The decline of the number of representatives of the American press abroad can, at least in part, be explained by organizational reasons. "Only a few newspapers," the IPI-study explains in detail, "and these few centered in but three American cities, maintain fulltime staffs of correspondents abroad – the *New York Times,* the *New York Herald Tribune,* the New York *Daily News,* the *Christian Science Monitor,* the *Chicago Tribune,* and the *Chicago Daily News.* Others (the Baltimore *Sun* is an example) make use of correspondents on special assignment abroad or station one or two men in leading foreign capitals. A few share special correspondents with other newspapers. These special foreign correspondents often compete with agency men in covering big spot news stories abroad. They do not work in exactly the same way, however . . . Most newspaper correspondents concentrate on interpretive aspects of foreign developments which the agencies, with hundreds of varied clients, do not cover in such detail."[32]

In view of the different weighing of foreign news in American newspapers it is small wonder that "in many small newspapers examined, foreign news was largely news of the Korean war. When the examination is limited to ten large newspapers, with foreign correspondents," the IPI-study goes on, "news from the Korean war theater also takes a large proportion of space, but about 82 per cent of the foreign news stories cover other areas."[33] It soon became apparent that the Korean War was not the only subject in those years worthy of a Pulitzer Prize. When in 1953 the Pulitzer Prize for International Reporting was awarded to Austin Wehrwein of the *Milwaukee Journal* "for his series of articles on Canada,"[34] the National Reporting award was given to AP correspondent Don Whitehead "for his article called 'The Great Deception', dealing with the intricate arrangements by which the safety of President-elect Eisenhower was guarded en route from Morningside Heights in New York to Korea."[35] In the 1954 term, the international prize was bestowed on Jim G. Lucas of the Scripps-Howard Newspaper "for his notable front-line human interest reporting on the Korean War, the cease-fire and the prisoner-of-war-exchanges, climaxing 26 months of distinguished service as a war correspondent."[36]

At about the time of the announcement of the prize Lucas confided to an American journalism researcher about his activity as a correspondent in the Korean war: "Quite frankly, I do not regard myself as a foreign correspondent. I can more accurately be identified, I believe, as a war correspondent. One of the more interesting sidelights in American journalism since 1941 has been the development of a corps of professional war correspondents. War is our business. We say we hate it – and I am genuinely convinced we do – but we

---

[30] Cf. Russell F. Anderson: News from Nowhere – Our disappearing Foreign Correspondents, op. cit.
[31] International Press Institute: The Flow of the News, Zurich: The International Press Institute, 1953, p. 16.
[32] Ibid., p. 17.
[33] Ibid., p. 22.
[34] Advisory Board on the Pulitzer Prizes (Ed.): The Pulitzer Prizes, 1917–1977, op. cit., p. 27.
[35] Ibid., p. 24.
[36] Ibid., p. 27.

International Reporting.

NO. 1   Here, in my opinion, is the most outstanding work submitted. Twenty-six related stories about Canada. I have read many articles about Canada --magazines --press services and special pieces. This writer's leg work, plus good writing and know-how, brings our neighbor on the north into the house.

Economics, politics, finance, "moose pasture stockateers," the St. Lawrence seaway, Canada's need for more people, aluminum--all these and more/subjects are brightly written and outlined.

Austin C. Wehrwein of the Milwaukee Journal is easy to read and easy to understand.

His work is distinctive.

* *

NO. 2   John Randolph of the Associated Press. He submitted 10 articles. He appears at home in any field. Best of the lot-- the piece on the third winter in Korea.

* *

NO. 3   Ray Cromley's pieces in The Wall Street Journal.

* *

NO. 4   Edward H. Hughes' articles in The Wall Street Journal.

NO. 5   John P. Leacacos' work in The Cleveland Plain Dealer.

NO. 6   Phillip Potter's series on Japan. Baltimore Sun.

W. C. Stouffer

Report of the 1953 International Reporting Jury

cannot do without it. In between wars, we may go back to our old jobs – to covering the State Department, the Pentagon or the State Capitol – but this we regard as kid's stuff. We are not happy at anything else. We are clannish. We know each other intimately. We know who drinks too much, who chases the native women and who isn't above faking a story. Few ever rose above junior officer [in the military services]. But now we are the confidants of admirals and generals and we dearly love to paint the big picture with a broad brush ... I want to make millions of people who have never been to Korea feel that they have. In war, nothing is unimportant. The things we, who are here, take for granted, are alien to millions ... I write for those who don't know and want to. Nor can I permit myself the luxury of writing [about] morale. Morale – as important as it is – is not my business."[37]

In this period, a change in the administration of the Pulitzer Prizes took place. Carl W. Ackerman, who had continously functioned as secretary of the Advisory Board since 1933 – in addition to his post as dean of the Graduate School of Journalism –, in 1954 "voluntarily gave up his responsibilities for the Pulitzer Prizes in view of his approaching retirement" and John Hohenberg, who had belonged to the professorial staff of the Graduate School of Journalism, Columbia University, since 1949 now "became the Board's secretary and the administrator of the awards, at the same time remaining a full-time teaching member of the Journalism Faculty ... Dean Ackerman retired from Joseph Pulitzer's school, which he had done so much to revive and expand into an all-graduate institution, in 1955."[38] "Throughout his adult life," Baker describes the multifarious impulses Ackerman had given to Columbia University, "his interests and his travels have been international ... Ackerman has always felt that the School of Journalism at Columbia has a world responsibility,"[39] – an attitude which surely applied to his engagement in the Pulitzer Prizes, too. Nearly simultaneously with the change in office of the Pulitzer Prize administrator from Ackerman to Hohenberg numerous retirements took place in the Advisory Board, too.

"The Board ... decided," Hohenberg describes the new situation, "to limit the service of its members to three terms of four years each. Under the resolution of April 23, 1954, an entirely new Board came into being within a relatively short time and some of the oldest and most influential figures in its history were phased out of membership ... At the 1954 meeting," Hohenberg goes on in another passage, "Joseph Pulitzer, Jr., the son of the chairman and the grandson of the donor of the prizes, had been invited to attend the 1955 session as an observer. But with the death of the second Joseph Pulitzer on March 30, 1955, the Board's chairmanship unexpectedly became vacant. Arthur Krock ... rose to the occasion by proposing a resolution within a few days under which Joseph Pulitzer, Jr., would succeed his father as the Board's chairman at the 1955 meeting. It was circulated by wire and unanimously adopted."[40] When the award committees, which were recomposed for the greatest part, had to decide about the bestowal of the International Reporting award in March/April 1955, the Korean War was over, so that the thematical interest could concentrate on other

---

[37] Jim Lucas: (Statement), in: J. William Maxwell (Ed.): The Foreign Correspondent. His Problems in Covering the News Abroad – A selection of reports by thirty-seven American correspondents, Iowa City/Iowa: The Graduate College and the School of Journalism, 1954, pp. 39, 42.
[38] John Hohenberg: The Pulitzer Prizes, op. cit., pp. 229 ff.
[39] Richard Terrill Baker: A History of the Graduate School of Journalism, Columbia University, New York: Columbia University Press, 1954, p. 113.
[40] John Hohenberg: The Pulitzer Prizes, op. cit., pp. 229 f.

A pass to Stalin's funeral, which reads: "Foreign correspondent Pass No. 013. Mr. Solsberi, Garrison [there is no letter "h" in Russian, so "h" is transliterated "g"] for admission to Red Square for the funeral of the Chairman of the Council of Ministers of the U.S.S.R. and the Secretary of the Central Committee of the C.P.S.U., Generalissimus JOSEF VISSARIONOVICH STALIN."

> ИНОКОРРЕСПОНДЕНТУ
> Пропуск № 013
> Г-ну Солсбери
> Гаррисон
> для ПРОХОДА на КРАСНУЮ ПЛОЩАДЬ
> НА ПОХОРОНЫ
> Председателя Совета Министров СССР и
> Секретаря Центрального Комитета КПСС
> Генералиссимуса
> Иосифа Виссарионовича
> СТАЛИНА

[*Source:* Harrison E. Salisbury: An American in Russia, New York 1955, p. 172.]

regions of the world. Both the jury[41] and the Advisory Board finally awarded the prize to Harrison E. Salisbury of the *New York Times* "for his distinguished series of articles, 'Russia Re-Viewed,' based on his six years as a *Times* correspondent in Russia. The perceptive and well-written Salisbury articles," the prize justification goes on, "made a valuable contribution to American understanding of what is going on inside Russia. This was principally due to the writer's wide range of subject matter and depth of background, plus a number of illuminating photographs which he took."[42]

As a consequence of the ending of the Korean War the interest of the Pulitzer Prize awarding committees focused again, as it had before 1950, on the Soviet Union, where the coverage of the post-Stalin era proved to be a profitable assignment for foreign correspondents. But as in the past, it turned out to be a difficult and even risky enterprise to gather background information about the new structures of power arising in the U.S.S.R. This problem had been pointed at already at the beginning of the fifties by a study of the International Press Institute.[43] Due to this circumstance, another IPI-study concluded, information from the Soviet Union played a minor role in American news agencies as well as in the

---

[41] Cf. Stanley P. Barnett/John R. Herbert: Report of the Jury on International Reporting nominations for 1955 . . . for work done in 1954, New York, March 15, 1955, p. 1 (PPO).

[42] Advisory Board on the Pulitzer Prizes (Ed.): The Pulitzer Prizes, 1917–1977, op. cit., pp. 27 f.

[43] Cf. International Press Institute: The News from Russia, Zurich: The International Press Institute, 1952, pp. 10 ff.

THE UNITED STATES MEDIA OF GENERAL INFORMATION ACCORDING TO LOCATION AND CITIZENSHIP OF CHIEF CORRESPONDENT

MEDIA	UK	FR.	IT	GER	SP	AU	CH	SW	BE	IR	DK	FI	HO	NY	PO	TR	YU
News Agency																	
Associated Press	u	u	u	u	u	u	u	n	n	—	n	n	n	n	n	—	u
International News Service	u	u	u	u	u	n	—	n	—	—	—	—	—	—	—	—	n
United Press	u	u	u	u	u	u	u	n	n	n	u	n	n	n	n	—	u
Macnens	—	u	—	u	—	—	—	—	—	—	—	—	—	—	—	—	—
North American News. Alliance.	n	—	—	—	—	—	—	—	—	—	—	—	—	—	—	—	—
Overseas News Agency	n	—	—	—	—	—	—	—	—	—	—	—	—	—	—	—	—
Newspaper																	
Baltimore Sun	u	—	—	—	—	—	—	—	—	—	—	—	—	—	—	—	—
Chicago Daily News	u	u	u	u	—	—	—	—	—	—	—	—	—	—	—	—	—
Chicago Tribune	u	u	n	u	—	—	—	—	—	—	—	—	—	—	—	—	—
Christian Science Monitor	u	u	u	n	—	—	—	—	—	—	—	—	—	—	—	—	—
Cleveland News Plain Dealer	u	—	u	—	—	—	—	—	—	—	—	—	—	—	—	—	—
Hearst Newspapers	u	—	u	—	—	—	—	—	—	—	—	—	—	—	—	—	—
Kansas City Star	—	u	—	—	—	—	—	—	—	—	—	—	—	—	—	—	—
Los Angeles Times	—	—	—	u	—	—	—	—	—	—	—	—	—	—	—	—	—
New York Daily News	n	n	u	u	—	—	—	—	—	—	—	—	—	—	—	—	—
New York Post	—	u	—	—	—	—	—	—	—	—	—	—	—	—	—	—	—
New York Herald-Tribune	u	u	u	u	—	—	—	—	—	—	—	—	—	—	—	—	—
New York Times	u	u	u	u	u	n	u	n	—	—	—	—	—	—	—	—	u
Philadelphia Bulletin	—	u	—	—	—	—	—	—	—	—	—	—	—	—	—	—	—
Scripps-Howard Newspapers	—	u	—	—	—	—	—	—	—	—	—	—	—	—	—	—	—
Toledo Blade	—	u	—	—	—	—	—	—	—	—	—	—	—	—	—	—	—
Washington Star	—	u	—	—	—	—	—	—	—	—	—	—	—	—	—	—	—
Magazines																	
Cowles Magazines	—	u	—	—	—	—	—	—	—	—	—	—	—	—	—	—	—
Newsweek	u	u	—	u	—	—	—	—	—	—	—	—	—	—	—	—	—
New Yorker	n	u	—	—	—	u	—	—	—	—	—	—	—	—	—	—	—
Time, Inc.	u	n	u	u	n	—	—	—	—	—	—	—	—	—	—	—	—
Saturday Evening Post	—	u	u	—	—	—	—	—	—	—	—	—	—	—	—	—	—
U. S. News	u	u	u	u	—	—	—	—	—	—	—	—	—	—	—	—	—
The Reporter	—	—	u	—	—	—	—	—	—	—	—	—	—	—	—	—	—
Radio Networks																	
American Broadcasting Co.	u	—	—	—	—	—	—	—	—	—	—	—	—	—	—	—	—
Columbia Broadcasting System	u	u	u	u	—	u	—	—	—	—	—	—	—	—	—	—	—
National Broadcasting Co.	u	n	u	u	—	—	—	—	—	—	—	—	—	—	—	—	—

SYMBOLS

u : United States Citizen
n : Non-U.S. Citizen
— : No full-time correspondent

Note: Specialized Media are not included in this study.

UK: United Kingdom
FR: France
IT: Italy
GER: Germany
SP: Spain
AU: Austria
CH: Switzerland

SW: Sweden
BE: Belgium
IR: Ireland
DK: Denmark
FI: Finland
HO: Holland
NY: Norway

PO: Portugal
TR: Trieste
YU: Yugoslavia

Location of American Foreign Correspondents in Western Europe in 1954

[*Source:* Theodore Edward Kruglak: The Foreign Correspondents – A Study of the Men and Women reporting for the American Information Media in Western Europe, Geneva 1955, pp. 136 f.]

daily papers, so that it did not reach quantitative significance in serveral testing sections in the 1952/53 period.[44] In that period, a strong concentration of American media representatives could be found, however, in the United Kingdom[45] and a certain massing of U.S. foreign correspondents in Middle and Western Europe, where the big American agencies and most of the newspapers quoted above maintained their own personnel.[46]

There had already been only six Western correspondents in the Soviet Union at the beginning of the fifties, among them four Americans (Eddy Gilmore and Thomas Whitney, AP, Henry Shapiro, UP, and Harrison E. Salisbury, *New York Times*);[47] "by the beginning of 1954, nine months after Stalin's death, the entire regular corps of Western correspondents in Moscow consisted of five men... They worked seven days a week, twelve to fourteen hours a day, and were dismayed at the smallness of their yield. Their main work was usually between 11 p.m., when they were able to pick up the *Tass* report, until as late as 5 a.m., when they were usually able to get a copy of *Pravda*."[48] In view of the nature of the flow of information from the Soviet Union it is small wonder that not only the American media suffered from a permanent deficit of reporting from the U.S.S.R., but that the Pulitzer Prize jurors, too, were steadily looking for outstanding journalistic products about the Soviet Union. Harrison E. Salisbury, the *New York Times* correspondent of long standing and a profound expert of the U.S.S.R. who had already received the Pulitzer Prize in 1955, was again awarded the honor for reports from and about the Soviet Union in the following year. This time, it was three American journalists at once on whom the prize for International Reporting was bestowed.

"Early in February, 1955," Hohenberg writes in describing the selection of the prize-winning press reports, "the canny Kingsbury Smith led his boss, William Randolph Hearst, Jr., and an associate, Frank Conniff, into Moscow on an exploratory mission. There had been no Hearst representative in Moscow for years. Smith picked an excellent time. The Hearst team enjoyed a world-wide press for its interviews with Krushchev, Marshal Nigolai Bulganin, Marshal Georgi Zhukov, and the crusty old diplomatic undertaker, Foreign Minister Zhukov, and the crusty old diplomatic undertaker, Foreign Minister Vyacheslav M. Molotov."[49] Evaluating this journalistic teamwork of three representatives of the Hearst press turned out to be a problem for the Pulitzer Prize jury in the International Reporting category. "This exhibit," the jury report says, "is in two sections: the interviews with Russian leaders by Mr. Smith and the impression stories of Mr. Hearst. If possible to do so," the Advisory Board was told, "we would recommend that the four interviews by Mr. Smith be given the award for international affairs reporting. Actually he interviewed... the four men who were to have the key roles for the Russians... It is our feeling that the four interviews

---

[44] International Press Institute: The Flow of the News, op. cit., pp. 214 ff.
[45] Cf. Theodore E. Kruglak: Correspondents of U.S. Media in the United Kingdom, in: *Journalism Quarterly* (Minneapolis, Minn.), Vol. 31/No. 3, Summer, 1954, pp. 324 ff.
[46] Cf. Theodore E. Kruglak: The Foreign Correspondents. A Study of the Men and Women reporting for the American Information Media in Western Europe, Geneva: Librairie E. Droz, 1955, pp. 130 ff.
[47] John Hohenberg: Foreign Correspondence. The Great Reporters and Their Times, New York–London: Columbia University Press, 1964, p. 401.
[48] Ibid., p. 402.
[49] Ibid., p. 404.

represent the most enterprising work by any reporter submitting an exhibit in the international category. Furthermore, the interviews were informative and well written. If the Advisory Board is not disposed to split an entry in the manner suggested we would recommend that the international reporting award be given to Mr. Smith, Mr. Hearst and Mr. Conniff for the entire entry as submitted."[50] The Advisory Board agreed and finally gave the prize to "William Randolph Hearst, Jr., Kingsbury Smith and Frank Conniff, *International News Service,* for a series of exclusive interviews with the leaders of the Soviet Union."[51]

Thus, a Pulitzer Prize had been awarded to members of the Hearst dynasty for the first time. Whether the awarding committees intended a retroactive conflict settlement on this occasion – there had been memorable competitive struggles between the donor of the awards, Joseph Pulitzer (sen.), and the founder of the competing press empire, William Randolph Hearst (sen.) –[52] must remain pure speculation in connection with the bestowal of the prize. "Some of the jurors and Advisory Board members," Hohenberg stresses, "argued against the selection of the Hearst team on the ground that resident correspondents, not traveling writers, should be honored. But the fight for the Hearst team was led by the chairman of the Advisory Board, Joseph Pulitzer, Jr., and that made the difference. The sons of the old New York newspaper rivals had met once or twice, by chance, but theirs was a bare acquaintance. In any event, the Hearst team won the 1956 International Reporting Prize on its own merit. And it finally disposed of the notion that Hearst entries were unwelcome in the Pulitzer competition."[53] In this connection, it should be pointed out that the nomination had not been sent in by the publishing house itself, but by a group of five persons, among them Basil L. Walters, executive editor, *Chicago Daily News,* who remarked in his letter accompanying the nomination of the Hearst team: "These men . . . did an outstanding job in reporting from Russia . . . Their dispatches appeared in a rival newspaper in Chicago. I was sorry about this but I was so impressed that I wrote to Mr. Hearst at the time complimenting him on the excellence of the enterprise and of the job being done. I am now formalizing that compliment by nominating the Russian series and its authors for the highest award in Journalism."[54] And Lee Hills, executive editor of the *Detroit Free Press*, had explained in a supplement to his nomination: "The reports from Russia were an exceptional example of news enterprise at a crucial turning point in the history of the Communist regime . . ."[55] It became apparent in the following years that the reports from the Soviet Union as from the other Eastern European countries had a certain fascination for the Pulitzer Prize jurors and the Advisory Board.

Another critical study of the International Press Institute about the governmental restric-

---

[50] John R. Herbert/Ralph McGill: Report of the Committee on International Reporting to the Board, New York, March 12, 1956, pp. 1 f. (PPO).
[51] Advisory Board on the Pulitzer Prizes (Ed.): The Pulitzer Prizes, 1917–1977, op. cit., p. 28.
[52] Cf. Don Carlos Seitz: Joseph Pulitzer. His Life and Letters, op. cit., pp. 210 ff.; Ferdinand Lundberg: Imperial Hearst. A Social Biography, New York: Equinox Cooperative Press, 1936, pp. 55 ff.
[53] John Hohenberg: The Pulitzer Prizes, op. cit., p. 247.
[54] Letter from Basil L. Walters, Knight Newspapers, Inc., Chicago Daily News, to the Secretary of the Advisory Board, Pulitzer Prizes (New York), January 24, 1956 (PPO).
[55] Letter from Lee Hills, Executive Editor, The Detroit Free Press (Detroit, Mich.) to the Secretary of the Advisory Board, Pulitzer Prizes (New York), January 24, 1956 (PPO).

> **CHICAGO DAILY NEWS**
> 400 WEST MADISON STREET
> CHICAGO 6, ILLINOIS
>
> January 24, 1956
>
> Secretary of The Advisory Board,
> Pulitzer Prizes in Journalism and Letters,
> 501 Journalism Building,
> Columbia University,
> New York 27, N. Y.
>
> ATTENTION: Mr. John Hohenberg
>
> Dear Sir:
>
> May I nominate William Randolph Hearst, Jr., Joseph Kingsbury Smith and Frank Conniff for consideration in Category 5 of the Pulitzer Prizes in Journalism in 1955.
>
> These men, working as a team, did an outstanding job in reporting from Russia in January and February 1955.
>
> Their dispatches appeared in a rival newspaper in Chicago.
>
> I was sorry about this but I was so impressed that I wrote to Mr. Hearst at the time complimenting the excellence of the enterprise and of the job being done.
>
> I am now formalizing that compliment by nominating the Russian series and its authors for the highest award in Journalism.
>
> Sincerely,
>
> *Basil L. Walters*
>
> Basil L. Walters
> Executive Editor
> Knight Newspapers, Inc.

Accompanying Letter for a Nomination in 1956

tions of journalistic activity in some countries[56] having aroused great interest in the 1955/56 period, all journalistic work done under aggravated conditions had to receive a certain bonus of attention – not only in the view of the Pulitzer Prize jurors. Another result was intensified occupation, in American press research, with the problems of the foreign correspondents.

---

[56] Cf. International Press Institute: Government Pressures on the Press, Zurich: The International Press Institute, 1955, pp. 115 ff.

Besides a study based on interviews with about 250 foreign correspondents in the U.S.A.,[57] an examination of the then about 450 full-time American correspondents abroad was performed, testing, among other things, their grade of professionalisation. "In general," the report states, "the foreign correspondents surveyed were a fairly seasoned group of news gatherers. More than nine-tenths had over five years of newspaper experience ... There was no respondent among the group who estimated his weekly output at fewer than 1,000 words, and one agency writer calculated his total at 30,000 words a week."[58] These quantitative indications of the output of foreign correspondents automatically raise the question concerning the quality of foreign correspondence. After all, this group as a whole consisted of potential competitors for a Pulitzer Prize in International Reporting. Regarding source quality and thus authenticity[59] of foreign news in American media, one must, as in other countries, start out from certain differences in standards.

When in 1957 the Pulitzer Prize for International Reporting was given to Russell Jones of the *United Press* "for his excellent and sustained coverage of the Hungarian revolt against Communist domination, during which he worked at great personal risk within Russian-held Budapest and gave front-line eyewitness reports of the ruthless Soviet repression of the Hungarian people,"[60] this was a decision of the Board. The jury, however, had ranked Ben H. Bagdikian of the *Providence Journal Bulletin* first in front of Russell Jones of *UPI* and J. A. Livingston of the *Philadelphia Bulletin*. Jones had achieved his second place, "(1.) because he was the only other newspaperman who did stay throughout the fighting, and (2.), because his vivid writing gave the reader the impression of being in on the brawl. Because of the difficulty that he must have had in filling his dispatches after the Russians had reinstated control we feel this was a distinct journalistic coup."[61] The *United Press,* Hohenberg writes, "having ended its boycott of the Pulitzer Prizes with the advent of the new directorate for the awards, promptly nominated Jones for the International Reporting Award of 1957 and he won it – the first Pulitzer honor for the wire service."[62] Here, too, one can only speculate whether the jurors and the Advisory Board were influenced by the first application for an award to UP, or whether it was the quality of the story alone that was decisive for the award. Incidentally, a member of the jury responsible for the preliminary selection and ranking of the competitors for the International Reporting award in 1957 was Herbert Bayard Swope,[63] who had won the first Pulitzer Prize for Reporting for his dispatches from Germany during World War I, exactly four decades ago.[64]

---

[57] Cf. Donald A. Lambert: Foreign Correspondents Covering the United States, in: *Journalism Quarterly* (Minneapolis, Minn.), Vol. 33/No. 3, Summer 1956, pp. 349 ff.

[58] J. William Maxwell: U.S. Correspondents Abroad – A Study of Backgrounds, in: *Journalism Quarterly* (Minneapolis, Minn), Vol. 33/No. 3, Summer 1956, p. 348.

[59] Cf. Wilbur Schramm: Quality in Mass Communications, in: John C. Merril/Ralph D. Barney (Eds.): Ethics in the Press. Readings in Mass Media Morality, New York: Hastings House, Publishers, 1975, pp. 37 ff.

[60] Advisory Board on the Pulitzer Prizes (Ed.): The Pulitzer Prizes, 1917–1977, op. cit., p. 28.

[61] Alan Hathway/Jenkin Lloyd Jones: Report of the team judging International Reporting, New York, March 12, 1957, p. 1 (PPO).

[62] John Hohenberg: The Pulitzer Prizes, op. cit., p. 247.

[63] Cf. the listing "Pulitzer Prize Jurors," for 1957 (PPO).

[64] For details cf. Erika J. Fischer/Heinz-D. Fischer: American Reporter at the International Political Stage. Herbert Bayard Swope and his Pulitzer Prize-winning articles from Germany in 1916, Bochum: Studienverlag Dr. N. Brockmeyer, 1982.

[Source: Editor & Publisher (New York, N.Y.), Vol. 90/No. 20, May 11, 1957, p. 3.]

The fortieth anniversary of the foundation of the Pulitzer Prizes, in the middle of 1957, was chosen by Joseph Pulitzer, Jr., the grandson of the donor of the prize, as an occasion for a general expression of thanks to the New York institution administering the prize. "On this anniversary," he explained, "congratulations are in order for Columbia University and the University's Trustees for the successful administration of the prizes for – forty years; to the Advisory Board on the Pulitzer Prizes for its key role in having recommended every prize winner to the Trustees during these four decades, and to the judges of the various juries and members of the Columbia Faculty for the work they have done to maintain and extend the influence of the awards. To all these who have served so selflessly for an ideal, may I gratefully express my thanks."[65] And the president of Columbia University and Advisory Board member ex officio, Grayson Kirk, underlined on this occasion the high value of the Pulitzer Prize Collection as a source. "It has been the cherished responsibility of the Libraries through the years," he wrote, "to preserve this unique compilation of records in the fields of American letters and in journalism, music, and art. The Graduate School of Journalism and the University Libraries have thus formed an effective partnership in establishing for the Pulitzer Prizes a permanent place in the history of our culture. In years to come I hope we shall be able to make the records more and more a significant and useful part of the American treasure house."[66]

At the time of the anniversary, the Advisory Board consisted – besides the president of the university, Grayson Kirk – of the following persons: Barry Bingham, the *Courier-Journal* (Louisville, Ky.); Hodding Carter, the *Delta Democrat-Times* (Greenville, Miss.); Turner Catledge, *The New York Times;* Norman Chandler, *Los Angeles Times;* Robert Choate, the *Boston Herald* (Boston Mass.); Gardiner Cowles, Cowles Magazines (New York, N. Y.); J. D. Ferguson, the *Milwaukee Journal* (Milwaukee, Wis.); John S. Knight, Knight Newspapers (Chicago, Ill.); Benjamin M. McKelway, the *Evening Star* (Washington D. C.); Paul Miller, Gannett Newspapers (Rochester, N. Y.); Joseph Pulitzer, Jr., *St. Louis Post-Dispatch,* (St. Louis, Mo.); Louis B. Seltzer, the *Cleveland Press* (Cleveland, Oh.), and John Hohenberg, Columbia University (New York, N. Y.), in his quality as the secretary of the Advisory Board on the Pulitzer Prizes.[67] John Herbert, who had belonged to the jurors in the International Reporting category of the Pulitzer Prizes the year before[68] and was the editor of the Quincy *Patriot-Ledger* in Quincy, Massachusetts, had this to say on the occassion of the fortieth anniversary of the awards, especially about the problems connected with the internationally-oriented Pulitzer Prizes:

"While a developing global sensitivity on the part of newspaper readers is all to the good," Herbert explained, "it poses a problem for Pulitzer Prize judges in the field of international reporting. When Joseph Pulitzer set up the newspaper awards forty years ago, foreign news coverage was pretty much the exclusive field of the foreign correspondents . . . Today foreign correspondents no longer have overseas news beats as their exclusive areas. News stories and feature material are being written from all sections of the world by traveling

---

[65] Joseph Pulitzer, Jr.: The Fortieth Anniversary of the Pulitzer Prizes, in: *Columbia Library Columns* (New York, N. Y.), Vol. VI/No. 3, May 1957, p. 3.
[66] Ibid., p. 4.
[67] Ibid.
[68] Cf. the listing "Pulitzer Prize Jurors," for 1956 (PPO).

The Pulitzer Family in 1954

The painted portrait in the background is of Joseph Pulitzer, who established the Prizes which bear his name. In the foreground are his son Joseph, the late publisher of the *St. Louis Post-Dispatch*, Joseph Pulitzer IV, and Joseph Pulitzer, Jr.

members of newspaper staffs —publishers or editors or reporters; even college professors with proper credentials from newspapers have served as correspondents during trips to Europe. A recent tabulation shows that 150 American newspaper, radio, and news agency reporters were at the Hungarian border during the 1956 revolt period. Many of these reporters were sent from newspapers not having their own foreign service and not in the habit of staffing overseas news. But here was a dramatic, human interest story and its location was not deterrent to staff coverage. As the world shrinks, this tendency toward home town coverage of global events will increase. This, in turn, creates problems for adequate judging of entries submitted to the international news category. For instance, should recognition be given to a hard-working reporter in Bonn who writes excellent, intelligent stories in providing day to day coverage of this critical area – or should the award go to an American newspaper publisher on a flying trip to Europe who happens to get an interview with a top Russian leader?"[69]

Herbert's last remark in his description of the problems connected with the International Reporting award quite plainly alluded to the prize given – with his own assistance as a juror – to William Randolph Hearst, Kingsbury Smith, and Frank Conniff in 1956, for interviews with leading representatives of the Soviet Union.[70] It is not known whether there had been controversial opinions about the submitted nominations among the jury members when the award was made. John R. Herbert, however, seems to have drawn certain conclusions from the selection problem, which caused him – within the article quoted above – to propose some reforms. "More realistically," he suggested, "shouldn't there be several categories for international coverage just as there are for domestic news so that the correspondent doing day to day work and the touring editor or publisher can get equal recognition for jobs well done? Just as a suggestion, here is a possible basis for recognition of good reporting in the international category: (1.) an award for distinguished correspondence by a foreign correspondent actually stationed overseas; (2.) an award for distinguished correspondence by a newspaperman visiting an area or areas. This would include the traveling editor or reporter and also the reporter who might be sent into an area to do a special story; (3.) an award for the newspaper making the best effort during the year to keep its readers informed of the international scene. In order to prevent larger newspapers from consistently winning this award, it might be possible to select one newspaper under 100,000 circulation and a second with more than 100,000 ciruclation. Frankly," Herbert added to his plea, "interest in this problem should be concerned primarily with increasing the number of entries in the international category."[71]

Finally, Herbert presented in his article the reasons which had induced him to submit these propositions. "Entires for international awards," he wrote somewhat regretfully, "come mostly from the East coast and the concentration of entries is from New York and Washington. The paucity of entries is most unfortunate at a time when more newspapers the nation over are carrying more foreign news than ever before (or should be!). A sharper definition of the International Reporting category by broadening the base for entries could stimulate new interest in this field."[72] It is not known wheter these suggestions were discussed in any way by the Advisory Board on the Pulitzer Prizes. If, however, a serious examination took place, it most probably led to the conclusion that – however right the analysis of the basic dilemma in the International Reporting category – the submitted propositions would have meant a considerable additional expenditure during the preliminary examination of the entries; moreover, the three internationally oriented prizes Herbert had in mind would not allow a completely unequivocal classification, as too many borderline cases would remain.

---

[69] John R. Herbert: International Reporting Awards, in: *Columbia Library Columns* (New York, N.Y.) Vol. VI/No. 3, May, 1957, pp. 20, 22.
[70] Cf. Advisory Board on the Pulitzer Prizes (Ed.): The Pulitzer Prizes, 1917–1977, op. cit., p. 28.
[71] John R. Herbert: International Reporting Awards, op. cit., pp. 22 f.
[72] Ibid., p. 23.

Heinz-Dietrich Fischer

When John Herbert again acted as a juror in the internationally oriented category in 1958,[73] his initiative seems to have been put *ad acta,* as there still existed an undivided category for International Reporting. Herbert Bayard Swope, the 1917 prizewinner who only the year before had acted as a member of the international jury, was at this time already suffering from a disease that threatened his life and that finally finished it on June 20, 1958.[74] Only a short time before, he had benevolently taken notice of the jury decision for the 1958 awarding term from his sick-bed, sending several letters of approval.[75]

Among the 32 nominations presented to the jury, eight of them entering the short list,[76] the *New York Times,* finally, was elected prize-winner "for its distinguished coverage of foreign news, which was characterized by admirable initiative, continuity and high quality during the year" of 1957.[77] The newspaper, the jury report gave as a reason for the decision, "should be recognized for distinguished coverage of foreign news, with special mention, in the opinion of the jurors, being accorded to: Herbert L. Mathews, for his daring and dramatic interviews with Fidel Castro, leader of the Cuban revolt; Turner Catledge and James Reston, for their lengthy, perceptive, and significant interviews with Nikita S. Khrushchev; Harrison Salisbury, for his reporting from Albania, Bulgaria, and Rumania – countries behind the Iron Curtain and beyond penetration by American newspapermen in routine operations; Sidney L. Gruson, for his reporting from Poland, which included the incredible scoop from Warsaw on June 12, and the two speeches of Mao Tse-tung in Peiping in February in which the Chinese leader admitted the liquidation of 800,000 people, outlined his views on self-criticism of the regime, on population controls needed, and criticized the Russian intervention in Hungary. But the *Times'* coverage was distinguished as much by its consistency and completeness as by its peaks. Such *Times* correspondents as William J. Jorden and Max Frankel in Moscow, Elie Abel and John MacCormac in the 'iron curtain' countries, and A. M. Rosenthal in India and southeast Asia provided readers with outstanding day-by-day coverage. Since 1942," the jury report continues, "awards for international reporting have been made to individuals. The rules stipulate that this award shall be 'for a distinguished example of reporting of international affairs.' On the basis of the entries which we have reviewed this year, it is our recommendation that the Pulitzer Prize for international reporting be given to the *New York Times.*"[78]

Despite this group award the reasons given for the prize reflect the influence of the reporting about a number of countries in Eastern Europe on the evaluation of the Pulitzer Prize committees. A study of the International Press Institute published in that period about the situation of the press in countries under authoritarian governments also focused on the communication control existing in some countries and its bearing on the freedom of the

---

[73] Cf. the listing, "Pulitzer Prize Jurors," for 1958 (PPO).
[74] Alfred Allan Lewis: Man of the 'World.' Herbert Bayard Swope – A Charmed Life of Pulitzer Prizes, Poker and Politics, Indianapolis – New York: The Bobbs-Merrill Company, 1978, p. 287.
[75] Cf. letters from Herbert Bayard Swope (New York, N. Y.) to Dean Edward W. Barrett (Columbia University), Relman Morin (The Associated Press), and Arthur Hays Sulzberger (The New York Times) of May 7, 1958, Herbert Bayard Swope Archive at Boston University (HBSA).
[76] Cf. Mort Stern/John A. Herbert/William P. Steven: Report of the Jurors on International Reporting, New York, March 11, 1958, p. 1 (PPO).
[77] Advisory Board on the Pulitzer Prizes (Ed.): The Pulitzer Prizes, 1917–1977, op. cit., p. 28.
[78] Mort Stern/John A. Herbert/William P. Steven: Report ..., op. cit., pp. 1 ff. (PPO).

The New York Times
Times Square

ARTHUR HAYS SULZBERGER
PUBLISHER

May 8, 1958

Dear Herbert:

You're always attentive and thoughtful. I thank you for your note of the seventh about the Pulitzer Prize.

All the best.

Faithfully yours,

Mr. Herbert Bayard Swope
745 Fifth Avenue
New York 22, New York

L

Columbia University in the City of New York
NEW YORK 27, N.Y.
GRADUATE SCHOOL OF JOURNALISM
OFFICE OF THE DEAN

May 13, 1958

Mr. Herbert B. Swope
745 Fifth Avenue
New York 22, New York

Dear Mr. Swope:

I am sure the Pulitzer Board, as well as Grayson Kirk, John Hohenberg and others, will appreciate your good note about the awards. I share your views that they were sound and discriminating.

Do let us see you some time.

All good wishes.

Cordially,

Edward W. Barrett

Letters to Herbert Bayard Swope in Answer to his Approval of the 1958 Pulitzer Prize Winner foreign correspondents stationed there to do their research and reporting. "The aim of this survey," the IPI declared in the introduction to the study, "is to give an account of the position of the press under all the authoritarian regimes existing since the Second World War. No enterprise of this kind has previously been attempted. It appears all the more opportune to fill this gap . . . in view of the fortieth anniversary of the Soviet regime in the U.S.S.R., the thirtieth anniversary of the Salazar regime in Portugal, the twentieth anniversary of Franco's rule in Spain, and the tenth year of the Peoples' Democracies of Eastern Europe."[79] While the study, in the main, referred to the Soviet Union, the Chinese People's Republic, Rumania, Czechoslovakia, Eastern Germany, Hungary, Poland, and Yugoslavia among the countries under Communist rule, "other authoritarian countries" were examined, too, especially Spain, Portugal, Latin America, Egypt and the Far East.[80] The IPI study also mentioned Cuba, where "constitutional guarantees (including Art. 33 on freedom of the press) were suspended in some provinces at the end of 1956 after the landing of Fidel Castro and his rebels. "From this date", the study goes on, "censorship has been applied for successive periods of 45 days, with varying periods of respite in between, as regularly as if impelled by clockwork. President Fulgencio Batista often assured representatives of IAPA (Inter-American Press Association) who have protested against these suppressions of guarantees that they are only due to the rebellion which had in fact dragged on for several years until the sudden fall of the Cuban strongman at the end of 1958."[81]

When the Advisory Board on the Pulitzer Prizes was making the 1959 award for International Reporting, pre-eminence was given to the situation of Cuba during the preceding year. The prize went to Joseph Martin and Philip Santora of the New York *Daily News* "for their exclusive series of articles disclosing the brutality of the Batista government in Cuba long before its downfall and forecasting the triumph of the revolutionary party led by Fidel Castro."[82] The jury, which obviously ranked its proposals based on a sort of classification by points for the first time, had placed a second nomination for the newspaper *Daily News*, and not for the two journalists finally honored, Martin and Santora.[83] The Advisory Board, however, changed not only the ranking on the list of recommendations, but it gave the prize to Martin and Santora and thus avoided the bestowal of a second honor on a newspaper within two years. Thus, Joseph Martin and Philip Santora were chosen prize-winners for their reports about Cuba written in teamwork, although they had not been nominated as candidates personally.[84] Not the least reason may have been the extraordinary working conditions under which Martin and Santora had to do their job.

"The series of articles submitted here," the newspaper's accompanying letter for the nomination of the Cuba articles at the end of January, 1959, reads, "might have been written a few short weeks ago instead of in April, 1958, when most people in the United States and

---

[79] International Press Institute: The Press in Authoritarian Countries, Zurich: The International Press Institute, 1959, p. 7.
[80] Ibid., p. 5.
[81] Ibid., p. 173.
[82] Advisory Board on the Pulitzer Prizes (Ed.): The Pulitzer Prizes, 1917–1977, op. cit., p. 28.
[83] Cf. Arthur C. Deck/Ben Maidenburg/John T. O'Rourke: Report of the jury of the International Reporting award, New York, March 12, 1959, p. 1 (PPO).
[84] Cf. the entry which only contains the nomination of the New York *Daily News*, signed by G. R. Shand, Managing editor of that newspaper (PPO).

elsewhere thought of Fulgencio Batista as a benevolent dictator. News reporters Philip Martin and Joseph Santora began their search for the truth behind the Batista regime early in March, 1958. They sought out underground contacts in Washington, Miami and New York. They spent weeks sifting facts from propaganda in Havana, Guanavo Beach and elsewhere in Cuba. During their stay in Havana, they were followed by Security Intelligence Police, their rooms were searched, their telephones tapped. Atrocity pictures – more than 200 of them – were obtained from secret sources and these had to be smuggled out. Martin and Santora were forced to memorize names, addresses, and telephone numbers so that if they were stopped and searched, the lives of these contacts would not be forfeited. Each point they covered in their series . . . has been authenticated by recent stories from Cuba. They predicted Manuelo Urrutia would head the provisional government. They stated flatly that Fidel Castro, while an excellent field chieftain, lacked certain qualities of statesmanship . . . The articles evoked widespread interest at the time they were published although in some quarters they were believed too incredible to be true. It was the first time that the real story behind the Batista dictatorship was made known to the American people."[85] With the award for the Cuba reporting, for the first time – leaving aside the U.S. – related prizes for Arthur Krock (1935, 1938) and the prize for Austin Wehrwein's coverage of Canadian problems (1953) – the Pulitzer Prizes focused on a foreign trouble spot that was close to home.

It is open to question, however, how fast and how thoroughly the Cuban story of Martin and Santora really spread among the American readership. For the newspaper the reports had been published in did not pass for a quality paper,[86] but was a New York popular paper in tabloid format. Thus, it would be interesting to find out which integral or condensed copies of these texts appeared in other papers. Without going into specific problems of selection and distribution research in detail,[87] an essay should be mentioned that was published in 1959 and deals with the problems of condensation or distortion of reports by foreign correspondents – expecially of agency correspondents: "Between the correspondent on the scene of a foreign news story and the receiver in his home there is an international chain of intermediaries who edit, rewrite, cut or eliminate . . . Communication research thus far has shed relatively little light on the operations of the intermediary communicators . . . Logical avenues of inquiry would include their career patterns, frames of reference, values and other characteristics, and how these factors influence the form and content of the news in various stages of its flow. Field and experimental methods might be used to test such hypotheses as these: International news stories tend to become more readable as they pass through the hands of successive intermediaries. A process of 'leveling, sharpening, and assimilation' takes place as the stories move through the international relay system. The more stages the intermediary communicator is removed from a news event, the less personal concern he feels about it and the more he thinks of it in terms of its 'marketability' to editors and readers."[88]

[85] Daily News: Cuba summary, part of the Pulitzer Prize-winning entry of the *Daily News,* New York, January 30, 1959 (PPO).
[86] Cf. Heinz-Dietrich Fischer: Die großen Zeitungen. Porträts der Weltpresse, Munich: Deutscher Taschenbuch Verlag, 1965; John C. Merrill: The Elite Press. Great Newspapers of the World, New York–Toronto–London: Pitman Publishing Corp., 1968.
[87] Cf. Alfred C. Lugert: Auslandskorrespondenten im internationalen Kommunikationssystem. Eine Kommunikator-Studie, Munich: Verlag Dokumentation, 1974, pp. 17 ff.
[88] John T. McNelly: Intermediary Communicators in the International Flow of News, in: *Journalism Quarterly* (Minneapolis, Minn.), Vol. 36/No. 1 (Winter 1959), pp. 24 ff.

Intermediary Communicators in Flow of News

FIGURE

This is a schematic representation of the step-by-step flow—through a series of gatekeepers, or intermediary communicators—of an international news story. A newsworthy event (E) comes to the attention of a foreign correspondent (C_1), who writes a story about it (S). The story goes to a regional bureau where an editor or rewriteman (C_2) may cut the story down (S') for transmission to the news agency's central bureau. There a deskman (C_3) may combine it with a related story (S_a) from another country. The resulting story (S'') goes to a national or state bureau where another deskman (C_4) prunes it down (S''') and relays it to the telegraph editor of a newspaper or to a radio or television news editor (C_5 in this example). He slashes it still further (S'''') and passes it on to the reader or listener (R). The receiver, if he chooses to read or listen to it, may be interested enough to pass on his oral version of the story (S-R) to family, friends or associates (R_1, R_2, etc.). Length of arrow represents length of story in each stage of its journey as determined by the intermediary communicators. Feedback, represented by broken lines, is infrequent and delayed—except in the case of direct feedback to the receiver from a person to whom he tells the story.

Graphic Design of a Typical Transmission Process of Foreign News

[*Source:* John T. McNelly: Intermediary Communicators in the International Flow of News, in: ›Journalism Quarterly‹ (Minneapolis, Minn.), Vol. 36/No. 1, Winter 1959, p. 25.]

The same exact research journalism exemplified by the reporting about Cuba, which had so much impressed the Advisory Board, was to be honored again in 1960 when A. M. Rosenthal, "one of a group of correspondents who brought the *New York Times* the 1958 Pulitzer Prize for International Reporting, won his own award in 1960 for his Polish dispatches, plus the additional material about the country that appeared in 1959 following his expulsion."[89] The official prize dealt with the quality of Rosenthal's dispatches in detail, not

---
[89] John Hohenberg: The Pulitzer Prizes, op. cit., p. 248.

only attesting him "perceptive and authoritative reporting from Poland," but adding this complement: "Mr. Rosenthal's subsequent expulsion from the country was attributed by Polish government spokesmen to the depth of his reporting Polish affairs, there being no accusation of false reporting."[90] The bestowal of the prize on Rosenthal obviously was not due to the vote of the 1960 International Reporting jury, but to a decision of the Advisory Board: Three out of 57 entries submitted (20 of them dealing "with Khrushchev, Russia, Russia–Poland or Russia–Berlin") were on the jury's final list, but Rosenthal was not among them.[91] But the jurors were not unanimous in their votes. While George B. Minot and Everest P. Derthick suggested Harrison E. Salisbury for the prize, Alan Hathway voted for Jules DuBois in his minority report. John Hohenberg added to the jury reports in his quality as Administrator of the Pulitzer Prizes the following handwritten "Secretary's Note": "The International Jury delivered three separate reports which speak for themselves."[92] Thus, the Advisory Board had to make a final decision in the spring of 1960, and it fell to Rosenthal.[93]

With its 1960 prize decision, the Advisory Board again had featured the Eastern Europe coverage by American neswpapers and agencies, which especially in the period of the Cold War was considered pre-eminent. In the following term, however, the awarding committees tried hard to take into consideration reports from other regions, too. If the prize for Will Barber in the mid-thirties, which was a special case, the author having received the international Pulitzer Prize for his reports from Ethiopia posthumously,[94] is left aside, no other journalist since then had won an award for reporting from African countries. "The reverberations of the East-West conflict," Hohenberg writes, "produced uprisings in Africa, Asia, and Latin-America as well as in Eastern Europe, all of them tough jobs for American correspondents. In the Congo, once the panicky Belgians withdrew in 1960 and chaotic fighting spread through the unhappy land, the veteran Lynn Heinzerling of the *Associated Press* so distinguished himself with his cool and accurate reporting that he won the Pulitzer Prize for foreign reporting in 1961."[95] The Pulitzer Prize jury had to select from no less than 61 entries in the international category and placed a journalist from the *Chicago Daily News* (for his "variety of coverage") together with AP correspondent Lynn Heinzerling at the top its list, ranking both equally. The jury report described Heinzerling's reports as an "outstanding example of pioneer reporting in the Congo. Mr. Heinzerling was there in the early days before the story had taken form and conditions of reporting were extraordinarily difficult."[96] As his entry also contained reports about other African countries, the Advisory Board included in its laudation, beside the Congo correspondence, also Heinzerling's "keen analysis of events in other parts of Africa."[97]

---

[90] Advisory Board on the Pulitzer Prizes (Ed.): The Pulitzer Prizes, 1917–1977, op. cit., p. 28.
[91] Alan Hathway/George E. Minot/Ernest P. Derthick: Reports of the Jurors, International Reporting award, New York, March 14, 1960, 6 pp.
[92] Ibid.
[93] For details cf. John Hohenberg: The Pulitzer Prizes, op. cit., p. 248.
[94] Cf. Advisory Board on the Pulitzer Prizes (Ed.): The Pulitzer Prizes, 1917–1977, op. cit., pp. 22 ff., 26 ff.
[95] John Hohenberg: The Pulitzer Prizes, op. cit., p. 248.
[96] Emmett Dedmon/Frank F. Orr/Ralph E. McGill: Report of the International Reporting jury for 1961, New York, undated, (March, 1961) p. 1 (PPO).
[97] Advisory Board on the Pulitzer Prizes (Ed.): The Pulitzer Prizes, 1917–1977, op. cit., p. 28.

Heinz-Dietrich Fischer

The Congo crisis was a sort of compensatory theater of war for the permanent East-West conflict; but in the early sixties, the Soviet Union again moved into the range of vision of the Pulitzer Prize committees. "Soon after Khrushchev's assumption of the Soviet premiership," Hohenberg reports about the trifling changes in the foreign press corps accredited in Moscow, "a few more foreign correspondents were permitted to enter the Soviet Union. But life still did not change materially for independent, foreign journalists behind the Iron Curtain . . . More than a score of Western correspondents, including seventeen Americans, were now in Moscow. In a gesture toward the foreign press, indicative of the lessons Khrushchev had learned abroad, the Soviet Union ended its formal censorship in March, 1961, and permitted foreign correspondents a limited amount of editorial discretion and travel. Those who interpreted this action to mean that they could do as they pleased soon discovered their error. Two West Germans and a Frenchman were expelled. Another German was barred for 'systematic slander of Soviet leaders' . . . The effect of the lifting of censorship was to place the burden entirely on the correpondent. A few were able to produce exclusive stories of a mild nature, the result either of Soviet favoritism or minimal enterprise. But there was no indication of when the Russians would permit the Western correspondents to witness a missile shot or an atomic test. 'Moscow,' concluded Earl J. Johnson, the editor of UPI, 'is no post for the hip-shooting cowboys of journalism.' The public confirmation of the ideological clash between the Soviet Union and Red China at the 22nd Congress of the Soviet's Communist Party[98] had to be covered by the foreign press corps from the basement. The correspondents were admitted to the first two sessions only and had to take the rest from the usual official Soviet sources,"[99] mainly the official news agency *TASS*.[100]

Beside *New York Times* veteran Harrison E. Salisbury, who had been expelled from the U.S.S.R. because of his well researched reports in 1954 and who in the following year won the Pulitzer Prize for International Reporting,[101] another journalist had become prominent for his analysis of the situation in the Soviet Union. He was not a foreign correspondent, but the distinguished columnist of the *New York Herald-Tribune* Walter Lippmann, who enjoyed considerable prestige in the U.S.S.R. as well and even had, to a certain extent, the confidence of some of its leaders, especially Khrushchev. Having already been received by Khrushchev for a two-hour interview in 1958, Lippmann again traveled to the U.S.S.R. in the spring of 1961 in order to have another talk with the most powerful man in the Soviet Union. "On this, our second visit," Lippmann reports about the journey, "my wife and I were taken on a long journey by plane and auto to Mr. Khrushchev's country place in Sochi on the Black Sea. Before we left Moscow, accompanied by two interpreters and an official of the Press Department, there was much mystery about all the details of the coming visit, such as when and where we were to see the great man. In fact, as it turned out, he had no other

---

[98] Cf. Hansjürgen Koschwitz: Pressepolitik und Parteijournalismus in der UdSSR und der Volksrepublik China, Düsseldorf: Bertelsmann Universitätsverlag, 1971, pp. 221 ff.; cf. also James W. Markham: Voices of the Red Giants. Communications in Russia and China, Ames/Iowa: The Iowa State University Press, 1967, pp. 146 ff.

[99] John Hohenberg: Foreign Correspondence, op. cit., pp. 406, 411 f.

[100] Cf. Theodore E. Kruglak: The two Faces of Tass, Minneapolis, Minn.: University of Minnesota Press, 1962, pp. 214 ff.

[101] Cf. Harrison E. Salisbury: An American in Russia, New York: Harper & Brothers, 1955, p. XI; Harrison E. Salisbury: A New Russia?, New York: Harper & Row, Publishers, 1962, pp. 1–11.

Columbia University
in the City of New York

NOMINATION FOR A PULITZER PRIZE IN JOURNALISM
To be filed with the Secretary of the Advisory Board on or before February 1

NOMINATION OF **Walter Lippmann**
(name in full of competitor)

HOME ADDRESS OF NOMINEE **3525 Woodley Rd., N.W., Washington 7, D.C.**

NOMINEE'S PRESENT OCCUPATION (if an individual) **Special writer for the Herald-Tribune**

Check Pulitzer Prize in Journalism for which nomination is made.

	Cross Here
1. For disinterested and meritorious public service rendered by a United States newspaper, published daily, Sunday or at least once a week, during the year, a gold medal.	1
2. For a distinguished example of local reporting in a United States newspaper, published daily, Sunday or at least once a week, during the year, the test being the quality of local news stories written under the pressure of edition time, One thousand dollars ($1,000).	2
3. For a distinguished example of local reporting in a United States newspaper, published daily, Sunday or at least once a week, during the year, in which the pressure of edition time is not a factor, written in the form of a single article or a series, due consideration being given to the initiative and resourcefulness and to the constructive purpose of the writer, One thousand dollars ($1,000).	3
4. For a distinguished example of reporting of national affairs in a United States newspaper, published daily, Sunday or at least once a week, during the year, One thousand dollars ($1,000).	4
5. For a distinguished example of reporting of international affairs, including United Nations correspondence, in a United States newspaper, published daily, Sunday or at least once a week, during the year, One thousand dollars ($1,000).	5 X
6. For distinguished editorial writing in a United States newspaper, published daily, Sunday or at least once a week, during the year, the test of excellence being clearness of style, moral purpose, sound reasoning, and power to influence public opinion in what the writer conceives to be the right direction, due account being taken of the whole volume of the editorial writer's work during the year, One thousand dollars ($1,000).	6
7. For a distinguished example of a cartoonist's work in a United States newspaper, published daily, Sunday or at least once a week, during the year, the determining qualities being that the cartoon shall embody an idea made clearly apparent, shall show good drawing and striking pictorial effect, and shall be intended to be helpful to some commendable cause of public importance, due account being taken of the whole volume of the artist's work during the year, One thousand dollars ($1,000).	7
8. For an outstanding example of news photography as exemplified by a news photograph or photographs in a United States newspaper, published daily, Sunday or at least once a week, during the year, One thousand dollars ($1,000). (This prize is open to amateurs as well as to photographers regularly employed by newspapers, press associations or syndicates.)	8

(Please check) Biography submitted **X**   Picture submitted **X**

Signature of person making nomination _____

Address **c/o New York Herald-Tribune**
230 West 41 St., New York 36

(Please see reverse side of this nomination form for Plan for Award of Pulitzer Prizes in Journalism and description of required exhibits and supporting material.)

Example of a Nomination Form of 1962

appointments after half past eleven in the morning, when he met us in the pinewoods near the entrance of his place . . ."[102]

The talks between Lippmann and Khrushchev, lasting eight hours, dealt with topics like nuclear weapons, disarmament, Cuba, China, Laos, Germany, and the United Nations. When the series of interview articles started in the *New York Herald-Tribune* on April 17, 1961, it was reprinted in about 450 papers all over the world. "What made Lippmann's articles required reading in foreign ministries," a Lippmann biographer states, "was Khrushchev's frankness on the Berlin issue."[103] When, in 1962, Lippmann was awarded the Pulitzer Prize for International Reporting "for his 1961 interview with Soviet Premier Krhushchev, as illustrative of Mr. Lippmann's long and distinguished contribution to American journalism,"[104] this was a kind of second Pulitzer award for the prominent journalist. In 1958, the Advisory Board on the Pulitzer Prizes had awarded him a "special citation" "for the wisdom, perception and high sense of responsibility with which he has commented for many years on national and international affairs."[105]

The reason why the honors for Lippmann by the Pulitzer Prize committees took place at such a late stage of his life is explained by John Hohenberg: During his long time on the Pulitzer paper *The World* Lippmann "refused to permit himself to be nominated and wouldn't even let himself be considered for membership in the Advisory Board . . . At least three times while he was on the *World,* Lippmann disqualified himself from consideration for a prize. And even while he was on the *New York Herald Tribune* thereafter, he asked Ralph Pulitzer not to nominate him. When Lippmann finally did win a Pulitzer special citation and a Pulitzer Prize, the Pulitzer papers and Pulitzer family had no dominant role in process."[106] And in another passage Hohenberg remarks about the bestowal of the Pulitzer Prize on Lippmann for his interview with Khrushchev: "Essentially, the interview merely provided a peg for the long overdue recognition of Lippmann's superior contribution to American journalism."[107] No wonder the jury's vote was unanimous: "It is the . . . judgement of the four jurors on the International reporting section that the Pulitzer Prize for 1962 in this field should be awarded to Walter Lippmann . . ."[108] The Advisory Board and the Trustees agreed.

Indirectly, the Soviet Union was the subject also of the 1963 Pulitzer Prize for International Reporting. Again, however, as in the case of the award in 1961 to Lynn Heinzerling for his reporting from the Congo, reports about a sort of "secondary war theater" were honored. The problems created by the situation of Cuba had been stressed for the first time in 1959 with the award to Joseph Martin and Philip Santora; now Cuba was to emerge in another connection. "In early October, 1962," Hohenberg states in analysing the genesis of a crisis

---

[102] Walter Lippmann: Khrushchev to Lippmann – Face to Face, in: *New York Herald-Tribune* (New York, N. Y.), Vol. CXXI/No. 41, 774, April 17, 1961, p. 1, col.1.
[103] Ronald Steel: Walter Lippmann and the American Century, Boston–Toronto: Little, Brown and Company, 1980, p. 527.
[104] Advisory Board on the Pulitzer Prizes (Ed.): The Pulitzer Prizes, 1917–1977, op. cit., p. 28.
[105] Ibid., p. 45.
[106] John Hohenberg: The Pulitzer Prizes, op. cit., p. 40.
[107] Ibid., p. 249.
[108] John S. Gillen/Harry Montgomery/William P. Steven/James A. Wechsler: Report of the International Reporting Jury to the Advisory Board, New York, March 8, 1962, p. 1 (PPO).

that was to reach global proportions, "Hal Hendrix of the *Miami News* published a story from his own sources that Russian military experts were building rocket bases in Cuba. The correspondent, however, could obtain no confirmation from official sources. The Kennedy administration had been stressing that it had no objections to purely defensive measures by the Castro regime, but now it took on an air of reticence about the whole business. However, on October 21, . . . the *Washington Post* reported an air of crisis in the capital. The *New York Times* also had information that something was up but didn't publish it after a personal appeal from President Kennedy himself. The Washington Press corps, however, had been alerted. It would have been a dull reporter, indeed, who could not see that there was extraordinary activity in the White House, Defense Department, and State Department. The wires were carrying reports of Army and Air Force movements toward Florida. As a climax to this activity, President Kennedy announced on the night of October 22 in a nationwide TV address that the Soviet Union was building offensive missile and bomber bases in Cuba in violation of its pledges not to do so. He ordered the imposition of a naval air 'quarantine', which was broadly interpreted as a blockade, on all further shipments of offensive weapons to the island."[109]

The *Miami News* nominated its correspondent Hals Hendrix for the 1963 Pulitzer Prize for International Reporting, adding to the entry the following reasons: "Each story was published by the *Miami News* before it appeared in any other paper in the country. With a single exception, each story was first denied comment by the appropriate authorities in Washington only to be confirmed later by the same authorities. The sum of the work . . . is impressive not only because of the accuracy, but also the enterprise of Mr. Hendrix. It would be something of an understatement to say that the usual sources of information for a reporter were not available to the reporter before, during or after the event which has become known as the Cuban crisis . . . Throughout the year, reporter Hendrix has consistently been ahead of the United States newsmen in reporting what was going on inside the island of Cuba."[110] The jurors in the International Reporting category also proved to be rather impressed by the dispatches of Hendrix. "It is the opinion of the members of the jury in this category," the jury report runs, "that the outstanding example of international reporting was submitted by the *Miami News* on behalf of Hal Hendrix. Mr. Hendrix's reports indicated that by hard digging he had confirmed the presence of large numbers of MIG-21s in Cuba days before President Kennedy's speech disclosing the extent of the Russian buildup in Cuba."[111] The Advisory Board unanimously agreed to this recommendation and explained that the honor had been bestowed on Hal Hendrix "for his persistent reporting which revealed, at an early stage, that the Soviet Union was installing missile launching pads in Cuba and sending in large numbers of MIG-21 aircraft."[112]

The 1963 awards ended another phase in the evolution of the internationally oriented Pulitzer Prizes. It includes the greater part of the Cold War period with its various international crises that sometimes – as in the cases of Korea and the Congo – resulted in hot wars.

---

[109] John Hohenberg: Foreign Correspondence, op. cit., p. 423.
[110] William C. Baggs: Summary of Nomination of Hal Hendrix for Pulitzer Prize, Category 5, Miami, Fla. (undated), (PPO).
[111] Arthur R. Bertelson/Howard H. Hays/Eugene S. Pulliam/Paul Schoenstein: Report of the International Award Jury to the Advisory Board, New York, March 8, 1963, p. 1 (PPO).
[112] Advisory Board on the Pulitzer Prizes (Ed.): The Pulitzer Prizes, 1917–1977, op. cit., p. 28.

> **THE TRUSTEES OF COLUMBIA UNIVERSITY**
> IN THE CITY OF NEW YORK
> TO ALL PERSONS TO WHOM THESE PRESENTS MAY COME GREETING
> BE IT KNOWN THAT
>
> LYNN HEINZERLING
>
> has been awarded
>
> THE PULITZER PRIZE IN JOURNALISM
> FOR DISTINGUISHED REPORTING
> OF INTERNATIONAL AFFAIRS
>
> IN ACCORDANCE WITH THE PROVISIONS OF THE STATUTES OF THE UNIVERSITY GOVERNING SUCH AWARD
> IN WITNESS WHEREOF WE HAVE CAUSED THIS CERTIFICATE TO BE SIGNED BY THE PRESIDENT OF THE UNIVERSITY AND OUR CORPORATE SEAL TO BE HERETO AFFIXED IN THE CITY OF NEW YORK ON THE FIRST DAY OF MAY IN THE YEAR OF OUR LORD ONE THOUSAND NINE HUNDRED AND SIXTY ONE
>
> PRESIDENT

Pulitzer Prize Document for the Winner of the International Reporting Award in 1961

The following list contains all prizewinners in the categories Correspondence, International Telegraphic Reporting, and International Reporting from the end of World War II up to the time of the Cuban crisis in the early sixties and the jurors involved:[113]

For Articles from 1946 – Awarded in 1947
Award Winners: Brooks Atkinson, *The New York Times,* New York[114]; Eddy Gilmore, *The Associated Press,* New York[115]
Jury Members (March, 1947):
   Carroll Binder, *The Tribune,* Minneapolis, Minnesota
   Erwin D. Canham, *The Christian Science Monitor,* Boston, Massachusetts
   Marvin H. Creager, *The Milwaukee Journal,* Milwaukee, Wisconsin
   Stephen, C. Noland, *The Indianapolis News,* Indianapolis, Indiana

---

[113] The listing is based on records in the Pulitzer Prize Office and has been completed in some points with the friendly help of Mrs. Robin Kuzen, Assistant Administrator of the Pulitzer Prizes, Columbia University, New York, N. Y.
[114] Prize-winner in the "Correspondence" category.
[115] Prize-winner in the "Telegraphic Reporting (International)" category.

For Articles from 1947 – Awarded in 1948
Award Winner: Paul W. Ward, *The Sun,* Baltimore, Maryland[116]
Jury Members (March), 1948):
    Marvin, H. Creager, *The Milwaukee Journal,* Milwaukee, Wisconsin
    Jenkin, L. Jones, *The Tulsa Tribune,* Tulsa, Oklahoma
    James Kerney, Jr., *The Trenton Times,* Trenton, New Jersey
    Stephen C. Noland, *The Indianapolis News,* Indianapolis, Indiana

For Articles from 1948 – Awarded in 1949
Award Winner: Price Day, *The Sun,* Baltimore, Maryland
Jury Members (March, 1949):
    Edward Lindsay, *The Decateur Herald,* Decatur, Illinois
    Burrows Matthews, *Buffalo Courier-Express,* Buffalo, New York

For Articles from 1949 – Awarded in 1950
Award Winner: Edmund Stevens, *The Christian Science Monitor,* Boston, Massachusetts
Jury Members (March, 1950):
    Wilbur C. Stouffer, *Roanoke World-News,* Roanoke, Virginia;
    Charles G. Wellington, *The Kansas City Star,* Kansas City, Missouri

For Articles from 1950 – Awarded in 1951
Award Winners: Keyes Beech, *Chicago Daily News,* Chicago, Illinois
    Homer Bigart, *New York Herald-Tribune,* New York
    Marguerite Higgins, *New York Herald-Tribune,* New York
    Relman Morin, *The Associated Press,* New York
    Fred Sparks, *Chicago Daily News,* Chicago, Illinois
    Don Whitehead, *The Associated Press,* New York
Jury Members (March, 1951):
    Virginius Dabney, *Richmond Times-Dispatch,* Richmond, Virginia
    Wilbur C. Stouffer, *Roanoke World-News,* Roanoke, Virginia

For Articles from 1951 – Awarded in 1952
Award Winner: John M. Hightower, *The Associated Press,* New York
Jury Members (March, 1952):
    Harry S. Ashmore, *Arkansas Gazette,* Little Rock, Arkansas
    Miles H. Wolff, *Greensboro Daily News,* Greensboro, North Carolina

For Articles from 1952 – Awarded in 1953
Award Winner: Austin C. Wehrwein, *The Milwaukee Journal,* Milwaukee, Wisconsin
Jury Members (March, 1953):
    Wilbur C. Stouffer, *Roanoke World-News,* Roanoke, Virginia
    Lawrence L. Winship, *The Boston Globe,* Boston, Massachusetts

For Articles from 1953 – Awarded in 1954
Award Winner: Jim G. Lucas, *Scripps-Howard Newspapers,* Washington, D. C.
Jury Members (March, 1954):
    Coleman A. Harwell, *The Nashville Tennessean,* Nashville, Tennessee
    Wilbur C. Stouffer, *Roanoke World-News,* Roanoke, Virginia

For Articles from 1954 – Awarded in 1955
Award Winner: Harrison E. Salisbury, *The New York Times,* New York
Jury Members (March, 1955):
    Stanley P. Bernett, *The Plain Dealer,* Cleveland Ohio
    Charles G. Wellington, *The Kanses City Star,* Kansas City, Missouri

For Articles from 1955 – Awarded in 1956
Award Winners: Frank Conniff, William R. Hearst, Jr., J. Kingsbury Smith, *International News Service,* New York

---

[116] In and after the 1948 awarding term there is only one new International Reporting category.

Jury Members (March, 1956):
>   John R. Herbert, *The Patriot-Ledger,* Quincy, Massachusetts
>   Ralph McGill, *The Constitution,* Atlanta, Georgia

For Articles from 1956 – Awarded in 1957
Award Winner: Russell Jones, *United Press,* New York
Jury Members (March, 1957):
>   Alan Hathway, *Newsday,* Garden City, New York
>   Jenkin L. Jones, *the Tulsa Tribune,* Tulsa, Oklahoma
>   Herbert B. Swope, free-lance journalist, New York

For Articles from 1957 – Awarded in 1958
Award Winner: *The New York Times,* New York[117]
Jury Members (March, 1958):
>   John R. Herbert, *The Patriot-Ledger,* Quincy, Massachusetts
>   Mort Stern, *The Denver Post,* Denver, Colorado
>   William P. Steven, *Houston Chronicle,* Houston, Texas

For Articles from 1958 – Awarded in 1959
Award Winners: Joseph Martin, Philip Santora, *Daily News,* New York
Jury Members (March 1959):
>   Arthur C. Deck, *The Tribune,* Salt Lake City, Utah
>   Ben Maidenburg, *Akron Beacon Journal,* Akron, Ohio
>   John T. O'Rourke, *Washington Daily News,* Washington, D. C.

For Articles from 1959 – Awarded in 1960
Award Winner: Abraham M. Rosenthal, *The New York Times,* New York
Jury Members (March, 1960):
>   Everest, P. Derthick, *The Plain Dealer,* Cleveland, Ohio
>   Alan Hathway, *Newsday,* Garden City, New York
>   George E. Minot, *Boston Herald,* Boston, Massachusetts

For Articles from 1960 – Awarded in 1961
Award Winner: Lynn L. Heinzerling, *The Associated Press,* New York
Jury Members (March, 1961):
>   Emmett Dedmon, *Chicago Sun-Times,* Chicago Illinois
>   Ralph McGill, *The Constitution,* Atlanta, Georgia
>   Frank F. Orr, *Register-Pajaronian,* Watsonville, California

For Articles from 1961 – Awarded in 1962
Award Winner: Walter Lippmann, *New York Herald-Tribune,* New York
Jury Members (March, 1962):
>   John S. Gillen, *The Philadelphia Inquirer,* Philadelphia, Pennsylvania
>   Harry Montgomery, *The Arizona Republic,* Phoenix, Arizona
>   William P. Steven, *Houston Chronicle,* Houston, Texas
>   James A. Wechsler, *New York Post,* New York

For Articles from 1962 – Awarded in 1963
Award Winner: Harold V. Hendrix, *The Miami News,* Miami, Florida
Jury Members (March, 1963):
>   Arthur R. Bertelson, *St. Louis Post-Dispatch,* St. Louis, Missouri
>   Howard H. Hays, *The Enterprise,* Riverside, California
>   Eugene S. Pulliam, *The Indianapolis Star,* Indianapolis, Indiana
>   Paul Schoenstein, *New York Journal-American,* New York

---

[117] By way of exception, the prize for International Reporting was not given to an individual journalist, respectively to serveral foreign correspondents mentioned by name, in this term, but to the *New York Times* collectively; for details see the introductory notes of chapter 30.

The second phase of development of the Pulitzer Prizes for International Reporting reveals even more clearly the interdependency between American engagements abroad and the themes of the American foreign correspondents' reports. There were, of course, differences in the jurors' interpretations of the originality of the annual entries.[118] The temporary similarity of interest between policy and press during the period of the Cold War[119] was a reason for American correspondents to function more and more as critical observers of other countries, but in some cases journalistic and political intentions still ran the risk of mingling with one another.[120] Despite these dangers U.S. foreign correspondents – with perhaps the exception of war correspondents in Korea – kept their journalistic autonomy as registras and analysts of foreign political, economical, and cultural constellations, while not refraining from criticism of measures and decisions of their own government.[121] The coverage of the Cuban crisis, which, in a way, was the climax of the Cold War, is an example of journalistic research which – employing investigative reporting methods – brought out results of world-political importance. The reports of Hal Hendrix, which brought him the 1963 Pulitzer Prize for International Reporting, certainly played a decisive part in the "opening phase of the great Missile Crisis of 1962 during which Khrushchev lost his nerve and eventually his power,"[122] as Hohenberg states.

About one year later – a few weeks after the presentation of the Pulitzer Prize for International Reporting to Hal Hendrix for his coverage of this highly explosive situation – the Cuba crisis indirectly influenced the improvement of *direct* communication between the two world powers. As early as march, 1963, it was felt in US governmental quarters "that the installation of a direct and sure communications link between Washington and Moscow 'would immediately reduce the danger of accidental war,'"[123] and in the first days of April "the Soviet Union accepted . . . the United States proposal for a direct 'hot line' communications link" between the two capitals.[124] At the same time, the *New York Times* reported from Washington, that the "administration is delighted with the prospect of opening a modern communications link with Moscow despite its belief that a primitive kind of sign language will continue to govern most East-West relations."[125] At the beginning of June it was learned that "the agreement to establish a sure and quick communications link between Moscow and Washington is ready for signature."[126]

---

[118] Cf. several respective examples in John Hohenberg: The Pulitzer Prizes, op. cit.
[119] Cf. James Aronson: The Press and the Cold War, Indianapolis–New York: Bobbs-Merrill Company, 1970, pp. 231 ff.
[120] Cf. Douglass Cater: The Fourth Branch of Government, Boston: Houghton Mifflin Company, 1959, pp. 178 ff.
[121] Cf. Richard R. Fagen: Politics and Communication, Boston–Toronto: Little Brown & Company, 1966, pp. 142 f.
[122] John Hohenberg: The Pulitzer Prizes, op. cit., p. 248.
[123] N. N.: U.S. Calls for Direct Link to Moscow to Avert War, in: *The New York Times* (New York, N. Y.), Vol. CXII/No. 38, 402, March 16, 1963, p. 1, cols. 6–7; p. 2, cols. 5–6.
[124] N. N.: Russia Approves 'Hot Line' to U.S. to Cut War Peril, in: *The New York Times* (New York, N. Y.), Vol. CXII/No. 38, 423, April 6, 1963, p. 1, col. 8; p. 2, col. 5.
[125] Max Frankel: Link to Moscow delights Capital, in: *The New York Times* (New York, N. Y.), Vol. CXII/No. 38, 423, April 6, 1963, p. 1, col. 7; p. 2, cols. 6–7.
[126] Max Frankel: U.S.-Soviet 'Hot-Line' Pact set for Signing in Geneva, in: *The New York Times* (New York, N. Y.), Vol. CXII/No. 38, 484, June 6, 1963, p. 1, col. 6; p. 5, cols. 1–3.

Members of the Advisory Board in 1964

Left to right: (standing) Newbold Noyes Jr., editor, the *Evening Star and Sunday Star*, Washington; Ralph McGill, publisher, the *Atlanta Constitution*; Paul Miller, president of the Gannett Newspapers; Turner Catledge, managing editor, the *New York Times*; John Hohenberg, the Graduate School of Journalism of Columbia; Erwin D. Canham, editor, the *Christian Science Monitor*; W. D. Maxwell, vice president and editor, *Chicago Tribune*; Kenneth MacDonald, vice president and editor, the *Des Moines Register and Tribune*; (seated) Barry Bingham, editor and publisher, the *Courier Journal* and the *Louisville Times*; Louis B. Seltzer, editor, the *Cleveland Press*; Joseph Pulitzer, Jr., editor, the *St. Louis Post-Dispatch*; President Grayson Kirk of Columbia and Norman Chandler, chairman and president, the Times-Mirror Company of Los Angeles.

U.S. and U.S.S.R. Sign Agreement for Direct Communications Link

TEXT OF AGREEMENT

Memorandum of Understanding

MEMORANDUM OF UNDERSTANDING BETWEEN THE UNITED STATES OF AMERICA AND THE UNION OF SOVIET SOCIALIST REPUBLICS REGARDING THE ESTABLISHMENT OF A DIRECT COMMUNICATIONS LINK SIGNED ON JUNE 20, 1963 AT GENEVA, SWITZERLAND

For use in time of emergency, the Government of the United States of America and the Government of the Union of Soviet Socialist Republics have agreed to establish as soon as technically feasible a direct communications link between the two governments.

Each government shall be responsible for the arrangements for the link on its own territory. Each government shall take the necessary steps to ensure continuous functioning of the link and prompt delivery to its head of government of any communications received by means of the link from the head of government of the other party.

Arrangements for establishing and operating the link are set forth in the Annex which is attached hereto and forms an integral part hereof.

Done in duplicate in the English and Russian languages at Geneva, Switzerland, this 20th day of June, 1963.

For the Government of the Union of Soviet Socialist Republics:

SEMYON K. TSARAPKIN

Acting Representative of the Union of Soviet Socialist Republics to the Eighteen Nation Committee on Disarmament

For the Government of the United States of America:

CHARLES C. STELLE

Acting Representative of the United States of America to the Eighteen Nation Committee on Disarmament

Annex to Memorandum

ANNEX TO THE MEMORANDUM OF UNDERSTANDING BETWEEN THE UNITED STATES OF AMERICA AND THE UNION OF SOVIET SOCIALIST REPUBLICS REGARDING THE ESTABLISHMENT OF A DIRECT COMMUNICATIONS LINK

The direct communications link between Washington and Moscow established in accordance with the memorandum, and the operation of such link, shall be governed by the following provisions:

1. The direct communications link shall consist of:

A. Two terminal points with telegraph-teleprinter equipment between which communications shall be directly exchanged;

B. One full-time duplex wire telegraph circuit, routed Washington-London-Copenhagen-Stockholm-Helsinki-Moscow, which shall be used for the transmission of messages;

C. One full-time duplex radio telegraph circuit, routed Washington-Tangier-Moscow, which shall be used for service communications and for coordination of operations between the two terminal points.

If experience in operating the direct communications link should demonstrate that the establishment of an additional wire telegraph circuit is advisable, such circuit may be established by mutual agreement between authorized representatives of both governments.

2. In case of interruption of the wire circuit, transmission of messages shall be effected via the radio circuit, and for this purpose provision shall be made at the terminal points for the capability of prompt switching of all necessary equipment from one circuit to another.

3. The terminal points of the link shall be so equipped as to provide for the transmission and reception of messages from Moscow to Washington in the Russian language and from Washington to Moscow in the English language. In this connection, the USSR shall furnish the United States four sets of telegraph terminal equipment, including page printers, transmitters, and reperforators, with one year's supply of spare parts and all necessary special tools, test equipment, operating instructions and other technical literature, to provide for transmission and reception of messages in the Russian language. The United States shall furnish the Soviet Union four sets of telegraph terminal equipment, including page printers, transmitters, and reperforators, with one year's supply of spare parts and all necessary special tools, test equipment, operating instructions and other technical literature, to provide for transmission and reception of messages in the English language. The equipment described in this paragraph shall be exchanged directly between the parties without any payment being required therefor.

4. The terminal points of the direct communications link shall be provided with encoding equipment. For the terminal point in the USSR, four sets of such equipment (each capable of simplex operation), with one year's supply of spare parts, with all necessary special tools, test equipment, operating instructions and other technical literature, and with all necessary blank tape, shall be furnished by the United States to the USSR against payment of the cost thereof by the USSR.

The USSR shall provide for preparation and delivery of keying tapes to the terminal point of the link in the United States for reception of messages from the USSR. The United States shall provide for preparation and delivery of keying tapes to the terminal point of the link in the USSR for reception of messages from the United States. Delivery of prepared keying tapes to the terminal points of the link shall be effected through the Embassy of the USSR in Washington (for the terminal of the link in the USSR) and through the Embassy of the United States in Moscow (for the terminal of the link in the United States).

5. The United States and the USSR shall designate the agencies responsible for the arrangements regarding the direct communications link, for its technical maintenance, continuity and reliability, and for the timely transmission of messages.

Such agencies may, by mutual agreement, decide matters and develop instructions relating to the technical maintenance and operation of the direct communications link and effect arrangements to improve the operation of the link.

6. The technical parameters of the telegraph circuits of the link and of the terminal equipment, as well as the maintenance of such circuits and equipment, shall be in accordance with CCITT [Comité consultatif international télégraphique et téléphonique] and CCIR [Comité consultatif international des radio communications] recommendations.

Transmission and reception of messages over the direct communications link shall be effected in accordance with applicable recommendations of international telegraph and radio communications regulations, as well as with mutually agreed instructions.

7. The costs of the direct communications link shall be borne as follows:

A. The USSR shall pay the full cost of leasing the portion of the telegraph circuit from Moscow to Helsinki and 50 percent of the cost of leasing the portion of the telegraph circuit from Helsinki to London. The United States shall pay the full cost of leasing the portion of the telegraph circuit from Washington to London and 50 percent of the cost of leasing the portion of the telegraph circuit from London to Helsinki.

B. Payment of the cost of leasing the radio telegraph circuit between Moscow and Washington shall be effected without any transfer of payments between the parties. The USSR shall bear the expenses relating to the transmission of messages from Moscow to Washington. The United States shall bear the expenses relating to the transmission of messages from Washington to Moscow.

[*Source: Department of State Bulletin* (Washington, D.C.), Vol. XLIX/No. 1254, July 8, 1963, pp. 50 f.]

Finally, a White House press release, dated June 20, announced: "Today (in Geneva) the representatives of the Governments of the United States and the U.S.S.R. at the 18-Nation Disarmament Conference signed an agreement which will establish a direct communications link between their respective capitals. This age of fast-moving events requires quick, dependable communications for use in time of emergency. By their signatures today, therefore, both Governments have taken a first step to help reduce the risk of war occuring by accident or miscalculation. This agreement on a communications link is a limited but practical step forward in arms control and disarmament."[127] Although this agreement seemed to have ended the critical phase of the Cold War it by no means mitigated the East-West antagonism, as was shown by the escalation of the Indochina conflict, which now became the main field of "veritable" war correspondence.[128]

Nearly parallel with the political events involving Cuba, a new dimension had opened up in the field of information technology with the orbiting of the American news satellite "Telstar 1" on June 10, 1962, which created new possibilities for foreign correspondence.[129] An exciting new era in the field of international communication began on July 23, 1962, when Europe and North America were linked by live television for the first time through the Telstar-1 experimental communication satellite orbiting high over the Atlantic. An estimated 100 million Europeans witnessed 22 minutes of live pickups of scenes of everyday life in a dozen North American cities from Quebec to the Mexican border. Later the same day, a North American audience of almost similar size became armchair tourists for 19 absorbing minutes as Eurovision cameras scanned from the Arctic Circle to the Mediterranean, and from the Danube to the Atlantic.[130] Despite these new technical possibilities and the general importance of television in the life of Americans[131] the print media still had more impact, especially in the field of foreign correspondence. "During the 114-day New York newspaper strike in 1962–63," Hohenberg quotes from a study in the 'Columbia Journalism Review,' "a total of 70.9 percent of so-called hard-core readers reported they missed international news 'very much.' Among readers with shifting attitudes, 58.1 percent in one category and 44.7 in another gave the same reply. One explanation was: 'TV is very brief on foreign affairs.' And another: 'A newspaper is my way of knowing what is going on in the world.'"[132] Could it be that these results, which of course must not be overestimated, open new future perspectives and encouragement for foreign correspondents of daily newspapers?

---

[127] From: White House Statement, June 20, in: *Department of State Bulletin* (Washington, D. C.), Vol. XLIX/No. 1254, July 8, 1963, p. 50, col. 1.
[128] Cf. Phillip Knightly: The First Casualty. From the Crimea to Vietnam: The War Correspondent as Hero, Propagandist, and Mythmaker, London: André Deutsch, Ltd., 1979, pp. 374 ff.
[129] Cf. Nancy Carol Jones: The Role of the United Nations in Communications Satellites, unpublished PhD dissertation, University of Missouri, Columbia, Mo., 1967, p. 206.
[130] Cf. Heinz-Dietrich Fischer: Eurovision and Intervision toward Mondovision, in: Heinz-Dietrich Fischer/John C. Merrill (Eds.): International Communication. Media–Channels–Functions, New York–Toronto: Hastings House, 1970, pp. 254 f.
[131] Cf. Gary A. Steiner: The People look at Television. A Study of Audience Attitudes, New York: Alfred A. Knopf, Inc., 1963, pp. 226 ff: Harry J. Skornia: Television and Society. An inquest and agenda for improvement, New York–London–Sydney–Toronto: McGraw-Hill Book Company, 1965, pp. 178 ff.
[132] John Hohenberg: Foreign Correspondence, op. cit., p. 433.

EDITORIAL REMARKS

The choice of internationally oriented Pulitzer Prize-winning texts had to be based on a number of compromises. Principally, it must be borne in mind that the prizes represent a continuum; although this is not true of the basic conditions under which the prize winners were determined. Although changing juries posited varying interpretations of the criteria for awarding the prize, compounded by changes in the awarding practices, the Advisory Board ultimately established its own priorities.

A volume of Pulitzer Prize-winning international reporting articles must of necessity be diverse despite certain factors imposed by the awarding committees. The talents and abilities of each prize winner are different and these differences are reflected in the articles. Nevertheless, it is not the task of the editor of this volume to look for differences in the quality of the texts, nor is there any intention of rating the prize winners.

Considering the difficulties and controversies connected with the awards, it is no small wonder that in some years awarding committees of the Pulitzer Prize had difficulty finding an acceptable and publicly justifiable compromise when and if problems arose during the selective procedure. These problems were not, however, relevant with regard to the selection of texts for this volume. Therefore, regardless of how the prize winners were eventually chosen, their inclusion in this volume was based solely on their individual merit. In order to maintain a cohesiveness within this volume, and to provide the reader with a fair representation of the author and his work, it was decided to select and reprint five articles by each prize winner.

This was done also for a practical reason: to meet the limitations of size of the individual volumes by the publisher. In many cases this selection process was rather difficult, especially given the varying number of contributions to the collection of each author. In the first years of the presentation of the Pulitzer Prizes, authors could submit as many articles as they wished. Thus, the entries often consisted of an entire year's output of the respective journalist, which in the case of newspaper or agency correspondents often amounted to a large quantity. However, in the last two decades the Advisory Board restricted that number to no more than ten articles per exhibit and author.

From the beginning, entries submitted to the Pulitzer Prize committees were rather diverse. Initially there were only few basic conditions to be fulfilled. Therefore, those nominating an author for one of the prizes (self-nominations were an exception) were not always interested in a complete and detailed representation of a subject area. Different subjects, usually from different regions, were provided the Pulitzer juries in order to make visible the thematical range of the respective journalist.

This was particularly true in the entries for agency correspondents. Here an additional problem arose to the editor of this volume. Because the Prizes were rarely awarded for journalistic raw materials, but for articles printed in the press of the year prior to the award presentation, the agency journalists often encountered the problem of not having any proof of their publications except for their teletype manuscripts. Thus, it was quite usual that the entries for agency correspondents contained newsclips from various papers – the published versions of their teletype manuscripts.

Different practices were also employed in the copyreading and editing of the materials. Thus, the text was often shortened or rewritten. One cannot assume therefore that in each case the newsclips represented verbatim the correspondent's original text. Nominators also selected reprinted agency bulletins from many different newspapers, employing a technique that might be described as an "appetizer principle." In many cases they submitted to the Pulitzer Prize committees only the opening passages of the published articles, so that many entries primarily consisted of segments from the front pages of American newspapers which were continued on the following pages but were not included in the submitted entry. Some entries thus contained only incomplete articles.

It was, therefore, necessary in these cases to contact those newspapers who had originally printed the stories in order to achieve a complete text. To eliminate artifacts of different editing practices, and to achieve a standard text it was important to submit copies of articles of each correspondent that – if at all possible – were published in the same newspaper. Again, a problem was encountered when different versions of the same article were published in two different editions of the same newspaper, e.g. in the morning and evening editions of a specific day.

Thus, for each selection the original newspaper was requested to provide exact citations of the articles. It was also necessary to determine the volume(s), number(s), page(s), and column(s) in order to present an exact reference for each article. This job was particularly taxing since microfilms of many American newspapers were not available in Germany, with the exception of the *New York Times,* the *New York Herald-Tribune,* and the *Washington Post.* Most of the information needed had to be obtained in the United States. In some cases it was necessary to verify the text since many of the passages in the Pulitzer Prize material were unreadable; quite a number of entries were several decades old and had turned yellow or were illegible.

Basically each reprinted article is an unabridged version of the original text and each provides the complete source of reference. The newspaper heading of the article is also cited so that the original version is identical with the reproduction in this volume. However, since most of the headlines, after several decades, do not contain sufficient information for the contemporary reader, all the headlines had to be reformulated and basic information about the content of each article had to be the subject matter could be accessible to the present-day reader of the articles.

In the reproduction of the original material, it was necessary to make the text readable without manipulating the original text in any way. Subheadings that occasionally appeared in the originals had to be eliminated in many cases; mostly, they provided only minimal information. Beyond this, however, no other adaptations seemed necessary or suitable. In the literal reproduction of the original texts only obvious errors (e.g. misspellings of names) were corrected.

Thus, this volume has been compiled both systematically and critically; editorial comments, however, are not included. Introductory notes which provide useful information on the genesis of the texts and short biographical notes about each author precede each chapter.

Each chapter also contains a list of supplemental readings which may aid the reader in achieving a more rounded perspective. Only few of the documents in the individual chapters are taken from the newspapers that served as sources for the texts, but they are often part of the secondary literature related to the respective chapter, and are referred to as such. The index at the end of this volume is confined to names appearing in the text. In some cases the names had divergent spellings, and some attempt was made to standardize the usage.

Prizewinners and Their Articles

1946

J. Brooks Atkinson

The New York Times

CHAPTER 19

REPORTS ABOUT THE SOVIET UNION IN 1946

The Post-War Situation and Some Typical Characteristics of the Country

   Introductory Notes
19.1 The Byrnes Plan and How Moscow Views It
19.2 America's Aims and Structure in the Soviet Press
19.3 A System of Permanent Distrust and Its Purpose
19.4 The Socialist Landscape and Its Climate
19.5 Russo-American Relations and Their Future Outlook
   Related Readings

Introductory Notes

When the Pulitzer Prize Jurors met in March, 1947, it was their delicate task to decide among the nominations to the two existing categories in the international field. While in the "Telegraphic Reporting (International)" category the Advisory Board finally gave the prize to Eddy Gilmore, Associated Press, *"for his correspondence from Moscow in 1946,"* in the Correspondence category the Pulitzer Prize went to the theater critic of the New York Times, Brooks Atkinson, *"for his distinguished correspondence during 1946, as exemplified by his series of articles on Russia."*

Justin Brooks Atkinson was born on November 28, 1894, in Melrose, Massachusetts. When he was eight years old he printed in rubber type a newspaper called The Watchout, *and about four years later, after he had joined the National Amateur Press Association he printed* The Puritan *in lead type. While a student at Harvard College, he wrote articles about George Bernard Shaw for the* Boston Herald. *Upon receiving his B. A. degree in 1917, he accepted an appointment to the faculty of Dartmouth College in Hanover, New Hampshire, as an instructor in English. After having served for several months in the United States Army during World War I he worked on a newspaper, the* Boston Transcript, *and from 1920 to 1922 held the additional position of associate editor of the* Harvard Alumni Bulletin. *Joining the staff of the* New York Times *in 1922 as a book reviewer, Atkinson edited this section of his paper for two years before devoting himself entirely to drama in 1925. During the following years, in addition to contributing reviews to his paper, Atkinson wrote a number of books. Atkinson always regarded himself as a newspaperman in the full sense of the term, not just a drama critic. Sharing this view, the* New York Times *sent him in 1942 as a war correspondent to Chungking, China. For two years he used that base, then during ten months in 1945–46 he was a news correspondent for his newspaper in Moscow. After he had returned to New York in July 1946 he wrote a series of articles for the* Times *about what he saw in the Soviet Union. Although they were denounced in* Pravda, *his reports on Russia won him the Pulitzer Prize in 1947.*

The following texts by Justin Brooks Atkinson, copyright 1946, are reprinted by kind permission of The New York Times, Inc., *New York, N. Y.*

19.1 The Byrnes Plan and How Moscow Views It

[*Source: Brooks Atkinson: Byrnes plan sham, Moscow implies. Tass story from Paris calls treaty proposal a blind for U.S. 'retreat' on Germany, in:* The New York Times *(New York, N. Y.), Vol. XCV/No. 32,242, May 4, 1946, p. 1, col. 6; p. 6, col. 4.*]

In the first reports of Secretary of State James F. Byrnes' proposal for a quadripartite treaty to be printed here, Tass, Soviet press agency, severely criticized its contents today.

The proposed twenty-five-year treaty for supervising Germany was described as a possible paper curtain to hide a retreat from agreements made at the time of Germany's capitulation last year, a possible attempt to divert attention from the Ruhr problems, a dangerous weakening of the machinery already set up to guarantee Germany's disarmament and one more maneuver that was introducing superfluous difficulties for the Foreign Ministers' Council in Paris. [A Paris dispatch said that the American delegation at the Foreign Ministers conference considered the Russian attack on the Byrnes treaty proposal an indication that the Soviet Union was unwilling to commit itself to the disarmament of Germany for the suggested twenty-five year term.]

Referring to the twenty-five-year term proposed by Mr. Byrnes, Tass commented in an article datelined Paris: "The experience of diplomatic relations of modern times proves that sometimes new argreements for any more or less long period are proposed by those who are doing everything possible to break existing treaties." The article put the Byrnes proposal in the same class as British Foreign Secretary Ernest Bevin's offer to sign a fifty-year treaty with the Soviet Union, which it said had been "put forward by British politicians who were by no means acting in the spirit of a treaty already existing between the two countries, concluded in 1942 for a term of twenty years."

In general, the Byrnes plan was regarded by Tass as unsatisfactory from every viewpoint. There was an implication that it was considered anti-Soviet in character when viewed in the light of "repeated statements on the part of the reactionary British and United States press about exactly which circles were interested in breaking up collaboration between the Allied powers."

Although Secretary Byrnes' proposal had been "expressed in cautious terms," the Tass article noted that it was the first official declaration concerning a cessation of the occupation of Germany. Instead of ending the occupation when the Allies have completed the demilitarization of Germany, Tass asserted, the Byrnes proposal makes termination of the occupation dependent on nothing except the willingness of German authorities to accept the disarmament terms. Since Germany has provoked two wars within the lifetime of one generation, the Tass dispatch declared, "the occupation of that country by Allied armies is the only guarantee against a possible rebirth of aggression until the demilitarization and denazification of Germany have been completely fulfilled."

In the Soviet view the Byrnes proposal looks like a first step toward disavowal of obligations that the Allies undertook last year to exterminate the roots and bases of German militarism. Since the Byrnes proposal was said to include nothing that had not been agreed upon a year ago and since the task the Allies undertook to fulfill had not all been completed, the Soviet writer inclined to the view that the proposal was a maneuver to escape previously assumed obligations "or, at any rate, to by-pass them."

The state of the disarmament of Germany is far from satisfactory, according to the article. It inquired whether all German military units in the British zone of occupation had been "really dispersed." It declared that camouflaged war enterprises had been preserved by the Germans in the western zones and that "for some reason or other the American side has not been displaying any concern over checking up the actual state of affairs."

The difficulties the Paris conference was encountering were explained, in the opinion of the Soviet writer, by the positions taken up by "reactionary circles inspired by Winston Churchill and their American friends, who in their shortsighted calculations are ready to ignore completely the interests of guaranteeing a durable peace."

19.2 America's Aims and Structure in the Soviet Press

[*Source: Brooks Atkinson: Soviet press turns guns on us. With Britain we are condemned now for imperialistic aims, in:* The New York Times *(New York, N. Y.), Vol. XCV/No. 32,250, May 12, 1946, section 4, p. 4, cols. 2–4.*]

To judge by the news that appears in the Moscow press, the course of events and current tendencies in the United States today confirm the theory that the Soviet Union has potential enemies abroad and that the danger of capitalistic encirclement still exists. Day by day the United States emerges as a strong, powerful nation torn by industrial strife between the workers and reactionary capitalists and also as a nation rapidly developing an imperialistic pattern and seeking to dominate the world with Great Britain.

For many months "imperialistic" Britain had a worse press here than the United States. But during the last few months – including the period of the Security Council meetings and the Paris Conference – the United States has begun to achieve full equality with Britain. There have been no more bitter attacks on the United States than in recent articles discussing Secretary of State James F. Byrnes' proposal for a twenty-five-year quadripartite treaty and the Iranian problem. By insisting on discussing the Iranian problem despite the Iranian-Soviet agreement, the United States and Britain represented two-faced imperialistic powers using the United Nations as a selfish political weapon and trying to settle world problems by private agreement behind the backs of other nations, the Moscow press has charged.

Mr. Byrnes' proposal of a twenty-five-year treaty is described as a maneuver to conclude the occupation of Germany before the Nazi influence is exterminated. As capitalist powers, the United States and Britain always are suspected of not being sincerely interested in exterminating Fascist individuals, industry and organizations. Considerable evidence is published on that point, tending to prove either that the Americans are encouraging the Fascists or that they are maintaining a complacent attitude of tolerance toward the Fascists. The Americans are reported to be encouraging the nationalistic sentiments of the Italians in Trieste.

J. Brooks Atkinson

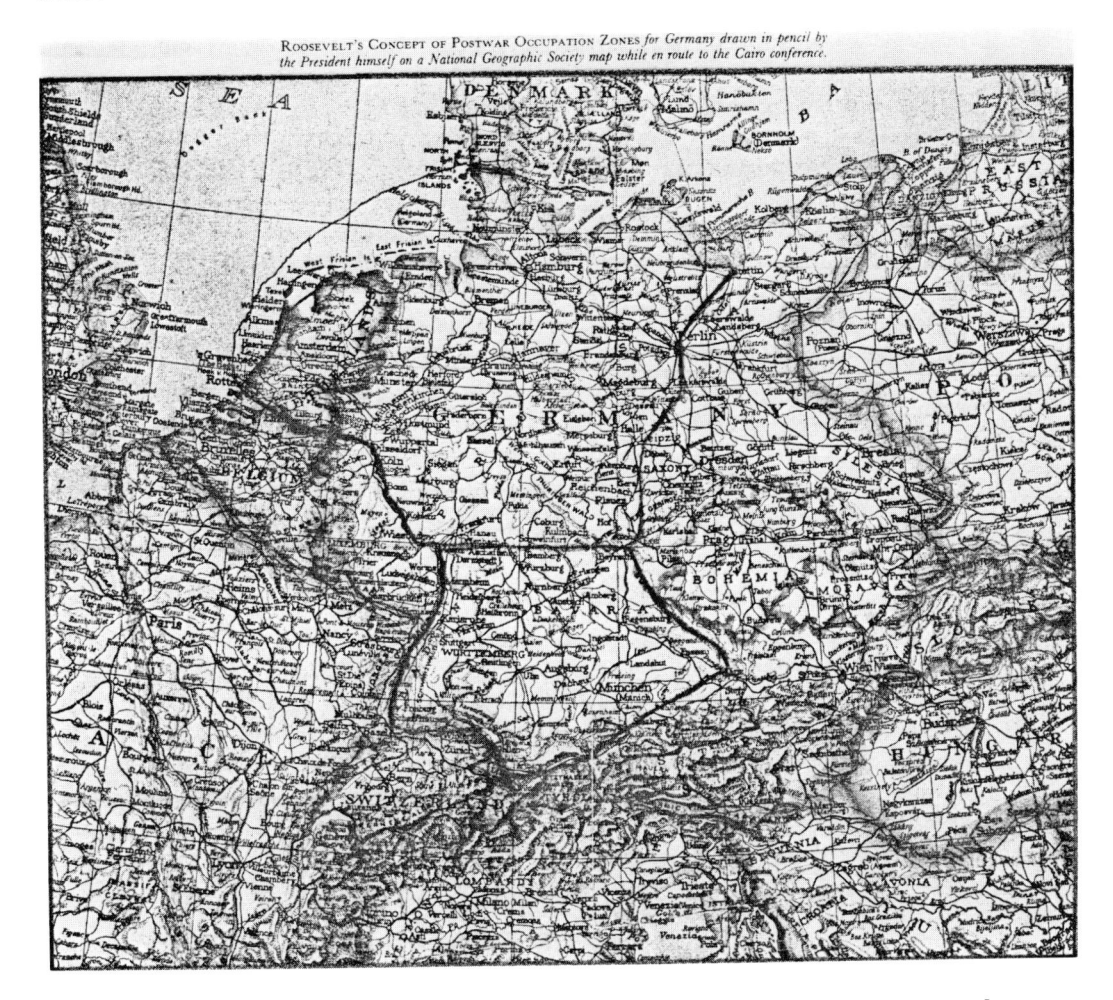

ROOSEVELT'S CONCEPT OF POSTWAR OCCUPATION ZONES *for Germany drawn in pencil by the President himself on a National Geographic Society map while en route to the Cairo conference.*

[*Source:* Jean Edward Smith: The Defense of Berlin, Baltimore, Md., 1963, opposite p. 18.]

Senator Glen H. Taylor, Democrat, of Idaho, is quoted as having said that failure to arrest 1,500 leading German industrialists in the United States occupation zone had strengthened the Hitlerites, who are said to be preparing a conspiracy for a return to power. A long review of Abel Plenn's "Wind in the Olives" presents the United States State Department's policy as directed toward strengthening Fascist power in Spain. "American capitalists have obtained control of Spanish industry, thanks to Franco's policy of transferring part of the Nazi assets in Spain to American big business," the review asserts. Although the American administration in Japan has not been specifically denounced, frequent news stories and articles from Japan dwell on the consolidation there of reactionary Japanese politicians and industrialists with odious Fascist records at the expense of the broad masses of the people. The Americans also have been reported looting Japan.

On the basis of innumerable Soviet news reports, there is evidence of the existence of many individuals and several organizations in America who criticize current tendencies in the United States and support policies that also are Soviet policies. These Russian dispatches also say that the logic of many Soviet policies frequently is endorsed by isolated individuals and groups in America.

But the weight of evidence is said to show vigorous expansionary tendencies in American politics and industry. It is reported that Americans are preparing to build air bases in Turkey and that American construction concerns have obtained huge contracts in Brazil. The vast extent of American military power is illustrated by reports of American refusal to evacuate the bases in Iceland and retention of bases in the Azores, of United States military units' participation in Mexican Army maneuvers and of United States preparations to integrate its military program with other American nations.

According to the Soviet viewpoint, the American press is part of the capitalistic tyranny. Discussions of the freedom of the press are regarded as pretentious humbuggery motivated by a desire to preserve the property of the newspaper proprietors. According to the New Times, printers do not have freedom of the press, since they print what they are told to print. Nor do reporters, editors and editorial writers, who the New Times says "write only what the publisher who hires them wants them to."

It concludes that "freedom of the press is enjoyed only by a small group of men who own the press and control ist." That is the accepted viewpoint here. In the midst of hosannas on "press day" last Sunday, Zaslavski joyfully asserted that "the army of Soviet journalists were proud of the fact that it has no other masters than its people, that it does not serve the interests of a bunch of magnates, bankers, etc."

Reading the Soviet press one gathers the impression that the United States is a country of strange contrasts. Women are being discharged from automobile plants. Widescale strikes are said to be crippling American economy. Yet the Americans are represented as expanding around the world, seeking new markets. On the whole the American pawn in the Soviet press confirms the current Soviet policy of keeping strong and vigilant.

19.3 A System of Permanent Distrust and Its Purpose

[*Source:* Brooks Atkinson: Russia bars amity with U.S., in: The New York Times *(New York, N. Y.), Vol. XCV/No. 32,306, July 7, 1946, p. 1, cols. 6–7; p. 6, cols. 2–3.*]

In the attempt to establish workable relations with the Government of the Soviet Union we have to abandon the familiar concepts of friendship. Friendship in the sense of intimate association and political compromise is not wanted, is not possible and is not involved. For the Soviet Government "apparatus," as the Russians use the word, is a political machine; and human approaches, like those implied in the word "friendship," are wide of the mark.

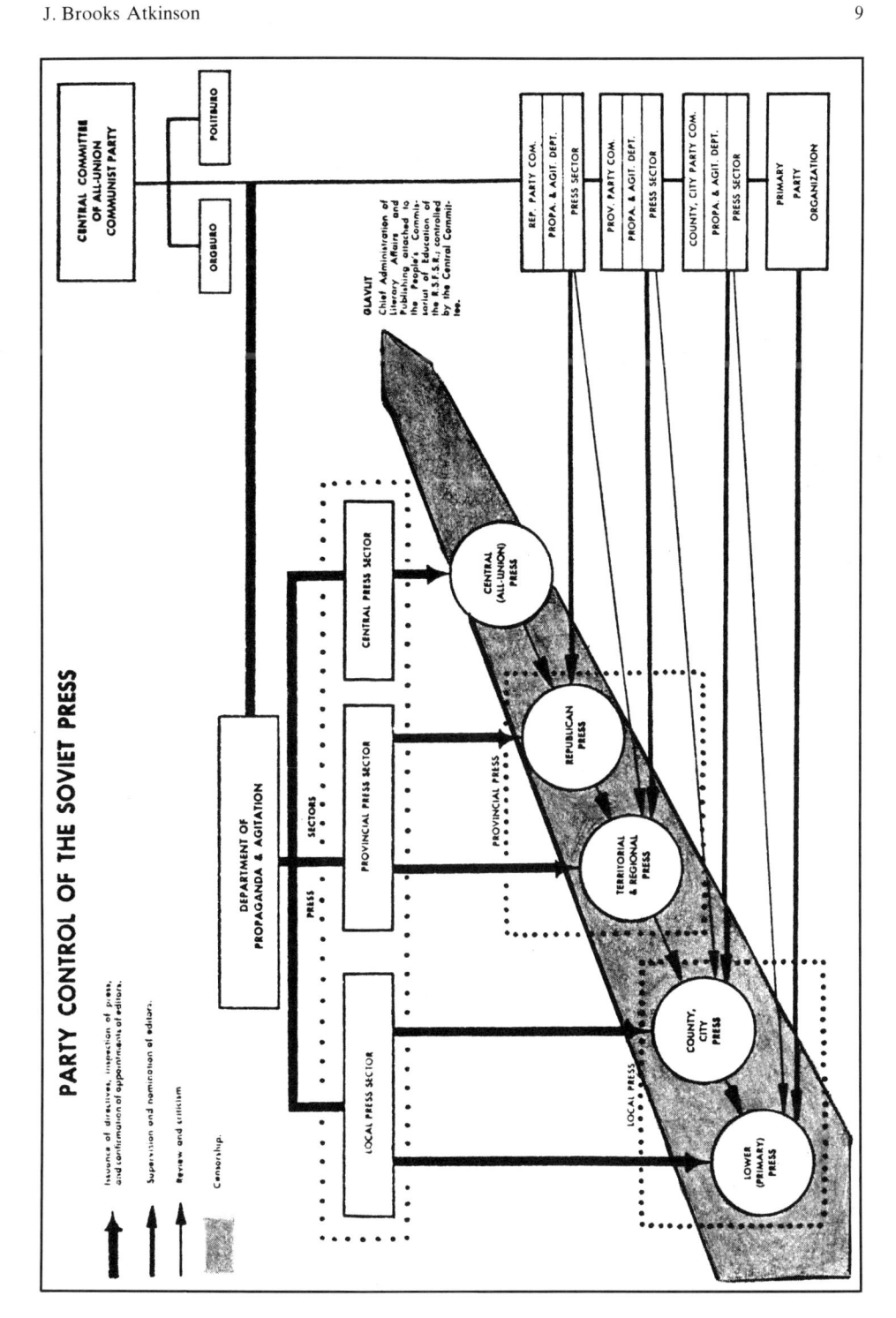

[*Source:* Alex Inkeles: Public Opinion in Soviet Russia. A Study in Mass Persuasion, Cambridge, Mass., 1951, opposite p. 208.]

On the whole, the Russian people are admirable people – genuine, hard-working and practical. You can trust their strength, native intelligence and courage. But between us and the Russian people stands the Soviet Government. Despite its sanctimonious use of the word "democracy," it is a totalitarian government. The familiar dictatorship of the proletariat is actually the dictatorship of the thirteen members of the Politburo of the Communist party.

There are no freedoms inside the Soviet Union. As far as I know, the Government is not imposed on the people against their will, nor is it a corrupt government that puts the personal interests of any one group ahead of what are regarded as the true interests of the State. Despite many internal disorders and disloyalties, like the factory frauds recently penalized and the treason of large groups in the Crimean and Chechen-Ingush Republics, my impression is that the people of the Soviet Union generally trust and respect the wisdom and integrity of their leaders. Like people everywhere, including the United States, the people of the Soviet Union are getting the government they deserve.

But, by nature, the Government is a machine for generating power inside the Soviet Union and as far outside as the power can be made to extend; and all attempts to deal with it in terms of friendship are doomed to failure. Although we are not enemies, we are not friends; and the most we can hope for is an armed peace for the next few years.

Where our interests lie, we have to apply equal power in the opposite direction. This is the most reactionary method of arranging world affairs. But the spirit of the Soviet Government is fundamentally reactionary, as its attitude toward defeated nations and the behavior of the Red Army in Manchuria suggest. Accustomed to the use of force inside the Soviet Union, the Soviet Government instinctively thinks in terms of force in its external affairs. Westerners who have seen that force in action are shocked by the mechanical power with which it crushes opposition, builds political bases and pushes people around. It recognizes no margin of tolerance between those who have submitted to it and those who have not. Without tolerance there can be no friendship in the Western democratic sense of the word.

Why are the Russians so difficult? There are a great many reasons. One reason is that their leaders have come up the hard way as professional revolutionaries trying to win power in a hostile environment, and they still believe in the methods that succeeded in 1917. In the Czarist state, which was also a tyrannical, police state, the professional revolutionaries maintained their organization by submitting to an austere discipline; and they developed to a high degree the technique of activity in secret. Vigilance and discipline got them to power; they believe that both are necessary to developing power today. Among other things, they agreed to the vicious doctrine that the end justifies the means – which, incidentally, may be the reason why the first Socialist state in the world has not released the workers from slavery but has reduced them to totalitarian slavery that includes the mind as well as the back.

The revolution was created in an underworld of planning, strategy, deceit, secrecy and violence. Since by force of circumstances the revolutionaries are not lawbreakers now but are law-givers, they can afford to relax, and they do. But much of the old tradition survives. They still conduct the affairs of state in secret. Soviet citizens have no more information about the current affairs of the Soviet Government than foreigners do. In some cases they have less, because information that is not commonly known inside the Soviet Union leaks out through foreign channels. Although the most violent period of the Soviet revolution has probably passed, a streak of violence persists. No one knows how many million political prisoners are now living in jail or in exile. The estimates run all the way from 10,000,000 to 15,000,000. No government in the world has so many internal crises and problems to face as the Soviet Government, which must conduct an industrial revolution simultaneously with its political revolution, and educate its people swiftly and effectively.

To survive, it believes that it must be free to conduct its affairs in secret and to act swiftly, by force if necessary. It naturally carries the same psychology into the satellite states where people are less used to that kind of treatment from a foreign source. In our relations with the Soviet Union we are dealing with men who have been conditioned in this revolutionary environment – some of them as active participants, all of them as adherents.

In view of the success of the Soviet Government inside the huge area of the Soviet Union, it is a little difficult for foreigners to understand the feeling of insecurity that the Soviet Union, it is a little difficult for foreigners to understand the feeling of insecurity that the Soviet leaders have. Premier Stalin is probably the most heavily guarded person in the world. Every Soviet citizen as well as every foreigner has to carry with him at all times his passport and personal identification papers, and he has to make frequent use of them. What we regard as wartime security methods are the daily security methods of the Soviet Union. To get to the Red Square for a celebration you have to show your special pass and ordinary passport to eight guards, all of whom read it thoroughly and compare the photograph with the bearer.

No foreigner knows much about what goes on throughout the length and breadth of the Soviet Union; as Paul Winterton has expressed it, there are only varying degrees of ignorance about the Soviet Union. But I know of no active, organized opposition to the government, although it is rumored that "certain circles" (a common Soviet newspaper phrase) in the Ukraine are restless and need watching. "Certain circles" there are said to believe that they have paid too high a price for the war and, no doubt irrationally, hold the present government responsible for their disasters. The imposing Communist headquarters in Odessa was burned last December in a fire that is thought to have been sabotage. There is active anti-semitism in the Ukraine. In other parts of Russia, not all the Moslems are satisfied with the Central Government. But the Central Government should be able to cope with dissident groups. As far as a foreigner can tell, the Soviet leaders are in a strong position. They have led their people to a remarkable victory over an efficient, modern foe; and the Communist party is naturally taking full credit for winning the war – in various degrees ignoring the contributions the other Allies made to the defeat of Germany, and taking credit for the knockout blow against Japan.

Apart from normal grumbling about the hardness of living, the people seem to believe in their government. But it is not in the nature of men like members of the Politburo to feel secure. As leaders of a backward, poorly fed, loosely organized country that is trying to lift itself by its bootstraps in a hurry, they have many unpleasant duties to perform and many labors to lay on the backs of their people. No doubt they feel that the circumstances require that they have freedom to act at the top without criticism, opposition or observation. Although their motives may be above suspicion, they behave instinctively like conspirators. Their behavior abroad is the same as it is at home, except that they do not have abroad the protection of a controlled press and the means of silencing opposition.

Part of our difficulties with the Soviet Union are owing to the ignorance of the Soviet leaders. Very few of them have been outside the Soviet Union. After many years of isolation, and also some bitter experiences with foreign countries, they have developed a phobia about the rest of the world. The spirit of the Soviet Government is anti-foreign. Ever since the bloody purges of 1936 there has been a nameless terror about foreigners, who are regarded as spies and enemies of the Soviet Union. Association with foreigners and active interest in foreign countries has in some vague way come to be regarded as treachery to the Soviet Union. Even the leaders are not immune. Leaders who get on too well with foreigners or who rationalize foreign points of view are treading on dangerous ground. They may find themselves in the doghouse before they know it. Even Mr. Stalin, who is regarded as having more common sense and balance than most Soviet leaders, does not understand freedom or democracy; in addition to his training in the doctrines of Marxism, he probably develops his ideas about foreign countries from prejudiced and incomplete information supplied by Soviet diplomats and journalists.

The Soviet leaders are the victims of their isolationism. Although they have access to an enormous mass of information from abroad, they lack the experience to analyze it. Having lived all their lives behind the "iron curtain" (a marvelously apt phrase) they cannot meet foreign problems or foreigners on what we regard as a normal basis. Contact with foreigners has in many ambiguous ways acquired the illusion of guilt. Since the peace of the world is at stake, the pity is that so many of our day-to-day frictions are unnecessary.

After the Moscow conference of last December, many foreigners believe that the Politburo made a deliberate decision to return to the status quo ante bellum and to regard foreign nations with a capitalist economy as inevitable enemies of the Soviet Union. Whatever the sincerity of such a point of view may be, it obviously creates inside the Soviet Union an atmosphere that is easier for a dictatorship to dominate. It is easier to rule a people who believe that a hostile world is organizing to exterminate them. As we have learned by our own experience during the war, people work better when they believe that they are working to save their national life.

19.4 The Socialist Landscape and Its Climate

[*Source: Brooks Atkinson: Socialist world Soviet aim, in:* The New York Times *(New York, N. Y.), Vol. XCV/No. 32,307, July 8, 1946, p. 1, cols. 6–7; p. 8, cols. 2–8.*]

The atmosphere of Moscow is abnormal. All normal communication being cut off with the outside world, the intellectual climate is stagnant. Behind the iron curtain of censorship, the emotional reactions to rumors and also to facts are neurotic. When news is removed from its normal background in the day's events and manipulated for the purpose of conditioning opinion, specific items often come as a shock.

The report of Mr. Churchill's speech at Fulton, Mo., was not published in the Soviet Union for a few days, presumably while the Soviet leaders were deciding how to handle it.

When finally they did publish it, with simultaneous political comment, Moscow received it hysterically as if the atomic bombs might start dropping before midnight. Where there are no safety valves to let off pressure every day, the emotional explosions are sudden, swift and disturbing.

After the shattering experience of two world wars we are all familiar with the arguments for political and commerical internationalism as the only means for avoiding military catastrophes. But Moscow also illustrates the necessity for intellectual and cultural association on a world scale. There are no new ideas in Moscow. All the old ones are reiterated with stupefying regularity. All the newspapers say the same thing in almost the same way, usually on the same day; with some refreshing exceptions, every man writes like every other man. During the long, enervating periods between microscopic changes in the official party line, even a foreigner could write a Soviet political article that could hardly be distinguished from the genuine polemics that appear in Pravda. Izvestia and the New Times. The prolonged policy of barring foreigners from Russia, of isolating the few who do creep in; of restricting their movements in the country and of censoring news and suppressing it has created a bloodless, old-fashioned, petit-bourgeois culture that is colorless and conventional.

Since I know nothing about science, I have unfortunately no way of judging the results of one of the most industrious acitivites of the Soviet Union, although I do know that the general level of medical practice is low. But from personal observation I feel competent to report that the general level of theatre, art and music is low – and I suspect that many writers, actors and musicians realize it. On the whole, there is no vitality in the arts; they are reactionary and moribund. Under the dead weight of political control there is little opportunity for individual enterprise and experiment. It would be logical to expect a new society, such as the Russians are trying to create, to be daring and bold in the arts. But it seems to me that Soviet art contains just as much hokum and bathos as ours, without producing occasional works of originality that compensate for the failures. The combination of isolationism and totalitarianism has resulted in the death of new ideas.

In an abnormal climate of this kind, group aberrations flourish. And it seems to me that the most conspicuous and also the most irritating abnormality in Soviet leadership is a group paranoia. The leaders imagine that every man's hand is against them; they imagine that they are surrounded. And, of course, there is no more cartain way of arousing first the bewilderment, then the contempt and finally the enmity of other nations. In view of the size, strength, courage and inexhaustible resources of the Soviet Union, this phobia about being trapped and cramped would be hilarious, if it were not so troublesome to foreigners who want to find some way of getting on with the Soviet Union.

As far as danger from abroad is concerned, the United States, with its highly integrated economy, is more vulnerable, even with the atomic bomb in the cellar. But differences of opinion and differences of interest in international affairs are interpreted by the Soviet leaders as agressive hostility to the Soviet Union, for that is how they would interpret differences of opinion and interest inside Russia. A Soviet citizen who opposed a Stalinist policy would be removed from society as an enemy of the State. The area of tolerance is invisibly thin.

In America, there is a kind of old wives' tale to the effect that the leaders of the Soviet Union are shrewd, cunning and realistic men who always know from one moment to the next where they are going. But I suspect that they are rather commonplace men who have had no experience of democracy at home and are confused by manifestations of democracy abroad. After succesfully destroying differences of opinion at home for the holiest Marxian reasons, they instinctively regard differences of opinion abroad as treachery to the Soviet Union and to the common people. Marxianism is a splendid science that has purged itself of the unscientific spontaneity of human nature.

The most formidable impediment to amicable international relations is the basic fact that the Soviet Union is a Socialist state developing and expanding in a capitalist world. According to the Communist party line, the Soviet is not secure from aggression so long as capitalist countries like the United States and Great Britain also hold dominant positions in the world. Russia has in the past maintained workable relations with capitalist countries, including Nazi Germany when Hitler was fighting the West. But the party line has now reverted to the theory that "monopoly capital," as the Soviet writers invariably describe it, is Fascist, is preserving the centers of fascism and is bent on the destruction of socialism. Since, according to Marx, "monopoly capital" is also destroying itself, there seems to be quite a lot of destruction going on, and the atomic bomb is obviously superfluous.

In the meantime, the United States is portrayed in the Soviet press as a violent, imperialistic nation that is extending its power throughout the world and is trampling on the rights of small nations, and the "monopoly capitalists" in the United States are portrayed as thwarting the "broad masses of the peace-loving peoples of the world," which is another daily idiom of the Soviet press.

During my ten months in Moscow, I never discovered in a newspaper or magazine any reference to the United States suggesting that, like the Russians, we also have creditable characteristics. Great Britain is portrayed in a baleful light, despite the fact that socialism has come to power at one time or another in England, New Zealand and Australia. This latter fact might throw some doubt on the theory that the trouble lies between socialism and capitalism. Perhaps the trouble lies elsewhere.

After my tour of duty in Moscow, I prefer the Western type of capitalism because it is more interested in individual men and women and places a high value on human freedom. The preservation of human freedom was the cause of the war; it remains the paramount issue in world society. Socialism is a rational approach to the problems of the world. And, as we are likely to find out in Britain, socialism does not necessarily involve the destruction of human liberties. In the case of so vast and varied a country as Russia, which has many nationalities to group together, socialism is probably the only system that can open the way to material progess. If there were any way of distinguishing between Soviet socialism and Soviet totalitarianism every man would watch with interest and hope the development of socialism inside Russia for the light it could shed on the problems of the rest of the world.

As a matter of fact, every thinking man will watch it with interest because, whatever else may be true of Russia, the achievements of socialism there so far have had the most profound effect on the rest of the world. People everywhere profoundly want to believe that some economic system is ideal, and, knowing nothing about the misery of life in Russia, they want to believe that Soviet Russia has found the ideal solution. By our standards, the Soviet Union has so far not solved any of the problems of freedom – including freedom from want and freedom from fear. To anyone who is attracted by the theory of socialism, the police regimentation of the Soviet people is not only disillusioning but frightening. But again, in my

THE PARTY PYRAMID

ORGANIZATIONAL LEVEL	REPRESENTATIVE BODIES	EXECUTIVE BODIES	
ALL-UNION	CONGRESS (ONCE IN 3 YEARS) / CONFERENCE (ONCE A YEAR)	SECRETARY-GENERAL / SECRETARIAT (DAILY) / POLITBUREAU — ORGBUREAU (SEVERAL TIMES WEEKLY) / CENTRAL COMMITTEE (ONCE IN 4 MONTHS)	PARTY SUMMIT
UNION REPUBLIC	CONGRESS (ONCE EVERY YEAR AND A HALF)	CENTRAL COMMITTEE (ONCE IN 3 MONTHS)	
TERRITORY OR REGION / AUTONOMOUS REGION / AREA	CONFERENCE (ONCE EVERY YEAR AND A HALF)	COMMITTEE (ONCE IN 3 MONTHS)	
DISTRICT / CITY	CONFERENCE (ONCE A YEAR)	COMMITTEE (ONCE IN 1½ MONTHS)	
PRIMARY ORGANIZATIONS IN RURAL LOCALITIES, ECONOMIC ENTERPRISES, PUBLIC INSTITUTIONS, ETC.	GENERAL MEETING	BUREAU OR SECRETARY	

PARTY MEMBERSHIP: 6,000,000

LINE OF FORMATION - - - - - - - →
LINE OF FORMAL ACCOUNTABILITY ～～～→
LINE OF CONTROL — · — · — →

THE SOVIET PYRAMID

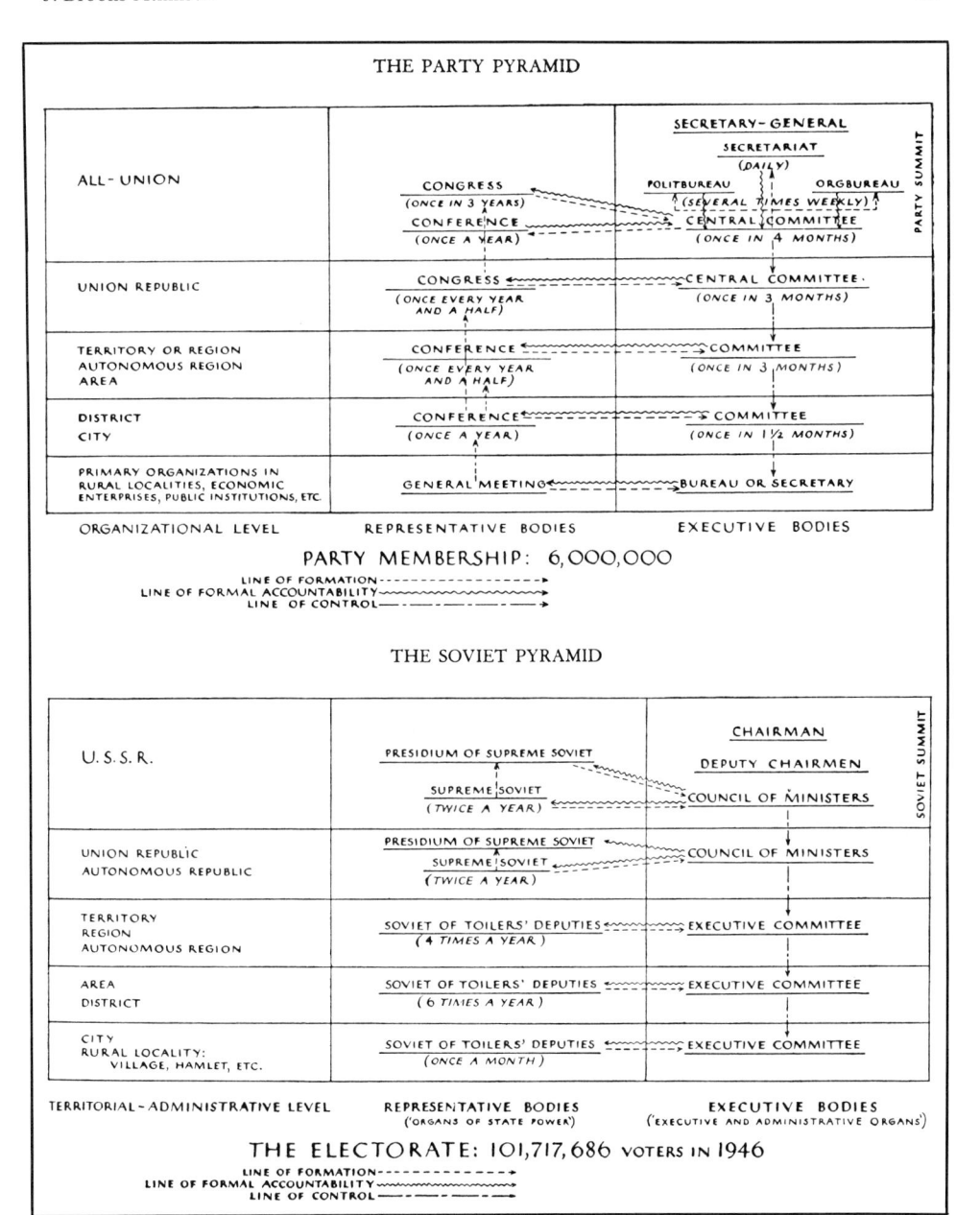

TERRITORIAL-ADMINISTRATIVE LEVEL	REPRESENTATIVE BODIES ('ORGANS OF STATE POWER')	EXECUTIVE BODIES ('EXECUTIVE AND ADMINISTRATIVE ORGANS')	
U.S.S.R.	PRESIDIUM OF SUPREME SOVIET / SUPREME SOVIET (TWICE A YEAR)	CHAIRMAN / DEPUTY CHAIRMEN / COUNCIL OF MINISTERS	SOVIET SUMMIT
UNION REPUBLIC / AUTONOMOUS REPUBLIC	PRESIDIUM OF SUPREME SOVIET / SUPREME SOVIET (TWICE A YEAR)	COUNCIL OF MINISTERS	
TERRITORY / REGION / AUTONOMOUS REGION	SOVIET OF TOILERS' DEPUTIES (4 TIMES A YEAR)	EXECUTIVE COMMITTEE	
AREA / DISTRICT	SOVIET OF TOILERS' DEPUTIES (6 TIMES A YEAR)	EXECUTIVE COMMITTEE	
CITY / RURAL LOCALITY: VILLAGE, HAMLET, ETC.	SOVIET OF TOILERS' DEPUTIES (ONCE A MONTH)	EXECUTIVE COMMITTEE	

THE ELECTORATE: 101,717,686 VOTERS IN 1946

LINE OF FORMATION - - - - - - - →
LINE OF FORMAL ACCOUNTABILITY ～～～→
LINE OF CONTROL — · — · — →

[*Source:* Julian Towster: Political Power in the U.S.S.R., 1917–1947, New York 1948, pp. 414 f.]

opinion, socialism in itself is not the source of the trouble between the Soviet Union and the United States and Great Britain. Other things being equal, the two Western democracies could get on with the Soviet Union more profitably than Nazi Germany did during the period of the fraudulent pact of friendship. Indeed, I expect that they will.

But that is not the point of view of the Soviet leaders. They regard themselves as custodians of the future of the world. In their opinion, everything is going their way; as leaders of a Socialist State with a Communist goal, they regard themselves as the advance agents of manifest destiny. In Poland and the Balkans they believe that they are helping manifest destiny along, although the resistance, is terrific from the "unenlightened," who are in the vast majority.

In their current relations with the Governments of the United States and Great Britain the Soviet leaders are not certain that they are dealing with the true representatives of the "broad masses of the peace-loving peoples." In their opinion, perhaps, these Governments are to one degree or another imposed on their people by political knavery, ignorance, inertia and the trickery of "monopoly capital."

Perhaps the Soviet Government, which champions the people at the same time that it pushes them around, will be able to get behind the facade of the American and British Governments into more direct contact with the people through trade unions and political pressure organizations. And, to continue looking at things from the point of view of the Politburo, perhaps the current representatives of the United States and Great Britain are only the old guard doomed to repudiation by the people when "monopoly capital" succeeds in cutting its own throat.

Whether the Soviet Government and the Communist party, which are virtually identical, are promoting revolutionary changes in the United States and Britain is not circumstantially known, although there is reason to believe that they are meddling in the politics of France by subsidizing and advising the French Communist party. But one of the causes of Soviet Russia's tenacity in international affairs is that it regards socialism as the most stabilizing factor in international peace. Any deviation from Soviet policy logically becomes a threat to world peace by reactionaries who are defending a dying economic organization. For communism is not only a political science but a religion, and its conduct is governed by dogma as well as by reason. The believers have to accept it without reservation. This religious fervor underlies the Soviet attitude toward foreign countries, and is assiduously cultivated at home. The modern ikons are the heroic statues and portraits of Lenin and Stalin in every public building and the huge portraits of the minor prophets carried by the believing multitudes on holidays. On great occasions the statues and images are decked with flowers or ribbons like the representations of the saints in the churches.

The literary style of Soviet propaganda overflows with religious expressions of love, gratitude, high resolves and sacrifice for a future life. Moscow is not only the capital of Soviet Russia but the holy city of the Communist faith; and Lenin is the father and Stalin is the son. Since the Soviet Government has done so little to solve any of the human problems of living, the holy attitude it takes toward its mission in the world may seem ludicrous and fatuous. But the parish letters to the faithful, which are the leaders on the front pages of the newspapers, solemnly declare that the Soviet Union is the most blessed nation in the world because it has embraced the one and only true faith, and that the future will overflow with love, joy and singing.

When the Soviet representatives meet ours at the conference table they are in effect meeting the last tottering princes of original sin, and they cannot give way to us without yielding divine principle. That is one reason why the Russians are so difficult to get on with in pagan assemblies that do not worship Marx, Lenin and Stalin.

19.5 Russo-American Relations and Their Future Outlook

[*Source: Brooks Atkinson: Soviet seen wanting peace despite its air of challenge, in:* The New York Times *(New York, N. Y.), Vol. XCV/No. 32,308, July 9, 1946, p. 1, cols. 6–7; p. 6, cols. 5–7.*]

In one respect, we and the leaders of the Soviet Union heartily agree: that the maintenance of peace depends upon peaceable relations between them and us. In view of their many problems, their war weariness and the wounds of the war that have not yet healed, they are eager for peace. They know more than we do about the horrors of war. Although they do not give us much credit for our share in the victory, that is no reason why we should withhold from them credit and admiration for their magnificent war record. Nor should we forget for a moment that their people have suffered painfully and are suffering still.

But, to eliminate as much as possible extraneous emotional factors, we should follow the Soviet leadership by ridding our minds of any assumption that peaceful relations are identical with friendship. Americans are likely to imagine that people in the rest of the world trust us, like us, envy us and probably want to borrow some money from us. Only the last of these things is true of the Soviet leaders. They do want to borrow money from us to accelerate the tempo of the current Five-Year Plan. Americans would probably regard a loan to Russia as a gesture in friendship. The leaders of the Soviet Union would have no such sentimental feeling.

Refusing a loan to them after making loans to Great Britain, China, France, Poland and other countries would probably be interpreted as an act of hostility on the part of a chaotic, irresponsible, spendthirft country dominated by reactionaries. Relief shipments to a country that has an anti-foreign government should reflect nothing more devious than the humanitarian impulses of the American people. The Russian people living in the areas devastated by the Germans sorely need help, get what is sent and are grateful for it.

But it should not be expected that relief shipments will alter in any way the austere and detached attitude of the Soviet Government, which, as a matter of fact, would like to be in a position to provide for its people without foreign assistance. Russia's isolationism cannot be broken down by munificence from abroad. For any man with self-respect in any part of the world resents, if he does not actually dislike, Father Bountiful who, to tell the truth, has a sort of smug expression. Father Bountiful cannot purchase friendship with his surplus food stocks and worn-out clothing; nor can Father Bountiful break down the stone wall of censorhip or establish the free exchange of scientists, professors, artists and students or promote free travel throughout the Soviet Union by footloose Americans. All these things seem to us casual and normal and the only basis for mutual understanding. But it is a matter of deliberate policy on the part of the Soviet Government to eliminate foreign influences during the period when it is trying to develop socialism in a conditioned climate.

Although the Soviet Union is challenging the rest of the world, it cannot afford to compete with the rest of the world or let its people know that in the Western democracies people not only have civil freedoms, but very much higher standards of living. The myth of persecution of the worker by "monopoly capital" would disappear if free association were permitted with the common people of the West.

Despite all these impediments to pleasant and easy relations – despite the truculence, the tenacity, the cries of persecution or the injured silences, despite the flamboyant retirements from unfavorable sessions of the United Nations – the Russians really do not want to lose friends throughout the world, nor build up resistance. They do not want to defy world opinion. Sometimes they are surprised by the vehemence of criticism from abroad. Accustomed to tyrannical police control at home, they are surprised when milder versions of totalitarian tyranny produce screams of protest in Poland and the Balkans and bellows of righteous indignation from such remote citadels of "monopoly capital" as England and the United States. Public opinion from abroad forced Russia to withdraw from Iran although there was nothing concrete then, and there is nothing concrete now, to prevent the Soviet from adding Iran to its satellite nations. Russia has the troops and the techniques to take Iran any time she wants to range the rest of the world solidly against her.

In the flush of victory last autumn the Russians opened a war of nerves against Turkey. Russia had enormous military strength in the vicinity, as she still has, and could have "liberated" Turkey from Turkish sovereignty, although not without fighting. But Turkey's nerves were strong, public opinion abroad began to grow restless, and the United States, taking a bland part in the war of nerves, sent a powerful battleship to Turkey bearing the ashes of a former Turkish Ambassador, as well as a few unspoken implications. It would be foolish to assume that the Soviet has written Iran and Turkey off the agenda. Some day the Soviet Government may be willing to pay the cost in world prestige, or consider that the price has fallen, for the whole Near East is shaky. But at present the Russians do not want to defy the rest of the world.

From time to time during my stay in Moscow I used to test the censor's alertness by unobtrusively inserting the following sardonic remark into my dispatches: "The Soviet foreign policy is very human. The Soviets want to remain on good terms with the whole world and meet with no resistance anywhere." The censor was always keen enough to remove those mischievous sentences. It was a game we played; he was always the winner. In spite of the ironic phrasing, there is a decent trace of truth in that assertion. Matters of right and wrong are not of much consequence in power politics anywhere at any time. But at present the Russians do not want to let loose the whirlwind that might blow up another war.

In these articles I have suggested some of the reasons why the Russians are so difficult to get on with in international affairs. If we are not friends, neither are we enemies. But whether we like it or not, we are competitors for influence on the rest of the world. Marxism is ultimately a program for the whole world. Being doctrinaire Marxists, the leaders of the Soviet Union naturally see our relationship in those terms, and we may as well keep the whole thing in perspective by looking at the future with their point of view in mind. There is no reason why we should feel complacent despite the backwardness of Russia and the low standards of living there. For Russia is potentially the most powerful nation in the world. She embraces a huge land mass that occupies the pivotal position between Europe and Asia. She has immense natural resources. She has comparatively unlimited manpower. As a totalitarian government, the Soviet leaders can make highly effective use of their manpower (which is also womanpower), and their workers ought to become more efficient as time goes on.

By and large, the Russian people are not only strong but decent, according to their standards of patriotism and devotion. The lack of what we regard as vital freedom does not distress them, for they do not know what Western freedoms are. As a matter of personal faith, I believe that freedom is more creative than dictatorship. Our record in the war, I think, proves it. Now that the war is over, there is no point in congratulating ourselves on our achievements in field and factory. But at least we have concrete evidence that under certain circumstances that threaten our freedoms the United States can organize and achieve a national goal. Although our manpower is more limited than the combined man and woman power of Russia, it is still very large.

We, too, have abundant natural resources, and our geographical position is also strategic. In international competition, our greatest asset is the high level of technical skill. Man for man, our population is infinitely more productive in the factory and on the farm. But in peacetime we are not organized for maximum production. Many other human considerations come first. Nor can we guarantee our people economic security. It is true that there is no unemployment in the Soviet Union, although work is not in any sense a matter of individual choice and every job is immensely overmanned. In competition with Russia, which is a dynamic force in the world, we have to maintain our supremacy by growth that is also dynamic. We have to increase production and raise standards of living on a dynamic scale. Our basic problem is how to organize for maximum production without infringing on the Bill of Rights. How thoroughly can we organize for the common good without curtailing human freedoms? Speaking as one American citizen, I don't know. What I do know is that the problem is there.

After ten months in Moscow I started for home a month ago very low in mind. On a basis of personal experiences and personal observations, I could see no prospect of cordial relations with the great Power of Europe and Asia. To put it in the simplest terms, that is a pity because it would be pleasant and enriching to have friendly association with these people.

My wife and I traveled in a Soviet plane from an excellent modern airdrome in Moscow to Odessa, by way of Kiev. The plane was a Russian version of our Douglas transport; and contrary to what many Americans report about Soviet flying, the whole flight was manged with a high degree of skill, comfort and dispatch. We enjoyed the other passengers, as we always enjoyed being with any group of Russian people. They had a warm family feeling toward each other; and it reached out a little to include us. Little courtesies were extended to us now and then; they proved that although we could not join the family, we were not excluded. These are small things, but they represent my experience with Russian people apart from officers of the Government; and they confirm my belief that the Russian people are sincere and good-hearted. It is a pity, perhaps it will be a tragedy, that as a nation we have to live with the Russian nation in an atmosphere of bitterness and tension. But we have to. There is no other way.

Related Readings

Browder, Earl Russel: War or peace with Russia?, New York 1947.
Burnham, James: The struggle for the world, New York–London 1947.
Byrnes, James Francis: Speaking friendly, New York 1947.
Carr, Albert H. Z.: Truman, Stalin and peace, Garden City, N. Y., 1950.
Dallin, David J.: The new Soviet empire, London 1951.
Dean, Vera Micheles: The United States and Russia, Cambridge, Mass., 1947.
Duranty, Walter: Stalin & Co. The Politburo – the men who run Russia, New York 1949.
Fainsod, Merle: How Russia is ruled, Cambridge, Mass., 1953
Fisher, Harold Henry: America and Russia in the world community, Claremont, Calif., 1946
LaFeber, Walter: America, Russia and the Cold War, 1945–1975, 3rd ed., New York 1976.
Lippmann, Walter: The Cold War. A study in U.S. foreign policy, New York 1947.
Meissner, Boris: Sowjetrußland zwischen Revolution und Restauration, Köln 1956.
Mosely, Philip Edvard: Face to face with Russia, New York 1948.
Reitzel, William/Kaplan, Morton A./Coblenz, Constance G.: United States foreign policy, 1945–1955, Washington, D. C., 1956.
Seton-Watson, George Hugh Nicholas: Neither war nor peace. The struggle for power in the postwar world, New York–London 1960.
Smith, Walter Bedell: My three years in Moscow, Philadelphia, Pa., 1950.
U.S. Department of State (Ed.): A decade of American foreign policy. Basic documents 1941–1949, Washington, D. C., 1950.

1947

Paul W. Ward

The Sun, Baltimore

CHAPTER 20

REPORTS ABOUT THE SOVIET UNION IN 1947

The Cultural Situation and How it is Formed by the Party

    Introductory Notes
20.1 The Russian Sense of Humor and Some of Its Products
20.2 The Idea of an Ethnic Plurality and Its Reality
20.3 Religion in Soviet Russia and the Various Churches
20.4 A 'Purge' in Arts and Its Consequences
20.5 'Socialist' Art and How It Is Produced
    Related Readings

Introductory Notes

As to the internationally oriented entries, the Pulitzer Prize committees in 1948 could again concentrate on one relevant categorie only, as the former Correspondence category, like the one in "Telegraphic Reporting (International)" created in 1942, had now been replaced by a prize category maintained continuously from then on: International Reporting. A correspondent of a newspaper that never before had been honored in one of the international categories, Paul W. Ward of the Baltimore Sun, *Maryland, was the first to win this new award which was a merger of the two previous categories. He won it "for his series of articles published in 1947 on 'Life in the Soviet Union.'"*

Paul William Ward was born on October 9, 1905, in Lorain, Ohio. Having studied at the universities of Akron (1921–22) and West Virginia (1923–24), Ward earned a B. A. degree at Middlebury College in 1925. After transitory employment at the Powers Photo-engraving Co. in New York during the 1925–26 period, Ward worked at a newspaper in New Bedford, Massachussetts, called the Standard, *from 1926 to 1930. In 1930 Paul W. Ward came to* The Sun *in Baltimore, Maryland. After three years on the staff in Baltimore, he was transferred to the Washington bureau to give him an opportunity for diversified experience in the coverage of congressional and departmental affairs and to lay a broad foundation for his development as a correspondent. He took advantage of this opportunity, preparing himself so thoroughly that in the spring of 1937 he became chief of* The Sun's *London bureau. In that capacity he covered the Nine-Power Conference in Brussels in the fall of 1937; Hitler's seizure of Austria in 1938; the Munich crisis in September 1938; Hitler's seizure of Czechoslovakia in March 1939; and Mussolini's seizure of Albania in April of that year. In May, 1939, Paul Ward was assigned to Moscow, then to Paris; in February 1940, he returned to his newspaper's Washington bureau where he concentrated exclusively on foreign affairs. In April, 1946, Paul Ward was assigned to Paris, from where he visited the British, French and American zones of Germany, plus Berlin, Vienna, Trieste and Rome. From February, 1947, on he had various assignments in Moscow, resulting in his series of articles on 'Life in the Soviet Union' which brought him the 1948 Pulitzer Prize for International Reporting.*

The following texts by Paul William Ward, copyright 1947, are reprinted by kind permission of The Sun, *Baltimore, Maryland.*

20.1 The Russian Sense of Humor and Some of Its Products

[*Source: Paul W. Ward: Russians jab in jest at woe of Russian life, in:* The Sun *(Baltimore, Md.), Vol. 220/No. 140 F, May 1, 1947, p. 1, cols. 4–5; p. 12, cols. 3–4.*]

One of the most revealing aspects of life in the Soviet Union is the jokes it produces. Not even the tight grip of Communist party zealots on Russian society has been able to throttle the Russian sense of humor. It has survived the dull evangels of the Soviet press, the repressions of the Soviet censorhip, and the menacing swoops by night of the Kremlin's secret police. Although the latter can mete out five years of forced labor in Siberia to any Soviet citizen caught telling stories that reflect on the present regime, Russians still tell them not only to each other but – in confidence – to visiting foreigners. The stories about to be recounted here were so acquired. They are merely samples from a large batch of Russian quips and yarns disclosing in a necessarily indirect way what Russia's current rulers call "remnants of capitalism in the consciousness" of their subjects.

There is only one facet of Soviet life that, in general, escapes the blade of Russian wit. Stalin seldom is the target of its irreverence. He figures in only five stories collected in the course of eight weeks, and none of the five reflects upon him. One does, however, reflect upon the pleasures of life under the collective-farming system that George Bernard Shaw recently urged be copied from the U.S.S.R. for the benefit of Britain's agriculture.

In this tale Roosevelt, Churchill and Stalin find the path of the limousine in which they are riding together blocked by an obstinate cow. The efforts of Roosevelt and Churchill to lure or prod her from the road are unavailing. But a word from Stalin, whispered in her ear, sends her bounding off in evident panic. Stalin then lets Roosevelt and Churchill in on the secret of his success: "I simply told her I'd put her on a collective farm if she didn't get out of the way."

Another yarn in which Stalin figures reflects the inadequacy of the Russian worker's food ration. Stalin, at a Kremlin banquet watches his henchmen gorging themselves on caviar, fish, game and beef put before them in gargantuan array. "My Ministers," he remarks in regal fashion, "are in good appetite." "Oh, this is nothing," one of the more naîve among them replies. "You should see some of your workers. They can eat a whole month's ration at one sitting."

There is also a tale which suggests the Russians do not completely credit the assurances of their leaders that the role Soviet authorities are playing in the "liberated" countries is pleasing to the citizens of those areas.

An admiring crowd gathered before a shop window in Bulgaria is split by an old peasant woman who elbows her way forward to see what the other have been staring at. She sees in the window a huge picture of a mustachioed man and asks who he is. Told it is a picture of Stalin, she is just as puzzled as ever, for, poor, simple peasant that she is, she never has heard of him. An astounded member of the crowd sets out to enlighten her.

"That," he says, "is the man who saved us Bulgarians, first, from the Nazis and then from the Fascists." "And will he," the peasant asks breathlessly, "also save us from the Russians?"

There is a political conundrum current in Moscow that belongs in the same category:

"What is the biggest country in the world?" "Poland, because it has no western frontier, its capital is in Moscow and most of its population is concentrated in Siberia."

Another yarn in which Stalin figures reflects the miserable housing conditions in Russia, where now, as before the war, several families must be crowded into quarters scarcely big enough for one and the angle under an apartment-house stairs is rated fit accommodation for husband, wife and two children.

In this tale a schoolteacher distributes pictures of Stalin to all her pupils and orders them to pin them up on the walls of their rooms at home. The next morning she quizzes the class to see whether her orders have been obeyed. Each little pupil answers in the affirmative until she gets to Natasha. Her reply, a stubborn negative, shocks the teacher into pressing questions that finally reduce Natasha to tears and a blurted explanation: "We live in the center of the room."

There is a brief tale that also reflects on present wages, living costs and the corruptions of the "black market" in the U.S.S.R. It is, in fact, no more than a humorous curse: "May you have to live on only your salary!"

The only story collected in Moscow that comes close to reflecting on Stalin himself is one which suggests in passing that objurgations from the Kremlin haven't been sufficient to wipe out interracial animosities within the Soviet Union.

Stalin is not a Great Russian but a Georgian and, trusting Russians will tell you, "speaks Russian like a bootblack." Their uneasiness about his broken Russian – rather like the uneasiness caused Berliners by Hitler's Viennese German – gains its point from the fact that Moscow's bootblacks are mostly from Georgia. And thereupon hangs the tale of a queue of bootblacks found waiting at a Kremlin gat one dawn. Asked what they were waiting for, one of them replied: "For the next vacancy in the Politburo."

It is a mean little joke, for, in reality, however much Stalin may favor his fellow Georgians over Russians, he has included only one beside himself – Beria – in the Politburo, which is the inner cabinet, or "palace guard," of his regime.

There are many Russian jokes that, taking no note whatever of Stalin, poke fun at the whole Soviet system. One of them rejects either the standard thesis of Soviet apologists – "Things are better now than they were 25 years ago" – or its counterpart: "Things will be better 50 years hence."

It is a cynical quip, wryly intoned: "Have we built socialism yet, or are things going to get worse?" It has as corollary based upon the constant assurance to the Soviet people that in another 25 years Russia will have "caught up with" the United States in its standard of living. "When we do, let me know, for that's where I want to get off," is a popular Russian commentary.

It is not only oldsters with memories of prerevolutionary days who confect such quips. Youngsters – students who have been crammed all their lives with dialectical assurances that life in the Soviet Union is sweeter than elsewhere – are responsible for a gag about one of the statues of Lenin that abound in Moscow. Lenin is posed with one arm outstretched, pointing westward. The founder of Bolshevism is saying "Get out of the Soviet Union," grinning students assert with the same zest that American teenagers, with eyes fixed on Hollywood, repeat Greeley's "Go west, young man; go west."

There are many jokes which indicate a cynical regard toward official propaganda in the

Soviet Union. In one a man is in heaven, finds it dull there, and gets permission to move to a quarter where he has seen people singing, dancing, playing cards and eating in Lucullan fashion. He finds himself, however, on the hot coals of hell when he asks about the comforts and pastimes he had observed, is told by a Communist devil: "Oh, that was just propaganda."

Another Russian jape that is whispered about Moscow jeers at the generals' wives who have been lifted to unaccustomed estate by the fortunes of war and find it slightly above their cultural level. It is a joke that also takes note of the influx of "liberated" goods from Germany.

A general's wife, moving into a new flat, has difficulty in getting the movers to put her recently acquired grand piano into the room she has chosen for it. The room, one of the movers tells her, would be a bad choice for "it has no resonance." "Oh, put it where I tell you," she responds impatiently. "I'll have my husband bring some resonance back from Germany."

There is also a quip that indicates Russians would like to enjoy some of the freedom of speech guaranteed them by the Soviet constitution. It is a quip about the recent drought in their country and employs a Russian pun. "Drought?" it goes. "Naturally, there was drought; 200,000,000 people had their mouths full of water."

To have one's mouth full of water means, in Russian, to be unable to talk.

Finally, all the misery of the Russian man-in-the-street is summed up in a tale built upon the fact that Lenin lies, embalmed and entombed, under glass in Red Square where hundreds queue up to gaze upon his remains each afternoon. In this story one Russian worker greets another, asking convivially: "How're they treating you?" "Just like Lenin," worker No. 2 replies. "They won't feed me and they won't bury me."

20.2 The Idea of an Ethnic Plurality and Its Reality

[*Source: Paul W. Ward: Russia still puts 'Jew' on passports, in:* The Sun *(Baltimore, Md.); Vol. 220/No. 142 F, May 3, 1947, p. 1, cols. 4–5; p. 5, cols. 1–2.*]

There is one hangover from Czarist times that Russia's current rulers have not tried to cure. The Soviet Government is probably the only major one left in the postwar world that still stamps the passports of a minority of its citizens with the word. "Jew." Just what the determinant is that puts that stamp on the identity papers of some Russians is as hard to ascertain as why the practice, begun under the Czars, has been continued under the Communists.

Certainly it is not based on any such religious definition as Hitler, for all his theorizing about blood and race, had to fall back upon for identifying the targets of his anti-Semitism. Many of those Soviet citizens whose passports are stamped "Jew" are young men and women nurtured in the aggressive atheism of the Bolshevik regime. They have never been devotees of Judaism. Nor can the practice of stamping "Russian" on the passport of one Muscovite

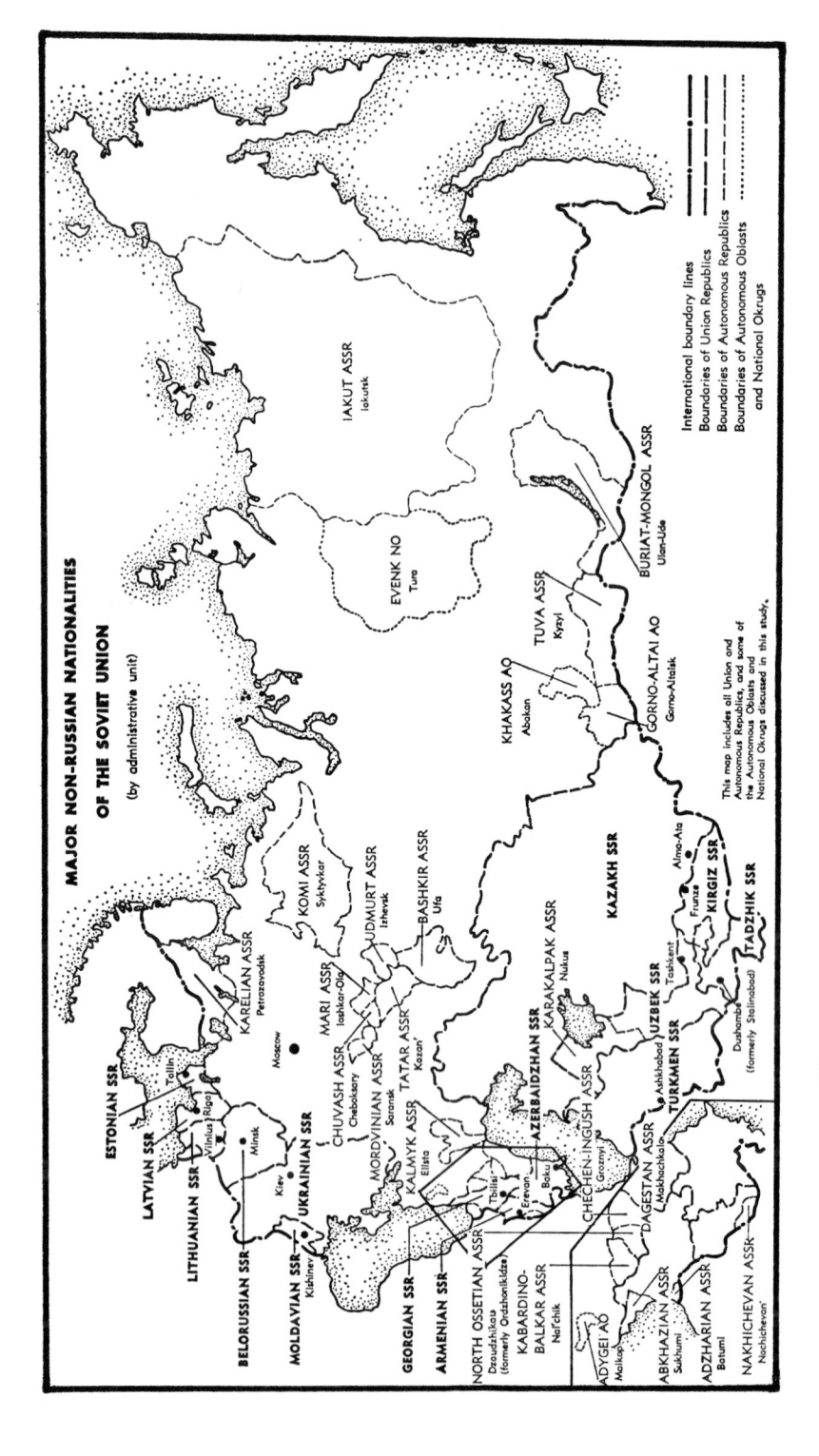

[Source: Lowell Tillett: The Great Friendship, Chapel Hill, N.C., 1969, p. XII.]

and "Jew" on that of his equally irreligious neighbor be based on any precise ethnic or national principles. The one may be indistinguishable from the other in customs and language or physical or mental traits.

Moreover, there exists within the "multinational" Soviet Union nothing distinguishable as a Jewish national group. The ill-fated Biro-Bidjan colony, which the Soviet Government set up on the fringes of Mongolia some twenty years ago as a counterpoise to Zionism, is the closest approach to that. It is believed to have absorbed at its peak no more than 15,000 Jews. To stamp the word "Jew" on the passport, or identity papers, every Soviet citizen must carry is not to subject him, to any particular onus. There has been no pale, no ghetto since the 1917 revolution. There are no property or other laws which place the bearer of papers so marked at a legal disadvantage in getting a job, schooling, food or housing accommodations.

The stamp does, however, put him at the mercy of whatever anti-Semitic prejudices may be harbored individually by the Soviet officials to whom he must show his papers every time he seeks an appointment, a job, additional ration coupons, or a better room. That may help to account for the fact that, according to residents, relatively few of the Jews evacuated from Moscow during the war have been able to get back into the town.

In an entertainment-starved city, where any sort of performance is a sell-out, Moscow's world-famous Yiddish Art Theater was able to draw one recent night an audience of only 62 persons. Ushers and cast together outnumbered the ticket buyers, who, a visiting American noted, spoke Russian, not Yiddish, as, in pairs, they promenaded about the lobby between the acts.

Certainly, despite all the official lecturing against it, there is still much anti-Semitic feeling among the people of the U.S.S.R. The Government itself has not done much to supplement its preachments with examples. Lazar M. Kaganovich is the only Jew left as a full member of the Politburo. No Jew has held a high post in the Foreign Office since Ivan Maisky and Maxim Litvinov got the gate. Jews also do not bulk large among the rank-and-file members of the Communist party. The prewar "purges" largely cleaned them out of the party hierarchy as well as out of the Soviet intelligentsia, where previously they had been preponderant.

There are still occasional violent outbreaks of anti-Semitism. They were sufficiently serious in the Ukraine after the Germans had been driven out to cause the Kremlin to dispatch a special unit of secret police troops to that "liberated" area. Nor does the nonpolitical Russian feel it necessary to conceal his anti-Semitism from foreigners. A Russian "intellectual" entertaining an American girl in Moscow's closest imitation of a smart New York night club complained to her that the place was "too full of Jews."

Similarly, in a recent Moscow court case, a judge, who was otherwise prone to lecture the parties on correct behavior expected from Soviet citizens, took no note of the plaintiff's charge that the respondent had called him "a dirty like." Nor did the respondent, who had also been accused of advocating the eviction of all Jews from the Soviet capital, feel it necessary to deny the charge. Instead he countered with an assertion, that the plaintiff had called him a "Hitlerite."

There is a double-edged joke that Russians tell which has some bearing upon this point. A Russian, finding a long line of Jews queued up at a point on the outskirts of the capital, asked what they were doing there. Told they were being evicted from Moscow, he protested that was an impossibility under the Soviet system, which barred any form of anti-Semitic discrimination. The people in the queue, however, were unimpressed. Eviction from Moscow did not seem impossible to them. "Have we not," one of them queried, "already been evicted from all the Moscow stories by the generals' wives?" The allusion is to the fact that old jokes which attributed grasping qualitites to the Jews have now been altered to be told at the expense of the spouses of loot-laden Red Army commanders.

A companion piece is a Moscow yarn about a Jew who sought a permit to emigrate to the United States. Why did he want to leave the Soviet Union, he was asked; did he not know it was the only country in the world "where a Jew can sleep in peace?" "Yes," he replied, "but lately I've developed an interest in eating, too."

There are so many tales of this sort told by Muscovites as to leave an indelible impression that the position of the Jew in the Soviet Union is less utopian than its fans abroad believe. They form part of a picture which also suggests that the Bolsheviks have been less successful in establishing intranational cooperation in their "multinational" state than their boasts would indicate.

Foreigners who have been permitted to travel into the fast eastern sections of the Soviet Union report with surprise that they found Great Russians living there in a fashion not unlike that of the British, French and American "imperialists" in prewar Shanghai or Hong Kong. The Great Russians, functioning like viceroys or minor satraps, live, they say, in settlements apart from and superior to the "native cities" and enjoy a kind of extraterritoriality. These reports are in line with a stream of articles in the Soviet press, emphasizing that the Great Russians are the superior people of the U.S.S.R. and adjuring party functionaries and bureaucrats to spare no effort to impress that fact upon the Uzbeks, Armenians, Ukrainians, Mongols and other breeds within the union.

There is another thing that casts doubt upon the Bolsheviks' boasts of having done away in the Soviet Union with the "inner conflicts that corrupt the bourgeois world." During the war, especially in the years 1941–43, the Soviet Union was rent by intranational clashes without equal in any other belligerent country. Such separatist tendencies, such anti-Soviet attitudes manifested themselves among national groups supposed to have been happily absorbed into the Bolshevik community of states that the Kremlin had to resort to violent means of repressing them. It acted, moreover, in violation of the constitution of the U.S.S.R. and of the constitutions of its constituent republics, which guarantee the right of self-determination and even of separation to the peoples concerned.

Four "autonomous" republics and one "autonomous national region" were obliterated by Kremling decree, which merged them into neighboring republics and ordered that their people be uprooted and moved en masse to Siberia. As though conscious that its action was arbitrary and illegal, the Kremlin kept the demise of all but one of the five secret. So, late as December, 1945, they were listed as "autonomous" units of the U.S.S.R. in a special edition of the Stalin constitution the Soviet Embassy then distributed here. The secret death of the other four was not publicly recorded until the 1946 election lists appeared.

The first to vanish was the Volga-German autonomous republic, which had a population of approximately 400,000 and was built around a colony of German emigrants dating back to the 1700's. Erased in August 1941, it was not only the sole republic to have its demise by Kremlin fiat announced but also the only one of the five made to vanish that had not been occupied by the *Wehrmacht*. The other three "autonomous" republics erased by fiat were the Crimean, Kalmyk and Checheno-Ingush. The "autonomous national region" that vanished overnight was Karachev. Their combined populations, subsequently scattered over Siberia, exceeded in number the 700,000 exiles sent to Siberia in Czarist Russia between 1823 and 1898.

20.3 Religion in Soviet Russia and the Various Churches

[*Source: Paul W. Ward: Religion in Russia tolerated, opposed, in:* The Sunday Sun *(Baltimore, Md.), Vol. 47/No. 18, May 4, 1947, p. 1, cols. 6–7; p. 14, cols. 5–7.*]

Religion is officially classified within the Soviet Union as a "survival of capitalism" and, as such, a thing to be obliterated. It is, however, the only "capitalist remnant" against which no ruthless campaign is currently being waged by Stalin and his henchmen.

A visiting American, looking at the candle-bearing crowds of youngsters and oldsters, male and female, that packed themselves in and around Moscow's churches on Easter, would be entitled to think no such campaign ever had been waged in the U.S.S.R. He could even be forgiven for going around to the Lenin Museum near Red Square to see whether to Marx's saying: "Religion is the opiate of the people" – which is graven on the museum wall – there had not recently been added: "And darn good for them, too!"

He would, in the first instance, be wrong, of course, for from 1917 until 1942 Russia's current rulers did their best to exterminate all forms of religion, including Judaism as well as Christianity. But in his second assumption the visitor would be less misguided. For there is ample evidence to indicate – if not to prove – that the Romanovs' successors in the Kremlin incline now to a belief that organized religion may be useful in helping them maintain and extend their sway over Russia's masses.

There are two things that make the evidence inconclusive. One is that the Soviet authorities have not removed all restrictions on religious activity, and those that have been removed can be quickly restored, for their removal was accomplished without any changes in Soviet law. The other is that the authorities have not halted but, instead, intensified anti-religious teaching of Soviet youth. Proof of the latter is to be found in the Soviet press. A recent issue of *Konsomolskaya Pravda,* offical newspaper of the Young Communist League, bespoke the need for "clear and firm atheistic views" on the part of Soviet youth.

In similar vein *Young Bolshevik,* another Communist party organ, quoted Stalin to the effect that the party must be anti-religious because its activity is founded on science and religion is "anti-scientific." "If a Konsomol believes in God and goes to church, he is not fulfilling his obligations," this journal declared. Teachers' newspapers and magazines contain similar declarations.

The principles of freedom of worship and separation of church and state were proclaimed at the beginning of the 1917 revolution. The second of these principles was, indeed, fulfilled. But the first was not except in technical measure. Russians were free to worship the gods of their choice, provided they could find churches that had not been smashed or turned into anti-religious museums; provided also that they could find priests not afraid to emerge from hiding and were not themselves intimidated by the risk of official displeasure.

Not until the 1936 constitution was proclaimed was the status of the clergy eased. In it they were given for the first time under the hammer and sickle equal rights with other Soviet citizens, including rights to rations as well as voting rights. But the campaign to turn all Soviet citizens into atheists – to extinguish the spiritual forces of religion which exalt the individual rather than his master, the Soviet state – continued apace.

Not until the German invasion of the U.S.S.R. in June, 1941, was the any material easing of the Kremlin's hostility to religion. Restricted toleration of the Russian Orthodox Church and of some other church groups began only as the Nazis advanced under a propaganda barrage to the effect that they were going to liberate Russia from its ahteist masters and restore Christianity there. They did reopen the churches the Bolsheviks had closed in the Ukraine, and some of the prayer books, feshly printed in Russian, that they brought with them are now on sale in Moscow. Moreover, such churches as they opened, and did not subsequently destroy, have stayed open, just as have, it is reliably reported, the small shops of private entrepreneurs they re-established around Odessa.

There are some foreign but on-the-scene students of Soviet affairs who believe that such activities on the part of the Germans, before they switched to tactics of barbaric terrorism, account for evidence that they were welcomed by a substantial part of the Ukraine's population. Such evidence is compounded of more than the fact that hundreds of thousands of Ukrainian troops deserted and joined the *Wehrmacht*. It includes and is bulwarked by the uneasiness Ukrainians exhibit when asked where they were during the German occupation.

All openly anti-religious papers ceased publication in the Soviet Union following the German attack in June, 1941. Moscow's anit-religious museum closed, and the Society of Militant Godless became at least dormant. Anti-religious propaganda had stopped entirely by September, 1941, and in 1942 there appeared the first religious publication printed in the U.S.S.R. since 1929. Designed as a counterblast to Nazi propaganda, it was a book entitled "The Truth Concerning Religion in Russia." It had a foreword by Acting Patriarch Sergei, of the Russian Orthodox Church, that began: "This book is above all an answer to the 'crusade' of the Fascists which has been undertaken by them allegedly for the purpose of 'liberating' our people and our Orthodox Church from the Bolsheviks."

Another corner was turned in September, 1943, when for the first time since the revolution the Kremlin's gates were thrown open to a delegation of clergy. Stalin received a group of leading Russian churchmen. Shortly thereafter the Orthodox Church was permitted to hold a council of bishops to elect a Patriarch. They chose Alexei, a classically educated cleric of extreme urbanity who had never been a parish priest. Last August, the Soviet press announced he had been awarded the Red Banner of Labor for his patriotic work during the war. One of his first acts had been to get the priesthood to sign a round-robin declaration of fealty to Stalin.

There are now about 25 churches open in Moscow, a city with a population which has swollen since the war to around 7,000,000. The clergy hopes that eventually 50 churches will be open there. Recently the Orthodox Cathedral at the historic church center of Zagorsk, which had been badly wrecked by revolutionists, was restored and reopened. The seminary there is also operating again, although hard-pressed to find candidates for the priesthood.

The churches of the Soviet Union, including the Orthodox Church, are still barred from engaging in missionary work or social welfare work. But they have been allowed to resume training such candidates for the priesthood as they can find among a Soviet youth into whom teachers have been pumping atheist doctrine for nearly a generation. They have also been allowed to publish, in the case of the Orthodox Church, a journal. But they are not allowed to engage in public education. No parochial or church schools have been reopened. The clergy, however, are permitted to give religious education to children at home or in their churches, whose approaches, as in the Czarist days, are once more jammed with beggars fantastically impoverished, maimed and diseased.

There is only one Roman Catholic church in Moscow. It is St. Louis's (it is more popularly known as the French Church). It is maintained by a single priest, Father Laberge, who arrived last year from Worcester, Mass. Although Moscow's Catholic population is estimated at 25,000, it is patronized largely by members of the foreign colony. An official Soviet statement, issued in August 1941, said there were 1,744 Catholic churches and 2,309 Catholic priests in the U.S.S.R. Most of them, foreign students conclude, were in the Baltic States and the parts of Poland that Russia annexed under the Hitler-Stalin pact, then still held, and has since regained.

These on-the-secene students also note that the Soviet regime is still markedly hostile to the Church of Rome, a fact they attribute, in part, to Catholicism's strong identification with Polish nationalism. They are also inclined to believe the Kremlin's current tolerance of the Orthodox Church is not unrelated to the fact that church has strongly attacked the Papal claim to supremacy in matters of faith and morals, a claim which runs counter to Communist necessities. The Government's favoritism toward the Orthodoxy Church was also evinced when the dissident "living church," which the Kremlin formerly supported in opposition to the Orthodox Church, was made to merge into the latter.

The Government's attitude toward the Orthodox Church as an instrumentallity of political power was hinted at when a governmental "Council for Affairs of the Orthodox Church" was set up during the war. It watches the church for the Kremlin but at the same time helps the church get financial and other assistance from the Government. It also helps to popularize the Soviet sway in Bulgaria, Serbia, Romania and Carpathia, as well as arranging such things as extending Patriach Alexei's authority to include the Orthodox Church in France after the death last year of the Paris patriarch who, until just before his death, had been a foe of the Soviets.

The Soviet Government's relations with non-Orthodox Church groups are conducted through a "Council for Affairs of Religious Cults," which was established in July, 1944. These groups include, besides the Roman Catholics, the "Old Believers," a schismatic orthodox denomination dating back to the Seventeenth Century; a large number of Lutherans in the Baltic States and Karelia; Seventh-Day Adventists, and some 4,000,000 Baptists. They also include Russia's Jews, who numbered slightly over 3,000,000 in 1939, according to the Jewish Statistical Bureau of the Synagogue Council of America. There is now at least one synagogue open in Moscow, whose prewar Jewish population was estimated by the same source at 131,747. Foreign investigators have found it difficult to get any information about Jewish religious activity in postwar Russia.

Next to the Russian Orthodox Church, the one with the biggest following in Russia is

	Soviet Worker		American Worker
	(A) Minutes	(B) Minutes	(C) Minutes
Beef (1 pound)	181	486	33
Lamb (1 pound)	466	473	30
Pork (1 pound)	273	740	31
Bacon (1 pound)	333		35
Smoked ham (1 pound)		1,333	41
Sausage (1 pound)	293	853	25
Chicken (1 pound)	167	527	25
Fresh fish (1 pound)	152	513	23
Butter (1 pound)	389	1,380	39
Lard (1 pound)	...	1,026	16
Cheese (1 pound)		1,026	31
Milk (1 quart)	138	264	10
Eggs (1 dozen)	136	307	30
Sugar (1 pound)	80	360	5
White bread (1 pound)	75	133	6
Black bread (1 pound)	21	173	9
Potatoes (1 pound)	16	73	3
Rice (1 pound)	115	306	9
Cabbage (1 pound)	...	73	3
Onions (1 pound)	18		3
Apples (1 pound)	72	320	6
Oranges (1 dozen)		1,500	17
Tea (1 pound)	573	2,267	50
Coffee (1 pound)	...	600	23
Chocolate (1-pound bar)		2,733	21
Cigarettes (20)	72	633	8
Beer (1 bottle)		216	8
Vodka (1 quart)	1,551	1,551	125
Wine (1 bottle)		700	63
Man's suit	10,666	36,000	1,225
Man's shoes	3,466	13,333	275
Man's socks	192	673	20
Man's shirt	1,333	4,000	100
Man's overcoat	12,800	66,666	1,225
Man's sweater	...	10,800	150
Woman's suit	5,066	33,333	825
Woman's woolen dress	5,066	16,000	500
Woman's slip	906	2,866	100
Woman's caracul coat	186,666	...	6,250
Woman's squirrel coat	53,333	...	3,997
Woman's rabbit coat	13,333		3,997
Woman's shoes	3,733	13,333	250
Woman's galoshes	...	5,333	125
Cotton sheet	666	2,666	110
Linen sheet	...	4,733	163
Radio (table model)		12,666	1,000
Dinner service	12,680	34,666	378
Telephone Serv. (min. chge. per mo.)		1,666	202
Rail sleeper (450 miles)	3,640	...	945
Trolley-bus fare	2	2	5
Gasoline (1 gallon)	50	...	10
Coal (1 ton)	2,000		700
Monthly rent (1 large room)	1,333	13,333	1,000
Firewood (per cord)	2,900		1,100

Columns A and B have been calculated on the basis of actual March list prices in the Soviet Government's "ration" and "commercial" stores in Moscow. They are not necessarily representative of conditions outside the capital. Travelers reported elsewhere bread sold for two and three times the Moscow price, whereas other commodities frequently were cheaper—if obtainable at all—than at the Soviet Union's hub.

[Source: Paul W. Ward: Life in the Soviet Union, Baltimore, Md., 1947, p. 63.]

probably the Church of Mohammed. There are about 20,000,000 Moslems in the Soviet Union. Mohammedanism existed under difficulties comparable to those imposed on Judaism and Catholicism until 1944, when, in the midst of the war, the first Moslem pilgrimages from the U.S.S.R. to Mecca were allowed. That development probably was not unrelated to Soviet efforts to woo the Arab world of the Middle East, which efforts are, in turn, undoubtedly responsible in part for the normally strong but sometimes wavering opposition of the Kremlin to Zionism.

20.4 A 'Purge' in Arts and Its Consequences

[*Source: Paul W. Ward: The arts in Moscow subject to 'purge', in:* The Sun *(Baltimore, Md.), Vol. 220/No. 144 F, May 6, 1947, p. 1, cols. 2–3; p. 14, cols. 4–6.*]

Current developments in the field of Russian arts and letters contrast sharply with Generalissimo Stalin's professions to Harold E. Stassen about Russo-American cooperation and with Vyacheslav M. Molotov's May Day assertion that he and his fellow Bolsheviks are "full of belief in our strength."

Visitors to Moscow these days find the Soviet intellectual world – which includes playwrights, actors, poets, novelists, movie producers and musicians – rent by a bloodless "purge" based on:

1. Patent fears that the ideas and institutions of Soviet authoritarianism seem less vital and attractive even to young Russians than the ideas and institutions of western, or "capitalist," liberalism.

2. A determination, accordingly to rid Soviet literature, drama and music of all "alien influences" and, besides making them ideologically pure, convert them into instruments of propaganda warfare against the western democracies.

Stalin and his Foreign Minister, Molotov, share responsibility for this campaign, which began as World War II ended. Both are members of the Communist party hierarchy, the Orgburo, which is superintending the purification of the intellectuals, and Stalin, kingpin of both the party and the Government, personally initiated the process. He is the man who on April 9 told the Republican presidential aspirant from Minnesota that "I am not a propagandist but a businesslike man." Then, professing faith in the possibility of Russo-American cooperation, he added: "Let us not criticize mutually our systems . . . One should respect the other system when approved by the people . . . If we start calling each other names, it will lead to no cooperation."

But Stalin is also the man who last August called the party hierarchy plus leading Soviet authors, theater directors and movie producers to the Kremlin and ordered them to devote their pens, cameras and voices to the extirpation of "western influences." Stage, screen and press were to concentrate on exposing capitalist "encirclement" and "imperialism" as threatening new wars.

The systematic manner in which they were assigned their tasks suggested that an ironic forecast the poet Mayakovsky made in the days of the first five-year plan had at last been fulfilled. He had dared to wonder then if, eventually, the Communist party hierarchy would put the pen on a par with bayonets and Stalin be found giving the Politburo reports on the production of "pig iron, steel and poems."

The campaign launched by Stalin and his henchmen to re-establish Communist party ideological orthodoxy in literature, drama, the movies and music already has resulted in the literary beheading of two of the Soviet Union's foremost writers and in the liquidation of one of its leading literary magazines. Naturally, it also has produced confusion and depression among the intellectuals, who find themselves damned for what, in wartime, they were praised for doing. The campaign, which is being pressed with such fervor as to suggest all is not quiet (below the surface) on the home front, is not confined to civilians or even to adults. The current "purge" extends to children's literature. The juvenile magazine *Pioneer* has been admonished for not publishing enough political, economic and social subjects. The Red Army press – *Krasnoarmeets,* in particular – has been assailed, too, for "bourgeois deviations."

To lead the campaign and act as a watchful supercensor over all aspects of Soviet culture, a new periodical was launched last summer by the "administration for propaganda and agitation" of the Communist party central committee. It is called *Culture and Life (Kultura i Zhizn)* and has set itself the task of combating any intellectual current distracting Soviet citizens from the "main task" of building communism. Its task is not an easy one, for the citizenry, despite 30 years of immersion in Communistic ideology, cling to tastes their leaders denounce as "bourgeois."

Into almost every ballet there is injected, irrelevantly, a Spanish dance featuring a swarthy young Russian toward whom Muscovite youth behaves precisely as American bobby-soxers conduct themselves in the vicinity of Frank Sinatra. There is the same screaming, the same swooning, the same rush toward the footlights by Muscovite youth when a fat but thin-voiced young tenor appears in opera at the Bolshoi. And one thing that is unmistakable is that Deanna Durbin and Bing Crosby are the reigning favorites of the Moscow screen. Moscow boys and girls love to talk about them, possibly with more ardor than their American counterparts, for they seldom get to see these favorites on the screen. The movie houses of the Soviet capital are so few and small that, if tickets were equitable distributed among the populace, each resident, it is estimated, would get to see only one film in two years.

The movie industry in the Soviet Union is, of course, a Government-owned affair. It has been bossed since the Spring of 1945 by I. G. Bolshakov, who proviously had been stationed in Sofia as Balkan representative of the industry. Later he held the same job in Poland while serving as chairman of the Soviet cinema committee which in March, 1946, was converted into the Ministry of U.S.S.R. Cinematography. Bolshakov's job is full of headaches. First, he had trouble getting the Communist hierarchy to approve his 1946–47 production plans. Then the exhibition of several of his features for this season was forbidden on ideological grounds and, for similar reasons, the editorial board of the industry's official organ, *Cinema Art,* had to be reshuffled. Finally, Bolshakov himself was called to account before the Government's budget commission on charges of wasting money.

At least 14,000,000 of the alleged 23,000,000-ruble loss was due to the banning of pictures whose production the party bosses previously had O.K.'d. It is possible that some of the pictures they banned will be shown outside if not within the Soviet Union. This is suggested by two recent experiences in Moscow. In one case a young Soviet actor pointed out in a night club what he said was a singing star of the Russian cinema and urged that we induce her to sing for us. Seeking a pretext for approaching her, we asked what film she had appeared in recently, and the young actor coached us in the pronunciation of some Russian title. But when he discovered what use we proposed to make of it, he protested: "You mustn't mention that picture in here; it has been banned in the Soviet Union." He promptly withdrew his objection, however, when we said we would tell the actress we had seen the film in London or New York.

In the other case, as guests of the Soviet Government, we were shown a new Soviet film, "Soloist of the Ballet." A "boy-gets-girl" picture, it so contravened the current party preachments as to what is proper in Russian films that one could not help suspecting that it, too, was for export only. The general line of those preachments is suggested by an article in one of the early editions of *Culture and Life*.

It declared "tear-jerkers, detective stories and pandering to the base emotions of backward people" were foreign to the Soviet cinema, which had to have "ideological purposiveness, political acumen and significance of themes." It deplored what it said had been a trend in Soviet film subjects away from the present to the past, toward old literary and dramatic productions, toward fairy tales and legends and petty everyday themes without "social significance." It inveighed against the low comedies and farees which Soviet theater audiences seem to prefer, and it noted that out of nineteen full-length films produced in the Soviet Union in 1945, eight were based on old plays or remote historical themes. It also noted that in six months 60 foreign films had been shown in the Soviet Union. *Red Star,* official newspaper of the Soviet Army, recently scored Soviet officers for showing foreign films in their clubs in Germany and Austria.

Two Soviet films were especially violently attacked. Sergei Eisenstein, who received the Stalin prize in 1945 for his "Ivan the Terrible" Part I, found his Part II of that film banned for what *Culture and Life* called its "cold, dispassionate historicism."

Eisenstein, who is about to revise the film to suit current party dictates, had not done right, it was charged, by the Sixteenth Century Czar whose sadistic bloodlettings gave the name "Red Square" to the space outside the Kremling where Stalin's subjects passed in review on May Day. Eisenstein, said *Culture and Life,* had shown Ivan not as a "progressive statesman" engaged in the "class struggle" but as a "maniacal evildoer surrounded by his gang of young cutthroats." A resolution subsequently adopted by the Communist party central committee repeated this denunciation verbatim except for changing the final phrase to read: "A band of degenerates like the American Ku Klux Klan."

P. Nilin's "Big Life," which was ballyhooed as a million-dollar production in real Hollywood style, suffered a similar fate. Initially well received, it was withdrawn when the Communist hierarchy decided it did not properly stress the deeds of the Bolsheviks in behalf of the masses. It celebrated the postwar reconstruction of the Donetz Basin, but gave the impression, they found, that this was accomplished by "brute force" and not by "modern advanced techniques and the mechanization of labor processes." They also did not like, on second thought, the fact that the Communist party secretary in one mine was shown risking expulsion from the party to help the miners. They were incensed, too, at finding the chief heroes of the film "hopeless drunkards" and the women miners depicted as housed in "dirty, half-ruined barracks." Their displeasure extended also to the fact that the whole film story was tied together by "cheap romances, erotic adventures, and nocturnal chats in bed."

The central committee of the Communist party of the U.S.S.R. has prescribed for the movie industry a 1947 production schedule that includes only one film on a prewar subject. It is to be about Taras Shevchenko, a Nineteenth Century Ukrainian poet. There are few comedies on the schedule and even they have "social ideas."

20.5 'Socialist' Art and How It Is Produced

[*Source: Paul W. Ward: Russia's musicians feel party's lash, in:* The Sun *(Baltimore, Md.), Vol. 220/No. 145 F, May 7, 1947, p. 1, col. 4; p. 13, cols. 3–8.*]

Although the nonverbal arts are not readily adaptable to Communist expression, musicians in the Soviet Union have not entirely escaped criticism for failure so to compose their scores as to inspire only Bolshevik emotions in the listening audience. Both Shostakovich and Prokofiev have recently felt the lash of official criticism to a degree which may have helped reverse their acceptance of invitations to visit the United States as guest conductors of the Boston Symphony.

It may also have had something to do with the facts that during the recent Big Four meeting in Moscow:

1. Shostakovich, making a personal appearance in a piano concerto at the Moscow conservatory, drew a less-than-capacity audience to the little auditorium set aside for him.

2. An English-speaking member of the capacity audience in a much larger auditorium across the corridor urged Americans, who had wandered into it by mistake, to stay because the Berlioz Requiem about to be presented there was "better" than anything Shostakovich might offer.

3. Shostakovich barely got "also ran" mention in the subsequent Soviet press reviews of that night's performances at the conservatory.

Until last October, Soviet music had escaped the attention of the "thought police" who comprise the "propaganda and agitation" division of the Communist party's central committee. Then, however, *Culture and Life,* the journal brought out last summer to whip Soviet culture back into the paths of Communist ideological orthodoxy, cracked down on the sharps and flats boys. Shostakovich was one of the first hit. It was not the first time that he had been singled out for official attack. In 1936 his ballet, "Limpid Stream," and his "Lady Macbeth of Mtsensk" had incurred the displeasure of the party bosses who decide what is good for Russians to hear as well as what they shall eat, wear, and make.

At that time, however, Shostakovich was criticized only on musical grounds; his music was assailed as cacophonous. Now the criticism is political. His latest, or Ninth, symphony was officially attacked in *Culture and Life* as showing ideological weakness and not reflecting the true spirit of the Russian people. It lacked "warm, ideological conviction" and revealed its author as under the influence of the self-exiled Igor Stravinsky, "an artist without a fatherland and without deep ethical principles."

Such attacks put Shostakovich and his music under a cloud; only an extraordinarily audacious concert or radio broadcast manager would, in their wake, include any of Shostakovich's recent works in a program for Soviet listeners. They do not, however, cost Shostakovich much more than mental anguish. He retains the apartment on Mozhaisk highway where he lives with two Steinway grands, his wife, Nina, a physicist specializing in cosmicray reserarch, and their two children, Galina, 11, and Maxim, 9. He also retains his posts as a legislator – he is a member of the Supreme Soviet of the R.S.F.S.R. from the Leningrad region – ans as a member of the Stalin prize committee. In addition, he continues to teach composition at the Moscow and Leningrad conservatories and to serve as musical adviser to the government's committee on arts and its Ministry of Cinematography. Moreover, he is currently engaged in correcting the error in his ways which *Culture and Life* detected.

The Moscow *News* announced a few days ago that "the story of the heroic struggle the youth of the Donbas town of Krasnodon waged against the German invaders during the Fascist occupation and their tragic fate told in Fadeyev's novel 'The Young Guard' has inspired Dmitri Shostakovich to write an opera on the subject." "He could hardly have chosen," this English-language biweekly continued, "a more grateful and momentous theme for his next major work."

The demands of the Communist hierarchy that music henceforth impart only the pure doctrine of Marx have not been addressed solely to composers of the stature of Shostakovich and Prokofiev. Even such musicians as Harlem-trained Eddi Rozner have had the Red light flashed in their faces. Rozner is director of the "Byelorussian State Jazz Band," which has been indicted for "triviality and banality" in its programs. The Kremlin's cultural watchdogs have not yet reverted to their prewar custom of embargoing jazz as "American slave music designed to lull the exploited masses into acquiescence." Their insistence, however, that in general Western music is an instrumentality of capitalism to be shunned lest it corrupt the dutiful souls of Soviet citizens is in sharp contrast with their propaganda outside the Soviet Union.

So recently as September the *Information Bulletin* of the Soviet Embassy here contained an article an "American Music in the U.S.S.R." Like previous articles in that publication, it conveyed an idea that the Soviet authorities take pains to make American plays and music available to the Soviet populace. In truth, a rigorous campaign to keep such things from the Russian masses has been under way since last summer. Through such media as *Culture and Life* theater directors are warned that they will be guilty of "sabotage" if they include Western society plays in their repertoires. Russian theaters are organized on stock-company lines and the Communist party's central committee ordered all of them last September to revise their programs. They were directed stop presenting merely "entertaining" plays or those which depicted the luxurious life of "czars, magnates and khans." Western society plays which take capitalism for granted and use "love themes aimed at sated and corrupt bourgeois tastes" were also put on the Kremlin's *index expurgatorius.*

Plays by Britain's W. Somerset Maugham and by the Hungarian exile, Ferenc Molnar, who now lives in New York, were specifically banned. Those of the American playwright, Lillian Hellman, however, escaped the ban. It is still all right for a Soviet citizen to like Miss Hellman's "The Little Foxes" or almost any of George Bernard Shaw's plays, as well as those of Shakespeare, Lope de Vega, Sheridan and Calderon. Nor is the young Soviet citizen resentful at having his theater-fare predigested for him in this fashion. After the recent opening performance in Moscow of Konstantin Simonov's "The Russian Question," an Intourist guide, serving as translator for a party of Americans in the audience, was asked whether she thought the Russian people would like the play. A governmental committee would appraise the play and decide "whether we should like it," she replied, adding: "If they do – we shall like it."

She said it not only proudly but just as though the play were a commodity which could be tested for gold content and specific gravity. It did not occur to her that there was anything strange about waiting for a government decree before deciding whether "we were amused." She, however, it needs be added, was a party zealot. Older Russians were not slow about confiding their dislike of the play which the Russians Sunday put on in Berlin and are preparing to put on in 500 theaters within the Soviet Union. The older Russians were not disposed to doubt the venality of the American press, which thy play emphasizes, or its central theme that an American journalist who tries to tell the "truth" about the Soviet Union will find himself out of a job. Their objections were that it was poor theater, that it got its propaganda across clumsily, that it was as dull and humorless as a prohibitionist tract.

That criticism would fit almost any Soviet production today. Except for presentations of prerevolutionary classics, the Soviet theater is a dreary affair. Even the ballet, which leads the world in technical perfection, is reactionary and moribund, lacking the imaginative verve of its British, French and American counterparts. Relieved of the profit motive, of the necessity of producing plays that pay their way, the Soviet theater, in Marxist theory, ought to be experimental. Actually it is less progressive than Broadway. The experimentalism that characterized it in the early 1920's has been curshed under the demands of the Kremlin that the theater devote itself to imposing Communist dogma on the masses. Its enforced isolation from any save the Bolshevik ethic has created, Brooks Atkinson, one of America's leading drama critics, found, "a bloodless, old-fashioned, petit bourgeois culture that is colorless and conventional."

That is not a distinctly American reaction. The Kremlin's cultural watchdogs agree with Mr. Atkinson that the Soviet theater is bourgeois, unoriginal and lacking in vitality. But they blame the situation on foreign influence rather than the lack thereof. Speaking through such media as *Culture and Life,* they charge that Soviet themes have been pushed out of the Soviet theater and that its directors have been catering to a public preference for low comedy and escapist themes.

Now all plays presented in the Soviet Union must have been approved in advance by the Government's Art Affairs Committee. Its members already have indicated – and the official press has served notice of – a preference for plays that assign credit for victory in World War II to a reformation of the Russian character and an industrial development of the country effected by the Communist party and the Soviet regime.

The campaign of which all this is a part started near the end of World War II during which the Kremlin had tolerated certain deviations from the Marxist fundamentalist thesis that the arts are weapons of political propaganda. The return to normalcy, to a tightening of party controls over intellectual life, began in 1944 when several prominent writers, including Ilya Ehrenburg, were castigated in the party press for ideological and artistic shortcomings.

One of the most significant attacks was directed at Sergeyev-Zensky, a painstakingly documentary historical novelist best known for his World War I trilogy "Transfiguration." The Bolshevik authorities had found his novels useful in exploiting the patriotic and nationalist rather than Communist line they fed the electorate during the last decade. Their appreciation was shown by an official celebration of his seventieth birthday in 1945. But his novel "The Cannons Are Moved Forward," published in 1944 with the approval of the censors, was attacked in *Bolshevik* two years later when the Communist bosses attitude toward nationalism was revised. The official organ of the party's central committee attacked Sergeyev-Zensky for paying in his novel too little attention to the rising revolutionary movement led by the Bolsheviki in World War I. They also attacked him for overemphasizing Russo-German antagonism in his book. By 1945 in the Kremlin lexicon Great Britain had replaced Germany as the real foe of Soviet policies and had become the Societ Union's Public Enemy No. 1.

Whether Sergeyev-Zensky's novel was historically correct did not matter. He found himself caught up in the same party-line snarls that Mikhail Zoshchenko, one of the most popular and at the same time audacious of Soviet writers, noted in his "What the Nightingale Sang." Undertaking to explain why he had hesitated to write a long novel on the "great theme" of the Soviet regime's achievements as all Soviet writers were urged to do in the middle 1930's, Zoshchenko said: "You just begin to write, and the critics surround you. 'This is not correct,' they say. 'It lacks a scientific basis in handling this problem. The ideology,' they say, 'is not the right one.' Well, you see, respected reader, it isn't easy to be a Russian writer."

He has better reason to say that now than when he wrote it. For Zoshchenko, who belongs to the older generation of Soviet writers, was among the first to feel the whip after Stalin last August launched his bloodless "purge" of the intellectuals. One immediate result of his meeting with the key men of letters was the reported banning of 120 manuscripts of books, plays, and movies then awaiting production.

The new line was set forth in an August 14 resolution of the Communist central committee, which *Culture and Life* revealed in a vehement article six days later. *Pravda* reprinted it the next day and *Konsomolskaya Pravda* August 27. Singled out for special attack were two Leningrad literary magazines, *Zvezda* and *Leningrad*. They were accused of exposing Soviet youth to dangerous literary influences and criticized, in that connection, for printing pieces by Zoshchenko and Anna Akhmatova.

The last-named was Russia's leading prerevolutionary poet. Her husband, Nikolai Gumilev, also a poet, was executed by the Bolsheviks in 1921 and her name vanished thereafter from the Soviet press until 1940 when an anthology of her old and new poems was allowed to be published. It had nothing to do with the Soviet system, yet it had an immediate success. So did her poem "Courage" which she wrote soon after the German invasion of June, 1941, and which became the *leitmotif* of Soviet wartime literature.

Now that the war is over, she is attacked for bourgeois-aristocratic estheticism and as a producer of "empty poetry, devoid of ideas, alien to our people." For publishing her poems and Zoshchenko's satirical stories on everyday life in the Soviet Union, the editors of both the Leningrad magazines were fired and the publication of one of them, *Leningrad,* forbidden. In addition, the central committee of the Leningrad Communist party was censured for "political error" and A. M. Yegolin, deputy chief of the National Communist party's "administration for propaganda and agitation," was installed as editor of *Zvezda*. The corrective work did not stop there. N. S. Tikhonov, chairman since 1944 of the praesidium of the Soviet Writers Union, was reprimanded, along with the whole praesidium for failure to halt harmful literary trends.

The party hierarchy sent a special emissary to Leningrad, A. A. Zhdanov, secretary of the central committee and member of the Politburo, to instruct the local Communist bosses in the new party line. His report, which denounced "burgeois culture," reflected profound anxiety over the susceptibility of the Russian people to "alien influences." The Writers Union praesidium echoed it in a resolution denouncing foreign influences which "poison the conscience of our people with ideas hostile to Soviet society."

Related Readings

Alt, Herschel/Alt, Edith (Eds.): Russia's children. A first report on child welfare in the Soviet Union, New York 1959.
Ashby, Eric: Scientist in Russia, Harmondsworth, Middlesex – New York 1947.
Bereday, George Zygmunt Fijalkowski/Brickmann, William W./Read, Gerald H. (Eds.): The changing Soviet school. The Comparative Education Society field study in the U.S.S.R., Boston, Mass., 1960.
Bereday, George Zygmunt Fijalkowski/Pennar, Jaan (Ed.): The politics of Soviet education, New York 1960.
Black, Cyril Edwin (Ed.): The transformation of Russian society. Aspects of social change since 1861, Cambridge 1960.
Brown, Edward James: Russian literature since the revolution, New York 1963.
Counts, George Sylvester: The challenge of Soviet education, New York 1957.
Fitzsimmons, Thomas et al.: USSR – its people, its society, its culture, London–New Haven, Conn., 1960.
Inkeles, Alex: Public opinion in Soviet Russia, A study in mass persuasion, Cambridge, Mass., 1958.
Kalinin, Mikhail Ivanovich: On communist education. Selected speeches and articles, Moscow 1949.
King, Edmund James (Ed.): Communist education, London 1963.
Kline, George Louis (Ed.): Soviet education, London–New York 1957.
Korol, Alexander G.: Soviet education for science and technology, Cambridge, Mass.–New York 1957.
Lazarevich, Ida Markovna/Lazarevich, Nicolas: L'école soviétique, enseignements primaire et secondaire, Paris 1954.
Maistrakh, Ksenia V.: The organization of public health in the USSR, Washington, D. C., 1959.
Makarenko, Anton Semenovich: The road to life. An epic of education, 2nd ed., Moscow 1955.
Parkins, Maurice Frank: City planning in Soviet Russia. An interpretative bibliography, Cambridge, Mass., 1949.
Sigerist, Henry Ernest: Medicine and health in the Soviet Union, New York 1947.
Simmons, Ernest Joseph (Ed.): Through the glass of Soviet literature. Views of Russian society, New York 1953.

1948

Price Day

The Sun, Baltimore

CHAPTER 21

REPORTS ABOUT INDIA IN 1948

The Country's Way to Sovereignty and the Cultural Impediments

    Introductory Notes
21.1 Britain's Influence on India and Its Remainders
21.2 Nehru as a Leader of Gentleness and Impatience
21.3 Pakistan's Situation and Her Future Outlook
21.4 The Cow and the Caste as Bars for Development
21.5 Undernourishment und Overpopulation as Main Problems
    Related Readings

Introductory Notes

After the interest of the Pulitzer Prize jurors and of the Advisory Board had been concentrated for a while on individual reports of series of articles by American foreign correspondents about the Soviet Union, the 1949 award concerned the political independence and sovereignty of a former British crown-colony. Price Day, staff correspondent of the Sun, Baltimore, Maryland, *was awarded the Pulitzer Prize for International Reporting "for his series of 12 articles entitled, 'Experiment in Freedom – India and its First Year of Independence.'" With the bestowal of the prize on Day the Pulitzer Prize committee for the second time in succession honored the outstanding foreign coverage of the* Sun, *Paul W. Ward having won the award the preceding year for this paper.*

Price Day was born on November 4, 1907, in Plainview, Texas. Upon receiving his B. A. degree from Princeton University in 1929, Day between 1929 and 1935 worked as a cartoonist and occasional free lance writer on various periodicals and then especially as a science fiction writer for the Saturday Evening Post, Colliers, *and other journals between 1935 and 1941. In 1942, Day moved to Florida where he worked for the* Fort Lauderdale Times *as a city editor; one year later he was sent to the Mediterranean battle areas as a war correspondent by the Baltimore* Sun, *where he performed his job from 1943 to 1945. He distinguished himself as a war correspondent of his paper by covering the 8th Air force, the Allied campaign in Italy including the Anzio beachhead and the liberation of Rome, the American invasion of southern France in the late summer of 1944, and the breaking of the German winter line in the Vosges Mountains. Day was the only reporter for an individual American newspaper present at the signing fo the German surrender at Reims. His postwar assignments included the Potsdam conference, the Nuremberg trials, and developments in Czechoslovakia, France and Germany and the Caribbean, culminating in his assignment to the leading role in the* Sun's *worldwide study of the British Commonwealth and Empire and the impact of its changes upon the life of the postwar period. In his function as a foreign and field correspondent in 1949 he received the Pulitzer Prize for International Reporting for his profound series on India.*

The following texts by Price Day, copyright 1948, are reprinted by kind permission of The Sun, Baltimore, Maryland.

21.1. Britain's Influence on India and Its Remainders

[*Source: Price Day: Imprint of England remains on India, in:* The Evening Sun *(Baltimore, Md.), Vol. 224/No. 11, November 29, 1948, p. 1, cols. 6–7; p. 12, cols. 5–6.*]

Where they can easily be obliterated, the outward marks of British rule are disappearing from India. The influence of Britain will remain for a long time. India's new monuments honor the martyred Mahatma Gandhi. There will be no more marble representations of heavily clothed British monarchs, staring unsquintingly into the alien sunshine. Hotels once almost exclusively British have become almost exclusively Indian. Clubs for Englishmen, where the only Indians were once bearers and waiters and watermen and laundrymen and sweepers, today are clubs for Indians. The panoply of the British *Raj* has vanished in the new day of *Swaraj,* self-rule.

Bombay, for example, still has a governor. But he is an Indian, Raja Maharaj Singh. And the office no longer entitles him to ride in a gilded coach, accompanied by a splendid bodyguard. And he does not have a band of his own, as his predecessors did. In time all the ikons of empire will be pulled down. All the Clive streets will be retitled. New spellings are already being given to the place names which were transliterated into English according to the way the British mispronounced them – they made Banaras into Benares, Commankanpore into Cownpore, Gange into Ganges.

When these processes have been completed, however, India will have much to remind her that the British were there. It is not only that foreign domination has left lasting scars, and some still-open wounds, which seem to be healing quickly. A measure of good remains, as well. The form of the new Indian Government is drawn form the West, above all from England. Its legal system is based on English law. Its great modern leaders went to school in England, though the influence of their education on Gandhi, Prime Minister Jawaharlal Nehru and Deputy Prime Minister Vallabhbhai Patel could be exaggerated. Even the language in offical use in India today is English: otherwise the introduction of new spellings would be unnecessary.

British engineers modernized and expanded India's irrigation system, which is the world's largest and on which the country depends for its very life. They developed her harbors. They directed the construction of her railways. India, of course, paid heavily for these works. More disinterestedly, British archaeologists discovered for India the glories of her ancient civilizations. British students of language rescued from oblivion the greatest of India's cultural treasures, Sanskrit literature. No less real is another and subtler legacy. The foreign rulers were arrogant in India; they were ineffectual in any higher meaning of the word "government" – but there did filter through to India the British spirit of liberalism, and that spirit played no small part in the achievement of independence.

The pattern is not neat. Nothing in India is neat, and nothing is simple. It is one of her charms. However, a general line of development can be discerned. Nehru has said that in the Eighteenth Century there were two Englands – on the one hand the England of political revolution and struggle for freedom, on the other that of the savage penal code. Nehru believes that it was the "wrong England" that came to India, and all but perpetuated there an outmoded system which England itself long ago discarded; though he adds that the two were not entirely to be separated.

An observer in India today, as he tries to evaluate the mixture of impulses that sent the British adventuring in the East, feels that they all must have developed originally from the same conditions of ferment and change at home. The British brought modern commercialism with them. They brought oppression. But they also brought a sense of the dignity of the individual which is one of the fundamentals on which the new India is based. This dignity has nothing to do with the air of superiority of the average imperialist. One of the deepest sources of resentment against the British has been that they considered themselves automatically the betters of all Indians – while to a high Brahmin, for example, Englishmen are crude and raw, with unspeakable personal habits.

Behind the imperialist, however, lay a country of greater and greater individual freedom, and the Indian leaders saw it and studied it. The freedom they fought for, and won, is the sort of freedom Englishmen understand. Because they do understand it, most people in England today perceive the justice of India's case, and think that India had the right to be free. London intellectuals think so because of their liberal convictions. The average Englishman thinks so because of his stubborn feeling for justice.

Britons in India as well, though in many cases with a great deal of reluctance, say that what has happened had to happen. It was such acceptance of historical necessity that made the transfer of power a step that could be taken with a minimum of ill-will, considering the past. Even Indians who are intensely nationalistic – and most Indians worth their salt are that – admit that at the last, and briefly, the "right England" took over. It is admitted further that the kind of economic and social progress India hopes for is based to a great extent on Western developments came to India through the British: in spite of the British, say some. They may add that it was a long time coming. Indians do not subscribe to the notion that through the past decades, or centuries, the British have been "training India for self-government."

At most they will acknowledge that British imperialism, for its own benefit and without thought of the long – range consequence for India-even without knowing what it was doing – destroyed the ancient village social and economic system, and so cleared the way for eventual, if painful, reconstruction on modern patterns. Now that freedom is a fact, thoughtful Indians recognize that their country still needs Britain commercially and technologically, and perhaps for defense. Understandably, India does not want to need anybody. It looks forward to full sovereignty and to an economic stability that will enable it to deal on equal terms with any other nation. The look, though, is a long look.

India today, conscious of the difficult way ahead, seeks to become fully independent and still remain in the Commonwealth to the extent that it may share the benefits of that group of nations. It appears ready, also, to share responsibility. Thus there is a tendency in India to acknowledge the better aspects of the association with Britain in a way that would have seemed impossible a year ago. The other side of the coin, the influence of India on England, is more difficult to make out, perhaps because the impress is so much lighter. For one thing, Britons exposed to India have been fewer than might be supposed. It is estimated that at its peak the British population of India, including troops, was a mere 135,0000, in a subcontinent of 400,000,000 people. An observer in India is struck by the thinness with which Britain held the country. For example, the Indian Civil Service had one British official to roughly each 1,000,000 of population.

Letters in the London papers in the winter before independence expressed grave concern over the fate of Britons in the I.C.S., but the problem was a minor one. Six months before independence only 477 names on the I.C.S. rolls were British, with only 316 non-Indians in the Indian police. The rich returns from India to Britain in the past were, in fact, obtained on a shoestring investment in personnel. Most of these people held themselves aloof from India and from things Indian. Individuals who did not do so laid themselves open to the grim charge of eccentricity, if not worse.

Orthodox imperialists were prone to gather with their own kind, after the day's business with Indians, and to put on a black tie and a cummerbund and sit under a fan and order a chota peg, a small whisky, before going in to their soups and their puddings. (In one matter, it might be noted, the British failed: they were never able to persuade Indians, other than Anglicized Indians, that a small armory of silver tools, manufactured in Sheffield, is necessary for the engorgement of food.)

Here and there a scholar, or a particularly sensitive business man, became fascinated by India and did his best to learn the country, but a more common attitude was that which saw Indian history since the advent of the British in terms of "the old days when chaps used to slay elephants with muzzle-loading rifles." This is caricature, to be sure – but the average Englishman of today, living in England, would be surprised an perhaps shocked to learn how very British the British were in India, to the end.

It may be that, for all their air of superiority, the British always felt lonely in this great, unruly, un-Western, overpopulated subcontinent, and huddled together for that reason. Certainly the town of Simla, with its English-village shops, its half-timbered houses and its English-Gothic church tower, was one of the earth's most beguiling examples of unashamed nostalgia. Also, to the end of British rule, fear remained present. The Mutiny of 1857 was still remembered, and Britons have always known that full Indian rebellion, though it might have been put down eventually, could have wiped out all of them in India at any one moment.

Such fears were more than mere memories of the past. One man, with more than 30 years in India, reports that as late as five months before independence his principal worry was "how the women were to be got out of Simla." The best plan, he thought, was to bring them under military guard to the Red Fort in Old Delhi, and try to get them out down-river from there. In justification of this seemingly romantic scheme, it might be noted that anti-British feeling was particularly high a that time, though it waned later. It waned to swiftly that by midsummer Mountbatten was cheered wildly by Indian crowds wherever he went; but in the midst of the adulation there were those who feared that hatred would rise again.

This was perhaps sufficient proof of the proposition that in three and a half centuries of association British and Indians never managed to meet in true mutual understanding, and that any important influence for good they had on each other came by accident, not design.

Today the situation is changed. India is free, and can deal with England not as a subject nation but as an equal. Reports from India indicate that the old touchiness of India on the question of its relationship with England is already beginning to go. In the United Kingdom, at any rate, the British also are less touchy on the subject of India. Those who hope for a great and strong Commonwealth, with India its eastern anchor, are heartened by these developments.

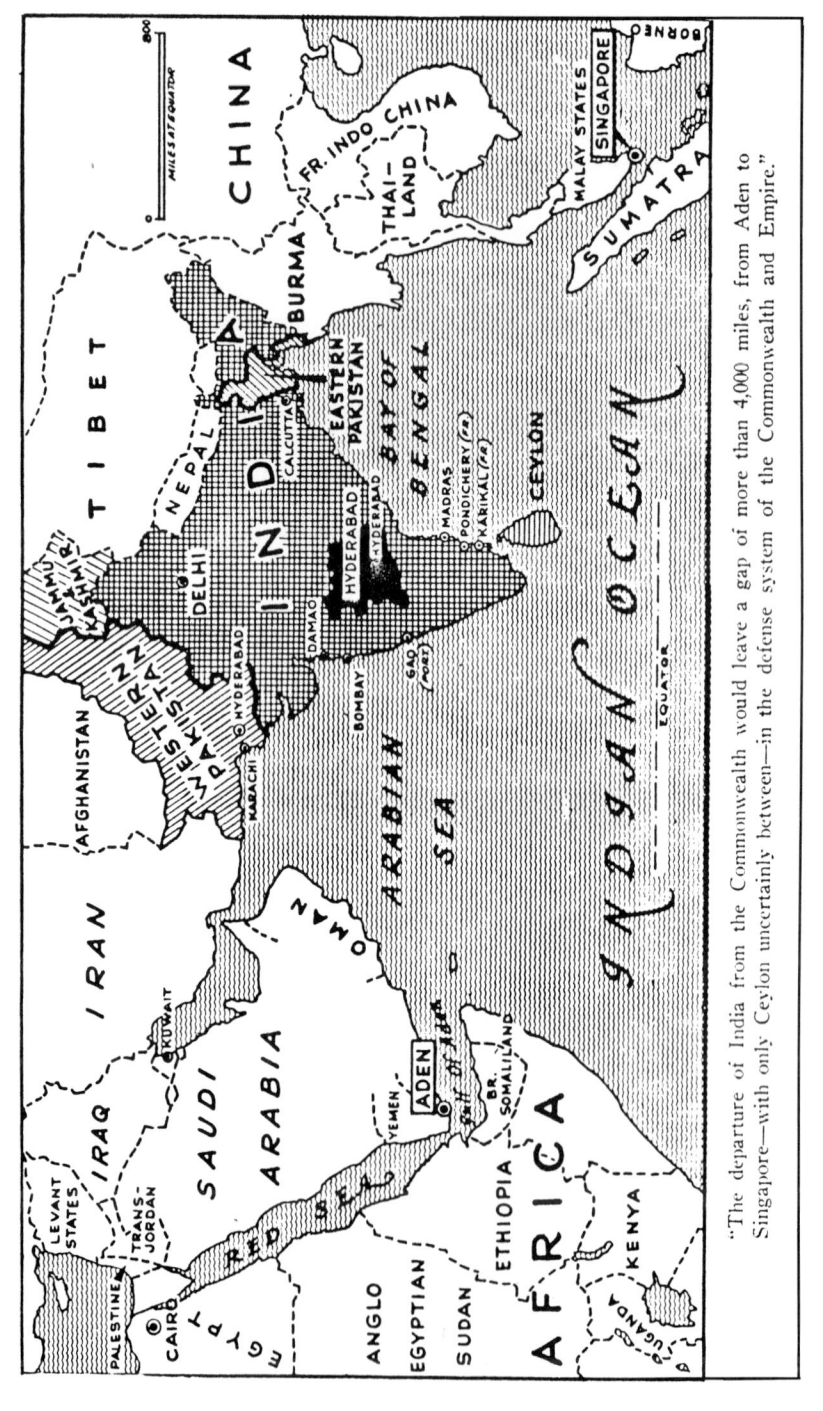

"The departure of India from the Commonwealth would leave a gap of more than 4,000 miles, from Aden to Singapore—with only Ceylon uncertainly between—in the defense system of the Commonwealth and Empire."

[*Source*: Price Day: Experiment in Freedom, Baltimore, Md., 1948, p. 2.]

21.2 Nehru as a Leader of Gentleness and Impatience

[*Source: Price Day: Nehru achieves place among world leaders, in:* The Evening Sun *(Baltimore, Md.), Vol. 224/No. 12, November 30, 1948, p. 1, cols. 4–5; p. 7, cols. 2–6.*]

India's first full year of independence, marred as it was by turmoil and tragedy, established one thing: the position of Jawaharlal Nehru in the front rank of world statesmen.

This came as no surprise to the East, where Nehru heads the nation with chief claim to present greatness. If the West had previously not quite understood his stature, it does so now, after this autumn's Commonwealth conference in London. There were times when the conference seemed to revolve around the slight, immaculate figure of the leader of the Indian dominion.

Stopping off in Paris after the London meetings, Nehru made a guest appearance before the General Assembly of the United Nations and, in his first public statement from an international platform since India became independent, warned the member nations that Asia was awakening and could not be ignored as in the past. He urged them also not to approach their objectives with "bloodshot eyes and minds clouded with passion." Observers in Paris found the occasion an impressive one.

Modern India has been fortunate in the moral strength of Mahatma Gandhi, and the practical shrewdness of Vallabhbhai Patel, Deputy Prime Minister and Minister for States, to whom goes much of the credit for the country's relative stability today. Many Indians believe that they have been most fortunate of all in Nehru. The recent phases of India's long story may best be observed, perhaps, through Nehru's complex personality. His journey of readjustment, from a background of wealth and encrusted tradition and high birth – he is a Kashmiri Brahmin – into the squalor and misery of India's 730,000 peasant villages and into a succession of prisons, from the role of leader in the struggle against the British to that of head of a vast sovereign state, can stand for the journey that India has made and is still making.

Nehru was born at Allahabad on November 14, 1889. He was educated at Harrow and Cambridge, and became a barrister of London's Inner Temple at the age of 23. After his return to India he came under the influence of Gandhi, who had also gone back to India following his invention of the method of nonviolent resitance in South Africa. In 1920 Nehru became an active member of the movement in India. Any one of three great influences – birth, England, Gandhi – might alone have determined the course of his life.

He could have remained within his caste and, in the words of Mr. H. N. Brailsford, one of the leading British students of India, "have spent his life in the paradise of Kashmir, writing books as notable for their grace of style as for their sweep of thought." He could have become Anglicized, to bask in the benefits the British would habe bestowed on a man of his position, charm und ability. He could have succumbed completely, as so many others did, to the almost overwhelming spell cast by Gandhi.

Nehru renounced his caste, with its prerogatives and its ritual and its landlords. He renounced all caste – but he did it without renouncing at the same time his background of Indian culture. No one ever mistook Jawaharlal Nehru for an Untouchable. No one ever mistook him for an Englishman, either, though he can wear fine Western clothes with an air of being born to them, and in casual conversation he speaks often in the limited jargon of the English upper classes.

Nehru took from the West the basis for his political thinking, a belief that progress is possible, and an affection for machinery and fast travel. But he managed to do it without losing any of his Indianness. He was Gandhi's most prominent disciple, and is his heir. He adored Gandhi personally, and recognized the political effectiveness of his methods. Gandhi's thinking has profoundly colored his own thoughts. He refuses to admit that anyone but Gandhi can stand as a symbol for Indian independence. Yet from their first meeting Nehru had doubts about the Mahatma. He could not share Gandhi's belief in a return to village industry, nor his asceticism nor his insistence that pacifism was the only proper credo under any possible circumstances. Nehru never relinquished his doubts, and never wavered in his loyalty.

By 1929, he was in the front line of the movement for independence from the British. In that year he succeeded his father, Pandit Motilal Nehru, who had also come down from the heights of birth and privilege, as president of the Indian Congress. The next eighteen years were a period of struggle and imprisonment, with some partial victories and many defeats. Toward its end, the pace stepped up until suddenly, almost too fast for anyone to realize what was happening, India was free, and Nehru was its first Prime Minister. He was far from happy about the conditions of independence. He wanted a united Indian subcontinent, with no partition between Indian and an Islamic state of Pakistan.

At the time, in India, it appeared probable that the peruasions of Patel were the principal factor in Nehru's final reluctant acceptance of Lord Mountbatten's partition plan. Even without the communal warfare that centered around the fact of partition – whatever its deeper causes – India when Nehru took the reins faced a mass of troubles on a scale commensurate with the upheaval that occurred when one fifth of the earth's people became their own masters. Industrial and agricultural production was falling ominously, food and clothing were in dangerously short supply, prices climbed dizzily and available foreign exchange was insufficient for the purchase of essential consumer goods and for the building and repair of the industrial plant.

All this was on top of India's normal dilemmas of near-famine, illiteracy still mounting to about 88 per cent, and a population growing so fast – despite an infant-mortality rate of 163 per 1,000 live births – that the present decade alone will see an increase approximately equal to the total population of Britain. The jubilant cries of "Jai Hind!" – Hail India – that greeted independence were cries of pride in the past and hope for the future. But the pride and hope were to fade sharply before rising again.

In his moment of triumph, Nehru was compelled by circumstances to consider first not the program of long-range reforms on which he had built his career, nor even the urgent daily administrative and diplomatic problems, but an outbreak of communal killing on a tremendous scale. First in the North West, then in the partitioned Punjab, then in the Indian capital at Delhi, Moslems killed Hindus and Sikhs, and Hindus and Sikhs killed Moslems. Deaths ran into the tens thousands, and then into the hundreds of thousands. No one will ever know the total. Whole villages were murdered on both sides. Millions of refugees took to the roads. Disease, including cholera, spread over the northern plains. Governmental administration limped almost to a halt. Communications were in chaos. No food moved on the railways, which were packed with refugees. Official telegrams from Lahore, in the Punjab, to

Karachi, capital of Pakistan, lay for days in the Lahore offices. With exceptional luck, a telegram from Delhi to Bombay or Calcutta would go through in three or four days.

Denied so much as an hour of pause and reflection, Nehru shuttled constantly between Delhi and the Punjab; and on no one day during its first weeks of office did the cabinet meet without that communalism was at the top of the agendum. The Prime Minister, already fatigued by the innumerable decisions that had to be made before the transfer of power, grew wearier. The skin of his mobile face stretched like parchment over the bones. The two extremes of his temperament, gentleness and quick impatience, became more pronounced, the one in regret at the tool of death and suffering and the blot on India's victory, the other in sharp anger at those Indians who encouraged murder and those foreigners who insisted on taking a patronizing attitude toward India in its time of distress.

Two pictures of Nehru come to mind. Both were at press conferences; the first, in a breathlessly hot room in the Council House in New Delhi, in the Summer of 1947. The Prime Minister had just flown back from the Punjab. He wore a white "Ghandi cap," something like an overseas cap, and tight white Indian trousers, and a wrinkled fawn-colored tunic. He sat on a big table, his legs swinging, and smoked cigarettes. He spoke for a long time, frankly and earnestly – and sorrowfully – and then his emotional voice hardened as he said that condescension from outsiders could not be tolerated. Some foreign reporters thought he was threatening them with censorship, but this turned out to be a false reading. It was simply that a story or two, suggesting that this was what happened when you turned Indians loose, had appeared in London, and that to Nehru they seemed intolerable. It was also suggested here and there that anarchy prevailed in India. It did not. If it had, the second picture might not exist.

The scene was India House in London this fall, on the day the Commonwealth conference came to an end. Nehru, wearing a dark blue double-breasted suit with a large red rose in the buttonhole of the lapel, was a few minutes late, and for a moment was confused. He said he had thought he was coming to a party. While Krishna Menon, Indian high commissioner in London, explained that it would not be proper for a participant in the conference to talk quotably to the press, Nehru sat at a table on the platform, before large matched portraits of himself and Gandhi, and had tea. When he talked, he spoke again frankly and at length; but this time showed no trace of the worries and the resentments that had marked the earlier occasion. He spoke, also, in much larger terms. He was no longer the troubled leader of a country on the edge of disaster: he represented the strong Government of a nation which, despite the magnitude of its continuing problems, had taken its place among the nations of the world.

Between those two appearances, Gandhi had been assassinated. Nehru has said many times that the Mahatma's death was an overwhelming tragedy, but the fact remains that his own strength is greater today than when Gandhi was alive, for he alone now stands for the moral power of India. He is aware of this, and convinced of its importance. He said recently, of moral values as applied to politics: "All this may seem fantastic and impractical in the modern world, used as it is to thinking in set grooves. And yet we have seen repeatedly the failure of other methods, and nothing can be less practical than to pursue a method that has failed again and again. We may not perhaps ignore the present limitations of human nature or the immediate perils which face the statesmen. We may not, in the world as it is constituted today, even rule out war absolutely. But I have become more and more convinced that so long as we do not recognize the supremacy of the moral law in our national and international relations, we shall have no enduring peace. So long as we do not adhere to right means, the end will not be right and fresh evil will flow from it."

This is the core of Gandhi's teachings, though Gandhi did in fact rule out war absolutely. It gains more weight – or has a different kind of weight – when it is presented by the undisputed leader of a large, free nation. Nehru is clearly worried about the future, but it is clear also that he sees for India, with its growing prestige in the West as well as in the East, a role as a force for peace. He certainly seems to have put aside the hatreds of the past; and reports from India indicate that his countrymen, too, are forgetting their old anger.

At the time of independence, one of the most important questions that could be asked of an Indian leader, or an Indian aspiring to leadership, was: "How much time have you spent in jail?" Prison sentences under the British were the quickest and surest measure of sincerity – even, in a nonviolent revolution, of actual effectiveness. An Indian today may still be justifiably proud of his prison record, but it no longer matters practically, only historically. It appears that Nehru's followers have joined him in realizing this.

21.3 Pakistan's Situation and Her Future Outlook

[*Source: Price Day: Pakistan does not wish to cut its British ties, in:* The Evening Sun *(Baltimore, Md.), Vol. 224/No. 15, December 3, 1948, p. 1, cols. 4–5; p. 7, cols. 2–5.*]

After an inauspicious beginning, the country of Pakistan now shows signs of future health, but at the moment it is still weak, and in need of any props it can find. Thus it is strenghtening its ties with other Islamic lands, of which it is the largest; and thus, also it intends to retain its status as a dominion in the British Commonwealth.

Liaquat Ali Khan, Prime Minister of Pakistan since it came into being and heir to the power of Mahomed Ali Jinnah, who died on September 11, said flatly in London this fall that no republican movement at all exists in his country. This is in strong contrast to the situation in India, whose Government hopes to retain ties of some sort with the Commonwealth but is determined that the nation become a sovereign and independent republic. "We have so many other problems," the Pakistan Prime Minister said, "that we have no time to think about this question of a link to the British crown, or about a republic." Pakistan, he added, perhaps with a touch of hyperbole, has had "such tragic difficulties that I can make bold to say that no other nation ever faced such difficulties."

The problems of the new nation have indeed been great, however, and it has shown some energy and efficiency in trying to solve them. The leaders of the Pakistanis have set in motion a full program for resettlement of the 6,600,000 refugees who came into the country as a result of last year's grim upheaval among the religious communities of the Indian subcontinent. They have also developed, from almost nothing, an operating administration, and have balanced a budget. They look forward to feeding themselves, even to exporting food, and might have done it this year but for the communal slaughter and a bad growing season.

Pakistan, however, labors under a number of disabilities that look strikingly permanent. The principal of them is geographical. It is a country of approximately 76,000,000 people, with an area of 357,683 square miles, carved out of the old British imperial India at the time of partition in the Summer of 1947. The carving was done in two pieces, to take in areas with heavy Moslem majorities.

Western Pakistan, with 303,583 square miles and 32,000,000 people, comprises the West Punjab, Sind, Baluchistan, North-West Frontier Province and some tribal regions and princely states. Its main centers are the capital, Karachi, in the humid lowlands at the mouth of the Indus, and Lahore, the important commercial city of the Punjab. Eastern Pakistan, sandwiched in between two sections of India, has a population of 44,000,000 and covers 54,100 square miles, with its subcapital at Dacca and its principal port at Chittagong, across the Bay of Bengal from Calcutta.

Though much of western Pakistan is covered by the lifeless and bony Thar Desert, the province also contains, in the Punjab and in the elaborate irrigation districts of Sind, some of the richest agricultural areas on earth. Eastern Pakistan is in Bengal, a famine area, perpetually on the edge of starvation; but it has a near monopoly on a major cash crop, jute, of which it produces three fourths the world's supply.

The map shows why this arrangement is not quite so happy a one as it sounds. The overland distance from Lahore to Dacca is about 1,150 miles, most of the way through a less-than-friendly India. The Pakistanis say, with a certain blitheness, that if land communications across India should ever become too difficult the two pieces of their country are still linked by sea, and that the distances between them is shorter than the much-traveled route between England and the port of India. This is true, but ships journeying from Karachi to Chittagong still have to traverse about 2,800 miles; and Pakistan's merchant navy is somewhat smaller than Britain's. Even with good communications and normal food production, at least one big problem would remain. Western Pakistan produces principally wheat. The Bengalis of eastern Pakistan are rice-eaters.

As to Pakistan's long-range prospects, two opposed views have been widely argued, and might be noted here. To begin with, Karachi in the early days of independence did not look like a capital. Its appearance caused one observer to remark, on the day Jinnah tools office as governor general, that "this isn't only a one-man country; it's a one-horse country, too." Officials of the Pakistan Secretariat had no phones, no *chaprasis,* bearers, except their personal *chaprasis,* no paper even to take notes on, no office furniture. Yet, within a month, "Operation Pakistan" had brought more than 7,000 officials and clerks by air to Karachi, makeshift housing was found for them and their families, tent cities were set up for single men, new construction was begun – in spite of the exodus of the city's carpenters and masons, who were Sikhs – and the Government was functioning as such. When evidence of Pakistan's administrative activity was brought to the attention of citizens of India, they had an answer: superficial efficiency is easy, under an authoritarian government.

If pressed, they might admit that Pakistan's retention of a relatively large number of trained British administrators, who got special consideration from Jinnah, could have something to do with it. The Indians insisted, nevertheless, that the Pakistanis, were in for a rough time. Pakistan, it was declared, could not but be backward. It had little industry and few persons experienced in commerce. Jinnah's dazzling success in securing the partition of India and preventing all-India unity would turn to dust in his mouth. Pakistan's financial resources,

PAKISTAN'S GEOGRAPHICAL DISABILITY—The map shows the distances by land and by sea between the western section and the eastern section of the newly-created Dominion of Pakistan.

[*Source:* Price Day: Experiment in Freedom, Baltimore, Md., 1948, p. 28.]

according to this point of view, were neither large enough nor diversified enough to meet the demands of the dominion, since they lay in the hands of a few landowners in the West Punjab, cotton merchants in Karachi and jute growers in East Bengal. Jute and cotton were admittedly of importance, but it was pointed out that the jute mills were in Calcutta and the cotton mills also in India.

On the other hand, a number of careful analyses decided, in their conclusions, that Pakistan's economic future looked better than India's even to the point of self-sufficiency. In addition to grain foods and cash crops, they found Pakistan with enough oil-seeds and salt, and declared that it need not depend upon India for sugar, which could be purchased more cheaply from Java, nor for coal, which could be supplanted by electric power, at least in Western Pakistan, with its swifter rivers and its dams. Pakistan cotton, which is of good grade and amounts to about 33 per cent of all cotton on the subcontinent, could be milled in Pakistan, it was contended; and leather works could be set up to handle the millions of hides that annually were fed through Lahore to be processed in southern India and then shiped to

Europe and America. Calcutta was seen as unimportant, a colonial excrescence: Chittagong could be developed as a port and processing center, and its harbor would not require constant dredging, as does Calcutta's.

Such prophecies have yet to begin to come true. If they are ever to come true, Pakistan must find capital, and a great deal of it. It may be able to do so. It has already managed to surmount a number of forbidding obstacles. It even seems to have succeeded in extracting a measure of loyalty from the hungry and short-tempered tribes of the frontier, and has not been forced to continue the expensive British policy toward the tribesmen, which has been described as a policy of "bribe and bomb." As noted, it has remained in close association with Britain and with the Commonwealth, though not without certain tensions.

Many Pakistanis believe that Britain is "anti-Pakistan," and are particularly resentful against Lord Mountbatten, who, as last Viceroy of India, was the agent through whom partition was effected. The charge is that Mountbatten was personally unfriendly to Pakistan while he remained in India as Governor General, after independence; and that he has continued since then to help India at the expense of Pakistan. Ghulam Mahomed, Pakistan Finance Minister, recently blamed Mountbatten in part for the Punjab massacres. Mountbatten, he said, had rejected advance warnings that the Sikhs were about to go on the warpath. Nothing was said about warring Moslems.

The truth seems to be that Pakistan would like Britain to accept in full its own version of all contested matters, including those of the Punjab terror and the Kashmir and Hyderabad disputes.

Lacking that acceptance, relations with Britain are reasonably good. Pakistan receives goods from Britain at the rate of about $ 8,000,000 worth a month, and the number of Englishmen in business in Pakistan is growing. Pakistan, of course, looks to Britain and to the Commonwealth for assistance in establishing security in the Indian Ocean, which Britain wants, too, and wants badly. So does India. For real security, India and Pakistan must have close co-operation. But there are as yet few signs of co-operation on any substantial scale between the two dominions.

Pakistan also looks elsewhere internationally. As a country with a population 80 per cent Moslem, it looks to the rest of Islam. Talk of any Pan-Islam movement stemming from the emergence of Pakistan as a nation is certainly premature. No military alliances are contemplated at the moment with the Arab League countries. But trade arrangements are under discussion, and most public statements by Pakistan officials contain a few phrases recalling that Pakistan is founded on religion.

It was on the basis of religion alone that the dominion's creator, Jinnah, the dapper, arrogant, brilliant Qaid-e-Azam, the "grand leader," demanded and got partition of India. That was a personal triumph, as Jinnah was well aware; and he seemed satisfied with that alone. Whether, behind his facade of cold, ascetic reserve, he ever doubted the wisdom of his course in openly fostering hatred between Moslem and non-Moslem, and in insisting on a separate dominion, cannot be said. The likelihood is that he did not. He declared once, before partition: "I have no ambition except to see with my own eyes the free Moslem state of Pakistan. With this I will die in peace."

When he did die, at the age of 71, the leadership of Pakistan passed into the plump, efficient hands of Liaquat Ali Khan, who had been general secretary to the militant All-India Moslem League since its reorganization by Jinnah in 1936, and deputy leader of the Moslem

League party since 1940. He is closely backed by Ghulam Mahomed, whose job it is to watch finances and create foreign investment confidence. The immediate future of Pakistan, bright or dark, is largely in the hands of these two.

21.4 The Cow and the Caste as Bars for Development

[*Source: Price Day: Sacred cows are safe despite India hunger, in:* The Sunday Sun *(Baltimore, Md.), Vol. 48/No. 49, December 5, 1948, p. 1, cols. 4–5; p. 15, cols. 2–3.*]

"Improve the plow and improve the cow, because there can be no plow without the cow."

"There is no such thing as an uneconomic cow."

Any Westerner who can understand these statements, without elucidation, may have made the first small step toward comprehension of the orthodox Hindu attitude toward the second most numerous of India's mammals. He may even have discovered the thread that could lead him into, though hardly through, the whole involved maze of Hinduism, with its twisting and circlings and doublings-back of caste and taboo and poetry, of lovely corridors and dark, dreadful tunnels.

Or he may not. It may be quite impossible for him to see how any people perpetually on the brink of famine can allow almost one third of the earth's approximately 700,000,000 cattle to roam uneaten. He may feel that no religious or historical considerations can explain the keeping alive of the ubiquitous Brahmin cow, hump-shouldered and dirty-white in color, fat or scrawny, sick or well, whole or crippled, which is the most privileged of all things in India. Again as to the whole of Hinduism, he may find forever inexplicable a system of social and occupational distinctions which renders it impossible for a man who makes a bed to sweep a floor – a system under which caste-Hindus would rather perish of plague than move their own garbage, which is a special job of the scavenger group of untouchables.

Powerful forces are at work to abolish at least the stronger taboos and divisions of Hinduism. Last Monday in Delhi the Constituent Assembly fulfilled a long-standing pledge by accepting an article for the draft constitution which legally abolishes untouchability. This step is an important one, but the abolition can hardly come overnight. Untouchability and its allied customs are not likely to vanish within this decade or the next, and perhaps not in this century or the next, or this millenium or the next.

It is this pull of tradition, above all else, that makes India basically not a revolutionary nation, as is thought by some, but the earth's most profoundly conservative country. It is a force for stability; and Hinduism, with its demonstrated vitality, its traditions of contemplation and its anti-materialism has much to teach the West, if the West would listen. Some Hindus are more than merely conservative, for independence in India brought a strong resurgence of militant Hinduism.

The insistence on the part of the Moslems – rather, on the part of the late Mahomed Ali Jinnah – for the partition of the old India into Pakistan and India was accompanied by a revival of a tight Hindu sense of community. When Jinnah succeeded in gaining partition, belligerent Hindus became all the more belligerent, and the communal madness of northern India last year was their madness, too, as well as that of the Moslems and Sikhs.

The murder of Mahatma Gandhi – by a Hindu – has caused a revulsion against militancy. But there is still a Hindu element, composed largely but not entirely of the reactionary Mahasabha, which believes that India should be a religious state, preferably called Hindustan, and that its laws should be based on Hindu doctrine. The program of this element calls also for preparation of the country on the basis of war against Pakistan, conscription of all young Hindus, treatment of all Moslems in India as fifth columnists and the declaring of the profession of Islam unlawful.

Prominent among further demands is one for the protection of cows. In the new constitution, it is declared, cow protection should be included as a fundamental principle, along with justice, the right to work, public assistance for the aged, the ill and the unemployed, free and compulsory education and special consideration for untouchables. A proposal to this effect was defeated at an early executive meeting of the Congress party, which is the party of government, by a margin of only nine votes, 49 to 40.

Most vocal of current opponents of cow slaughter is Seth Ram Krishna Dalmia, who provided the statements quoted earlier. Mr. Dalmia, a thin, nervous little man, is probably India's second richest individual – second by far behind the Nizam of Hyderabad and below such large families of industrialists as the Tatas and Birlas, but nevertheless second. He is proprietor of air lines, investment agencies, factories of a dozen sorts, particularly cement factories, and a string of newspapers, among them the *Times of India,* once British-owned. He lives in a heavily furnished house in New Delhi, and presses upon visitors a maginificent array of fruits and cold soft drinks – Dalmia is, and all India is rapidly becoming, prohibitionist – from delicate lemon concoctions to fine, thick, black iced coffee, with whipped cream floated on top.

When Jinnah left Delhi for his capital at Karachi, Dalmia bought his house, for a reported $100,000, and announced that the place would become the headquarters of the Anti-Cow-Slaughter League, flying the sacred flag of the cow; but the Government requisitioned the building. Dalmia says that he is "prepared to prove in due time that mankind cannot exist without the abolition of cow slaughter," though when pressed as to whether he intends his movement to become international, he's not yet quite sure. He points out, however, that he is interested in two major projects – prevention of cow slaughter and the creation of "one world." To promote his campaigns, he has been buying up newspapers, and he made a missionary trip to the States this fall.

When he insists that there can be "no plow without the cow," Dalmia means that the bits and pieces of soil worked by India's peasants are too small for cultivation by tractor. In this he has a case. He does think that the ancient stick with which the peasant scratches the surface of the ground could stand improvement, and the breed of draft animals as well. The latter should be done, he believes fervently, only through nonbreeding of poor cattle, not through their destruction. He claims, or rather his expert on the subject interposes for him, that all cows, even the diseased and lame, are "economic," since, says the expert, even the worst cow eats food worth 108 rupees a year, and produces manure worth 110. In terms of dollars, the two figures come to about $34.56 and $35.20, respectively.

The chief economic argument against cow slaughter is not, however, the need for draft animals or the fabrication of fertilizer, but the production of milk.

Proponents of nonslaughter declare that India's most pressing need is for cheap milk and milk products. Nutritionists agree with them, but argue that enough milk will be forthcoming only as a result of drastic measures to improve the quality of India's livestock. Partly because of insufficient fodder and straw, India's cows, though as noted they number about one third of the world's cattle, produce only about one eighth of the world's milk.

While Mr. Dalmia and his group may, and do, argue in public in terms of economics, it is over the religious aspects of cow slaughter that they become really serious. Dalmia himself says hotly that "Hindus who are not against cow slaughter do not unterstand Hinduism." In orthodox Hinduism the cow is regarded as the source of well-being, the originator of life; actually as the mother of all. "Would you kill your mother?" asks many a Hindu, in terms of stern reproach, when the subject of cows is raised. Even Gandhi, writing in this weekly, the *Harijan,* to advocate improvement in the quality of India's herds, used to title his remarks: "How to Serve the Cow."

Reverence for cows is a part, though merely a part, of the doctrine of *ahimsa,* universal compassion, which also extends to the protection of sacred monkeys and peacocks, and indeed to most other life. The trouble taken by the Jains not to swallow the smallest gnat is well known. Most other Indians have at least a trace of the same reluctance. This is true not only of Hindus. Many Moslems, on principle killers and eaters of cows, will blanch if asked to destroy a mouse – partly because innumerable Moslems doctrines of Hinduism is difficult for any Indian.

The strongest of the doctrines, or, more accurately, practices, is that of caste. In fact, Hinduism is more than anything else a matter of caste, but once that is said, new vaguenesses and interminglings appear. Originally, in the far, indefinite past, the caste system may have arisen from racial discrimination – a desire on the part of Aryan conquerors to set themselves permanently above the earlier, and darker, inhabitants of India. Even that may have been based on still earlier divisions having to do with division of work and, on a higher plane, reciprocity of obligations. The four historical castes are those of the Brahmins, scholars and priests; the Kshatriyas, soldiers and administrators; the Vishyas, merchants, and the Sudras, servants and manual workers.

These classes still exist. Gandhi was a Vishya. The princes are mostly Kshatriyas. Nehru is a Brahmin, though an heretical one. Then there are numberless subcastes, and below them all are some 60,000,000 to 70,000,000 outcastes, untouchables, who perform all the lowest and hardest and filthiest jobs of India. These are the *Harijans* – "beloved of God" – of Gandhi. But Gandhi gave many indications that he was more interested in raising their lot, in effect in giving them caste, than he was in abolishing caste altogether. In all castes, and even among the untouchables, who are forbidden entrance to caste-Hindu temples and are often not allowed to draw water from village wells, further subdivisions according to function exist. And new ones constantly develop, until the result is a tangle in which no one on earth can find his way around.

Within the caste system, all depends on birth. You are what you are because of what your parents were, and can hope to become nothing else, nor can your children. The only way out is through reincarnation. This belief is one definite thing that can be singled out in the Hindu maze of credos. If a Hindu conducts himself properly in one life, he may hope to be reborn to a better, and so on until the final attainment of nirvana. This is a system which makes not only for acceptance of lack of change, but for stubborn resistance to change.

In spots, and slowly, it is breaking down. Intellectuals among the Hindus no longer insist that their children marry within their own caste. The urbanization of hundreds of thousands of former villagers, gathered now in industrial centers where the important thing ist to have a job, and where the eyes of the village do not penetrate, is a potent factor, and will become more potent with further industrialization. Untouchability is going, too, especially in the cities. The announced policy of the new Indian Government is for its abolition, and the Maharajah of Travancore, who may serve here as a straw in the wind, opened his state's temples to untouchables some time ago.

The end of caste, and of cow veneration, and of many kindred things, may come in time, but today they are still an important part of the fabric of the past that lies over India. It is a fabric strong in color and heavy with richness, but to a Westerner it feels like a pall.

21.5 Undernourishment and Overpopulation as Main Problems

[*Source: Price Day: India's limited land and burden of births, in:* The Evening Sun *(Baltimore, Md.), Vol. 224/No. 18, December 7, 1948, p. 1, cols. 2–3; p. 7, cols. 1–4.*]

India today is alive with the hopes and plans that have burgeoned with freedom. It is also, as it has been immemorially, a land of famine and poverty and pestilence.

At any time, the failure of the wet monsoon in one area, or too much rain in another, is capable of causing disaster on a scale with which the new Government is not yet equipped to cope. A touch of bad luck in the weather, or a breakdown in distribution, could bring on another calamity like that of 1943, when – quietly, uncomplainingly, uncomprehendingly and almost unnoticed – about 3,000,000 Bengalis starved to death or died of disease as the direct result of hunger. The fault lies not altogether in poor land and poor weather. Much of India's land is of fair quality, and some of its weather generally favorable, if uncertain. The real trouble is that there are too many people for the soil. There is not enough land, at least not the way it has been exploited, to support almost one fifth of the population of the globe.

Rural Bengal, packed with people almost to bursting, offers a case in point. "If you gave the people of Bengal proper medical care," says a health officer, "you would condemn them all to certain starvation." That is, the higher the death rate of the Bengali peasants, the better chance the survivors have of not dying too soon. Most visitors to India are struck first by the antlike massing of people in the loud, dusty, odorous, colorful cities, where large families live in tiny dark boxes, or simply inhabit the streets; but the real problem of overcrowding is rural.

If there must be said to be only one true India, it can be found not in the cities, but in the approximately 730,000 villages of the subcontinent – typically collections of mud and straw, with a well or tank and a wallow outside the mud walls where the water buffalo lie all but submerged, the tops of their massive heads and backs showing like dark, smooth rocks. With antique plows to scratch the soil, and buffalo or bullocks to pull the plows, the villagers till tiny plots of land sometimes no bigger than a large room, und often fragmented all around the villages. In total cultivated land, these plots come to about three quarters of an acre per person in all of India, and the figure diminishes inexorably with the growth of the population. In calories per person per day, the yield averages 600 to 800. Germans in the Ruhr in the postwar years have slowly starved on twice that.

For the great mass of citizens, in fact, India's main problem is not how to prevent religious hatreds, or how to avenge communal murder, or what political direction the country is going to take. It is simply, for a brief while, to keep from dying. Malnutrition, not counting actual starvation, accounts for millions of India's more than 8,000,000 deaths a year, though no one can say how many millions, since the cause of 85 per cent of all deaths is listed as unknown. People just die, and are carried by their families and two or three friends to the burial ground, if they are Moslem, or the burning ground, if they are Hindu, and that is that.

These simple funeral are as constant a feature of Indian life as is the Brahmin cow, or the *pan* seller, squatting on his haunches and dispensing his concoctions of betel leaf, lime and bright spices – and they are noticed but little more. The bodies under the shrouds are, with great frequency, small. In India the expectation of life is 27 years, as compared with 61 in the United States and 63 in Australia. Professor Gyan Chand, one of the most thoughtful of Indian economists, once called his a "death-ridden" country, and added: "We might well adopt the human skull as our national emblem, not to proclaim that we do not fear death or to carry it to other lands in pursuit of our national aims, but to drive into the minds of our people the fact that death in its most gruesome forms is our common lot, the badge of all our tribe."

Yet for every person who dies in India, more than two are born. Officially, the birthrate is 35 or 36 per 1,000, and has remained approximately the same for the past 60 years. It has been guessed, however, that one-third of all births are unreported. India's birthrate is certainly the hightest in the world. Too many deaths and too many births are the twin horns of India's dilemma, and on whether it can be solved or not depends the future of the nation.

The leaders of independent India are aware of this, as none of the foreign rulers of the country has ever been quite aware. Noting that "neither freedom nor life itself can exist without food," a Delhi spokesman says, "there is no disentangling this theme from the future politics and economics of our country." The Government is attacking the problem vigorously – though even the most vigorous initial attack can only nibble at the edges – in the main fields of irrigation, mechanization, land-tenure reform and increased productivity. For India's existing irrigation systems, much credit goes to the British, but not all: extensive irrigation dates indefinitely from the dim past, and no one knows who built many of the canal systems still in use.

At the time of partition of the subcontinent between India and Pakistan, more than 75,000 miles of canals watered about 70,000,000 acres of land. Pakistan, by far the smaller of the two dominions, came out of partition with one-third of the irrigation complexes, measured in land, and one-half, measured in volume of water. Thus India today contains approximately 48,000,000 acres of irrigated foodproducing soil. Projects now contemplated – some have been started – would increase that by about 56 per cent. An increase of that extent lies well in the future.

Much is hoped also from mechanization, where mechanization is possible, and work in this field is under way. As a sample, American tractors have brought a total of more than 121,000 acres under new cultivation in a number of regions, while a central tractor pool has operated elsewhere. Annual yields from these lands are expected to exceed 12,000 tons. Much as India needs tractors, however, their use is limited. They cannot replace bullocks, and still operate economically. Estimating that the minimum area of land for cultivation by a small tractor is 150 to 200 acres, and the minimum economical operation 1,800 hours a year, and noting that this would mean full irrigation and double annual cropping, a Government agricultural report says plainly: "Bullocks must continue to be the main source of power for cultivation in India for all time, unless there is an economic revolution in the country."

Revolution as used here means revolution – the full development of methods of growing food otherwise than from soil. The Indian Government is determined upon an agricultural revolution of another kind, and one which it can set in motion – land reform. If carried out logically, land reform will mean abolition of the *zamindari* system, under which *zamindars*, owners of large collections of villages and farmlands, have not only charged their tenants back-breaking rents, but have often exacted further payments for weddings, houses and other personal whims. The actual cultivators have received, in kind or in cash, as little as 20 per cent of the products of their labor. They are all in debt to the money lenders. Debt with interest running as high as 100 per cent per annum is often all that the Indian *ryot*, peasant, is able to bequeath to his heirs. Many Indians blame this situation on the British, who, it is charged, destroyed the ancient system of autonomous and self-contained villages.

How much additional land could produce food under greater irrigation and mechanization, and under a corrected system of tenure, is an unanswered question. Some estimates place the figure at four or five per cent, but much of this might prove to be submarginal. Indeed, much of the land farmed now is submarginal. Indian rice paddies, for example, bring forth about 800 pounds of grain per acre. An acre in rice in China yields, 1,400 pounds, in Italy, 3,000. According to once recognized authority, India's long-worked agricultural soil has reached "a stabilized condition, and a low but permanent standard of fertility has been established." This apparently means that, short of the washing away and blowing away of the land completely, things could not be worse.

It is also said that the Indian method of a shallow tilling of the soil is not, as it appears to be, inefficient and lazy, but is a result of the *ryot's* shrewd understanding of his land. This also may be true, in the sense that the peasant has learned that he had better not plow too deep. Proper use of fertilizer is being taught, and fertilizer plants stand high on India's crowded list of priority. But long education will be necessary to break down the superstitious conservatism of the peasant, who believes, among thousands of other such things, that artificial fertilizer cannot be good. Not only that. He is apt to look askance at the use even of natural fertilizer. Intensive natural fertilizing, as it is practiced in China, is all but unknown in India. Something of the difficulties of peasant education may be judged from the fact that millions of peasants have never heard of artificial fertilizer, just as they have never heard of Jawalharlal Nehru or even Mahatma Gandhi.

If there is a way out of India's inability to feed its people, it has not yet become apparent.

Hopeful signs appear – wheat production per acre is substantially up this year, and the Government seems to have real hope of achieving its target of 10,000,000 additional tons of food grains a year – but the trend continues ominously the other way. One brief statement, with its implications, suggests the whole picture: Taking 1931 for reference, with an index of 100, food production for all the Indian subcontinent rose five points, to 105, by 1947. Between the same two years, the population grew from index 100 to index 120. Only in Sind, now part of Pakistan, and in the Punjab, also in Pakistand, did agriculture and population roughly keep pace; and even that balance was heavily disturbed in last year's troubles, and has not yet been restored.

The trend may be reversed, in time, and with great effort. It will have to be, if India is ever to achieve the greatness hoped for it by its leaders. Meanwhile, the symbolic validity of the skull – and the vulture, and the carrion crow, and the scavenging pariah dog – cannot be denied.

Related Readings

Bazaz, Prem Nath: Whither India after independence?, New Delhi 1970.
Bettelheim, Charles: L'Inde indépendante, Paris 1971.
Bhatia, Balmokand M.: India's food problem and policy since independence, Bombay 1970.
Bhatia, Krishan: The ordeal of nationhood. A social study of India since independence, 1947–1970, New York 1971.
Chakrabarty, Atulananda: Nehru, his democracy and India, Calcutta 1961.
Collins, Larry/Lapierre, Dominique: Um Mitternacht die Freiheit. Indiens dramatischer Weg in die Unabhängigkeit, Reinbek bei Hamburg 1978.
Dutt, Vishnu: Ghandi, Nehru and the challenge, New Delhi 1979.
Embree, Ainslie Thomas: India's search for national identity, New York 1972.
Ghosh, Kalyan Kumar: The Indian National Army. Second front of the Indian Independence Movement, Meerut 1969.
Gopal, Sarvepalli: Modern India, London 1967.
India (Republic), Ministry of Information and Broadcasting (Ed.): India since independence, New Dehli 1971.
Kulkarni, Venkatesh Balkrishna: British Dominion in India and after, Bombay 1964.
Mansergh, Nicholas (Ed.): The transfer of power 1942–47, 2 vols., London 1970.
Mohan, Jag (Ed.): Twenty-five years of Indian independence, Delhi 1973.
Rawding, F. W.: Gandhi and the struggle for India's independence, Cambridge 1981.
Schütz, Wilhelm Wolfgang: Unteilbare Freiheit. Nehrus Politik der Selbstbestimmung, Göttingen 1964.
Sinha, Sasadhar: Indian independence in perspective, New York 1964.
Wolpert, Stanley A.: Tilak and Gokhale. Revolution and reform in the making of modern India, Berkeley, Calif., 1977.

1949

Edmund W. Stevens

The Christian Science Monitor

CHAPTER 22

REPORTS ABOUT THE SOVIET UNION IN 1949

The Structure of the Government and the Way It Acts on the People

Introductory Notes
22.1 The Supreme Soviet and What It Symbolizes
22.2 Stalin's Secret Police and a Bitter Paradox
22.3 The Order of Ascendency and the Favoured Candidates
22.4 Bureaucracy and the Reversal of an Idea
22.5 Trade Unions and Their Effects on Production
　　Related Readings

Introductory Notes

The bestowal of the International Reporting award for reports about India turned out to be only a thematical interlude, for in the course of the cold war the Pulitzer Prize committees again focused on the U.S.S.R. as they had already done in 1947 and 1948. This time the honor went to Edmund W. Stevens of the Christian Science Monitor *"for his series of 43 articles written over a three-year residence in Moscow entitled, 'This is Russia – Uncensored.'" The prize-winning materials were an accumulation of Russia-related dispatches of which, however, only a part were written in the year relevant for the bestowal of the prize, that is 1949.*

Edmund William Stevens was born on July 22, 1910, in Denver, Colorado. His parents took him to Rome as a child and remained there during World War I. He returned to the United States as a youth and attended Dwight School in New York City and Columbia University where, in 1932, he received his B.A. degree. Postgraduate studies in the fields of government and international law followed in 1932-33. Since he was educated in part in France and Italy, he learned the languages of those countries in addition to German and Russian. In 1934 he continued his studies in Russian at Moscow University. From 1934 to 1939, Stevens lived in Moscow, acting as a correspondent for the Manchester Guardian, *the* Observer *and* Reuters. *He also worked for the American-Russian Chamber of Commerce, specializing in research on Soviet production. From 1937 to 1939 he was special representative for the Cunard-White Star Line in Moscow. In 1939 Stevens began to write extensively for the* Christian Science Monitor. *He attained prominence as a war correspondent during World War II, and was an eye-witness of some of the most stirring events. When the sudden German attack on Norway began, he was one of three American newspapermen in Oslo and was able to describe in detail the ensuing operations. As the war progressed, he kept one jump ahead of the Nazis through the Balkans, Greece, the Middle East, and North Africa. Between 1946 and 1949 Stevens served as the Moscow correspondent of the* Christian Science Monitor, *where he wrote his Pulitzer Prize-winning series of articles which "cut a window in the Iron Curtain, giving a detailed view of every facet of Soviet life" during that period.*

The following texts by Edmund William Stevens, copyright 1949, are reprinted by kind permission of The Christian Science Monitor, *Boston, Massachusetts.*

22.1 The Supreme Soviet and What It Symbolizes

[*Source: Edmund Stevens: Dullest parliament – Soviet is 'supreme', in:* The Christian Science Monitor *(Boston, Mass.), Vol. 41/No. 300, November 17, 1949, p. 1, cols. 1–2.*]

"We Russians," a friend once remarked to me, "can claim one priority that nobody ever will challenge. We have invented the world's dullest Parliament." My friend was giving an average citizen's opinion of the Supreme Soviet of the U.S.S.R., defined by the Soviet Constitution as "the highest law-giving organ in the land."

The best indication of what the Kremlin bosses really think of their sovereign Parliament is the fact that the Supreme Soviet is the one government section whose proceedings are open to foreign correspondents and diplomats. In the Soviet Union this is a sure sign that no state matters of consequence are to be dealt with.

For a fortnight each year, usually in February or March, some 1,800 Supreme Soviet deputies converge on Moscow from all corners of the country. They are a colorful crowd, central Asiatics and Caucasians in their native costumes. Gilded marshals and generals with chestfuls of shiny medals. In the Great Hall of the Kremlin, where the last Romanovs were crowned, they sit through endless speeches and vote when called on to do so. With punctilious adherence to parliamentary procedure, the chairman calls first for a show of those in favor – a forest of hands shoots up. Next he asks for those opposed. Not one hand is raised, and so the chairman announces: "Nyet!" Finally, he asks for the abstentions. Again not a single hand, and again the same announcement. The chairman then declares that the measure or law up for vote has been unanimously adopted and moves on to the next item.

The main business of every Supreme Soviet session is the adoption of the annual budget. Just how the budget happened to be chosen for these deliberations, or some other field of government activity, is a Kremlin secret. The Soviet Constitution, which sets forth the Supreme Soviet's functions, says nothing about its concentrating on the budget. Yet for the better part of a week, after approving the agenda for the session, the delegates listen first to the draft of the budget presented by the minister of finance, next to speeches by various delegates proposing minor changes and amendments, and then to the final draft again presented by the finance minister, substantially the same as the initial draft, save that a few minor changes and recommendations have been incorporated.

The presentation of the draft is made at a joint session of both houses. This is when Prime Minister Joseph Stalin and the other members of the Politburo put in an appearance. They sit on a raised platform at the far end of the hall behind the speaker's stand, in the shadow of a tall white marble Lenin. After the first half hour or so, Stalin usually saunters out, and gradually the others follow suit. Thereafter the "highest law-making organ in the land" continues its deliberations without the party leaders, save that the marble Lenin always is there.

Just how much relation these deliberations have to the actual conduct of affairs is indicated by the circumstance that the budget for 1946 was not debated and approved until October, when the fiscal year was almost over. Nor do the billions of rubles dealt with in the budget give any clue to the actual state of the country's economy in view of the highly nebulous value of the ruble.

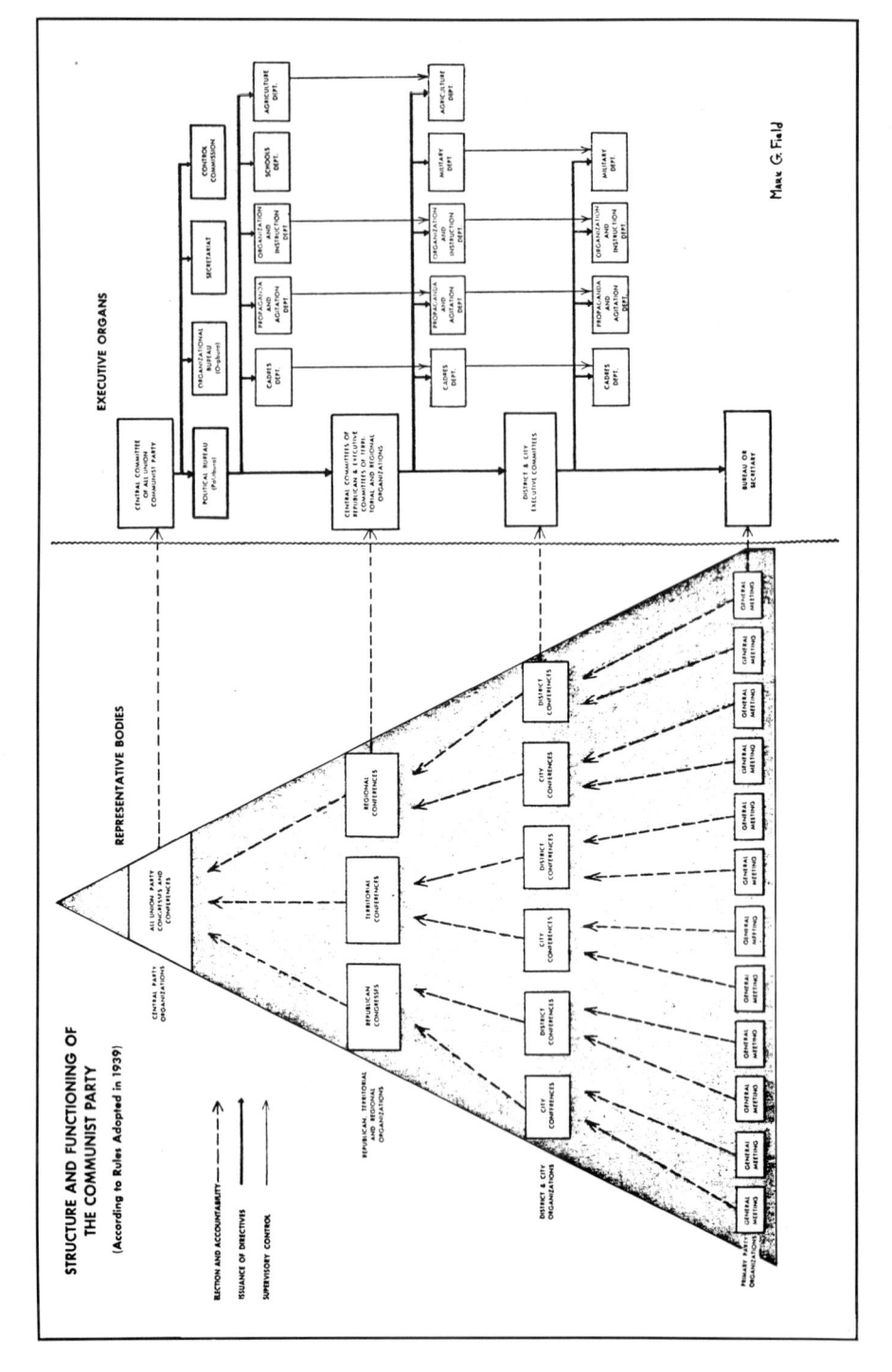

[*Source:* Alex Inkeles: Public Opinion in Soviet Russia. A Study in Mass Persuasion, Cambridge, Mass., 1951, opposite p. 28.]

After the initial joint sitting, the two chambers of the Supreme Soviet hold their meetings separately. The finance minister submits his final draft, first to one chamber for approval and then to the other, which means that he makes virtually the same speech three separate times. Having passed the budget, in the last half hour of its final session, each chamber hears the reports of the Supreme Soviet Presidium and of the Council of Ministers on ukases and decrees, appointments and dismissals during the time elapsed since the previous session. This is as close as the Supreme Soviet ever gets to the actual substance of government. Everything is approved in rapid-fire succession. Never has the Supreme Soviet let the presidium or the council down by vetoing any measure passed between sessions.

Only on one occasion in its history was the Supreme Soviet's unanimity record ruffled – and that was easily ironed out. Once when the agenda was up for approval at the opening meeting, a woman delegate raised her hand as "opposed." Then, to a flabbergasted assembly, she explained that she objected to a proposed meeting Sunday, and she was sure other out-of-town delegates agreed with her, as this would prevent them from seeing the ballet Swan Lake. The matter was arranged to suit her convenience, harmony was restored, and the agenda speedily approved – unanimously. But everyone present somehow felt a genuine blow for democracy had been struck. Thereafter the arrangements invariably have provided the delegates with plenty of time to look around and enjoy the sights and amenities of the Soviet capital. This was easy, since the two chambers, using the same hall, meet alternately. When not meeting, the delegates are out on the town. The best blocks of ballet and theater seats are reserved for them. Before rationing was abolished, they were provided with coupons to the best stores, serving high government and secret police officials. At present they all have liberal expense allowances, in addition to free board at Moscow's three best hotels and to free transport.

So eager is the Kremlin to confirm the impression that the Supreme Soviet, like the Soviet people whom they claim to represent, is just one big happy family that the least reference to serious difficulties or disagreements by some individual delegate is generally deleted from the stenogram. The Supreme Soviet in all respects faithfully images the one-party ballot system that elected it. As for the Supreme Soviets of the R.S.F.S.R. (Russia proper), and other union republics, they simply approve budgets under the amounts assigned to each republic through the all-union budget. Their proceedings are correspondingly less eventful and shorter than those of the U.S.S.R. Supreme Soviet.

The determination to keep all genuine debate out of the Supreme Soviet may seem puzzling. Surely a little lively discussion, a bit of dissent, a clash of opinion even on nonessentials, would lend at least a semblance of plausibility of the performance. As matters now stand, while the Supreme Soviet may serve to confirm fellow travelers abroad in the belief that the Soviet Union is a democracy, it impresses few thinking individuals inside the country. From the internal propaganda standpoint, the Supreme Soviet is something of a liability, since its threadbare, humorless parody of parliamentary forms serves as a constant reminder to the Russians of how unfree they are.

A likely answer is that here we are dealing with one of the Soviet inconsistencies. When the constitution establishing the present parliamentary system was written, Stalin and his assistants may well have honestly envisaged the gradual introduction of democratic features. The police state, however, operates and evolves according to an inner logic of its own, a logic that not even Stalin can alter. In a sense not even he can control the Frankenstein he helped to fashion. And the police state eyes even the least hint of genuine freedom and democracy with adherance and dread.

22.2 Stalin's Secret Police and a Bitter Paradox

[*Source: Edmund Stevens: Minister of 'Justice' bares MVD cruelty, in:* The Christian Science Monitor *(Boston, Mass.), Vol. 41/No. 304, November 22, 1949, p. 1, cols. 1–2.*]

The powers and functions of the MVD (secret police) are not set forth in the Soviet Constitution, that same constitution which describes the rubber-stamp Supreme Soviet as the highest law-giving body in the land. The MVD does not feel slighted by this omission. On the contrary, it doubtless would resent any attempt to define its authority, since definition implies limits.

This deliberate avoidance of any set statutory framework is the clue to the MVD's central position in the Soviet system. It is unfettered, omnipotent police power reduced to practical organizational form – the state in the full sense of Lenin's definition of the state as "a machine for suppression." The MVD is not a subject the aspiring young Soviet student would be likely to choose for his master's or doctor's thesis. The MVD prefers the light of high-wattage incandescent bulbs in shut-in places to the light of day. It shuns publicity, and its feelings generally are respected. Consequently, commentaries by Soviet sources on the nature, structure, methods, and powers of the MVD are rare.

We therefore are all the more indebted to K. P. Gorshenin, Soviet Minister of Justice, for a brief but englightening description of the MVD's origin and early evolution. In December, 1917, Gorshenin explains, when the Soviet regime was but a few weeks old, a special commission was established under the chairmanship of Felix Dzerzhinsky.

Its purposes, as set forth at the time, were:

"1. Circumvention and liquidation of all counterrevolutionary and saboteuring attempts and actions throughout Russia, regardless of who the authors were."

"2. Turning over to the court of the military-revolutionary tribunal all saboteurs and counterrevolutionists and drafting measures for the struggle with these [elements]."

This initial decree further imposed specific limitations on the authority of the new organization: "The commission conducts only the preliminary investigation and only insofar as required for circumventive purposes." In other words, at this early stage the commission had no power to pass judgment and impose sentences. It simply conducted its investigation and turned its findings over to the court of the revolutionary tribunal. A semblance, at least, of due process of law was thereby preserved.

On Dec. 13 (old style), 1917, the Council of People's Commissars officially designated the new body as the All-Russian Extraordinary Commission for Struggle With Counterrevolution and Sabotage, specifying that it was directly responsible to the Council of People's Commissars. Thereafter the body was commonly known by its Russian initials VChK, rendered colloquially as Cheka. The first major step expanding the Cheka's original restricted character followed a few months later. Quoting Gorshenin: "In March, 1918, the All-Russian Extraordinary Commission proposed to all local soviets the immediate organization of local extraordinary commissions. At the same time the VChK stipulated that after the organization of local Chekas, the right to carry out all arrests, all searches, requisitions, and confiscations connected with counterrevolutionary crimes, speculation, crimes of office (presumably graft and dereliction of duty), and through the press (publication of anti-Soviet material) belongs exclusively to organs of the Cheka."

The comprehensive character of this list of functions is self-evident. But this tremendous expansion of its organization and its competency only whetted the Cheka's appetite. According to Gorshenin: "At the end of 1918 the VChK was reorganized from an organ of investigation into an organ that also resorted directly to extra-juridical (i.e., without reference to the courts) measures of coercion, assuring swift and, of necessity, cruel repression of the enemies of the Soviet state." In this candid definition Gorshenin has provided, let us hope for his sake unwittingly, a damaging exposé of the fraudulent, phony character of the "rights" and "guarantees" of the individual written into the Soviet Constitution.

The fact that Gorshenin ranks second only to Foreign Minister Andrei Y. Vishinsky among Soviet legal authorities lends added weight to his words. As head of the Ministry of Justice, which in the past on all-too-rare occasions (and even then only lower local officials were involved) has blown the whistle on the MVD, Gorshenin knows whereof he speaks when he describes its methods as "cruel." Mr. Gorshenin was dealing with the initial period of the Soviet police state. Since then the Cheka has been successively renamed GPU, NKVD, and finally MVD. And with every change of initials its organization and functions have expanded. Within a few years it had organized and trained a compact, highly disciplined, well-armed, well-paid internal army whose members were fanatically loyal to the party leadership – this in addition to an all-pervading network of part-time and full-time undercover agents, with untold numbers of spies and contacts in every walk of Soviet life.

The GPU proved an indispensable ally to the Stalin leadership in the intra-party struggle, first with the Trotskyites in 1925–27 and with the "Rightists" in 1930. Without the powerful arm of the GPU and its "extrajuridical measures of coercion," the regime never could have embarked on its stupendous campaign to drive the Russian peasantry into collective farms. Likewise, for many of the vast industrial construction projects of the successive Five-Year Plans, starting with 1927, the GPU provided an ample supply of forced labor.

In addition to its internal security functions, the GPU was placed in charge of all Soviet intelligence work, thereby extending its activities to other countries, particularly those with important Communist minorities. In 1934 the GPU was transformed into the NKVD or Ministry of Internal Affairs, with control over the civil and criminal police concentrated in its hands. Thereafter even dog licenses were issued by the NKVD.

One of the greatest paradoxes of all time is the fact that H. G. Yagoda, who headed the GPU through its period of greatest expansion, and who for years literally held the lives of Stalin and other Kremlin leaders in the palm of his hand – together with the lives of millions of plain citizens – ended as the victim of the very instrument he had helped to fashion: shot by one of the firing squads he had trained, convicted as a traitor under the same procedure he had devised and used against thousands of others.

Regardless of whether he was guilty or innocent of the charges against him – including the alleged killing of Maxim Gorky and a plan to assassinate Stalin – the implications for the Soviet police state system are equally devastating. For if he was, as Vishinsky insisted as prosecutor at the 1938 purge trial in which Yagoda figured, a depraved, cold-blooded criminal with a lust for power, then how about the hundreds of thousands dragged off to forced labor camps or shot by GPU firing squads during Yagoda's decade of incumbency? That is one question I have never heard a Soviet apologist try to answer.

22.3 The Order of Ascendency and the Favoured Candidates

[*Source: Edmund Stevens: Stalin sits as legend – Malenkov sits tight, in:* The Christian Science Monitor *(Boston, Mass.), Vol. 42/No. 4, November 29, 1949, p. 1, cols. 1–2.*]

"Stalin is the Lenin of today."

This recent formula, which Soviet editorial writers use with recurring frequency, sums up the postwar apotheosis of the Kremlin leader. As one time, Stalin claimed to be no more than the humble apprentice of Lenin the great revolutionary master. The very term "Stalinism" was coined as a derogatory epithet.

Seldom in history has a man become a legend in his own lifetime. Yet Stalin the man already has been totally replaced by Stalin the legend where the Russian public is concerned. The legendary Stalin is a mellow, unclelike character, who loves to accept bouquets of flowers from little girls in token of thanks for their "happy childhood." He radiates gentle patience and benevolent wisdom. All this bears little resemblance to the sharp, ruthless politician who gained control of the party machinery as Lenin's hand faltered and who, by a series of deft moves, not only consolidated his own position but outmaneuvered the entire group of Lenin's close associates, who finally were disposed of during the purges of 1934–1938.

Chief promoter of the Stalin legend is Stalin himself. His mode of life, his every public act of utterance, is calculated to fit this role. Having divorced himself largely from the everyday business of government, he descends from the Olympian remoteness of his semiretirement only at rare intervals to make history with a few well-chosen words, usually in the form of a press release.

Stalin has not made a public speech since February, 1946, when he addressed his constituents during the Supreme Soviet election campaign. From year to year, he lengthens his vacations at his Sukhumi villa on the Black Sea shore, leaving Moscow in August and returning only just in time for the May Day parade. Meanwhile, responsibility for running the state gravitates increasingly to Stalin's lieutenants, the members of the Politburo. This is the level at which the struggle for personal power takes place.

The order of ascendancy at a given time always can be ascertained from the alignment of portraits displayed on Soviet holidays. When Andrei A. Zhdanov was alive, Stalin, in the center, was flanked invariably by Vyacheslav M. Molotov on the right and Zhdanov on the left. Next to Molotov came Georgi M. Malenkov and next to Zhdanov Laurenty P. Beria, but at one time Beria was alongside Molotov. The demise of Zhdanov disarranged the pattern and for a time Beria and Malenkov appeared to be running neck and neck while Molotov continued to hold first place. The race was so close that I recall how, during the Nov. 7, 1947, festivities, the positions of Malenkov and Beria portraits where shifted twice in the course of a single day.

Within the past year, a major readjustment has occurred. Beria, a powerful figure by virtue of his control of the MVD (secret police) and close personal relations with Stalin, does not appear to aspire to further advancement. Molotov, since he relinquished the foreign ministry, has gone into partial eclipse. Russians say that Molotov, even in his prime, was important only as the appendage or reflection of Stalin and was never a personality in his own right. His present decline, they add, is simply the result of Stalin's increased retirement.

The rivalry between Zhdanov and Malenkov was long an open secret. It was a struggle between antithetical temperaments rather than opposing political views. Zhdanov was the brilliant intellectual, inclined to brashness, but with a keen instinct of leadership, the only spellbinder in the Politburo. His intense party zeal was flavored strongly with Russian nationalism. He was a man of considerable cultural background, thoroughly versed in Russian literature and with a rich command of his native language. He was, in addition, an accomplished amateur pianist. Like other Soviet leaders of his generation, his knowledge of the outside world was negligible.

Malenkov is the typical product of the party apparatus, in which he has spent his entire adult life. Lacking mass appeal, he dislikes the limelight and prefers to pull wires behind the scenes. Cautious where Zhdanov was impetuous, plodding where Zhdanov was brilliant, Malenkov has a brain closely akin to the vast party card index which he keeps as chief of the party organization. He thus occupies today much the same strategic post that Stalin held when Lenin was failing. He has the same talent for party-machine manipulation that stood Stalin in good stead in the days of the struggle for Lenin's mantle. Zhdanov, by comparison, had more of Trotsky's characteristics.

During the past year, Malenkov has used his position to carry out a quiet but thorough purge from key posts of Zhdanov's protégés and appointees, the most important of whom were Nikolai Voznesensky, member of the Politburo and chairman of the State Planning Commission, and Alexander Kuznetsov, trade-union chairman, both products of Zhdanov's Leningrad party organization. While Zhdanov sometimes was inclined to overreach himself, as in the 1939 attack on Finland, the expulsion of Tito from the Cominform, and the Berlin blocade, Malenkov favors consolidation of present holdings before attempting further expansion. It would be utterly wrong to construe this as meaning a softer policy more "friendly" or conciliatory toward the West. There is nothing soft or "friendly" about Malenkov. At home, Malenkov's consolidation policy has meant whole-sale collectivization of the Balts, deportation of "unreliable" elements from border and coastal areas, and renewed discrimination against the Jews, including ruthless suppression of Zionism.

There has been no letup in the party indoctrination campaign in all spheres of learning and culture which Zhdanov initiated. Part of the Malenkov policy has been to intensify the anti-American campaign, to expend enormous efforts and resources on blacking out the Voice of America radiocasts in Russian. Abroad, the Malenkov consolidation policy has meant tighter control of Cominform countries, ruthless elimination as "Titoists" of all Communists with the slightest spirit of independence, universal and arbitrary imposition of the Soviet economic pattern, including collectivization of the peasantry and destruction of the middle classes, using the "extrajuridical" technique of the MVD, as well as the "model" trials with their self-accusations.

Malenkov's caution is reflected in the lifting of the Berlin blockade and in the fact that the campaign against Tito has so far stopped short of actual invasion. But such things are a matter of cold judgment and tactics and do not express any genuine desire for friendship with the West, which Malenkov despises just as Zhdanov did and understands even less. The emergence of Malenkov marks a major historic milestone. The party helm is passing into the hands of a generation of party members who have no clear personal recollections of the old order and who did not themselves take part in the revolution.

Malenkov and his contemporaries reached maturity and have spent their entire active lives under the Soviet system and are its products, whereas the older Bolsheviks, including Stalin, were not. This profoundly affects their thinking and attitude.

22.4 Bureaucracy and the Reversal of an Idea

[*Source: Edmund Stevens: One party, one voice, one tongue – or none, in:* The Christian Science Monitor *(Boston, Mass.), Vol. 42/No. 10, December 6, 1949, p. 1, cols. 1–2.*]

No All-Union Congress of the Soviet Communist Party has been held since 1939, though party rules prescribe that these congresses must be called at least once every two years. Technically, it could be argued therefore that the present party leadership's mandate expired more than eight years ago and that the Soviet leaders have been acting illegally ever since. To date, however, no party member has tried to raise the issue.

People in Russia have learned to attach no importance to such technicalities. I once pointed out to a Russian acquaintance that Article 46 of the Soviet Constitution provides that the Supreme Soviet (parliament) shall sit twice yearly, whereas in practice there usually is only one session a year, which promptly adjourns after approving the budget. My friend was frankly surprised at my comment. "But think of the extra trouble and expense involved if they met twice yearly," he objected. "And besides, what on earth would they do?"

The All-Union Party Congress is the supreme assemblage of the Communist Party, with technical powers to shape or reshape party policy and select or reject party leadership. It elects the Central Committee which in turn elects the Politburo from among its own numbers, as well as the Orgburo, and the Central Committee secretaries. Technically, the Party Congress is free to change the top party leadership. From any standpoint, it is high time for a party congress. Not only has the mandate of the present party leadership technically lapsed, the entire composition of the party rank and file has changed.

By 1939, as a result of the purges, party membership had shrunk from a prewar high of around 3,000,000 to less than 2,000,000. Today, after mass induction of younger elements

Higher Educational Institutions in U.S.S.R. by Types, September, 1949 *

Type	Number of Institutions	Number of Students
Universities	32	87,836
Technical institutes	167	239,310
Agriculture and animal husbandry	90	78,652
Law and economics	32	37,964
Pedagogical and teachers	379	212,001
Medical	72	99,850
Arts	51	13,119
Physical culture	14	5,746
TOTALS	837	774,478

* Excluding correspondence students and institutions.

Higher Educational Institutions of All Types in Each of the Union Republics of the U.S.S.R., September, 1949 *

Union Republic	Number of Institutions	Number of Students
Russian	480	474,795
Ukrainian	159	137,160
Uzbek	35	29,281
Georgian	19	24,745
Kazakh	23	18,117
Belorussian	28	17,870
Azerbaijan	19	17,361
Armenian	14	10,124
Latvian	9	10,063
Lithuanian	11	9,625
Estonian	8	6,801
Kirghiz	7	5,257
Moldavian	8	4,728
Tajik	9	4,247
Turkmen	6	3,390
Karelo-Finnish	2	714
TOTALS	837	774,478

* Excluding correspondence students and institutions.

The Soviet Higher Education System

[*Source:* George B. de Huszar et al.: Soviet Power and Policy, New York 1955, p. 214.]

from the army as a wartime morale-building measure, the figure has soared to beyond 5,000,000. The new members never have had an opportunity to vote for representatives to the higher party organs. The major preliminaries to a party congress took place last winter, when local party congresses were held in the regions, territories, autonomous and union republics.

According to the theory of "democratic centralism," the lower level elects its representatives to the next higher level, and so forth, the source of authority being the rank-and-file membership at the base of the pyramid. In current Soviet practice it works exactly the other way around. Authority emanates from the Politburo at the peak and is delegated downward. The lower party levels simply carry out directives from above. Under this dispensation, initiative and originality are not encouraged within the party apparatus. Party members are judged by the readiness with which they obey or transmit orders from above. The result is an amazing uniformity not only of policy, but even of thought and verbal expression.

This was strikingly apparent in the reports of the party secretaries to the local party congresses. Though delivered in different languages and in widely separated areas, they all sounded as though written by the same hand. On January 25, 1949, in Kiev, Nikita Khrushchev, in his capacity of secretary of the Ukrainian Communist Party (he also is a member of the Politburo), began his report to the local party congress as follows: "Comrades: Since the 15th Congress of the Communist Party of the Ukraine, more than 8½ years have elapsed. This period was replete with events of worldwide historic importance."

Khrushchev spoke in Ukrainian. That very same afternoon, more than a thousand miles away in Tbilisi, Secretary Charkviani of the Georgian Communist Party was telling delegates to the Georgian Party Congress: "Comrades: Since the 13th Congress of the Communist Party of Georgia, nearly nine years have elapsed – a period replete with the greatest historic events."

Simultaneously, in Baku, Secretary Bagirov told the Azerbaijan Party Congress: "Comrades! Since the 16th Congress of the Communist Party of Azerbaijan, almost nine years have elapsed. During those years extremely important events took place." Some days later, on February 10, Party Secretary Bogolyubov told the Kirghizian Party Congress: "Comrades: Since the Sixth Congress of the Communist Party of Kirghizia, almost nine years have elapsed. This was a period replete with the greatest worldwide historic events."

So on down the party line ad infinitum. Allowing for differences in local problems, much the same uniformity prevailed throughout the proceedings of all the local party congresses. Identical uncomplimentary remarks were everywhere passed about the West. Identical flattering references were made to Stalin, followed by time out for "thunderous applause."

There are good indications that the Kremlin would like to impose a similar uniformity and unanimity on the 195,000,000 nonparty members of different languages and nationalities under its rule. One significant thread running through every local congress was a new stress on the close ties between the non-Russian nationalities of each republic and the great Russian people, everywhere exalted as the universal standard bearers of civilization.

Uzbekistan Party Secretary Yusupov (himself Russian) even dug up a quotation from Friedrich Engels, dated 1851, lauding Russia's role in the Orient as "progressive." At the same time, Yusupov sternly warned against any notion that the close similarity between Uzbek and Turkish languages signified any cultural or historic kinship. This, he said, was "pan-Turkism," which was anti-Marxist and a tool of Anglo-American imperialism.

Azerbaijan Party Secretary Bagirov urged all Azerbaijanians to master Russian, »the language of our big brother, the native tongue of our multimillioned, multinational Soviet family." He illustrated his argument with, a quotation from a local 19th-century poet:
My son, know you Russian science
And master you that language.
We need them. Without them the world is dark.
Without this learning there's no road to light.

The secretary of the Kazakhstan Party told his congress that all textbooks on the history of Kazakhstan were being rewritten, since, he said, the authors had wrongly pictured Kazakh history as a long struggle for independence and had failed to deal adequately with the historic and economic ties between the Kazakhs and the Russians.

It follows that the Kremlin would much prefer that the Kazakhs and other members of the Soviet family concentrate on learning Russian, "the language of our big brother," rather than studying the history of their own struggles for independence from Russia. Stalin himself has always stressed that knowledge is a guide to action.

22.5 Trade Unions and Their Effects on Production

[*Source: Edmund Stevens: Trade Union chant – work, work harder!, in:* The Christian Science Monitor *(Boston, Mass.), Vol. 42/No. 27, December 27, 1949, p. 1, cols. 1–2.*]

The postwar period has brought little relaxation to the Russians. Everyone who works, down to the last ditch digger, is being prodded and cajoled constantly into working at a faster pitch. Gone is the prewar prating about cutting the prevailing eight-hour day to seven hours. Today the man who refuses to "volunteer" for overtime is looked upon as "unpatriotic," and nobody likes to be called that.

One of the main agencies, but by no means the only agency, for getting the Soviet worker to work harder and longer is the Soviet trade union. The Soviet trade union has nothing in common but the name with trade unionism as conceived and practiced in western countries. The sole similarity is with some old-time company unions. While, on paper, the Soviet trade unions are pledged to represent and defend the workers' interests vis-à-vis management in all disputes including wage issues, and while all sorts of clauses on rights of appeal and arbitration are written into the charters, these provisions have about as much meaning and application as the civil liberties guaranteed in the Soviet Constitution. The actual power of decision resides elsewhere, beyond recourse. The strike weapon, labor's effective defense against arbitrary power, is as utterly outlawed as it was in Nazi Germany or Fascist Italy.

As against this fictitious purpose, the real purpose of the Soviet trade unions is to assist the government in getting as much work as is humanly possible out of Soviet workers. They function primarily as an enormous, well-oiled, nationwide machine for transmitting to the great working masses the endless official ballyhoo campaigns aimed at keeping the worker constantly pepped up so that he will exert his utmost effort.

The trade unions are the organizers and sponsors of the Stakhanovite or "socialist competition" movement, the principle of which is to get the workers competing with each other to work better and harder. Trade-union meetings are held where speeches are made, resolutions passed, challenges issued from one brigade or worker to another to outdo each other. To keep things from lapsing into routine, a whole military vocabulary is employed. One constantly is regaled with "victories" on the production front, of "battles" for lower production costs, for economy of raw materials, fuel, or electricity, and now, in particular, for improved quality. The whole effort is stage-managed by local trade-union leaders acting on directives from the trade-union center.

The scale of this sustained effort is indicated by the official claim that 90 per cent of all Soviet industrial workers and technicians take part in "socialist competition." The Literary Gazette, with a flair for literary phrase, enthuses: "In our country the Stakhanovite movement has flowered with a lush bloom – a great army of people tasking with their souls, with ardor, making their daily contribution to the common cause."

Every year produces its new crop of much-publicized stars of socialist competition, individuals who are built up as shining examples for the working rank and file to emulate. Some years the emphasis is on quantity, other years on quality. Last year's campaign stressed quality, and its main hero was a Moscow textile-loom operator named Alexander Chutkikh. He was credited with having achieved spectacular improvement in the quality of his cloth. The Soviet press promptly took him up and he was blazoned from Kaliningrad to Vladivostok as "Initiator of the struggle for high-grade weaves." Soon he was showered with honors, including a Stalin Prize.

Pressed by admirers for the story of his signal success, Chutkikh confided in a published article that "it was all quite simple." One morning, saddened by the news that consumers were grumbling about the quality of cloth, he decided to investigate for himself. He made the rounds of the shops. In one place a woman flung a bolt of cloth down on the counter and walked out. Chutkikh examined the bolt and found himself agreeing with the disgruntled customer. The cloth was of curious hue, with an ugly pattern. Then and there Chutkikh had his flash of inspiration. "It suddenly came to me that competition for increase in quantity of manufactured goods must be supplemented with competition for excellence of quality. At a meeting of factory Stakhanovites I suggested organizing brigades for excellent quality. I was seconded. My unit became the first in the plant to produce first-grade cloth. The newspapers wrote it up."

That was all there was to it. Thereafter, continued Chutkikh, the letters started pouring in. "People I had never met wrote in asking advice, wanting to know what they should do in order to produce only high-quality goods. There were hundreds of such letters. Boatmen, roadbuilders, buttermakers, and metalworkers all wanted the same thing – to turn out excellent products so as not to blush before the Soviet consumer."

Just what magic "open sesame" Chutkikh dispensed in reply to these queries is not clear either from his own statement or from the voluminous press publicity. Perhaps it is a state secret. At any event, overnight almost, the Soviet press reported "Alexander Chutkikh Brigades" were being formed spontaneously all over the country, and even in Bulgaria, by his ardent emulators. Though Chutkikh held the center of the limelight, he did not monopolize it. Numerous other model workers got their names and pictures in the papers, all of which moved the Literary Gazette to contrast this "Soviet glorification of the toiling man" with America, where it charged only gangsters like Al Capone are so celebrated. Presumably there is no intent to imply that racketeering was involved in both cases.

The stars of "socialist competition" are strictly one-season wonders retired to oblivion as soon as the novelty wears off. Year before last a similar fuss was made over Alexander Matrosov, credited with achieving no less sensational improvements in the production of shoes by leather- and time-saving proposals which, when described, sounded elementary to the point of naïveté: Today Matrosov is as forgotten as other model workers before him.

A salient and laudable aspect of the "Stakhanovite" or "socialist competition" campaigns is their stress on the importance of developing and encouraging "innovations." But the campaigns themselves seem sadly in need of a bit of innovating. Though the stars change and the focal point shifts from one industry to another, the methods, slogans, and clichés have scarcely altered since the whole movement was initiated in 1935 with the Donbas miner, Alexei Stakhanov.

This does not imply that the concerted ballyhoo fails in its purpose of making people work harder. But the attempt to present the whole performance as "spontaneous" and initiated by the rank and file is as fishy as a can of caviar. The result – in greater output or better quality – is achieved by the sheer concerted drive and overwhelming impact of a mighty and unopposed propaganda machine. The Soviet trade unions, backed by the Communist Party, the Soviet Government, and the entire press, comprise its vital cog. The workers, engineers, and technicians conform, though the whole thing is, of course strictly "voluntary." They well know the price of nonconformity.

Related Readings

Berman, Harold Joseph: Justice in Russia. An interpretation of Soviet law, Cambridge, Mass., 1950.
Cantril, Hadley: Soviet leaders and mastery over man, New Brunswick, N. J., 1960.
Chambre, Henri: Le marxisme en Union Soviétique. Idéologie et institutions, leur évolution de 1917 à nos jours, Paris 1955.
Dallin, David J.: The changing world of Soviet Russia, New Haven, Conn., 1956.
Deutscher, Isaac: Russia in transition and other essays, New York 1957.
Granick, David: The Red executive. A study of the organization man in Russian industry, Garden City, N.Y., 1960.
Gunther, John: Inside Russia today, rev. ed., New York 1962.
Inkeles, Alex/Bauer, Raymond A.: The Soviet citizen. Daily life in a totalitarian society, Cambridge, Mass., 1959.
Leites, Nathan Constantin: A study of bolshevism, Glencoe, Ill., 1953.
Meek, Dorothea L. (Ed.): Soviet Youth. Some achievements and problems – excerpts from the Soviet press, London 1957.
Mehnert, Klaus: Der Sowjetmensch. Versuch eines Porträts nach dreizehn Reisen in die Sowjetunion 1929–1959, 6. ed., Stuttgart 1959.
Miller, Wright Watts: Russians as people, New York 1961.
Moore, Barrington jr.: Soviet Politics – the dilemma of Power. The role of ideas in social change, Cambridge, Mass., 1954.
Moore, Barrington jr.: Terror and progress USSR – some sources of change and stability in the Soviet dictatorship, Cambridge, Mass., 1954.

Morton, Henry W.: Soviet sport – mirror of Soviet society, New York 1963.
Pipes, Richard (Ed.): The Russian intelligentsia, New York 1961.
Sosnovy, Timothy: The housing problem in the Soviet Union, New York 1954.
Timasheff, Nicholas Sergeyevitch: The great retreat – the growth and decline of communism in Russia, New York 1946.
Vakar, Nicholas Platonovich: The taproot of Soviet society, New York 1962.

1950

Marguerite Higgins

New York Herald-Tribune

CHAPTER 23

REPORTS ABOUT KOREA IN 1950

America's Fight Against Communism and the Conquest of Seoul

    Introductory Notes
23.1 Korean Resistance and the American Way of Breaking It
23.2 Vignettes of Terror and the Liberation of Seoul
23.3 Crowds Cheer and Liberators Inspect Conquered Area
23.4 Works of Reconstruction and the Communist Practise
23.5 The Victor's Ceremony and Further Casualties
    Related Readings

Introductory Notes

The outbreak of the Korean War in the middle of 1950 was followed by a strong concentration of American war- and foreign correspondents in this region. Among the U.S. journalists reporting from Korea who covered action continuously there were the six who received the 1951 Pulitzer Prize for International Reporting for, as it was put flatly, "their reporting of the Korean War." The prize-winners were Keyes Beech and Fred Sparks of the Chicago Daily News, *Relman Morin and Don Whitehead of the* Associated Press, *and last but not least Homer Bigart and Marguerite Higgins of the* New York Herald-Tribune.

Marguerite Higgins, the only woman in this group and only the second female journalist to win a Pulitzer Prize for International Reporting since the award for Anne O'Hare McCormick in 1937, was born on September 3, 1920, in Hong Kong. After receiving her early education in France and England, "Maggie" Higgins returned to the United States with her family. She was graduated with honors in 1941 from the University of California. During the summer she was a cub reporter on the staff of the Vallejo Times-Herald *in California. The following semester she entered the School of Journalism at New York's Columbia University to work for an M.A. degree in that field, which she received in 1942. As a student she held a job as a campus correspondent for the* New York Herald-Tribune, *which employed her as a member of its city staff upon her graduation, and in 1944 she was sent to the* Tribune's *London bureau. From London Marguerite Higgins was transferred to the Paris office of the newspaper because of her fluency in French. In those last days of World War II she accompanied the Seventh Army deep into Austria, and in 1945, at the age of twenty-four, she became chief of the Berlin bureau of the* New York Herald-Tribune. *For her stories on Buchenwald, Dachau, and the occupation of Munich, she received the New York Newspaper Women's Club award as the best foreign correspondent in 1945. Later on she covered numerous international conferences and other events before she became the paper's Tokyo correspondent in 1947. From there she was one of the first reporters to get to Korea when the war started. In her own words, "getting to Korea was more than just a story, it was a personal crusade . . ."*

The following texts by Marguerite Higgins, copyright 1950, are reprinted by kind permission of the International Herald-Tribune, *New York, N.Y.*

23.1 Korean Resistance and the American Way of Breaking It

[*Source: Marguerite Higgins: Reds in Seoul Forcing G.I.s to Blast City Apart*, in: New York Herald-Tribune *(New York, N.Y.), Vol. CX/No. 37,934, September 25, 1950, p. 3, cols. 1–3.*]

The red clay ridges and pine groves on the northwest outskirts of Seoul shuddered in the last twenty-four hours with one of this war's most sanguinary battles as tired but dogged marines inched their way toward the center of the South Korean capital, a point still some three miles away. Spectacular artillery duels in what was certainly the worst phase of the battle for Seoul took place in the suburb of Sinchon, where a famous Korean landmark, the American-founded Chosen Christian University, was being blasted to bits. It is victim of a stubborn determination on the part of the North Korean Communists to fight to the end, and to bring Seoul down in ruins about them if necessary. The university was founded in the 1890's by Horace G. Underwood, a Presbyterian missionary who was among the first Christians to arrive in Korea.

Late this afternoon the marines were advancing on the university, where the North Korean 17th Division headquarters has been reported housed. Fresh American troops had to be put into the battle to advance through the lines of South Korean Marines who earlier suffered heavy casualties from enemy artillery. The artillery fire had also been reaching to the back of the entire front-line area. It was with wry comments that Marines waiting to go into a new attack the afternoon waved copies of Friday's "Stars and Stripes," the army newspaper. The edition bore a headline which read: "Yanks Enter Seoul From Two Sides!"

Stalled on the outskirts of Seoul for more than twenty-four hours, Marines all along the front reported, in the words of Maj. John Canney, a battalion executive officer: "We've been running up against a different breed of cat here in the past day or so." The major, whose battalion was dug in on a strategic hill overlooking the city, added: "The prisoners we've been taking in the last twenty-four hours seem better fed, taller in stature and far more fanatical. For instance, we had our tanks up blasting the hell out of mortars dug in on a hilltop. We blasted out the mortar position, but a while later they just brought mortars back up and started shooting at us all over again."

The North Koreans, who as it later turned out had a forward observer right in the American lines, were murderously accurate with their high-velocity weapons and mortars. Searching out troop concentrations, the Reds' mortars a number of times scored thirty to forty casualties with one burst. As we traveled to different headquarters, from battalion to company and even back to regiment, we could find no place free of the whine and whistle and thump of enemy shells. The enemy would not give up even when the marines got to the top of the ridges and dug in. Able (A) Company, trying to get to the top of a ridge already occupied by Charlie (C) Company, was pinned down for eight hours by snipers and machine gunners who had sneaked around the mountainside to come at the troops from the rear. When A Company finally reached their objective they had only one officer left – the company commander.

If the Americans had ever had any idea of going easy in the shelling of Seoul in order to save buildings, it became clear today that the Communists were not going to give them a chance. The Reds hat obviously saved everything for this final blast and in self defense the Americans had to answer back with everything they had. It is one of the ironies of this war that some of the artillery and even machine guns that the Communists are using so effectively are pieces captured in the days of the American retreats.

The enemy persistence in sniping and machine gunning of all positions has made the evacuation of wounded tragically difficult. On one ridge close to the Han River, wounded had to lie in the hills for four hours before medical corpsmen could get their heads up high enough to carry them out. The artillery duels were taking a terrific toll of Korean civilians. All day and all night women, little children and old men were being brought by pushcart, oxen or litter into the regimental command post in the pathetic hope that the frantically busy doctors could pause long enough to tend to them. First-aid teams helped when they had time, but that was not so often.

Shortly after noon, the Marine artillery and air power let loose. One of the strongest artillery barrages of this war literally tore up the hillside ahead, where the enemy was crouched, and the planes came in for a final blow with fire bombs. Then the Marines started to move forward again.

23.2 Vignettes of Terror and the Liberation of Seoul

[*Source: Marguerite Higgins: Inside Seoul: Marines Gain Inch by Inch, in:* New York Herald-Tribune *(New York, N.Y.), Vol. CX/No. 37,936, September 27, 1950, p. 3, cols. 1–3.*]

Flames and smoke wreathed downtown Seoul today as Marines battered and burned their way forward in slow house-to-house fighting. With the main hotel and government districts of the South Korean capital still in Communist hands, the Marines edged forward by ferreting out the enemy from cellars and roofs, culverts and chimneys.

American flame-throwing tanks stabbed at the flimsy Korean houses, igniting whole blocks, but still the enemy fought on, bringing tanks, grenades and self-propelled guns to support their last-ditch-fight. Eight-foot-high sandbag barricades were encountered with increasing frequency as the Marines slogged toward the main part of Seoul, and big American tanks had to be called in to blast them away with their 90-mm guns.

By late this afternoon, no place in the western part of Seoul was yet free from the hum of sniper bullets or safe from sudden attack by riflemen or machine-gunners hidden in the cellars or hill-side buildings. Creeping behind the forward Marine troops, this correspondent entered the downtown area at the main Seoul railroad station. It was exactly three months ago that I had been chased out of this city by the Communist invaders who, on the night of June 27, had pushed in even as I and the sixty members of the American Military Mission were escaping by ferry and raft across the Han River.

I found the sprawling railroad station a scared and flaming ruin with twisted, blackened

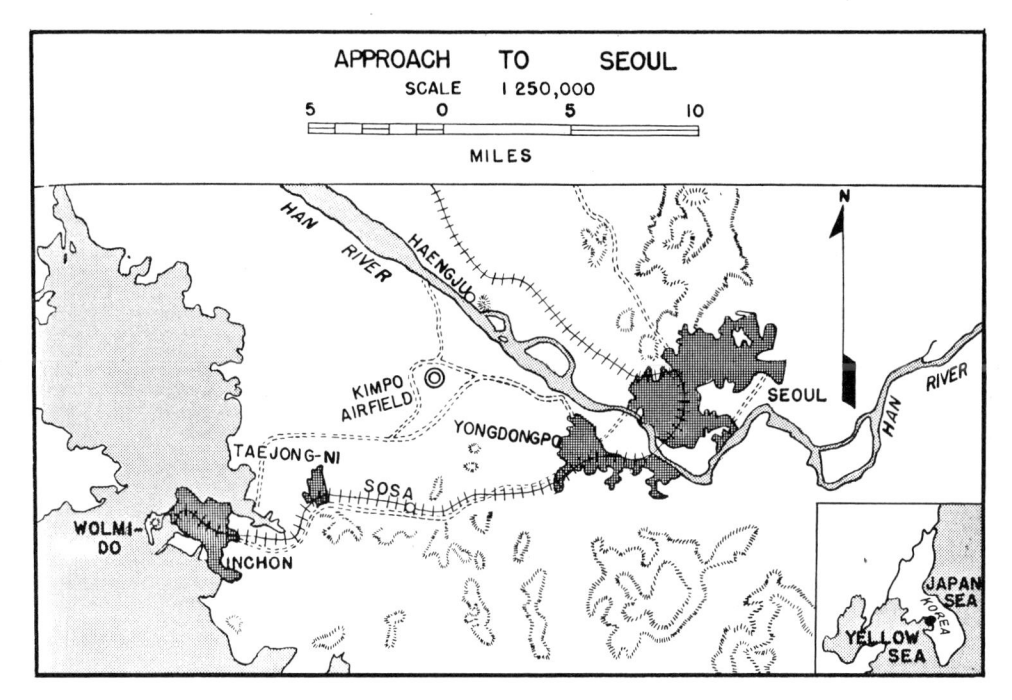

[*Source:* Lynn Montross: Cavalry of the Sky. The Story of U.S. Marine Combat Helicopters, New York 1954, between pp. 128/129.]

cars and locomotives strewn in disorder across the tracks. Most of the houses on the hillside directly in back of the station had been razed in the crossfire. By standing on a bluff near the station I could see the main hotels and government buildings about 1,000 yards away. They appeared intact, but the district in which they are located was encircled by smoke and flame.

The flash of bursting artillery was rapidly approaching the central downtown area. The state of the buildings will depend on the Communists themselves. Orders are to damage Seoul as little as possible, but if the North Koreans take cover in the buildings our big guns and rocket-firing planes will have to go after them just as they have had to blast out other areas in the city. Up to now, the Communists have exacted the maximum penalty for every yard gained.

Among the buildings that still appeared untouched were the Chosen Hotel and the big Banto building, which formerly housed the Economic Co-operation Administration and part of the American Embassy. The Seoul City Hall and the domed capitol also stood out clearly and seemed undamaged.

Despite the pounding of our artillery and the shelling with white phosphorus, the enemy was not only still willing to fight but also to counterattack. Late this afternoon a platoon, marching four abreast and dragging an anti-tank gun, marched right into the position of a forward Marine company. There have been many American casualties, for the street fighting gave the North Koreans the opportunity for close-range firing at the Marines as they raked through the tenements and back alleys looking for the dug-in foe.

THE KOREAN WAR JUNE–NOVEMBER 1950

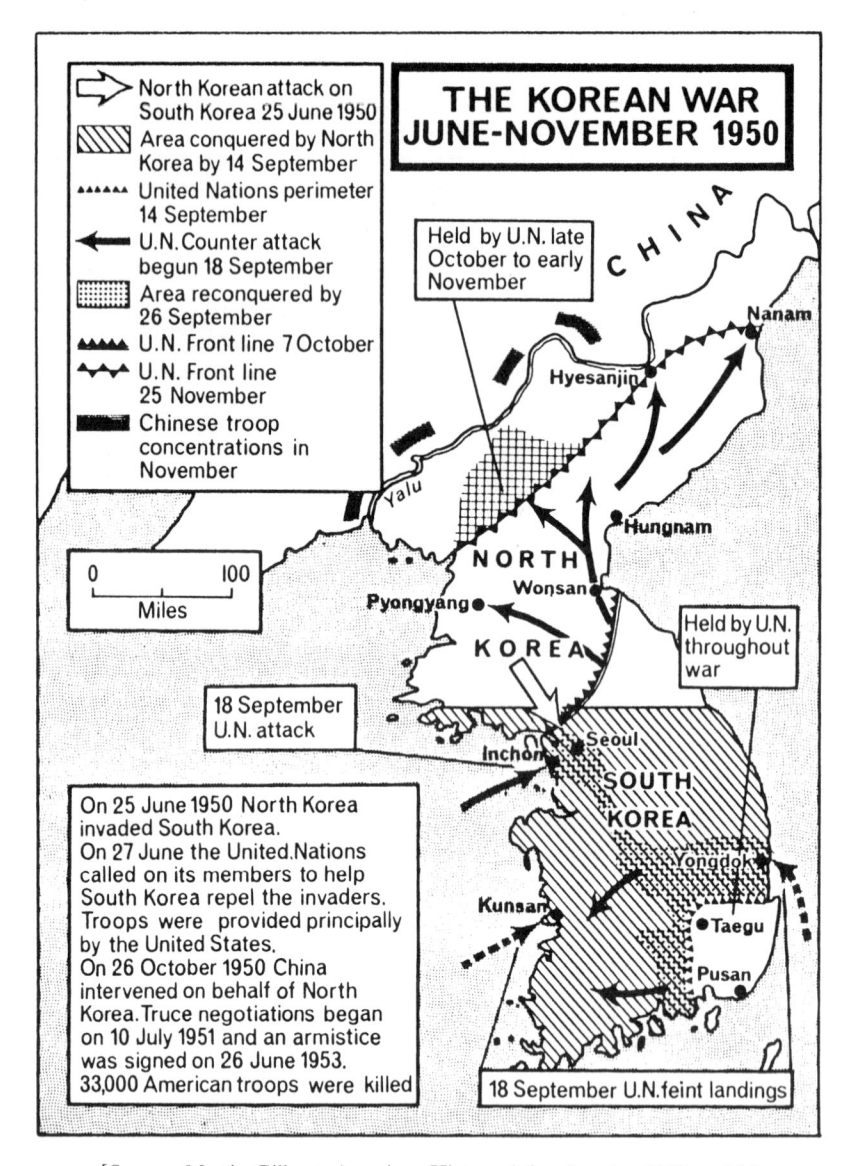

Legend:
- North Korean attack on South Korea 25 June 1950
- Area conquered by North Korea by 14 September
- United Nations perimeter 14 September
- U.N. Counter attack begun 18 September
- Area reconquered by 26 September
- U.N. Front line 7 October
- U.N. Front line 25 November
- Chinese troop concentrations in November

Held by U.N. late October to early November

18 September U.N. attack

On 25 June 1950 North Korea invaded South Korea. On 27 June the United Nations called on its members to help South Korea repel the invaders. Troops were provided principally by the United States. On 26 October 1950 China intervened on behalf of North Korea. Truce negotiations began on 10 July 1951 and an armistice was signed on 26 June 1953. 33,000 American troops were killed.

Held by U.N. throughout war

18 September U.N. feint landings

Places marked: Nanam, Hyesanjin, Hungnam, Pyongyang, Wonsan, Inchon, Seoul, Kunsan, Yongdok, Taegu, Pusan

[*Source:* Martin Gilbert: American History Atlas, London 1968, p. 94.]

The chatter of machine guns and the explosion of big guns was so steady that the occasional lulls were startling. Korean civilians, especially children, would not take cover properly and thousands have been carried by all sorts of improvised litters to the aid stations. Children foraging for empty Marine ration cans along the hilltops were perfect targets for stray bullets.

Capt. George Westover, commander of George (G) Company, told us: "I guess we did not push forward as fast as the high brass wanted us to. But what we have been through in the last forty-eight hours has been hell on earth." G Company last night withstood an enemy tank-led counter-attack and finally came out of the line this afternoon. They had two days of steady fighting with no sleep. As the lead company of the battalion, Capt. Westover's men late yesterday pushed deep into the smoking town a mine-laden street. Their aim was to reach the American Consulate. "We could not pause to check every side street and house," Capt. Westover explained, "and about 1,000 yards south of the consulate machine gunners and riflemen – some of whom we must have by-passed – but loose with big, waist-high, grazing fire."

For four hours Communist and American heavy machine guns duelled. A patrol of five men, including two wounded, could not get back to the company's lines. When orders came for G Company to pull back, Capt. Westover refused to desert them. All rescue attempts failed until two Marines rushed forward and exploded smoke grenades which gave cover for the evacuation. 1st Sgt. Rocco Zullo, of Claremont, N.H., and his men found forty North Koreans holding out under cover and killed them all with hand grenades. Sgt. Charles L. Daniels, of Moorehaven, Fla., refused to be evacuated after being wounded in the back and the leg. He was taken out of the line only after he lost consciousness.

Capt. Westover, who broke into tears from fatigue and emotion as he told us of his company's experience, said: "I think you could say without wasting any adjectives that nearly every man in our company was a hero last night."

23.3 Crowds Cheer and Liberators Inspect Conquered Area

[*Source: Marguerite Higgins: Flaming Seoul Cheers Weary G.I. Liberators, in:* New York Herald-Tribune *(New York, N.Y.), Vol. CX/No. 37,937, September 28, 1950, p. 4, cols. 2–3.*]

Thousands of Koreans stood for hours in the flaming streets of Seoul tonight to cheer their liberation by the United States Marines, who at dusk plunged triumphantly through the heart of the South Korean capital. By the light of a reddened moon and leaping fires, American and South Korean flags could be seen flying over Seoul's tallest and most important buildings. At the American Consulate, which suffered minor damage, the North Korean flag was hauled down and the Stars and Stripes hoisted at 3:37 p.m. (1:37 a.m. E.S.T.)

The long-awaited fall of Seoul began at about mid-afternoon, when the hard core of Communist resistance crumbled. Weary Marines, who had been fighting house-to-house and cellar-to-cellar warfare, suddenly gained momentum and, behind tanks, crossed the enemy barricades to their objectives to the northeast of the city. There was occasional sniper and automatic-weapons fire, but, with a few exceptions, that was about all.

Until this afternoon, the Communists put up a stubborn rear-guard action that forced American artillery and flame-throwing tanks to burn down many acres of the city. Tonight, as I drove back across the town, flames were licking four and fivestory structures on both sides of the main street, making the area a suffocating, acrid-smelling inferno of heavy smoke and flames. Buildings crashed into the rubble-laden streets where tangled power lines, overturned streetcars and potholes grimly recalled the desperate fighting of the battle for Seoul. Once the Communist resistance began disintegrating, events moved so fast that even correspondents helped out in the liberating. Keyes Beech, of the "Chicago Daily News," and I, "captured," somewhat by accident, the Chosen Hotel, which is the landmark best known to foreigners.

This capture was the outcome of a lonely jeep drive past the ruined railway station and down Seoul's main street while searching for Charlie (C) Company, which was spearheading the 1st Battalion's drive through the city. As we rode carefully in the tracks of tanks to avoid the possibility of hitting mines, we reached within a block of the Chosen Hotel. Despite reports at battalion headquarters that the Chosen Hotel still housed enemy troops, seventy-five Korean civilians who flocked around our jeep assured us that "Imingun (Korean for Communist soldier) all gone away." Self-appointed Korean resistance fighters, waving American flags and carrying stolen guns, offered themselves as escorts.

We parked the jeep, marched a block-and-a-half down a side street to the hotel and were greeted with clapping and assurances of undying regard for democracy by Wang Han Sok, assistant manager of the hotel, and some twenty-odd of the establishment's staff members. Mr. Sok told us that the Communist North Korean manager brought down from Pyongyang by the "Korean People's Army" had absconded with most of the hotel records and keys. He had assured Mr. Sok that the Communist army would be back within a week to throw the Americans out. Mr. Sok did not seem very worried about this possibility. The assistant hotel manager told us that a handful of Russian and Chinese journalists had occupied the hotel until five days ago, as did two Russian officials whom he could not identify. North Korean big-wigs made the hotel their hangout, he said, observing bitterly that they had a great fondness for dry English gin and that they had consumed the hotel's entire stock without paying for it. Kim Il Sung, Communist leader of North Korea, had twice visited the hotel, according to Mr. Sok, and shared his countrymen's fondness for gin and whiskey. As the first Americans in the area, we signed the register at 5:15 p.m. with a flourish as the entire staff and Mr. Sok stood by. We did so with considerable satisfaction, for both Mr. Beech and myself had been run out of Seoul by the Communist advance on the night of June 27. It was a good feeling to be back on the winning side.

After we had finished writing our names in the register we heard a commotion outside the hotel. Poking our heads cautiously outside the door, we saw that a South Korean Marine unit had arrived. About twenty soldiers were crouched at the main gate, their guns turned menacingly on the hotel's front door. The Southern Korean Marines were unimpressed by the welcoming clap of the hotel staff and ordered them, at bayonet point, to put their hands above their heads and to get on the move. Mr. Beech and I, to the astonishment of the South Koreans, emerged at this point to motion them into the hotel grounds. It took some energetic gesturing to convince them that we were Americans and to prevent them from marching us off, too. After a few exchanges of pidgin Korean and pidgin English, we straightened matters out and were all liberators together.

At the hotel we picked up an English-speaking journalism student who guided us around the downtown areas. Huge pictures of Prime Minister Stalin and Kim Il Sung were plastered all over. Anti-American posters were almost as prominent. The Banto building, around the corner from the hotel, which had housed the Economic Co-operation Administration mission, was undamaged, as were most of the steel and concrete government buildings. Unfortunately, the greatest damage was to flimsy Korean homes and small office buildings. At the railway station we saw from close up a smoking hillside where thousands of buildings were gutted and charred ruins. We talked there to First Lt. Jack N. Lerond, twenty-five, of Stockton, Calif., who was in charge of the tank platoon that burned the hillside down.

"We came to this city with humanitarian motives," Lt. Lerond said, "and we found that humanitarian motives landed you in a large, rectangular wooden box." The lieutenant added: "The groups were hidden all over the buildings by the railyard, from roof to cellar. The only way we could get them out was to burn them out."

23.4 Works of Reconstruction and the Communist Practise

[*Source: Marguerite Higgins: Seoul Taking Revenge on Its Fifths Column, in:* New York Herald-Tribune *(New York, N.Y.), Vol. CX/No. 37,938, September 29, 1950, p. 3, cols. 1–2.*]

Marine bulldozers began scraping the streets of Seoul free of barricades today as the dazed and battered capital emerged from a seven-day siege to assess its damage and to go on a splurge of revenge against pro-Communists. As dawn broke without the familiar reverberations of battle, Koreans, some of whom had been in hiding for months, thronged the streets searching for a return to their pre-Communist way of life.

To the Roman Catholic Cathedral on the hill came the Rev. Li Thomas, still in the working man's uniform in which he disguised himself on June 28 when the North Koreans captured the city. To the Seoul newspaper office returned Lee Sung Poa, a reporter, who escaped the fate of his comrades tried as "American collaborators." Faithful clerks who had to hide their association with the United States on pain of sudden arrest filtered back to the American Embassy.

Throughout the still flaming city the hunt for any one tainted by association with Communists was on in a spirit of ruthlessness and strong emotion born of three months of Communist oppression. The streets were cluttered with Communists and Communists suspects kneeling on torn pavement with hands behind their heads – the customary posture of prisoners taken by Koreans. Among those kneeling were screaming mothers with babies tied to their backs, old and young men, even seventeen-year-old girls. In a number of cases the Marines had had to take over the guarding of the political suspects because the "working over" given them by South Korean police and officers had been too enthusiastic, even for the tough American Marines.

The Communists left Seoul a hungry city. Young children foraging for food trailed all Americans about the city. Kindly Marines kept them in good supply of combat rations. But today many youngsters were able to distinguish one can from another, showing a notable preference for the cookie and cracker units. Most of the Marines were dispersed on high ground outside the city. Some headquarters personnel were esconced in such historic landmarks as the grounds of Duk Soo Palace, by now inevitably dubbed "duck soup" by every Marine. They passed the day in scrounging with the usual objectives of beer and eggs. About all they got was beer.

The big question is, "After Seoul, what?" Aggressive combat commanders like Col. Lewis B. Puller of the 1st Marine Regiment are caring to go and would start a race to the 38 Parallel, former boundary between North and South Korea with gusto.

23.5 The Victor's Ceremony and Further Casualties

[*Source:* Marguerite Higgins: *MacArthur Turns Over Republic to Rhee in Ceremony at Seoul,* in: New York Herald-Tribune *(New York, N.Y.), Vol. CX/No. 37,939, September 30, 1950, p. 1, cols. 6–7; p. 2, cols. 4–6.*]

General of the Army Douglas MacArthur restored war-battered Seoul to the Republic of Korea today, even as American Marines repulsed a counter-attack on the city's outskirts and started northeast toward the 38th Parallel, the boundary between North and South Korea. Glass and debris crashing from the torn roof of the South Korean Capitol punctuated the brief noontime ceremonies, adding a realistic reminder of the war being waged only a few miles away.

Before an impressive array of generals and admirals, the United Nations supreme commander formally turned over this hard-won capital to South Korea's President Syngman Rhee with these words: "On behalf of the United Nations Command, I am happy to restore to you, Mr. President, the seat of your government. It is my fervent hope that from the travail of the past there may emerge a new and hopeful dawn for the people of Korea." Gen. MacArthur then led the assembled group in the Lord's Prayer.

White-haired President Rhee, who is seventy-two, then stepped to the rostrum bedecked by the flags of the U.N., the United States and Korea, to call for unification of his country and for a "victory in which we must and shall show magnanimity." Referring probably to the splurge of anti-Communist activity in the city, the President pledged: "We will not follow a policy of unconsidered revenge. There will be no witch hunts."

Then, as if words could not possibly express his deep feelings, the South Korean President, with tears in his eyes, looked at the audience of generals and colonels, soldiers and sailors who had helped fight his war, and stretched out his hand toward them, clenching and unclenching his fist as he said: "How can I ever explain my own undying gratitude and that of the Korean people?" At the close of his speech, President Rhee conferred on Gen. MacArthur the South Korean Order of Military Merit.

The Communist counter-attack against Seoul struck at American Marine battalions dug in on high ground some 8,000 yards from the partially ruined Capitol Building. The enemy

The War in Korea

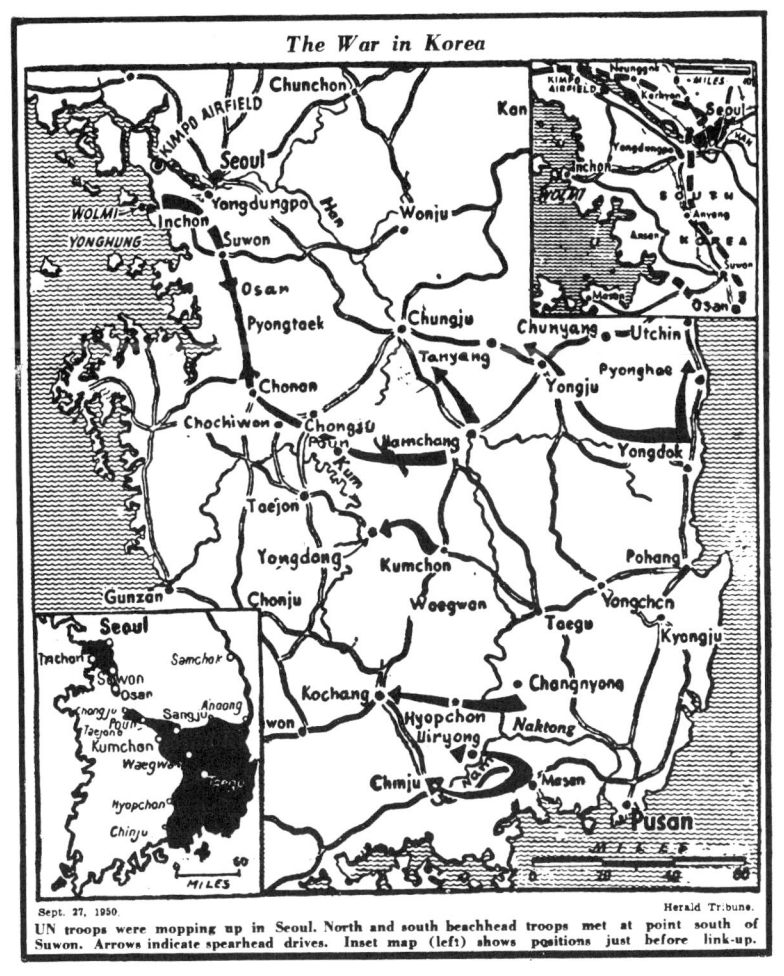

Sept. 27, 1950.   Herald Tribune.
UN troops were mopping up in Seoul. North and south beachhead troops met at point south of Suwon. Arrows indicate spearhead drives. Inset map (left) shows positions just before link-up.

[*Source: New York Herald–Tribune*, European Edition (Paris), 63. Year/ No. 21,048, September 27, 1950, p. 1, cols. 5–7.]

threw a force of 500 men at the Marines and suffered seventy-two known dead before the three-hour battle was over. They killed and wounded a substantial number of Marines.

As the ceremonies in the gilded Assembly room of the Capitol were taking place, the bulk of the Marine forces which had taken Seoul were moving out again to objectives only a few miles south of the 38th Parallel. The ruined and charred South Korean capital, about 60 per cent of which suffered damages in the seven-day siege, was by no means completely free from the enemy. Snipers last night inflicted some thirty casualties on the American forces.

Gen. MacArthur and the top commanders of Army, Navy and Air units in the Far East started gatherings at Kimpo Airport at 9:45 a.m. The Supreme Commander, clad in summer uniform, stepped off his new plane, the Scap, into a black Buick, which led a caravan of cars and jeeps at least a mile long. A Bailey bridge, flown in piece by piece by the Air Force, had been thrown across the Han River only a few hours before Gen. MacArthur's arrival. Marine bulldozers worked twelve hours to clear Seoul's main streets of sandbag barricades and burned-out vehicles. Hundreds of Koreans lined the sidewalks to stare and clap as Gen. MacArthur's procession passed.

President Rhee, who with his entire Cabinet flew to Seoul from Pusan in Gen. MacArthur's second plane, the Bataan, was greeted at the gates of the Capitol by Gen. MacArthur, who personally guided him to the rostrum. It was shared with American Ambassador John G. Muccio and Mrs. Rhee, among others. Representing the Marines were two regimental commanders, Lt. Col. Ray Murray, of the 5th Marines, and Col. Lewis B. Puller, of the 1st Marines. Col. Puller, whose motto is, "Get two battalions abreast and go like hell," and the handful of actual combat veterans present were unshaved and dirty – in conspicious contrast with the spit-and-polish brass from Tokyo and points south. Taking off for the front immediately after the ceremonies, Col. Puller remarked, "My job is to capture cities, not to return them."

Among the high officers in the audience were Air Force General George C. Kenney, Vice-Admiral Charles T. Joy, commander of Far East naval forces; Vice Admiral Arthur D. Struble, chief of the 7th Fleet, Lt. Gen. Walton H. Walker, 8th Army commander. Gen. Walker later told reporters, "The enemy is now in complete rout. The job ahead is exploitation of our advantage to destroy the enemy. We have flushed the covey, now we have to get the single shots." Maj. Gen. Eric Partridge, of the 5th Air Force, who was also on hand, said that airmen were working round the clock to cut off the escape route of the Reds, most of whom are now busy changing out of army uniforms into civilian clothes. The general reported that Air Force planes yesterday caught a group of 500 enemy soldiers in the act of changing clothes and "strafed them hard."

Gen. MacArthur, during today's proceedings, acted very much his usual role of man of destiny. When whole panes of glass would come cascading down from the roof, the others on the rostrum would involuntarily cover their heads for protection. Gen. MacArthur disdained to give the menacing cascade any notice whatsoever. After the ceremonies, Gen. MacArthur, as he proceeded down the main aisle, clasped Gen. Walker on the shoulder, and, with a smile, asserted, "I think events are supporting my old contention that there is no substitute for victory."

Related Readings

Bromberger, Serge et al.: Retour de Corée. Recits de quatre correspondants de guerre français sur le front de Corée, Paris 1951.
Dzélépy, Eleuthère Nicolas: La guerre n'est pas pour demain. La leçon de Corée, Paris 1952.
Fehrenbach, T. R.: The fight for Korea. From the war of 1950 to the Pueblo incident, New York 1969.
Fehrenbach, T. R.: This kind of war. A study in unpreparedness, New York 1963.
Flint, Roy Kenneth: The tragic flaw – MacArthur, the Joint Chiefs, and the Korean War, PhD dissertation, Duke University, Durham, N.C., 1976.
Gaddis, John Lewis: The United States and the origins of the cold war, 1941–1947, New York 1972.

Higgins, Marguerite: War in Korea. The report of a woman combat correspondent, Garden City, N.Y., 1951.
Karig, Walter/Cagle, Malcolm W./Manson, Frank A.: Battle report, Vol. 6: The war in Korea, New York 1952.
Kwak, Tae-hwan: United States – Korean relations. A core interest analysis prior to U.S. intervention in the Korean War, PhD dissertation, Claremont, Calif., 1969.
Lai, Nathan Yu-jen: United States policy and the diplomacy of limited war in Korea, 1950–1951, PhD dissertation, Amherst, Mass., 1974.
Leckie, Robert: Conflict – the history of the Korean War, 1950–53, New York 1962.
Matray, James Irving: The reluctant crusade – American foreign policy in Korea 1941–1950, University of Virginia, Charlottesville, Virg., 1977.
O'Ballance, Edgar: Korea 1950–1953, thesis, Hamden, Conn., 1969.
Paige, Glenn D.: 1950 – Truman's decision. The United States enters the Korean War, New York 1970.
Poteat, George Howard: Strategic intelligence and national security. A case study of the Korean crisis (June 25 – November 24, 1950), thesis, St. Louis, Mo., 1973.
Rougeron, Camille: Les enseignements de la guerre de Corée, Paris 1952.
Schnabel, James F.: Policy and direction – the first year. Vol. 3: United States Army in the Korean War, Washington, D.C., 1972.
Stemons, James Samuel: The Korean mess and some correctives, Boston, Mass., 1952.

# 1951

John M. Hightower

The Associated Press

CHAPTER 24

REPORTS ABOUT KOREA IN 1951

The Final Stage of the War and the Conditions for Peace

    Introductory Notes
24.1 America's Educational Aim and Her Main Apprehension
24.2 MacArthur's Policy and the Consequences at Home
24.3 Plans for an Armistice and America's Precautions
24.4 Negotiations for Peace and Communist Hospitality
24.5 Early Negotiations for Peace and Their Main Issues
    Related Readings

Introductory Notes

In 1952, too, Korea was to play an important role, even if this was only due to the Truman-MacArthur controversy about the general strategy of the war. When the prize for International Reporting was given to John M. Hightower of the Associated Press *"for sustained quality of his coverage of news of international affairs" during 1951, the approval referred to all the dispatches submitted to the Pulitzer Prize jury, including reports about general aspects of American foreign policy or the Japanese peace conference; the focus, however, was on the description of the arguments about American strategy in Korea.*

John Murmann Hightower was born on September 17, 1908, in Coal Creek, Tennessee. He attended public schools in Knoxville and then studied at the University of Tennessee for two years (1927–28) prior to becoming a reporter for the Knoxville News-Sentinel. *Not long after joining the* Associated Press *in Nashville in 1933, he was advanced to the position of Tennessee State editor of the AP, and in 1936 he was transferred to the Washington bureau of his news agency. As a news analyst for the AP in the nation's capital, Hightower was assigned first to the Navy Department and then, in 1943, to the State Department. Here he covered many of the most important diplomatic events of the time including the Roosevelt-Churchill meeting in Quebec, the chartering of the United Nations at San Francisco, the early U.N. meetings in New York and London, the Marshall Plan and the North Atlantic Treaty Pact. In the course of his years at the State Department, Hightower reported the activities of five successive Secretaries of State. It was during his assignment to the Navy Department that Hightower is said to have developed his explanatory-interpretative method of reporting. Especially mentioned for citation when he was selected as a Pulitzer Prize winner for International Reporting in 1952 was Hightower's interpretative reporting of the events leading up to the dismissal of General of the Army Douglas MacArthur. The increasing conflict between MacArthur and the Truman Administration was clearly depicted by Hightower about three weeks before the General's dismissal, and six days prior to MacArthur is being relieved of his United Nations command, Hightower alone among journalists had found this out.*

The following texts by John Murmann Hightower, copyright 1951, are reprinted by kind permission of The Associated Press, *New York, N.Y.*

24.1 America's Educational Aim and Her Main Apprehension

[*Source: John M. Hightower: MacArthur's chances of getting power to win declared slim, in: The Evening Star (Washington, D.C.), 99th Year/No. 45**, February 14, 1951, p. A 7, cols. 4–6.*]

Officials here see little chance that Gen. Douglas MacArthur will get the power and authority he considers necessary to achieve complete victory over the Chinese Communists in Korea. The expected dispatch of American troops to Western Europe, a widespread desire in high places here for a reasonable Korean settlement if possible, the determination to avoid spreading the war – all these factors seem certain to work against fulfillment of the conditions described by Gen. MacArthur as essential to success.

In a Tokyo statement following a battlefront visit, the Allied commander yesterday described the situation this way: Recent U. N. advances have been merely tactical successes; it is academic now to talk about a massive drive across the 38th Parallel into North Korea; such a drive would require offsetting the numerical superiority of the Communists with their protected bases in Manchuria.

From the blunt summary he made and his insistence on the point that there are decisions beyond his province which only governments can make, it is apparent that Gen. MacArthur is calling for a definition of United Nations objectives in Korea now and the decision to pay the price necessary to win them.

His own estimate indicated that steps necessary to a military victory would require:

1. A substantial enlargement of U. N. forces to more nearly equal those of the foe.
2. Authority to bombard positions and communications of the Chinese troops in Manchuria.

On the first point, while Gen. MacArthur's forces are being given replacements now and brought up to full strength the State and Defense Departments are anxious to build up as fast as possible divisions for assignment to Gen. Eisenhower's new Atlantic pact command in Western Europe. Gen. MacArthur is understood to have sought permission to use Chinese Nationalist troops from Formosa, but that has been denied on grounds they were needed to defend that island.

On the issue of bombing by U. N. planes in Manchuria, Washington sees difficulty on two counts. In the first place this country's allies, notably Britain, are anxious to keep the Korean war in strict limits. They have objected to possible crossing of the 38th Parallel as it appeared last weekend U. N. forces soon might do. In the second place military authorities here have ruled out bombing in Manchuria because it might bring a Communist far Eastern Air Force into the fight. Obviously, the Manchurian situation would be changed if Red planes from Manchurian bases got into the fight in large numbers anyway. In that event, there seems to be no doubt that bombing of Manchurian air bases would be quickly authorized.

But as for the overall purpose of the present Korean operation military and diplomatic authorities here alike regard it as a limited fight capable of making the Communists pay heavily for their aggression and of diverting them from new adventures for the time being.

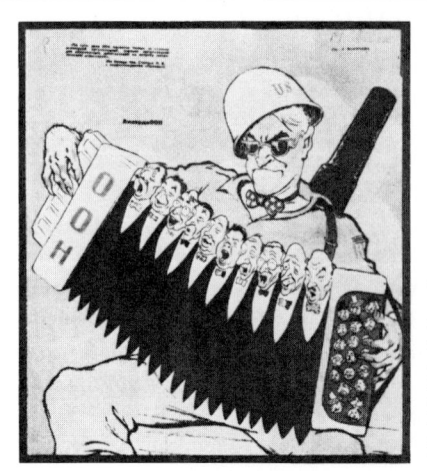

Soviet view of the cold war. Left, during the Korean War in 1951 the United Nations were regarded as the instrument of US policy. Below, the accusation of germ warfare. American imperialism in the form of an aeroplane scattering bugs over the countryside. Bottom, from the White House the United States reaches out to encircle the USSR in Korea, Iran, Turkey, Formosa and Vietnam

Soviet Cartoons on the Korean War
[*Source:* J. P. Nettl: The Soviet Achievement, London 1967, p. 177.]

Officials decided some time ago that neither the Communists nor the U. N. forces could win a clearcut, decisive victory in Korea. The Chinese have too many men and the U. N. troops too much fire power, according to this estimate. What is hoped for here is that the Chinese Reds will come to the same decision and so agree to negotiate what the western nations could accept as a reasonable settlement. At a minimum this would require the freeing of all South Korea from Communist forces – Chinese or Korean. If the Chinese are not interested in negotiating a settlement the war may go on indefinitely, with the American purpose being to destroy as much of the enemy at as low a cost in U. N. lives as possible.

Officials concede the Chinese may be so much under the domination of Moscow that the Russians will be able to compel them to go on fighting. If that happens the present United States idea of limiting the war in the hope of peace undoubtedly will be subjected to a new look.

24.2 MacArthur's Policy and the Consequences at Home

[*Source: John M. Hightower: MacArthur may fly back to U.S. next week, Martin says, while Truman foes hit policy speech, in:* The Evening Star *(Washington, D.C.), 99th Year/No. 102**, April 12, 1951, p. 1, cols. 2–3; p. 12, cols. 3–5.*]

President Truman personally concluded that Gen. MacArthur had to go as soon as he saw a copy of Gen. MacArthur's letter to House Republican Leader Martin. That was last Thursday afternoon. Mr. Truman's conclusion did not become an official decision, however, until several days later – after the President had consulted his most trusted advisers in his own official family and in Congress.

These and the related events and decisions were told to this reporter by supporters of Mr. Truman, close enough to see the whole picture emerge. Their account, which of course reflects administration thinking, follows:

Mr. Truman first learned of the MacArthur letter to Mr. Martin when an aide carried a news ticker account of it into the Chief Executive's oval office and laid it on the President's desk. The letter was a direct challenge of presidential policies on two points – use of Chinese Nationalist troops and the relative importance of Asia in the conflict with Communism.

There had been a long buildup of MacArthur incidents before that and Mr. Truman had become increasingly annoyed. His hope that the general would shut up had given way to irritated wonder at what he would say next. The President and his closest advisers felt the general did not intend to comply with various orders that he stop what the administration considered political talk. Instead, he seemed to be seeking opportunities to assert his independence of administration policy.

In short, in the President's view, Gen. MacArthur had not been playing on the team.

Gen. MacArthur was pushing his policy line so hard – advocating expansion of the war beyond Korea – that the President wondered whether Gen. MacArthur wanted to come home in a blaze of controversy, martyred by his dismissal. America's Allies in the Korean fight were getting extremely restive and the State Department feared the United Nations coalition might begin to pull apart.

Furthermore, the chief policies which Gen. MacArthur advocated, use of Chiang Kai-shek's troops and enlargement of the war against China, were beginning to gain support. The President felt he could not directly fight the idea of a general subordinate to him, but he and his top officials could combat the proposals of a former subordinate. He could only fight Gen. MacArthur openly if he fired him first. It was against this background of his own thinking, as known to persons close to him, that the President "hit the ceiling" when he saw the news account of the letter to Mr. Martin. Shortly afterward he began his consultations.

He talked with many cabinet members aside from Secretary of Defense Marshall and Secretary of State Acheson, his two principal confidants. He enlisted the opinion of the Joint Chiefs of Staff, headed by Gen. Omar Bradley. Friday morning there was a cabinet meeting, devoted to a briefing by Gen. Bradley about the Communist buildup for an offensive in Korea. When it ended Gen. Bradley and Gen. Marshall stayed behind and talked with the President 45 minutes.

Saturday morning those two were closeted with the President again, discussing the way to remove Gen. MacArthur, the successor, the timing of action and announcement and what the announcement should say. Sunday the Joint Chiefs of Staff met at the call of Gen. Bradley, their chairman, at 3 p.m. There was little doubt even then that they were talking about the MacArthur problem but enormous doubt as to what solution they favored. The official silence was deliberate since there could be no hint of the President's intentions until he was ready to act.

On Monday Mr. Truman talked the situation over with his congressional leaders. That session was followed by a cabinet meeting at which the MacArthur problem was raised and advice sought from the members. The President did not in all cases indicate to those whose counsel he solicited that he was already determined to act. He wanted arguments pro and con.

Tuesday night, when the climax came, the President's staff had collected the documents to be put out showing pertinent orders sent to Gen. MacArthur to clear political statements and covering some other subjects which had figured in the controversy. Mr. Truman called in Gen. Bradley and Assistant Secretary of State Dean Rusk, director of Far Eastern Affairs, and conferred by telephone with Secretary Acheson. The orders went out through military channels to Gen. MacArthur, Lt. Gen. Matthew B. Ridgway and Lt. Gen. James A. Van Fleet, the three men directly involved in the shakeup. The President then let his Press Secretary, Joseph Short, go forward with plans to announce the action at 1 a.m., which was estimated to be the time Gen. MacArthur would be getting the official word in his Tokyo headquarters.

Mr. Truman made his final, unchangeable, official decision sometime Monday when the whole plan of timing and press releases had been worked out. The President knew he was going into a tough fight, he wanted to hit the first punch sharply and solidly.

The fight is just beginning. Gen. MacArthur is now freer than ever to speak his own mind. And administration men will feel free to engage the general and his supporters in another "great debate."

24.3 Plans for an Armistice and America's Precautions

[*Source: John M. Hightower: U.N. check role – as guard against trickery, in:* The Kansas City Times *(Kansas City, Mo.), Vol. 114/No. 156, June 30, 1951, p. 1, col. 8; p. 2, col. 4.*]

The United States is prepared to insist that any armistice with the Communists in Korea should provide for United Nations observation of armed forces on both sides of the truce line. Informed officials gave this word today as General Matthew B. Ridgway, U. N. commander in the Korean war, formally offered the Communists a chance to attend armistice talks.

Emphasizing the American position that any effective armistice must be as secure as possible against violation, officials here said there are only two real guarantees:

1. Full information about the activities of the military forces on the other side once the armistice begins to make sure they are not engaged in a build-up or planning a surprise attack.

2. The military capacity to do something about the situation if information indicates that the opposing force is up to some trickery.

Authorities familiar with the whole background of the Ridgway statement said:

Ridgway's proposition was backed up not only by the American government but by the other fifteen governments with armed forces in Korea. The other governments – whose diplomats met at the State department this afternoon – gave general approval to the step which Ridgway took, but the U. S. took responsibility for preparing the instructions sent to him before he issued his message. The South Korean Republic government, which has been bitterly critical of the idea of ending the war short of the unification of all Korea, apparently was informed of the proposed action at some point before it was taken but responsible officials here did not know precisely when.

Washington does not expect serious trouble with the South Korean government. It takes the position that the South Koreans certainly could not be expected to give up their goal of unification. That is also the announced goal of the U. S. and the U. N.; they want to seek it by political means, however, if the war now can be brought to an end. The South Koreans will have a better opportunity of express their views from now on because the sixteen nations which meet here on the Korean situation twice weekly have invited them to join the group and they will do so at the next meeting next week.

Ridgway's terse message raised many questions, the foremost being how will the Communists react? Top authorities here profess to be without any clues. They did not know whether the Reds would even reply.

The message was addressed to the commander in chief, Communist forces in Korea, but no person or nationality was given. The reason for this is that American government officials know there are two top level Communist leaders in Korea but they do not know whom the Reds prefer to consider the commander in chief, if either. The two Red leaders are Marshal Kim Il Sung, who is also North Korean premier, and Chinese General Pen Teh-huai. Under Sung on the North Korean side is General Nam Il, who operates as a field commander.

The basic United States position on "reasonable" terms for a cease-fire arrangement in Korea are understood to follow the line laid down in a December 15, 1950, memorandum of a United Nations cease-fire group. This memorandum specified that "supervision of the cease-fire shall be by a United Nations commission whose members and designated observers shall insure full compliance with the terms of the cease-fire. They shall have free and unlimited access to the whole of Korea." It was also provided that all governments or "authorities" involved in Korea should cooperate with the cease-fire commission and its observers in its duties.

Other matters covered in the December 15 memorandum provided (1) that the stop in hostilities should apply to all Korea, that a 20-mile-wide demilitarization zone in the vicinity of the thirty-eight Parallel should be created, (2) that forces on either side would carefully respect this zone, (3) that reinforcements and replacements for forces should promptly cease, (4) that prisoners of war should be exchanged man-for-man and that proper provision should be made for such matters as refugee handling and the civil government of the demilitarized zone.

On Capitol Hill, Congress members generally welcomed the direct action taken by Ridgway. Typical comment:

Senator McFarland (D-Ariz.), the Senate majority leader: "I hope the fighting can be stopped on a basis where war won't break out again."

Senator Connally (D-Tex.), chairman of the Senate foreign relations committee: "I am highly gratified, I hope it means a cease-fire and peace."

But Senator Ferguson (R-Mich.) cautioned that "it all depends on the terms" worked out if an armistice meeting is, in fact, held. "There will still be much to be done after this meeting to determine whether the Reds are sincere," Ferguson said.

24.4 Negotiations for Peace and Communist Hospitality

[*Source: John M. Hightower: Tougher policy at start may have speeded truce, in:* The Roanoke Times *(Roanoke, Va.), Vol. 130/No. 15, July 15, 1951, p. 1, cols. 3–4; p. 4, cols. 6–7.*]

United States officials ruefully relearned this week one of the basic lessons of past years in dealing with negotiators from Communist lands – don't politely take anything for granted. The record of Korean truce talks, from the beginning through the breakdown, suggests to some authorities here that a tougher policy at the outset in demanding detailed agreements on arrangements might have forestalled the breakdown and would have blocked some of the Red propaganda gains.

Conceivably it may turn out in the end that the North Korean and Red Chinese negotiators overplayed their hands in taking control of the truce city. It may be that the patience of Vice Admiral Charles Turner Joy's UN delegation in the face of Red provocations will exert a favorable influence on public opinion in the free world.

Yet there have been some anxious hours in Government quarters here over Red propaganda uses of their show of strength at Kaesong. And Gen. Matthew B. Ridgway's switch from a policy of cool politeness to one of stern command clearly reflects decisions reached in determination to regain some control of the situation. Today, a Pyongyang radio broadcast reported Communist acceptance of Ridgway's ultimatum. It said "we agree to your proposal of fixing the Kaesong area as a neutral zone" and "we now agree to your proposal to include the 20 UN news reporters of your side as a part of the personnel of your delegation."

The initial specific issue which caused the breakdown was Red refusal to permit newsmen cleared by Ridgway to go to the conference city. However, Ridgway and Secretary of State Acheson have made clear that, in this Government's view, the fundamental issue was equality of the negotiating teams. In other words, the UN negotiators finally decided, presumably on consultation with Washington, that they will not be controlled in their movements of personnel by the Reds. Any other course would represent some knuckling under.

The point is considered of utmost importance because the peace at issue is supposed to be not a dictated but a negotiated peace. This is in line with the military view held in Western capitals – and assumed to be held by the Reds also – that neither side is willing to pay the price for a total victory in Korea. Hence, neither side is in position to dictate and enforce terms. Whatever power advantage there is in the Korean situation, in fact, seems to be with the UN force which has repulsed the heaviest Red attacks and driven on into North Korea.

Three assumptions on the part of the United States apparently had a lot to do with the way the situation developed. These were:

1. If the Communists really wanted to end the war, they would be willing to do so on terms acceptable to this government and its allies, but they would want to find some way to save face in the process.

2. The United States and its allies were ready on their part to pay a reasonable price for peace and as part of this were willing to go along with some Chinese face-saving moves if necessary.

3. If the Communists were sincere about peace they would want secret negotiations; therefore, the UN side would enter the talks intent on every precaution to insure secrecy. One of the first things which each side had to find out when the negotiations opened was whether the other sincerely wanted to end the war or was merely seeking political or military advantage. Each side also had to determine how badly the other wanted peace.

Ridgway's acceptance of the Red proposal to meet at Kaesong rather than on a neutral hospital ship at Wonsan, and his later acquiescence in the presence of Communist armed guards at Kaesong was in line with Washington's assumptions about the need for Chinese face saving as well as an evidence of good faith on the UN side.

Similarly, his early prohibition against newsmen going to Kaesong and the cautiously generalized reports given out after the early meetings were in line with the belief that secrecy on important matters was essential to successful negotiation and that good faith could be demonstrated with such action. Some officials described the United States-UN behavior in

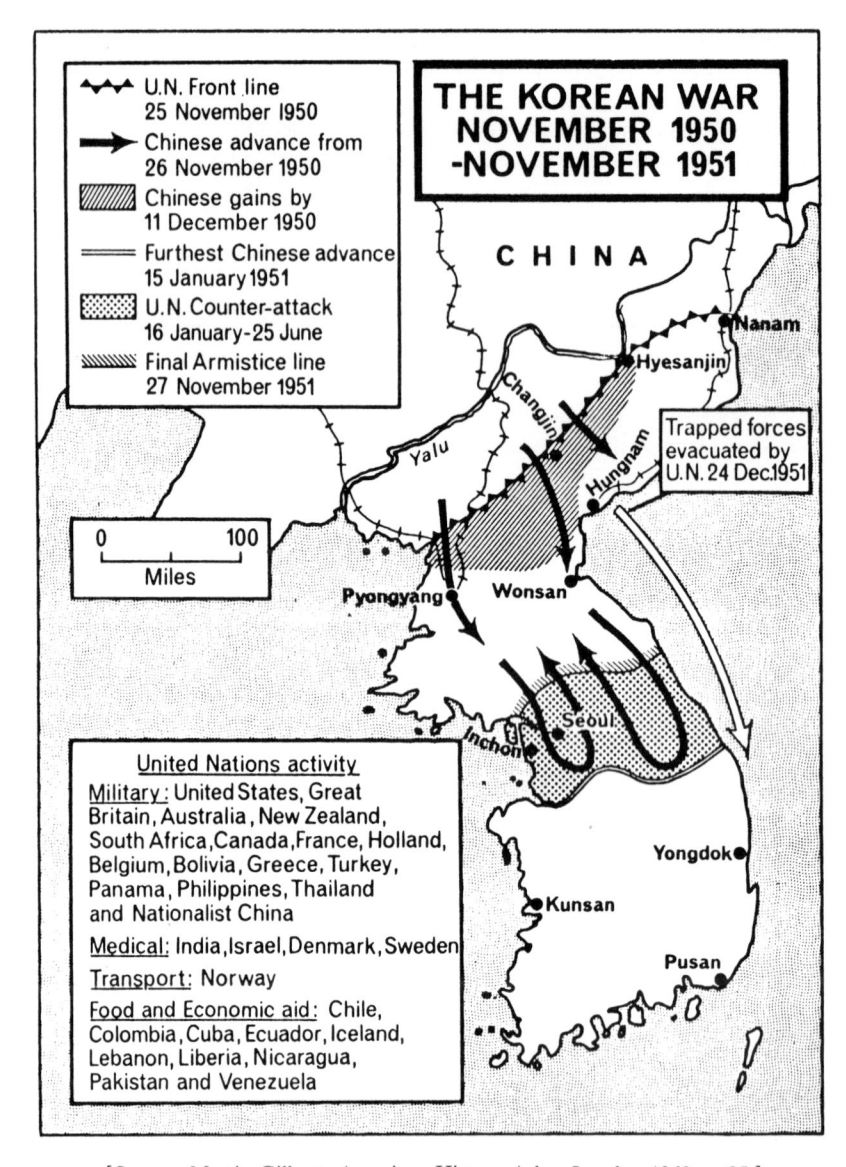

[Source: Martin Gilbert: American History Atlas, London 1968, p. 95.]

these respects as generous. It was at least motivated in part by a polite assumption that the other fellow could also be counted upon to avoid tough handed or extreme action because he too wanted to end the fighting.

The Red response to these moves was to take full charge of the City and the meeting place with their armed guards. Apparently to the surprise of some authorities here, they also proclaimed themselves in their propaganda to be hosts in the manner of victors receiving a vanquished foe. Then they announced officially their terms for an armistice, which implied that they were dictating the terms, and they attempted control over the UN delegation by barring newsmen.

These moves left Ridgway no alternative, in his view and that of Washington, except to break off the talks and demand full equality of treatment from here on.

24.5 Early Negotiations for Peace and Their Main Issues

[*Source: John M. Hightower: 5-point Korea truce agenda agreed on, in:* The Evening Star *(Washington, D.C.), 99th Year/No. 207**, July 26, 1951, p. 1, col. 4.*]

Military and diplomatic officials here consider that United Nations negotiators got everything they fought in the first round of the Korean armistice talks without making any concessions on vital issues. In fact it was the Communists who gave ground by backing down twice from positions they had taken. Yet despite these initial successes, responsible officials here are only mildly optimistic about the chances that the negotiations will actually produce an armistice. Many difficult problems remain to be solved in the round now starting.

Gen. Matthew B. Ridgway's announcement of the agreement on an agenda noted there are numerous basic points on which there is "presently wide diversion of views" between the Reds and the U. N. command. That cautionary note is fully indorsed here by officials familiar with all the problems facing the negotiators. Some authorities believe it may be as much as a month before the negotiations are concluded, and said it must still be determined how high a price the Reds are willing to pay in what Washington considers "real concessions" in order to end the fighting.

The two most serious problems now foreseen here are those having to do with the mapping out of a buffer zone between the Communist and U. N. armies, and with the arrangements for supervision or enforcement, of an armistice once it is established. The agreement on an agenda was possible only because the Reds abandoned yesterday their previously insistent demand for an agreement, prior to an armistice, on removal of all foreign troops from Korea. That broke the week-long deadlock of the Kaesong meetings.

The price the United Nations paid for this apparently is covered in Point 5 of the agenda. The point provides that the negotiators can later make recommendations to the governments on both sides.

It is understood that in accepting the modified Red proposal on the troop withdrawal issue, the United Nations agreed to discuss arrangements for coming to grips, after an armistice, with the whole problem of withdrawal of outside forces from the Korean peninsula. This was in line with the basic American policy position, that troops would be pulled out some day but no time could be fixed now.

Previously, the Communists had given in on a procedural point when they agreed that the area where the talks are held at Kaesong should be treated as neutral territory. They agree, too, that Gen. Ridgway's right to send any one he wished, including newsmen, into this area, was beyond question.

When Gen. Ridgway went into the truce talks, according to informants here, he had instructions to seek in the first instance substantially the agenda now adopted. This provides for discussion of the demarcation line, armistice arrangements and prisoner of war arrangements without commiting either side to any particular line of action. The real arguments therefore are now to begin.

In connection with the location of the buffer zone, the Reds have made clear they will insist that it be precisely on the 38th Parallel. Gen. Ridgway's instructions are to work it out along the present battle line – most north of the parallel. Argument on this could go on for many days.

As to enforcement of armistice terms, Gen. Ridgway has instructions to seek a firm system of inspection all over Korea by international truce teams. The argument runs that this would make preparation of a surprise attack or other truce violations by either side impossible.

On the third point of substance, arranging for exchange of prisoners of war, the difficulty will come over the ratio of exchange. However, many more Communists are held prisoner by the U. N. forces than the other way around. A one-for-one exchange would free all U. N. troops held captive without freeing all Red soldiers. So it is expected that the Communist negotiators will insistently demand an agreement for each side to release all its prisoners.

Related Readings

Cagle, Malcom W./Manson, Frank A.: The sea war in Korea, Annapolis, Md., 1957.
Davis, Larry: Mig alley, Warren, Mich., 1978.
Deagle, Edwin Augustus jr.: The agony of restraint – Korea 1951–53. A study of limited war and civil-military policy processes, Cambridge 1970.
DeWeerd, Harvey Arthur: The Korean War – political limitations, Santa Monica, Calif., 1960.
Higgins, Trumbull: Korea and the fall of MacArthur. A précis in limited war, New York 1960.
Kim, Chum-kon: The Korean War. The first comprehensive account of the historical background and development of the Korean War (1950–53), Seoul 1973.
Langley, Michael: Inchon landing – MacArthur's last triumph, New York 1979.
Lowitt, Richard: The Truman-MacArthur controversy, Chicago, Ill., 1967.
MacArthur, Douglas: Reminiscences, New York 1964.
Miller, John jr./Carroll, Owen J./Tackley, Margaret E.: Korea 1951–53, Washington, D.C., 1956.
Oliver, Robert Tarbell: Verdict in Korea, State College, Pa., 1952.
Rovere, Richard Halworth/Schlesinger, Arthur jr.: The MacArthur controversy and American foreign policy, New York 1965.
Spanier, John W.: The Truman-MacArthur controversy and the Korean War, Cambridge, Mass., 1959.
Stone, Isidor Feinstein: The hidden history of the Korean War, 2nd ed., New York 1969.
Thomas, Robert Cyril Wolferstan: The war in Korea, 1950–1953. A military study of the war in Korea up to the signing of the cease fire, Aldershot, Hampshire, 1954.
U.S. Marine Corps: U.S. Marine operations in Korea, 1950–1953, Washington, D.C., 1955.
Whitney, Courtney: MacArthur – his rendezvous with history, New York 1956.

1952

Austin C. Wehrwein

The Milwaukee Journal

CHAPTER 25

REPORTS ABOUT CANADA IN 1952

The Country's Great Fortuness and How They Are Exploited

    Introductory Notes
25.1 Raw Materials Grow and Industry Expands
25.2 The Canadian Stock Market and the Problem of Fraud
25.3 Canada Starts on Seaway and America Missed the Boat
25.4 Population Problems and How They Might be Solved
25.5 A Province of Superlatives and Its Riches
    Related Readings

Introductory Notes

It was really a surprise when, while the Korean War was straining the nerves of the American public, the 1953 Pulitzer Prize for International Reporting was awarded for the coverage of a subject totally unconnected with one of the major international crisis. When the Pulitzer Prize committees honored Austin C. Wehrwein of the Milwaukee Journal *"for a series of articles on Canada," it was the first award for reporting about a country which because of its geographical neighborhood with the U.S.A. had hardly been covered by American foreign correspondents so far.*

Austin Carl Wehrwein was born on January 12, 1916, in Austin, Texas. He was educated in the public schools of Madison, Wisconsin, and graduated from the University of Wisconsin in 1937 with a B.A. degree in economics. He became a reporter of the Milwaukee Journal *after graduation until he entered the Columbia University Law School, from which he graduated in 1940 with a LL. B. degree. Afterwards he became a member of the Wisconsin Bar, but instead of practicing law he returned to newspaper work. Between 1940 and 1943 when he volunteered for the army he worked for the* Associated Press *and the* Milwaukee Journal *in Madison, Wisconsin, and in the Washington, D.C., bureau of the* United Press *news agency. Next he was on the Shanghai edition of* Stars and Stripes, *and after the war he returned to the* United Press *in Washington, resigning in 1948 to go to England where he attended the London School of Economics. He subsequently joined the Economic Co-operation Administration (ECA), working on the ECA information staff in London, Copenhagen, and Oslo. Wehrwein resigned from ECA in 1951 and joined the* Milwaukee Journal *as a reporter, assigned to the financial page of that newspaper. His series of articles written for the newspaper in 1952 about the economic, political, and cultural aspects of Canada was published as a booklet entitled, "Canada's New Century," and it sold 5,000 copies. "A number of bulk orders have been received," a promotion manager of the* Milwaukee Journal *wrote to Dean Carl W. Ackerman, secretary of the Advisory Board, adding "we have no way of knowing what the ultimate distribution" of the booklet may be.*

The following texts by Austin Carl Wehrwein, copyright 1952, are reprinted by kind permission of The Milwaukee Journal, *Milwaukee, Wisconsin.*

25.1 Raw Materials Grow and Industry Expands

[*Source: Austin C. Wehrwein: Canada forges ahead on the economic front, in:* The Milwaukee Journal *(Milwaukee, Wisc.), Vol. 70/No. 328, October 12, 1952, p. 1, cols. 2–3; p. 2, cols. 5–7.*]

"The 20th century belongs to Canada." That prophecy was made about 50 years ago by one of Canada's great statesmen, Sir Wilfrid Laurier.

Today as the world plods wearily into the second half of the century it is coming true. Not in the sense that Canada expects to become a great military conqueror, with its tiny population of 14 million now and perhaps 40 million in the year 2000. Rather in the sense that she commands the economic resources that are essential to the United States and the free world in war or peace.

Equally as important, Canada shares our belief in freedom and will use her power as a decent neighbor and partner on this continent. But we must face the fact that while we grow poorer by the hour in natural resources Canada grows richer. Although we use up half of the world's production of raw materials we produce only a fraction of what we need. We totally lack some of the most vital materials, and even import iron ore and oil.

But here is Canada, with a population not much bigger than that of New York city and its metropolitan districts, on an area one-third bigger than the United States, with this record:

Supplying 90% of the free world's nickel and 70% of the asbestos; leading in production of uranium and platinum and nonferrous metals; ranking second in gold, zinc and in other mysterious metals that are the key to modern industry. Her iron ore deposits are probably the world's largest and her crude oil reserves, also among the biggest, increased 34 times in the last six years. Yet, the potential is still virtually untapped.

Nor should it be forgotten that Canadian wheat feeds 100 million mouths, nor that her forests supply the paper on which nine out of ten American – and three out of five worldnewspapers are printed – including the one you hold in your hand at this moment.

Just as sure as the Canadian winter winds that sweep down over Milwaukee, our country must depend upon Canada. And by the same token, Canada needs us. We are wedded, for better or for worse, for richer or for poorer, in sickness and in health.

Yet, Canada's mushrooming progress is not confined to basic commodities. Although the government refused to encourage "hothouse" industries that need tariff protection, Canada has in the last three decades become a highly industrialized nation, tripling manufacturing volume. Here, too, we have a tremendous stake, perhaps more than Canadians would like, although the government welcomes our participation. There are more than 3,000 branches of United States firms here, double the number in 1939, of which 347 entered since 1946. Among the new arrivals are 13 which have their home offices in Wisconsin, including three from Milwaukee. They are Automatic Products Co., Ladish Co., and Globe-Union Corp. The branch plants do a quarter to a third of Canada's manufacturing business.

From January, 1950, to mid-1952, Americans invested nearly one and one-half billion dollars here, and it is estimated that reinvestment of Canadian profits added a sum equal to more than one-half of that figure. Americans have invested close to eight billion dollars all-told in Canada. Our people own one-eighth of all the government and corporate bonds, a quarter of all the business capital and 37% of the manufacturing. In 1950 American investment in all branches of the oil industry was 54% of the total book value, and is undoubtedly higher now. Last year, 378 million dollars went out of Canada for interest and dividends to Americans.

At the same time, since 1946, Canadians themselves have set aside some 20 billion dollars for new investment, or more than one-fifth of their total production. Government economists here point out that large as it is, American investment is only about 10% of the total, with perhaps another 5% coming from Europe, the remainder being home grown.

Just as important as our money is American willingness to go into risky fields and bring in experts to help speed development. A case in point is oil. Another bonus that comes with American investment is the assurance that the Canadians will have a market. Case in point: Iron ore mined for our steel mills.

No doubt, the oil and natural gas discoveries in western Canada, the opening up of the high grade iron ore reserves on the Quebec-Labrador border and in northern Ontario, and the big aluminum projects both in Quebec and British Columbia have been the most spectacular. Capital investment in such projects alone is expected to be a billion dollars in the next three years. But nearly every industry and region has been touched with the magic wand. No longer is Canada confined to the area which lies 100 miles north of the 3,000 mile border. Many of the projects are in the northern frontier country, and the boom has given new depth to Canada, both in geography and diversification of industry. Steel production, for example, is triple prewar and the country is on the road to self-sufficiency. With but a fifth of the potential harnessed, hydroelectric production is half of ours. And a host of new industries in growing up around the oil discoveries on the prairies.

Although the economies of the United States and Canada are complementary, Canadians are willing to compete with us when they can. At Malton, Ont., near Toronto, the Avro Canada Co. is building one of the world's most powerful jet engines and is laying the groundwork for the capture of the jet air liner market across the border. The firm has already built its first commercial jet aircraft and when its defense output eases off will be ready to supply them in volume to our air lines.

Of interest to Americans in the market for stocks is the fact that the Toronto Stock Exchange is now the biggest on the continent in volume. On Bay st., Canada's Wall Street, they joke that the day the volume hit the record of 7,500,000 shares (Oct. 19, 1951) was the day that "America discovered Canada." In the past American-Canadian relations have been strained by the "stockateers" and "moose pasture" salesmen who worked out of Bay st., selling Americans millions of dollars worth of worthless stocks by mail and telephone. Now, however, the brokers' association and the Ontario authorities are working closely with our securities and exchange commission to stamp out the evil.

As far as the individual coming into Canada is concerned, this country's coming of age is immediately brought home as soon as he changes his American money into Canadian. The American dollar, once the undisputed champion of the world, no longer weighs in at 100c or more in Canadian money. Today a visitor gets but 95c for each buck. "It's too bad we don't call our dollar a 'sheaf' or a 'shoat' or something," one economist remarked. "Then our American friends who do not understand why their money isn't 'just as good' as ours wouldn't be so put out about it."

Another statistic must be cited to complete the picture. We are each other's best customers. Last year Canadians bought goods from us worth more than 2.3 billion dollars, and we sold them even more, or 2.8 billion dollars worth.

"It might not be too far fetched to compare Canada today to that stock character in fiction – the young girl who for years tries vainly to attract the attention of the big boy next door," Finance Minister Douglas Abbott commented. "When he suddenly becomes aware that she has grown into a beautiful young woman and begins to pay her a lot of attention, she doesn't quite know how to handle the situation. But of course she enjoys it, and like most young girls today, learns pretty quickly how to take it in her stride. So do we!"

25.2 The Canadian Stock Market and the Problem of Fraud

[*Source: Austin C. Wehrwein: Stockateers' business not what it used to be, in:* The Milwaukee Journal *(Milwaukee, Wisc.), Vol. 70/No. 333, October 17, 1952, p. 20, cols. 1–5.*]

Have the "moose pasture stockateers" gone the way of the dodo bird? The official story on Bay st., the Wall Street of Canada, is that the "buccaneers of Bay st.," who fleeced American suckers out of millions, are on the decline.

Privately, brokers admit that some of the worst – many of them Americans – are still on the scene. But they haven't broken Canadian law, and if the American government has something on them for past performances it is up to the Yanks to extradite them, authorities here say. The extradition treaty was broadened last August to deal with the situation, but so far there has not been a single case brought under its provisions.

"Moose pasture stockateers," it should be explained, are rapid conversational types attracted to this financial center by the possibility of a fast buck from the country's big oil and mineral discoveries. Using long distance telephone calls and hyperthyroid literature they sold millions of dollars worth of low priced but worthless securities to Americans. How much is a matter of sheer guess. Our securities and exchange commission once estimated the loss at 10 to 50 million dollars a year. But Oswald E. Lennox, the mild mannered chairman of the Ontario securities commission who has two Bibles on his desk, estimated that the top was about 10 million dollars. And Clarence H. Adams, one of the SEC commissioners, said last month that the swindle had "come to a virtual halt."

This jibes with information from Wisconsin sources. The Milwaukee Better Business Bureau has reported a sharp drop in complaints; in the period January to August, the Wisconsin department of securities issued only five stop orders, compared with 18 in the like period last year. Lennox said in an interview that he had canceled about 60 licenses in the last two years, a rate far exceeding any other period except for 1946, when there was a general cleanup.

"I can truthfully say that to my knowledge there are no 'boiler rooms' operating," said

John Rogers, chairman of the Ontario Broker-Dealers' association. He is a partner in one of the leading securities houses, Doherty, Roadhouse & Co., whose senior partner, D'Arcy M. Doherty, is president of the Toronto Stock Exchange. In the language of the trade, "boiler rooms" are outright thieves' dens – crooks who do things like selling nonexistent stocks. Actually, the moose pasture boys have real live companies with land, but the prospects are usually imaginary.

As for such remaining operators, Rogers said: "In all businesses there will be some crooks. We think we've made great strides in rectifying various evils which existed in the past." The problem is attacked on two fronts. Ultimate power is in Lennox's commission – there is no federal body, regulation being left to the provinces, which correspond roughly to our states. On the day to day policing level is the Broker-Dealers' association, which was given its powers by law about four years ago. Stock listed on the exchange must also meet that body's requirements.

In general outline, the securities law follows our securities and exchange act and requires "full disclosure" of the facts surrounding a proposed stock offer. The association requires salesmen to pass a written examination, has financial requirements for members, and audits their books. The commission also makes surprise audits. The association sets the ceiling profits a broker can make, judging each stock separately and allowing a wider spread on speculative issues than on industrials. It reviews all literature sent out by association members, and does its best, Rogers said, to cut out misleading and flamboyant statements. It often orders a rewrite job.

This is probably its most important function as far as an American is concerned, because most of the suckers were caught on that kind of bait. The commission reviews the formal "prospectus" – but many stock buyers do not have sense enough to ask for one, and, anyhow, it takes an expert to understand what they say – like the fine print on an insurance policy. In general, the association can keep shady character out of the brokerage business, fine erring members up to $1,000, or kick them out. It can also ask the commission to cancel their license to do business.

But there are loopholes. One is the fact that Canadian law does not permit tapping telephones, and while Rogers said that flamboyant telephone conversations have been the grounds for discipline, such cases are hard to get evidence on. That goes right to the heart of the matter because the telephone was the chief "gimmick" in the wholesale frauds. "The vicious thing is the reported telephoning," Lennox admitted. "It's something we don't understand in this country. People here don't buy that way."

The stockateers operated mostly on Americans. Lennox recalled a case of a salesman who sold some stock one day and then called the American customer again the next day to say the mine had "come in" – in manifest impossibility – and sold $10,000 more of the stock. "But we can't prove the calls," he said.

Another difficulty is that the commission does not have a staff big enough to make spot checks on properties, some of which may be as far away as the Yukon. Commission approval of a prospectus is not, therefore, a guarantee of its accuracy, as it would be with the SEC. However, if lies were discovered, the guilty would be prosecuted. And in fact, authorities say, most of the prospectuses are accurate because they are gotten up with the aid of reputable engineering firms. And not even the SEC will guarantee the merit of a stock or promise that it will make money.

Another loophole is that there is a whole group beyond the reach of both the commission and the association. They are what is known as "promoters." They buy stock directly from the treasury of a company. Because they are the owners of the stock – just as John Jones could own stock – and not brokers, who act as agents buying and selling for others – they do not have to register or be members of the association. The theory is that a man can do as he likes with his own property. Thus, their literature is not subject to review, nor are their ethics scrutinized. However, if they tie up with a broker, asking him to sell their stock, that broker must be a member. If there is a skulduggery, the "front" man may get caught, but the promoter behind is safe. He has no license to lose.

The prospectus is supposed to list everyone with a 5% or more interest in an offering. But by simply creating a second front company, the identity of the real owner can be concealed. Thus, some of the most notorious characters are still in business. There are at least four or five promoters who have been the subject of a number of exposes in the United States still doing business, often through reputable firms.

Bay st. brokers shrug their shoulders, observing that the stockateers' current operations may be on the level. Then add that it is, anyhow, very hard to trace ownership. Unmasking the source of a buck, they say, is hard any place. And they say that the commission, if it can, will force the promoters' names to be made public. One of these is Albert Edward De Palma, who started his career as a St. Louis necktie salesman, a bail jumper on a United States mail fraud indictment and reportedly on the SEC's most wanted list. He is said to be one of the richest men in town. Any broker here can mention others.

Canadian susceptibilites were deeply wounded by "unfavorable" publicity when the swindles were at their height. Observers contend that when the SEC was most critical not a single concrete instance of fraud was called to the attention of the government here.

Now, however, Lennox said that the SEC has sent him information on about a dozen complaints in the last year. "We are working in close cooperation with the SEC – hand in glove," he said. "And we are working with the other provinces." This intra-Canadian cooperation may be very important for us, because the word in Bay st. is that some of the "bad boys" are setting up shop in Montreal, the No. 2 financial center.

Some brokers insist that many things labeled "fraud" are the result of a misunderstanding on the part of American customers. For example, the profit margin between what a promoter pays and what he sells the stock for may seem too high. But, authorities here argue, speculative oil and mineral stocks can't be marketed on the same basis as industrials. And, in fact, there have been almost no complaints about industrial offerings.

Another technical difference that looks bad on paper is that a stock seller does not have to "stabilize the market." That is, he may sell you a stock for 30c a share, and then offer the next block at 40c. In the meantime, he will tell you that he still has some of the 30c stuff left, but that the "price is going up." Here's your chance to get some at the "old price," he says. Now, that is true in a sense – but not in the sense that the market price has gone up, because there is no market. He is not obligated to buy it back from you at his price – that is, to stabilize the market. And you may find that you can't sell it so anybody.

But, brokers here point out, many stocks offered by legitimate firms are like that. They are speculative, and in some cases they grow up to be big strapping $20 shares. "Where oil and minerals are involved, there is speculation," Rogers pointed out. "Nobody really knows what's in the ground. I think the public should realize that the odds are against any one

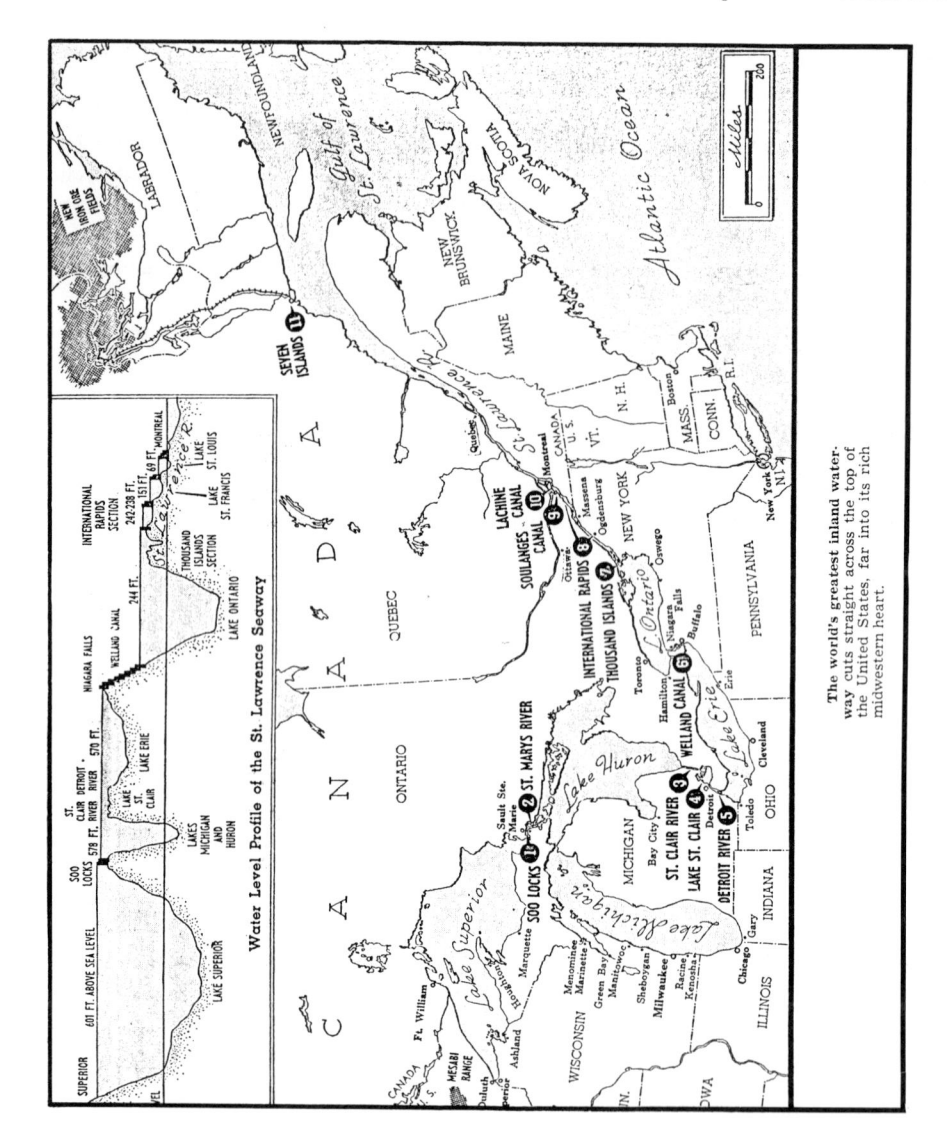

[*Source:* Austin C. Wehrwein: Canada's New Century, Milwaukee, Wisc., 1953, p. 24.]

property starting from scratch – from the green grass – and becoming a producing mine ... So if you buy a cheap stock and it does come in – you're well rewarded. But the odds are against you." But Rogers added he did not think that anybody in his association was "knowingly selling moose pasture."

So all in all, the securities industry represented by men like Rogers and Lennox feel that there are real opportunies in Canada, and that the American purchaser who uses common sense should be able to buy stocks without tears. But they counsel patience because even projects that appear to have excellent prospects won't pay off overnight. And if a salesman on the telephone tells you otherwise, hang up. Finally, Canadian securities men and the commissioners in the various provinces are ready to take a step which is unprecedented, according to the SEC.

Although Canadians don't like to put it this way, it boils down to an agreement to enforce the laws of the United States in Canada. The SEC plans, after long discussions with Canadian authorities and the Broker-Dealers' association, to permit Canadians to file issues up to an aggregate of $300,000 a year under the so-called "short form," which means with a minimum of red tape. In return for this right, the provincial commissions will take action against any Canadian who does not avail himself of the privilege. This amounts to writing that SEC regulation into Canadian law. Issues of more than $300,000 would have to be registered under normal procedures.

This goes a long way. A few years ago, all Canadians in the business, good and bad (plus the American fringe group), railed against the SEC for "expecting us to enforce your laws." But the problem isn't cleared up, because most states – including Wisconsin – also require registration. And in the past, the complaint has been made here that good stocks were labeled "fraudulent" simply because they weren't registered with state securities agencies. The point Canadians make is that the use of that nasty word "fraud" to describe "technical violation" was too sweeping.

In any event, this pending SEC action may prove far more important than the broadening of the extradition treaty, which so far has netted nothing, despite wide claims when it became effective. There is no magic about an extradition treaty. It does not mean that a Milwaukee policeman can fly up here and make a pinch if he thinks he's got the goods on a stockateer.

What actually happens is that our law enforcement officials ask Canada to send a man back. But – and here's the catch – the accused is entitled to a hearing, and the judge has to be satisfied that the alleged crime fits the Canadian interpretation of the fraud provision in the treaty. Nor does he find the man guilty – he only decides where there is a prima facie (at first sight) case. The Milwaukee cops might think it is fraud on Wisconsin av., but the judge here will ask himself whether it is fraud on Bay st.

25.3 Canada Starts on Seaway and America Missed the Boat

[*Source: Austin C. Wehrwein: Canada looks eagerly to starting on seaway, in:* The Milwaukee Journal *(Milwaukee, Wisc.), Vol. 70/No. 337, October 21, 1952, p. 40, cols. 1–6.*]

Fed up after 50 years of fruitless dickering for a joint project, Canada is itching to get going on the St. Lawrence seaway on her own. Nothing – not even the fact that her "overweight" dollar is now worth more than ours – has stirred national pride more than the decision that Canada is powerful enough to "go it alone." It is a dramatic example of the country's rapid postwar economic growth and the decision is one which will have a direct impact on Milwaukee. Thanks to Canada, we will see more foreign flags in our port and, too, a growth in water borne trade between Milwaukee and Canadian and world ports.

Canada plans to start work this spring. A whole floor of a downtown building here has been taken over by the project staff. Barring a last minute hitch, contracts will be let soon after New Year's day. The government has made it clear that wherever possible the work will be given to Canadian and British firms – which means that some heavy industries in Milwaukee may see additional sales go out the window. It is expected that Canadian firms will expand to meet the demand. On the other hand, American companies with Canadian subsidiaries or branch plants, such as Allis-Chalmers Manufacturing Co., may benefit indirectly.

Officially, the Canadian government still takes the position that it would prefer a cooperative development. Reports that the big Detroit automobile manufacturers will urge such a course were received in Ottawa with "interest," according to government spokesmen. But if our congress doesn't act immediately after it meets next January – Canadians doubt that it will – the door will be closed forever on a mutual navigation channel in the key international section of the big river.

Canada is ready, willing and able to build the navigation facilities in Canadian territory. But it is not generally realized in the United States that our cooperation is required for the basic electric power development in the international section. So one hurdle remains.

The proposed Great Lakes-St. Lawrence seaway is a 1,200 mile channel, 27 or more feet deep, from Montreal to the head of the Great Lakes. Together, with the St. Lawrence ship channel, already built by Canada, it will create a 2,200 mile route from the Atlantic to the heart of the continent. The present channel will be deepened and widened so that ships drawing 25 feet of water can carry their cargos through the St. Lawrence to the lakes and conversely permit large lake freighters to reach Montreal. At present small ships can get through, but there is a bottleneck between Prescott, Ont., and Montreal, where the channel is only 14 feet deep. So reloading is now often necessary at Prescott and Montreal for the voyage across the Atlantic from or to Europe. The improvement will permit most of the world's shipping to get to Milwaukee and our midwest heartland.

Coupled with this is the development, on a joint United States-Canadian basis, of a hydroelectric power project in the international section of the river. The cost of this 2,200,000 horsepower project will be split 50-50. Canada also plans to deepen the Welland ship canal. This would provide a 27 foot waterway from Montreal through to Lake Erie. Unless there are some legal tangles growing out of the necessity for joint Canadian-American action on the power dam question, Canada is on the mark for a spring beginning.

The full job will take about five years. It will cost Canada about half a billion dollars, 300 million dollars for the navigation part and about 200 million dollars for the power. The power works on our side would cost about the same. The only difference between this project and the joint plan is that in the joint undertaking the navigation works would have been on our side of the international boundary.

Going it alone will cost the Canadians 35 million dollars extra. But – and this is another point neglected in the United States – the whole thing will be self-liquidating as far as Canada is concerned. It won't cost the taxpayers a thin Canadian dime!

There will be two autonomous agencies in the picture – the St. Lawrence Seaway authority on the navigation side, and the Ontario hydroelectric power commission on the power side. The seaway body, roughly similar to our TVA, will sell bonds which will be paid off from the tolls, and the Ontario power body will either sell bonds or pay for the installation out of its profits. The tolls, by the way, will be the same for our ships as for Canadian – that is provided for in a treaty. And they may be smaller than they might have been under the joint plan, because Canada is allocating less of the total cost to the seaway than a 1941 joint agreement did. It is expected that the tolls will clean up the cost in about 50 years.

Specifically, this is what the Canadians plan to see started next spring:

1. A dam in the Long Sault rapids and the two powerhouses a short distance below this, one on each bank, each capable of generating 1,100,000 horsepower. This dam will flood communities on both sides of the river, on the Canadian side for a distance of about 30 miles and a width of one to four miles.

2. A control dam near Iroquois point (just about across from Ogdensburg, N. Y.), to protect down river interests at Montreal.

3. A side canal to carry navigation past the Long Sault dam and another to circumnavigate the Iroquois control dam, and dikes where necessary along the way.

4. The bottleneck section between Prescott (directly opposite Ogdensburg, N. Y.) and Montreal of the present channel will be deepened to about 27 feet, from the present 14 foot depth. The canals in this area cover a distance of about 68 miles.

It should be remembered that this is but the last link in the seaway system – Canada already has spent about a billion dollars on other stages of the St. Lawrence-Great Lakes navigation route. The United States has spent about 93 million dollars, including a 31 foot lock at Sault Ste. Marie.

When completed, the seaway will carry traffic equal to that on the Panama, Suez, Manchester and Kiel canals combined. Among the cargos that will travel the seaway are wheat from Canada's central provinces; oil from her new central fields; iron ore from the newly found deposits on the Labrador-Quebec border, which will come to the rescue of American steel furnaces when the high grade ores of Minnesota's Mesabi range give out. The power is also of tremendous importance. Ontario has had a power shortage for some time, and the International Rapids section is the only remaining large block of undeveloped water power in the southern part of the province."

But the project will not only offer new industries to that region – it also will force the relocation of seven villages and one town which will be under about 20 feet of water. Obviously, roads and railway tracks also will have to be moved to higher ground and this difficult task of moving people – and graveyards – will cost Ontario about 75 million dollars. There are fewer settlements on our side, so the problem is not as difficult.

The project itself is expected to require 150,000 tons of steel and eight million barrels of cement. About 136 million cubic yards of earth and rock will be needed, and six and one-half million cubic yards of concrete will be poured. The pay roll will average 15,000 persons. How much of this construction has been lost by American firms by Canada's "go it alone" decision is anybody's guess, but obviously we may have, in a very real way, missed the boat.

While the average Canadian's growing sense of nationalism is titillated by the spectacle of a nation of 14 million showing up a neighbor of 150 million persons, the government has no desire to give us the "razzberry" publicly. The official position was summed up in a statement to The Milwaukee Journal by Transportation Minister Lionel Chevrier in these words: "The St. Lawrence project is one that neither Canada nor the United States can afford to do without. It is urgent for our mutual economic development and for our mutual defense. This double urgency applies both to the power, an immediate demand on both sides of the border, and to the navigation facilities, which will permit us to make the most of the iron ore deposits of Labrador and which will save many millions of dollars a year in the cost of moving grain, coal and other products. Our two countries must act together so that, to use the words of a great British statesman, in the days to come the Canadian and American peoples will, for their own safety and the good of all, walk together in majesty, in justice and in peace."

In a recent public speech, William M. Benidickson, parliamentary assistant to Chevrier, put it a little more bluntly: "When Canada comes to a decision today, it is not prepared to be hamstrung by what it regards as unreasonable delays. Canada is now seizing the issue by the forelock . . . a clear clue to the changed status of Canada in the western hemisphere, a result of its rapid economic growth and . . . a sharp change in outlook of the Canadian people. (The seaway) is the basic essential of growth. Without it, frontiers more than 1,000 miles removed from the lakes or the St. Lawrence, but of which the water highway is a vital communications link, could not be cracked open. The fullest possible development of that God given, natural 2,200 mile, cheap communication system is vital to our continued national growth."

Chevrier and Benidickson didn't say so, but in this instance, we have been badly out of step and stumbling far behind our good – if smaller – friend and neighbor.

25.4 Population Problems and How They Might be Solved

[*Source: Austin C. Wehrwein: Canada's biggest need – people and more people, in:* The Milwaukee Journal *(Milwaukee, Wisc.), Vol. 70/No. 345, October 29, 1952, p. 33, cols. 1–4.*]

What this country needs is more Canadians. Here is a great continental expanse, one-third greater than the United States, with a population of only 14 million persons, less than a tenth of ours.

Most of the population today is strung along the 3,000 mile border, roughly within 100 miles of that unfortified line. This is natural, because the north is still largely wilderness and is not an inviting area for settlement. But if Canada is to consolidate her current economic expansion, she must be willing to pioneer into the bleak north where much of her new mineral wealth has been found.

As Canada enters her new century, she has more than enough agricultural lands to feed a bigger population and some rich soil still unbroken. Her natural resources are vital to the United States and the rest of the free world. Her rushing streams promise more and more hydroelectric power, and when the atomic power age dawns she'll be there, too, with the world's biggest supply of uranium. But she needs people to continue her expansion. Already labor is scarce on her big construction projects, with more – such as the St. Lawrence seaway

– to come. And she must "import" experts, engineers and supervisors from the United States and Britain. And while her boom is real and her economy sound, the country has a very tender Achilles heel: To thrive, Canada needs an expanding market in the United States and the rest of the world. Canada is free – and dependent.

So, aside from the brain and muscle new residents would provide, they would also help build up a bigger internal market. This would diversify the economy, provide new opportunities for individuals, and cushion business against the ups and downs of the world market.

Even allowing for the difficulties in settling the north, which is akin to our difficulties in "planting" a population in Alaska, the disparity between our internal market and Canada's can be seen in the fact that Canada has hardly four persons a square mile on the average, compared to our 50. And we, too, have some wide open spaces. Prime Minister Louis St. Laurent said last week that the country needs 40 million persons by the year 2000. Other leaders have spoken of doubling the present population within a generation.

Last year 194,000 immigrants arrived, the most since 1914. This year, because of a cutback which has been fiercely criticized in the press, the total will be between 150,000 and 165,000. To reach the 40 million goal, Canada would have to have at least 225,000 immigrants annually for the next 48 years. This takes into account the annual baby crop and is based on the fond hope that only 10,000 Canadians will leave. Actually, some authorities think that at least 240,000 immigrants would be needed each year.

Using the larger figure, that would mean something more than 11 million foreigners, which is only three million fewer than the present population. The United States, by comparison, welcomed 39 million immigrants in the 174 years between 1776 and 1950. In 1950, the last year for which figures are available, our intake was 249,000. The biggest immigration year was 1914, when we got 1,218,000.

So Canada faces a tremendous digestive process in the years ahead. It is complicated by the tacit official policy favoring British, Irish and (to a lesser extent) north European peoples, whereas Italy, for example, has the biggest and most anxious to move surplus population. The official policy has been to attempt to preserve the "fundamental character" of the country, which means, to some extent, the hope that the bulk of the new citizens will come from the British isles. But often the "citified" British make poor immigrants; sometimes they're too "smart aleck," regarding the proud Canadians as "colonials."

Because of the French speaking third of the population, largely concentrated in Quebec, French immigrants also are welcomed, but they are not numerous and are not popular with the French Canadians, whose traditions date back to the 17th century. Although they have clung to their own culture, they have been out of direct contact with France and, among other things, they dislike the modern French attitude toward the Catholic church, which is the root of life here in Quebec province but is not in France itself. Too, their language is a patois – a corruption of the original tongue.

Another factor is that Canadians have only recently "discovered" themselves. Nationalism is growing now, but the country wasn't really unified until 1867, and Newfoundland broke away from England only in 1949, creating for the first time a confederation "from sea to sea." The lack of good roads and thin population tended to make each province, which has far more "state rights" than our states, somewhat "insular." Canadians go south to the United States more often than they go east or west.

All this has added up to a feeling in the past that an individual is "French" or "Scottish" or "English," rather than "Canadian." Such awareness of race, intensified by a lack of intermarriage (partly because of religious differences) between the French and the other groups, has made many Canadians a bit uneasy about foreigners or "new Canadians," as the government propaganda calls them. This is less true in the west, where the population is generally like that of our middle west, with many persons of (for example) German, Polish, Swiss, Lithuanian, Dutch and Croatian descent. There are also many Ukrainians and some Russians whose numbers include the Doukhobors, a few of whom belong to the weird sect which sometimes parades in the nude.

But while the French Canadians are making rapid progress, the dominant influence in Canada is still British, and with that there is often a touch of snobbishness. As a representative citizen of Toronto, which prides itself on being one of the "most British" of Canadian cities, told the writer: "We still raise our eyebrows when we hear a non-Anglo-Saxon name."

Canadians lack – even now – the counterpart of what we call "Americanization." While the concept has sometimes been abused in the United States, it has provided a driving force which has speeded up assimilation and made an immigrant want, often desperately, to "become Americanized." As explained to the writer, the Canadian theory is "integration" rather than "melting pot." This is based on the idea that foreign cultures often have value, which, preserved, can enrich the society. But it has tended to segregate some groups.

In practice, the mechanics of their immigration policy is much like ours. While there are no set quotas, a "selective screening" process to eliminate paupers, undesirables, and subversives and otherwise to pick and choose has resulted in the same thing. Asiatics, except for a token allowance of 150 from Indian, Pakistan and Ceylon (which are in the British Commonwealth), are excluded. That our system is similar to Canada's does not tell the whole story. For one thing, there is less than total agreement in the United States as to the desirability of our policy, and second, Canada needs population to keep her date with destiny, while we have met and married that allegorical yound lady.

The more advanced thinking about "new Canadians" was expressed last week by Rene B. Perrault of Montreal, president of the Canadian Chamber of Commerce. "With a wealth of virtually every vital resource, Canada is short of the most important resource – people," he told the annual chamber convention at Toronto. "The answer is immigration, more immigrants – many more!" More people, he told the assembled businessmen, are necessary for defense and will raise the standard of living. "We should be aware of the danger of trying to keep so rich a land all to ourselves," he said. "Our moral sense urges us to provide sanctuary and opportunity. The advisability of continued immigration has been challenged in recent months and the government a few months ago tightened up its selective program. But I believe, and the Canadian chamber believes, that the needs outweigh the difficulties foreseen in immigration at the rate of the last year."

When Premier St. Laurent suggested the year 2000 goal as 40 million, which was five million more than the previous target, it was assumed that a new policy was being worked out. The point is that starting last July, the brakes were put on immigration from Italy, Germany, Austria, Greece and Finland. Labor union pressure, caused by the fear of job competition in some areas, was believed to be one of the factors. But in the press, at least, the policy was roundly criticized and the door is expected to open again next year.

As part of the policy, set in 1947, of increasing the population "with due regard to the absorbtive capacity and the fundamental character" of the country, most immigrants are either placed in jobs before they leave Europe, or are required to work a year on farms. This is often a waste of skill, but, on the other hand, if an immigrant breaks his agreement, nothing is done to penalize him.

Yet this points up another problem. Today's immigrants are usually city people. Everywhere there is a trend away from the land, and if Canada is to open up her north, she needs men and women willing to live close to the land, just as did the Europeans who hacked away our wilderness during the last century. Even native Canadians are slow to plunge into the north, and Canadians joke that the country needs a modern Horace Greeley, saying, "Go north, young man, go north."

Closely related to this is the fact that perhaps the most important long range problem Canada has faced in trying to fill up her vast space is the steady drain of her best brains and most ambitious youth south to the United States. Up to now the country simply hasn't offered the opportunities available in the United States. And even today wages and professional salaries are often as much as 30% below ours.

Contrawise, today Canada draws heavily on our industrial and business manpower to help "staff" her boom. "Let's Stop Exporting Canadians," was the heading on a recent editorial in the Montreal Gazette. Since 1945, Canada admitted 582,700 immigrants, but in the same period it lost 314,600 persons for a total net gain of only 268,100. The total net loss of immigrants and native Canadians runs about 1,000 a month, according to immigration minister W. E. Harris. Canadians like to reel off the names of American leaders who originated here. Right in Wisconsin, our lieutenant governor, George Smith, is an ex-Canadian.

This correspondent met a German youth who arrived recently and after he said that he was glad he had a job in an Ottawa department store stockroom rather than working in the "bush," he asked eagerly, "Don't you think I should go to the States? I hear you can make a lot of money there." But Canadians hope that the tide is turning. Said Harris: "I do not want to minimize the loss. It is a regrettable one – but far less serious than some would have us believe. And to offset it, over the last seven years, our intake from the United States has been at an average of about 8,500 a year or a total of almost 60,000. Returning Canadians have added another 25,000 to this total so that the traffic north across the border has been at the rate of about 12,000 a year."

Canadians hope that this will increase. They are particularly happy to see the prodigal sons return, and they point out that some of the big expansion – particularly in the western oil fields – has been manned by Americans on the top executive level. The welcome mat is out for the Yanks, and Canadians hope they'll stay.

25.5 A Province of Superlatives and Its Riches

[*Source: Austin C. Wehrwein: Busy British Columbia is the 'Texas' of Canada, in:* The Milwaukee Journal *(Milwaukee, Wisc.), Vol. 71/No. 31, December 16, 1952, p. 33, cols. 1–6; p. 37, cols. 1–3.*]

British Columbia, which boasts that it is in the midst of a "billion dollar boom," is the "Texas" of Canada. Although its population is 70% British by extraction, the natives have forgotten the tradition of understatement associated with their forefathers. They will lay on the superlatives at the drop of a Douglas fir, the felling of which is one of their major industries.

B. C., as the Canadians call the province, is big. It is larger than California, Oregon and Washington together, and it is the living link between those states and Alaska. B. C. is rich in resources. It has tremendous stands of timber; gold, silver, lead, zinc, asbestos, iron, tungsten, copper and coal. Big schools of salmon, halibut and other fish swim in its coastal waters. Its lands produce fruit, vegetables and grain, and feed dairy and beef cattle. It has natural gas and oil. It has an immense electricity potential in its rushing rivers. And it is a crossroad of commerce, north and south, east and west. B. C. has a varied climate, ranging from the subarctic to a summer span of semitropical weather in the lush Okanagan valley.

B. C. is growing. Although its population of 1,625,000 is still about one-half of Wisconsin's, averaging three persons to a square mile, it increased 42,5% in the last 10 years. This was a greater percentage increase than any comparable North American area except for California, Nevada and Arizona. (California 53,3%; Nevada, 45,2%; Arizona, 51,1%.)

Vancouver, the nerve center and financial sluice gate for B. C.'s rushing wealth, claimed six years ago, when the community celebrated its 60th birthday, that it was the only city on the continent which multiplied more than 200 times in two generations. One of its suburban real estate developments is a project in which the Guiness brewing family of Ireland has sunk a reported 40 million dollars.

A visitor's impression is that of a thriving and prosperous city. The picturesque city on a peninsula, ringed by mountains, seems to have a higher percentage of well dressed women than any other Canadian city, with the possible exception of Calgary, which is oil rich and full of Americans in the upper reaches of the petroleum industry. Figures of the Vancouver Board of Trade (Chamber of Commerce to Americans) show that since the war the province's total pay rolls have nearly doubled; the output of basic industries has more than doubled; agricultural production has increased 25%; fisheries production nearly doubled, and forest production has nearly tripled. The Board of Trade estimates that the billion dollars invested in the province since 1950 is double the total investment in manufacturing in 1943. But forestry is still the No. 1 business, with annual production worth more than half a billion dollars.

The climate is kind to trees, and the province is one of the world's few remaining areas with large exportable surpluses of quality soft woods. Although wasteful cutting in bygone days (now corrected by conservation laws) reduced the stands of big timber, B. C. still abounds in Douglas fir, hemlock, spruce and cedar. Conservation has encouraged the cutting of smaller trees suitable for pulp wood, and the pulp and paper industry has a 325 million dollar expansion program. It is estimated that 40c out of every dollar earned in the province comes from the forests directly or indirectly.

A new development is cellulose production. The Celanese Corp. of America has built a 30 million dollar pulp mill near Prince Rupert, on the coast, and plans a 75 million dollar integrated forest industry at Castelgar in the southern interior. Natural gas from the neighboring province of Alberta will be used by the company in this new industry for B. C. Over the Rockies from Alberta an oil pipe line is being built which will serve Vancouver and the northwestern part of the United States. Natural gas will follow within a few years. Giant diesel motors from the Nordberg Manufacturing Co. of Milwaukee will pump the oil over the great divide.

Miners and lumbermen laid the foundations for the B. C. economy, and agricultural development lagged until about 1910 when improved transportation opened new markets. But there still are vast areas awaiting settlement. Only about a fifth of the arable land (more than five million acres) is being used, and some experts think about another 20 million acres might be developed for grazing. At the same time, almost half of this great province is unfit for much of anything except black flies in summer. Of the 234,403,000 acres, close to half consists of water, muskeg, swamp and barren lands. Of the remainder, 72 million acres, or 30%, is good only for forest – but, of course, that isn't bad.

In the area near Vancouver there are dairy farms, and specialty crops like small fruits, bulbs and hops. In the southern interior there are tree fruits – especially apples. There is mixed farming north of that area, and in the central interior big cattle ranches. Vancouver is also one of the key transportation centers of the hemisphere, with a magnificent harbor serving both oceangoing and coastal shipping. The two Canadian transcontinental railroads end here, and the Great Northern railway comes up from Seattle. Vancouver claims the fastest growing airport in Canada, although it is often plagued by fog.

In trying to sum up these and other developments, British Columbians find themselves constantly using adjectives ending in "est." For example, B. C. has:

The world's largest cattle ranch – bigger than the famed King ranch in Texas.

Canada's highest per capita wealth, per capita production and purchasing power as well as the largest percentage of taxpayers.

The world's largest smelter. (At Trail, which is the world's largest lead and zinc producer and Canada's largest chemical fertilizer producer.)

The finest softwood stand in the British Commonwealth and some of the biggest and oldest (more than 1,000 years old) trees in North America. (The California redwoods are, however, bigger and older.)

The world's largest tungsten mine.

The world's biggest pulp and paper industry expansion programs.

One of the greatest sources of accessible untapped hydroelectric power in North America.

What will be the largest aluminum smelter anywhere, the Alcan Kitimat project, now building.

The adjectives don't end there. B. C. claims to be one of the most beautiful parts of the western hemisphere, and the total tourist take of more than 38 million dollars a year tops some of its manufacturing industries. The tourist literature reads like a love letter. Some samples from a current publication: "Lush meadows ... snowcapped mountains rising

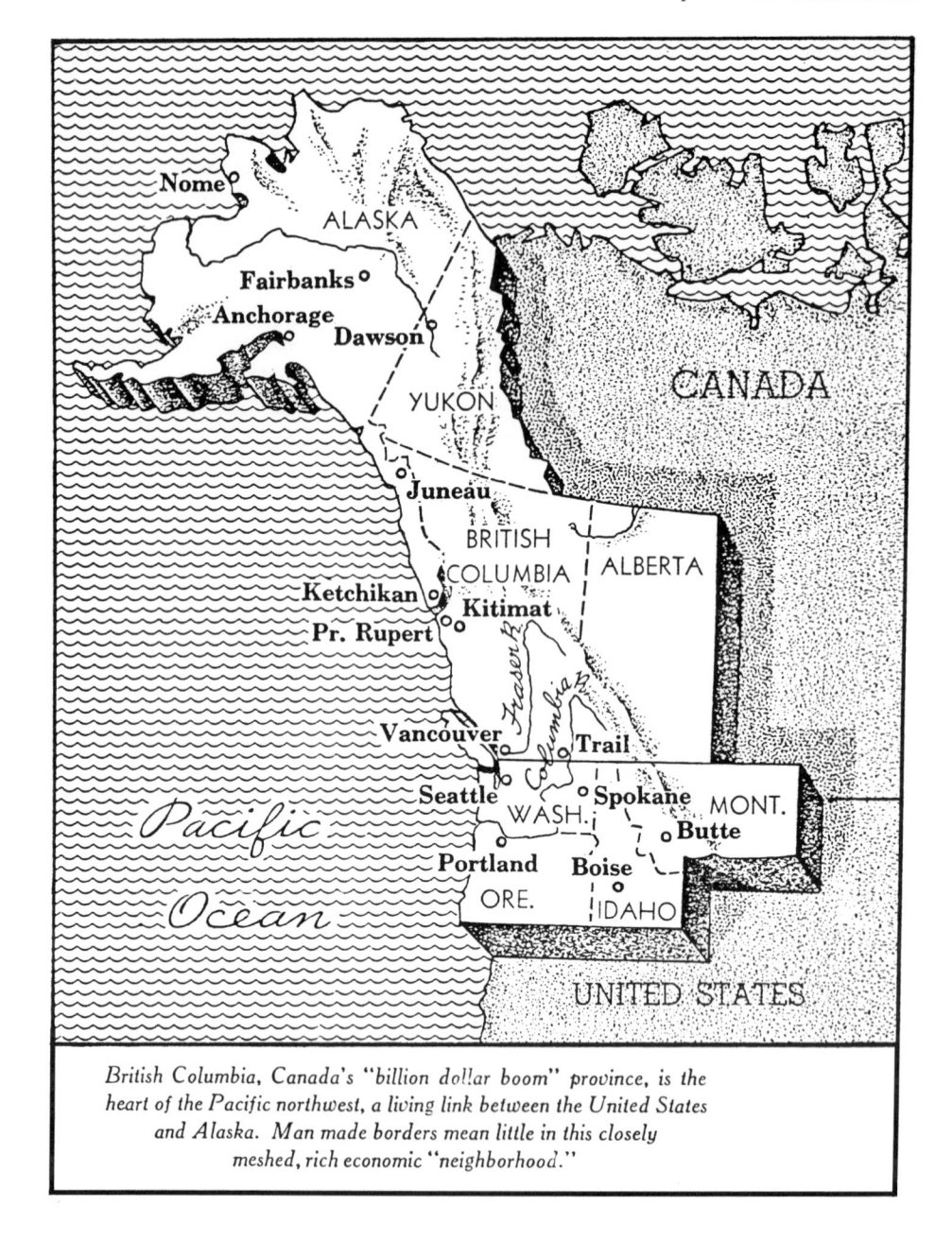

British Columbia, Canada's "billion dollar boom" province, is the heart of the Pacific northwest, a living link between the United States and Alaska. Man made borders mean little in this closely meshed, rich economic "neighborhood."

[*Source:* Austin C. Wehrwein: Canada's New Century, Milwaukee, Wisc., 1953, p. 71.]

grandly from their green foothills ... parklike valleys ... frowning canyons ... tumbling rivers toss their white manes, broad lakes lie lambent ... wild reaches of the sea." The fish are described as "matchless," the big game hunting as the best in Canada. The adjective machine runs down only when it comes to game birds. They are "not so remarkable."

The ocean winds moderate the west coast climate, giving it moist, often foggy, weather, much like England, a circumstance which attracted many Englishmen. Elsewhere, in the predominantly mountainous province, which includes nearly the entire width of the western North American mountain belt, the weather varies with the altitude and geographical location.

In this, and many other things, it is like Washington and Oregon, and if there is a friendly rivalry between Vancouver and Seattle, Wash., there is also a community of interest which ties the whole Pacific northwest together. On the south B. C. flanks Washington, the northern tip of Idaho and eastern Montana. The Alaskan panhandle reaches down like an arm on the west, curtaining the northern part of B. C. from the sea.

The businessmen of the area have already taken steps to make this geographical propinquity more productive. They have organized the Pacific Northwest Trade association (PNTA), which acts as a super, international trade association and chamber of commerce. The president is Ralph Baker, American born head of Standard Oil Co. of British Columbia. The association believes, according to its leaders in Vancouver, that one of its jobs is to explain not only the needs of the northwest (meaning Oregon to Alaska) to the rest of North America, but also to explain Canadians to non-northwest Americans and Americans to non-northwest Canadians.

Nevertheless, a visitor gets the impression that the Vancouver businessman is somewhat more nationalistic than, say, his counterpart in Winnipeg. At best it is a patriotic pride in Canada's achievements, at worst a supercilious sense of superiority in the British fashion.

Aware that the timber lands on both sides of the border are the same that the interior agricultural regions grow the same crops; that they share some of the same rivers and the island sheltered sea lane to Alaska; that further development of Canadian oil and natural gas awaits an American market; that the same schools of salmon swim all along the coast; and that as a region the lines of commerce run north and south because of the mountain barrier; aware of these things, the association has set its goal as the need "to do something together." For example, the recent PNTA session in Yakima, Wash., came up with a resolution against higher tariffs. The Alaskan, Canadian and south of the border Americans see eye to eye on other subjects such as tourists, reasonable solutions of joint water power developments, mutual military defense, and even education.

Nor should it be overlooked that the middle leg of the Alaska highway runs across the northeast corner of British Columbia, making another tangible United States-Canadian tie. Historically, the Canadian part of the region has been closely tied to the United States. What is now, roughly, Washington, Oregon and British Columbia, was jointly occupied by Britain and the United States from 1818 to 1846. During this period John Jacob Astor's northwest fur business laid the foundation for the family fortune. James Polk was elected to office in 1844 on the slogan "Fifty-Four Forty or Fight." This meant that he was willing to go to war with Britain to establish the northern United States boundary out here at what is now the southern tip of Alaska's panhandle. But when the campaign oratory was over, the present boundary line at the 49th parallel was set by treaty. Britain in turn gave up its claim to the

Columbia river. Since then, the United States-Canadian border has been the longest unfortified boundary in the world.

Separated from eastern Canada by 100 miles of prairie and a mountain wall 500 miles wide, British Columbia was first settled early in the 19th century by Englishmen who came by ship around South America or overland by way of Oregon and Washington. Like California, British Columbia got its first running jump with the discovery of gold in the 1850's. The arrival of the Canadian Pacific railway in 1886 marked the beginning of modern British Columbia. Lord Shaughnessy, the Milwaukee born son of an Irish immigrant, was one of the builders of this railroad, and when he got his title the punsters said that he was "the peer who made Milwaukee famous." It was his railroad that created a continental Canada because British Columbia, a British colony, would not join the Canadian confederation until steel rails met tidewater.

Today British Columbia, still somewhat isolated from eastern Canada despite the railroad an airplanes, calls itself such names as "The Gateway to the Pacific," "Canada's Industrial Empire" or just "Amazing British Columbia." Vancouver is the "Queen of the Coast."

In language unrestrained for a government agency, the provincial department of trade and commerce said: "British Columbia, once more generally appreciated as the vast playground which it still is, has within the last few decades attained an important industrial status in the economic world. Today, its potential recognized by the investor, industrialist, agriculturalist and laborer alike, the province is developing at an unprecedented rate, with opportunities still apparently unlimited."

"Unlimited" is a big word, but that's Canada today, in the midst of its new century.

Related Readings

Aitken, Hugh G. J. et al.: The American economic impact on Canada, Durham, N. C., 1959.
Archer, Maurice: Canada's economic problems and policies, Toronto 1975.
Armstrong, Muriel: The Canadian economy and its problems, Scarborough, Ont., 1970.
Barbeau, Raymond: Le Québec est-il une colonie?, Montréal 1962.
Barber, Joseph: Good fences make good neighbors. Why the United States provokes Canadiens, Toronto 1958.
Brunet, Michel: Canadians et Canadiens. Etudes sur l'histoire et la pensée des deux Canadas, Paris 1954.
Callahan, James Morton: American foreign policy in Canadian relations, New York 1967.
Clarkson, Stephen (Ed.): An independent foreign policy for Canada?, Toronto 1968.
Conant, Melvin: The long polar watch. Canada and the defence of North America, New York 1962.
Craig, Gerald Marquis: The United States and Canada, Cambridge, Mass., 1968.
Crispo, John H. G. (Ed.): Wages, prices, profits and economic policy, Toronto 1968.
Deutsch, John J. et al. (Eds.): The Canadian economy. Selected readings, rev. ed., Toronto 1965.
Garigue, Philippe: L'Option politique du Canada français. Une interprétation de la survivance nationale, Montréal 1963.
Gordon, J. King (Ed.): Canada's role as a middle power, Toronto 1966.
Heeney, A. D. P./Merchant, Livingston T.: Canada and the United States – principles for partnership, Ottawa 1965.

Lamontagne, Maurice: Le fédéralisme canadien – évolution et problèmes, Québec 1954.
Pal, I. D. (Ed.): Canadian economic issues. Introductory readings, Toronto 1971.
Robert, Jean-Claude: Du Canada français au Québec libre. Histoire d'un mouvement indépendantiste, Paris 1975.
Russell, Peter (Ed.): Nationalism in Canada, Toronto – New York 1966.
Stovel, John A.: Canada in the world economy, Cambridge 1959.
Thomson, Dale C./Swanson, Roger F.: Canadien foreign policy – options and perspectives, Toronto – New York 1971.

1953

Jim G. Lucas

Scripps-Howard Newspapers

CHAPTER 26

REPORTS ABOUT KOREA IN 1953

The Front and How the Soldiers Face It

    Introductory Notes
26.1 'Our Town' and Its Social Order
26.2 A Basic Rule of War and Changes It Brings Along
26.3 Nights of Terror and No End to be Seen
26.4 Replacements Face Strange Country and 'Fear Future'
26.5 Death-Bringing Planes and a Special Sort of a Bomb
    Related Readings

Introductory Notes

After the bestowal of the Pulitzer Prize for International Reporting for the coverage of Canada the year before, the rough realities of Korea were returned to in 1954. The year's prize went to Jim G. Lucas of the Scripps-Howard Newspapers "for his notable front-line human interest reporting of the Korean War, the cease-fire and the prisoner-of-war exchanges, climaxing 26 months of distinguished services as a war correspondent." As in the case of Edmund Stevens four years before, the prize for Jim Lucas was based on his reporting during several years, although it was only the articles published in 1953 that should have been taken into consideration.

Jim Griffing Lucas was born on June 22, 1914, in Checotah, Oklahoma. He received his first journalistic experience as editor of the high school paper in that community. After only a year at the University of Missouri in 1932–33, he quit college to work at a salery of $12 a week for the newspaper Daily Phoenix, *Muskogee, Oklahoma, and for the* Times-Democrat *of that city. Between 1936 and 1938 he worked as a news broadcaster for the station KBIX, Muskogee, Oklahoma; from 1938 to 1942 Jim Lucas was a reporter and feature writer for the* Tulsa Tribune, *Tulsa, Oklahoma. From 1942 to 1945 he served as a combat correspondent in the Marine Corps; he experienced seven bloody island campaigns (Guadalcanal, New Georgia, Russel Islands, Tarawa, Saipan, Tinian, Iwo Jima) and emerged in 1945 as a first lieutenant, winner of the Bronze Star medal and the National Headliners award for a brilliant job of reporting at Tarawa. For three days at this island he had been listed as "killed in action". Jim Lucas started working for the* Scripps-Howard Newspapers *after World War II, spezializing in military reporting. He went to Korea immediately after the outbreak of hostilities there and spent 26 of the 36 months of the Korean War reporting from the front lines. Jim Lucas was made an honorary member of the American Seventh Division in a citation which described his dispatches as "mellowed by uncommon understanding of the sacrifices and hardships endured by men in the line". In February, 1953, Jim Lucas received the Veterans of Foreign Wars' General Omar N. Bradley gold medal for his "outstanding accounts of combat . . ."*

The following texts by Jim Griffing Lucas, copyright 1953, are reprinted by kind permission of the Scripps-Howard Newspapers, *Washington, D. C.*

26.1 'Our Town' and Its Social Order

[*Source: Jim G. Lucas: GI outpost battles foe and own rear, in:* New York World-Telegram and The Sun *(New York, N.Y.), Vol. 120/No. 103, January 3, 1953, p. 4, cols. 1–2.*]

Our Town atop Pork Chop Hill is in a world of its own. Its contacts with the outside world are few – but imperative. Its immediate concern is the enemy on the next ridge. That's "His Town." To "His Town" Our Town gives grudging respect. But if possible, His Town is going to be wiped out.

Our Town's business is war. It produces nothing but death. To exist, therefore, it must rely on others. Food, mail, clothing – even the weapons of destruction – are shipped in. These items are sent in from that part of the outside world which the men of Our Town call "rear." As often – and far more passionately – they are at war with "rear" as they are with the enemy. "Rear" – which includes anything beyond the foot of Pork Chop – is populated, Our Town is convinced, by idiots and stumblebums.

Physically, Our Town – while hardly attractive – is not uncomfortable. Much municipal planning went into it. The streets are six to eight feet deep. At times after dark, Our Town's streets are invaded by men from His Town. The citizens of Our Town invariably expel these interlopers. To assist in maintaining law and order on such occasions, the shelves along streets of Our Town are liberally stocked with hand grenades.

There are 30 to 50 houses in Our Town. They are referred to as bunkers. Each street and each bunker is numbered. After a few days, it is comparatively easy to find one's way. Half of Our Town's bunkers are living quarters. The others are stores – storage bunkers, that is. From these, you can obtain a wide assortment of ammunition, sandbags, candles, charcoal or canned rations. Our Town's buildings are sturdy. The typical building is at least six feet underground. It is made of four-by-ten-inch logs to which are added many sandbags. It's almost impervious to enemy shelling.

Our Town is not without its social life. I went visiting this morning at 19 Third Street in Our Town. Entering Number 19, one gets down on his hands and knees. The front door is low. My hosts were First Lt. Pat Smith of Hollywood, Calif., Cpl. Joe Siena of Portland, Conn., Pfc Eddie Williams of Brooklyn and Pvt. Don Coan of Anadarko, Okla. Don had coffee brewing in an old ration can. He opened a can of sardines. Eddie was heading for the rear on a shopping trip. His list included candles, a coffee pot (which he'd had on order for a month already) and a reel of communications wire. He also was taking a field telephone for repairs. Our Town, like others, enjoys small talk. Over coffee, the group discussed what a man should do if a grenade-wielding Chinese suddenly appeared at the door. There was no unanimous decision.

Our Town has its own banker – Warrant Officer James W. Cherry of Jackson, Tenn. He came up the other afternoon. Within 300 yards of the enemy, be distributed $23,411. Many men didn't want their money really. Money is an almost valueless commodity up here. Three days from now, the postal officer will come up the hill, selling money orders.

If money has no value, other things do. Things like candles, fuel, and toilet tissue. There's never enough charcoal for the stoves which heat the bunkers. To stay warm, you can climb into your sleeping bag – if you're a fool. The men refer to sleeping bags as "coffins." Too many soldiers have been killed before they could unzip their sleeping bags.

Our Town's "Mayor" is a tall, gangling Texan – Capt. Jack Conn of Houston. He's company commander. The Vice Mayor is his executive officer – First. Lt. Bill Gerald, also of Houston. Bill Gerald is a Negro. The Battalion Commander, Lt. Col. Seymour Goldberg of Washington, D. C., is convinced Our Town is a pig sty. Our Town's residents think Colonel Goldberg is a martinet. Colonel Goldberg always arrives in a foul mood – to be expected, since high-up officials usually are blind to local problems. The Colonel expects miracles overnight. (Privately, he concedes this is an act – "If I didn't raise hell, they wouldn't take me seriously.")

Our Town endures this outsider stoically. The Colonel says the men need haircuts. "When would they have time to get haircuts?" say Our Town's citizens. He says the bunkers need cleaning. "They look all right to us," fume Our Towners, "and we live here." He says ammunition isn't stored properly. "Let up on these all-night patrols and we'll store it right," retorts Our Town – not to the Colonel's face, of course. Invariably, the Colonel corrals a hapless private and demands he be court-martialed for one thing or another. Our Town's Mayor dutifully notes the boy's name and then throws away the notes when the Colonel leaves. But the Colonel expects this.

There was much glee the other day when the Colonel issued an order that any man found outside a bunker without a bullet-proof vest on be punished. A moment later, the Colonel left a bunker – and forgot his vest. There's method in the Colonel's madness. He deliberately sets out to make Our Town hate him. "If I didn't," he says, "it would go to pot."

You see, the Colonel once was a company commander who hated "rear." But on Bloody Triangle Hill, he won a promotion. Now he's part of "rear." He knows he must prod the men up front, so that their outfit will remain – despite the presence of death itself – a proud, disciplined, organized Army fighting unit.

26.2 A Basic Rule of War and Changes It Brings Along

[*Source: Jim G. Lucas: One misstep spells death in Korea, in:* New York World-Telegram and The Sun *(New York, N.Y.), Vol. 120/No. 106, January 7, 1953, p. 8, cols. 3–6.*]

This is such a miserable country to die in. It's not just that it's Korea. It would be miserable country if it were Ohio, Texas, Indiana or Pennsylvania. War is universal and battlefields are the same.

Three of our men got it last night. Old timers say it was their own fault. They say it gruffly – because they know it could have been them – as if that explains everything. It was their own fault, they say, because the guys let themselves get trapped. One enemy patrol deliberately exposed itself and the kids chased it up a draw where another was waiting in ambush. Our people heard the shooting, saw the flashes and, after the survivors got home, went out and recovered the bodies.

Jim G. Lucas

North and South Korea After the War

[*Source:* AP Map of 1955, locating the one-time armistice town of Kaesong and the north bank of the lower Han River.]

One foul out here and you're through. Every man here remembers at least once when he almost fouled out. They sit around bunkers at night and talk about it. It is pitiless self-examination and it isn't pretty to hear. The patrols they talk about are those which didn't come off. Those are the ones they remember. Each man blames himself for something he didn't do – some oversight he fears cost some buddy his life.

A few minutes ago, we looked over some cards those kids filled out before they were killed last night. They filled them out so division public information men could write hometown newspapers and the home folks could see their boys' names in print. Take the lieutenant. He wrote with a firm strong hand. A young man whose gold bars were still new. He was graduated from a small southwestern college last August. Korea in October. Dead in January. And the two enlisted men killed with him. One had been a hotel desk clerk, a draftee. The other had just finished high school and enlisted to beat the draft. They were killed near a bend in the Imjin River between two hills we've named Chink Baldie and Pork Chop.

Six months ago, not one of those three ever heard of the Imjin, probably. And when they went out last night, all they knew about the countryside was what they had learned from a map. Military maps – to me anyhow – are a confusing conglomeration of curlicues and squares. They tell me men like Eisenhower and Bradley can look at a map and actually see the countryside. But for most of us, maps never quite prepare us for the real thing. You could put those three boys back home of course and never have lost them. But they weren't back home. They were in a draw between two hills near a bend in the Imjin River north of the 38th Parallel in Korea. And there was an ambush waiting for them.

This country around the Imjin was not always a miserable place to die in. For some, it was once a good place to live. The sides of the hills we are fighting and dying for still bear the outlines of rice paddies. The village in the valley that now is No Man's Land was the village of Kungmal. It's hard to say how many lived here, because only a few houses are standing. But it was home for someone. These people loved their land and homes fiercely. It had been handed down from generation to generation. They asked only to be let alone to live their lives as they had always lived them. But who ever heard of Communists letting other people alone?

Now these people are gone – dead or pushed aside by the current of war – and we've come in. Because we had to. And – by necessity – we've altered the face of this part of Korea. We've cut roads through rice paddies, sliced huge chunks out of their mountains, made bunkers of their trees and burned or destroyed their homes, because they might conceal snipers. There are deadly land mines lurking like rattlesnakes in their paddies. Along their roads there's barbed wire wherever you turn. There are smoke pots in their valleys and there is seldom a minute when guns are not firing.

So it is an unfriendly, sullen, alien land here around the frozen Imjin. Miserable country to die in. Some day, perhaps, the Koreans who've always lived here and found the living god will come back to their bend in the river. Then perhaps they'll patiently rebuild their villages, smooth over the scars of war, dig up the mines und resume peaceful, ageless living. But it's not that way tonight.

26.3 Nights of Terror and No End to be Seen

[*Source: Jim G. Lucas: Up front-waiting – with dead radio, in:* New York World-Telegram and The Sun *(New York, N.Y.), Vol. 120/No. 112, January 14, 1953, p. 29, cols. 1–4.*]

This is the picture as I write: We're sitting in a bunker up front. Out in No Man's Land are the broken remnants of an ambushed patrol. We don't know if our missing men are alive or dead. Our radio link with the patrol has been knocked out by the Commie mortars. So we wait ...

It had been an ill-fated patrol from the start. Capt. William P. Haynes of Knoxville had outlined the plan back at battalion headquarters. The enemy, he said, had been creeping gradually closer to our defences. Now, the enemy was dug in some 300 yards away, on a hill called "Fanny." First Lt. William P. Jones of Aberdeen, Miss., would lead the patrol. Its mission: to wreck the Red defenses and take prisoners. The infantry company furnishing the patrol members was commanded by Capt. W. B. Tuttle of New York City. Captain Tuttle had lost 14 men to ambushers in his unit's last two patrols. The ambush last time had come near a creek at the foot of Hill Fanny. Today, Captain Tuttle had the artillery drop shells in that area until dark – to make it too hot for the Reds.

At 5:30, Lieutenant Jones had his patrol ready to move. Just then, the enemy opened up with mortars. No one was hurt. But it was a bad sign. It meant the enemy knew something was up. The patrol left. At 7, from the valley below Lieutenant Jones reported crow calls. We heard them, too – eerie and out of place in the darkness. The explanation was obvious. The Reds were signalling one another. At 9:30, Master Sgt. Cecil Williams of Laurel, Miss., led a small advance guard of the patrol to that creek where our men had been ambushed before. But nothing happened. Sergeant Williams placed his men along the creek bank, ready to protect Lieutenant Jones' group when it moved up to cross the frozen stream. Suddenly all hell broke loose.

Back in the bunker, Captain Tuttle had been keeping in touch with the patrol by radio. Then, through the loudspeaker, had come that murderous din. Machine guns chattered, rifles cracked, men shouted. Over the bedlam, we heard Lieutenant Jones shout to Sergeant Williams: "What did you hit out there?" There was no answer; only gun fire and the grunting of men working their rifles fast. "Medic! Medic!" came a cry through the loudspeaker. Then: "We ran into an ambush, sir." (That apparently was Sergeant Williams explaining to Lieutenant Jones.) Lieutenant Jones to Sergeant Williams over the radio: "How's your ammunition?" Sergeant Williams in reply: "Getting low, sir. Can you pull up, sir, and let us get behind you? Our ammo's about gone, or I wouldn't ask, sir."

In the bunker, you kept thinking – This isn't a movie. It isn't a radio serial. It is men you ate supper with, getting hell shot out of them a few hundred yards away, and you can't raise a finger to help. Now over the radio came another sound we'd expected and dreaded. Chinese mortar fire. Sergeant Williams, shouting to his men: "We gotta get the hell out of here!" The mortar shells were falling like dew. Sergeant Williams to his men: "Spread out! I never saw such a bunch of people for bunching up and holding hands. Spread out, dammit!" Then Lieutenant Jones' voice came in: "Captain Tuttle! Captain! Can you get me tank fire?" Captain Tuttle could and did – immediately. Our mortars began sounding off, too. Sergeant

Williams called in to the Captain: "Captain, those mortars are still coming in. They're ruining us. We – –" That's when the radio went out.

So here we are, sitting in the bunker. Waiting. Now it's midnight. And here comes Sergeant Williams. "Kinda hot in the valley tonight, sir", he says, trying to be casual. But he can't hide his anxiety. He shucks off his parka and sits – rigid and stiff backed – on the edge of a bunk. Then Sgt. Richard Padgett of Evansville, Ind., enters. He and Williams greet each other wildly. Each had figured the other dead. "Is the Lieutenant in yet" asks Padgett, making no attempt to conceal his concern about Jones. "You were with him last," says Captain Tuttle. "Where'd you see him last?" "It was at the foot of the hill," replied Padgett. "The mortars began dropping all around. He yelled at me to take off. That's the last time I saw him. Sergeant Randall was with him."

There's a new chill in the air. Master Sgt. Edwin Randall hadn't been assigned to this patrol originally. But he was headed home and had begged for the job – wanted to say he'd been on patrol. Now if he'd gotten hit, so close to rotation . . . There's heavy silence. Then the phone rings. Tuttle grabs it. The caller is in an outpost down the hill a way. We all heard his voice, verging on panic, ask: "Is Padgett there? Has ANYONE seen Padgett?"

It was Lieutenant Jones. "He's here!" Captain Tuttle shouted. "Where's Randall?" "He's here with me," said Lieutenant Jones. "What about Padgett? Is he okay?" Padgett takes the telephone. "Here I am, Lieutenant!" he yells. "You okay? You okay, sir?" What Jones answers isn't clear. But it sounds like: "Thank God." And anyone who says he is crying is a dirty liar.

26.4 Replacements Face Strange Country and 'Fear Future'

[*Source: Jim G. Lucas: Korea is like end of time, in:* New York World-Telegram and The Sun *(New York, N.Y.), Vol. 120/No. 124, January 28, 1953, p. 21, cols. 1–3.*]

Vernon Coleman – who is 25, a native of Clute, Texas and the father of two – will not soon forget the hollow despair of his first 24 hours in Korea. Korea can seem the end of the world to such a man as Vern Coleman. He first set foot on it at 3:30 in the morning.

There were no welcoming bands. They put Vern Coleman in a truck with 50 other bewildered young Americans, hauled them through stinking, dark streets to the repple depple (replacement depot), pointed to a bunk and told him it was his. This morning, someone woke him and said if he was interested in breakfast he'd better get a move on. Since then, no one has told him a thing.

Because he is older than most and a father, Vern Coleman has had more time to think than probably is good for him. He wonders, among other things, what he's doing in Korea. He begged for a chance to enlist earlier and no one would take him, although he was single then. Thus, he wasn't particularly worried later on, when he got his greetings. He had a good

[*Source:* Walter Lefeber: America, Russia and the Cold War, 1945–1971, 2nd ed., New York–London–Sydney–Toronto 1972, p. 98.]

job as a riveter, three dependents and the same disqualifications he'd always had. But they took him. Suddenly, here he was in Korea.

Korea can also seem like the end of time to younger men like Walter Simmons of Roanoke, Va., and Charles Gage of Chicago. Both are 23. Both are married; each the father of one child. Walter was a farmer. He was making his farm pay. Now, he says, his father and brother will farm it for him. But they have their own farms. Young Gage, a major in business administration, had finished his third year at Illinois University. His baby was two weeks old. He'd sent his family to his wife's parents in Iowa.

Vern Coleman tries to get interested in a game of hearts. Privately, he admits he's thinking about his family, now moved in on his wife's sister in San Antonio. Walter Simmons is too whipped to care; he lies in his bunk and stares at the ceiling. Charles Gage tries to treat it as a joke. All have some things in common – their frustrations, their fears and their terrifying insecurity. Uprooted – for many it was their first long trip away from home – they find themselves in a strange land. Ahead lies a war they have read about for three years.

It is difficult to describe their feelings to anyone who has not lived through it. Old ties have been cut and they have not had time to make new ones. They have no sense of belonging to anything. Eventually, they will acquire a sense of belonging to a division, regiment, battalion or company. But that comes later.

These men come from all over our country. They are as typically American as chocolate sodas. Day by day and week by week they come here – frightened and uprooted. Look at the list:

Tom Lamond, 22, Osage City, Kansas. An apprentice lineman for Santa Fe. Richard Pickford, 22, Philadelphia. A television tester. Milton Britto, 24, Brooklyn. Married. Truck driver. Stanley Northcutt, 21, Cynthiana, Ky. Married with three stepchildren. A tenant farmer, he lost his farm when he was drafted.

Edward Love, 21, Columbus, Ind. Spot welder. Robert Stiles, 20, Indianapolis. Machinist. Hubert Sneed, 23, Edgewood, Tex. Married. A recent graduate of East Texas State College.

That isn't the whole list. They range in age from Bob Stiles' beardless 20 to Earl Harris' white-haired 60. No one – least of all Pop Harris – knows why this veteran of 27 years Army service was sent to Korea. His medical records show he is on the downgrade and unfit even for moderately heavy work. But here he is.

The man over them understand their fears. "I know they're bewildered," says Lt. Col. Edmond J. Padgett of Lebanon, Ind., who commands the replacement battalion. "They feel they haven't a friend in the world." But these men don't know Colonel Padgett. They know him only as arbiter of their futures. They know only that – from the moment they arrived – they have been prisoners of an imposing list of "don'ts." They can't leave the old schoolhouse where they're quartered. Wherever they turn, signs bar them – "Off Limits to Casuals" . . . "No transients beyond this point." Casuals. Transients. That's them.

All this is necessary. The handful of officers and men responsible for them worked all night. They're tired. They see these men not so much as men but as problems: As persons who have an uncanny knack of getting under foot; who misplace their records or fail to show up at train time.

But because this is Korea, the replacements are full of unanswered questions. How close is the front? Was that artillery we heard last night? How about casualties? Is it as bad as they say on Sniper Ridge? The blood and thunder yarns spun by a handful of old-timers going back for a second hitch don't help. These boys – understandably – are scared. Bad scared. Maybe, some day, Vern Coleman will be able to laugh and tell his kids about it. Soldiers and ex-soldiers are like that. But, wherever he goes and whatever he does, he is not likely soon to forget the hollow despair of his first 24 hours in Korea.

26.5 Death-Bringing Planes and a Special Sort of a Bomb

[*Source: Jim G. Lucas: Star grazing, in:* New York World-Telegram and The Sun *(New York, N.Y.), Vol. 120/No. 136, February 11, 1953, p. 31, cols. 1–2.*]

The night was less than an hour old, but already the North Korean sky was full of our planes. This was the first shift. Ours had been the first ship off the runway. The first shift usually is unrewarding. The enemy hasn't had time to warm up the trucks and locomotives he's kept hidden all day. You usually make your big kills in the later shifts.

The ether crackled as a dozen pilots argued over who would bomb the juicier targets. There were bomb blasts lighting up the enemy's main supply route between Pyongyang and Kaesong. But tonight, our particular plane wasn't out to kill. Ours was a leaflet drop. The bays were loaded, not with bombs, but with pamphlets, books, surrender cards and – most precious of all – news. Free, uncensored news sheets from our side of the Bamboo Curtain.

We had two targets. One was directly below Sariwon, the second between Chinnampo and Pyongyang. We intended dropping two bombs on each. A thousand feet above ground, they'd come open with a muffled pop, spraying the countryside.

Most of the emphasis in our briefing had been on escape. The walls of the closely guarded war room were plastered with posters illustrating how to survive, how to find food, shelter, etc. Briefers spoke of good areas in which to hide, areas where helicopters could land, etc. I was loaded down with survival gear – extra flares, flashlights, rations, compasses. As I listened, it became alarmingly clear to me that none of these people seriously expected me to return. I wished now I'd taken my Boy Scout training more seriously.

"We've got to be careful," Capt. Howard Mix of Battle Creek, Mich., my pilot, said as we walked to chow. "They claim we're not entitled to the protection of the Geneva Convention as POW's."

This was a new angle.

"Why?" I asked.

"It's those shells we use for the leaflets," he said lightly. "They say we use them for germs."

As we roared away, the control tower warned us to stay away from another airfield, 10 miles away. It was under attack. Ahead, a searchlight sent a shaft up into the clouds. "That's the Holy Land," Capt. Howard Dunham of Vallejo, Calif., the navigator, explained. That's what pilots call the Panmunjon neutral area. We climbed past 10,000 feet, noting the cabin temperature down to 21 below zero. There was no cabin heat, and I was dressed like a mummy. "Keep an eye peeled for strange aircraft," Howard Mix nudged me. Whereupon, the United States Air Force acquired its most conscientious sky scanner.

Friendly little stars suddenly became objects of deep suspicion. There was one big star – I think it was Venus – which gave me a particularly hard time. Whenever I turned my head, it invariably shifted position. This I regarded with acute misgivings. But if I tried to stare it down, it dove at me like a runaway jet, guns blazing. I found this even more upsetting.

We headed for Sariwon.

"That's where we would have drawn flak if we were going to get it," Howard Mix said.

"It'll come later tonight," Howard Dunham said. This crew had other assignments before dawn.

After Sariwon, we cut in between Chinnampo and Pyongyang. In the North Korean capital, searchlights were stabbing the sky. By midnight, Howard Mix said, "You can read a newspaper up here." Our bomb bays ground open and we dropped our leaflet bombs. The big doors whined as they closed again. We turned sharply and headed south. Below, around Big and Little Nori a battle raged. An air strike was dropping napalm bombs. Artillery bursts lit the countryside.

Back on the ground, I gratefully peeled off my Buck Rogers suit and looked up at the stars, once again twinkling in friendly fashion. I could even forgive Old Venus.

"How was it?" Howard Mix asked.

"All right," I said, "but I suspect you gave me your sissy run."

"Want to go again?" he asked.

I was on my third cup of coffee and second sandwich when he put his B-26 down the runway to start his second mission.

Related Readings

Acheson, Dean Gooderham: The Korean war, New York 1971.
Caridi, Ronald J.: The Korean war and American politics. The Republican Party as a case study, Philadelphia, Pa., 1968.
Collins, Joseph Lawton: War in peacetime – the history and lessons of Korea, Boston, Mass., 1969.
Gardner, Lloyd C. (Ed.): The Korean War, New York 1972.
George Alexander L.: The Chinese communist army in action. The Korean war and its aftermath, New York 1967.
Heller, Francis H. (Ed.): The Korean War. A 25-year perspective, Lawrence, Kans., 1977.
Jackson, Robert: Air war over Korea, London 1973.
Lo, Clarence Yin-hsieh: The Truman administration's military budgets during the Korean War, Berkeley, Calif., 1978.
Marshall, Samuel Lyman Atwood: The military history of the Korean War, New York 1963.
Montross, Lynn: Cavalry of the sky. The story of U.S. Marine combat helicopters, New York 1954.
Oglobin, Peter: The Korean War, Cambridge, Mass., 1958.
Rees, David: Korea – the limited war, London – New York 1964.
Ridgway, Matthew Bunker: The Korean War – How we met the challenge. How allout Asian war was averted. Why MacArthur was dismissed. Why today's war objectives must be limited, Garden City, N.Y., 1967.
Russ, Martin: The last parallel – a marine's war journal, Westport, Conn., 1957.
Stewart, James T. (Ed.): Airpower – the decisive force in Korea, Princeton, N.J., 1957.
Toner, James Hugh: Candide as constable. The American way of war and peace in Korea, 1950–1953, Ph. D. dissertation, University of Notre Dame, Notre Dame, Ind., 1976.
Vatcher, William Henry: Panmunjom – the story of the Korean military armistice negotiations, New York 1958.
Wu, James Su-tien: Korean War and Sino-American relations, Hwakang 1976.

1954

Harrison E. Salisbury

The New York Times

CHAPTER 27

REPORTS ABOUT THE SOVIET UNION IN 1954

The Post-Stalin Era and Important Events Connected With His Death

    Introductory Notes
27.1 A New Regime and Tactical Political Changes
27.2 The Death of Stalin and an Avoided Disaster
27.3 Beria's Coup and Why It Brought Along His End
27.4 Numerous Intrigues and a Toast to Justice
27.5 The New Junta and How It Works Together
    Related Readings

Introductory Notes

When the war in Korea was finished, the Pulitzer Prize committees again concentrated on the Soviet Union. Harrison E. Salisbury, the New York Times's *Moscow correspondent of long standing, was awarded the prize for International Reporting in 1955 "for his distinguished series of articles, 'Russia Re-Viewed,' based on his six years as a* Times *correspondent in Russia." As in the cases of the awards for Edmund Stevens (1950) and Jim G. Lucas (1954), the decision was based on materials written during several years, although only those reports from the preceding year should actually have been taken into account.*

Harrison Evans Salisbury was born on November 14, 1908, in Minneapolis, Minnesota. While still a college student at the University of Minnesota, he became a reporter for the Minneapolis Journal *from 1928 to 1929. He was a correspondent for the* United Press *in St. Paul, Minnesota, in 1930, the year in which he received his B. A. degree. After graduation he worked for the* UP *in Chicago and Washington, D. C., then moved to its foreign desk in New York City. In 1943 Harrison Salisbury became manager of the London* UP *office; he visited Algiers as well as Cairo and, in January, 1944, also Stalingrad. When, in October 1944, Salisbury became the agency's foreign news editor shortly after his return to the United States, he published a series of articles on his Russian observations which also came out as a book. During his time as foreign news editor of* UP, *Salisbury from 1945 through 1948 covered the founding of the United Nations and U. N. sessions. In January, 1949, he joined the* New York Times *as its Moscow correspondent; the newspaper had had no correspondent in the Russian capital since 1947, when another* Times *correspondent left for a vacation and was refused reentry. Salisbury held his Moscow post until September, 1954, when, at his own request, he was replaced. In his more than five years as "the* Times *man" in the Soviet Union, Salisbury wrote several series of widely read and frequently controversial dispatches. In the summer of 1954 Salisbury returned to New York to accept an assignment on the* Times *city staff. His series of articles, 'Russia Re-viewed', was published in the* New York Times *in September and October, 1954, and was expanded to a book, 'An American in Russia', published in 1955.*

The following texts by Harrison Evans Salisbury, copyright 1954, are reprinted by kind permission of The New York Times, *Inc., New York, N. Y.*

27.1 A New Regime and Tactical Political Changes

[*Source: Harrison E. Salisbury: Under new management, Soviet tactics change, in:* The New York Times, *International Edition (New York/Amsterdam), Vol. CIV/No. 35,302, September 19, 1954, p. 1, cols. 4–5; p. 3, cols. 2–7.*]

The death of Joseph Stalin has given Russia a new regime with a new way of doing business that has already achieved notable successes at home and abroad.

Let's agree firmly and quickly that the ultimate, long-term objectives of the Soviet Union remain the same under the present administration as they did under Stalin and Lenin. And let it not be thought from what is reported here that an era of sweetness and light has suddenly descended upon Communist Russia. It has not. In the past year this correspondent has seen in the far-flung reaches of Russia first-hand evidence of the horrors of life in the world's greatest police state.

Those horrors are shocking and important. But they are not new. What is new and what is immediately important, and likely to be more so as time goes by, is that Russia has passed into the hands of a group of men who are displaying striking flexibility and adaptability in their handling of domestic and foreign problems. The new rulers of Russia are demonstrating effective and even attractive approaches to many of the problems of the day. They are drawing strength from a frank facing up to some harsh and unpleasant realities of the Stalin epoch. At many points they have broken sharply, dramatically and decisively with the sterile and rigid precepts of Stalin's era. "When you talk to these new men," a Western diplomat reports, "they speak so pleasantly, so apparently openly and with so much common sense that you must constantly remind yourself whom it is you are talking with. That's why, in a way, they are more dangerous than Stalin."

By abandoning Stalin's bludgeon for more graceful tactics, Russia's new leaders have managed to bring the Soviet Union a considerable distance out of the blind alley into which Stalin's stubborn and unchanging policies had led it. Undoubtedly, possession of the hydrogen and atomic fission bombs, a fine fleet of jet aircraft, including continental bombers, and reasoned knowledge of the ability of Russian scientists and Russian industry to match paces with the United States, have given the new men of Moscow a large measure of confidence. On this foundation the present Government has demonstrated a remarkable mobility and freedom of maneuver that have produced a series of successes, at home and abroad. More seem likely to follow.

This situation obviously confronts the United States with new problems and new dangers. Many thoughtful diplomats in Moscow doubt, that the United States has fully taken into account the nature of the changes that have followed Stalin's death. They believe that American policy is suffering severely from a failure or inability to adjust realistically to Moscow's "new look," or even to acknowledge that the "new look" exists.

In this connection it might be well to note that the broad essentials on which this and subsequent dispatches in this series are founded have been faithfully reported to Washington by United States diplomatic observers on the scene in Moscow. This correspondent believes that his conclusions for the most part do not differ in fundamentals from those that the State Department has received from its own experts.

The truth is that observers in Moscow in the past year and a half have watched the launching of the Soviet system into a new era, just as sharply distinguished from its Stalinist predecessor as Lenin's famous N. E. P., or "New Economic Policy," differed from his policy of "war communism." The Stalin system with its peculiarly Florentine qualities of secrecy, duplicity, terror and pettifogging readings of the Marxist gospel did not survive its founder's death. Nor did the quasi-religious iconostasy, or reverential display of the portraits in the fashion of Orthodox church icons.

Not that the secret police or the labor camps have vanished. They persist as a horrible stain on the face of the Russian soil and an indictment of the Russian conscience. Nor can it be said that the hands of Russia's new rulers are free from the tinge of blood. They struck down Lavrenti P. Beria ruthlessly. And the precise manner of Stalin's own death is an open question. But, generally speaking, the successor regime has broken with many of Stalin's ways. In method, in conduct and in specific policies it has adopted a radical "new look," the essence of which is moderation of the worst Stalin excesses at home and caution abroad.

Lenin defined his N. E. P. as a temporary tactic designed to enable the Revolution to consolidate its forces for future advances. He said the ultimate goal remained unchanged. Today there is no reason to suppose that Russia's present leaders disagree with him. But the present group has a different way of conducting its business and, so far, it is proving to be a successful way. Methods that the United States found appropriate in dealing with the Stalin regime often prove to be duds or even boomerangs in the new situation. To employ a football analogy Russia is still trying to win the ball game. But her new coaches have substituted a tricky forward pass offensive for Stalin's traditional pile-driving line play. Russia's objective – to win the world ball game – hasn't changed but her style has and if we go on playing Russia for a drive through tackle when she has shifted to end zone passes we shouldn't be surprised to see her rack up some long gains down field.

The new Soviet regime appears to have achieved a striking degree of internal stability with the disposal of Beria. The new chiefs may fall to quarreling tomorrow, but so far as available evidence goes that does not seem likely. To persons who have wachted the progress of events in Moscow in recent months, speculation over "a struggle for power" between Premier Georgi M. Malenkov and Nikita S. Khrushchev, First Secretary of the Central Committee of the Communist party, seems to be wishful thinking and dangerously wishful thinking, since it suggests tensions and weaknesses that do not appear actually to exist.

The new Russian era has the following characteristics:

It is not a one-man dictatorship. Instead, it represents rule by a group, or "junta," of political leaders who have the active support of the chiefs of the Soviet Army. In this junta Premier Malenkov is first, but only "first among equals." "Collective leadership" is no mere catchword. These men are seriously trying to make it work.

"Reformism" in domestic affairs, a tendency to subordinate ideology to common sense, an effort to put some moral content back into trite party shibboleths, tentative efforts toward certain greater freedoms and, particularly in Moscow, a big increase in consumer goods and services.

Maintenance of the political police system and the labor camps, but subordination of police to civil power, curtailment of police policy-making and some amelioration of the worst police abuses.

Continuance of Stalin's emphasis on expansion of heavy industry and further development of advanced Soviet military striking force as epitomized by the atomic and hydrogen bombs and the fine Soviet jet aircraft.

The first major effort to repair the damage to agriculture inflicted by the Revolution, Stalin's forced collectivization program and World War II. Peasant profit motives are being revived. And a vast new network of state farms, highly mechanized and staffed with vigorous young people, is being set up on new lands.

A foreign policy generally intended to reduce the possibility of Soviet military involvement, to ease the severe overextension of Soviet military commitments insisted upon by Stalin, to improve relations with America's principal allies, Britain and France, and, if possible, achievement of some kind of modus vivendi.

An effort to convince the world at large and the Russian people themselves that the Soviet union is now ruled by a group of "reasonable men" with tangible standards of conduct in foreign as well as domestic affairs.

By no means the least interesting result of Russia's new course is that, in its initial phases, it seems to have had more effect upon Soviet relations in Western Europe than upon the relations of Soviet citizens to their new rulers.

Perhaps the Russians are more skeptical. True, they crowd into the big new G. U. M. department store in Red Square to buy the Government's new aluminum saucepans and cotton textiles. Peasants are rapidly multiplying their home-owned pigs, cows and chickens to profit by the new Government deal. Writers have even begun to experiment with new forms and musicians are talking, at least, about Stalin's anathema – jazz. But with all this there is a kind of Missouri show-me attitude and even an apathy toward the Government's experimentation with greater freedom.

Ordinary Russians are not rushing to make friends with foreigners, although they may talk a little more easily on trains and in theater lobbies. Wait-and-see seems to predominate. After twenty-five years of Stalin terror, it is going to take some time to convince Russians that it is safe to take the new Government at its word.

The apathy is almost exactly the kind that first greeted the reforms of Czar Alexander II, who came to the throne in 1855 after the death of the tyrannical Nicholas I and brought an end to serfdom. Cowed by twenty-five years of oppression by Nicholas, the Russian public of the mid-nineteenth century was supine in its acceptance of Alexander's reforms. Much the same is true today – and for the same reason.

On the other hand, diplomats in Moscow, and elsewhere, who are in contact with the Russians, as well as the rising number of visitors to Russia, both Soviet-invited and self-invited, are increasingly impressed with the "new look." And, unpleasant as it must be for United States policy makers, the plain truth is that the "new look" has begun to pay off internationally. The new Soviet regime, under the expert guidance of Foreign Minister Vyacheslav M. Molotov, has achieved a series of striking successes.

Rightly or wrongly, the convening of the Berlin and Geneva conferences, the settlements in Korea and Indochina and the final defeat of the European Defense Community are regarded by the United States' best friends in Europe as feathers for the cap of Mr. Molotov – feathers plucked from the ruffled tail of the American eagle. And the new regime is working industriously to create an atmosphere that will make possible more successes.

A whole series of harassing abuses and practices designed to make life unpleasant for foreigners in Moscow has been eliminated. Many bureaucratic stupidities, including a ridi-

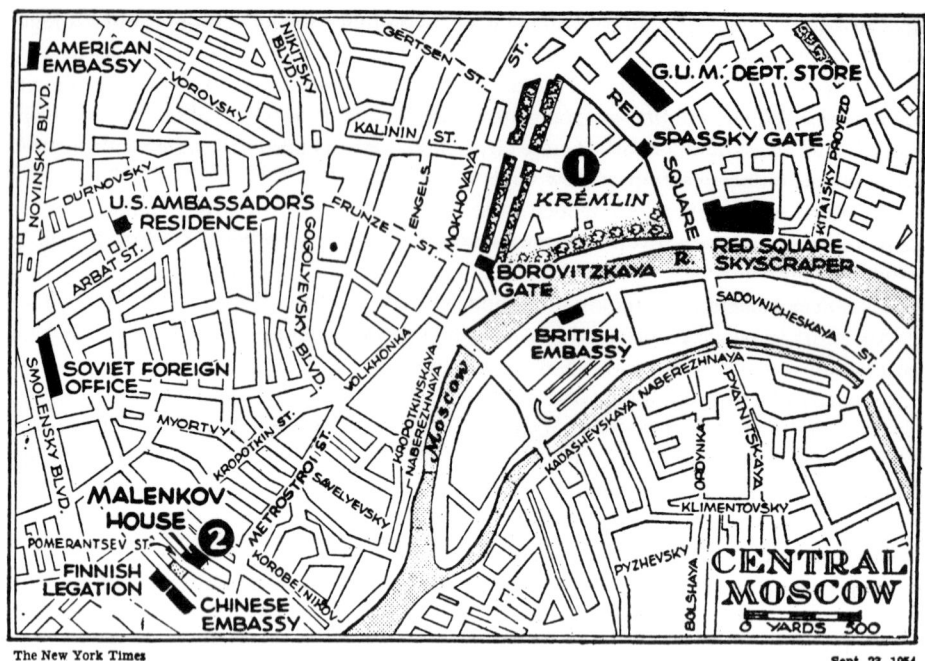

The New York Times   Sept. 23, 1954
NEW DEAL: The Kremlin (1), which served Stalin as living quarters, is being reopened to the public. Premier Georgi M. Malenkov now resides on Pomerantsev Street (2).

[Source: *The New York Times* (New York/Amsterdam), International Edition, Vol. CIV/No. 35, 306, September 23, 1954, p. 3, cols. 3–5.]

culous ruble exchange rate, remain. But major restrictions have been lifted on travel. Open surveillance has been notably reduced. Diplomatic contacts have become courteous and often warm. The first steps toward wider social intercourse between Russian and foreign diplomats have been taken. Capricious arrest and disappearances of Russian servants and employes has virtually ceased and hundreds, if not thousands, of foreign nationals, whose basic crime was merely that they were foreign, have been released from arbitrary imprisonment. All this has cost Moscow nothing – and brought substantial returns.

It has been said often enough that Russia deserves no special credit for stopping doing many things that no decent or civilized country should ever have done in the first place. Nonetheless, the new Government, by methodically seeking to improve the morals of its administrative behavior, has made a decided impression. The fact that for many years Russia automatically turned down almost every visa application made to it is forgotten when her new rulers liberalize the visa policy. And when, at the very time Russia begins to admit a few token groups of American students, the United States refuses visas to some Soviet students because they are Communists, Pravda does not have to raise a cry about an American "iron curtain." The British and French make the point themselves without any Soviet prompting.

As to why Stalin's successors have adopted this new approach, many explanations have been advanced. One thing, of course, is basic. Stalin ruled Russia single-handed for more than twenty-five years. The system he created was an image of his own personality traits – Georgian suspicions, a mountaineer's narrow hatreds, the bourgeois dreams of a poor shoemaker's son, the midnight habits of a proscribed revolutionary, the wolf-like morals of a hunted bank robber. Stalin's Russia came to resemble Stalin almost more than it did Russia. Both within Russia and without, the identification of man, method and regime became almost complete.

But Russia's new rulers are not a group of little Stalins, even though they worked for the master for years and even though they are of almost identical height – about five feet four inches, just an inch shorter than the old Generalissimo. They are, in fact, a highly interesting and diverse group of men with individual and differing personalities, which they have been at some pains to exhibit to foreigners in recent months. But perhaps most important of all is the fact that they are a group and that they are practicing group government. Premier Malenkov, his pictures to the contrary, is full of old-fashioned grace and courtesy. Mr. Khrushchev is hail-fellow-well-met. Mr. Molotov is quiet, patient and reasonable. Lazar M. Kaganovich likes his liquor. Marshal Nikolai A. Bulganin is handsome and witty. And Anastas I. Mikoyan is probably the sharpest and cleverest of all.

Since they are all Communists, it can be assumed that all of them wish, eventually, to arrive at the same goal as did Stalin. But not necessarily by the same route or with the same methods. The firmness by which they are sticking to group principles is one example of this. In fact, the vigor with which this group has repudiated some of the most striking symbols of Stalin and his era; the ruthlessness with which they have cut Stalin's image down to life-size or even smaller; the hardly concealed contempt they have shown for many of Stalin's idols – these suggest that few people hated Stalin more deeply and thoroughly than his own right-hand men.

That Russia's new rulers are alive today well may be thanks only to the fortuitous death of the old Generalissimo. Stalin had not been in his grave ten days before his name disappeared from Pravda. Previously it often was mentioned 125 times or more on one front page alone. Quotations from the master disappeared as well, and only recently have they crept back, but only as a pale second to Lenin.

Some of the few old Bolsheviks who had survived Stalin's purges of the Nineteen Thirties were ostentatiously resurrected from the obscurity that, in many cases, had been the chief means of their survival, and presented with medals. For many others, long since dead in Siberia, the Far North and Central Asia, the change came too late. But it was a gesture whose significance few Russians failed to note.

Since the Kremlin had become synonymous with Stalin and his terror and secrecy, the new Government sought to erase such an impression and dissociate itself from it. The leaders moved their residences away from its grim walls and now they say that soon they will give it up as a seat of government as well, and reopen the great iron gates to tourists and ordinary passers by as in Czarist times. Stalin had let the curious, yet lovely, turrets and bulbs of St. Basil's Cathedral in Red Square deteriorate. The New Government ordered them gilded with real gold and painted in brilliant organe, vermilion, purple, crimson, yellow, green and blue, the like of which has not been seen in Russia in modern times. And, as a parallel move, the pride of Stalin's stuffy, baroque architectural taste, the grandiose forty-four-story skyscraper he had started to build in the lower reaches of Red Square, and by which he would have placed the mark of his personality upon this historic place by destroying the medieval architectural affinity of the Kremlin and St. Basil's, has been abandoned and will not be completed.

Stalin's bad luck in his attempt to perpetuate the memory of his regime with a building of dramatic height has an almost Babel-like quality. His first effort in the late Nineteen Thirties was to construct a "Palace of Soviets," which would have been the world's tallest building, taller than the Empire State. His wreckers tore down the Church of the Saviour, Moscow's most impressive cathedral, to provide a site for the new structure. But World War II broke out before the steelwork had risen more then three stories. It was never completed. The steel was ripped out and sent to the plants for scrap to make tanks, and the huge vacant lot remains today as an impressive testimonial to Stalin's vanity. Now the same fate has overtaken his postwar effort to overshadow Red Square with another giant building. Red Square itself has been turned back to the people, whom Stalin would never permit freely to stroll there. And the great G. U. M. department store has been reopened along one side of the Square in violation of Stalin's edict that "trade" and crowds of shoppers did not befit the dignity of the scene on which he gazed from his Kremlin windows.

No Stalin prizes for literature, science and the arts – Russia's equivalent of the Nobel and Pulitzer awards – were made in 1953. And if this year they are quietly resumed, it will surprise no one if Stalin's name no longer accompanies them. Stalin's industrial pride was the great Stalin Auto Works in Moscow, which turned out the enormous Zis limousines in which the dictator always rode. Production of the Zis limousine has been brought to a halt except for a few custom-made machines used for ambulances. The assembly line that used to make Stalin's favorite car now turns out bicycles – 1,200 a day – for the multitudes.

Under Stalin, every factory manager, every first, second and third-string bureaucrat sat up half the night, drowsing at his desk "in case the Kremlin calls." For Stalin was a night worker and the Harun al-Rashid of the telephone, ranging far and wide across his empire. Siberia was the reward of the executive who did not lift the receiver when the Kremlin called. When, a year ago, the new Government ordered all offices on a 9-to-6 schedule and forbade night work, every bureaucrat, every party worker in the country knew that the Stalin era had really ended.

Ostentatiously, clumsily and self-consciously, the new rulers are trying to persuade Russia's intellectuals to discuss and disagree on questions of art and science. The effort has been marked by some notable regressions, particularly in the field of literature. But progress has been made, especially in the sciences, where much damage was done by Stalin in his later years. The biological sciences had suffered particularly and the key field of nuclear physics was threatened.

A notable "pilot" project in this cause has revolved around Prof. Trofim D. Lysenko, the unorthodox Soviet biologist whom Stalin had set up as the Marxian high priest of science, the man who made or broke the reputation of his scientific betters, the man whose word could and did cost scientists their jobs and even send them off to the East. In an effort to demonstrate that the new policy of open discussion is not a mere matter of lip service, Professor Lysenko's sharpest scientific critics have been encouraged to open fire upon him with a full-scale and well-documented attack on the falsity of his theories and upon his dictatorial personal conduct. At the same time to demonstrate that the Government does not wish merely to substitute one "czar of science" for another, Professor Lysenko has been given full freedom to reply to his critics (such as he never permitted during his reign) and the Government has gone out of its way to lend encouragement to Professor Lysenko's perfectly sound activities in the field of practical agriculture.

The object lesson inherent in this Lysenko discussion is supposed to be that it is possible to argue questions out, vigorously and even acrimoniously, without, in the end, sending the losing side to Siberia.

It must, however, be reported that, while seeking to assuage fears of Siberia, the new regime has not abolished Siberia and the police reign it symbolizes. In many thousands of miles of traveling through the Soviet North, Far East and Central Asia – from one end of Siberia to another – this correspondent in the last twelve months time and again encountered the terrible Soviet prison labor system. It is sufficient for the moment to say that few of the horrors of the M. V. D. (Ministry of Internal Affairs), of which we have heard have been exaggerated, although perhaps the most shocking fact is the similarity of life and living conditions of prison and slave labor and so-called free labor working in the blighted areas of the east and north, where the M. V. D. is supreme. In the West, people often speculate over the possibility of internal risings and anti-regime troubles in Russia. It is assumed that the resentment and bitterness that must be felt by so many millions of victims of Soviet police brutality must, somehow, be translated into action.

After crisscrossing the areas in which most of these embittered people are forced to reside, this correspondent has found small grounds to believe that any important results may be expected in this direction. Only rarely does one encounter an individual whose spirit and energy have sufficiently survived the hardships and ordeals to which he has been subjected so that he manages to avoid the abyss of apathy and resignation that is the usual result of laborcamp life or forced residence in the East. The ordinary Russian, sent to the East, turns to vodka rather than thoughts of revolution or revenge, and with Slav fatalism sinks quietly and dully into the gray morass of M. V. D.-land.

But, even in this most horrible excrescence of the Soviet system, the new rulers of Russia are seeking to turn over a new leaf. They have released a considerable number of persons from the camps. They are investigating the matter of freeing some more and, in some places at least, they have actually improved the conditions of life of the prisoners.

There is no sign, however, that the new regime has the slightest intention of abolishing the camps or the police system in general. Amelioration is the key word, just as it is in so many other areas, such as censorship and facilities for foreign correspondents. The censorship, also, has been eased. But not to the point of permitting any discussion of prison camps or the M. V. D.

27.2 The Death of Stalin and an Avoided Disaster

[*Source: Harrison E. Salisbury: Was Stalin put to death to avert blood purge?, in:* The New York Times, *International Edition (New York/Amsterdam), Vol. CIV/No. 35,303, September 20, 1954, p. 1, cols. 6–7; p. 3, cols. 2–7.*]

It is by no means impossible that Stalin was murdered on or about March 5, 1953, by the group of his close associates who now run Russia. There is, naturally, virtually no way of proving this, since all the final events in Stalin's strange life are shrouded in mystery. However, many people in Moscow believe it is possible that the old dictator was "assisted" in his exit from mortal life.

There is considerable circumstantial evidence to support this belief. While it is not possible to prove that murder occurred, it seems plain to one who watched the events in Moscow that a powerful incentive to murder existed. This incentive was lodged in the increasingly plain signs that something akin to dementia was taking hold of Stalin and that the country stood on the brink of a reign of terror beside which that of the Nineteen Thirties would have seemed trivial. What appeared to be brewing inside the secret walls of the Kremlin was a new massacre of the Streltzi – a blood purge of the men standing closest to Stalin, similar to that in which Peter the Great struck off with his own hand the heads of the men who had been his firmest supporters. Or like the mad blood orgies of Ivan the Terrible.

There is still to be seen at Zagorsk, an ancient monastery forty miles outside Moscow, a great fat book of parchment pages, about the size of an oldfashioned family Bible. On these pages were written down at the orders of Ivan the names of all the men he had ordered executed – the hundreds of burghers of old Novgorod, the chiefs of the dread Oprichnina and all the rest. The bulging book is only a partial list. No such book lists the victims of Stalin's purges. Even the records of the M. V. D. are far from complete. Yet there is strong reason for believing that the bloodshed of the Thirties would have been eclipsed by the slaughter that was being prepared in the weeks before the old dictator met his death.

All this does not mean that Stalin did not meet a natural end. He was 73 years old. He had suffered from a heart ailment for several years. There are fairly reliable indications that he had had at least one slight stroke in recent years. However, he had consistently given the impression of robust health and clarity of mind to foreigners whom he received. This was true even within three weeks of Stalin's death. In the month before he died, Stalin received three foreigners – Leopoldo Bravo, Argentine Ambassador in Moscow; K. P. R. Menon, Indian Ambassador in Moscow, and Dr. Kitchlu, an Indian active in the "peace movement," who had been invited to Moscow.

Señor Bravo saw Stalin on Feb. 7 and the two Indians saw him Feb. 17. Each of them commented on his apparent good health. The only clue possibly bearing on the state of Stalin's mind was noted by Mr. Menon. Stalin doodled on a pad of paper throughout the interview, an old habit of his. Mr. Menon noticed that he was drawing wolves – one wolf after another. And Stalin apparently had wolves on his mind because presently he was saying that Russian peasants knew how to deal with wolves – they shot them and exterminated them. And, added Stalin, the wolves know this and act accordingly. Mr. Menon recalls being slightly puzzled by this reference to wolves. He was not sure whether it was a reference to capitalist "wolves" of America or an olbique criticism of the Indian doctrine of nonresistance.

It might, however, have been a tiny visible evidence of a mind that, behind a facade of seeming brightness and normality, was only too preoccupied with the subject of "eliminating wolves." However, except for this somewhat disconcerting reference, the testimony of Stalin's three foreign visitors is unanimous. He seemed fit and healthy.

Even so, a cerebral hemorrhage would not have been uncommon for a man of his type and age and strenuous life. On the other hand, if Stalin just happened to be struck down by a ruptured artery in his brain on March 2, it must be recorded as one of the most fortuitous occurrences in history. It saved the lives of some thousands of Russians and, in particular, it almost certainly spared the lives of the little group of men who stood closest to Stalin.

To understand the witches' brew that had been stirred up in Moscow and something of the atmosphere of the immediate weeks before Stalin's death, it is necessary to turn back a few pages in the extraordinarily complex and terrifying sequence of events that led up to the end of that thirty-year period in Russian history that, even in his lifetime, began to be known as the "Stalin epoch." The true start of the story goes back a long way – to the Eighteen Seventies when a small boy named Joseph Djugashvili was beginning his life in the poverty-stricken village of Gori, back in the remote but history-laden mountains of Georgia. Joseph's father was a shoemaker who drank too much. His mother was a handsome, intelligent woman who bequeathed to her son pride, stubbornness and determination to rise in the world. Joseph's mother sent him to the ecclesiastical seminary. He was a bright student, or so the old Patriarch of the Georgian Church told me three years ago. It was probably Georgian nationalism and resentment against the Great Russians that turned Joseph's thoughts to revolutionary channels. Czarist police and exile to Siberia may have helped to make him remorseless and bitter. He probably was suspicious by nature. Othello is a favorite Georgian play because the motives of suspicion and jealousy are so close to Georgian hearts.

The boy Djugashvili became the revolutionary Stalin and, eventually, the ruler of all Russia. He won Russia by ruthless use of the most sinister weapons and he maintained his hold in the same fashion. Now rich in years but, apparently, little softened in character he was approaching what should have been the golden years of retirement and contemplation. But fate had other events in store. The immediate story opens with the calling of the Nineteenth Congress of the Communist party, summoned to assemble in Moscow in October, 1952.

For thirteen years there had been no congress of the party, although in earlier days such meetings had been held almost every year. The summoning of this long-delayed session as Stalin was approaching his seventy-third birthday was expected to provide a strong clue to the party succession. Although Stalin had given indication enough that, as with many elderly men, the thought of death was almost too repugnant for mention in his presence (the enormous and unusual concentration of Soviet medical work in the field of longevity and the frequent press articles about persons in the Soviet Union who lived to the age of 120 and even 140 were no accident) it was generally felt that he would not, at long last, have summoned the party to meet if he did not propose to give it a clear line as to whom he wished to inherit his mantle.

But nothing of the kind happened. No successor emerged, no crown prince, no favorite son. If it had seemed for a short time that the great roles at the party congress were to go to

Georgi M. Malenkov and Nikita S. Khrushchev, such ideas were quickly dispelled. The great role, the only important one at the congress, was played by Stalin himself. In fact, he transformed the actual congress into a mere claque by issuing a "masterwork," the new Stalin version of economics, a kind of Stalinesque gloss on Karl Marx's "Das Kapital," a few days before the congress met. After this act all the congress had to do was to praise Stalin's new economic principles and quote from them extensively. It reduced the speeches of Mr. Malenkov and Mr. Khrushchev to the customary level of party hackwork and Stalin displayed his own contempt for the body he had called to Moscow by issuing his declaration in the form of a pamphlet before the congress men and limiting his congress speech to a few rambling remarks about the role of the foreign Communist parties.

Moreover, the personnel changes ratified by the party congress were designed to conceal and confuse the lines of succession rather than clarify them. For the twelve-member Politburo, which at least had the virtue of being a compact and recognizable body of leaders, there was substituted an amorphous "presidium" with twenty-five full members and eleven alternates, so big a body that it obviously could play no role in government. But it was an excellent device for diffusing the leadership picture.

The same thing was done with the party secretariat, which had always been a tight little group and was, in fact, the means that Stalin himself had utilized to climb to supreme power. In recent years the secretariat had, in so far as Stalin ever let any strings out of his own fingers, come more and more under the day-to-day direction and operation of Mr. Malenkov. Now the secretariat was suddenly expanded to a total of ten members, headed by Stalin. It included Mr. Malenkov and Mr. Khrushchev, but there were so many new and comparatively unknown secretaries that it was difficult to visualize how such a body could function.

In fact, the net effect of the party congress and the personnel changes was to give the impression that someone was deliberately shuffling the cards in such a way that only he would know who was to come out on top. And the person who shuffled the deck, of course, was Stalin. The question was: Why the mystification and whom was he fooling? Within a few weeks of the close of the congress there occurred two curious events, difficult to interpret at the time, but, as it happened, portents of what the future held in store.

The first was the way in which the pictures of Government leaders were displayed in Moscow in the days of the annual November Seventh holiday. These displays of portraits were always watched with interest, by foreigners and Russians alike, as a barometer of changes in political fortunes. It was the absence of Nikolai Voznesensky's portrait from such a display in March, 1949, that gave the first hint that he had lost his job as top state planner. Now, when the portraits went up on the Moskva Hotel, the Maly Theatre, the Central Telegraph Office and other prominent buildings in the center of town, a significant change was observed. Lavrenti P. Beria, who had long occupied the No. 4 spot, below Stalin, Mr. Molotov and Mr. Malenkov, suddenly dropped to position No. 6. Marshals Klimentiy E. Voroshilov and Nikolai A. Bulganin, the two military members of the top hierarchy, moved up ahead of the Secret Police chief.

At the big Bolshoi Theatre party meeting on the eve of the Nov. 7 holiday, and the next day on the podium of the mausoleum in Red Square, Beria was closely watched. But no change in his demeanor was observed. As was his custom in late years, he appeared the most jovial member of the top leadership, talking and joking and, most of the time, directing his conversation to Mr. Malenkov. However, the fact that he had slipped to No. 6 could not be ignored. It immediately recalled a priviously unexplained event. Six months before there had been a purge in Beria's private satrapy, the Georgian party and Government. Henchmen whom he had installed when he came to Moscow in 1938 to take over the secret police job and bring the great purges of the Thirties to an end were ousted and new men were installed. Although Beria himself went to Tiflis and apparently supervised the housecleaning, and although the new Georgian party leaders paid him tributes, the suspicion was inescapable that strong tides were running against him.

Before the full significance of these events could be assessed another and still more curious thing happened. A newspaper in Kiev, capital of the Ukraine, announced suddenly that a special military court had sentenced three men to death by shooting and had ordered long prison sentences for a group of others on charges of "counter-revolutionary wrecking." Such mouth-filling charges are only too common in Russia. But the Kiev case was in some ways unique. The men who were executed were not traitors in the ordinary or even in the farfetched Russian sense. They were, as far as the charges went, a group of executives in the Kiev retail and wholesale trade networks who apparently had engaged in fairly wide-scale black marketing, theft and other forms of commercial skulduggery.

It was difficult to see that their activities, however reprehensible, constituted any threat to the security of the state. Moreover, there were some strange circumstances about the case. The Russian criminal code makes no provision for military trial of persons accused of the type of commercial crime involved in this case. The code makes no provision for death sentences for persons found guilty of such crimes. Most of the persons involved in the case appeared, from their names, to be of Jewish extraction. While for the moment this was to be a single unlovely blossom, within six weeks it was possible to see more clearly what it signified.

At the time it could only be noted that the victims were mostly Jewish (in the Ukraine, where anti-Semitism ignites most easily); they were fairly prominent members of trading organizations directed by Poliburo Member Anastas I. Mikoyan; they were fairly prominent in a party organization still largely dominated by Mr. Khrushchev, and their prosecution appeared to have been taken out of the hands of Police Chef Beria and vested in an unusual, temporary, military body.

It seemed apparent that strong and unpleasant forces were on the move in Russia. But, so far, like the cards of the party congress, the pattern was too mixed for intelligent interpretation. And by this time (in fact, before the whole strange phantasmagoria began to unfold) one of the few foreigners capable of intelligent assessment of such phenomena, the then United States Ambassador George F. Kennan, had been declared persona non grata and barred from a ringside observation post in Moscow. In December the wheel was given another confusing spin. Just before Christmas, Pravda voiced a sudden and unexplained demand for a new round of "mea culpas" from persons prominent in the party, particularly in the fields of ideology and economics. These men had been so incautious nearly five years before as to praise a study of Russia's economy during World War II that was issued by Voznesensky not long before his downfall as chief party planner.

Since the views for which apologies were now demanded had been on public record during the entire period, the motivation behind Pravda's call was hard to perceive. It was evident, however, that someone, in the typical Florentine fashion of Kremlin politics, had set in motion a curious weapon that was bound to do considerable damage to reputations in high party positions, persons concentrating on organization, such as Mr. Malenkov, and upon economy, such as Lazar M. Kaganovich.

This was followed almost immediately by the most deadly and sinister event to occur in Russia, in all probability, since Stalin had murdered his way to power – the announcement on Jan. 13 of the arrest of a group of nine doctors, six of them Jews, who were charged with having plotted against the lives of a group of members of the Soviet Government, including several high military chieftains. The group was said to have connections, through Zionist organizations, with British and American intelligence and to have carried out its operations through the slackness of the Soviet security organs.

It was immediately apparent that this was to be not a mere flash in the pan, but the basic scenario of a desperate and deadly plot that, had it not been halted in the early stages of its unfolding by the death of Stalin, could well have blossomed into a purge more deadly than that of the Thirties and a blood bath more terrible than any of Ivan's, 350 years ago. It was now only too plain that what had gone before – the confusing party congress and the rest – was only by way of setting the stage for this new and more horrible drama. It was designed to create an atmosphere of uncertainty and bewilderment in which terror could strike without end. There were two obvious and immediate targets of this plot – Beria, as chief of security, and the Jews.

It was equally obvious that, regardless of who had concocted the precise ingredients of this poisonous broth, its creator, sponsor and guiding genius could only be one man, Stalin himself. No such plan could have been drawn without his authority. No such announcement could have been made except with his approval. Moreover, the fatal hallmarks of Stalin's hand, the same touches that marked the purges by which he rose to power, were only too plain. As one cynical American said: "The old man has reached for that bottle again – look out!" It was quickly obvious that there was no intention to limit the focus of the purge to Beria (himself half Jewish) and Jews in general.

Like the black plague, the germs of the new purge raced through the Soviet body politic. Each fresh batch of provincial newspapers reported new scandals, new exposures, new arrests. Almost invariably the first victims were Jews, in trading organizations, in professional posts, doctors, lawyers, writers, actors. Any Jew was a fair target.

The heaviest run of cases was in the Ukraine – in Mr. Khrushchev's territory. And quickly the fire turned from the Jews to the party organizations that had permitted such "scandals." The target broadened. Mr. Khrushchev was involved because his party lieutenants were being attacked. Beria was involved from the start because of his security responsibilities, Mr. Mikoyan because of his trading organizations, Mr. Malenkov because his party organizations in one city after another were implicated. Most deeply and dangerously involved of all was that dry and pedantic little man who had survived so much before, Vyacheslav M. Molotov. For, in the central press itself, reports began to filter through of arrests and confessions of persons closely connected with the Foreign Office; persons who worked in the Foreign Office; persons once connected with foreign correspondents.

Even the military were not entirely immune although generally it could be said that, of all the branches of Soviet power, the military seemed least affected. It had, after all, been military men who were the supposed targets of the "Jewish doctors." And it was a military court that had set the ball rolling in Kiev. If one wanted to make a pattern, one could suggest that the military were cast in the role of "victims" of the plot and the "saviors" of the country as well. But a horrible thought arose. In the Thirties every facet of Soviet life was racked by this disease. Then, finally, the madness was brought to a climactic end with a grand purge of all the chief generals of the country. It is not likely that any general with a memory as long as the hair on his shaved head could have felt much confidence about his fate once this horrible plague began to strike.

The terror steadily deepened in Moscow. People began to go about with furtive and downcast faces. Where would it stop this time? Was there no end of the blood sacrifice that Stalin demanded? Rumors circulated. Nobody knew at the time which ones were true and which were false. There had been arrests in Tass, the news agency. The head of Tass, Nikolai Palgunov, a man known for years to be very close to Mr. Molotov, had vanished . . . Mme. Molotov had disappeared . . . Banished to Siberia . . . Arrests in Moscow University . . . Arrests in the Academy of Sciences . . . More Jews . . . Protectors of Jews . . . Arrests in the Central Committee . . . The Jewish jazz band leader Utesov had been arrested . . . Mekhlis, Jewish security administrator, who had been ill for several years, died. Kaganovich (a Jew) led the funeral procession . . . Window dressing, Moscow said . . . By the middle of February there was not a man in that little group commonly referred to as the Politburo who could not feel the hot breath of the purge on his neck. Perhaps he would survive, but only Stalin knew.

As never before, Stalin now had an iron hold on the party and on the succession, for he had made it plain to every man in the Kremlin that few would survive this purge, and only those whom Stalin spared. Every man in the inner circle was threatened – except Stalin. Molotov . . . Malenkov . . . Beria . . . Voroshilov . . . Bulganin . . . Khrushchev . . . Kaganovich . . . Mikoyan . . . There wasn't a safe name on the list. Over the whole scene could be sensed the ghost-like, sinister presence of the man who was so seldom mentioned and so seldom seen – Stalin's chef de cabinet, the silent, inscrutable General Poskrebyshev – the man who vanished without a trace with the death of his chief.

Is it possible that these powerful and able Soviet leaders, together with their colleagues in the Army, stood idly by and took no step to halt this creeping terror that was certain to destroy almost all of them before it finished? It is possible, certainly, since no one was able to halt the terror of the Thirties until it had eliminated most of the prominent leaders of the Bolshevik party. But there was a difference this time. The plot was not aimed at men with whom Stalin had ideological or leadership quarrels. It was aimed at his own trusted and respected lieutenants. A person who has at least second-hand knowledge of some of these events has said frankly that the story of the Nineteenth Party Congress and the events that culminated in Stalin's death will never be written, for good and sufficient reasons.

In any event, it was apparent to all in Moscow in February that great and sinister events were in the making. This correspondent quietly made preparations for covering big news. I did not know what it would be, but I was certain it was coming. I arranged with my colleagues for an allnight watch at the telegraph office. I arranged to get Pravda and Izvestia at the publishing houses and I sought to persuade New York of the necessity for setting up special telephone dictation circuits to London for transmitting the big news. But, so heavy was the Moscow censorship, so drastic were the cuts in any dispatches that sought to convey the true atmosphere of events in the Russian capital, that even on the very day Stalin's illness was announced I received a telegram from New York questioning the need for a telephone circuit to London.

Stalin's death brought all this and much more to an end. To repeat – if Stalin died a natural death in March, 1953, it was the luckiest thing that ever happened for every man who was close to him. And probably for Russia as well.

27.3   Beria's Coup and Why It Brought Along His End

[*Source: Harrison E. Salisbury: Beria's troops held Moscow, but he hesitated and lost, in:* The New York Times, *International Edition (New York/Amsterdam), Vol. CIV/No. 35,304, September 21, 1954, p. 1, cols. 5–6; p. 3, cols. 2–6.*]

For about seventy-eight hours, in March of last year, Lavrenti Pavlovich Beria held Russia in the hollow of his pudgy hand. He was supreme. There was no one who could challenge him – not Malenkov, not Khrushchev, not Molotov, not the Army. At any moment within those fateful hours, Beria might have proclaimed himself dictator, all-supreme ruler of Russia, heir of Stalin.

He did not do so, and in that failure to act he sealed his own fate. The life that came to an end last Christmas Eve, probably in the blood-stained cellars of the Lubyanka Prison, was doomed from that moment when Beria did not act.

The story of the March days of 1953, just before and just after the death of Stalin, has never been publicly told. Much of it was concealed and suppressed by the Moscow censorship. Many details are not yet and possibly never will be known outside the tight little circle of men in the Kremlin who were the chief actors in one of the great dramas of modern times. Enough is known, however, so that the factors that led to Beria's removal and execution can be traced with almost crystal clarity, in an otherwise Florentine labyrinth of intrigue and counter-intrigue, plot and counter-plot.

These factors were so obvious at the time that this correspondent could confidently note in his private correspondence that a showdown over Beria's power was inevitable. To see why this was so it is necessary to turn back to the story of the events of Stalin's death in March, 1953 – the real story, not the emasculated one that was all that fearful censors permitted correspondents to cable at that time.

The first announcement of Stalin's fatal illness was made in Moscow about 8 A. M., on March 4, 1953. It said the Generalissimo had suffered a massive cerebral hemorrhage early Monday morning, March 2, two days previously. It was apparent to everyone in Moscow that this was the end for Stalin. The only question was how long the end would be in coming. It did not seem likely to be long. This anticipation proved correct. At 4 A. M., on March 6, the Moscow radio, in its shortwave broadcasts, overseas and to provincial newspapers within Russia, announced that Stalin had died at 9:50 the previous evening.

This correspondent was at the Central Telegraph Office in Moscow at the time the flash on Stalin's death came through. The office is in Gorky Street, just two blocks from the

Kremlin. At frequent intervals that night I circled the Kremlin by car and toured central Moscow. All was quiet in the city. There were lights burning late in the Kremlin, but that was not unusual. About 1 A. M. a number of Kremlin limousines pulled into the Kremlin garages, as if returning from taking home the participants in some midnight conference. About 3 A. M. three big Zis limousines parked in front of the Moscow City Soviet building. This was the first indication of anything unusual. A few minutes later a woman at the Izvestia distribution desk said the papers would be "very, very" late.

These details are cited to show how quiet was the center of Moscow on the night of Stalin's death. Nor was there much drama in the way the news reached the Moscow correspondents. My chauffeur, sitting at the car radio tuned to the Tass dictation-speed broadcast, heard the announcement at 4 A. M. He shambled in and whispered in my ear. I filed a bulletin I had already prepared and within a few minutes the other correspondents had filed theirs. But there the matter ended. An iron censorship clamped down. The cables about Stalin were not passed. Neither was a message about office accounts that this correspondent tried to file.

Not only were no messages passed, but a telegraph clerk flipped all the jack cords out of the switchboard through which international calls are placed. While the switchboard lighted up and correspondents frantically shouted to be connected with London and Paris and Stockholm, the operator sat quietly with folded hands. The censors ordered her not even to touch the board. A few minutes later a sleepy mechanic hurried in, ripped open the back of the switchboard and yanked the main cable. It was three and a half hours before communications were resumed from Moscow. The world got its first news of Stalin's death, not from Moscow correspondents but from London pickups of the Soviet radio. However, thanks to the hiatus imposed by the censors, this correspondent is in possession of an almost complete picture of what occurred in Moscow in the hours immediately after the official announcement of Stalin's death. And that account is the key to the Beria story.

Seeing that no copy was likely to be passed for hours, I got into my car and made several tours of the city. As late as 5 A. M. the center was absolutely quiet. Outside of the City Soviet, where obviously some arrangements connected with the death were going forward, there was no sign of unusual activity. No more militia (as the Russians call their police) were on duty. Only a few lights dimly burned in the Kremlin. Nothing extraordinary.

But shortly before 6, a difference became apparent. Whereas before that hour traffic was sparse, possibly even sparser than is customary in those predawn hours, smooth-running, quiet convoys of trucks began converging on the center of the city. They rolled quietly down Gorky Street. They slipped noiselessly down Lubyanka Hill. More appeared from beyond the Moscow River and slowly crossed through the Red Square. In each of these trucks, sitting silently, arms folded, on wooden cross-benches, was a detachment of twenty-two soldiers of the special battalions of the M. V. D., or to translate its initials, the Ministry of Internal Affairs, Beria's ministry.

For the first hour or so the disposition of these troops was not apparent. The truck convoys crossed and recrossed the center of the city without obvious pattern. Slowly little knots of trucks congregated at various intersections and began to accumulate in the enormous open squares that are so numerous in the heart of Moscow. Around 7:30 A. M. the censorship on Stalin's death was lifted and it was about 9 o'clock before I again emerged from the telegraph office. Vast changes met my eyes. By that time there were thousands of troops in the central part of the city and great lines of trucks. Columns of tanks had also made their appearance on upper Gorky Street. All the trucks, all the tanks, all the troops bore the familiar red-and-blue insignia of the Ministry of Internal Affairs. They were Beria's forces.

I went over into Red Square. The way was still open and a curious spectacle was revealed. A thousand or two thousand persons were standing in a cigarshaped crowd toward the main Spassky Gate of the Kremlin. The crowd was quiet and well-mannered and had not yet been interfered with by the police. Obviously these people expected (correctly, as it turned out) that Stalin's body would be brought out through this gate. It was extraordinary to see a crowd freely collected right in the middle of Red Square. I had never seen such a thing before. While I watched, however, freedom of movement into and within Red Square gradually was brought to an end by a giant pincers operation of the M. V. D.

First, light lines were thrown across the streets giving access to the Square. Persons were allowed out, but not in. Then, rapidly growing bodies of troops were introduced into the lower end of Red Square and began to press the crowds back away from the Spassky Gate and toward the State Historical Museum end. Drifting back with the crowds, I saw that the troops intended to clear not only Red Square but Manezhny Square and Theater Square, the big adjacent open spaces, as well. During the next hour this great pincers operation continued and the movement of both pedestrians and traffic in the heart of the city was brought to a total halt.

Moscow is constructed like a series of expanding rings. The Kremlin is the innermost ring. About a mile out is a second ring, a tree-lined boulevard constructed on the site of an old city wall. Perhaps half a mile farther out is a second broad asphalted boulevard, the Sadovaya Circle, built on the base of another old wall. Avenues radiate through these circles, like the spokes of a wheel, giving access to the heart of the city. The military movement that had occurred clamped an iron band on each of these circles and spokes. Not only were thousands of troops deployed across all these streets and along their sides to form cordons, but tens of thousands of trucks were brought into Moscow and formed, bumper-to-axle and tailboard to radiator, into impenetrable barricades. At all key points the truck and troop barricades were reinforced by phalanxes of tanks, drawn up three deep.

There was an iron collar around Moscow's heart and from about 10 or 11 A. M. of March 6, 1953, until 4 P. M. on March 9 it was not removed. During those hours not one person entered or left the center of Moscow without leave of the M. V. D. command, Beria's command. There was literally no traffic movement in the center of the city. The New York Times offices were right in the heart of this dead area, in the Hotel Metropole. Since The Times' car was operating on the morning of March 6, it was within this area and, by one of those strange quirks of fate, it continued to operate within the closed ring during all those hours, molested and threatened repeatedly by the M. V. D., but somehow continuing to pass through the seven police lines that barred the way from the Metrople through Theater and Manezhny Squares and the back door of Gertzen Street to the telegraph office. This fantastic military operation had steel tentacles that rammed their way back through the city to its outskirts. Nor was this the limit of the M. V. D.'s grip on Moscow.

On Sunday, March 8, this correspondent decided to investigate rumors that thousands of persons were arriving in Moscow from all over the country to view Stalin's body, which was then lying in state. There were reports that the trains were so crowded that persons had ridden the roofs of trains all the way from Leningrad in sub-freezing weather. There was no way of getting to the railroad stations, all of which lie at or beyond the second circle, except by walking through the countless military barricades. The metro (subway) system was working, but not to the sealed-off center of the city.

Not long after dawn, I left the Metropole Hotel and made my way past sleepy sentry lines, past curbside campfires where some troops were whiling away the hours, playing accordions and stamping out tunes with their soft leather boots, to the Kursk railroad station. There the true state of affairs was considerably different from the rumor. Notices, handwritten, were posted at the ticket offices. All trains out of Moscow were running, but no trains into Moscow within the suburban radius or other near-by points. Moscow was a city truly sealed off – not only on the inside, but from without as well.

Later that day, by dint of simply walking past the sentry posts with a resolute air, I strolled right into Red Square. It was a strange feeling. The huge square was deserted. Troops were on guard at all the entrances to keep everyone out. But in the center, at the famous Mausoleum, there were power cables running out from inside the Kremlin and power chisels and hammers were busy. Fifteen or twenty workmen were busy chiseling the name of Stalin into the stone beside that of Lenin and making arrangements in the tomb's inner chamber. A colonel of the M. V. D. was supervising the work, Beria's colonel. I strolled over

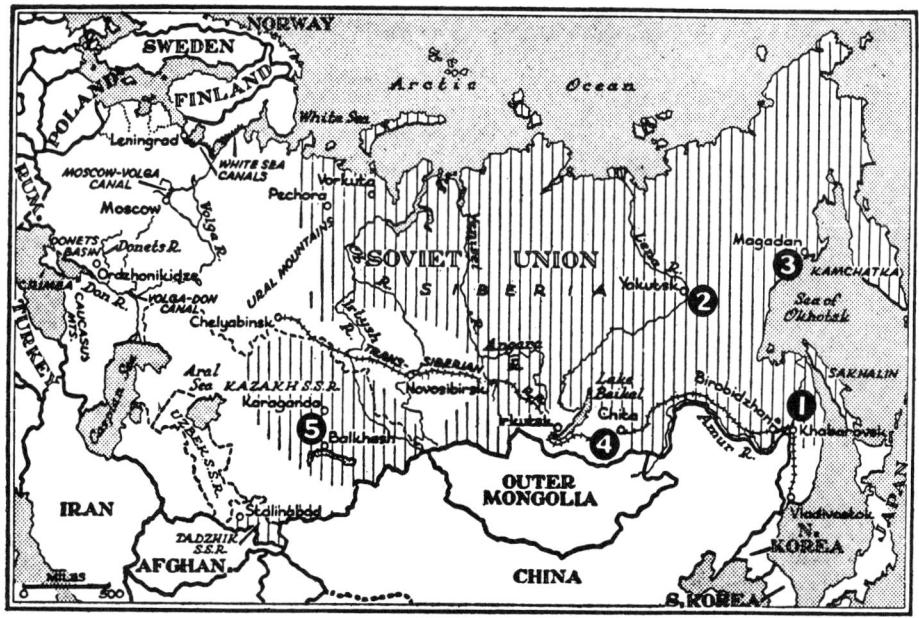

The New York Times   Sept. 27, 1954

M. V. D.-LAND: The empire ruled by the secret police is shown approximately by vertical shading. Its capital is Khabarovsk (1). Among the more notorious prison areas are those at Yakutsk (2), Magadan (3), Chita (4) and Karaganda and Balkhash (5).

[*Source: The New York Times* (New York/Amsterdam), International Edition, Vol. CIV/No. 35, 310, September 27, 1954, p. 3, cols. 3–5.]

and watched idly. No one paid any attention. It probably seemed to them that I had a right to be there, otherwise the sentries would not have admitted me. It was deathly quiet in Red Square except for the intermittent sound of hammers and chisels. The quiet must have been noticeable to the men inside the Kremlin walls. It was then that the thought struck home so sharply.

What troops were these that held the city? M. V. D. troops. Were there any other troops in the city? No. Could any other troops enter the city? No. The closest military camps were all M. V. D. camps. Other troops could enter only with M. V. D. permission or by fighting their way street by street through the barricades. What of the Air Force? Perfectly useless. Even if it bombed the whole city to rubble, it could not break the grip of the M. V. D. upon every strategic position in Moscow. And what of the Kremlin? The men who were there were there because the M. V. D. permitted them to pass through the lines. Or, if they wished to leave the Kremlin, they could leave only by M. V. D. permission. Beria's permission.

It was not likely that the men in the Kremlin had failed to note that they were, in effect, the prisoners of the M. V. D. They were men trained to think in military terms and, particularly, in terms of civil war and street fighting. To the military leaders the realization of their position must have been even more forcible. Because the M. V. D. was not just a group of initials. It was not just a department of the Government. It was an individual. A powerful, ruthless man of extraordinary ability named Lavrenti Pavlovich Beria. And it was Beria's troops and Beria's tanks and Beria's trucks that had accomplished this small miracle and taken over the city of Moscow while the radios were still blaring out the news of Stalin's death to the startled citizenry. Using the basic movement plans that twice a year for many years had been employed on May Day and on Nov. 7 to control traffic movement in the center of the city, and simply extending the plan back to control the whole city and its environs, Beria had with the smoothness of clockwork put Moscow into his grasp. It was too smooth and too complete and too good. No military man could see that exhibition and feel a moment's safety – unless he trusted Beria completely or unless Beria was the top boss. It was too plain and too obvious that Beria had a machine that, before dawn any morning, could take over the Kremlin, take over Moscow and, having done this, have a crack at making Beria master of all Russia. There is not much doubt that Beria himself was fully aware of his power at that moment. It is also likely that he had only in the final hours of Stalin's life regained full and unchallenged control over the M. V. D. He and his command of this vast police army had been one of the targets of machinations that generally are described as the so-called "doctors' plot," which had a vital role in the events leading up to Stalin's death.

But in the coalition of forces that occurred at or about the time of Stalin's death, Beria got back his M. V. D. Perhaps that is why he overplayed his hand so badly at a moment when he was not prepared to strike for full mastery of Russia. Perhaps he did not fully realize the impression he would make on his colleagues.

Whatever the explanation, on the next day, Monday, when Stalin was formally laid to rest beside Lenin, Beria spoke at the funeral bier along with Georgi M. Malenkov and Vyacheslav M. Molotov. There was an undercurrent in Beria's speech that could have flowed only from his knowledge of his power. He sounded just a little condescending toward Mr. Molotov and Mr. Malenkov – perhaps more in his delivery than in his language. What was more interesting, he sought to convey without exactly saying so that he spoke for the Army as well as the police. It took only three and a half months to demonstrate that condescension was not exactly called for on Beria's part and that he had shown the Army, only too plainly, the power and danger of his position. There can be no shadow of a doubt that, from the moment Beria sealed off the Kremlin and Moscow with his troops, he signed his own death warrant.

He was not strong enough to rule. But he was too dangerous to any other ruler or rulers. In the unstable coalition of party, police and Army, Beria had too much sheer military power that could be too quickly applied at the center. He was too big for the triumvirate, but not big enough to be dictator. The only real surprise about Beria's end was that it came so soon. It was a measure of the real weakness of his position (once his troops were out of Moscow) that his colleagues were able to deliver the coup de grace so quickly and with hardly a ripple on the surface of the Moscow waters.

A legend has arisen in some quarters outside Russia in the months since Beria's downfall that he was a great "liberal." It is recalled that the announcement of the exposure and reversal of the so-called "doctors' plet" was made in the name of his ministry. It is said that he advocated more liberal measures for Russia's multitudinous and usually mistreated minority nationalities.

Some color, perhaps, is lent to such tales by the fact that Beria was a minority man himself, coming from Georgia and being partly of Jewish ancestry and from the small mountain area known as Mingrelia. While he bossed Georgia before going up to Moscow in 1938 at the end of the purge period he did a good deal for the Georgian Jews, sponsoring a charitable Jewish aid society, various trade and farm schools and even opening a museum of Jewish culture, which still survives.

However, as Stalin's police chief he was the man who carried out the deportation of hundreds of thousands of minority nationals from their home places, Balts to Central Asia, Byelorussians to Siberia, Jews to the Far North, and so on. It is hard to find in his record as M. V. D. chief any trace of "liberalism." Nor did I ever hear anyone in Russia suggest that the chief of the secret police was really a kind and liberal man. One piece of so-called evidence that was cited to bolster the case for Beria's "liberalism" was the fact that, whereas the man he installed as chief of special investigations of the M. V. D. after the reversal of the doctors' case in April, 1953, was executed along with Beria last December, the previous chief inquisitor, a man named Ryumin whom Beria had blamed for fabricating the doctors' plot evidence, had not, apparently, been punished.

Six weeks ago, however, a brief announcement in the Soviet press revealed that Ryumin had been executed for his role in the notorious conspiracy. That demolished about the only remaining pin supporting the case of "Beria the liberal." Naturally, hardly a word of any of the foregoing was ever permitted to pass the Moscow censorship.

27.4 Numerous Intrigues and a Toast to Justice

[*Source: Harrison E. Salisbury: Army playing a major role, with Zhukov key figure, in:* The New York Times, *International Edition (New York/Amsterdam), Vol. CIV/No. 35,305, September 22, 1954, p. 1, cols. 2–3; p. 3, cols. 2–7.*]

The exact role of the Soviet Army in the events attending the death of Stalin and the arrest and execution of Lavrenti P. Beria remains somewhat unclear. But one thing is certain. The influence of the Soviet Army in the day-to-day management of Soviet policy and, particularly, the influence of the dominant group around Marshal Georgi K. Zhukov in the Army has greatly increased in the post-Stalin era. When all the facts become known – if ever – it may well be established that the dominant role at the time of Stalin's death and again at the time of the Beria crisis was played by the Army.

Most of the few tangible pieces of evidence that support the thesis that Stalin's death was not entirely natural are linked in one way or another with the Army. And some of this evidence concerns a rather obscure young general named Sergei Matveyevich Shtemenko, who was Soviet Chief of the General Staff until about twelve days before the announcement of Stalin's fatal illness and has not been seen or heard of since that time. Perhaps Shtemenko is still alive, serving in some obscure army capacity. Perhaps not. His fate is one of the many missing minor pieces in a fascinating jigsaw puzzle.

Not much is known about this ambitious young general, but enough has come to light to arouse a great deal of interest. He was not a prominent officer in World War II, but served on the General Staff and at the end of the war was rewarded with the Order of Suvorov, First Class, and, like dozens of other officers of his rank, his picture was published in Pravda. Shtemenko was not heard of again until November, 1948, when, in a general shake-up of top Army posts, he succeeded Marshal Alexander M. Vasilevsky as Chief of Staff. He held that post for a little more than four years. Then, a few days before the annual Red Army Day celebration, Feb. 23, 1953, he was removed without any public notice and replaced by Marshal Vasily D. Sokolovsky, a close associate of Marshal Zhukov.

Although Moscow has always been scrupulous in announcing any change in the post of Chief of the General Staff, Shtemenko's removal was secret and became public only accidentally. The chief of staff traditionally holds a reception on the evening of Feb. 23 to which foreign military attachés were invited. The first and only indication that Shtemenko had gone came when these invitations were issued in Marshal Sokolovsky's name. Possibly Shtemenko's sudden removal was quite unconnected with the events that were so quickly to follow – the announcement of Stalin's fatal illness and death. But perhaps not. Shtemenko was one of five military figures named as intended victims of the infamous "doctors' plot" – the phoney anti-Semitic mechanism that was set going in January, 1953.

As previously noted, there were signs that this "plot" had been constructed in such a way as to be used as a weapon against all of Stalin's closest aides, with the possible temporary exception of the military, or at least a group of the military. In other words, the favor of the military was solicited while a purge was conducted of all other elements in the Soviet ruling circle. What arouses suspicion as far as Shtemenko's role is concerned is the fact that the four other supposed "victims" of the plot were all veteran senior military figures. And each of them has kept his job in the period that has followed Stalin's death.

If this recitation sounds complex and labyrinthian, it is because the facts are complex and labyrinthian. The forces that activated the "doctors' plot" and were set in motion by Stalin's death and in the Beria affair were not simple. Events in the Kremlin under Stalin usually had the intricate design of a Brussels tapestry and were often seen from the wrong side or only in part.

One thing, however, is certain with regard to the military. Because of a fortuitous or planned change in the Soviet High Command, the post of Chief of Staff at the time of Stalin's death was occupied by Marshal Sokolovsky, who has been more closely associated with Marshal Zhukov than any other Soviet officer. Another point, equally certain, is that from the moment of the announcement of Stalin's death the military (and this means the real military and not "political" military, such as Marshal Nikolai A. Bulganin, or old cronies of Stalin like Marshals Kliment E. Voroshilov and Semyon M. Budenny) has played an important and prominent role in Soviet affairs. This was shown symbolically in the first picture published in Moscow after Stalin's death. It showed twelve men standing beside Stalin's bier – six in civilian clothes and six in uniform.

Such symbolic pictures in Russia are carefully and thoughtfully prepared and executed, in simple fashion, to convey to the Soviet public some political truth. The lesson of this picture is obvious. The civilians occupy the most prominent positions, but the military bulk is larger than at any time during Stalin's power. If anyone in Moscow failed to get the significance of the picture, he could read in the announcement of the reorganization of the Government that Zhukov, whose name had been missing from the Soviet press since 1946 and who had himself been "exiled" from Moscow to the provincial military command of the Odessa region, had emerged from the shadows and, with a single stride, regained his old prominence. He was named with Marshal Vasilevsky as Deputy Minister of Defense.

The drama of Zhukov's return to power is not inconsiderable. He and the younger and more handsome Marshal Konstantin K. Rokossovsky were the two real military heroes to emerge in Russia in World War II. Zhukov's popularity with the masses was genuine and considerable. The fact that he immediately emerged into the public spotlight with twenty-four hours of Stalin's death not only suggests the depth of his hold upon the Army leadership and the stability that his association with the new Government would suggest to the public, but also raises certain questions that are still unanswered. For instance, Marshal Zhukov would seem to have been waiting in the wings for this call back into the spotlight – naturally enough, if the February change in the Chief of Staff was a curtain-raiser for the events of March.

Curiously, or perhaps not so curiously, there was another important military shift just a few days before the anti-Government Berlin riots of June 17 and the arrest of Beria on June 26. In this shift the tough, hardbitten commander of the Sixty-second Army at Stalingrad, Army General Vasily I. Chuikov, was suddenly "transferred to responsible work in the Ministry of Defense" from the post of Commander in Chief, Germany, which he had held for five years. The shift occurred June 6, eleven days before the riots, twenty days before Beria's arrest. He was replaced by an active young general named Andrei Grechko, a Ukrainian who had held the important Kiev command under the watchful eye of wise old Marshal Konev. A leading member of the Ukrainian branch of the Communist party, Grechko, while an Army man, was also a protégé of Mr. Khrushchev.

This was a very important shift. It would appear to mark the first – but by no means the last – occasion in which the political forces represented by the Army and by Mr. Khrushchev joined hands. It was these two elements, the Army and Mr. Khrushchev's Ukrainian and Moscow party organizations, that, standing side by side with Mr. Malenkov, gave the present ruling clique the power to deal with Beria. Grechko was a young general, but his political reliability was vouched for by Mr. Khrushchev. He was put into Berlin at a moment when great events were in the making, while General Chuikov was brought back, probably to report to the General Staff regarding conditions in Germany.

Possibly as a riposte in reply to the Grechko move, Beria six days later raided deep into Mr. Khrushchev's territory and obtained the removal of Leonid G. Melnikov, whom Mr. Khrushchev had installed to run the Ukrainian party apparatus. It was a pyrrhic victory. Five days later the Berlin riots broke out and within less than a fortnight Beria's game was up.

Apparently no one outside the intimate Kremlin circle knows exactly how the Beria affair was actually brought to a climax, but the dominant role of the Army was clear to everyone in Moscow. It has been reported that a column of Army tanks was seen, moving around the Sadovaya Circle Boulevard and turning toward town at Kachalova Street, where behind tree-shaded high walls Beria's residence stood.

However, it is almost certain that the tank column was observed on the day following, rather than the day of Beria's arrest. It is probable that the mechanics of arresting the Secret Police chief were somewhat more simple – a pair of Army officers may quietly have stepped forward and taken him into custody when he entered the usual conference room in the Kremlin where the Government members met. Confirmation of the Army's key role and, in particular, of the participation of Marshal Zhukov in the Beria crisis was provided by the recent revelation that the same plenary meeting of the Central Committee that denounced Beria elevated Zhukov from candidate to full membership in the committee.

Although the Army had never really played an independent political role during the Stalin era, it was now recognized as such an entity. The announcement of Beria's arrest was made on July 10 and was followed immediately by a series of meetings at which the Government's action was approved an Beria was denounced as a traitor. The biggest of these meetings was one held by all the top Army commanders. Marshal Bulganin spoke as Minister of Defense. Those who stood beside him were Marshals Zhukov, Vasilevsky, Sokolovsky, Govorov and many others. It was clear to everyone that the "Zhukov group" was 100 per cent behind the Government if, in fact, it had not dictated the Government's action.

The importance of the military was further enhanced when the Moscow meeting was followed by a similar one in Beria's personal bailiwick in Georgia. Army General Alexei I. Antonov, a former Chief of Staff closely associated with Zhukov who had been quietly running the important Trans-Caucasus Command through one Georgian political upheaval after another, was the principal figure at this meeting. The meeting was notable for the absence of political and M. V. D. generals, who usually crowded the platform of any party meeting in Georgia. Later it developed that most of these "generals" had been arrested along with Beria.

In the months that followed, the role of the Army in the Government appeared to harden into a permanent and accustomed routine. It did not seem in Moscow that the Army or the Zhukov group, specifically, was seeking to dictate Government policy. Rather, it seemed to be holding a watching brief, but to be participating in discussions of both foreign and domestic policy. There is little doubt, for example, that the Army sought successfully to obtain modifications in foreign policy that tended to reduce the swollen commitments of the Stalin era and, in general, sought to lessen immediate possibilities of a shooting war. It is certain that the Army strongly supported the Government's policy of improving the consumers' goods position and relaxing the harsh strains on Russia's internal economy. The Army, with its millions of raw levies every year, was probably in the best position to judge accurately the real economic strains and moods of the people.

It was not until November that the Army felt called upon to show its hand publicly, but when it did so the action was significantly in the form of a nudge to the civilian leaders to get on with the business of meting out to Beria the fate that the Army felt he deserved. The nudge was public and it was administered by Marshal Zhukov in a fairly dramatic way at the big diplomatic reception that is traditionally held by the Foreign Minister on Nov. 7. All of the Government chiefs, except Malenkov, Khrushchev and Voroshilov, were present when Marshal Zhukov was invited to the inner-room table by Mr. Molotov. The principal foreign ambassadors, including Charles E. Bohlen of the United States, were present and toasts were flowing freely in the Russian tradition. Mr. Bohlen, who is something of a veteran in this game, had offered a toast to justice. Then Marshal Zhukov was called upon to speak. He said he desired to support the toast that had just been drunk, he wished to drink again "to justice." This was an unusual thing to do. In Russia it is the custom to offer your own toast and Mr. Mikoyan rather rudely reminded Marshal Zhukov of this fact. Zhukov persisted and when he was heckled he stolidly and a bit angrily repeated that he proposed a toast to justice. The toast was drunk.

The significance of this demonstration was lost on no one present. Justice, in the context in which Zhukov spoke, could mean only a decision in the still pending Beria case. He was publicly, and in the presence of diplomats of many countries, calling on the Government to speed up the adjudication of Beria. Why he felt this necessary is not known. Perhaps someone in the Government was temporizing. But, regardless of his reason, he got results. Within six weeks Beria and a group of his associates had been executed. The justice demanded by Marshal Zhukov had been done by a tribunal headed by an Army man. Five days later the papers published a two-paragraph item, reporting that a statue of Marshal Zhukov had been erected in his home town, an unusual form of public honor and one that had been denied him during Stalin's lifetime.

But a more unusual tribute was paid to Marshal Zhukov and to the role of the Army in the present Government when the quadrennial elections to the Supreme Soviet were held last winter. The customary appeal to the electors was signed by twenty persons, the first five of them being Marshals of the Soviet Union – Budenny, Bulganin, Vasilevsky, Voroshilov and Zhukov. It was an accident of the Russian alphabet that the five marshals were listed first. But it was no accident that for the first time onequarter of the names on the election list were those of military figures.

As far as can be judged, the influence of the Army and of Marshal Zhukov continues to be conservative and moderate. Zhukov gets along well with Westerners. This is not merely the impression he made on General Eisenhower. It is the impression he consistently makes on foreigners. He is a big, rather handsome man with a smile not unlike that of General of the Army Omar Bradley, except that his face is squarish where General Bradley's is longish.

Moreover, Zhukov obviously is a man with his own ideas – ideas that not necessarily always coincide with those of the other top figures in the Soviet Government.

The relationship, however, appears to be a smooth-working and generally successful marriage of convenience. The prestige and weight of the Army grow steadily and most recently were seen in the stripping of uniforms and epaulettes from the army of Soviet civil servants who had donned them in recent years.

Marshal Zhukov gave an insight into his ideas with his nudge to the Government on the Beria question. He gave a broader and more interesting insight on the ninth anniversary to the capitulation of Germany last May. He contributed an article to Pravda on that occasion that was not just the usual piece of propaganda handed out by the party to a general for publication under his signature. But Zhukov's article was different. It paid tribute, for example, in an honest and straightforward fashion to the role played by the Western Allies, and particularly the United States and Britain, in the war. It had a few gracious words to spare for General Eisenhower and Field Marshal Viscount Montgomery. It did not in the usual fashion that has been the recent Moscow style claim that only the Soviet Army won the war and that Germany was defeated by Russia, in spite of, instead of through the help of, the United States and Britain.

In this respect Marshal Zhukov's article was sensible, polite and reasonable. But along with these words he appended some sharp phrases, too, directed against United States foreign policy, which he blamed for having caused a deterioration of relations between the United States and Russia after the war, and for intensifying world tensions. He warned that Russia was not a country to be meddled with lightly, and he said some harsh things about American bankers, who he seemed to think were more interested in profits from war orders than in world peace. Despite these rather unoriginal sentiments, there was over the whole of his statement an aura of decency and good sense that inevitably recalled an idea that was considerably discussed by some American diplomats just after the war ended.

The idea was that Marshal Zhukov would play an important role in post-war Soviet government and that he and General Eisenhower were the sort of men who talked each other's language and that if the two of them could get together a great many obstacles in the path of Soviet-American relations might be removed.

This hunch never had a chance for a practical test, although it played a fairly important role in the thinking that led to the choice of Gen. Walter Bedell Smith as the first postwar United States Ambassador to Russia. Now that Marshal Zhukov is actually drawing a long oar in the Soviet Government, it might not be a bad idea to put that war's-end hunch to a little test.

Harrison E. Salisbury

27.5 The New Junta and How It Works Together

[*Source: Harrison E. Salisbury: Members of the ruling clique are depicted close up, in:* The New York Times, *International Edition (New York/Amsterdam), Vol. CIV/No. 35,306, September 23, 1954, p. 1, cols. 2–3; p. 3, cols. 2–7.*]

In Moscow today the party is over when Premier Georgi M. Malenkov starts for the door. But, often enough, Nikita S. Khrushchev, first secretary of the party's Central Committee, lingers behind for one last word.

When the Soviet Premier and the party secretary went to the British Embassy last month to dine with Clement R. Attlee, former Prime Minister, it was nearly 1:30 A. M. before Malenkov finally rose and moved toward the door. Foreign Minister Vyacheslav M. Molotov and Minister of Domestic Trade Anastas I. Mikoyan got up, too, and began to make their farewells. But Khrushchev, deep in a discussion with Aneurin Bevan, went on talking. "Znachit ***" ["that means ***"] said the compact little Ukrainian, repeating the word "znachit," as is his habit, two or three times in every sentence, "znachit.***"

Malenkov was by now standing at the door. He smiled a little tiredly as he watched Khrushchev jabbing a pudgy finger in Mr. Bevan's chest to drive home his points. "Po'yekhali," Malenkov said, quietly. "Let's go." Bidding his hosts a courteous good-by, Malenkov went down the stairs. Mikoyan had already left and Molotov followed closely. A moment later, still talking, Khrushchev hurried after them. By the time he got to the door, his colleagues had already clambered into the waiting Zis limousine, with its bullet-proof windows and heavy bomb-proof steel body. Mikoyan and Malenkov were sitting in the back seat and Molotov on the jump. Khrushchev pulled down the second jump-seat, a security colonel popped into the front beside the driver, and the new Soviet junta, complete in one car, pulled off down the Sofiskaya embankment.

That typifies how the junta behaves in Moscow and the kind of impression it makes on outsiders. The "junta" is what the ruling group, consisting of Malenkov, Khrushchev and Molotov, is more and more often being called in Moscow. This triumvirate, with the strong support of Marshal Georgi K. Zhukov's group of the Army, and assisted by a secondstring line-up of Marshal Nikolai A. Bulganin, Lazar M. Kaganovich and Mikoyan, is running Russia.

With the elimination of Lavrenti P. Beria the secret police no longer has a direct policy voice in the Government. Sergei N. Kruglov, the new M. V. D. chief, and Col. Gen. Ivan A. Serov, the security boss, are old-line non-political-style police workers whose principal duties for many years were in the so-called "industrial" section of the M. V. D. Quite recently, and in fact only since so many rumors started to circulate abroad concerning rivalry between Malenkov and Khrushchev, the junta has taken to showing itself to foreigners in Moscow.

The more often the top figures have come in contact with Westerners, the stronger has grown the impression that the most important factor about the junta is how well it works together (now that Beria has been eliminated), rather than any question of rivalry. So far, every foreigner who has met both Malenkov and Khrushchev or has seen them together will give you odds that the former is top dog and that he would take Khrushchev in any showdown.

One experienced Western diplomat who has spent a good many hours in the company of both men puts it like this: "Both of them are shrewd, able men, but there is this difference. When Khrushchev starts a sentence, he doesn't know how it is going to end and he doesn't care too much. But Malenkov never starts a sentence without knowing exactly how it is going to come out."

Malenkov early this year moved out of the Kremlin into an old remodeled merchant palace in Pomerantsev Street, only a few blocks from Spaso House, the residence of the United States Ambassador. Khrushchev may occupy the house next door, but that is just a guess. A handsome block of six new houses is being rushed to completion by military construction workers on the Lenin Hills, formerly Sparrow Hills, just below the site of the new Moscow University. While these residences may be intended for Moscow faculty members, their size, the height of the walls being put up around their compounds and the fact that special dredges are deepening the landing area on the Moscow River just below them suggest that the houses may also be designed for members of the Government. In any event, no members of the Government live in the Kremlin any more. Malenkov, Khrushchev and Molotov still have their office suites there, but Khrushchev recently confirmed the persistent rumor that they are moving out and plan to reopen the Kremlin to the public, as it was before the Revolution.

With the new emphasis on group leadership some of the more moribund Communist party organizations have been revivified and given an active function. For example, the Central Committee of the party, which Stalin never convened for years on end, now meets regularly every three months. It provides an important forum for reports by Malenkov and Khrushchev. The denunciation of Beria was made by Malenkov in the form of a report to a July plenary session of the Central Committee. Khrushchev's big new farm program has been outlined and reported on at a series of Central Committee meetings.

The easing of Kremlin restrictions has been a symbolic gesture on the part of the junta to dramatize to the Russian public that it has greater freedom than under Stalin. Under Stalin, ordinary persons never got into the Kremlin. A few of the privileged went on sight-seeing excursions. A handful, mostly friends of the M. V. D. security guards, got tickets to the gallery of the Supreme Soviet. Restrictions in Red Square were equally tight. No strolling was permitted. Loitering was discouraged. For hundreds of years the square had been a meeting and assembly place for Russia, but in Stalin's time, except for the formal and controlled spectacles of May Day and November Seventh, it was like Siberia. No one went there who did not have to.

The new regime has changed all that. Nowadays Red Square is again a favorite strolling and loitering ground. Up to 150,000 or 200,000 persons go to the square every day, just to visit the huge new G. U. M. department store, and the Kremlin itself has become a kind of town hall for Russia. Almost every week there is a convention or a congress in the Great Kremlin Palace, and beautiful St. George's Hall, with its walls of white marble and its gold and crystal chandeliers, has been turned into a sort of Moscow assembly hall, where high school and college youngsters are invited for holiday dances at New Year's and during the June graduation days.

The Premier's decision to abandon the Kremlin as a place of residence apparently came not long after the new Government took over. A little more than a year ago a large-scale remodeling, refurbishing and rebuildung job was launched in a quiet little "pereulok" or side street between Metrostroi and Kropotkin Streets, in a quarter of the city that used to be known as the "old stables." This is an area about seven or eight minutes' drive from the Kremlin, adjacent to the well-known Arbat quarter, where many wealthy families had their homes in pre-revolutionary days and where most of the foreign embassies are situated. It is about six blocks distant, through winding lanes and back alleys, from Spaso House. The site is only about 100 yards distant from the modernistic Finnish Legation and the adjoining Chinese Embassy. It occupies the area from 2 to 6 Pomerantsev Street, extending through the block to Yeropkinsky Street. In the narrow block in front of the Premier's residence, from Pomerantsev Street through to Kropotkin Pereulok, where the Finnish Legation stands, some ugly old barns and sheds were torn down and a small park was built.

Nearly 200 feet of frontage in Pomerantsev Street, involving at least two good-size houses, has been set aside for the Premier's establishment. The plot includes a four-story mansion in late nineteenth-century baroque, flush with the street. Large, full-grown lime and poplar trees have been transplanted into the grounds and into the garden in front of it. Work to complete the set-up proceeded by day and night under floodlights, and the Premier apparently moved in shortly after Jan. 1.

New traffic rules, barring bicycles from Kropotkin and Metrotroi Streets and prohibiting passing and left turns into the lanes adjacent to the Premier's residence, were established and police posts were erected in both Kropotkin and Metrostroi Streets at the ends of the pereuloks. But – and this was no doubt done purposely – no uniformed police or military guards were stationed at the establishment. Instead, two plainclothes men loiter inconspicuously on the sidewalk across the street from Malenkov's home. About 100 feet from the back gate, however, there is a militia (police) station.

The houses that have been thrown together for the use of the Premier are not particularly ostentatious. They are typical of the homes of wealthy merchants of the nineteenth century. This whole quarter at the end of the eighteenth and beginning of the nineteenth century was the most aristocratic in Moscow. In Kropotkin Street, then known as Prechistenka Street, there were forty-nine palaces in the Eighteen Fifties, eleven belonging to princes, counts and generals. By 1914 there were fifty-one, only two belonging to princes and sixteen to middle gentry and thirteen to merchants.

It is a quick and easy drive from the Kremlin to the Premier's establishment, involving a minimum of stir along the street, in sharp contrast with the elaborate precautions that Stalin insisted upon along his famous "route" leading from the Kremlin to his dacha, or villa. Stalin's route led through Arbat Square and then into narrow, twisting Arbat Street, one of the oldest and narrowest streets in Moscow and also one of the busiest shopping streets. This halfmile stretch was generally regarded as the best-policed street in the world. Traffic policemen were stationed every 100 paces down the center line and there were two or three officers at each corner.

When Stalin drove down the Arbat his cavalcade – one security car ahead of his bulletproof limousine and two behind – moved at such a rapid pace that it created a minor whirlwind in the narrow old street. Hats were whisked from the heads of passersby and in winter it took five minutes or more for the snow to settle down. There were so many plainclothes detectives on the sidewalk that ordinary citizens sometimes had to walk off the curb. Every resident and every employe in the buildings along the Arbat had to go through special M. V. D. inquiry and his passport had to bear a special stamp. After Stalin died, the Government withdrew most of the policemen from the Arbat. It was an act just as significant to Muscovites as the new freedom in Red Square.

Malenkov's dacha and those of most of the Government members are situated on the same Mozhaisk highway, west of Moscow, where Stalin's was. Malenkov's is at Barvikha, twenty-five miles from Moscow. It used to belong to the fabulously wealthy Morozov family and in the early Thirties the writer Maxim Gorki lived there. Malenkov has established the custom of going south, to the Black Sea coast, for a month in late summer. He and Molotov and Khrushchev have villas at Matsesta, just south of Sochi in the North Caucasus.

In general, the members of the junta are traveling a good deal around the country. The first such jaunt was taken by Malenkov about a year ago. A tornado hit the ancient town of Rostov Veliki, 125 miles north of Moscow, and did much damage. The next Sunday Malenkov turned up to inspect the wreckage and promise aid to the inhabitants. He has made other similar visits – all unpublicized – and Khrushchev has traveled even more widely, twice going out to Southwest Siberia and Kazakhstan to see how the farm program is getting on.

There are many contrasts between Malenkov and Khrushchev. The Premier is eight years younger than the party secretary and has a grace and charm that belie the impression given by his photographs of a fat, gross man. He has a boyish smile and just a touch of little Lord Fauntleroy in his manner that startles Westerners. Malenkov, for instance, captivated Dr. Edith Summerskill, one of the recent British Laborite visitors, first by picking her a bouquet of lovely posies from his own garden, second by the warmth of the feminist sentiments he expressed, and third by the fact that when he proposed an old-fashioned toast, "to the ladies," he rose and walked to one end of the table to clink glasses with Lady Hayter, wife of the British Ambassador, and then to the other end to clink glasses with her.

A few weeks ago, at a reception in the Polish Embassy, he interrupted the toasts while he saw, personally, to a waiter's bringing a chair for 82-year-old Dr. Olga Lepeshinskaya, whose soda-bath technique was supposed to keep Stalin eternally youthful. When Malenkov and his colleagues paid a surprise backstage visit to the Comédie Française last spring, it was the Premier who sought to put the women artists at ease by assuring them they need not worry at being surrounded by Communists because, after all, Communist was just an old French word. "Malenkov has a very attractive personality," said one Briton who has had a chance to see the Premier often. "In fact, he worries me rather more than the rest because he is so pleasant."

Malenkov has other winning mannerisms. It has been noted that, when the discussion begins to get tense or sharp, it is the Premier who cuts in with a little joke or deft change of subject. For example, during a meeting with the Britons, Khrushchev started to hammer away on the subject of British support for entry of Communist China into the United Nations. Although the British showed more and more displeasure, Khrushchev plodded ahead unheedingly until Malenkov intervened and changed the subject.

Neither Malenkov nor Khrushchev knows English. Malenkov knows a little French, Khrushchev a little German. But Malenkov's Russian is perfect and his pronunciation and style are what the Russians call cultured. This has strengthened the impression that his family had middle-class origins and that he learned to speak and use good language at home in

Samples of Censorship

Following are deletions typical of those made by Soviet censors in dispatches recounting a trip to Siberia and the Soviet Far East

The deleted material was varied—sometimes economic, sometimes political, sometimes quasi-military, sometimes sociological. The deleted sections are printed in bold-face type.

From a dispatch date-lined Novosibirsk: "The mighty Novosibirsk dam which is scheduled to produce upward of 700,000 or 800,000 kilowatts of power is the first effort to turn its [the River Ob's] vast energy to a useful purpose. * * *"

From dispatches from Yakutsk:

"They drink a special kind of brown vodka called hunter's vodka and also straight spirits with or without a beer chaser. **Drunkenness is a real problem. And not all residents of Yakutia are happy with their lot. To many this is an alien countryside and they would much prefer their native Kiev or Odessa or Tiflis.** As is inevitable when a considerable fraction of the population has been directed to a particular region, not everyone adapts himself. And, there is plenty to adapt one's self to in Yakutia.

"Housing is another problem. Even miners get tired of barracks life and it is not suitable housing over the long term for families, especially with children. In work camps, of which Yakutia has many, of course this form of housing is normal. But in Yakutsk a big drive is now being launched to provide better building * * *"

From a dispatch from Kirensk:

"This country virtually provided its own punishment although if the climate and living conditions were not enough the police were handy to make things worse for the prisoners. **It is easy to see why this region has an inevitable attraction for a police administration looking for a place to send persons from more civilized areas. While it seems doubtful that camps would hold any particular terror for local residents accustomed to a grim life already it would be a different matter to persons from Russia's more effete west.**"

From a dispatch from Chita (the introductory sentence):

"Perhaps every third person you meet in the street in Chita is in uniform—the uniforms of the Soviet land forces, of the air force and civil air service and of the railroad enterprises and mining enterprises. This is natural because Chita is one of Russia's eastern 'watchdogs.' * * *"

From a dispatch from Khabarovsk:

" 'Of course we are a very young city and things are not as well fixed up as they will be later on.' This kind of remark is designed of course as an excuse for all sorts of bad conditions and abuses—huts and barracks for housing, unpaved dirty streets, poor municipal facilities, inadequate sewers, almost any evil you can name."

By deleting unfavorable material and leaving the favorable material, the whole impression of the article often is changed and distorted.

From *The New York Times*, October 2, 1954

[*Source:* Harrison E. Salisbury: An American in Russia, New York 1955, p. 287.]

Orenburg before the revolution. This is borne out, also, by his official biography, which is as severe and restrained as Stalin's was florid and ornate. It merely says that he comes from an "employe family." This means Malenkov's parents were not peasants and not workers and, in all probability, his father was a Czarist civil servant.

Another clue to Malenkov's origin is concealed in his patronymic, Maximilianovich, which shows that his father's name was Maximilian, a very unusual name for a Russian. It is not on the calendar of the Orthodox Church and no Orthodox priest can have christened Malenkov senior. Evidently, Malenkov's grandparents were somewhat unconventional and not devout church believers. The name Maximilian suggests Maximilien de Robespierre, a famous figure of the French Revolution. Thus it seems possible that Malenkov comes from a family strongly influenced by reforming, liberal or even revolutionary ideas.

Malenkov has good table manners and so do his associates. He eats in the European rather than the American style, wielding his knife with the right hand and the fork with the left and not transferring the fork from hand to hand as we do. His clothes are well tailored of excellent material and his light summer suits of tropical worsted stood up well under Moscow's record summer heat this year. He is not so heavy as his photographs make it appear, and is very light on his feet. He and Khrushchev are the same height, about 5 feet 4 inches. When the entire junta walks into a room, it makes a startling impression because of its uniform height and the revelatory insight into Stalin's refusal to have men taller than himself around him.

Malenkov has been married for many years, but not to a sister of Khrushchev as has sometimes been reported. His wife, a pleasant, plain woman about his age, has not yet appeared with the Premier at any public social event, although she was shown in a newsreel last spring accompanying her husband to the Soviet polling booth. The Malenkovs have two children, a boy and a girl.

In contrast with Malenkov's suavity, Khrushchev presents himself as a diamond in the rough. He is a bluff, open, frank one-time miner, who blurts out things that the Premier is too tactful to mention. Khrushchev, for instance, told the British Laborites that, while they represented only the working class of Britain, his party, the Communists, represented the workers not of just one little country but of all countries. He told the British Ambassador, Sir William Hayter, that the best international relations in the world were those between the Soviet Union and China and that Britain should take a tip from the Chinese in her relations with Moscow.

Where Malenkov proposes few toasts and drinks most of them in white wine, Khrushchev proposes many and drinks them in vodka. He likes to indulge in the old Russian custom of drinking "do dna," or bottoms up, and the more he drinks the more he talks. At Molotov's reception for Chou En-lai, Chinese Communist Premier, Khrushchev talked on and on to Sir William. Finally Malenkov left and he was still talking. At that point Kaganovich took Khrushchev by the elbow and gently but firmly steered him along in Malenkov's wake.

Khrushchev's language is rough and ready, constantly interspersed with "znachit" this and "znachit" that, often marked by verbs that do not agree with subjects, full of dangling clauses and uncompleted ideas, and all spoken with a soft Ukrainian accent. Khrushchev is a buttonhole talker. He likes to put his hands on the man he is talking with, not infrequently grasping a lapel with one hand and gesticulating with forefinger jabs to the chest with the other. He looks his listener straight in the face with eyes so wide open and baby-blue that one diplomat reported that he had to look away because "in another moment he would have had me believing he was just as honest and open-hearted as he looked."

Members of the junta frequently interrupt, correct and contradict each other. Mikoyan makes rather a specialty of this. Both he and the heavy-handed Kaganovich cut in on Khrushchev when, as often happens, the Secretary overstates or misstates himself.

In this company Molotov is the quietest, most reserved and dignified. However, he has thawed notably since Stalin's death and there is no doubt that at long last he has become an initiator of foreign policy and not merely an instrument for carrying out orders. He is treated with marked respect by his colleagues.

Junior members of the junta, like Maxim Z. Saburov and Mikhail G. Pervukhin, listen quietly and say little. Saburov is the only member who speaks English. He spent some time in the United States in the Thirties, studying engineering. Mikoyan frankly regrets his inability to speak English.

At big public events Marshal Georgi K. Zhukov almost always is also present, sometimes at the head table and sometimes not. But he is never far away and his public conduct permits some inferences to be drawn. Sometimes Marshal Zhukov sits with the junta and expresses his opinions forcefully and bluntly, as on the occasion of the last Nov. 7 reception. Other times, as at the reception for Chou En-lai, he spends the evening in a room adjoining that in which the guest of honor is being entertained.

That evening he chatted quietly most of the evening with the Navy Chief, Admiral Nikolai G. Kuznetsov, munching new Crimean apples. After he had eaten four, he treated himself to two large green cucumbers. Occasionally he glanced into the room where the junta was entertaining Chou En-lai, as if to satisfy himself that all was in good order. Then he returned to his conversation and his cucumbers. He gave the impression of a man who was confident that his affairs were in good hands and going well. As far as anyone in Moscow can tell, he has every reason for such confidence.

Related Readings

Arnold, Theodor: Sowjetrußland von Stalins Tod bis Chruschtschows Sturz (1953–1964), München 1964.
Avtorkhanov, Abdurakhman: Stalin and the Soviet Communist Party. A study in the technology of power, New York 1959.
Crankshaw, Edward: Russia without Stalin – the emerging pattern, New York 1956.
Dallin, David J.: Sowjetische Außenpolitik nach Stalins Tod, Köln 1961.
Deutscher, Isaac: Russia after Stalin, London 1953.
Embree, George Daniel: The Soviet Union between the 19th and 20th Party Congresses, 1952–1956, The Hague 1959.
Lazareff, Hélène/Lazareff, Pierre: The Soviet Union after Stalin, London 1955.
Leonhard, Wolfgang: The Kremlin since Stalin, New York – London 1962.
Meissner, Boris: Das Ende des Stalin-Mythos. Die Ergebnisse des XX. Parteikongresses der Kommunistischen Partei der Sowjetunion. Parteiführung, Parteiorganisation, Parteiideologie, Frankfurt/Main 1956.

Meissner, Boris: Die Kommunistische Partei der Sowjetunion vor und nach dem Tode Stalins. Parteiführung, Parteiorganisation, Parteiideologie, Frankfurt/Main 1954.
Nove, Alec: Was Stalin really necessary? Some problems of Soviet political economy, London 1964.
Salisbury, Harrison Evans: Moscow journal – the end of Stalin, Chicago 1961.
Salisbury, Harrison Evans: Stalin's Russia and after, London 1955.
Shulman, Marshall Darrow: Stalin's foreign policy reappraised, Cambridge, Mass., 1963.
Ssachno, Helen von: Der Aufstand der Person – Sowjetliteratur seit Stalins Tod, Berlin 1965.
Steininger, Alexander: Literatur und Politik in der Sowjetunion nach Stalins Tod, Wiesbaden 1965.
Stipp, John L. (Ed.): Soviet Russia today – patterns and prospects, New York 1956.
Young, George Gordon: Stalin's heirs, London 1953.

1955

J. Kingsbury Smith

International News Service

CHAPTER 28

REPORTS ABOUT THE SOVIET UNION IN 1955

Changes in the Leadership and Several Important Statements by Its Members

    Introductory Notes
28.1 Molotov Judges Chinese Conflict and Charges the U.S.
28.2 Russia's View on Peace and Coexistence With America
28.3 The Fall of Malenkov and Communist Democracy
28.4 How Stalin Used to Relax and the Fall of His Brother
28.5 Soviet Policy and the Role of the Journalists
    Related Readings

Introductory Notes

After the Pulitzer Prize for International Reporting had been given to six American foreign correspondents stationed in Korea collectively in the early fifties, it was three journalists in 1956 on whom the coveted award was bestowed, namely Frank Conniff, William Randolph Hearst, Jr., and Kingsbury Smith of the International News Service, *the news agency of the Hearst newspaper chain, "for a series of exclusive interviews with the leaders of the Soviet Union." Though the prize had been given to all three* INS *correspondents, the prizewinning articles were published in the Hearst papers under the exclusive byline of Kingsbury Smith.*

Joseph Kingsbury Smith was born on February 20, 1908, in New York City. He attended public and private schools in New York and New Jersey and at the University of London. Smith joined the Hearst company's International News Service *in July, 1924, and after a training period in the New York headquarters was assigned to the* INS *London bureau in 1927. He was transferred to the Washington bureau in 1931 and later became chiefs* INS *State Department correspondent. His forecast of developments throughout the period leading to Pearl Harbor won him the George R. Holmes Memorial Award for the best* INS *reporting in 1941. Smith received a National Headliners Club Award the same year. In 1944, Smith returned to London as* INS *European Manager. From there he directed the* INS *D-day coverage, and later he was chosen by lot to represent the American press at the Nuremberg execution of the top Nazi war criminals. His coverage of Soviet encroachment in Eastern Europe was highlighted by the last statement made by the late Jan Masaryk of Czechoslovakia only a day before his death, in which Masaryk revealed the hopeless situation of his country under Russian domination. Smith received four major journalistic awards for a doublebarrelled scoop early in 1949. On December 31, 1953, Smith again made journalistic history in a telegraphic interview with the then Soviet Premier Malenkov on prospects of improved relations with the United States. In January, 1955, Smith accompanied W. R. Hearst and F. Conniff to Moscow for a series of exclusive interviews with Soviet Premier Bulganin, Communist Party boss Khrushchev, Marshal Zhukov, and Foreign Minister Molotov, and with Svtlana Allitueva, Stalin's daughter.*

The following texts by Joseph Kingsbury Smith, copyright 1955, are reprinted by kind permission of Hearst Newspapers, New York, N.Y.

28.1 Molotov Judges Chinese Conflict and Charges the U.S.

[*Source: Kingsbury Smith: Soviet may be willing to aid in cease-fire, in:* New York Journal-American *(New York, N.Y.), No. 24,418, January 29, 1955, p. 1, cols. 1–8; p. 2, cols. 1–4.*]

Soviet Deputy Premier and Foreign Minister Molotov told William Randolph Hearst Jr. today that the situation in the Formosan area constitutes a threat to peace and indicated that the Soviet Government might be willing to ask Communist China to agree to a temporary cease-fire.

Molotov made this important statement in the course of an 80-minute exclusive interview with the American publisher and this correspondent in his office in the Kremlin. In response to a question, Molotov said: "The Soviet Union is interested in reducing international tension everywhere." He added "everything that contributes to that end will find support on the part of the Soviet Union."

It was pointed out to Molotov that the immediate and acute problem in the Formosan area seemed to be to prevent the existing situation from developing into an extended conflict. Molotov was asked whether, if no agreement could be reached next week at the UN Security Council meeting for a permanent cease-fire between the Chinese Communist and Chinese Nationalist forces, what could be the attitude of the Soviet Government to the possibility of a temporary cease-fire to facilitate the withdrawal of Nationalist Generalissimo Chiang Kai-shek's forces from those islands close to the mainland which now are under attack. It was explained to Molotov that this might avert heavy casualties which would be bound to be suffered by both sides if an attempt were made to take those islands by force.

It was also stated it might avert the danger of an extension of the conflict. Molotov replied: "I can provide a short reply to that question. If Chiang Kai-shek should desire to withdraw his forces from any islands hardly anyone would try to prevent him from doing so." We asked whether that meant that Molotov thought the Communist Chinese forces on the mainland would not attack a withdrawal or ships which might facilitate a withdrawal. Molotov said: "I am not authorized to speak for the Chinese Peoples Republic. That question should be asked of them."

We inquired whether the Soviet Government would be prepared to ask the Chinese Government that question. Molotov, gazing intently at us, said: "Is the Government of the United States asking us to do that?" Hearst quickly answered: "We are not speaking for the American Government in any way. We are simply journalists." Molotov then said: "I'm taking note of that." Hearst again said he wished to make it clear "we are simply asking a journalistic question; we are not representing and not speaking in any way for the American Government."

Molotov's implied willingness to consider as request to ask the Chinese Communist Government to agree to a cease fire permitting withdrawal of the Chinese Nationalist forces from Tachen and other offshore islands seemed to be somewhat more advanced than the reply he gave yesterday to British Ambassador Sir William Hayter. Sir William informed

Molotov that the Security Council is meeting Monday and was understood to have expressed the hope that the Soviet Government would urge Peiping to accept an invitation to send a representative to attend a council session bringing about a cease fire in respect to the Tachens. British sources in Moscow have said Molotov's reaction to Sir William was "pretty limited."

Hearst opened the conversation by telling Molotov he was pleasantly surprised by the friendliness of the Russian people in the streets and wherever he encountered them. He said this encouraged him to hope that relations between the Soviet Union and the United States could be improved. Molotov replied that "relations between our two governments are such there is room for improvement but relations of our peoples towards Americans is quite good."

Hearst then raised the question of the Formosa crisis. He said it appeared to be overshadowing all other international issues at the moment and asked whether Molotov felt the situation which had developed there constituted a serious threat to peace. Molotov answered: "The situation in the area of Taiwan, or Formosa as you call it, is of course such as to draw everybody's attention to it because it creates tension in the Far East and reacts negatively on the whole international situation. It presents a threat of war and a threat of violation of peace. It cannot be considered otherwise than one which intensifies international tension and creates a threat to war. I cannot fail to add that in my view the responsibility falls on the United States in view of its interference in Chinese internal affairs in Formosa, which is an integral part of China."

We called Molotov's attention to British Foreign Secretary Sir Anthony Eden's statement that China did not control Formosa for more than 100 years. Molotov cited the Cairo declaration, the Potsdam agreement, the Japanese surrender terms, and a statement which Molotov said was made by the President of the United States in 1950, all of which Molotov added made it clear that Formosa belonged to China.

(The Allies in the Cairo declaration in 1943 said that all the territories Japan has stolen from the Chinese, such as Manchuria, Formosa, and the Pescadores, shall be restored to the Republic of China," Nationalist Generalissimo Chiang Kai-shek then was in power.

(The Potsdam declaration in 1945 said "the terms of the Cairo declaration shall be carried out," and at the San Francisco conference on the Japanese peace treaty, which Russia refused to sign, Japan renounced claims to Formosa and the Pescadores.

(On Jan. 5, 1950, President Truman said the United States stood by its Potsdam pledge to give Formosa back to China. This was just after the Chinese Communists had driven the Nationalists off the mainland and before the Communists invaded South Korea, later to be joined by the Chinese Reds).

"The present situation," said Molotov, "arises from the fact China was deprived of the island first by Japan and now by the United States." We said Molotov was noted for being one of the greatest realists in the world and we were sure he realized there was no likelihood of the United States withdrawing protection from Formosa until peace was secured in the Far East. Therefore the problem was to find a solution within the framework of reality, even if only a temporary solution.

Hearst then said: "The Soviet government sought at the Geneva Conference to avert an extension of the Indochinese conflict. Is it prepared to do likewise in respect to the Formosan situation?" Molotov answered: "There is a considerable difference between the problems of

Indochina and China. In one respect the position of the Soviet Government is the same as far as Indochina, China, or any other area is concerned. That is, the Soviet Government is interested in reducing international tensions everywhere. Everything that contributes to that end will find support on the part of the Soviet Union insofar as it does contribute to that end. What is needed is that measures proposed should be directed toward reduction of international tension."

Molotov made the usual reference about interference of one state in the affairs of another as not contributing to a reduction of tension. He said he was looking at the situation from a realistic point of view and it must be recognized that the Chinese (Communist) Government controls the whole mainland of China and the Chinese people feel they have achieved not without difficulties a great national victory.

Therefore, he added, Communist China is bound to insist on respect for its national territory and interests. "As far as the U.S.S.R. is concerned," he said, "it is developing its relations with China on a basis of equal rights and friendship, taking into consideration the mutual interest of the two countries. We consider this realistic."

This correspondent said that we understood the Soviet position in respect to Communist China but the important and immediate problem was to find a solution which would prevent the current situation from developing into a general conflagration that might endanger the peace of the world. Molotov replied: "China does not threaten anybody and it would be well if nobody threatened China." Hearst said he wished to stick to the question and not get involved in a debate. He then asked: "If the American Government would use its good offices to urge its Chinese friends to seek a peaceful solution of this problem would the Soviet Government be disposed to do likewise with its Chinese ally?" Molotov answered: "It must be realized that the two parties are not the same. There can be no comparison between the governments of the Chinese Peoples Republic and the so-called Chiang Kai-shek Government." Molotov said the latter Nationalist Government should move to some other spot.

Turning to the European situation Hearst inquired whether as a first step toward disarmament the Soviet government would be prepared to join with the Big Three Western Powers in evacuating military occupation forces and bases from all of Austria pending conclusion of an Austrian peace treaty. The Western Powers already have agreed to withdraw their military forces from Austria simultaneously with Russian forces when a peace treaty is concluded. Molotov went into a lengthy exposition on the Soviet government's well-known position about American defense bases around the world, asserting their existence constituted an unfriendly attitude toward the Soviet Union and was threatening Russia.

This correspondent said we could not agree that measures which the American Government had taken and which were supported by the American people and North Atlantic Treaty Organization nations were unfriendly. I emphasized that they had been prompted in the interest of security and the maintenance of lasting peace. Molotov then asked that if everybody agrees to withdraw military bases from Austria could it be done elsewhere and if so, how.

This correspondent answered it might prove to be contagious. We said we did not wish to become involved in a dialectical debate with Molotov over the question of American bases. The meeting then came to a conclusion. We shook hands with Molotov and departed from the ancient Kremlin building.

Gross National Product of the USSR by Use in Current Prices, 1928-55
(billions of rubles)

Outlay category	1928	1937	1940	1944	1950	1955
Household purchases in retail markets						
In government and cooperative shops and restaurants	—	110.0	160.0	111.0	328.0	412.0
In collective farm markets	—	16.0	26.0	30.0	47.0	51.0
Total	12.10	126.0	186.0	141.0	375.0	493.0
Housing; services	2.79	17.4	26.2	20.1	50.4	65.7
Consumption of farm income in kind	6.70[a]	25.0	42.0	25.0	61.0	85.0
Military subsistence	0.25	2.5	6.6	25.7	14.1	17.2
Household consumption outlays	21.84	170.9	260.8	211.8	500.5	660.9
Communal services						
Health care	0.54	7.9	11.6	12.6	25.0	34.0
Education	0.87	17.0	23.8	20.9	59.0	69.3
Other	0.14	0.7	1.0	0.7	1.5	1.7
Total	1.55	25.6	36.4	34.2	85.5	105.0
Government administration, including NKVD (OGPU; MVD and MGB)	0.82	7.4	13.9	14.0	36.9	27.6
Defense (as recorded in budget[b])	0.76	17.4	56.5	135.7	80.8	105.4
Gross investment						
In fixed capital	6.00	35.2	53.9	38.9	156.5	239.6
Other	1.32	24.2	13.7	14.7	51.5	45.4
Total	7.32	59.4	67.6	53.6	208.0	285.0
Gross national product	32.29	280.7	435.2	449.3	911.7	1,183.9

[a] Includes 0.30 billion rubles of farm wages in kind.
[b] Exclusive of pensions to officers, et cetera, that are included in published budgetary defense figures.

Note: Here and in succeeding tables the dash (—) means not applicable or not available.

Gross National Product of the USSR by Use in 1937 Prices, 1928-55
(billions of rubles)

Outlay category	1928	1937	1940	1944	1950	1955
Household purchases in retail markets						
In government and cooperative shops and restaurants	—	110.0	127.0	68.0	148.0	260.0
In collective farm markets	—	16.0	13.0	1.6	23.0	23.0
Total	105.0	126.0	140.0	70.0	171.0	283.0
Housing; services	10.3	17.4	19.1	13.3	21.6	32.1
Consumption of farm income in kind	35.6[a]	25.0	30.0	18.0	28.0	32.0
Military subsistence	0.8	2.5	5.0	17.2	6.0	9.6
Household consumption outlays	151.7	170.9	194.1	118.5	226.6	356.7
Communal services						
Health care	2.1	7.9	9.5	8.8	11.0	15.8
Education	3.9	17.0	19.9	14.1	24.6	28.1
Other	0.6	0.7	0.8	0.5	0.7	0.7
Total	6.6	25.6	30.2	23.4	36.3	44.6
Government administration, including NKVD (OGPU; MVD and MGB)	3.0	7.4	10.8	8.5	14.8	10.5
Defense (as recorded in budget[b])	1.9	17.4	45.8	118.0	42.4	62.0
Gross investment						
In fixed capital	10.9	35.2	39.4	24.2	66.5	112.2
Other	7.8	24.2	11.5	11.7	24.2	23.8
Total	18.7	59.4	50.9	35.9	90.7	136.0
Gross national product	181.9	280.7	331.8	304.3	410.8	609.8

[a] Includes 1.6 billion rubles of farm wages in kind.
[b] Exclusive of pensions to officers, et cetera.

National Income of the U.S.S.R. in Prevailing Rubles

[Source: Abram Bergson: The Real National Income of Soviet Russia since 1928, Cambridge, Mass., 1961, pp. 46, 48.]

28.2 Russia's View on Peace and Coexistence With America

[*Source: Kingsbury Smith: Russia's views on peace, in:* New York Journal-American *(New York, N.Y.), No. 24,426, February 6, 1955, p. 1, cols. 1–8; p. 37, cols. 3–8; No. 24,427, February 7, 1955, p. 1, cols. 5–6; p. 2, cols. 2–6.*]

Nikita Khrushchev, one of Russia's top leaders, told William Randolph Hearst Jr. today the Soviet government is prepared to join other interested countries in trying to prevent the Formosan conflict from developing into a major war.

In a two-hour 45-minutes interview with the American publisher, Khrushchev, considered in Western circles the No. 2 man in the Soviet hierarchy, said: "We are interested in peace and we are prepared to do what we can to find a solution to this issue and prevent the conflict from developing into war. If America shows common sense – and I have no doubt about the common sense of the Chinese – I believe that with the participation of other countries interested in peace it may yet be possible to avert war."

This correspondent – who with Frank Conniff, editorial assistant to Hearst, attended the long conference – asked if the Soviet Union would be one of the countries participating in efforts to avert war. Khrushchev nodded his head and replied affirmatively "that is not excluded." Khrushchev's statement seemed to reflect the same desire to avert extension of the Formosan conflict as was indicated by Soviet Foreign Minister V. M. Molotov in an interview with Hearst last Saturday.

This attitude by Khrushchev, the first secretary of the Russian Communist party and a member of the Soviet presidium, was combined with a strong defense of Communist China's policy in respect to Formosa. Recalling Khrushchev's visit to Peiping when he concluded a new pact with the Chinese Communist government, Conniff asked how he estimated the chances of preserving peace in the Far East. Khrushchev emphasized he could not speak for the Peiping government but could only express his personal views. "How the situation will develop under present conditions it is difficult to say. How it develops depends on the United States. I must say I was surprised by the position taken by the United States. We have known Gen. Eisenhower as our partner during the war and we respect him, but I should think the present position taken by the American government would not be understood by the American people themselves."

Khrushchev spoke at length about what he described as American interference in the internal affairs of China and referred to the Korean war, which he called "another instance of flagrant interference in a civil conflict." He added: "Interference did not serve to enhance the prestige of the United States. It is well the end has come to that war and that the fire was put out. We do not want a fire to start anywhere else."

Khrushchev reiterated the Soviet view that Formosa belonged to China and should be under the Government controlling China. He said Communist China cannot yield in its demand to gain control of Formosa because China is a proud, great country. "It is none of my business, of course," he said, "but if the United States found itself in a similar position I think it, too, would not allow itself to be humiliated." He added he thought America's attitude reflected hatred toward the Chinese people.

I recalled Molotov's conversation with Hearst last week in which the Soviet Foreign Minister said the President of the United States had stated in 1950 that Formosa belonged to China. I further said American policy in respect to Formosa was based simply on consideration of security and maintenance of peace in the Far East. I recalled that America withdrew its military forces from Korea in the interests of peace and within a relatively short time thereafter there was fighting which threatened peace in the Far East and the entire world. Therefore, this correspondent continued, the United States was reluctant to withdraw protection from Formosa until peace had been secured in the Far East. I told Khrushchev that the American people have no hatred for the Chinese people, which was borne out by help during the war and during the great flood and other disasters in the past.

The conversation with the short, stocky, strongwilled boss of the Russian Communist party and its 7,000,000 members covered a wide range of subjects, including the question of coexistence and military balance of power between Russia and the West, and the Soviet Union's new economic plan for greater emphasis on the production of heavy industry. Although Khrushchev spoke in a serious vein during most of the interview and his brow was knitted from time to time as he touched on delicate subjects, he displayed a genial attitude. He joked and winked about capitalists and Communists sitting around a table talking together and at times his blue eyes twinkled. At other times they became sharp and shrewd and the lids almost closed as he stressed the point about Communist China's alleged right to Formosa and attacked American policy. Tiny strands of white hair popped up from an almost bald pate and the sides of his round head were fringed with close cropped white hair.

In his opening remarks with Khrushchev, Hearst said he had noted that the Soviet leader had recently praised American agricultural methods and had said that they should set a good example for Soviet agriculture." Khrushchev replied: "There are a great many good things in America which merit our copying. And I think Americans could find many good things in the U.S.S.R. That refers not only to agriculture but to industry and other fields as well. In those fields, too, there are a great many things in America that merit our copying."

During the discussion of Soviet economy Khrushchev said Russia did not like to be spending so much money on armaments but felt compelled to do so under present international conditions. "You believe," said Khrushchev, "that we are to blame and we believe you are to blame for these conditions because you are establishing bases around our territory and trying to talk from positions of strength. It is a concept proclaimed by (British Prime Minister Sir Winston) Churchill and repeated by (U.S. Secretary of State John Foster) Dulles and others. I believe the production of guns or atomic bombs is the result of abnormal relations that have developed and I must say that they do not form the wealth of the countries."

Khrushchev asserted it was "dangerous" to pursue a policy based on a position of strength. "It is dangerous," he said, "because in accordance with that policy both one side and the other have to increase their forces as each side tries to make itself stronger than the other. That of course might lead to exhaustion and it also leads to stockpiling the means of warfare, and when enormous materials are reserved for war or piled up, it of course is possible that some spark might set off war."

Khrushchev told Hearst there were "no points of issue with America which cannot be solved. America is a good country," he said, "with good people and we want nothing from them. On the other hand, is there anything America wants from Russia? It is impossible to get anything from the U.S.S.R. by blackmail or through threats. If it is possible to get something from us, it can be done by trade and normal relations. We should seek to develop normal, business-like trade relations so that in time they might be strengthened and transformed into friendly relations. A conflict of any kind is certainly not in the interest of our nations. I am convinced that we shall find the strength and common sense to achieve an improvement in our relations."

We took issue with Khrushchev concerning the responsibility for existing international conditions. We said our leaders sought to negotiate a settlement of world problems with the Soviet Union when the West was in a position of weakness and they found it impossible to do so. Therefore they felt it necessary to establish an equal position of strength. Hearst reminded Khrushchev of America's wartime lend-lease aid and postwar offer of Marshall plan assistance. We also said there was no intention on the part of our leaders to try to blackmail the Soviet Union into giving us anything. We added that what the American government and people want from the U.S.S.R. is peace, friendship and understanding.

Hearst pointed out there was nothing in the American Constitution or in the writing or utterance of America's great leaders saying our two systems were incompatible or that one or the other must go down as there was in the teaching of Marx and Lenin. This correspondent said that the fear that those teachings may still be the basis of Soviet long-range policy is something that causes concern to the American people.

Khrushchev appeared to take our vigorous dissent to his remarks without irritation and launched into a long analysis of the relationship between strength and weakness. The Soviet leader said: "We do not believe it would be right for us to be stronger than America or the bloc America has formed. We recognize that each nation has the right to think of its security and build up its forces in order to guarantee that security. That might be termed balance of power and I should think that the conception is more or less correct. But Churchill and Dulles have put out the concept of positions of strength and not balance of power. That means that one position should be stronger than another and that one of the parties forms positions of strength in order to enforce its will on the other side by constantly developing and building up its forces, and that would simply raise the temperature. I believe this is a vicious kind of policy because within it there always is the possibility of a showdown through war."

Speaking of lend-lease, Khrushchev conceded it was "of great assistance to us during the war." "It would be silly to deny that," he added. "But we paid with our blood for that assistance." Hearst said he was not suggesting repayment but citing lend-lease as evidence of American goodwill.

The long interview broke up in friendly fashion. Khrushchev said he felt such frank talks served a useful purpose and congratulated Hearst for defending his country's position so well.

Nikita Khrushchev, the blunt, rugged boss of Russia's Communist Party, ridicules the Western reports that a split might be developing between him and Soviet Premier Malenkov. In the course of a long interview with American Publisher William Randolph Hearst Jr., the Number Two man in the Soviet hierarchy also made the following points:

1. Russia's rulers believe communism will in the long run gain the "upper hand" in the world.

2. However, Russia wants no war and Soviet leadership wants to see the global struggle between communism and capitalism confined to long-range competitive coexistence.

3. How long this coexistence will last "no one can tell."

4. Soviet leaders believe Russia and the West can live together without fighting.

5. The development of heavy industry to strengthen Russia will be given priority in the future.

6. As for American airmen imprisoned by Communist China, Khrushchev said, "I can well understand the feeling of countrymen of those fliers," and "personally, I would like to see a favorable settlement of that issue."

Khrushchev described as "wishful thinking" reports which have appeared in the Western press indicating a struggle for power might be developing between him and Malenkov. He related the story of a professor who gave his blindfolded students a glass of liquid and asked each one to describe the smell. "Each gave a different answer," Khrushchev said. "The professor told them it was the same liquid – ink – and it smelled to each as each wanted it to smell."

In response to Hearst's inquiries as to what, exactly, Soviet leaders meant by coexistence, Khrushchev said: "The question of coexistence is a very wide one, but it is a fact that capitalist countries like America and Britain on one hand and Socialist countries like the U.S.S.R. on the other exist today in the same world. We are living on one and the same globe and there is no place where we could step out of it. What is the conclusion to be drawn.

"You are against socialism. We are against capitalism. You want to build up your economy on a capitalistic basis. We want to build up ourselves on the basis of socialism. There is no reason why you should not do so. The only thing necessary is that you should not try to prevent us from building up our economy on principles we think best. Some people might say it is the will of God. We believe it is due to facts of historical development that these two systems have come into being. You believe capitalism is something that cannot be shaken. We believe the same about our own socialist system. These of course are opposite solutions. But how can solutions be reached. For hotheads, war is a solution. That is a silly kind of solution. We believe, as Lenin said, the solution lies in coexistence. In other words we can live together without fighting. Lenin spoke of long term coexistence. How long no one can tell. It would depend on historical conditions. If the American people prefer to live under capitalism, there is no reason why they should be prevented from doing so. I sympathize with Communism. You sympathize with capitalism."

Dropping his furious tone momentarily, the heavy set, bald little Soviet leader leaned over the conference table at his office, headquarter of the central committee of the Communist Party, near the Kremlin. Patting Hearst's arm, his beady blue eyes twinkling in a smile, he remarked: "You are a capitalist yourself, but we are having a peaceful talk here. If we can coexist around this table, I should think we could exist around the globe." Hearst replied: "We coexist daily in the United Nations."

Khrushchev then resumed a serious mien and continued: "You believe capitalism will have the upper hand. We believe Communism will in the long run. When that will happen, it is impossible to tell. As far as the United States is concerned, it depends on the American people. No one else can decide the question for them. If you had asked Czar Nicholas II ten years before the revolution in Russia how long his system would last, he would have said it will stand for ages. But ten years later it no longer existed. In the United States, the working class is very strong and some day will raise its voice."

Hearst pointed out: "The working class is the American people right now. It raises its voice at every election." Khrushchev answered: "You believe in the stability of the capitalist system. That it is much better to live under. That is your internal affair." "It is not the words themselves that are important," Hearst said. "It is understanding what those words mean that is important. When you speak about leaving it up to the American people, I can assure you we do leave it up to the American people at every election. If you would leave it up to the Russian people in the same manner, we think it would be a good thing."

Hearst said he noted with interest the decision by the Soviet government to place greater emphasis on production of heavy industry. He asked whether it meant it was now felt necessary to concentrate on strenghtening the military potential of the Soviet Union or whether the new program was aimed at development greater means of production for consumer goods as well. Khrushchev said he thought "we (the Russians) were misunderstood abroad when we adopted decisions on development in production of consumer goods. Some people misunderstood us to mean we would reduce development of heavy industry. That is a misconception. We always considered and we will continue to consider in the future that various branches of industry should develop parallel to each other but with heavy industry being just a bit in advance. Why is that necessary? Because heavy industry creates the means of production.

"In order to raise the standard of living, it is necessary to create the means of production. At the recent plenary session, the Central Committee adopted the decision to increase stockbreeding. What is stockbreeding but production of consumer goods? However, development of stockraising is impossible without necessary heavy industry because it needs tractors, agricultural machinery, and so on."

Questioned as to whether the international situation and defense also had a bearing on the decision to give priority to heavy industry, Khrushchev replied: "As for the use of our industry for peaceful or defense purposes, we do not oppose one to the other." He reiterated that Russia did not like to spend so much money on armaments but felt compelled to do so under existing conditions.

In response to questions, Khrushchev said he would like to visit the United States some day and inspect American agricultural methods. But with an ironical smile, he added: "I should think it would be difficult to find any influential person in America who would dare invite the first secretary of the Communist Party in the Soviet Union. Would it not be said I am going there to subvert or blow up something."

Khrushchev left the meeting of the Supreme Soviet for the interview with Hearst, who was accompanied by Frank Conniff, his editorial assistant, and this correspondent. Western envoys in Moscow agreed the interview was one of the most revealing and important any Soviet leader has ever given to foreign journalists.

28.3 The Fall of Malenkov and Communist Democracy

[*Source: Kingsbury Smith: Malenkov quits; army boss Bulganin in, in:* New York Journal-American *(New York, N.Y.), No. 24,428, February 8, 1955, p. 1, cols. 1–8; p. 9, cols. 1–8.*]

Georgi Malenkov, 53, resigned as Soviet Premier today with a confession of "guilt for shortcomings in agriculture." He was succeeded by Defense Minister Marshal Nikolai A. Bulganin, 60.

Nikita S. Khrushchev, 60, Deputy Premier and Communist Party Frist Secretary, was the central figure in the sensational shift of power which may have far reaching consequences in Soviet internal and foreign policy. For the time being it was not clear what additional posts, if any, he would assume. Western diplomats had thought Khrushchev, regarded as No. 2 man in the Soviet Union, would succeed Malenkov, but the post went to Bulganin, who has been in charge of all Soviet armed forces.

A bellicose attack by Foreign Minister Molotov on the United States was the first statement of policy following the juggling of the Soviet hierarchy. Molotov accused the U.S. of preparing "for a new war – an atomic war," demanded the U.S. "withdraw its forces" from the Formosa area, and claimed Russia is ahead of the U.S. in atomic developments, including the hydrogen bomb. [At the United Nations, in Washington and in London, Western diplomats who have served in the Soviet Union said Khrushchev has become the real ruler of the Soviet Union, with "army boss" Bulganin a mere "figure head."]

This correspondent was among those spectators in the Soviet Parliament who heard a statement by Malenkov read by the Parliamentary Chairman A. P. Volkov. Malenkov's statement said the premiership required "great experience in state work ... I am conscious of my inadequate local experience and the fact that I have never had any experience of management." The man who had held office for nearly two years and is the youngest of the top Soviet leaders added: "A person possessing more experience should be appointed to the post. I see especially clearly my guilt for shortcomings in agriculture since I took responsibility in that sphere."

Khrushchev, the energetic, bald Ukrainian who has plugged for greater agricultural production and stress on heavy industry, strode to the speaker's stand as Parliament reconvened, following a first session today at which Malenkov resigned. He nominated Marshal Bulganin to be the chairman of the Soviet Council of Ministers, or cabinet – that is, Premier.

The second session began at 4 p. m. (8 a. m. N. Y. time). The first session began shortly after 1 p. m. (5 a. m. N. Y. time). Malenkov sat silent during both sessions. Bulganin's nomination was approved unanimously. Khrushchev, in proposing Bulganin, told Parliament: "We are confident that a Government headed by Bulganin will secure the development of heavy industry, and on this basis the development of light and food industries and agriculture, and will insure the well-being and cultural level of the Soviet people."

Malenkov, who took over after the death of Premier Stalin in March, 1953, had inaugurated a policy of more goods for the masses. The pudgy, 250-pound Malenkov, in his letter or statement read for him, offered his continued services to the Soviet Union. He said that if given a new post, he would do his best to serve the State. But no announcement of acceptance of this offer was made. A month ago Minister of Trade Anastas Mikoyan, who had been long identified with the campaign to produce more consumer goods for the Soviet people, resigned his post. He also was present at the momentous session today.

Khrushchev was given a standing ovation as he and other Ministers entered the chamber for the second session, also witnessed by this correspondent. Deputies remained silent when Khrushchev, after nominating Bulganin, asked whether there were any other suggestions. There was none – and the deputies went on to the voting. Everyone raised his right arm in approval of Bulganin. This brought a new round of applause.

As soon as the first session ended, Western envoys such as America's Bohlen, Britain's Hayter and France's Joxe went into a huddle in the diplomatic corridor to discuss the significance of Malenkov's resignation. The diplomats felt the statements which Khrushchev, Molotov and Deputy Defense Minister Marshal Zhukov have made to William Randolph Hearst Jr., during the past ten days assumed greatly increased importance in the light of this new shift of power in the Soviet regime. Western ambassadors felt Khrushchev's emphasis to Hearst on the desirability of long-range competitive coexistence between Russia and the U.S. indicates that that will continue to be the basis of Soviet Foreign policy under the new set-up. It was pointed out that the removal of Malenkov must have been decided by the Central Committee of the Communist Party which was meeting shortly before Hearst's interview with the First Secretary of the Central Committee.

Some diplomats felt the manner in which Khrushchev and Zhukov stressed Russia's desire for coexistence may have been prompted by the desire to reassure the Western world that this change in governmental leadership would not mean any drastic shift in Soviet foreign policy. One of the leading Western envoys in Moscow had predicted yesterday that if Hearst was not received by Malenkov during his current visit after having been received by Khrushchev, Molotov and Zhukov it could indicate that Malenkov was in political eclipse.

Malenkov sat in the front row of the top Soviet hierarchy as the announcement of his resignation burst upon the joint session of the two houses of parliament. But the seat in which he had sat at the opening of the Supreme Soviet Parliament last Thursday was occupied at today's momentous meeting by Khrushchev. It also was Khrushchev who led the parade of government leaders into the hall. Khrushchev sat next to Marshal Klementiy Voroshilov, president of the Soviet Union; who occupied the left end seat of a five-man row.

Bulganin, attired in his uniform of a Marshal and so soon to become Premier, sat on Khrushchev's right. Malenkov sat between Bulganin and deputy premier Lazar Kaganovitch. In nominating Bulganin, who although a Marshal has never commanded an army in the field, Khrushchev said at the second session: "He possesses great experience in political and state economic activities which testifies to the fact that he will successfully cope with his task as chairman of the council of ministers." Bulganin, red-faced and jovial, has a reputation as a businessman, "political general," and diplomatist.

Immediately after Bulganin's appointment was confirmed, the Supreme Soviet, or parliament, began discussing foreign affairs. Foreign Minister Molotov made an introductory speech. In his review of the international situation, Molotov praised what he called the "international authority" of India as "an important new sister in the strengthening of peace." This was a reference to Indian Prime Minister Nehru's efforts to get a settlement of the Formosan situation, his policy of neutrality in the East-West conflict, and his friendly terms with Russia and Communist China. Molotov said great changes in the international position had occurred since World War II, and Russia no longer is "internationally isolated." He told the applauding deputies that the camp of "capitalism and imperialism" was opposed by the camp of "socialism and democracy" led by the Soviet Union and the Chinese (Communist) Peoples Republic. "Countries in the Socialist camp," he said, "are getting much more support from Russia, the basis of whose power is heavy industry and the development of agriculture."

This new emphasis on heavy industry and agriculture was begun by Khrushchev early last December and was endorsed by the Communist Party Central Committee at its meeting late last month. The public stress on this had clashed sharply with the emphasis on consumer goods initiated by Malenkov in August, 1953.

As the joint session of Parliament convened, the parliamentary chairman immediately announced he had a statement from Malenkov. He then began reading the statement in which the Premier asked to be "allowed" to resign. With the conventional self-criticism practiced by Communist Party members, Malenkov blamed himself for the failure of attainment of high agricultural production goals. The statement took less than five minutes to read.

There was no doubt the delegates, some 1,300 of them from all parts of the Soviet Union, were surprised. A rumble of astonishment swept the assembly when the chairman finished reading the statement. The chairman then quickly recognized a Presidium representative, who obviously had been chosen to rush the acceptance of Malenkov's resignation. This man, Deputy A. M. Puzanov, walked briskly to the rostrum and said: "On behalf of the Presidium I wish to say we think Comrade Malenkov's request to resign is justified and I move we adpot a resolution accepting his resignation."

Then the chairman, Volkov, read a prepared resolution stating that Parliament "decrees the adoption of the appeal of Comrade Malenkov that he be allowed to resign. "We will vote," he asserted. "Who is for the resolution?" The hands of the delegates shot up automatically. This correspondent noticed only one woman who failed to raise her hand, perhaps because she had not yet recovered from the shock of what she heard. Volkov immediately said there were no dissenters and no abstentions and the resolution was adopted. The chairman then suspended the session until 4 p. m. Malenkov did not speak for himself. No one spoke in his defense. The delegates simply on the decision of the ruling group at the top as being the right one. Soviet democracy was in action.

Purging of Malenkov, and Mikoyan, who resigned before him, did not appear to be in the cards. In fact, immediately after the end of the first session, Moscow radio, in broadcasting the news to the nation, said Malenkov's resignation would be misinterpreted by the bourgeois press, meaning that in Western nations. Malenkov was quoted as saying: "We can expect those slanders but we are Communists and we don't care what they say."

28.4 How Stalin Used to Relax and the Fall of His Brother

[*Source: Kingsbury Smith: Stalin's daughter tells Hearst her brother is 'very, very ill', in:* New York Journal-American *(New York, N.Y.), No. 24,430, February 10, 1955, p. 1, cols. 1–8; p. 23, cols. 1–2.*]

Svtlana, the only daughter of Russia's late ruler Joseph Stalin, lives today as a married woman with two children in a small apartment in the center of Moscow. Before leaving Moscow for Leningrad, William Randolph Hearst Jr., this correspondent, and Charles H. Klensch, INS representative in Moscow, visited this woman who now is about 35 years old.

It was the first time she had ever granted an interview, and she told us: "You are the first Americans to have been in my apartment." She revealed to us that her brother, Vassily Stalin, who was a high-ranking officer in the Soviet air force is "very, very ill," and no longer on active duty.

When Hearst asked her about her brother, tears swelled in Svtlana's eyes as she replied. She seemed extremely emotional. She said Vassily had not been working for some time, but after a moment's hesitation added quickly: "I hope he will be well again soon." It was obvious she did not wish to talk about her brother's illness. We did not press her as to the nature of it, especially since we had been told by Western envoys in Moscow that nothing had been heard of Vassily since his father's death. There were rumors that he was being kept in a sanatorium. Vassily formerly led the Soviet air force flight over Red Square during Nov. 7 anniversary celebrations of the revolution.

Svtlana said Vassily was her full brother by Stalin's last and second wife, Alilueva. Svtlana also seemed deeply moved when she spoke of her father. She appeared reluctant to talk about any private views he may have expressed within the family circle concerning Russian or international affairs. When asked whether he had expressed to her his thoughts concerning the future of Russia and the world, she replied: "His views were the same as those expressed in his public speeches."

Svtlana said she did not think her father had left any memoirs, adding: "He was too busy to write memoirs." She further said Stalin's only forms of relaxation during the latter years of his life were reading and puttering around the orchard and garden of his country home on the outskirts of Moscow. Asked if he read light fiction, such as detective stories, for relaxation, Svtlana replied: "No, he was not interested in fiction. He preferred historical works, especially about ancient times. He liked to work nights and he also read late at night."

The daughter of the man who ruled Russia for nearly 30 years and who after the last war probably was the most powerful single individual in the world lives in what would be considered in America as a modest working-class type apartment. It is located in the interior of a block of flats that looked almost like an American tenement. It is a drab, gray building about 10 stories high with gloomy walls, stone stairways, dim lighting and an elevator that takes people up only. We were told by Western diplomats that these buildings, which are located near the Kremlin, are occupied by the elite of Soviet aristocracy – such as high government officials, leading artists and literary personalities.

As far as Svtlana's apartment is concerned, there was no sign of the Western conception of luxury, except perhaps for the neatly-clad maid who opened the door and an upright piano in a rather cramped little room that served as both sitting and dining room. Behind the maid at the door stood Svtlana, a red-haired woman with a fair complexion, a rather pretty face and a pleasant smile. She is much more slender than most Russian women and looks more Irish than Russian. Her hair was cut short in a fluffy fashion. She wore a pink and beige pullover sweater, a brownish-tweed skirt, and good-looking pumps.

She led us into her dining-sitting-room and invited us to be seated. A white cloth covered the table, on which there was a plate of oranges, apples and nuts. In one corner of the room stood a combined radio-television set. Crystal and glassware, typically Russian, adorned a chest on a side wall. Svtlana spoke little English and understood it much better. She said she learned it from tutors and in school. She told us she now was teaching Soviet literature at the Moscow Academy of Social Science.

In response to questions, she said she was married and had two little children – one boy aged ten, named Joseph after his grandfather. The other child a five-year-old girl. She asked if we would like to see them and when we replied affirmatively, she went out into another room and brought them back. The boy was wearing a sweater and dark brown trousers. He had on a red bandana neckerchief which is the emblem of the Soviet Boy Scouts. The boy was polite, but a little bewildered. His sister, however, was smiling and by no means shy. We asked if we could take a photograph of Svtlana with her daughter, and she agreed willingly.

Throughout our visit, however, she was tense and seemed almost apprehensive. Nevertheless, she was very gracious and friendly. She told us she had inherited her red hair from her Georgian grandmother on her father's side. We bade her farewell after she had shown us her small, booklined studio in which there was a large photograph of her father in a relaxed mood, lighting his pipe.

28.5 Soviet Policy and the Role of the Journalists

[*Source: Kingsbury Smith: 'Peace policy' is unchanged, Bulganin tells W. R. Hearst, in:* New York Journal-American *(New York, N.Y.), No. 24,432, February 13, 1955, p. 1, cols. 1–8; p. 21, cols. 1–8.*]

Marshal Nikolai Bulganin, Russia's new Premier, told William Randolph Hearst Jr., today that the Soviet Government's policy of seeking to improve relation with the United States remains unchanged despite the sharp attacks on America made at meetings of the Supreme Soviet (Parliament) this week.

In the first interview he has ever granted to Western journalists, the long-time member of the Soviet hierarchy, who replaced Georgi Malenkov four days ago as head of the government, parried questions as to how the Soviet Government reconciled these protestations for improved relations with the warmongering accusations against the United States. He said:

"Our assurances of our desire to have good normal relations with the United States Government are quite sincere."

Bulganin agreed that it would be "useful" if government officials made fewer public statements which tend to whip up sentiment against other countries. He also indicated that the Soviet Government does not want to limit experimental explosions of nuclear weapons. He further said that the committee form of collective leadership would continue to prevail in the Soviet regime. He added that his promotion to the Premiership and of Marshal Georgi K. Zhukov to the Defense Ministry did not mean an increased military influence in the conduct of governmental affairs.

Bulganin received the American publisher in the Kremlin office he already occupied as a Vice Premier. He wore civilian clothes and looked less bulky than he does in the uniform of marshal – the title Stalin bestowed on him during the war. He was neatly dressed in a dark business suit with black shoes, gray shirt, and dark blue tie. At 59, Bulganin has a full shock of white hair topped by prominent waves which curl back over the right side of his head from a high forehead. A trim gray goatee and moustache added to his non-military appearance. He answered questions with neither the rapidfire assurance of Communist Party Secretary Nikita S. Khrushchev nor the positive dogmatism of Soviet Foreign Minister V. M. Molotov. He chose his words carefully and spoke in a low, well modulated voice. He described himself as a "young Prime Minister" who feels "just like anybody else does when picked for a job like this."

Hearst, who was accompanied by Frank Conniff, his editorial assistant, and this correspondent, told Premier Bulganin that he had been talking with his brother, Randolph, in his New York office last night. Hearst said his brother had told him that the speeches which Bulganin and Molotov had made in the Supreme Soviet – speeches which contained violent attacks on the United States – had caused a good deal of speculation in America. The American people, Hearst added, are wondering whether the change in governmental leadership in Russia means that the attitude of the U.S.S.R. toward the United States will be any different from what it was under Malenkov. Bulganin replied quickly: "No, it does not."

Conniff then reminded Bulganin that Khrushchev told Hearst he thought it was silly and unfair for people in the West to whip up sentiment against the U.S.S.R., and to give the impression that the Soviet Union wants war. Yet, Conniff added, that was the impression the Premier and Molotov gave about the United States in their speeches to the Supreme Soviet. "Our people are bound to feel that is silly and unfair," said Conniff. "Does the Premier think it would serve the cause of peace better if there was no whipping up of sentiment by government officials against each other's country?" Bulganin said: "Yes, I think that would be useful although the speech made by Mr. Molotov to which Mr. Conniff made reference did give quite an objective appraisal of facts and it fully reflects the views of the Soviet Government."

This correspondent pointed out that Molotov in his statement made frequent references to what he described as the aggressive intention of the United States Government and asserted that the United States is preparing for war. "The American people are confident that their government has no aggressive intention and does not want war," I said. "They know President Eisenhower refrained from action in Indochina and in the Formosa area that might have precipitated an extension of those conflicts. When they read such statements as those made before the Supreme Soviet about the American government's intention they can only assume that the Soviet Government is misinformed about the American Government's intention or deliberately wishes to turn the rest of the world against the United States. It is concerned over the latter that makes the American people think they must look to their defenses and makes them think they need military bases. How does the Premier reconcile these attacks on the United States with assurances which have been given us that the Soviet Government want an improvement of relations between Russia and the United States?"

Bulganin, who was toying with a penknife, opening and closing the blade, leaned over the conference table and speaking slowly and seriously answered: "Our assurances of our desire to have good normal relations with the United States Government are quite sincere. Both Foreign Minister Molotov and I in our statements spoke of our desire and our belief that the present tension in international relations should be reduced. That is perfectly true. We do desire that, and we believe that all nations in the world share that desire.

"As for any sharp points in Mr. Molotov's speech, I might say that Mr. Molotov spoke only of things that are taking place. Mr. Kingsbury Smith said just now that his (Molotov's) speech might have given rise to a sentiment which might be taken as strengthening the desire of the American people to have military bases. I must say those bases were created long before the speeches of either Mr. Molotov or myself were made and of course the creation of those bases cannot be connected in any way with the speeches made by the representatives of the Soviet Government. Therefore, I believe it is incorrect to pose questions in that way. Furthermore, I would like to repeat that the establishment of more normal relations as I indicated in my speech is what we want. I pointed out that during the war against the German Fascists we did have good relations with the United States, Britain and also France, and we would be very satisfied now to have those good relations reestablished."

Hearst pointed out that today was the anniversary of one of America's great governmental "and one might say, spiritual leaders, Abraham Lincoln." He recalled that at the conclusion of the Gettysburg Address Lincoln said it was his resolve and the country's resolution that government of the people, by the people, for the people, should never perish from this earth. "I wondered," Hearst asked, "if the Premier would like to comment on that, and especially whether he shares that view." Bulganin said: "I think that is a very good quotation. It was a fine statement by a great man." Hearst asked if Bulganin had been familiar with that statement of Lincoln's before. Bulganin said "no."

We mentioned how we were about to board a plane in Leningrad for Helsinki when we received word that Bulganin would receive us and we hastened back to Moscow. This correspondent said Hearst in the course of his conversation with leaders of the Soviet Government had thought to make some suggestions which might have some positive results in helping to improve relations between our two countries. In this connection I said we noted Molotov's statement to the Supreme Soviet that Russia has now surpassed the United States in the development of the production of Hydrogen weapons. I added that we had also noted frequent references, made to us and in the Supreme Soviet, that the Soviet Government wants to see an end to the armaments race. I further said we were all aware of the fears expressed by scientists concerning the effect on humanity of a continuation of unlimited explosions of nuclear weapons for experimental purposes.

I explained that Hearst would like to make a specific suggestion, and Hearst said: "In view of the possible danger to humanity of unlimited thermonuclear and atomic bomb explosions for experimental purposes, would the government of the U.S.S.R. be prepared, pending prohibition of the production of these weapons, to consider concluding with the Government of the United States and other Western powers an agreement to restrict the number of such experimental explosion each year? This would not require any system of control since both sides would immediately know if there were any violations. In other words, this could be one and perhaps the only way of making a start in the direction of atomic disarmament without the necessity of control."

Bulganin said: "I am very glad to hear those remarks by Mr. Hearst, remarks that are directed towards humanitarian objectives, but I believe that we should follow the more radical path proposed by us. We should go further. We are prepared to discuss a prohibition of the production of the means of mass destruction, and a prohibition of the storing of atomic weapons, and to destroy everything we have created in that field. If we look at the suggestion just made from a practical point of view we shall come to the following conclusions: If we limited or discontinued altogether the experiments in that field what would that give to the people? In fact nothing, because both sides would retain in storehouses all the means that have been previously produced and all these means at any moment could be dropped on the heads of the people. The nations of the world have frequently heard statements by one side and the other that they have a sufficient number of these means of mass destruction. I can state quite seriously and definitely that our proposal is to prohibit the use and storage of these means of mass destruction. That is the direction in which in our opinion we should work. We should seek for such an agreement if we want peace and if we want to avoid war.

"People might say that storing of these means of mass destruction is now sufficient and that is the reason why the question has been raised of discontinuing further experimental explosions. That might increase the anxieties of some nations. Some people would say that before there were insufficient stockpiles but now sufficient stockpiles have been created so that experimental explosions can be discontinued. We feel we must go along our road first and that production of these means must be prohibited. That is all I want to say on that subject."

This correspondent said that he thought the Premier misunderstood Hearst's question. We were not suggesting complete discontinuance of these experimental explosions. We understood that the Soviet Union may wish to continue them and our government may wish to do the same thing. But in view of the warnings of scientists concerning the dangerous effect on humanity that a continuance of unlimited experimental explosions could have, we felt that the Soviet Government might be prepared to consider an agreement limiting the number to five, or 10, or even 20 a year. I added that the unwillingness of the Soviet government to do so was disappointing.

Bulganin then changed his attitude towards this suggestion of Hearst and said: "We would not refuse to consider any proposal that is directed at reducing the dangerous use of these means of mass destruction if that proposal is in fact directed towards that end. That is all I wish to add." Bulganin showed a restrained and friendly attitude throughout the interview. He seemed to be eager to answer our questions in a conciliatory manner. Once or twice he raised his hand or waved a finger for emphasis. He reflectively stroked his goatee or fingered one of the pencils from a big pile at his right when not toying with the penknife. At other times he folded his hands across his stomach and smiled at certain phrases of the conversation.

The room in which the interview took place was a high, white-ceilinged, partly panelled

Table I

Number of pupils and teachers in thousands in schools of three levels in the specified years

	1914–15	1927–28	1940–41	1950–51	1955–56
Pupils in schools of general education	7,896	11,589	35,528	34,752	30,070
Pupils in schools of middle vocational education including correspondence	36	189	975	1,298	1,961
Pupils in schools of higher and professional education including correspondence	112	169	812	1,247	1,867
Teachers in all schools	231	341	1,237	1,475	1,733

Table II

Total output of specialists of schools of middle and higher qualification in thousands in the specified years

	First Five-Year Plan 1929–32	Second Five-Year Plan 1933–37	Third Five-Year Plan 1938–40	The War Years 1941–45	Fourth Five-Year Plan 1946–50	Fifth Five-Year Plan 1951–55
From higher schools	170	370	328	302	652	1,121
From middle schools	291	623	678	540	1,278	1,560

Table III

Mass libraries and moving-picture establishments

	1913	1940	1950	1955
Mass libraries	13,880	95,400	123,100	147,200
Moving-picture establishments	1,510	28,000	42,032	59,285

Table IV

The press

		1913	1927	1940	1950	1955
BOOKS	Titles	27,000	33,400	45,800	43,100	54,700
	Copies in millions	89	226	462	821	1,015
JOURNALS	Titles	1,472	1,645	1,822	1,408	2,026
	Copies in millions	–	229	245	181	361
NEWSPAPERS	Titles	1,055	1,197[1]	8,806	7,831	7,246
	Copies in millions	3.3	9[1]	38	36	49

[1] For 1928.

Education and Media, 1914–1956

[*Source*: George S. Counts: The Challenge of Soviet Education, New York 1957, pp. 309 f.]

one with the inevitable conference table covered with green balze. Behind Bulganin's desk were pictures of Lenin and Stalin. A single telephone sat on the left side of the desk. This contrasted sharply with the half dozen phones of different color which were evident in Communist Party Secretary Khrushchev's office when we interviewed Khrushchev last week.

We asked the Premier on what level it was first decided to "allow" Malenkov to resign. Bulganin answered that the decision first was taken by the Central Committee, then brought before the Supreme Soviet "by authority of the Central Committee and a bloc of Communist and non-party members." In response to another question Bulganin said that Malenkov still is a member of the all-powerful nine-man Presidium of the Central Committee, which indicated he still retains an important position in the Soviet hierarchy. Bulganin further said there was no doubt that the manner in which he replaced Malenkov as head of the government meant that the principle of collective leadership is not being altered.

Conniff said the view still prevailed widely in Western governmental circles that the ultimate objective of Soviet foreign policy remains the achievement of predominant Communist influence in the world, and asked if this was so. Bulganin said he had nothing to add to what Khrushchev had said to us on that subject. [Communist party secretary Khrushchev said in a Feb. 5 interview with Hearst and Smith that Russian rulers believe Communism will in the long run gain the "upper hand" in the world. But he said Russia wants no war and wants to see the global struggle between Communism and capitalism confined to long-range competitive coexistence. Khrushchev said how long that coexistence would last "no one can tell."]

This correspondent asked how Bulganin estimated the chances of agreement for establishment of an effective system of international control of all armaments, including atomic weapons, with continuous inspection in all countries. Bulganin answered: "We favor disarmament. We favor controls." He added that the Soviet Government had made proposals which were well known and he had nothing to add.

Conniff returned to the question of Hearst's telephone conversation with his New York office and said our people have emphasized the serious concern aroused by the strong tone taken by the speakers of the Supreme Soviet in regards to the United States. "Is there anything we can, as journalists, say to clarify or to alleviate this situation?" Conniff asked. Bulganin answered: "What Mr. Hearst, Mr. Kingsbury Smith, and Mr. Conniff could do is to transmit through the press and by any other means our real desires. That is the desire to seek reduction of international tension, to preserve peace among nations, and to improve relations with the United States. By conveying that in an objective and correct manner a great deal could be done. Especially by the kind of journalists with whom I am speaking today. A great deal depends on journalists."

Hearst said: "I am of a second generation of journalists in my family and I am fully aware of the responsibility of journalists." Conniff asked how Bulganin felt personally when the great authority of leadership and its enormous responsibilities were conferred on him. Bulganin said: "I feel as people always feel in similar cases." With that the hour and 10-minute interview ended.

Related Readings

Alexandrov, Victor: Khrushchev of the Ukraine – a biography, New York 1957.
Allilueva, Svtlana: Twenty letters to a friend, New York 1967.
Biagi, Enzo: Svtlana – an intimate portrait, New York 1967.
Boettcher, Erik et al. (Eds.): Bilanz der Ära Chruschtschow, Stuttgart – Berlin – Köln – Mainz 1966.
Boffa, Giuseppe: Inside the Khrushchev era, New York 1959.
Bromage, Bernard: Molotov – the story of an era, London 1956.
Brzezinski, Zbigniew Kazimierz: The permanent purge. Politics in Soviet totalitarianism, Cambridge, Mass., 1956.
Crankshaw, Edward: Khrushchev's Russia, Baltimore – Harmondsworth 1959.
Kulski, Wladyslaw Wszebór: Peaceful co-existence. An analysis of Soviet foreign policy, Chicago 1959.
Löwenthal, Richard: Chruschtschow und der Weltkommunismus, Stuttgart 1963.
MacGregor-Hastie, Roy: The life and times of Nikita Khrushchev, London 1959.
Malenkov, Georgi Maksimilianovich: Report to the Nineteenth Party Congress on the work of the Central Commitee of the C.P.S.U. (B)., Oct. 5, 1952, Moscow 1952.
Meissner, Boris: Rußland unter Chruschtschow, München 1960.
Pálóczi-Horvath, György: Khrushchev – the road to power, London 1960.
Rush, Myron: The rise of Khrushchev, Washington 1958.
Seton-Watson, George Hugh Nicholas: From Lenin to Khrushchev. The history of world communism, 2. ed., New York 1960.
Wolfe, Bertram David: Strange communists I have known, New York 1965.

1956

Russell Jones
United Press

CHAPTER 29

REPORTS ABOUT HUNGARY IN 1956

The Civil War and the Exposition of Communism

    Introductory Notes
29.1 The Ten-Day Revolution and Its Violent End
29.2 A Ship Named 'Liberty' and Her Harbour
29.3 Hope For Western Aid and Widespread Disappointment
29.4 Masses Fight Fearlessly and Russia Now Sends Planes
29.5 Hungarian 'Capitalism' and Why It Cannot be Extinguished
    Related Readings

Introductory Notes

After several Pulitzer Prizes for International Reporting had been awarded for coverage of the Soviet Union, suddenly one of the U.S.S.R.'s satellites, in this case Hungary, became the focus of interest. One of the few American correspondents who watched the Hungarian uprising from close up in Budapest and had reported it for his news agency was Russell Jones of the United Press. The Advisory Board on the Pulitzer Prizes bestowed the International Reporting award in 1975 on Russell Jones "for his excellent and sustained coverage of the Hungarian revolt against Communist domination..."

Russell Jones was born on January 5, 1918, in Minneapolis, Minnesota. He went to school in Minneapolis and was graduated from high school in Stillwater, Minnesota, in 1935. Almost immediately he began his newspaper career as a reporter for the Post Messenger, *Stillwater, Minnesota. Two years later he joined the* St. Paul Dispatch *and remained there until 1941, when he entered the U.S. army. He was assigned to Europe, thus beginning what was to be a stint of fifteen years on that continent. Jones served a year in the infantry, then became one of the founders of the European edition of* Stars and Stripes. *Subsequently he worked as a combat correspondent in England, North Africa, France, Belgium, and Germany. Jones was discharged from the Army in 1945 with the rank of technical sergeant. The following year he became a reporter for the* Stars and Stripes, *assigned to cover news in both New York and Europe. He accepted a post as editor of the* Weekend Magazine, *a European publication, in 1948, and this took him to Paris and Frankfurt. In 1949 Russell Jones became a United Press correspondent and was assigned to London. Shortly after, he was named UP bureau manager in Prague, and was in that post when an Associated Press correspondent was jailed in 1951 on a charge of spying. The State Department warned that it would be only a matter of time before Jones, too, was arrested, but the correspondent begged to be allowed to stay. Finally United Press ordered him to Frankfurt for a "conference", and he was not permitted to return to Czechoslovakia. Later, working as the chief Eastern European correspondent for the United Press, Russell Jones did not even have a visa when he drove into battered Budapest in the final days of October, 1956, to cover the Hungarian revolt.*

The following texts by Russell Jones, copyright 1956, are reprinted by kind permission of the United Press International, *New York, N.Y.*

29.1 The Ten-Day Revolution and Its Violent End

[*Source: Russell Jones: Did reds touch off Hungary revolt? Evidence hints answer is yes, in: The Chicago Daily News (Chicago, Ill.), Vol. 81/No. 339, December 10, 1956, p. 1, cols. 1–2; p. 12, cols. 1–4.*]

A final spark is always needed to inflame men to the point where they are willing to lose their lives in a fight for liberty. People the world over are asking whence came that spark in Hungary.

What could move Hungarian men, women and children to claw with bare hands at Communist tanks and troops? Now that I am out of Hungary and free of censorship, I can write what many people in Budapest believe to be true: Communist rulers of Hungary provoked an anti-Communist demonstration. Their idea was to kindle a small fire, to release some of the smoldering passion and then to stamp it out so ruthlessly no one would dare try again. But it flamed instead until it engulfed all of Budapest, then the whole of Hungary and, until its tongue was scorching, even the Kremlin. It has been damped down – but it is not out yet.

The man believed behind it was Ernoe Geroe, the hated "Stalinist" dictator of Hungary, close friend of Lavrenty Beria. There is evidence Geroe plotted with the Russians to start the revolt and kill it. As a Bolshevik since 19, trained in Moscow as late as 1944, he had the experience for it.

I can cite these facts:

– The first Budapest demonstration came on Oct. 23.

– Yet on Oct. 21 – two days earlier – Soviet tank forces that later appeared in Hungary started moving out from the Kiev area of Russia.

– A Russian mechanized division that fought in Hungary left its barracks near Rimosoara, Romania, on Oct. 22.

– Soviet troops in Hungary itself were alerted at 2 p. m. on Oct. 23 and were on the road to Budapest by 6 p. m., four hours before the massacre at Parliament Square.

– That night Geroe himself went on the radio to assail the demonstrators as "counter-revolutionaries." In that stroke he condemned what he knew was a popular uprising, removed any hope for an easing of the regime – and guaranteed a violent showdown.

Geroe met an appropriate end. The Budapest radio reported on Nov. 4 that he had been "murdered in a barbarous fashion" by the revolutionaries. He was attempting to escape to Russia. No one had better motive for getting away. And no one knew better that Hungary was ripe for a "small" revolt, but he had so suppressed the nation that its mood was one of desperation. Prices were impossible. Stores were barren. The secret police had curtailed more liberties with each year for 10 years. And then – standing before them – was the example of the successful protest of the Poles against the Warsaw regime and the Russians.

The greatest shock to the Hungarian Communists and their Russian masters must have been the type of people who fought the hardest. Believe none of the stories that this was a misguided uprising formented to restore the great estate owners of the Horthy regency or the

SUMMER

Rakosi is replaced by Gerö as First Party Secretary after Suslov's and Mikoyan's visit to Budapest.

AUTUMN

University students break away from the Communist youth organisation and set up their own Association of Hungarian University and College Students.

OCTOBER

6   Gerö goes to Moscow.

10 Gyorgy Lukacs, widely-known literary critic and party theoretician of long standing, long time in disgrace, now re-instated, at a press conference at Budapest University demands complete freedom for writers and the abolition of censorship.

14 Rehabilitation of Imre Nagy, former Hungarian Prime Minister, deposed and expelled from the Party in 1955.

19 Min. of Education yields to students' demand to abolish the compulsory tuition of Russian in schools and universities.

20—22 Soviet troop moves reported from Soviet-Hungarian frontier areas; assembly of floating bridges; recall of officers on leave.

20—21 Open-air meetings are reported to have taken place in Györ demanding withdrawal of Soviet troops from Hungary and the release of Cardinal Mindszenty.

22 Budapest students draw up a list of 16 demands and call a demonstration in support of them and to express sympathy with Poland and Gomulka's election as Party leader. Students' demands include those for the withdrawal of Soviet troops, reconstitution of the Government under Imre Nagy, free elections, freedom of expression, improvements in the standard of living.

23 Mass demonstration in Budapest. Gerö's speech over the radio attacking the demonstrators. Clashes with the Hungarian secret police (AVH); shots fired by AVH.

23—24 Imre Nagy appointed Prime Minister; Gerö — First Secretary of the Party.

24 7.45 a.m. State of emergency proclaimed.
    8.00 a.m. Radio announces appointment of Imre Nagy as Prime Minister.
    8.30 a.m. Summary jurisdiction ordered. Decree signed by Nagy, Chairman of the Council of Ministers.
    9.00 a.m. Radio reports that the Government had appealed for support of Soviet troops to help restore order.
    (The first Soviet tanks had made their appearance in Budapest at about 2 a.m.).
    11.00 a.m. Government proclamation granting exemption from summary jurisdiction for all those laying down arms before 13.00 hours.
    12.30 a.m. University Students' Association appeals to all students to support Imre Nagy.
    1.00 p.m. Time limit for the surrender of arms extended until 5 p.m.
    7.45 p.m. Kadar, Party Secretary, declares that only surrender or complete defeat awaits those who continue their 'murderous and hopeless fighting.'

    During the day fighting spread to other parts of Hungary. Soviet troops, including tanks, reported to be in action in Budapest.

    11.00 p.m. Radio Budapest announces that 'the situation has generally improved. The rioters have been isolated, though in some places they have made sudden attacks.'

    Rail and air communication with Budapest practically at a standstill.

    Workers' Councils Spring up all over the country.

25 Minister of Defence appeals to troops to report back to their units.—In an Order of the Day he states that heavy losses have been inflicted on the rebels, and that with the brotherly aid of the Soviet troops the 'People's Democracy' has been saved.

    Population of Budapest greatly embittered by Soviet tanks guarding the Parliament Building opening fire on unarmed demonstrators in support of the AVH.

    Reported that Mikoyan, Soviet First Deputy Prime Minister, and Suslov, secretary of the CPSU arrived in Budapest and left at noon.

    At 11 a.m. Radio Budapest announces the appointment of Janos Kadar as First Secretary of the Party in place of Erno Gerö.

    In the afternoon, Kadar broadcasts a promise of greater democratisation and of the opening of negotiations with the USSR.

Chronology of Events in Autumn 1956

[*Source:* Hugo Dewar/Daniel Norman: Revolution and Counter-Revolution in Hungary, London 1957, pp. 61–63.]

industrial magnates. I saw with my own eyes who was fighting and heard with my ears why they fought.

The first armed resistance came from students, the youths who had been so carefully selected as the party elite of the future. The fiercest fighters were the workers, the proletarians in whose name communism had ruled. Even the Hungarian army, purged and re-purged a dozen times, joined the battle for freedom or sat on the sidelines. The two big names that came out of the revolt were Communist – Imre Nagy, a lifelong party member, and Lt. Col. Pal Maleter, who had deserted to the Russians in World War II and returned as a Red partisan. Yes, wherever came the spark, it found its tinder among the common people.

The areas of destruction, the buildings most desperately defended and the dead themselves are the most eloquent proof of this. It was the workers' tenements that Soviet siege guns smashed, factory buildings that became forts and the tired shabby men with broken shoes and horny hands of the laborer who died by the thousands. A 17-year-old girl, twice wounded at Corvin theater, told me she fought because "it isn't right that my father with four children to feed should get only 900 forints ($80) a month." The chairman of the workers council at the Csepel iron and steel plant with 38,000 workers, biggest in the country, said: "These are our factories? We will fight to the death to hold them. But we will continue plant maintenance because we want to work here again."

In Dorog, one of the coal centers, miners continued to work despite the general strike. But not to produce coal. They didn't want their mines ruined by flooding. The same attitude is true in the country. The farmers want to get out of the collectives but they do not want the restoration of the landlords. They think everyone should have the right to own and till his own land. Something like 100 acres a family would be fair, they think.

It was for these simple, basic things that the Hungarian people fought. These and the right to speak and think freely, to elect men of their own choice and to raise their children in their own way. They will go on fighting for them.

29.2 A Ship Named 'Liberty' and Her Harbour

[*Source: Russell Jones: While world watches – Mindszenty awaits fate. Prisoner-Cardinal is symbol of Hungary's hope for freedom, in:* The Chicago Daily News *(Chicago, Ill.), Vol. 81/No. 340, December 11, 1956, p. 18, cols. 3–7.*]

At about 10 each morning in the American legation in Budapest, a small Hungarian woman scurries from the kitchen in the basement to a room on the third floor. She knocks on the door, deposits a tray on a chair just outside. It bears a typical American breakfast – scrambled eggs, toast, fruit juice and coffee. The man in the room who takes the tray over to a desk that serves as his breakfast table is short, slight and bowed with his 64 years – the last eight in Communist prisons.

He is Josef Cardinal Mindszenty, Prince Primate of Hungary, a priest without a pulpit, a leader who cannot speak to his people. The whole world is watching to see what happens to this man. He has become the symbol of a free Hungary. Mindszenty's own freedom lasted only five days, from the morning of Oct. 31, when Hungarian soldiers freed him, until Nov. 4 when he took sanctuary in the American legation as Russian tanks slaughtered the freedom fighters in the streets.

If he steps from that building he faces almost certain return to the Communist jails where, as he puts it, he endured "things which are unspeakable and defy the imagination of every man." His secretary, the Rev. Egon Turcsanyi, left the legation and tried to reach the West on Nov. 10. He was arrested immediately. Opinion in Budapest is that the Red regime of Janos Kadar and the Russians will not try to force their way into the legation and seize

Mindszenty. "Why should they?" one Hungarian asked me. "The situation now is the same as when the secret police had him – but now the Americans run the jail."

There is grim truth in the remark. The cardinal's life, although comfortable enough, is that of a prisoner. What the future holds is not clear. Some legal experts believe the United States cannot continue to shalter him if the puppet government takes formal steps. Legation officials will not discuss eventualities, and they have been very careful in the manner of his asylum. No messages from or to the cardinal are delivered. Visitors are politely but firmly turned away.

For Cardinal Mindszenty, each day is much like the last. He rises about 7 a. m. and prays and meditates for several hours before breakfast. Then he works on the memoirs to which he is devoting his main energies. The room in which he works and sleeps is the private office of U.S. Minister Thomas P. Walles. His bed is the minister's leather couch. The desk he uses for both work and as a dining table also serves as an altar when he celebrates Mass. At one of his Masses during the height of the fighting, 15 American correspondents were present.

Mindszenty was arrested the day after Christmas, 1948. In the weeks before, his anti-Communist rallies had drawn crowds so large they could hardly be accommodated. He was convicted Feb. 8, 1949, of treason, disloyalty to the government and currency-law violations. He was sentenced to life. For almost eight years he was dragged from one Communist prison to another – seven in all.

"Sometimes I did not know where I was," he said.

His liberation came at the height of the success of the Hungarian revolt. A Hungarian army squad led by Maj. Josef Palinkas broke into the old manor where he was held at Felsoe Peteny 65 miles from Budapest. They barely beat a group of the AVH secret police who were going for Mindszenty, too. At that time the AVH was in terror of lynching by the populace and their plan was to drive Mindszenty through Budapest to show the people that they, too, were with the revolutionaries.

Only five days later the cardinal had to seek sanctuary in the legation. One of his first acts was to write a letter to President Eisenhower, describing himself as "a shipwreck of Hungarian liberty." It concluded: ". . . I beg of you, do not forget, do not forget this small, honest nation enduring torture and death in the service of humanity."

29.3 Hope For Western Aid and Widespread Disappointment

[Source: Russell Jones: The burden of U.S. flag was too much, in: Washington Daily News *(Washington, D.C.), Vol. 36/No. 30, December 12, 1956, p. 2, cols. 2–5.]*

I put away the American flag on Nov. 12. For 15 days it had covered the hood of my small Ford. And at first I was more than proud of the cheers and applause it brought from Hungarians in the streets. But as the days wore on, the cheers turned to stares of bewilderment and, sometimes, expression of bitterness.

I took the flag down because I could no longer bear the burden of representing America to the Hungarian people, of trying to answer the question. "Why don't you help us?" Worse, I couldn't bear the sympathy, and courtesy with which they listened to my stumbling, inadequate answers. When the Russians launched their second attack on Nov. 4 and crushed the young democracy, the West stood by, seemingly helpless.

On Csepel Island where the workers fought for the seized Hungary's greatest complex of factories, a simple workman said: "President Eisenhower said the United States had never encouraged a revolt against a legitimate government. What does he mean? What have you been telling us all these years? What did the 'policy of liberation' mean?" What does an American say to questions like that? I didn't know and I still don't know. One man in Miskole, 160 miles northeast of Budapest, pushed his head into our car to say: "You Americans. You gave us a lot of help when we needed it. Drop dead." Much harder to take was the kindness of an old woman. She too asked why the Americans didn't help. I told her, "But I am only one person." She patted my shoulder.

Most blame in Hungary is aimed at Radio Free Europe and the Voice of America. They have been successful in reaching the Hungarian people. So much so that over and over again, Hungarians would ask. "Why do you bother talking if you are not going to do anything?" But the problem goes deeper than radio broadcasts. The mere example of free societies in the West was an encouragement for Hungarians to attempt, and almost achieve, the impossible.

The United States was not the only target. Britain and France were accused time and again of having exploited the revolution to cover their attack on Egypt. A worker in Csepel said, "Britain has roasted the chestnuts of Suez in the fires of Budapest." Another said more bluntly, "Eden has stabbed the Hungarian revolution in the back." But the United States drew blame, too, for its Suez policy. "If Eisenhower can threaten war when the Russians talk about volunteers, why can't he do the same when they send 5000 tanks into Hungary?" asked a miner in Dorog. "Are we less important than the Egyptians and the Israelis? Is the blood we shed less red than theirs?"

Despite the inability of the Hungarians to understand the reasons why they were not helped, the West and America in particular, has a great reservoir of good will. On the simple human side, the Hungarians are grateful for the help the West has given them over the years. Time and again, anonymous little people would come to me to ask that I help send messages to friends. Not requests for aid, just assurances they had survived. The messages were left in the hotel, slipped in our pockets, left under the windshield wipers of our cars or handed over openly under the noses of Soviet soldiers. I remember one. It read: "Tell Louie we are living. Tell him we mess (sic) them."

The Vienna license plates on my car brought the repeated query, "Are you going to Vienna?" But no one ever asked that I take him along. It was in a feeling of utter inadequacy that I took the flag off my car on Nov. 12. The burden of being a representative of all America was too much.

Budapest, 1956
Many street-names have changed

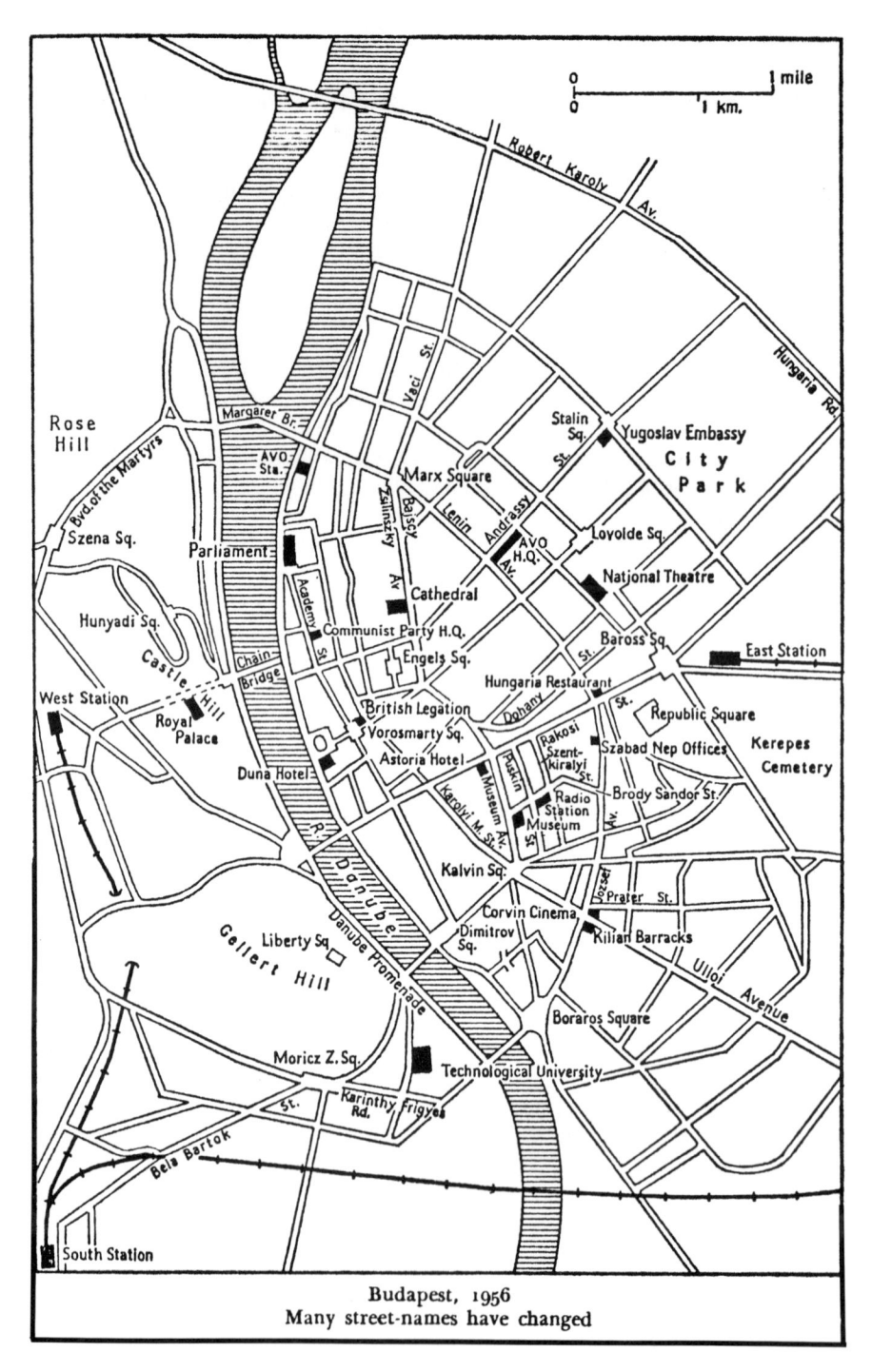

[*Source:* Noel Barber: Seven Days of Freedom. The Hungarian Uprising 1956, London 1973, p. 15.]

29.4 Masses Fight Fearlessly and Russia Now Sends Planes

[*Source: Russell Jones: To name a hero is to insult a people, in:* Washington Daily News *(Washington, D.C.), Vol. 36/No. 31, December 13, 1956, p. 2, cols. 2–5.*]

Heroism is an overworked word, but if I were handing out Congressional Medals of Honor they would go to the entire Hungarian people. Never has an entire nation fought with such desperate courage, for such unselfish motives and against such overwhelming odds. The workers, the students, the women and the children of Hungary fought and won the revolution of Tuesday, Oct. 23. They fought and died in resisting the Soviet return. And when their weapons proved weaker than their spirit, they simply refused to work for their Moscow masters.

To choose any Hungarian as the hero would insult the thousands of those who fought. But there were these individuals who stand out in my memory: The 14-year old girl who turned herself into a human torch to set fire to three Russian trucks and the guns they towed. She died with half a dozen Russian soldiers caught in the flames. I never saw her in life, but I saw the charred remains of her body outside the Kilian barracks, covered with a Hungarian flag and a pathetic bunch of artificial flowers. An elderly man wept as he translated a note pinned to the flag: "Here lies a Hungarian girl of 14 years. She died for her country. All Hungary mourns her."

The 13-year-old boy with the shaved head. He had fought in both the revolution and the Soviet attack of Nov. 4. The Russians herded him along with some other 2000 young Hungarians into cattle cars for deportation. He had escaped and walked all the way back to Budapest. He was ashamed because the Soviets had shaved his head and his cap slipped down on his ears. He was literally as tall as the rifle he carried as he patrolled in front of the Corvin theater. I thought of America's Andy Jackson who fought our revolution at 12. The children – and I mean children – who spread the sloping streets leading into Moscow Square with heavy oil and soap so Soviet tanks skidded and went out of control as they attempted to charge the barricades.

With the few weapons they had taken from the police, the Hungarians fought the Soviet army. With Molotov cocktails – bottles of gasoline – they knocked out so many of the Soviet T-34 tanks that the Russians never again used them against organized resistance. With a handful of antiquated 85-millimeter anti-tank guns, they knocked out more tanks as the huge 152-millimeter Red Army siege guns. In the Kilian-Corvin area alone, they destroyed two siege guns and at least six tanks. But finally, courage, ingenuity and old weapons were not enough.

In their second attack, the Russians brought in their T-54 tanks. They were virtually invulnerable to fire. Unlike the 34s, their gasoline was carried in internal tanks. I took a long hard look at these new land-going Soviet dreadnoughts. It was the first time they had gone into action before Western eyes. The sleek turrets and closely joined body seams of the T-54s gave little opportunity for flaming gasoline to cling or penetrate. Exhausts were protected by flaps and pillows were put in the engine louvers to filter out gasoline fumes. Shells from the

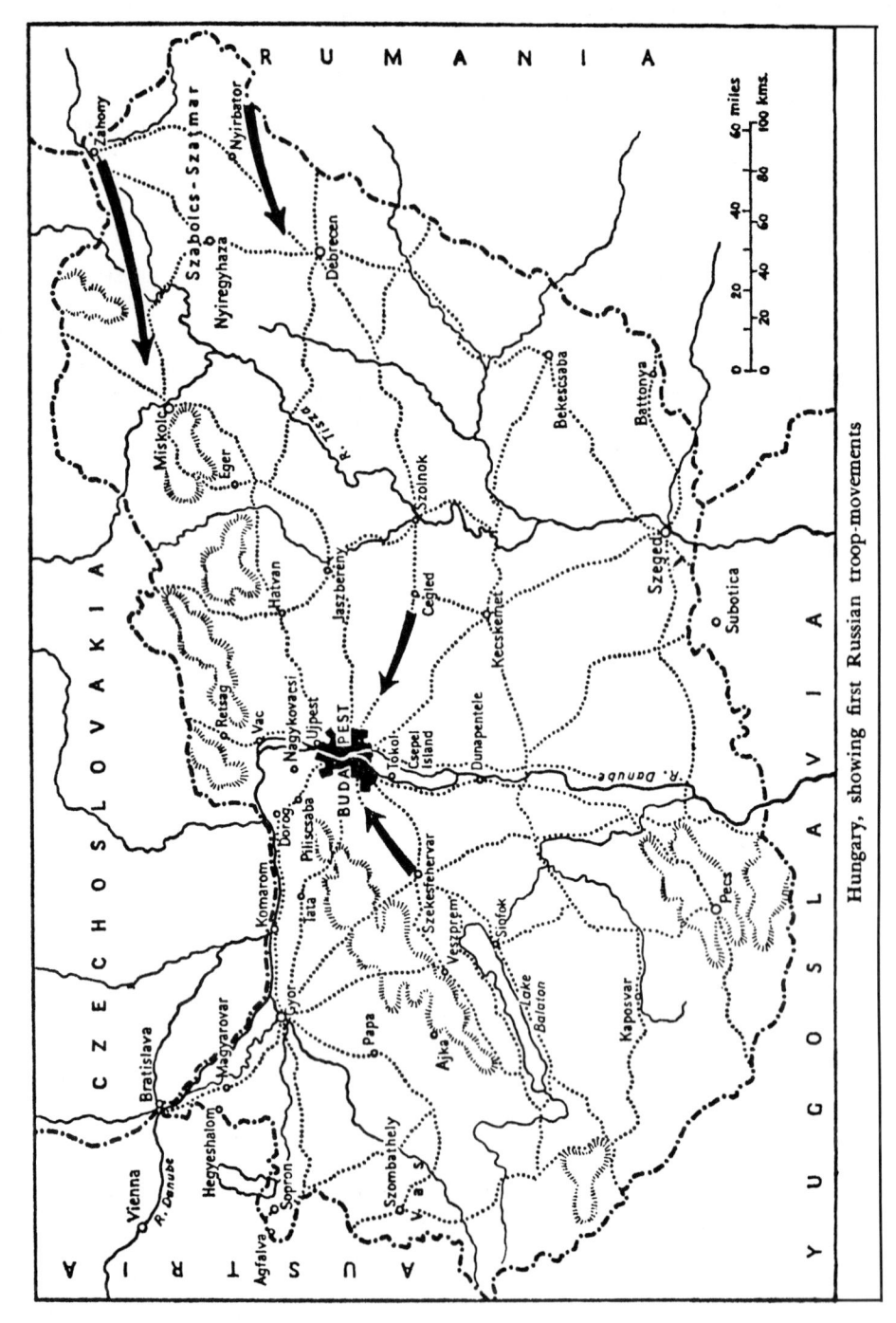

Hungary, showing first Russian troop-movements

[*Source:* Noel Barber: Seven Days of Freedom. The Hungarian Uprising 1956, London 1973, p. 16.]

World War II 85s bounced harmlessly off the most modern tank in mass production on either side of the Iron Curtain. Unlike the first attack, in the second the Soviets used planes. The MIG 15s and 17s and the IL 28s, to bomb strong points. Long rifle 152-millimeter guns on Gellert hill fired down into the resistance areas.

But the Hungarians fought on. Men holding out in the postoffice telephoned Josef Cardinal Mindszenty in the U.S. Legation to ask. "Bless us, Father, before we die." They died on the second day. The Russians took no chances. A single shot from a sniper brought a salvo from the heaviest artillery to kill one man. Church steeples were systematically shelled because they were choice spots for a sniper. The last areas to hold out were the great iron and steel plants on what was once called "Red Csepel," and the industrial suburb of Ujpest. They stopped fighting only when it became clear the Russians would destroy the entire works that the men consider their own. Even after the crushing of resistance in Budapest, the struggle went on in the country. Students at Sarospatak college near Satoraljauhely, not far from the Soviet border, took to the hills as partisans, confining the Russians to the main roads.

As I write this, reports from Budapest indicate fighting may break out again. If it does, I will hope, against all logic and reason, that a people who have taught the world a lesson in courage will win. A British diplomat said to me one night in Budapest: "These are a people who must be especially beloved of God." I subscribe.

29.5 Hungarian 'Capitalism' and Why It Cannot be Extinguished

[*Source: Russell Jones: The battle of Hungary – in the end, the Soviets will lose, in:* Washington Daily News *(Washington, D.C.), Vol. 36/No. 32, December 14, 1956, p. 2, cols. 2–5.*]

Ten million Hungarians, armed with little more than courage, have handed Russia and communism the most shattering defeat. Never again can the Kremlin claim it represents the poor, the downtrodden, the exploited. The naked and brutal force that holds communism together has been exposed for all the world to see.

Whatever terrible punishment the Soviets inflict on Hungary, in the end they will lose – as few empires in history ever lost before. For all their charges of "counter-revolution," white terror and fascism, the unconcealable truth is that workingmen and women, intellectuals and youth arose spontaneously and unanimously against them. One of the small satisfactions the Hungarian people had during the revolt was to learn from foreign radio stations of the turmoil their uprising caused in Communist Parties throughout the world. Peter Fryer, correspondent of London's Daily Worker, reached the end of his communist rope in Budapest. His paper refused to print his blunt dispatches about the Soviet attack. So one night, seated in the British legation, he worte his resignation while Russian tanks patrolled the street outside. And I know that even hardened communists like Sam Russell, who replaced Fryer, and Andre Stil of the French communist paper, L'Humanité, were deeply embarassed by the hatred of the Hungarians for the Soviets and all things communist.

What must the masses of Asia and Africa think now? And in the other East European satellites – What do they think now of Nikita Khrushchev's "separate roads to socialism?" The whole world knows that the roads lead to the same place. It has taken the Hungarians to point out that all signposts point to Moscow.

Nothing so infuriates the Hungarians now as the feeble communist efforts to portray their uprising as the work of capitalists and Fascists. I remember the iron worker who said to me: "Look, I'm the capitalist trying to take back his factory." His coat was held togehter by string. The knees of his trousers were patched and patched again. He wore no socks.

Or the women who defied Soviet tanks and machineguns to lay flowers at the tomb of the unknown soldiers. These were the women who marched alone, who insisted their men stay indoors, and dared the Russians to shoot them. Or the Hungarian soldiers who, under orders, stood with Red army men at road checkpoints. One took our papers out of a Russian's hands, saying: "This bastard doesn't understand. He can't even read." As we started away, he called: "Run over the bastard." At another road check, I was accompanied by a Hungarian woman and her daughter. The Hungarian soldier examined my papers, then started to ask about the women. His gaze caught mine, and he suddenly said: "Your wife and daughter are all right. Get going." He elbowed his Soviet companion out of the way and let us pass.

What can the Soviets do about people like these? They can continue their present policy of military occupation, hoping the Hungarians will starve themselves into submission. They can institute a reign of terror to drive the people back to work. They can take over the plants themselves, using slave labor or even Soviet soldiers to work the machines. Which they will try I do not know. Even the bravest man must have goods for his family and even the finest spirit can be broken. Perhaps the Soviets can force a semblance of order.

But, having seen what I have seen, I must believe against all logic and reason that the Hungarians will win. So much of the impossible already has happened that it could end in a way that now seems impossible – in freedom for a people who have shown so clearly they are second to none in their love of it.

Related Readings

Aptheker, Herbert: The truth about Hungary, New York 1957.
Arnet, Edwin (Ed.): Aufstand der Freiheit. Dokumente zur Erhebung des ungarischen Volkes, Zürich 1957.
Bain, Leslie Balogh: The reluctant satellites. An eyewitness report on East Europe and the Hungarian Revolution, New York 1960.
Barber, Noël: Seven days of freedom. The Hungarian uprising 1956, London 1974.
Beke, Laszlo (pseud.): A Student's diary. Budapest, October 16–November 1, 1956, London 1957.
Davidson, Basil: What really happened in Hungary? A personal record, London 1957.
Dewar, Hugo/Norman, Daniel: Revolution and counter-revolution in Hungary, London 1957.
Fryer, Peter: Hungarian tragedy, New York – London – Toronto 1956.

Gleitman, Henry: Youth in revolt. The failure of Communist indoctrination in Hungary, New York 1957.
Hofer, Walther: Die weltpolitische Bedeutung des ungarischen Freiheitskampfes, Zürich – St. Gallen 1958.
Király, Béla K./Jónás, Paul (Eds.): The Hungarian revolution of 1956 in retrospect, New York 1978.
Kopácsi, Sándor: Die ungarische Tragödie. Wie der Aufstand von 1956 liquidiert wurde, Stuttgart 1979.
Méray, Tibor: Thirteen days that shook the Kremlin, New York 1959.
Strasser, Peter: Ein Atemzug Freiheit. Volksaufstand und Konterrevolution in Ungarn. Bericht der Sonderkommission der Vereinten Nationen, Wien 1957.
Vasari, Emilio: Die ungarische Revolution 1956, Ursachen, Verlauf, Folgen, Stuttgart 1981.
Zathureczky, Gyula von (Ed.): Der Volksaufstand in Ungarn. Berichte und Zeittafel, Köln 1957.
Zinner, Paul E.: National communism and popular revolt in Eastern Europe. A selection of documents on events in Poland and Hungary, February–November, 1956, New York 1956.

1957

Elie Abel

The New York Times

CHAPTER 30

REPORTS ABOUT YUGOSLAVIA IN 1957

Tito's Brand of Communism and Quarrels With Moscow

Introductory Notes
30.1 Yugoslavia's Illusion and How It Is Destroyed
30.2 A Promised Credit and Its Political Implications
30.3 Tito's Refusal to Changes and Rumors About a Meeting
30.4 Soviet Fulfills Promise and Opens a New Phase
30.5 A Secret Meeting and Its Impact on the Future
Related Readings

Introductory Notes

In contrast to the previous custom of the postwar period to award Pulitzer Prizes for International Reporting to individual correspondents, it was decided in 1958 to give the award to the New York Times *in total "for its distinguished coverage of foreign news" during 1957. The newspaper's prize-winning entry – which was originally nominated for the Meritorious Public Service category – shows clearly, however, that the materials submitted did not by any means represent world-wide coverage of events, but that they had been filed exclusively from East European countries, namely Albania, Czechoslovakia, Hungary, Poland, Rumania, the Soviet Union, and Yugoslavia. The submitted articles came from the following foreign and/or special correspondents of the* New York Times: *Elie Abel (Belgrade, Budapest, Bucharest, Prague, Warsaw), Turner Catledge (Moscow), Max Frankel (Moscow), Sydney Gruson (Warsaw), William J. Jorden (Kiev/Moscow), John MacCormack (Budapest/Warsaw), James Reston (Moscow, Warsaw), Harrison E. Salisbury (Belgrade/Sofia/Tirana). Among these eight journalists who had contributed to the entry, Elie Abel was probably the most important one, since his articles came from a number of countries.*

    Elie Abel was born on October 17, 1920, in Montreal, Canada. After he had received a B.A. degree at McGill University in 1941, Abel did graduate studies at Columbia University, New York, where he received an M.S. degree in 1942. Since 1941, Abel had already been working as a reporter for the Windsor Star *in Ontario, Canada. During World War II he joined the Royal Canadian Airforce abroad. In the 1945–46 period Abeld continued his journalistic work on the* Montreal Gazette *in the Canadian province of Quebec as an assistant city editor. From 1945 on, Abel was stationed as a foreign correspondent in Berlin, Germany, for a news ageny, the* North American Newspaper Alliance, *before functioning as UN correspondent for the* Overseas News Agency *between 1947 and 1949. In 1949, Abel changed to the* New York Times, *first working mainly in Washington, later reporting also from Eastern Europe. His dispatches from East European countries were filed in his function as a special foreign correspondent of the* New York Times. *In this capacity he wrote, among other things, those dispatches constituting the Pulitzer Prize entry of his newspaper.*

    The following texts by Elie Abel, copyright 1957, are reprinted by kind permission of The New York Times, *Inc., New York, N.Y.*

30.1 Yugoslavia's Illusion and How It Is Destroyed

[*Source: Elie Abel: Khrushchev talk alarms Belgrade. Return to Soviet campaign of criticism against Tito is seen in Yugoslavia, in:* The New York Times, *International Edition (New York/Amsterdam), Vol. CVI/No. 36,329, July 12, 1957, p. 3, col. 1.*]

President Tito's hopeful assumptions about the dawning of a new day in Moscow got a rude jolt today. For the last week Belgrade officials had been jubilant over Nikita S. Khrushchev's purge of Old Guard Stalinists in the Kremlin. This happy development, the Yugoslav public was told time and again, could only lead to improved relations between Belgrade and Moscow and to relaxation between the Soviet Union and the Western powers.

Tonight there was shocked silence in the Yugoslav capital. Although early editions of tomorrow morning's newspapers carried brief news items on the Soviet leader's visit to Prague, their reports did not mention his criticism of the Yugoslav brand of communism.

If Mr. Khrushchev had set out with deliberate intent to offend the proud Yugoslavs, he could not have chosen his words with greater care. He mocked at the worker councils, which the Yugoslavs regard as their uniquely important contribution to the theory and practice of modern communism. He announced Moscow's determination to bring Yugoslavia back into the Soviet camp. And he had some barbed things to say about Communist countries that receive aid from the West.

Marshal Tito was away from the capital on his Brioni Island retreat. Vice Presidents Edvard Kardelj and Alexander Rankovic were at Sochi in the Soviet Union. The Yugoslav Foreign Ministry had closed for the day, hours before word of Mr. Khrushchev's Prague comments reached Belgrade.

The few officials who could be reached tonight would say nothing. Their dismay was obvious. Nor did any of the Belgrade officials appear to know anything about an impending Tito-Khrushchev meeting. Noting that MM, Kardelj and Rankovic were already in the Soviet Union, they said it would be logical if the two Vice Presidents talked with Mr. Khrushchev on his return from Czechoslovakia.

It has been obvious to Western diplomats in this capital that the Yugoslav, who used to pride themselves on their expert understanding of Soviet developments, had no advance information about the dismissal of Georgi M. Malenkov, Lazar M. Kaganovich, Vyacheslav M. Molotov and Dimitri I. Shepilov. When the news was published the Yugoslavs fell back on their faith in Mr. Khrushchev's good intentions and their conviction that the removal of the Stalinists could only be a step forward.

Mr. Khrushchev's blunt talk today was bound to shake this faith somewhat. In criticizing the worker councils and Marshal Tito's ties with the West, the Soviet party chief returned to the two main themes of the recent Soviet propaganda campaign against Yugoslavia.

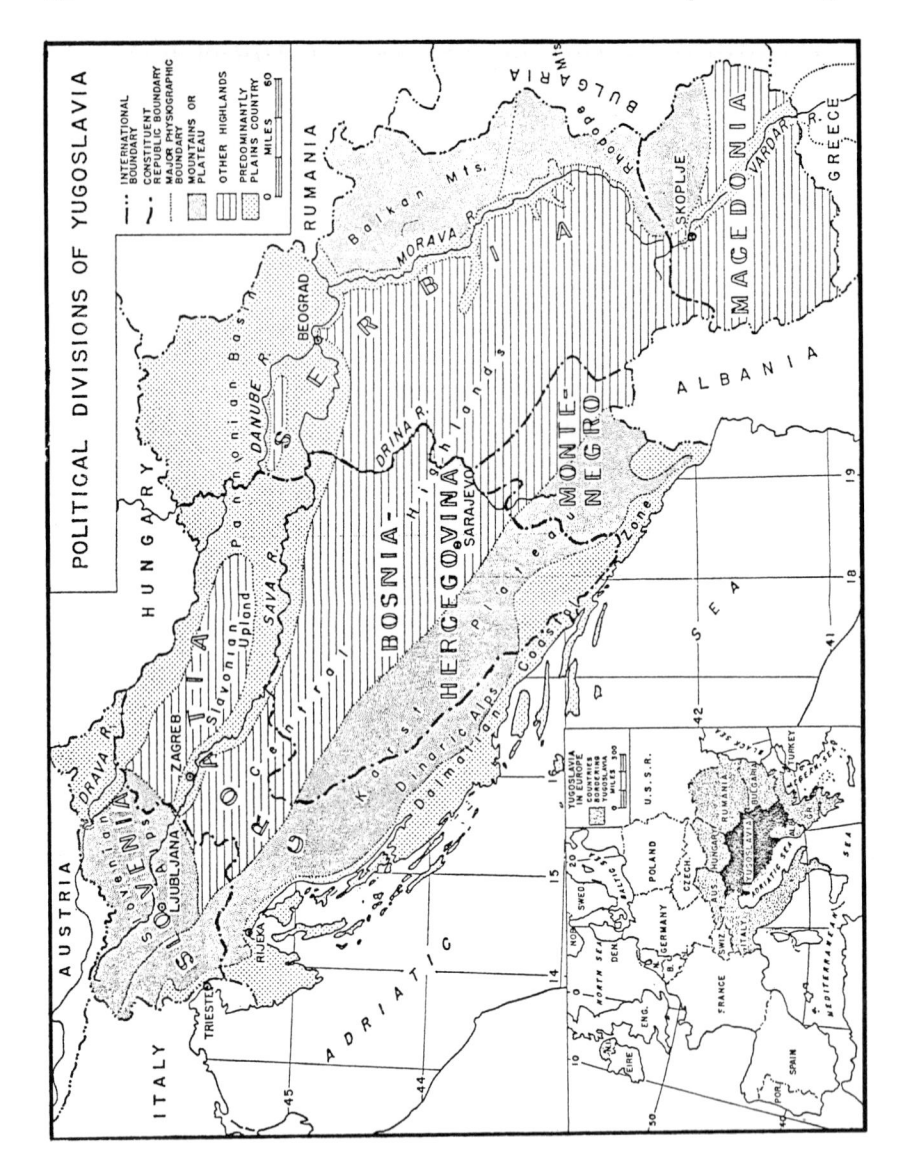

[*Source:* Fred Warner Neal: Titoism in Action. The Reforms in Yugoslavia after 1948, Berkeley-Los Angeles 1958, last cover p.]

30.2 A Promised Credit and Its Political Implications

[*Source: Elie Abel: Yugoslavs seek Soviet renewal of pledge of aid. Mission going to Moscow to urge a reinstatement of $250,000,000 promise, in:* The New York Times, *International Edition (New York/Amsterdam), Vol. CVI/No. 36,331, July 14, 1957, section 2, p. 1, col. 1; p. 6, cols. 2–3.*]

A Yugoslav economic delegation will leave for Moscow in a few days to seek a reinstatement of a $250,000,000 aid commitment on which the Soviet Union reneged last winter.

News of the mission was disclosed this afternoon in a special bulletin issued by Yugopress, the semi-official news agency. It said that the Belgrade delegation, headed by Hasan Brkic, president of the Foreign Trade Committee, would discuss with Soviet representatives the "execution of previously agreed investment arrangements."

Under the original agreement announced last Aug. 3, the Soviet Union was to furnish Yugoslavia with a long-term credit of $175,000,000 for the construction of an aluminum and hydroelectric project at Niksic, in Montenegro. In addition, the Russians were to have contributed about $75,000,000 toward the building of a fertilizer plant and an electric power station in Yugoslavia.

The history of this arrangement can be traced in the chart of Belgrade–Moscow relations over the last year. It was concluded during the first flush of reconciliation following President Tito's state visit to Moscow in the spring of 1956. Moscow backed out of the deal after its suppression of the Hungarian revolt had brought into the open a clash of opinions between the Soviet leadership and President Tito.

The Kremlin's present willingness to reconsider the aid program is regarded as a token of the interest of Nikita S. Khrushchev, the Soviet Communist party chief, in realigning Yugoslavia with the Soviet bloc. Belgrade has never balked at accepting economic and even military assistance from countries with differing viewpoints, for example, the United States. Marshal Tito has said publicly more than once that United States aid was extended without political conditions.

The fact that ideological differences with the Soviet Union remain unresolved should not, in the Yugoslav view, be an obstacle to the fulfillment of the original aid commitment. For the moment, however, the Tito regime is being careful to softpedal these differences.

Borba, the organ of the Yugoslav League of Communists, published a sketchy account today of the Khrushchev speech in Prague, Czechoslovakia, on Thursday in which the Soviet party leader said some unpleasant things about the Yugoslav brand of communism. These remarks, reported at length by a Yugoslav correspondent published, although his account was circulated privately in Government and party officials and to editors of leading Yugoslav newspapers. What Borba carried instead, and a day late, was a brief report from which all the sting of Mr. Khrushchev's words had been removed.

There was no mention of Mr. Khrushchev's announced determination to bring Yugoslavia back into the Soviet orbit. The biting things he said about Yugoslav workers' councils, about Marshal Yugo Tito's stand on the Hungarian revolt and about Yugoslavia's ties with the United States were toned down with a censor's pencil. All that survived was this passage: "He [Khrushchev] then spoke about workers' councils in Yugoslavia, noting that workers'

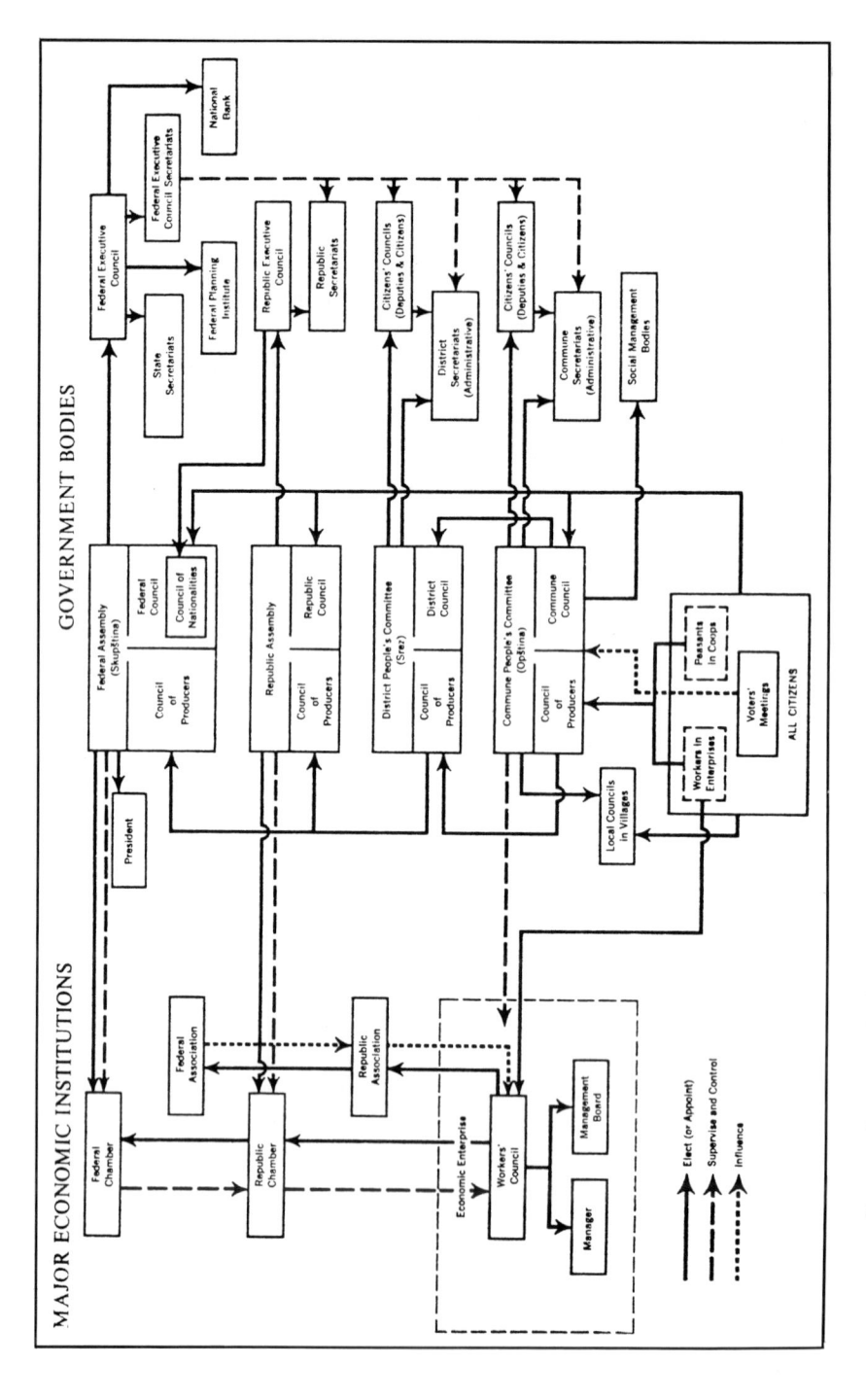

[*Source:* George W. Hoffman/Fred Warner Neal: Yugoslavia and the New Communism, New York 1962, p. 215.]

councils were not the only organizational form available. In the end Khrushchev spoke critically of the economic aid, received by Yugoslavia from the United States as well as of the Yugoslav attitude toward the events in Hungary."

It appeared that the Yugoslav leadership was not prepared at this stage to dispel the officially fostered impression among the public that Mr. Khrushchev's victory in the recent Kremlin shake-up meant a revolutionary change in Soviet policy toward Yugoslavia and the West.

30.3 Tito's Refusal to Changes and Rumors About a Meeting

[*Source: Elie Abel: Yugoslavs weigh Soviet accord. Tito seen refusing any changes, in:* The New York Times, *International Edition (New York/Amsterdam), Vol. CVI/No. 36,338, July 21, 1957, section 2, p. 2, cols. 2–3.*]

Yugoslav Communists are cautiously exploring the prospects for reconciliation with Moscow, though not on Nikita S. Khrushchev's terms. Under no circumstances, authoritative Belgrade sources insist, will President Tito rejoin the Soviet bloc or weaken his independent ties with the West.

The blunt insistence of Mr. Khrushchev, the Soviet Communist party chief, during his visit to Prague last week that the Yugoslavs must do these two things caused Yugoslav leaders to discount their high hopes of a truly revolutionary change in Kremlin policy. There is some disposition here not to take at face value all the harsh things Mr. Khrushchev says about the Yugoslav brand of Communism. For the moment, however, no one in authority here pretends to know the Soviet party leader's real intention with respect to Yugoslavia.

Political discussions between Belgrade and Moscow leaders may take place in the fall, when Marshal Klementiy Voroshilov, President of the Soviet Union, comes to Yugoslavia on a state visit. Meanwhile, Belgrade looks on the Soviet-Yugoslav economic negotiations, which started in Moscow this week, as the first test of Mr. Khrushchev's present attitude. The Yugoslavs are asking the Russians to honor belatedly the economic aid commitments they made to Yugoslavia a year ago. These originally provided credits amounting to about $250,000,000 for the construction of an aluminum plant in Montenegro, as well as an electric power station and a fertilizer plan elsewhere in Yugoslavia. Moscow reneged on the commitments last winter at the height of its ideological squabble with Marshal Tito over the Hungarian uprising. What the Yugoslav leaders want is the re-establishment of reasonably cordial relations that would respect each country's rights to interpret and apply Communist teaching in its own way.

Yugoslav officials say that the long-postponed visit of Marshal Voroshilov almost certainly will take place before the end of the year, possibly as early as September. It seems not to have been decided so far whether other members of the Moscow Presidium will accompany the nominal Soviet chief of state. If Mr. Khrushchev or Deputy Premier Anastase I. Mikoyan were to come along, the visit would certainly be more than a protocol affair.

The Belgrade press has played down the brief Moscow talks last Thursday between Mr. Khrushchev and Marshal Tito's chief lieutenants, Edvard Kardelj and Alexander Rankovic. The two Yugoslav Vice Presidents, ostensibly vactioning in the Soviet Union, also talked at a villa outside Moscow with Enver Hoxha and Todor Zhikov, Communist party chiefs of neighboring Albania and Bulgaria respectively. This meeting had its social side, as the wives of all four were present. If, in addition, anything of political importance occurred, the Yugoslavs are saying nothing about it.

Many Belgrade Communists are skeptical about the Kardelj-Khrushchev meeting. They interpret official Soviet reports of the "frank and friendly" conversations to mean that both sides were outspoken to the point of a sharp exchange, which probably settled nothing. Yugoslavia's differences with her Communist neighbors and with Mr. Khrushchev are not susceptible of settlement in one convivial evening, these sources say. Moreover, they point out that Mr. Kardelj and Mr. Rankovic left Moscow the following day for Leningrad en route to Finland and Western Europe. It is felt here that they might have stayed a few days longer for further talks if these had seemed worth while.

30.4 Soviet Fulfills Promise and Opens a New Phase

[*Source: Elie Abel: Soviet grants Yugoslav aid on which it had reneged. Signs pact for the full 250,000,000, in:* The New York Times, *International Edition (New York/Amsterdam), Vol. CVI/No. 36,348, July 31, 1957, p. 1, cols. 6–7; p. 2, col. 2.*]

The Soviet Union has agreed to honor belatedly the $250,000,000 economic aid commitment to Yugoslavia on which it reneged last winter. A compromise agreement, signed yesterday in Moscow and made public here this afternoon, reinstates the full amount of the aid program.

With technical assistance from East Germany and Soviet financing, it provides for construction of an aluminum and hydroelectric project in Montenegro and a nitrogen fertilizer plant and a second electric power station elsewhere in Yugoslavia.

The Yugoslavs, who had insisted last winter that the four-year postponement demanded by Moscow was unacceptable, nevertheless settled for less than the immediate start of construction provided in the original agreement. Hasan Brkic, head of the Yugoslav Foreign Trade Committee, outlined the new terms on his return from the Soviet capital today. The fertilizer plant is to be built according to the previous schedule, Mr. Brkic said, with preliminary work completed by 1959. But the start of the aluminum-power combine, which accounts for 70 per cent of the Soviet credit, is to be delayed until next year, with construction stretched out until 1964. That is three years later than originally planned.

Yugoslavia boasts abundant bauxite and potential hydroelectric power. Her lack of financial resource has delayed exploitation of these riches. Up to now Belgrade's efforts to interest Western Governments in financing the newborn aluminum industry have elicited no ready response.

The Soviet commitment, which seems to have been part of a political design to realign Yugoslavia with the Communist bloc, dates from 1956. The fertilizer plant was approved in January of that year and the aluminum project in August. At the height of last winter's ideological squabble between Belgrade and Moscow, both agreements were nullified. The Soviet Union requested a delay until the end of the current Five-Year Plan in 1960. The Yugoslavs, interpreting this move as an effort to punish their heresy, rejected the postponement with a show of indignation.

The compromise announced here today marks the formal opening of a new phase in Soviet-Yugoslav relations. There is no evidence that President Tito made the slightest ideological concession to the Russians. The present agreement is in fact being interpreted here as a vindication of Marshal Tito's thesis that state relations between the Soviet Union and Yugoslavia can and should be cordial, despite their long-standing differences over the theory and practice of communism.

30.5 A Secret Meeting and Its Impact on the Future

[*Source: Elie Abel: Tito, Khrushchev confer and agree to a closer bond – Wide accord set, in: The New York Times, International Edition (New York/Amsterdam), Vol. CVI/No. 36,352, August 4, 1957, p. 1, cols. 7–8; p. 2, col. 5.*]

The leaders of the Soviet Union and Yugoslavia hammered out a working agreement for closer interstate and party cooperation at a secret meeting in Rumania. News of the meeting, held for the last two days, the first between President Tito and Nikita S. Khrushchev since their conferences on Brioni Island and in the Crimea last September, was confirmed tonight in a statement by the Yugoslav Government. It had been announced by the Moscow radio earlier in the day.

Both parties pledged themselves to work toward the "removal of obstacles" that hinder the improvement of relations between them and to strengthen the "unity of the international workers' movement." There was, however, no suggestion in the communique that Marshal Tito had budged from his refusal to rejoin the Soviet bloc. [An attempt to settle some of the deep-seated Soviet-Yugoslav differences had been expected by authorities in Washington. Some officials speculated that the meeting seemed thus far to have produced no tangible rewelding of the uneasy Belgrade-Moscow relationship.]

In addition to Marshal Tito, the Yugoslav delegation consisted of Dr. Edvard Kardelj and Col. Gen. Alexander Rankovic, the two Vice Presidents who had prepared the ground for the meeting during their recent visit to Moscow, as well as Veljko Vlahovic, Central Committee member in charge of liaison with foreign Communist parties, and Veljko Micunovic, Ambassador to Moscow. Mr. Khrushchev was accompanied by Anastas I. Mikoyan, Deputy Premier and member of the Presidium; Otto V. Kuusinen, another Presidium member; Nikolai Ponomarev, the Soviet party's liaison man with foreign Communists, and Ni-

TYPES OF AID, 1945-1959

A — UNRRA (1945-1948) — 16.2%
B — Economic assistance (1950-1959) — 47.5%
C — Specific projects (1949-1950) — 4.0%
D — Military assistance — 32.3%

ECONOMIC ASSISTANCE, BY COMMODITY, 1950-1959

A — Foodstuffs — 56.2%
B — Feed and fertilizer — 1.5%
C — Fuel and raw materials — 23.2%
D — Miscellaneous capital equipment — 0.7%
E — Special projects — 7.9%
F — Miscellaneous — 1.9%
G — Ocean freight — 7.9%
H — Technical cooperation / technical exchange — 0.7%

ECONOMIC ASSISTANCE, BY PROGRAM, 1950-1959

A — Technical exchange / technical cooperation — 0.6%
B — Defense support — 34.3%
C — Special assistance — 1.7%
D — Emergency relief — 4.3%
E — Title I — 33.9%
F — Title II — 4.1%
G — Title III — 11.9%
H — Specific projects — 9.2%

UNITED STATES AID TO YUGOSLAVIA

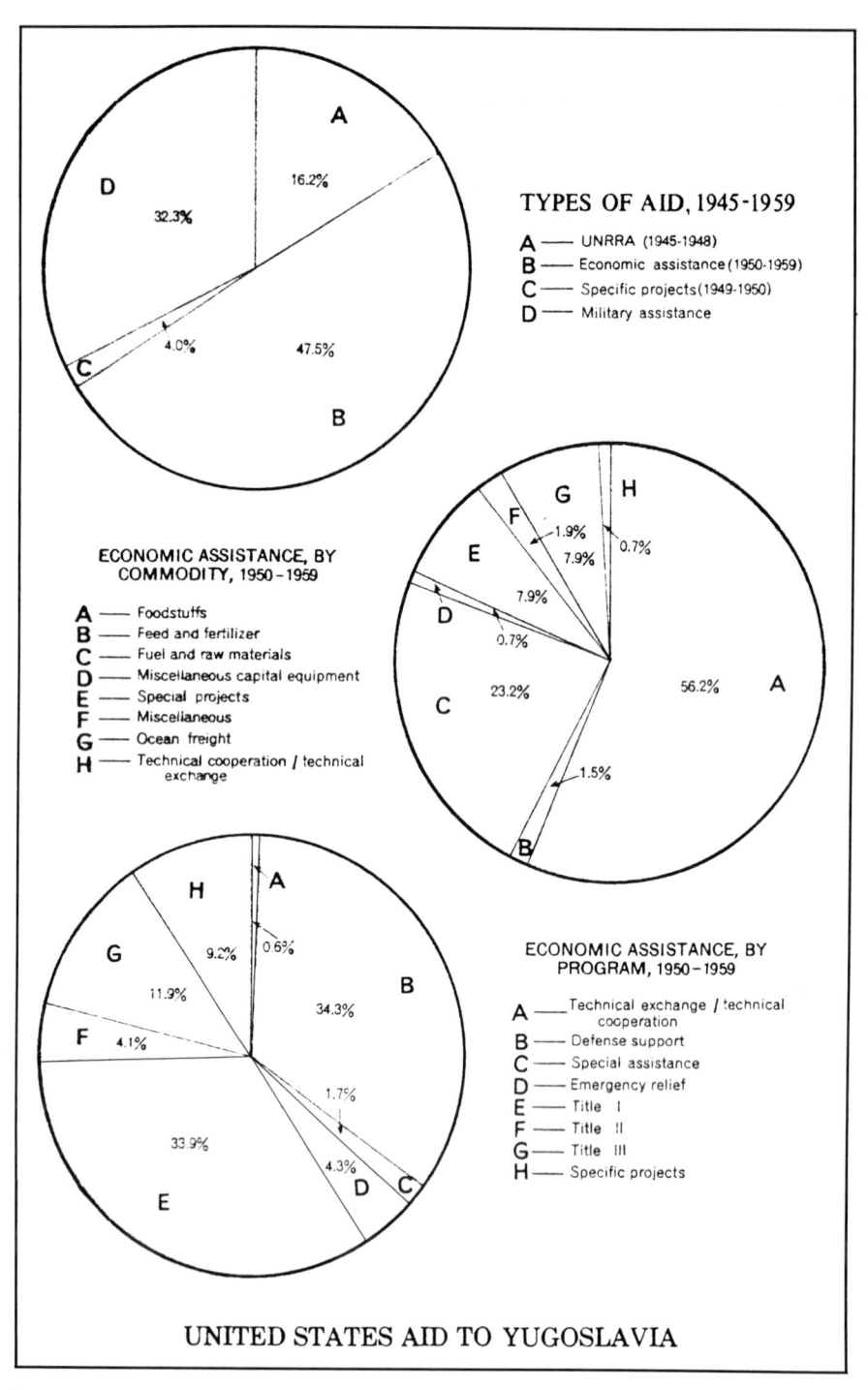

[*Source:* George W. Hoffman/Fred Warner Neal: Yugoslavia and the New Communism, New York 1962, p. 350.]

kolai P. Firyubin, Soviet Ambassador to Belgrade. Mr. Firyubin is the husband of Miss Yekaterina A. Furtseva, a protégé of Mr. Khrushchev and the first woman ever elected to the Soviet Presidium.

The latest Tito-Khrushchev conference followed the conclusion this week of a new agreement under which the Soviet Union staked Yugoslavia to a $250,000,000 economic aid program for the construction of aluminum and fertilizer plants over the next seven years. The Kremlin's agreement to reinstate this program, upon which it had reneged last winter, appears to have been the first major step toward breaking the ice that had crusted Yugoslav-Soviet relations since last winter.

This was part of Marshal Tito's price for a reconciliation with the Soviet leadership. In addition, the Kremlin agreed to reaffirm the Belgrade declaration of June, 1955, and the Moscow declaration of June, 1956. These state and party instruments acknowledged the right of Yugoslavia – and by extension of all other Communist countries – to find their own way to socialism, free of Soviet interference and dictation.

What Marshal Tito may have given the Russians in exchange is not entirely clear from the language of the Yugoslav communiqué. It speaks of "conrete forms of cooperation" between the two parties, mentioning exchanges of delegations and of publications. The communiqué also emphasizes the "special significance" of unity and "brotherly cooperation" among the Communist parties and countries. What may be meant by this phrase is the establishment of an international coordinating body of Communist parties, along with an international party journal.

At the Brioni meetings last autumn, Mr. Khrushchev proposed both these measures and Marshal Tito, with painfully vivid memories of the Cominform in mind, turned him down. This time there is some reason to suspect that the Yugoslav chief of state may have been more receptive. But it must be emphasized that nothing is known here so far about the detailed forms this cooperation would take.

Related Readings

Bass, Robert Hugo/Marbury, Elizabeth (Eds.): The Soviet–Yugoslav controversy, 1948–58. A documentary record, New York 1959.
Clissold, Stephen (Ed.): Yugoslavia and the Soviet Union, 1939–1973. A documentary survey, London–New York 1975.
Dedijer, Vladimir: Tito, New York 1953.
Djordjević, Jovan: La Yougoslavie démocratie socialiste, Paris 1959.
Farrell, Robert Barry: Jugoslavia and the Soviet Union, 1948–1956. An analysis with documents, Hamden, Conn., 1956.
Halperin, Ernst: Der siegreiche Ketzer. Titos Kampf gegen Stalin, Köln 1957.
Hoffman, George Walter/Neal, Fred Warner: Yugoslavia and the new communism, New York 1962.
Johnson, A. Ross: Yugoslavia in the twilight of Tito, Beverly Hills, Calif., 1974.
Jukić, Ilija: Tito between East and West, London 1961.
Maclean, Fitzroy Hew: The heretic – the life and times of Josip Broz-Tito, New York 1957.
Mollet, Guy: Le Socialisme selon Tito, Paris 1971.
Naegelen, Marcel Edmond: Tito, Paris 1961.

Neal, Fred Warner: Titoism in action. The reforms in Yugoslavia after 1948, Berkeley, Calif., 1958.
Smole, Jože: Yugoslav views on coexistence, Beograd 1961.
Vucinich, Wayne S. (Ed.): Contemporary Yugoslavia. Twenty years of Socialist experiment, Berkeley, Calif., 1969.
Wilson, Duncan: Tito's Yugoslavia, Cambridge–New York 1979.
Zaninovich, M. George: The development of Socialist Yugoslavia, Baltimore, Md., 1968.

1958

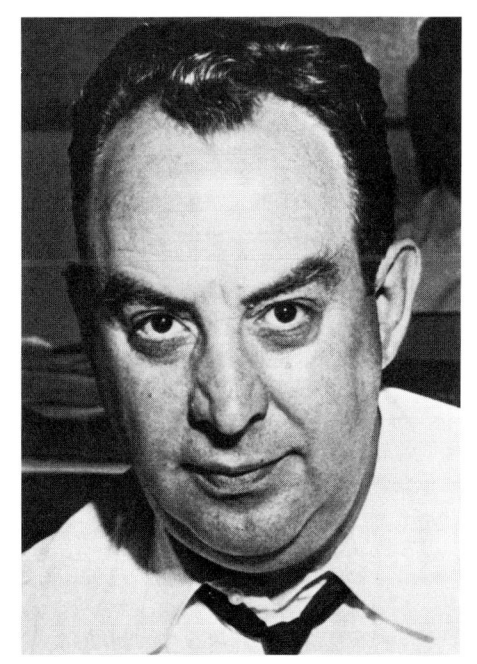

Joseph G. Martin/Philip J. Santora, *Daily News*, New York

CHAPTER 31

REPORTS ABOUT CUBA IN 1958

The Batista Rule and Rumors About Revolution

    Introductory Notes
31.1 Batista's Reign of Terror and the Fight for Freedom
31.2 Official Sadism and Its Various Exponents
31.3 The Batista Coup and the Fruits of Temptation
31.4 Cuba's Captive Press and How It Is Run
31.5 The Dictator and His Counterpart Castro
    Related Readings

Introductory Notes

Probably encouraged by the preceding year's award to the New York Times, *the New York Daily News submitted an entry for 1959 with the intention to win a prize for the newspaper as a whole, too. The Pulitzer Prize committees did rank first the materials presented by this newspaper but awarded the prize to two journalists of the* Daily News, *Joseph Martin and Philip Santora, the News entry consisting exclusively of their collective articles. Martin and Santora received the International Reporting award "for their exclusive series of articles disclosing the brutality of the Batista government in Cuba" from 1958.*

Joseph George Martin was born on May 9, 1915, in New York City. In the depths of the depression, he quit high school in Queens and roamed the town looking for jobs in warehouses, factories and on the docks. He never got a job as a laborer, but somebody was able to place him on the New York Daily News *as a copyboy in 1933. Within a year he was advanced to reporter, working out of Brooklyn police headquarters and on general assignment until he entered the Army Air Force in 1943; he was discharged early in 1946. Back to work at the News, Martin shortly uncovered a large scale-building racket on Long Island which defrauded hundreds of ex-GIs and developed other stories that won him awards from veterans' groups.*

Philip Joseph Santora was born on July 29, 1911, in New York City. He was educated at Syracuse University (1929) and received a B.A. degree from New York University in 1933; then he was a graduate student at the Sorbonne, Paris. During World War II, Santora was assigned to Military Intelligence with Patton's Third Army. Before he took up newspaper work on the New York Daily Mirror *(1936–1943, 1946–1954), Santora had a varied career: boxing instructor, clerk at Bellevue Hospital, etc. In 1954 he came to the New York* Daily News *as a special feature writer.*

Martin and Santora began their search for the truth behind the Batista regime in Cuba early in March, 1958. They sought out underground contacts in Washington, D.C., Miami, and New York. Through hundreds of interviews they learned the secrets of a terror-ridden island. It was the first time that the real story behind the Batista dictatorship was made known to the American public by a newspaper, The New York Daily News.

The following texts by Joseph George Martin and Philip Joseph Santora, copyright 1958, are reprinted by kind permission of the New York News, Inc., New York, N.Y.

31.1 Batista's Reign of Terror and the Fight for Freedom

[*Source: Joseph Martin/Phil Santora: Batista's foes seek reckoning, in:* Daily News *(New York, N.Y.), Vol. 39/No. 245, April 7, 1958, p. 2, cols. 3–5; p. 26, cols. 1–5.*]

Tortured, enslaved Cuba is teetering on the brink of the bloodiest revolution in its strife-ripped history, with most of the crocodile-shaped island's population awaiting the call to death or liberation with almost cheerful fatalism. The Cubans hope the outside world will understand.

They want others to understand, for instance, that when a young girl is raped by a police chief while his grinning cops hold back the heartbroken father, the day of reckoning can include no mercy. That the police official who produced a bullet-riddled body and sneered, "There's the answer to your habeas corpus" cannot be dealt with in the ordinary legal way.

These are merely random samples of atrocities committed in the name of president Fulgencio Batista. Murder, rape, corruption in low and high places, the torture methods employed by police, the systematic plundering of a rich country, the reduction to enslavement of what was once a gay, happy people – these are merely a few of the scores Cubans must settle. Is this a one-sided picture? It might seem so. But it's the picture we found – and we went to Cuba to get both sides of the story.

During the past six years, over 4,000 anti-Batista Cubans have met death by violence – victims of a reign of terror that ranks with Heinrich Himmler's Gestapo in Nazi Germany, the OGPU in Soviet Russia and even the Spanish Inquisition. Friends and relatives of the victims have not forgotten. They want the slate wiped clean, and if it can be wiped clean only with blood – well, that's the way they want it. "We won't even try to hold them back for the first three days," said a responsible member of the underground. "It would be like trying to hold back the ocean. They have waited a long time – and a blood bath is the only way to make a fresh start."

The present reign of terror is taking place less than 100 miles from the mainland of the greatest democracy in the world. It is being conducted with ruthless efficiency and the people of Havana – no matter what their sympathies – don't go out at night unless it's absolutely necessary. The dreaded SIM, the Security Police, patrol the streets in their olive-colored cars and uniforms and shove machine guns under the chins of citizens. They're merely asking for identity cards, but the machine guns are always present. More than any other weapon, the machine gun is the symbol of Cuban rule.

There are two types of censorship in Cuba. There is the ridiculous, arbitrary type imposed by the government. And there is the self-censorship imposed by the newsmen, both domestic and foreign, who have sold out to the Batista government. Except in rare cases, the things that filter through this palmetto curtain are thoroughly distorted. "Please tell the rest of the world what's going on here," begged a Cuban lawyer.

Our trail began with the underground in New York and led to Miami, where more than 2,000 exiles are fighting to extricate their beloved Cuba from the grasp of its oppressors. It led to Havana, where foreigners who carry typewriters and cameras are viewed with suspicion and kept under constant police surveillance.

What really goes on in Havana? At night, for one thing, strange things happen in cemeteries. A woman who went out one morning to pray at the tomb of her husband, thought the slab on the above-ground mausoleum seemed off-center. Her son investigated and found three bodies had been dropped in during the past two nights. The wife of an important banker was sent out of the country by her husband because a police official became smitten with her – and what the police want in Cuba, they take.

Rumors have spread that the Communists have been supporting Fidel Castro, military leader of the revolutionaries in Oriente Province. One report states that Russian submarines have been landing arms in the Santiago sector. The insurgents deny these reports. Even though the Communist Party last week announced its support, they say, it is neither needed nor wanted. They add that the Reds are a weak party in Cuba, without resources to buy munitions. They further point out that Batista was on the Red ballot and legalized the party out of gratitude. Since then, however, Batista has outlawed the Reds.

These is a great deal to be said for the rebel argument. The great middle class of Cuba is anti-Red and extremely powerful and respected. There is a saying that when Cuba's middle class takes a hand in politics something happens. More than that – they are completely selfless. Many of these doctors, lawyers, teachers and accountants could find employment in the U.S. if they chose to emigrate. They could bow to Batista and their fortunes would be intact and their families safe from the SIM. But to them this is unthinkable. They are Cubans and they would rather stay and fight – even at the risk of having their families annihilated. Chivatos – spies – are everywhere. The bootblack may be selling information. Taxi drivers keep their ears open. The room boys at the hotel. Waiters. For a few pesos the spies sell their neighbors to the secret police. Phones are not to be trusted even when used by non-political U.S. tourists and businessmen. Cables and mail are subject to censorship.

There are 6,000,000 people in Cuba. They are a proud race and they are being held captive by a brutal minority that rules by atrocities, murders, and plunder. Batista is reputed by the revolutionaries to have $300 million in Swiss banks. Gen. Francisco Tabernilla, head of the Cuban army, is the man behind a chain of discount houses. His son, Gen. Francisco Tabernilla Jr., by sheerest coincidence head of the Air Force, flies in electric appliances and household goods in military planes, avoids the customs inspectors and thus undersells legitimate dealers. Eusebio Mujal rules Cuba's workers with an iron hand and an elastic conscience. He's one of Cuba's most feared and hated men. He even outranks Batista as a man to be eliminated. He is slated for execution at the first opportunity.

The last six years have been a nightmare for those Cubans who do not belong to the Batista group. "The island smells of death," said a Cuban doctor, "the earth is soaked with the blood of Cuban martyrs. We cannot leave it. We must win – whether it is tomorrow or next week or next year. With Castro or with someone else." Batista would like to impose martial law, he said, but this would wreck the already badly-hit tourist trade and ruin the business at the gangster-operated casinos. Schools are closed. Children are kept off the streets. Sugar cane workers are taking lessons in sabotaging the crops – they would rather go hungry than have the profits filter into the pockets of Batista and his insatiable followers.

Batista's informers operate widely in Miami and Mexico. They spy for pay, giving the time and place of arms shipments destined for Castro's forces in the Sierra Maestra mountains or for Faure Chomon's insurgents in the Sierra Escambray or for the Directorio Revolucionario. Or for other, smaller groups. "If all of these groups could be placed under one command, said a rebel wistfully, "we could take over the government within a matter of days. Much of the army would come over to us." But there is no unified command. Nevertheless, there is help for Castro's forces. Arms are hidden everywhere in Havana. Occasionally, through torture, a captive rebel discloses the hiding place of a cache of grenades or machine guns or carbines, rifles and dynamite. But there is more where those came from. Rich men are behind the movement. Even middle-class Cubans give until it hurts.

And there is sabotage. Cuba's rich sugar cane fields, the backbone of her economy, are particularly vulnerable. The rebels distribute pamphlets showing workers how to tie phosphorous to the rats which infest the fields and thus start fires. There are the bombs that set oil storage tanks afire. Rails are ripped from the railroads that penetrate the interior of the island. Could bloodshed be avoided if Batista consented to free elections? Batista, say the rebels, would merely put up his usual straw men and knock them over and retain power. There can be no solution, they insist, while Batista is in power.

Cubans who had been hurt and puzzled by the U.S. policy of sending arms to Batista, are a bit mollified by the recent embargo on munitions shipments to the Cuban dictator. The embargo became known only when the U.S. suspended shipment two weeks ago of 1,950 Garand riffles ordered by the Cuban government in 1956. "We hope that this action will continue," said an insurgent, "and that your country will not give Batista more arms with which to fight us. We cannot fight your country and our oppressor. Give us only the chance to resolve our differences by ourselves. We Cubans emulate you Americans in every way. We try to imitate your dress, your manners. We go to watch your movies. We try to learn your language. Our homes and our lives and even our schools are patterned after yours. Don't force us to cast aside our respect and admiration for you."

Havana has a population of 1,200,000. But only in the dirty side-streets and alleys do the people venture out in numbers after dark. Because these are the people who have nothing more to lose – except their lives. And lives aren't held too dearly by those who have to beg for a living, by those who have to walk the streets selling themselves into prostitution or by the wispy women who hold infants in their arms and beg coins from the dwindling tourist population. The one thing all seem to have is boundless courage. It takes courage for an underground contact to walk through a crowded hotel lobby and telephone the room of visiting newspapermen. For he doesn't know if the elevator man has decided to sell out. Or if the telephone operator is a chivato working for the SIM.

A few weeks back, a spy in Miami sold the sons of a Cuban patriot to the secret police. The Cuban had asked the secret Batista agent for the best way of sending his sons to Cuba to take part in the fight for freedom. He was told that the boys could go by plane directly to Havana and that they would be well taken care of there. The father said he didn't want the boys to go, but that they were insisting and he could not forbid them. He wanted them safe. Was the agent sure this was the best way? The agent assured him that was the ticket. The contact would be made in a Havana restaurant, he said. The boys were greeted by the SIM when they landed. They were missing for several days. Then their bullet-riddled bodies were found in a Havana suburb. Back in Miami, the informer was badly beaten. He wasn't killed. "We didn't want a major crime on our hands," said a rebel. "No international incident to

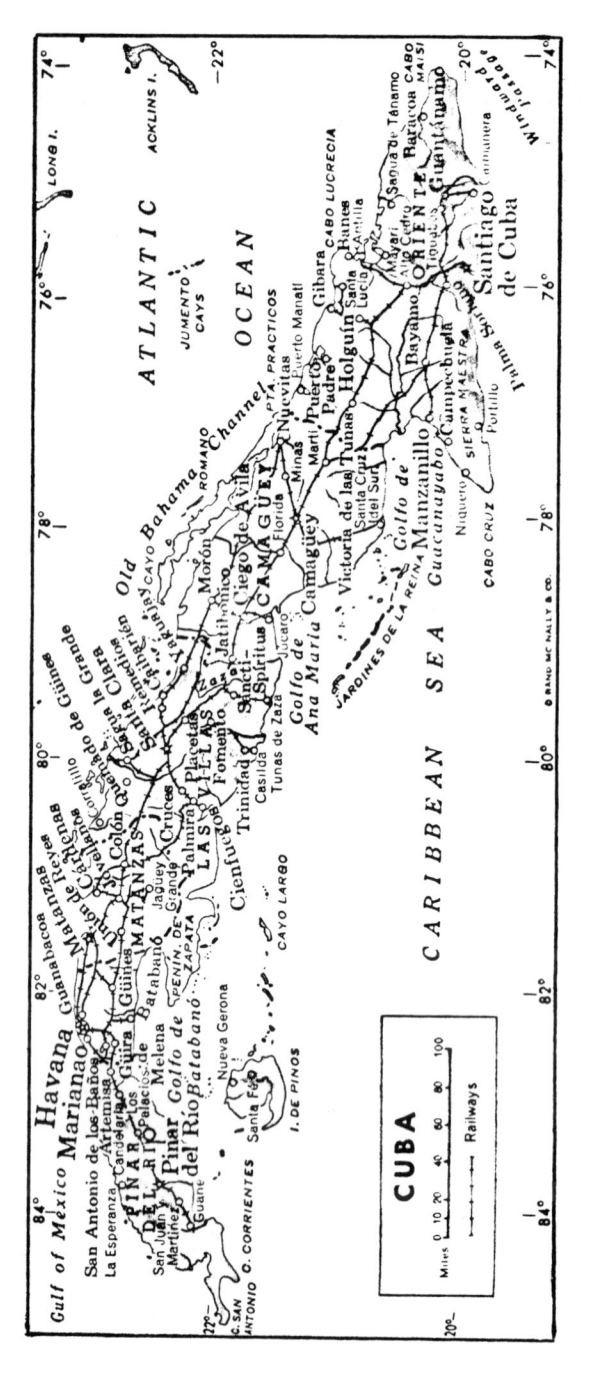

[*Source:* Collier's Encyclopedia, Vol. 7, New York–London 1969, p. 539.]

undo the work we're doing. But some day the deaths of those boys will be avenged." One more score to be wiped off that slate.

A general strike is the greatest weapon of the men who follow Castro and his insurgents. In every revolution in Cuba's history, the organized force of workers has been a decisive factor in the fall of the regime. The second weapon is the power held by the great middle class – the lawyers, doctors, small bankers and students. The students of Havana University – 18,000 strong – have a history of fighting tyranny that goes back over 80 years. Hundreds of these have been arrested recently. Hundreds of others have disappeared.

American gamblers and hoods who took over the casinos at the Riviera, Hilton and Capri are trying to laugh off a revolution. They insist that "Castro is a nut" and that Batista is too strong to be overthrown. They are whistling past the graveyard. It is well known that Castro and other insurgent leaders are against gambling, particularly gambling controlled by shady characters from the U.S. Castro is quoted as saying: "Gambling is the cancer that has been eating at my country; it must be cut out."

"But that's a secondary item," said one of our contacts. "The regime must go. We must have free elections. We must have our real plight described to the world by journalists who can't be subsidized or bought. Just tell the true story, that's all we ask."

31.2 Official Sadism and Its Various Exponents

[*Source: Joseph Martin/Phil Santora: Batista rules by death, terror, in:* Daily News *(New York, N.Y.), Vol. 39/No. 246, April 8, 1958, p. 2, cols. 3–5; p. 26, cols. 1–5.*]

This is a grim rollcall of Fulgencio Batista's chief terrorists – killers so brutal and ruthless that even the man who helped create the monsters seems afraid of trying to control them. These are the men whose names are whispered with fear and hate, whose incredibly sadistic deeds read like pages torn from the records at Dachau.

Maj. Estaban Ventura Nobo dislikes dull evenings. When one comes along, he sends his police out to pick up unfortunates who stray into one of the three police districts technically under his control – actually, he operates throughout Havana. Then he beats a selected victim into insensibility just for the kicks. Ventura's name has become a lewd epithet throughout Cuba. He is an avid student of torture, having been tutored in the fine points by Angel Borlenghi, who was minister of the interior in Argentina under ex-dictator Juan Peron.

Recently, Ventura used a Borlenghi invention – putting two electrodes on the genitals of a 16-year-old boy and shocking him into what he hoped would be a confession of "his crimes against the state." The electrodes touched and the boy was electrocuted, cutting short Ventura's fun for the day. Another Ventura gimmick is a basket made of piano wire which is fastend about the genitals. Two wires draw the basket shut, causing indescribable pain. He has been known to rip the ear off a subject when a beating with fists failed to get results.

Ventura goes under psychiatric care at intervals. But in between treatments he roams the streets of Havana with up to a dozen heavily armed bodyguards, looking for victims to assuage his thirst for torture. He loves expensive white suits and keeps one or two in each of the precincts under his command. He's also nuts about publicity and when the photographers show up, Ventura dons a fresh white suit, sprinkles a bit of cologne on his hair and pencil-thin moustache and holds a press conference. Lean, about 160 pounds, 40 years old, married and the father of two young daughters he was born in Pinar del Rio Province in the western part of Cuba. Those are the so-called vital statistics. Ventura has mistresses throughout the area of his command. He can well afford them with the money he gets from business men who either get up the monthly assessment or find themselves answering questions in the cellar of a stationhouse.

Batista turns a deaf ear to pleas – and some of these come from his top aids – to remove Ventura from his post. Even the Gerardo Abreu incident failed to away him from loyalty to the terrorist who swaggers through Havana instilling fear in the most innocent of Cubans. Gerardo Abreu's death resulted in the only indictment ever handed up against Ventura. Abreu was a 20-year-old pianist-student who was socially popular among young people in Havana. Ventura ordered him arrested on charges of terrorism – an ironic touch – and sentenced him to jail. He was released on a writ of habeas corpus. Less than a week after his release, he was again arrested by Ventura.

Immediately, there were cries for "justice" from social and student groups. A witness gives the conclusion of the grim story: "I heard noises on the street in front of the Palace of Justice. Guards from the palace were there and they were discussing something in loud tones with other men. It was about 11 P. M. A few minutes later, I heard the chatter of a machine gun. I saw three men get into a car and drive off." Abreu's body was found there the next morning. No one dared approach the spot during the night. Ventura was quoted later as saying: "They wanted justice – and I gave them justice, with interest." The dreaded, dapper killer is also the author of the phrase, "Here's your habeas corpus." It was uttered when the lifeless body of a suspected terrorist was dumped at the feet of the lawyer who had obtained the writ.

Ventura was an obscure lieutenant in charge of the 5th Precinct five years ago, before he distinguished himself by working over a priest, the Rev. Ramon O'Farril, who had plotted to have President Batista ambushed on one of his infrequent visits to church. Father O'Farril was so badly beaten that he suffered fractures of two ribs, internal injuries and is permanently deaf in one ear. In Miami, the exiled priest admitted his part in the plot to have Batista assassinated. "It is high time," he said, "that the UN stepped into the Cuban case. They should step in if for no other reasons than the reasons of humanity. The bloodiest drama in the gory history of Latin America is now taking place in Cuba. There have been thousands of deaths – murders by the Batista regime. There are the countless tortures and humiliations. These and the exiles who have been ousted from their homeland are more than sufficient reason for international intervention in the Cuban problem. Not even the highest prelates of the Roman Catholic Church have escaped terrorist action under the Batista regime. The Cuban people are in immediate need of the help of all the Catholics of the world and also of the moral and physical support of all the upright and wholesome people of the free world."

Ventura's closes rival in the brutality sweepstakes is Capt. Julio Laurent, in charge of naval intelligence. Laurent was an unknown bush-leaguer before he murdered his first Cuban. The victim was a supporter of ex-President Carlos Prio Socorras. He was arrested in a house in the swank Vedado section, dragged out into the street where Laurent, then a lieutenant, was waiting with a submachine gun in hand. While two men held the suspected terrorist, Laurent pressed the tommygun against his body and cut him almost in half with three long bursts. Then he turned to the crowd of horrified spectators and shouted: "And anyone who accuses me will die a similar death." He was charged with murder, but no witnesses would appear against him. Along with Ventura, he was accused of the murder of a captain involved in the Cienfuegos uprising last Sept. 5. The captain, Alfredo Gonzales Brito, was brought to Havana after his arrest in Cienfuegos. In the home of the second ranking commander of the Cuban navy, he was beaten and kicked into unconsciousness. Revived, he was tortured with cigars and cigarets that burned hole over more than half of his body. The finale came when Laurent and Ventura ordered the captain and a close friend taken to a castle tower overlooking the sea. There, the two were gagged, trussed and thrown into the sea.

An incident that has caused the greatest indignation concerns a 50-year-old schoolteacher, Mrs. Esther Milanes. Mrs. Milanes was a teacher in a Catholic school and had a minor part in the underground movement. She was picked up, along with a student from Colombia, South America, by men under the command of Capt. Jose Sosa, another of the sadists who pretend to administer justice in Havana. The woman was beaten with fists and the flat feet of Sosa and his henchmen in an attempt to make her talk. They threatened to have her raped by a particularly repulsive-looking member of the precinct force. When threats and heatings failed, they took an iron bar and inserted it forcibly into her body.

Mrs. Milanes might never have been released alive had it not been for the Colombian ambassador, who went looking for the student. She and the boy were released in his custody and she was rushed to the hospital. She revealed that they tortured the boy in front of her in an attempt to break her down. Then there is Col. Manuel Uglade Carrillo, who likes to sit in the third degree room and watch prisoners being given a working over. Uglade, who was the first chief of the SIM (secret police) when Batista came into power, laughs heartily while the girsly torture goes on. The new chief of police in Havana is Pilar Garcia, who got his reputation by quelling a riot at Matanzas two years ago this month. After the uprising had been put down Garcia made "examples" of 11 rioters. He had them shot.

There is, in Santiago de Cuba, a lieutenant colonel named Jose Maria Salas Canizares who, along with his brother, gained notoriety throughout the island for violence. Canizares, 6-foot, 200-pound thug, likes to lead his men into battle with the visor of his legion-style cap turned up. Sort of a trade mark. He carries an ox goad with which he strikes people during demonstrations. When he was assigned to Santiago, he promptly ordered a blackout and then riddled a few houses with machine gun bullets so that the "people in this city will know who's boss." Then he went out to pick up the local leader of Castro's July 26 movement. He picked up two young men. He had an idea that one of them was the real thing but didn't know which one. So he killed them both to make sure.

When the weeping widow of one remonstrated, Canizares laughed and volunteered that he and his men could take care of her sexual wants.

These are the chiefs. But the men under them can be equally brutal. In some instances, they surpass their leaders because they feel that is the way to success and recognition under Batista. Another killer was Col. Fermin Cowley, who won his spurs in Holguin, in the northern port of Oriente Province on Christmas Day, 1956. On that day, Cowley hanged 14 students, supporters of the Castro movement. One of the victims was the brother of Rep. Eugenio Cusido, who is still in office. On the day the victims were being buried, Cowley showed up and said he didn't like the way the ceremonies were being conducted. He ordered the funerals suspended. Early last year, rebels stopped a bus on the main road into Oriente. They ordered the passengers out – with their luggage – and then set fire to the bus. Cowley demanded that the passengers and driver identify the rebels. They said they couldn't. When four suspects were brought in, Cowley asked the driver to identify them. He said he couldn't because he hadn't seen their faces. Cowley hanged all four, "just in case they were all guilty."

A year ago this month, a World War II paratrooper went to Oriente Province with 27 men. The veteran, Calixto Sanchez, was one of those suspected of having taken part in the March 1957, attack on the presidential palace in Havana. In mid-April, he was surrounded by government forces and surrendered to a lieutenant who offered him the guarantee of a formal trial. When Cowley learned of the surrender he personally machine-gunned all 28 to death. The "mad colonel" was married seven times. He had no children, but he collected German-made toys with a sort of psychopathic intensity. His career came to an abrupt halt several weeks later when Fidel Castro sent two men out of the Sierra Maestra with orders to liquidate the colonel. Cowley – traveling confidently with a small bodyguard – showed up at a store one day to buy light bulbs. The clerk said he didn't have the type on hand and suggested Cowley return the next day. Cowley came back the following day and was shot to death by the Castro executioners waiting in ambush.

On March 24 – two weeks ago – a woman was arrested in a Havana hospital only two days after bearing a child. The charge was not made clear and she hasn't been seen since. The baby is still in the hospital. In the little town of San Juan Martinez, a local magistrate sent his sons off to the movies. The boys, Luis Saiz, 16, and Sergio Saiz, 14, got into an argument with a soldier. He shot them to death. When the funeral was held the next day, the angry townspeople had words with soldiers and police. The police opened fire and killed eight with machine-gun fire.

These are but a few of the incidents sworn to by Cubans of highest integrity but smothered by the Cuban press, which is firmly under Batista's thumb. And with such things taking place less than an hour's plane ride from Miami – less than 100 miles from United States soil – these Cubans want their democratic neighbors to know.

31.3 The Batista Coup and the Fruits of Temptation

[*Source:* Joseph Martin/Phil Santora: Batista coup boss regrets it, in: Daily News *(New York, N.Y.), Vol. 39/No. 249, April 11, 1958, p. 2, cols. 3–5; p. 38, cols. 1–5.*]

Swarthy, solidly-built Gen. Jorge Garcia Tunon is a man who – through an error in judgment – helped write one of the bloodiest chapters in Cuban history. Today, in Miami, he's a bitter, disillusioned man, reluctant to talk about it. For Gen. Tunon is the man who engineered the coup d'etat that put President Fulgencio Batista into power six bloody years ago. It is something that the general, a completely honest man living in poverty, will always have on his conscience.

"You must understand the reasoning behind the coup," he said. "Batista just 80 days before the June 1 elections of 1952, was a beaten man. He was being backed by the Partido Accion Unitaria, the PAU, or United Action Party. Less than 10% of the votes were his." Dr. Roberto Agramonte was the candidate of the Orthodox Party, or Partido del Pueblo Cubano. He had about 60% of the votes, according to a straw poll. Carlos Hevia was the choice of the Authentic Party, Partido Revolucionario Cubano. Carlos Prio Socorras was president and high-ranking army officers were unhappy with his corrupt regime.

"The army has always been strong in politics," said Gen. Tunon, "and we were concerned with the fact that those around Prio were weak, that our country needed a group of honest men in office. We had no ambitions for ourselves – or at least at that time, I believed this was so. "We felt that Batista was the best man of the three. We wanted a strong man who would clean up the situation and begin a new, better period of history with liberty and order. I was a captain at the time, in charge of a company in Columbia barracks at Military City."

"We remembered that when Batista had been president eight years earlier, he had wielded real authority. We talked to him and he told us in many beautiful phrases of his love for Cuba, that he could do many things now that he could not do in the past when so much confusion had been present in his regime. He told me that he was penitent about the reforms he could not carry out in his previous term. The talk took place in the house of his mother-in-law. He told me that he had some young officers already on his side. You must understand that when people spoke of him in those days, they did so with respect. People said that the killings in the streets would be eliminated if Batista were in power – that he would bring peace to our Cuba. What an irony!"

"Originally, the plan was to make Batista prime minister. The president, at that time, was scheduled to be Alonso Pujol. I headed a military junta. But Pujol was too intelligent to be under the thumb of Batista. Pujol backed out. He not only refused to be part of the scheme but he denied he had been in on early conferences. Batista spoke of the main problems facing the new government: (1) an honest administration free as much as possible of corruption; (2) getting rid of the gangster element supported by the civilian government, and (3) to respect all the institutions of the country, such as civil guarantees, free speech, free elections, etc."

The climax of the coup was a thing out of a play. The coup was almost ruined because Batista ordered his car out of line en route to the Columbia barracks so that he could meet a friend and put on his good-luck leather jacket, one which he had worn as an army sergeant. "We prepared a plan," Gen. Tunon continued, "whereby 11 officers in Columbia barracks, eight in La Cabana, three in the air force and eight in the navy prepared the men under them. No one else knew of the plot. Early on the morning of March 10, four officers went to the Batista farm, Kuquine, on the outskirts of Havana. I was to bring him to the garrison, where he would take over in a bloodless coup. There were seven cars by this time – with army officers and police. I was in the first car. Batista didn't cooperate. He told us to go on ahead and he would come along later. He wasn't afraid, he was being cautious."

"He finally consented to take his place in the motorcade. Then he did something that almost ruined our chances. When we neared the garrison his car cut out from the caravan. I ordered the rest of the cars to stop because I thought he might have changed his mind. We looked for him and found that he was changing his civilian jacket for a leather windbreaker he had worn as a sergeant. It was either superstition or ego – or a combination of both. The brown jacket was brought to him by an officer who should not have even known of our mission and moreover, an officer I did not trust. Batista even changed cars, going the rest of the way with that officer. We were supposed to be at the garrison at 2:40 A. M. sharp. The stop made us three minutes late and those three minutes almost cost us our coup, for when we arrived the officer we had expected to be in charge of the gate had gone to another part of the garrison and a new one was confronting us. An alarm could have been sounded but fortunately, the trusted officer returned and talked briefly to the sentinel and we passed through the gates. I had taken the precaution of posting the men of my own company as security guards. A driver and two men went to the home of Gen. Ruperto Cabrera, chief of the army. He lived on the post and was routed out of bed and taken to Batista's farm as hostage. Batista had given his wife a sleeping pill earlier, so that she would not awaken during the night and worry about his absence – one of the few considerate things I have ever known him to do."

There were 4,000 men in the Columbia garrison, but so complete was the coup that not a drop of blood was shed. As each new shift reported for duty, they either joined the movement or were disarmed and put into cells.

Batista called newspaper friends with the scoop. He took over completely that first day. "His old friends began appearing," said Gen. Tunon. "He had his claque and our group was being eased out of the picture." An accused embezzler, Marino Lopez Blanco, was made secretary of the treasury. He had been trying to buy his way into the previous Prio government. Gen. Francisco Tabernilla, who had been kicked out by President Grau San Martin eight years earlier, was put in charge of the army. Juan Rojas, then a captain, became a general in the Batista government. The members of the junta went over to him.

Today all of the officers who took part in the coup – with the exception of Gen. Tunon – are rich and powerful members of the Cuban hierarchy. "I came from an old army family," said Tunon, "and the men unter me liked me. I was made a brigadier general earlier because I was head of the junta. This was a popular decision with the men. I didn't realize that this didn't set well with Batista, but he reasoned that anyone who could organize one coup might be tempted to create another. I was put under constant surveillance. The men under me were told to disregard my orders. A captain was assigned to my section to countermand any orders I might give. Then guards were put around my house – one was a gardener whom I never hired and the other a sort of handyman. I went to Batista's home to protest and ended up by resigning."

No action is too petty for Batista. Gen. Tunon was retired – and exiled to Miami – with a pension of $331 per month. Charges of conspiracy were made after he left the country and the pension was declared forfeit. What does Gen. Tunon think of Batista? "I think that he cannot remain in power too much longer," he said hopefully. "He has hurt too many people and revoked too many institutions dear to the people of Cuba. His principal support comes from the repressive groups. But his spies are everywhere. The morale of the army is at a new low despite what you hear about salaries and other inducements. "The only way to unseat him is either through the army or through the church. The U.S. government could help by

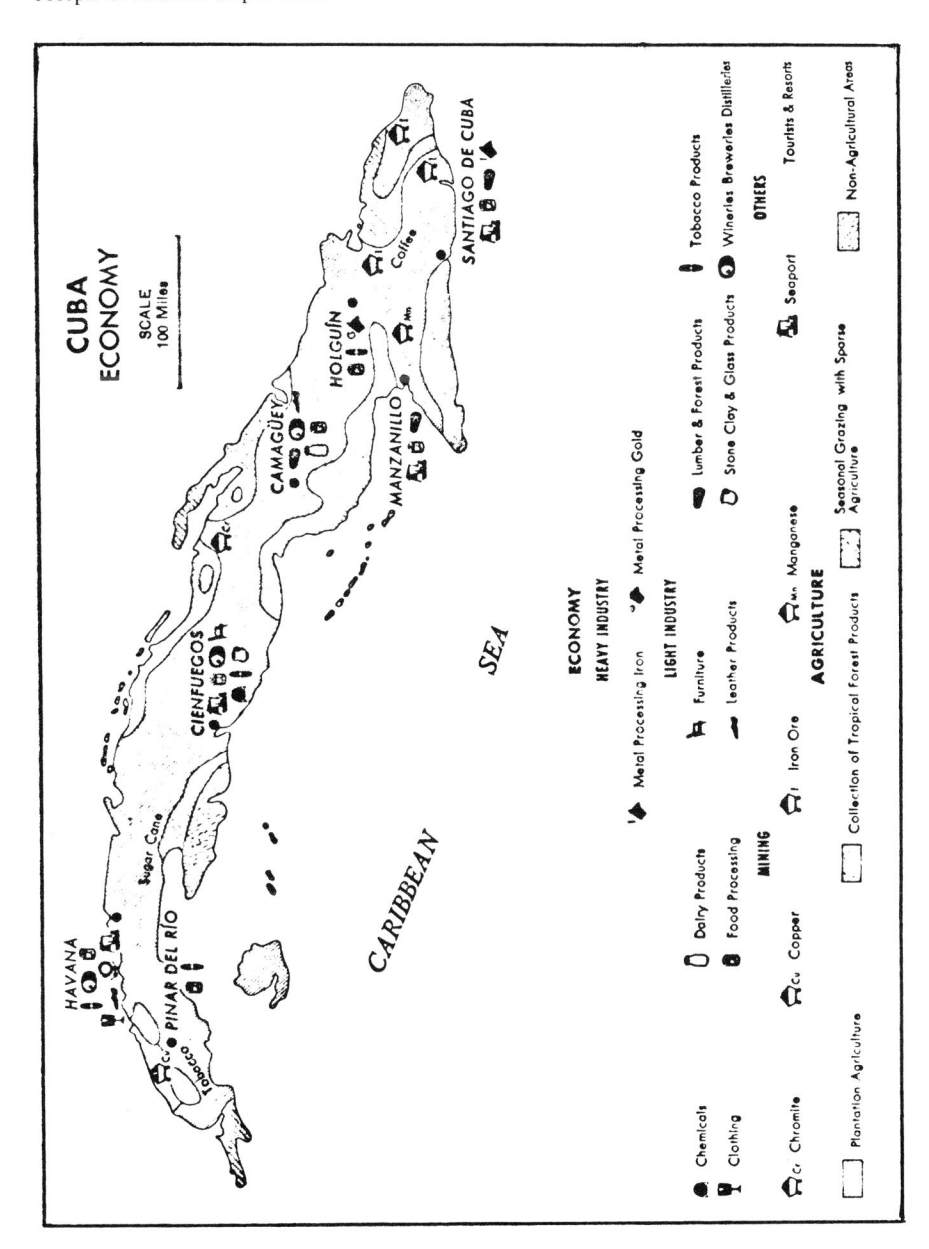

[*Source:* Collier's Encyclopedia, Vol. 7, New York–London 1969, p. 536.]

acting as an interested third party – or by just sitting on the sidelines and alowing Cubans to settle their own quarrels."

Whether you hear it from the general who helped Batista to power or from a waitress now working in Miami or from a real estate man, the story of Batista's reign is an unlovely thing. Batista is not the first to plunder Cuba. Virtually every government head since Cuba gained its independence has lined his pockets and then gone off the live in sumptuous exile. Those in power cannot resist the temptation of easy money. Batista's brother-in-law has charge of the slot machine racket. A close friend said that the right contractors get the road and building construction jobs and that the proper kickback comes back to the palace. There are the atrocities and the loot and the prostitution and the censorship. These are the things that Batista stands for, no matter how he attempts to disguise them.

And an hour's flight from the palace in Havana, the man who helped create Cuba's Frankenstein monster cringes beneath the weight of his conscience. The fact that he has a conscience automatically disqualifies him as a Batista man.

31.4 Cuba's Captive Press and How It Is Run

[*Source: Joseph Martin/Phil Santora: Batista is in control of subsidized press, in:* Daily News *(New York, N.Y.), Vol. 39/No. 251, April 14, 1958, p. 24, cols. 1–5.*]

Dictator Fulgencio Batista, who likes to call himself an old newspaperman, maintains iron control over virtually all of the Cuban press through a feudal system of subsidies without which most of the major newspapers would cease to exist. This is a normal procedure even when insurgent forces aren't creating little incidents. Now that civil guarantees have been tossed down the drain and censorship has been imposed, control of the press is complete.

Not a dissident whisper filters into Cuba's newspapers. And newsmen aren't as indignant – at least not openly – as they would be in this country because they, too, are subsidized and without the added money they would scarcely be able to subsist. The result is darkness and ignorance of the true state of affairs for the great majority of the 6,000,000 peole of Cuba as well as a fuzzy picture for the outside world. Censorship, enforced by economic necessity, is the great weapon in Batista's arsenal. No atrocity picture is printed. The press doesn't dare to criticize the inhuman Maj. Esteban Ventura Nobo or the other psychopathic characters who enforce Batista's decrees.

Technically, Batista has imposed official censorship some eight times since 1953. Before that, censorship had been imposed only once, by Machado back in 1931 to 1933. Chief of his censors is Evangelina de las Lleras, a member of the underground movement that ousted Machado in 1933. She's a shade over 50 and, purposely or not, unable to see any point of view but her own. Her decisions, however devoid of reason, are final. There are 40 censors in all, one for each of the 16 newspapers in Havana and the others for telephone, magazines, radio stations and the island's four TV stations.

Subsidizing began in 1933, when people within the newspapers were bought. Presidents

Grau San Martin and Carlos Prio Socorras followed suit when they came to power. But it was found that a general subsidy was more effective. Batista's tab for purchasing the integrity of newspapers and newsmen runs into millions of dollars each year. The subsidies run from $4,000 per month to as high as $1,000 per day and many of Havana's newspapers could not possibly make ends meet without this largesse from Batista, the boy who wears a button describing him as Newspaperman No. 1. The button entitles him to hold a job with a guild minimum wage of $22.08 per week, despite or because of which he has managed to accumulate what revolutionaries estimate as $300,000,000.

Any sparks of rebellion among editors are quickly extinguished. Luis Ortega Sierra, a veteran Cuban newsman, was baldly beaten and exiled to Miami and his newspaper, Pueblo, was sold for peanuts. Five papers are controlled or owned directly by the government. One of these is Pueblo, operated by Andres Domingo Morales, a close friend to Batista. On the rolls of Pueblo appears the name of Fulgencio Batista as a reporter. It's an evening paper with a circulation of about 2,000.

Tiempo en Cuba is operated by the strong-armed Sen. Rolando Masferrer. A brilliant lawyer. Masferrer has distinguished himself by his services to the present regime. He commanded a battalion in the Spanish Civil War and is an extreme liberal, though not a Red. He has organized his own police force. He carries a gun and is known as a rough customer. Tiempo en Cuba is the Pravda of the Batista government. Masferrer constantly harasses those around Batista, making them feel insecure and thus keeping them on their toes. The censors don't bother him because they have no need.

Alerta is an evening paper with a circulation of 3,000. It was formerly the property of Minister of Communication Ramon Vasconcelos, a Batista supporter who fell from grace and is now living in Spain. No more patriotic newspaper exists in Cuba than Ataja. It features blue and yellow headlines on white newsprint. The colors of the national police are blue, those of the army yellow, and the Navy, white, and Ataja, which means attack, is circulated in barracks all over the island. Even then, its circulation is only 12,000. It is operated by a pompous little man. Alberto Salas Maro, who stretches out to a height of five feet and has a habit of chinning himself on casino roulette tables for hours at a time.

Repulica is owned by Julia Elisa Consuegra, in her fifties and an old friend of Batista. The newspaper has a circulation of 1,000 and was started by former police chief Rafael Salas Canizares – who is a better story than Replica. Canizares clubbed a student to death in 1951 and was indicted in Havana. He was to face the court the same week Batista took power in 1952. Batista had the case taken care of and made Canizares a general in charge of the national police. At the time Canizares was poor. But he took control of gambling until 1956 and upon his death left $14,000,000 to his widow. His death was almost accidental. After the March 13, 1957, attack on Batista's palace, four rebels of the Directorio Revolucionario were executed. Out of retaliation, they shot to death Security Police Chief Blanco Rico in a cabaret, the Montmarte, of which hoodlum Meyer Lansky owned a sizable portion. Canizares heard the killers were at the Haitian embassy and raced off to intercept them. There were a dozen refugees there, but none of them was involved in the Rico killing. Canizares was hunting for them out in the garage when he was met by a young man with a gun. They both opened fire but Canizares fell, mortally wounded. Irindido Martinez, the boy who fired the fatal shot, is still in hiding.

There are the "independent" newspapers that get money and other favors from the government. The 125-year-old Diario de la Marina, once the voice of the church and the Spanish colony, is a morning paper with a circulation of 35,000. Today it gives Batista no cause for worry. Informacion is run by the Claret family, which is close to Batista. El Mundo was born with the republic 57 years ago and once had a great tradition as an independent liberal newspaper. The owner of record is Amadeo Barletta, an Italian who went to Cuba 20 years ago and – in between visits to other countries and deals with other dictators – has done very well indeed under the Batista regime. Former President Prio is reported to have put up more than half of the purchase price for El Mundo. Barletta was once Mussolini's consul to the Dominican Republic. When Barletta was thrown into jail there, Mussolini threatened to send his fleet to free him. Barletta has also done business with Peron, as well as with Prio and Grau San Martin. He has had a hectic life. On one occasion, Batista assigned SIM men to guard him and the El Mundo plant, which didn't do much to help the newspaper's reputation.

Another morning newspaper, Excelsior, has a circulation of 28,000 with the help of a plan whereby they print lottery numbers. The owner is Alfredo Hornedo, almost 80 now, a man with a Texas complex. He has the world's largest theater in the Miramar section of Havana – so big that it's rarely opened because of the expense of operating it. Hornedo also owns El Pais, a lottery paper with a circulation of 40,000. The Havana Post is owned by Clara Park, 55, of New Orleans. It is Havana's only English daily and during the Little Rock, Ark., incident, heavily played up the cause of Gov. Faubus and attacked the stand of President Eisenhower. Mañana is owned by Jose Lopez Viloboy, president of Cubana Airlines, in which Batista is deeply interested.

The great Cuban newspaper, Prensa Libre – Free Press – is not subsidized. It has a circulation of over 85,000 and is headed by Sergio Carbo, a newsman with an excellent reputation. The censorship is evident when you pick up a copy of the usually fearless Prensa Libre. With incidents breaking loose all over the place, with threats of total war by Castro, seizure of arms shipments, the front page heavily played up a chit-chat column which wanted to congratulate one Jose Sierra on his birthday. Reporters are poorly paid. Scale is $22.08 per week, but there is something called the botella. The botella is a government job of doing nothing as a rule. A reporter can have several of these, bringing his salary up to $1,000 per month for the man covering the palace, and somewhat less for those on less important beats.

Stories of U.S. mobsters allied with Batista in the gambling racket were so muffled by the purchased press in Havana that the news of the alliance wasn't exposed until THE NEWS uncovered the story last January. Not only does the subsidized press suppress the news, but reporters working for Batista don't hesitate to attempt to slander legitimate newsmen coming into the country to do an honest job.

31.5 The Dictator and His Counterpart Castro

[*Source: Joseph Martin/Phil Santora: Summary: Castro? Maybe – Batista? No, in:* Daily News *(New York, N.Y.), Vol. 39/No. 254, April 17, 1958, p. 36, cols. 1–5.*]

There are more than 2,000 Cuban exiles in Miami, which has been called the Siberia for Latin-America, and the reason most of them are battling the Batista regime is simple – they want to go home. They want to go back, however, with the guarantee they won't be dragged out of their beds during the night by the dreaded SIM (Security Police) and forced to submit to torture and worse.

There's the pianist who says: "Even here, I can feel the hand of Batista. His spies are everywhere in this city – even in New York and other places where Cubans have gone for refuge. I listen to the shortwave broadcasts from Fidel Castro's headquarters in the Sierra Maestra two or three times a week and they give me hope – even though I am not 100% for Castro, either." You hear that often – Cubans who hate Batista are not necessarily in love with Castro. There is a mistaken idea that if you talk or write about the regime's terrorism you have to be for Castro. A large share of the exiles in Miami are for Cuba only. The insurgents, be they Castro's or Faure Chomon's or followers of other rebel leaders, are merely the weapons by which the anti-Red middle class hopes to free its homeland.

There's the exiled newspaperman who says: "Batista is a murderer, but Castro is an ambitious man, and who knows if things will be any better when and if he takes over? Our best hope is a third party – preferably the army – under a non-political man like Gen. Jorge Garcia Tunon, also exiled by Batista." Revolutionaries are common in Miami. They seem to collect in the same places night after night. "I have a family in Havana," said one, "and my sole aim is to go there to live with them again. I saw them eight months ago, but it's too risky for me to make frequent trips. I can only fight against those who keep me from my mother and two brothers."

Portly Dr. Roberto Agramonte, a former sociology professor; his wife, daughter and son – who fought with Castro in the Sierra – are exiles living in a cramped "efficiency apartment." Suitcases are scattered about the place and there is little furniture – the mark of the transient who hopes this is only a temporary stop. Agramonte, Dr. Manuel Bisbe and others in the "26th of July Movement" spoke March 16 at a commemorative meeting at the Flagler Theater in Miami. It was a Sunday morning, but there were about 300 present to pay tribute to the memory of Dr. Pelayo Cuervo, slain as a suspect in the March 13, 1957, attack on the Presidential Palace. Cuervo had no part in the uprising, but he had been a marked man because he couldn't be bought. He was taken from the home of a friend, pushed into a car and shot to death in a Havana suburb.

The people at the Flagler were middle class. Some of them arrived late, making excuses to friends that they had to attend church first. Batista likes to call them Communists, but Reds aren't in the habit of putting church services before revolutionary meetings. Inside, there was emotion-drenched oratory. Batista, say these sober, well-educated people, "has drunk the blood of the Cuban people." The current theme – "Liberty or death." Cuba's martyrs are remembered in Miami – and there are many martyrs, with new ones created by each abortive uprising. "But it's like a chain letter," said a Cuban attorney, "Each person who dies for Cuba inspires a dozen others to take his place in the movement against Batista. Some day – be it this month or this year – we will return to our homes in Cuba." The revolutionaries and exiles don't always find jobs. But they seem to get along – mostly from the bounty of those who have plenty of money and are willing to share it.

Castro has his followers. So does ex-President Carlos Prio Socarras. So do others. Curiously, Batista and Castro profess the same aims for Cuba. They don't want to run the country personally, they say, they merely want a strong, honest group to take over – with free elections, civil rights and all the other benefits the Cubans don't have. Batista turns on his ever-ready charm and tells the world he would like nothing better than to turn over the reins to some deserving characters. In the next breath, he indicates he would like to retain control of the army in case anything goes wrong. Castro has said he doesn't want to be president of Cuba, not even a high officer of the government. He wants to sit on a park bench in the background and make like an elder statesman. "I would act only as the conscience of the administration," he said.

The consensus among the more highly-educated exiles is that Cuba would be better off if neither Castro nor Batista ruled the island. "There are many misconceptions," said an exile. "There is, for instance, a popular belief in the U.S. that if Batista relents in his reign of terror, takes it easy on his enemies, there will be peace. This is not so. There can be no peace while he directs any phase of the government. But on the other hand, I do not believe that Fidel Castro is statesman enough to rule Cuba as it should be governed."

Batista has ruled Cuba for 17 of the last 25 years. The past six years have been the goriest in Cuba's history. How did he get started? Fulgencio Batista y Zaldivar was born of humble parents and was a laborer in a sugar mill, a farm worker, a tailor and eventually a stenographer. He joined the army at the age of 20 and attained the rank of staff sergeant because of his knowledge of shorthand. He came into power through a coup in Sept. 4, 1933, ending the reign of tyrannical President Gerardo Machado. But, though he was now Cuba's strong man, Batista didn't become president until 1940 when a coalition – including the Communist Party he now denounces – elected him. When he was barred by the Cuban constitution from running for a second term in 1944, he put up his own candidate – who was defeated. Batista retired to Daytona Beach to lick his wounds and plan a comeback. When he regained control in 1952 through a coup d'etat, he was hailed as the savior of the people. But the people were soon to find out that this was a different Batista than the one they had known. This one was out to make a fortune and a place in history. He has done both.

Castro is now 32. He is a brilliant lawyer, has three university degrees and comes from a wealthy family in the sugarcane business. However, he has a reputation as a young man who likes to run off in the direction of a revolution. In 1946, he was a member of an expedition against President Rafael Trujillo, of the Dominican Republic. The invasion fell through and Castro escaped by leaping into the sea from a ship. He also took part in a revolt in Colombia. Is he Communist? One of his severest critics says: "Castro may have used Reds to gain the ends he seeks, but he's not a Red. He may have associated with them but I'm sure that he was not aware of the political inferences. He has suffered from nothing more serious than adolescent political growing-pains." The Castro "26th of July Movement" originates from his attack on the army barracks in Oriente Province. From that day on, even though Castro's losses were heavy and he had to flee for his life, his name became synonymous with Superman and Robin Hood. There are those who don't believe that Castro will ever really come

PRODUCTION OF MAIN CROPS
(Thousands of metric tons)

	1958	1959	Percent change
Sugar	5,778.6	5,964.2	+ 3
Tobacco	41.6	41.2	− 1
Coffee	29.1	49.2	+68
Rice (unpolished)	222.7	295.5	+32
Cotton	0	1.4	—
Black and red beans	30.0	35.0	+16
Corn	147.0	190.0	+29
Peanuts	7.0	11.0	+42
Potatoes	101.0	113.0	+11
Pineapples	100.0	98.0	− 2
Oranges	73.0	81.0	+11
Cucumbers	18.0	18.0	0
Tomatoes	69.3	73.1	+ 5

CUBA'S CURRENT ACCOUNT
(Millions of dollars)
Aggregates for seven years, 1952-1958

	Receipts	Expenditures	Balance
1. Merchandise	4,818.1	4,636.4	181.7
2. Tourism	247.7	232.9	14.8
3. Transportation	49.7	480.7	−431.0
4. Insurance	5.5	11.8	− 6.3
5. Dividends & interest	51.7	369.1	−317.4
6. Gov't transactions	12.0	9.7	2.3
7. Other services	138.5	33.8	104.7
8. Gifts	17.1	36.5	− 19.4
9. Total (1 through 8)	5,340.3	5,810.9	−470.6

The Cuban Economy in 1958

[*Source:* Leo Huberman/Paul M. Sweezy: Cuba – Anatomy of a Revolution, 2nd ed., New York–London 1961, pp. 138, 141.]

out of his beloved mountains – that when he does venture out too far he'll be cut to ribbons.

You have to try to divorce the distortions from the realities in any analysis of the Cuban situation. You have to discount the enthusiasms of Castro's followers as well as the propaganda dished out by the Batista regime. The best way is to talk to the solid, substantial men who have never before entered into a revolutionary movement, who refused to go into politics. These men comprise the great middle class of Cuba. They speak with wisdom and authority. They had made great sacrifices – leaving their beautiful homes in Havana to live in airless little rooms in Miami, New York and Chicago. Dr. Manuelo Urrutia, who will head the provisional government if Castro wins out, is in New York. He was an honored magistrate for 31 years before he was exiled for daring to indict a police official for murder. Men who have known violence only through hearsay form the nucleus of the underground that goes from New York to Miami and Cuba.

It is work to which they have become accustomed. They don't complain – they merely keep the guns going over to the Sierra Maestra and the Sierra del Escambray. One of them said: "Castro is almost a prisoner in his mountains. Batista is virtually a prisoner in the barracks at Columbia Military City. But the Cuban people are the real prisoners."

Related Readings

Batista y Zaldivar, Fulgencio: The growth and decline of the Cuban Republic, New York 1964.
Batista y Zaldivar, Fulgencio: Respuesta, Mexico 1960.
Bonachea, Rolando E./Valdés, Nelson P. (Eds.): Cuba in revolution, Garden City, N.Y., 1972.
Chester, Edmund A.: A sergeant named Batista, New York 1954.
Dewart, Leslie: Christianity and revolution – the lesson of Cuba, New York 1963.
Enos, John Lawrence: An analytic model of political allegiance and its application to the Cuban revolution, Santa Monica, Calif., 1965.
Foner, Philip Sheldon: A history of Cuba and its relations with the United States. Vol. 4: From the revolution of 1933 to the Cuban socialist revolution, New York 1964.
Goldenberg, Boris: The Cuban revolution and Latin America, New York 1965.
Green, Gilbert: Revolution – Cuban style. Impressions of a recent visit, New York 1970.
Huberman, Leo/Sweezy, Paul Marlor: Cuba – anatomy of a revolution, New York 1960.
Karol, Kewes S.: Guerrillas in power – the course of the Cuban revolution, New York 1970.
Mills, Charles Wright: Listen, Yankee – the revolution in Cuba, New York 1960.
Morray, Joseph P.: The second revolution in Cuba, New York 1962.
Nelson, Lowry: Cuba – the measure of a revolution, Minneapolis, Minn., 1972.
Ruiz, Ramón Eduardo: Cuba – the making of a revolution, Amherst, Mass., 1968.
Seers, Dudley (Ed.): Cuba – the economic and social revolution, Chapel Hill, N.C., 1964.
Smith, Robert Freeman (Ed.): Background to revolution. The development of modern Cuba, New York 1966.
Smith, Robert Freeman: The United States and Cuba. Business and diplomacy, 1917–1960, New Haven, Conn., 1960.
Suárez Núñez, José: El gran culpable. Cómo 12 guerrilleros ani quilaron a 45.000 soldados?, Caracas 1963.

1959

Abraham M. Rosenthal
The New York Times

CHAPTER 32

REPORTS ABOUT POLAND IN 1959

The Gomulka Government and the Structure of the Warsaw Pact

Introductory Notes
32.1 Gomulka's Move to Russia and the Polish Communism
32.2 A Historic Event and Its Interpretation
32.3 Poland's New Territory and How It Develops
32.4 A Warsaw Pact Discussion and Its Premises
32.5 Communist Diplomacy and Its Tactical Function
Related Readings

Introductory Notes

Attention having been fixed on a satellite of the Soviet Union for the first time with the Pulitzer award given to Russell Jones for his reports from Hungary, and the New York Times *having received its 1958 prize for coverage of East Europe, the International Reporting Prize in 1960 was awarded according to the same pattern. The Advisory Board on the Pulitzer Prizes bestowed the award on Abraham M. Rosenthal of the* New York Times *"for his perceptive and authoritative reporting from Poland" in 1959.*

Abraham Michael Rosenthal was born on May 2, 1922, in Sault Ste. Merie, Ontario, Canada. He moved with his family from Canada to New York City as a boy (1926), and he attended elementary and high school in the Bronx where he graduated in 1939. At the City College of New York, which A. M. Rosenthal attended after illness had interrupted his education for two years, he was editor-in-chief of The Campus, *the undergraduate newspaper, and college correspondent for the* New York Times. *In February, 1944, while still an undergraduate, he joined the city staff of the newspaper as a reporter. He completed his college courses at night and received a B.A. in social science in 1948. After two years of local reporting for the* Times, *he was assigned to the United Nations bureau of the* New York Times *in Lake Success, New York. He was a member of the* New York Times *staff that covered the general assembly session in Paris in 1948. In 1951 A. M. Rosenthal became a United States citizen, and after eight years of covering U.N. proceedings, he was assigned to New Delhi in 1954 as the* New York Times *correspondent in India and Pakistan. For four years Rosenthal covered those nations. His perceptive reporting earned him a citation from the Overseas Press Club. In June, 1958, Rosenthal traveled extensively in Pakistan, Ceylon and Afghanistan. He also carried out specific assignments in Malaya and Netherlands New Guinea. His reporting again earned him a citation from the Overseas Press Club. In June, 1958, Rosenthal was transferred by the* New York Times *to Warsaw, from where he covered Poland and other Easter European countries. He remained there until November, 1959, when he was ordered by the authorities to leave the country for "exposing too deeply the internal situation in Poland."*

The following texts by Abraham Michael Rosenthal, copyright 1959, are reprinted by kind permission of The New York Times, *Inc., New York, N.Y.*

32.1 Gomulka's Move to Russia and the Polish Communism

[*Source: A. M. Rosenthal: Gomulka's way – Communist, but different, in:* The New York Times *(New York, N.Y.), Vol. CVIII/No. 36,940, March 15, 1959, Section 4, p. 4 E, cols. 1–4.*]

This was a week of triumph for Wladyslaw Gomulka, the kind of triumph he likes best and very much like the man himself – intricate, painstaking and fervently non-dramatic. From all over Poland came Communist delegates to testify that the party was now cast in the mold of the man they had seen reviled and disgraced a decade ago.

From Moscow and Peiping came representatives to state solemnly that Poland was well and truly following the master pattern of Socialism. Not a word was said about the fact that many of the Polish Communist achievements praised so lavishly were possible only because M. Gomulka knew the people would rise unless the master pattern were slashed to fit the Polish cloth. It is M. Gomulka's party, and the congress of the Polish United Workers (Communist) party held in the Russian-built skyscraper that dominates Warsaw was M. Gomulka's congress.

M. Gomulka returned to power in 1956 at a time when the Polish explosion against Stalinist repression had shattered the party. He has spent the last two and a half years picking up the pieces. The first and indispensable job was to face down the Russians and convince them that the price for trying to bottle up Poland completely was civil war. He went ahead – and in response to pressures of the people at least as much as the party – agreed to those conditions which, to this day, set Poland sharply apart from the rest of the Communist countries: peasant-owned land, a truce with the Roman Catholic Church, the removal of police terror. Then M. Gomulka set about recreating the party in his own image. He is a man who by nature and politics loathes communism's extremes – the Stalinists and the "radical" revisionists.

The party apparatus is still full of the old-line party men who hate the new ways, and they have influence in communism's bureaucracy. But they cannot try seriously to threaten M. Gomulka because they know their return to power would dangerously stir Poland again. The Left-Wing revisionists, the party's spark in 1956, M. Gomulka dismissed almost contemptuously. He threw them out or told them to shut up. They have.

But the work of the party and M. Gomulka – the two had almost merged – was just beginning. The party had to bring the upsurge of 1957 into conformity with the maintenance of Communist power and Communist discipline. The party knew that there were conditions that could not be tampered with, and the fact is, most party members were happier to live with those conditions. One was the privately-based farming system. Occasionally, as with a start, Poland's Communists recall that they are supposed to be for collectivazation, but nothing much is ever done about it. The second condition for the minimum amount of acquiescence the party needed to rule as a Polish party, rather than a branch office of Moscow, was the outlet provided by the removal of police terror. A Pole cannot take political action outside the approved sphere, and he cannot write his mind. But he can talk without fear of arrest; and talk he does.

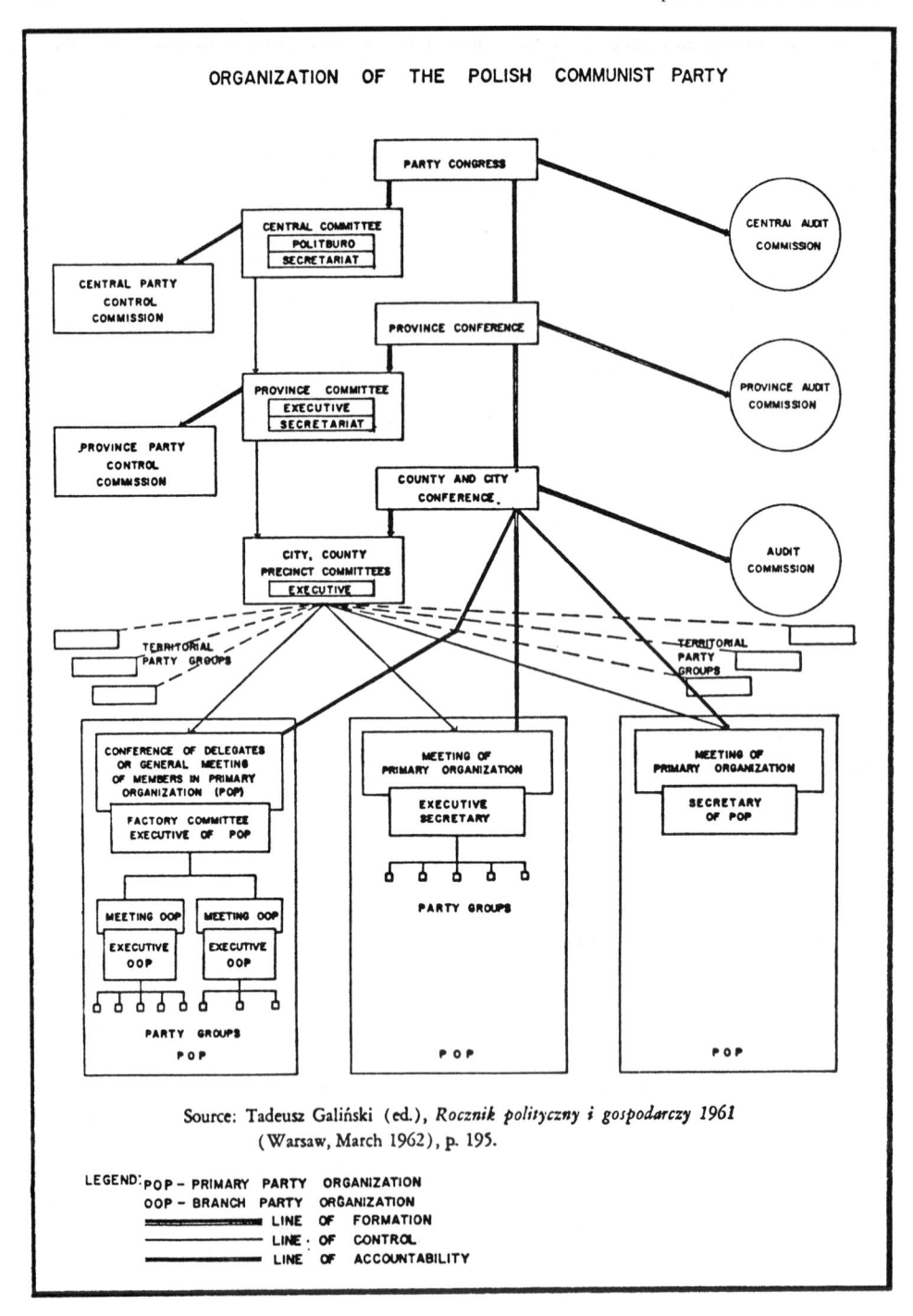

[Source: Richard F. Staar: Poland 1944–1962. The Sovietization of a Captive People, Baton Rouge, La., 1962, p. 148.]

That does not mean things have not changed in Poland. From a Communist viewpoint, they had to change. One of the most important changes – and one of the easiest – was to pull the reins on the intellectuals. Inside the party, the spark of criticism almost flickered out. At the congress this week, they were reciting a rhyme, which in rough and cleaned-up translation goes: "No matter what is said, sit on your seat and nod your head." There was no sudden wiping out of all freedoms, no imprisonments. There still are Western plays performed in Warsaw and still an occasional political satire. But satire is getting weaker and economic pressures on writers heavier. It is not 1984; but most definitely neither is it 1956.

While the intellectual tightening was going on, the party made another important change by moving closer and closer to the Soviet Union. This was not simply the opportunism of the moment. The world may insist on thinking of M. Gomulka as a brave Polish David always fighting the Soviet Goliath, but he insists on thinking of himself as a Communist. When he talks of the need for unity among the Communist countries, he means it. He knows that, without a strong Soviet Union, the Polish Communist party would cease to exist. But although the Polish Communist party has been restored as a political mechanism and its ties with Moscow re-established, the party now must face the fact that, in great areas of Polish life, its influence is hardly felt at all.

Closing the gap between the Communists and a population cold and indifferent to them becomes the party's biggest task. There is no magic formula except the fist, and this the party will not yet chance. Instead, the party concentrates on trying to come into contact with the people by increasing its role in the factories, cultural affairs, in social organizations, in clubs of all kinds. The objective is to make the influence of the party part of the daily life of the people of Poland.

The people of Poland so far have managed to restrain their enthusiasm for this process. Looking to the future, there are few of M. Gomulka's men who would predict that the chilliness of the country will be replaced by enthusiasm. But, still looking to the future, the Communists have a certain security in the Gomulka way. Because nobody can think of another method of satisfying the two essentials for maintaining power in present-day Poland: Keeping the people quiet and satisfying the Russians.

32.2 A Historic Event and Its Interpretation

[*Source: A. M. Rosenthal: Roles rewrite 1956. Red party seeks to shed 'Romantic' notions of the October Revolution, in: The New York Times (New York, N.Y.), Vol. CVIII/No. 36,943, March 18, 1959, p. 8, vols. 4–5.*]

The history of Poland's political upheaval of 1956 is being drastically rewritten in a concert hall in a Warsaw skyscraper. The job is being carried out in the speeches of high-ranking delegates to the third national congress of the Polish United Workers (Communist) party. Bit by bit it is emerging as one of the most important aspects of the congress and it tells considerable about the Polish Communist party, its shape, its tone and its plans.

There is a variety of objectives behind the process of change in the perspective on the political revolution that gave Poland more liberties than any other Communist country.

Possibly the most important is to present the revolution and its benefits entirely as the result of action of the party itself and not as a response to pressures of aroused workers, peasants, students and intellectuals outside the party. Another objective is to strike out of the ideological history of the party the memory that the Soviet Communist party and its leaders tried to throttle the upheaval and saw it as a danger to themselves. Another important objective is to give a measure of ideological rehabilitation to the "reformed" Stalinists who opposed the revolution and to deny completely the importance of the "revisionists" inside the party who helped spark it.

All these objectives are vital to the kind of party that Wladyslaw Gomulka, its leader, is creating. M. Gomulka is building a party that has completely shed any "romantic or bourgeois" ideas that 1956 was a step on the road to social democracy, that will tighten discipline in its ranks and in the country and that will draw closer to the Soviet Union. At the same time M. Gomulka wants a party that will retain a measure of political initiative independent of Moscow and will recognize that to stay peacefully in power some of the gains of 1956 must be preserved. M. Gomulkas' particular problem is that he wants the party to be as orthodox as possible but knows that whatever popular strength it has in the country rests on its deviations from orthodoxy.

The rewriting is carried on by the standard process of emphasizing the factors the party considers suitable and dropping mention of the others. October was the month in 1956 when the upheaval reached its height and the word has become synonymous in this country with hope. But the party now never refers to "October" and simply refers to the period as the "time of the eighth plenary meeting of the Central Committee." In speech after speech delegates refer enthusiastically to the inspiration given to the revolution by the twentieth congress of the Soviet Communist party in February, 1956 at which Nikita S. Khrushchev denounced Stalin and called for an end to the "cult of personality." Most students of Communist history recognize that the twentieth congress did give rise to hopes and restlessness in Eastern Europe. But at the current Polish meeting not a word is said about the fact that eight months later Mr. Khrushchev came storming into Warsaw and tried to arrange a coup to put down the Polish turmoil and eliminate M. Gomulka. When they allude to the turbulence of those days, Communist delegates present it as a sort of intramural affair. Pressures of an aroused people on the party are referred to only occasionally and glancingly and then as a reaction to administrative errors rather than to basic policy.

Among the most fascinating aspects of the rewriting is the sort of reversal of roles assigned to the "dogmatists," who opposed the revolution, and the "revisionists" who fought for ist. The "dogmatists" – Stalinists they were called in the old days – are no longer a major threat to M. Gomulka. But after clipping their claws he made peace with them because they were the core of the party bureaucracy and basically he respected them more than he did the revisionists.

At today's meeting, for instance, Deputy Premier Zenon Nowak, counted a dogmatist in 1956, in effect blamed the revisionists for making the Stalinists more Stalinist. He said the revisionists had muddled things by supporting the changes of 1956. Actually, he said, they were just trying to re-establish capitalism, but their support for the changes confused a lot of "devoted comrades" and "prompted their dogmatist reservations."

Although both dogmatism and revisionism are criticized by the delegates there is a world of difference in the language used. Dogmatism is merely a tendency and "no real problem," as M. Nowak said today. But revisionism is the "greatest danger," the "venomous fang" of reaction. There is "an old Polish proverb" that has just been made up in Warsaw to cover the congress: "It is safer to write history than to make it."

32.3 Poland's New Territory and How It Develops

[*Source: A. M. Rosenthal: Poles now say they are in the region to stay, in:* The New York Times *(New York, N.Y.), Vol. CVIII/No. 36,952, March 27, 1959, p. 3, cols. 2–4.*]

For Poland and for Central Europe important news is developing almost unnoticed in the cities and farmland where the Polish eagle replaced the German swastika at the end of World War II. It is not an event but an attitude. "We are not sitting on our suitcases any more," said a Pole, casually, in the Club of the Scientists. "We have unpacked. This is ours – but now we feel it, we feel we are staying." At a time when most of the world talks about a foreign ministers' meeting and a summit meeting the Poles talk about them too. But they talk about them mostly in terms of the arc-shaped slice of eastern Germany turned over to Polish control by the Allies in one of the major territorial changes of the war. The slice now makes up the western and northern third of Poland. This land is ours, fully and finally, the Poles say. Only when the peace treaty is signed, the West replies.

It is now fourteen years since the street called Adolf Hitler-Strasse in the smoking shell of Breslau became Ulica Powstancow Slaskich in what is now Wroclaw, since the burning port of Stettin became the still jagged Polish port of Szczecin, since the wagons of Polish peasants first moved on to the land of German farmers and Prussian Junkers. For most of those fourteen years the Poles – because of Western policy, mistakes of their own Government and the rootless nature of the new population – sat on their suitcases and it held up development of the new territories. The cities and many towns of the west still shock the eye and stagger the mind in their devastation. The Poles did not inherit the fat and smooth East Germany of before the war but a near wasteland, and this they plead with foreigners to remember.

When the Poles started going west – there is a population now of about 7,500,000 Poles compared with a prewar German population of about 9,000,000 – they found that more than half the houses were burned to the ground or stood, gutted, open to the sky. More than 60 per cent of the industry was wrecked – and the Russians helped themselves to a part of what remained, as war booty. The land was virtually without livestock, the railway lines were often twisted wreckage, the bridges were down and the water mains were empty. Reconstruction was painful and slow – too slow, the Poles say now. There are miles of hideous emptiness still in Wroclaw, but there are also new houses and factories. In Szczecin the foreigner can choose to concentrate on the piers that lie in wreckage or the six miles of piers rebuilt.

The feeling of uncertainty that gripped the western territories came in part from Western refusal to recognize the Polish borders as final. But the Government in Warsaw also added to

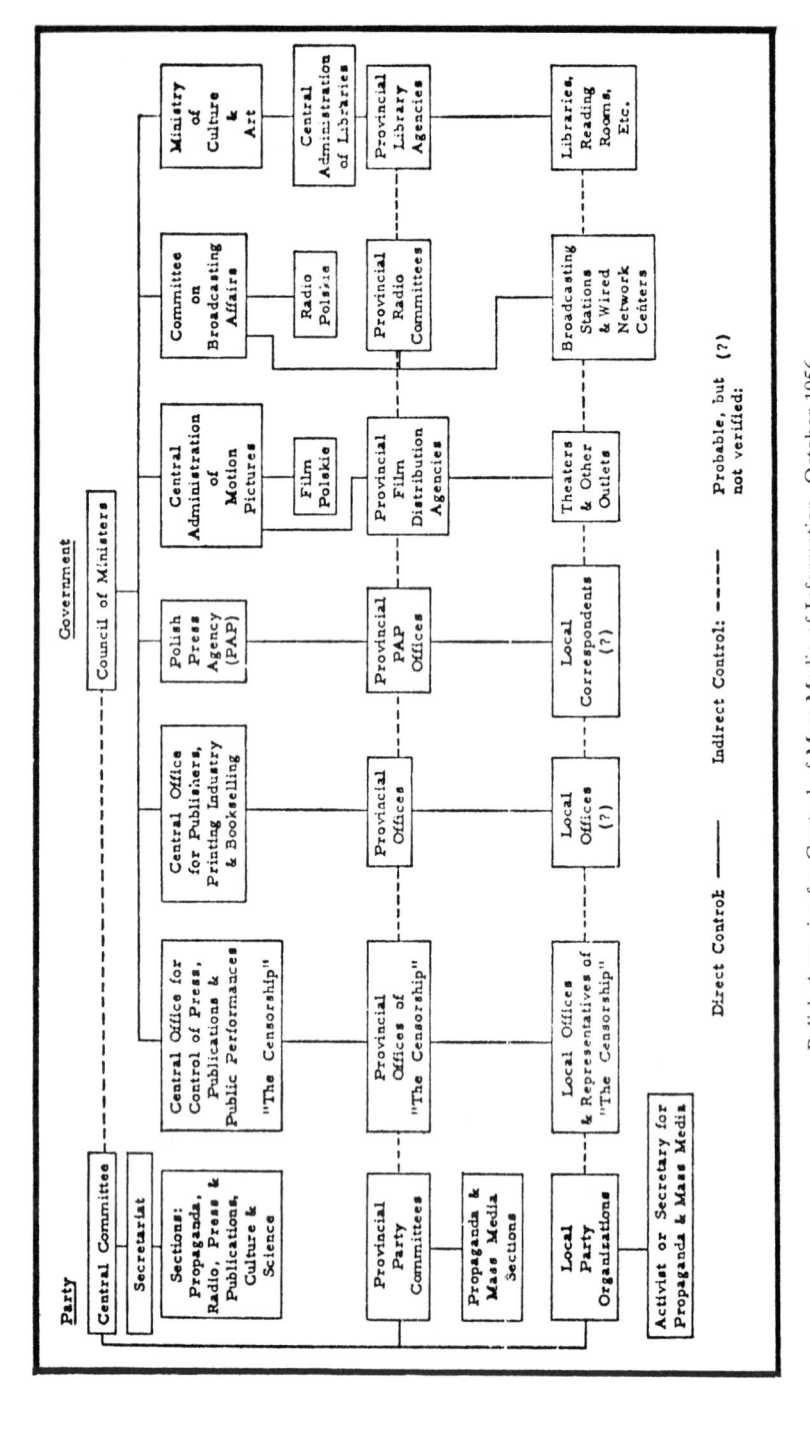

Polish Agencies for Control of Mass Media of Information, October 1956

[*Source:* Clifford R. Barnett: Poland – its people, its society, its culture, New York 1958, p. 145.]

the unease by underinvesting in the western regions. The unease has not totally disappeared, but it is going. The Poles are coming to think that come what may at foreign ministers' meetings the borders will remain. Warsaw is putting more money into the west – twice as much this year as nine years ago. And the new territories now have the highest birth rate in the country. More than one-third of the people in the area by now have been born here.

The state has stopped trying to put pressure on the peasants to join the collectives and is urging them to buy land. The Roman Catholic Church in Poland also has contributed to the growing feeling of stability. Stefan Cardinal Wyszynski, the Primate of Poland, came to the west and told the people that the Holy See took account of the fact that "Poland has come here, plows and sows here, kneels and prays, believes and loves here."

32.4 A Warsaw Pact Discussion and Its Premises

[*Source: A. M. Rosenthal: Summit: How the East prepares. Warsaw Pact goes through motions, in:* The New York Times *(New York, N.Y.), Vol. CVIII/No. 36,982, April 26, 1959, Section 4, p. E 5, cols. 6–8.*]

The Soviet bloc has organized a preview, a sort of road company try-out, for its role in the big Geneva foreign ministers' show. It will open here on Monday for a one or two day stand.

In one of Warsaw's handsome palaces the foreign ministers of that marvelously uncomplicated military and political alliance called the Warsaw Pact will get together to discuss Germany, Berlin and Geneva. The foreign ministers of the Western alliance have been busy too with rounds of pre-Geneva meetings, busy trying to settle or at least subdue differences, trying to find a policy for Geneva and then trying to agree on it.

Such problems are not on the agenda of the Warsaw Pact foreign ministers. Any questions on the minds of the foreign ministers – such as the advisability of insisting on going ahead with a separate East German peace treaty, about which the Poles are most dubious – are discussed outside the formal talks. The purpose of the meeting will not be to determine or agree upon policy but simply to reiterate it or announce any new developments in it. The objective is one of communiqué. But formal and pre-determined though it may be, the meeting in Warsaw gives the world a chance to take a look at the workings of Communist bloc diplomacy. Attending the session will be the Soviet Union and the Eastern European countries – the signatories to the pact. Communist China, apparently in a bloc move to impress the West, will also send a representative, although it is not a member.

The Warsaw securtiy pact was set up in the spring of 1955. It was the Communist bloc's formal counter-thrust to the remilitarization of West Germany and its integration into the West's military picture. The treaty is a simple document. Contracting parties agree to come to each other's aid in time of attack. Joint command of forces assigned to the pact is set up.

It is quite plain that the instrument of power in Eastern Europe is not the Warsaw Pact but the strength of the Soviet Union. The Warsaw Pact did not in any way change the military or political picture in Eastern Europe, as the North Atlantic Treaty changed it in Western Europe. But it did provide the Russians with a legal justification for stationing troops in Eastern Europe. And officially the troops are there with the consent of the government involved. It seems true that the present governments of East Germany and Hungary would be in no great hurry to be without the comforting presence of Soviet troops.

The Poles in 1956 wrung from the Russians an agreement to remove part of the Red Army detachments in this country. There is probably no wild enthusiam among Polish Communists for the presence of the remaining Red Army troops. But they accept their presence, almost unnoticeable except in bivouac areas, as part of the price of maintaining a relationship with the Soviet Union that is the basis of their own power in their own country. Just how significant the treaty pledges of cooperation and consultation and respect for sovereignty are can be seen in recent history. Only twice were Red Army Warsaw Pact detachments moved into action positions. Once was in Poland, when Soviet tanks moved to the Warsaw gates to put down the political upheaval. They were called off by a Moscow unwilling to face a war with the Polish people and the Polish Communist party. The second time was in Hungary when Red Army troops crushed the 1956 revolution. In other words, the only times Warsaw Pact forces moved militarily was against Warsaw Pact governments.

The country that makes the decisions in the Warsaw Pact, of course, is the Soviet Union. The only question is to what extent these decisions can be influenced by the junior partners. The answer is that the governments of Eastern Europe as such do not have much of an influence in shaping Moscow's foreign policies but that the political situations in those countries do have a role. The Kremlin may not be swayed, for instance, by the opinions of the East German Government. But if the East German Government obviously needs shoring up, that becomes a political consideration Moscow has to take into account. Premier Krushchev may still burn with anger at the memory of Poland's defiance but he recognizes that the Polish Communist party, to stay peacefully in power, must, at least for the time being, be allowed a certain latitude. Poland wants to keep her comparatively polite relations with the West. That is one reason for her antipathy toward a separate East German peace treaty. Moscow may take that into account, not because of "pressure" from Warsaw but because Poland's relationship with the West could be of some use to the bloc.

It is easy enough to see through the facade of "political consultation" of the Warsaw Pact. But it would be a mistake to assume that the talk of "solidarity" in the Communist camp, particularly as concerns the current negotiations, is a sham. There is a large degree of solidarity, based on the self interests of the Eastern European governments and the fears of the people. As seen in this part of the world the whole purpose of Soviet strategy at the moment is to gain recognition for the long-term division of Germany through Western acceptance of the existence of East Germany.

Eastern European Communists think that to reach that goal Moscow will threaten and bluster but will not go to war. They believe Moscow's principal card is Berlin and that it will put it forward as a variety of poker hands.

The division of Germany is a situation that presents problems to the Eastern European governments. But it is plain they think a reunified Germany would present bigger ones. For Poland, for example, a reunified Germany under Western influence might present threats to the former German territories now part of Poland. And any reunified Germany – neutral,

PZPR CENTRAL APPARATUS, 1962

First Secretary
† W. Gomułka

Secretaries
† E. Gierek   W. Matwin
W. Jarosiński   † E. Ochab
† Z. Kliszko   R. Strzelecki
† R. Zambrowski

Bureaus, Groups, Institutes, School (6)

- Cadres' Bureau (Z. Kliszko, Dir.) •†
- Central Party Group to Combat Corruption (J. Albrecht, Dir.) •
- Institute of Social Science (A. Schaff, Dir.) •
- Letters & Inspection Bureau (E. Pełowska, Dir.) ••
- Party History Institute (T. Daniszewski, Dir.) •
- Press Bureau (A. Starewicz, Dir.) •

Departments (10)

- Administration (K. Witaszewski, Dir.) •
- Agriculture (E. Pszczółkowski, Dir.) •
- Culture (W. Kraśko, Dir.) •
- Economic (J. Olszewski, Dir.) •
- Foreign (J. Czesak, Dir.) ••
- General (B. Bendek, Dir.) ••
- Military (W. Jaruzelski, Dir.)
- Organization (M. Marzec, Dir.) •
- Propaganda & Agitation (L. Stasiak, Dir.)
- Science & Education (A. Werblan, Dir.) •

Commissions (16)

- Construction (J. Bogusz, Chmn.)
- Coops, Local Ind. & Handicrafts (S. Kuziński, Chmn.)
- Education (W. Jarosiński, Chmn.) •
- Employment & Wages (J. Kulesza, Chmn.) •
- Heavy Industry (J. Olszewski, Chmn.) •
- Justice (J. Hessel, Secr.)
- Light Industry (M. Peć, Dpty.)
- Market Supplies (J. Kujda, Secr.)
- National Minorities (W. Szachelski, Chmn.) •
- Publishing (L. Kasman, Chmn.) •
- Peoples' Councils (R. Zambrowski, Chmn.) •†
- Social (W. Nieśmiałek, Secr.)
- Sport & Tourism (W. Reczek, Chmn.) •
- Transport (L. Puzoń, Secr.)
- Workers' Councils (F. Blinowski, Chmn.) •
- Youth (M. Renke, Chmn.) ••

NOTES: † member, Politburo
         • member, Central Committee
         •• candidate member, Central Committee

[Source: Richard F. Staar: Poland 1944–1962. The Sovietization of a Captive People, Baton Rouge, La., 1962, p. 160.]

Western or Socialist – would raise again the possibility that the Soviet Union and Germany, as the two most powerful European states, would settle things between themselves. Historically, Poland pays the bill.

The Soviet denunciations of rearmament in West Germany also meet a warm political and emotional response here. It does not take a great deal of imagination to understand that an Eastern European does not have to be a Communist to be deeply upset at the thought of a militarily powerful Germany – East, West or unified.

And among the governments of Eastern Europe, it is important to realize, there is a sort of class solidarity. Polish Communists do not much admire Czechoslovakian Communists, Hungarian Communists are not full of love for Rumanian Communists and nobody likes the East German Communists. But just the same the governments do have a mutual interest in each other's strength and most of all in the strength of the Soviet Union. All they have to do is think where they would be without it.

32.5 Communist Diplomacy and Its Tactical Function

[*Source: A. M. Rosenthal: Red Bloc meets in Poland today – Aims to exploit 'Breach' in West, in:* The New York Times *(New York, N.Y.), Vol. CVIII/No. 36,983, April 27, 1959, p. 1, cols. 7–8; p. 7, cols. 3–7.*]

The Communist world's foreign ministers, who will meet here tomorrow, are plainly convinced that a breach exists in Western diplomacy and that they can widen it. Almost every technical detail of the meeting between the Warsaw Pact states – the Soviet Union and seven Eastern European Communist countries – and Communist China is being treated as a great secret. But the purpose apparently is the publicity the final communiqué will get.

It will be the Communist bloc's reply in advance to the meeting in Paris Wednesday of Western foreign ministers. It will also be designed to set the stage for the Big Four foreign ministers' conference in Geneva next month. It has been something of a task to find out that the Communist ministers will meet here in a governmental conference hall and that they will dine on salmon, caviar and poultry. Warsaw newspapers are printing only a minimum about the talks. On this Sunday, most of the people of Warsaw seemed to have their minds on other things – walking in the greening parks, sitting in the suddenly blossoming outdoor cafes and raising their faces to the spring sun that is lifting the winter's grayness.

Although technical details are soberly hushed, the strategy of Communist diplomacy in preparation for the Geneva conference has been taking rather clear shape. That strategy is based on a strong belief that many Western European powers, particularly Britain, are afraid of the growing strength of West Germany. The Communists also believe that there is pressure in the United States for a negotiated settlement with Moscow and that the departure of John Foster Dulles has cut down the United States' role as the binding diplomatic force in the Western alliance. Some of these things are being said, publicly and privately, for propaganda purposes. It also seems clear that the Communists believe they will have an opportunity at Geneva to exploit the differences they are convinced exist.

In the Communist alliance there are diplomats who believe that the best course for the Soviet Union to follow would be to strengthen the hand of "reasonable" Western diplomats – they think particularly of Prime Minister Harold Macmillan of Britain – by presenting themselves as reasonable. The expected communiqué may give some idea of how far Moscow is willing to publicize this "soft" tactic at the moment.

The theme of divisions in the Western alliance was emphasized in a speech April 22 by Adam Rapacki, Polish Foreign Minister. It was published last night.

He said Bonn had "aggressive" designs not only against the East but also against Western Europe. He said, "speaking frankly," that the idea of a unified Germany under Bonn's domination aroused fears in France, Britain and the smaller nations of Western Europe and in some circles in North America. The frankest comments have come from a newspaper owned by Pax, a stanchly pro-Government Roman Catholic organization that does not have much popular support but often speaks quite bluntly. The newspaper, Slowo Powszechne, said in its week-end edition that the Warsaw meeting "without doubt" would try to take advantage of differences in the Western alliance by "adding arguments to those circles that believe in the necessity of negotiation."

The most important delegate to the Warsaw conference, Andrei A. Gromyko, Soviet Foreign Minister, arrived from Moscow tonight. Also here are the foreign ministers of Albania, Rumania, Bulgaria, East Germany and Czechoslovakia and the deputy ministers of Hungary and Communist China. It is being noted here that officially the Warsaw meeting will not be simply a session of the Warsaw Pact, the Communist world's military and political alliance. It will be a meeting of the foreign ministers of the pact countries and of Communist China. It is believed here that this terminology was designed to emphasize Red China's participation in discussions of European problems.

In part this seems to be meant as a bow in the direction of Peiping. In at least equal part it is apparently also meant as evidence to the West that in Geneva the Soviet Union will be speaking not only for itself and its sphere in Eastern Europe but also for Communist power in Asia.

Related Readings

Alton, Thad Paul: Polish postwar economy, New York 1955.
Barczyk, Georg: Die Organisation der landwirtschaftlichen Betriebe in Polen und den deutschen Ostgebieten. Ihre Umgestaltung nach 1956 und die Auswirkung auf die Produktion, Giessen 1962.
Barnett, Clifford R. et al.: Poland – its people, its society, its culture, New Haven, Conn., 1958.
Bielecki, Franciszek et al.: Pologne – réalités et problèmes, Warszawa 1966.
Bronska-Pampuch, Wanda: Polen zwischen Hoffnung und Verzweiflung, Köln 1958.
Dziewanowski, Marian Kamil: The Communist Party of Poland – an outline of history, 2nd ed., Cambridge, Mass., 1976.
Feiwel, George Richard: The economics of a socialist enterprise. A case study of the Polish firm, New York 1965.

Hartmann, Karl: Polens Geist zwischen Ost und West. Eine Betrachtung zur geistigen Lage in Polen nach dem Zweiten Weltkrieg, Hannover 1962.
Hiscocks, Richard: Poland, bridge for the abyss? An interpretation of developments in postwar Poland, London – New York 1963.
Korbonski, Andrzej: Politics of socialist agriculture in Poland, 1945–1960, New York 1965.
Lammich, Siegfried: Das sozialistische Parlament Polens, Köln 1971.
Lewis, Flora: The Polish volcano. A case history of hope, London 1959.
Montias, John Michael: Central planning in Poland, New Haven, Conn., 1962.
Morrison, James F.: The Polish People's Republic, Baltimore 1968.
Raina, Peter K.: Political opposition in Poland, 1954–1977, London 1978.
Staar, Richard Felix: Poland, 1944–1962. The Sovietization of a captive people, Baton Rouge, La., 1962.
Szyr, Eugeniusz et al. (Eds.): Twenty years of the Polish People's Republic, Warszawa 1964.

1960

Lynn L. Heinzerling

The Associated Press

CHAPTER 33

REPORTS ABOUT THE CONGO IN 1960

A Period of Unrest and Lumumba's Struggle for Unity

    Introductory Notes
33.1 Lumumba's Aims and a Change of Direction
33.2 Secessionist Movements and the Role of the U.N.
33.3 Lumumba's Fight for Unity and Pressures From Without
33.4 A Two-Hour Coup and Its Reported Details
33.5 The Premier's Comeback and Several New Plans
    Related Readings

Introductory Notes

A quarter-century after William C. Barber had won the then Pulitzer Correspondence award, in 1936, for his reports about Ethiopia, an African country for the second time was brought into the focus of the International Reporting Prize. Again the occasion was an unpleasant one. For this time the award went to Lynn L. Heinzerling of the Associated Press *"for his reporting . . . of the early stages of the Congo crisis" in 1960.*

Lynn Louis Heinzerling was born on October 23, 1906, in Birmingham, Ohio. After attending Akron University (1924–25) and Ohio Wesleyan University (1925–27), he joined the Cleveland Plain-Dealer *in 1928 and stayed at this newspaper until 1933. In December, 1933, Heinzerling entered the service of the* Associated Press *at Cleveland, and in 1938 he transferred to the foreign news desk of* AP *in New York prior to transfer abroad. From 1938 to 1945 Heinzerling's byline stories came from virtually every important European news center, including Berlin, Helsinki, Copenhagen, Paris, Madrid, Lisbon, London, Cairo, Rome, and Vienna. He was in Danzig on September 1, 1939, when the German battleship 'Schleswig-Holstein' turned her batteries against the small Polish garrison on the Westerplatte, a Polish munitions dump and fort in the harbor area, to start the war. Heinzerling also helped to cover the early phases of the German occupation of Denmark and the Nazi invasion of the Netherlands; later he was with the British Eighth Army and the U.S. Fifth Army in Italy. He was assigned to Germany before his appointment in 1948 as chief of the* AP's *Geneva bureau. In January 1957, Heinzerling was named chief of the Johannesburg bureau of his news agency and in that post he traveled widely over the African continent. Twice in 1960 African events changed the course of* AP's *orderly plans for Heinzerling. Early in the year he was to exchange posts with another* AP *correspondent to become chief of the bureau in Vienna, when heavy rioting broke out in South Africa and he had to stay there. Then, in late spring, Heinzerling was moved to London to be coordinator there for all news from Africa, when the Congo erupted. So Heinzerling, as* AP's *top African specialist, was sent again to Africa to head up the staff there. He remained in the Congo until November, 1960.*

The following texts by Lynn Louis Heinzerling, copyright 1960, are reprinted by kind permission of The Associated Press, *New York, N.Y.*

33.1 Lumumba's Aims and a Change of Direction

[*Source: Lynn Heinzerling: Lumumba is off for U.S., Canada – Cancels Russ troop call, seeks world capital, in:* The Times-Picayune *(New Orleans, La.), 124th Year/No. 181, July 23, 1960, section 1, p. 1, col. 6.*]

Premier Patrice Lumumba turned from his flirtation with the Soviet Union and took off Friday for the United States and Canada in search of capital for the Congo's crippled economy. He said he wants to be friends with everybody.

Lumumba abondoned his threat to call in Soviet soldiers to force out Belgian soldiers. He told a news conference in this United Nations-guarded capital there is no longer any need for Soviet military intervention. The lanky Congolese leader, who only a few days ago was calling Western nations imperialist and issuing ultimatums to the United Nations, signed one agreement with an American financier for development of mineral and power resources of the former colony Belgium freed June 30. Lumumba also held out a hand to the Belgians. He gave the Belgians credit for helping to build the Congo and said he considers them "our friends." He insisted only that Belgian soldiers evacuate the Congo, including the treaty bases of Kamina and Kitona, and that Belgian Ambassador Baron Jean van den Bosch leave the country immediately. Lumumba said the ambassador, because of the reports he sent home, and Gen. Emile Janssens, former commander of the Congolese army, were the two Belgians who damaged the Congo most.

"We have political independence and now we need economic independence. We need bread and happiness for our people," Lumumba said. "We want the assistance of all the world, but we do not want charity. We offer, to all those who want to help us exploit the country, equitable remuneration on their investment and all necessary guarantees."

"The shift in Lumumba's diplomatic stand was abrupt. He expressed profound thanks to the United Nations for its quick action in the Congo, although the Security Council set no deadline in renewing its call for the withdrawal of Belgian soldiers. He had been threatening to call in the Soviet Union and soldiers of the African-Asian bloc nations if the Belgian units did not leave immediately.

Lumumba set out for New York aboard a jet airliner in a hunt for international capital, technical and medical help to put this backward young African nation on its feet. The British-built plane was supplied by President Kwame Nkrumah of Ghana. L. Edgar Detwiler, American president of the Congo International Management Corp. (CIMCO), founded just two months ago, signed a 50-year development pact with the Premier. The agreement is subject to ratification by the Congo's Parliament now in recess. Detwiler, who accompanied Lumumba on the plane, said his corporation will supply capital and management and training for Congolese who are expected to take over key positions.

He reported in an airport interview that the Congo government has received attractive offers from the Soviet Union. "We had to fill the vacuum before the Russians did," he said. "We think we are doing the Belgian interests this way. Suppose the reserves of the Congo fell into other hands – if they were lost to the free world?" He said crude mineral reserves of the Congo are extimated by his experts to be worth two billion dollars.

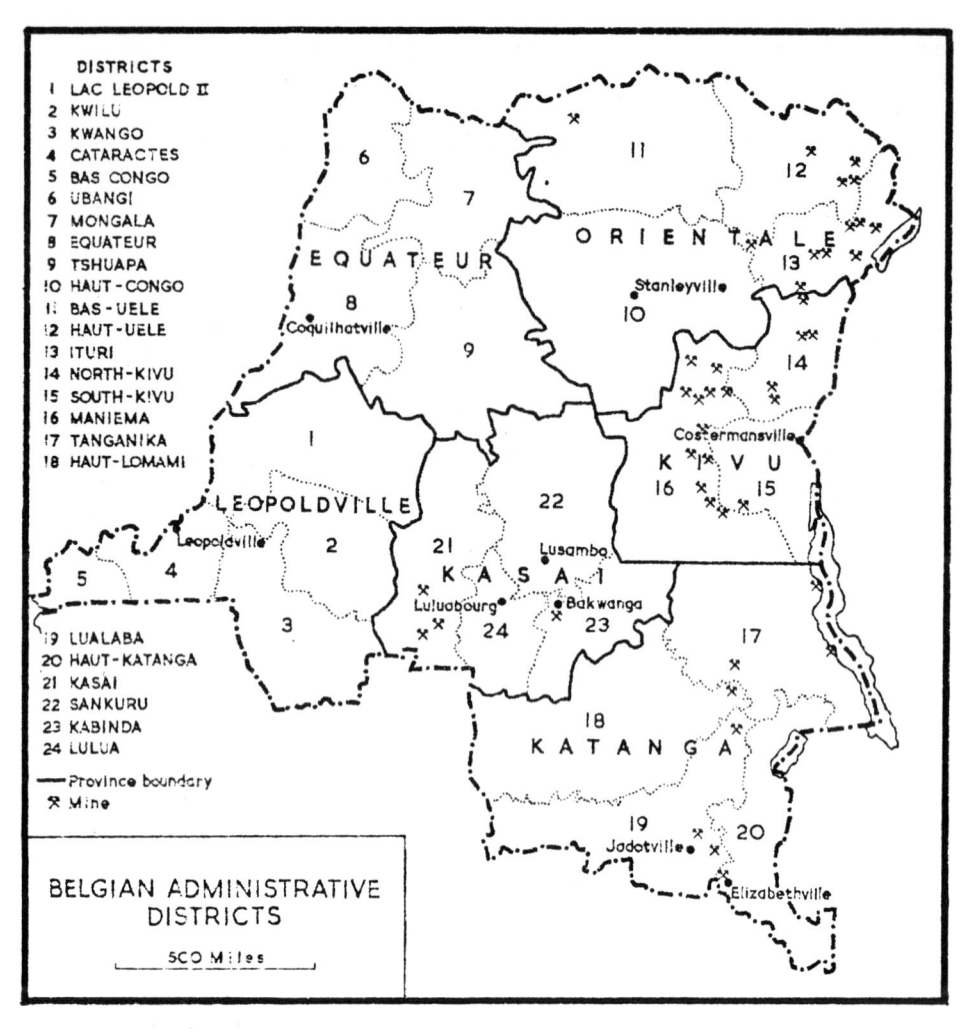

[Source: Catherine Hoskyns: The Congo. A Chronology of Events, January 1960–December 1961, London 1962, frontispiece.]

33.2 Secessionist Movements and the Role of the U.N.

[Source: Lynn Heinzerling: Lumumba returns to find regime shaken by dissent – Move for Federation gains strength, in: The Times-Picayune (New Orleans, La.), 124th Year/No. 198, August 9, 1960, p. 4, cols. 4–5.]

Premier Patrice Lumumba came home Monday night to find his government shaken by dissent and parading youths shouting "down with Lumumba." Returning from a two-week tour of North America and Africa, Lumumba learned the Leopoldville capital province had joined secessionist Katanga in demanding strong autonomy for the Congo's six provinces with a federation within a federation to replace his central regime.

"I made an excellent and fruitful trip to the United States as well as to Africa," Lumumba told newsmen at the airport. "All I can tell you is that Africa from east to west and from north to south is on the side of the Congo government." He said he would first have to talk with other members of his regime before making additional statements.

In Lumumba's absence during a critical period of his young nation's life, sentiment against his central government and his method of running it hardened. With economic distress spreading, the influential Bakongo tribesmen of western Congo were reported rising in indignation against his leadership. Belgian sources said separatist movements were growing in Kasai province to the east and Equator province in the northwest.

Lumumba returned to find still unsatisfied his demands of two weeks ago that all Belgian troops leave the country and that Baron Jean van den Bosch, head of the Belgian mission, go with them. Before leaving Accra, the capital of Ghana, Lumumba announced he and Ghana President Kwame Nkrumah had agreed to establish a combined high command to speed the withdrawal of Belgian soldiers from this former Belgian colony, if the U.N. fails.

The main concern of Lumumba has been the defiance of rich Katanga province, which has declared itself independent of his rule. But now Katanga's cry for a federation of self-ruling provinces was taken up by Leopoldville province, which controls the Lower Congo. Gason Dioni, vice president of the province, announced the provincial government had sent its demand for a federation of Leopoldville, Oriental, Equator, Kasai, Kivu and Katanga provinces to the United Nations Security Council. Furthermore, Dioni told the U.N. the big Mukongo tribe he heads "rejects the unitarian, centralized government."

The youth demonstrations against Lumumba were led by Jabako, the youth organization of Congo President Joseph Kasavubu, a political foe of the Premier. Hundreds of them, including girls in colorful dresses, chanted. They passed out leaflets demanding that Guinea and Ghana units of the U.N. leave the Congo. Leaders of Guinea and Ghana have offered troops to help drive the Belgian soldiers from Katanga province. Jabako also issued a communiqué demanding a plebiscite under U.N. auspices to permit each people or tribe in the Congo to determine its own political destiny. The youth group Sunday night voted no confidence in Lumumba. Before the demonstration broke up, dozens of Congolese and Ghana soldiers were rushed to the square in front of the new Stanley Hotel, where many U.N. employes live, to maintain order. Swedish soldiers patrolled the main boulevard.

President Kasavubu's Abako party speaks for the Bakongo tribe, which inhabits the province of Leopoldville and dominates its political and tribal life. Although he was often at Lumumba's side during the dangerous early days of independence. Kasavubu has had little to say publicly about the unhappy position of the new nation. As President, Kasavubu has little to do with its political leadership, taken over by Lumumba when he won out over Kasavubu as Premier. Kasavubu has always been for a loose central government and strongly autonomous provincial governments but he has not expressed any views publicly concerning the demands of his followers.

But unlike Katanga, Kasavubu's followers want the Belgian soldiers to get out of the Congo. U.N. forces, moved into the Congo at Lumumba's request last month after violent antiwhile disorders, are replacing the Belgians in five provinces. But the U.N. forces were withheld from Katanga on U.N. Secretary general Dag Hammarskjold's orders last Friday when it became apparent the secessionist government there was determined to fight to keep them out. In Elisabethville, the provincial capital, Katanga Premier Moise Tshombe declared his stand for a federation of the six Congo provinces was gaining increasing support. Without mentioning the action of Leopoldville province, he said Dioni and leaders in Kasai and Equator province favored a federation instead of a central government.

In the midst of all the troubles Congolese officials showed little concern about what the U.N. Security Council was doing in New York. While the U.N. Command here has been roundly criticized for slowness in forcing the Belgian withdrawal and from avoiding a showdown in Katanga, some Congolese officials said the U.N. must stay here for a long time. Otherwise, they said, the Congo will disappear as a modern nation.

33.3 Lumumba's Fight for Unity and Pressures From Without

[*Source: Lynn Heinzerling: Council blunt with Lumumba – Stop harassing U.N. is Africa States Order, in:* The Times-Picayune *(New Orleans, La.), 124th Year/No. 221, September 1, 1960, p. 2, cols. 1–3.*]

African neighbors bluntly told Premier Patrice Lumumba's government Wednesday to stop harassing the United Nations and cooperate in U.N. efforts to end the chaos within this two months old nation.

A Lumumba setback in the conference of independent. African states coincided with a report from Elisabethville of reverses for his troops in their campaign against rebels in Kasai Province. Albert Kalonji, the Baluha chieftain who proclaims himself president of a Mineral state in southern Kasai, claimed his troops have recaptured Bakwanga, his capital, and three other towns that Lumumba's men occupied last week. Independent confirmation was lacking.

Lumumba was on hand for the windup of the 13-nation conference of independent African states which he opened at the Palace of Culture last Thursday while his police outside used warning shots and wielded gun butts to break up a demonstration against him. The Premier, who has attacked the United Nations off and on and spread the suspicion that its motives are imperialistic, sat quietly as the resolution calling for Congolese cooperation was read. But he bounded back a little later with a complaint the Congo had not been consulted about U.N. moves. He suggested "incidents would have been avoided if from the beginning a spirit of cooperation had existed between representatives of the United Nations and those of the government of the republic."

The conference pointed out that the United Nations entered the Congo "at the express request of the government of the Republic of the Congo" and intended to safeguard her independence, her unity and her territorial integrity." The resolution noted that the U.N.

PARTY STRENGTH IN NATIONAL ASSEMBLY, BY PROVINCE, MAY, 1960

Party	Leopold-ville	Equa-teur	Orientale	Kivu	Katanga	Kasai	Total
MNC-Lumumba	1	2	21	5	—	4	33
PSA	13	—	—	—	—	—	13
Abako	12	—	—	—	—	—	12
Cerea	—	—	—	10	—	—	10
PNP	—	2	3	—	—	3	8
Puna	—	7	—	—	—	—	7
Conakat	—	—	—	—	7	—	7
MNC-Kalondji	—	—	—	—	—	8	8
Balubakat	—	—	—	—	6	—	6
Independents	1	—	1	1	1	1	5
Reco	—	—	—	4	—	—	4
UNC	—	—	—	—	—	3	3
Luka	3	—	—	—	—	—	3
Local interests	—	2	—	—	—	—	2
Association Ngwaka	—	2	—	—	—	—	2
Mederco	—	2	—	—	—	—	2
Customary chiefs	—	—	—	1	1	—	2
Coaka	—	—	—	—	—	2	2
Front Commun	1	—	—	—	—	—	1
Abazi	1	—	—	—	—	—	1
RDLK	1	—	—	—	—	—	1
Unimo	—	1	—	—	—	—	1
Cartel MNC-Lumumba-Unebafi	—	—	—	1	—	—	1
Cartel ARP-PRC	—	—	—	1	—	—	1
Atcar	—	—	—	—	1	—	1
Cartel MNC-Lumumba-Coaka	—	—	—	—	—	1	1
Total	33	18	25	23	16	22	137

SELECTIVE LIST OF PARTY NEWSPAPERS PUBLISHED IN 1960

Name	Place of publication	Frequency	Political group
Notre Kongo	Leopoldville	Weekly	Abako-Kasa-Vubu
Kongo Dieto	Leopoldville	Weekly	Abako-Kasa-Vubu
Kongo Dia Ngunga	Leopoldville	Weekly	Abako-Kasa-Vubu
Vigilance	Leopoldville	Bimonthly	Jabako
Congo	Leopoldville	Weekly	Abako-Kanza
La Voix du Peuple	Leopoldville	Weekly	MNC-Kalondji
Emancipation	Leopoldville	Bimonthly	Parti du Peuple
Solidarité Africaine	Leopoldville	Weekly	PSA
La Nation Congolaise	Leopoldville	Weekly	PUNA
La Liberté	Leopoldville	Weekly	PNP
L'Indépendance	Leopoldville	Weekly	MNC-Lumumba
La Vérité	Leopoldville	Irregular	Cerea
Congo Libre	Leopoldville	Irregular	Interfédérale
Uhuru	Stanleyville	Weekly	MNC-Lumumba
Rédemption	Stanleyville	Irregular	MNC-Lumumba
La Lumière	Lulaubourg	Weekly	PNP
Franchise	Luluabourg	Weekly	Lulua-Frères
L'Abeille	Luluabourg	Weekly	MSM
Le National	Elisabethville	Irregular	Cartel
Congo d'Abord	Elisabethville	Irregular	Balubakat
La Voix du Katanga	Elisabethville	Irregular	Conakat
Conakat	Elisabethville	Weekly	Conakat
Le Phare	Coquilhatville	Weekly	Unimo

Development of Political Groups and Newspapers

[*Source:* René Lemarchand: Political Awakening in the Belgian Congo, Berkeley–Los Angeles 1964, pp. 224, 268.]

mission was designed to prevent the Congo from becoming involved in the cold war. The United Nations was praised for "the work of peace it brings to the Congo" and for promotion of the withdrawal of Belgian troops.

Lumumba, who has repeatedly called for the withdrawal of U.N. white troops, and who has harassed Secretary-General Dag Hammarskjold, reasserted confidence in the United Nations and its members. But he added: "Our great hope is that this organization pursues its objective with more efficacy for the great happiness of humanity." The Premier asked that Congolese and U.N. troops join forces to pacify the country. His troops, he said, are burning with impatience and "obsessed with the idea of immediately entering Katanga to liberate their brothers." The southeast province of the Congo, Katanga, has proclaimed its independence. It is allied with Kalonji's Mineral state. Lumumba, charged that colonialists meaning Belgians, had created a general staff of "saboteurs of our national independence" in Katanga. He said the withdrawn Belgian troops have been replaced in Katanga by Belgian gendarmes disguised as "technical advisers" to train Katanga Premier Moise Tshombe's police.

Lumumba, who is relying more and more on the promises of the Soviet Union and its satellites while his government is being infiltrated by agents of the East, said the African conference has taught the West a lesson. "The Western world has understood," he said, "that it is no longer possible to continue its play without risking the complete loss of Africa's friendship." He added that peace will not be complete in Africa "until the West puts an immediate end to its colonial enterprises."

In New York, Hammarskjold disclosed he has protested to Belgium for failure to get its last combat troops out of the Congo by Monday midnight as promised and announced. He said nearly 600 soldiers, some of them parachute troopers, remain. Loridan said the Belgians had fallen behind a timetable they expected to meet but that Hammarskjold exaggerated the situation. He said the remaining soldiers will head home as soon as planes become available.

A Belgian Defense Ministry spokesman in Brussels declined to confirm or deny the reported Belgian failure to get its troops out of the Congo. He said, however, "If there were some delays they probably were due to the lack of necessary planes to evacuate our soldiers from the Kamina base in time on Monday night."

33.4 A Two-Hour Coup and Its Reported Details

[Source: Lynn Heinzerling: Lumumba back free man soon after arrest – Rides through streets shouting 'Victory', in: The Times-Picayune (New Orleans, La.), 124th Year/No. 233, September 13, 1960, p. 1, col. 1; p. 3, cols. 5–8.]

Patrice Lumumba came roaring back through the streets of Leopoldville shouting "victory" from a military jeep Monday night only two hours after he was arrested and then freed.

The ousted premier sped to Leopoldville radio station after a tour of the African communes but was not allowed to speak.

What happened at Camp Leopold, where Lumumba had been taken by army troops, could not be learned immediately. Lumumba was in custody less than two hours. When he reached the radio station he said, "I'm not arrested. The people are with me." There were reports – all unconfirmed – that troops of Lumumba's Batatela tribe had somehow managed to free him from Camp Leopold.

At the moment it appeared that Lumumba had won a round in his continuing battle for power with president Kasavubu. The United Nations position meanwhile appeared to be weakening. Reports circulated here that the United Arab Republic had decided to withdraw its U.N. forces, including a paratroop battalion that had just arrived. In Cario a government spokesman contended the U.N. had violated the Congo's sovereignty by seizing the radio and airfields. There were rumors – unconfirmed – that Ghana might also withdraw its U.N. force. While a V.A.R. withdrawal probably would not affect the U.N. operation greatly, the Ghana force has been a mountain of strength to the U.N. in preserving order. Guinea's mission here announced Sunday its troops had been withdrawn from the U.N. command, but this has not been confirmed.

But it was the steadfast U.N. guard at the radio station that turned Lumumba back again. The radio station guard was greatly strengthened and barbed wire was strung after Lumumba's visit. Six or seven military jeeps loaded with armed soldiers in camouflaged helmets came racing through the city with Lumumba, sirens sounding. Lumumba occasionally raised his voice above the din through a loudspeaker to shout "Victory, Victory." But whether it was a victory or not could not be determined in the confusion. One or two newsmen in the radio station at the time Lumumba appeared asked him what he intended to do. Lumumba claimed he was the victim of a coup d'etat and said: "I decree this evening a general mobilization. We must tell the people."

Later he said: "I accuse the United Nations of being responsible for all." Even the most hardened observers of Congo life were astonished by the day's events. Lumumba had been taken out of the residence by armed soldiers. He was followed by his wife and children and a car piled high with baggage. Two hours later he was free again.

Lumumba did not return to the official residence of the premier after his unsuccessful visit to the radio station. Instead he went to the villa where he had lived before independence on Boulevard Albert. There, both Congolese troops and Ghana police and troops of the U.N. force were on guard. A newsman who approached a group of Congolese before the villa was told, "we don't need the press today." The Congolese soldiers roughly beckoned correspondents with their rifles to move on.

Lumumba's arrest and release took place so swiftly it left even the United Nations unclear as to exactly how it was accomplished. U.N. officials said they knew nothing in advance about the action. Apparently two different factions of the army were involved. Troops loyal to President Joseph Kasavubu apparently made the arrest and troops backing Lumumba brought out his release. Army chief of staff Col. Joseph Mobutu was believed to have played a role in getting Lumumba freed.

Lumumba exulted over his swift release and openly called for the arrest of Kasavubu. "It's Kasavubu's turn to go to jail now", he declared. A U.N. official said "anything can happen now. Absolutely anything." Lumumba later made a statement claiming the "ill-fated attempt" to arrest him was made by disloyal troops with a warrant issued nearly a week ago.

The statement charged that Kasavubu forced the Congo republic's Belgian attorney-general, Rene Rom, to sign the arrest warrent Sept. 6 – one day after Kasavubu fired Lumumba as Premier. The statement did not explain why it took nearly a week to carry out the warrant. Lumumba said Rom was taken to Camp Leopold after the arrest and admitted to senior army officers that the warrant was a plot hatched by Kasavubu.

Lumumba's statement claimed that this "aroused such anger among the soldiers that they wanted to go down into the town to arrest all Europeans and all those who where the cause of my arrest." Lumumba said he managed to calm the excited troops and later circulated in the native African quarters to appeal to the population to refrain from any hasty ill-considered action. "Wherever I went I was received with shouts of "Long live the liberator," Lumumba declared.

In another action following his release, Lumumba appealed to the Afro-Asian states for immediate and powerful military aid over the heads of the United Nations. Unless he received such help quickly Lumumba said, he would address his appeal to what he called another quarter. He did not identify the quarter, but observers recalled Lumumba previously had threatened to seek direct military aid from the Soviet Union.

In all the excitement, the power struggle between the left-wing Lumumba and the Congo's moderate president, remained unresolved.

Kasavubu, as chief of state, named a new 23-man government to replace Lumumba's red-backed regime and halt what Kasavubu has called a drift to chaos and communism. Kasavubu's premier designate is Senate President Joseph Ileo. Whatever the outcome, the Congo is certain to remain an issue in the cold war. The Soviet Union backed Lumumba with a fleet of planes, 100 trucks and scores of technicians, all sent in outside U.N. channels.

The first announcement of Lumumba's detention was made by his own chief of security, Charles Muzungo. About 200 soldiers of the Congolese army, being swiftly coordinated with U.N. forces, made the arrest. They met no resistance when they surrounded Lumumba's luxurious villa overlooking the Congo River. "I do not want any bloodshed", said the lanky, goateed Negro who became government chief when Belgium freed the Congo June 30" I will come with you." He was taken to Camp Leopold II, headquarters of the capital's 1,000-man government. Lumumba made a trip in a baggage-laden government limousine, accompanied by his wife and two children. Members of Lumumba's staff and a limousine with his belongings followed soon afterwards.

About three hours later Lumumba appeared in downtown Leopoldville. He demanded that he be allowed to speak over Radio Leopoldville, which the U.N. Command controls. Though the U.N. had put the station back in service Monday morning after silencing it for a week, Lumumba was told it could not be used to air his views. U.N. Ghana soldiers said they had orders to fire if he tried to get into the station again. Lumumba had tried to seize the station Sunday. He was turned back at gunpoint then by a British lieutenant of the Ghana forces. There was no explanation for Monday's surprising change of events. Fifty cars with Europeans gathered around the radio station. Congolese soldiers in camouflaged vehicles chased them away.

Earlier it had appeared that the United Nations had the situation firmly in hand. Gen. Victor Lundula, the ex-sergeant who commands the Congo's 20,000-man army, had a talk

Locations Where Congo Fighting was Reported

[*Source:* AP Map of July 6, 1959, locating Kisangani (Stanleyville) and Bukavu where the Congolese Government claimed foreign mercenary soldiers had landed.]

with Swedish Maj. Gen. Carl von Horn, U.N. military commander in the Congo. A U.N. spokesman said they discussed reorganization of the Congolese forces and continued cooperation between the Congolese and U.N. armies. Then Kasavubu conferred with the U.N. special representative in the Congo, Rajeshwar Dayal of India. Presumably the U.N. will speed supplies to the Congolese forces sent into the interior by Lumumba and left stranded there by the U.N. grounding of Soviet transport planes.

The U.N. spokesman also said that soldiers in the field would be paid, as were those in the Leopoldville garrison, through the cooperation of the U.N. The Lumumba forces in the interior are to maintain a truce negotiated in the field Saturday and now supervised by a 14-officer group led by Swedish Colonel S. M. Millersward. The cease-fire still is being observed throughout the nation, the U.N. spokesman said, though there have been minor violations. Aburst of gun fire wounded two followers of Albert Kalonji, a military foe of Lumumba, and the firing of an arrow slightly injured a Siberian soldier of U.N. Command in Kasal Province.

In Elizabethville, capital of secessionist Katanga Province, a government spokesman charged that Congolese soldiers exchanged fire with Katanga forces in the north and then retreated into adjoining Kivu Province. He said another detachment crossed the border from Kasai and advanced toward the town of Katanga.

33.5 The Premier's Comeback and Several New Plans

[*Source: Lynn Heinzerling: U.N. protection for Lumumba – Reappers, places self under guard, in:* The Times-Picayune *(New Orleans, La.), 124th Year/No. 239, September 19, 1960, p. 2, cols. 1–3.*]

Fiery Patrice Lumumba, who dropped from sight when his Communist-supported Congo collapsed, reappeared Sunday and immediately placed himself under the protection of United Nations troops. The ousted Congolese premier, defiant as ever, moved back into his official residence. The road in front of the residence was quickly blocked and U.N. Ghana troops deployed through his garden. They set up a command post beside the garage.

He disappeared shortly after Col. Joseph Mobutu, the Congo's emerging army strongman, seized power last Wednesday and announced "neutralization" of Lumumba and President Joseph Kasavubu. Lumumba apparently had been hidden for the last two days by the Guinean mission here. His disappearance had led to a spate of rumors, including some that he was dead. Only a few Congolese and a small group of newsmen saw him move back into his imposing residence overlooking the Congo River but they agreed he was still talking big.

Lumumba came out on the front balcony soon after he returned. Mobutu, who now runs the Congo along the lines of a military dictatorship, is "not important," Lumumba called down in answer to a newsman's question. Lumumba said he had summoned Parliament for Monday and that Mobutu would be fired then. Lumumba had called a meeting of parliament for Sunday but a handful of Mobutu's troops firmly turned back the two dozen senators and deputies who appeared. It was all done politely and without the bayonet displays which marked the relations between soldiers and civilians under Lumumba.

Although he was not as talkative as usual, Lumumba answered a few more questions called up to him. It was "not right" for Kasavubu and Mobutu to order Soviet officials out of the Congo, he said. The Soviets, who have been trying to get a grip on the mineral-rich Congo for weeks, pulled down their embassy flag Saturday and departed by plane for Moscow.

Lumumba insisted he was still premier and denied he had been arrested. He said he had asked the United Nations to furnish air transport so he could go to New York and head the Congolese delegation before the General Assembly. He said he has received no answer. He said if a U.N. plane is supplied, "I will present plans at the United Nations for re-establishing law and order." Referring again to Mobutu's expulsion of Communist diplomats from the Congo, he said: "I will take steps soon to put this right." He did not elaborate.

Military attaches here said 10 Soviet planes in Stanleyville would be flown back to Moscow. They have been prevented from aiding Lumumba's military undertakings by a U.N. ban on any flights which might provoke civil strife. What will be done with the 100 Soviet trucks and drivers provided Lumumba is not known.

Related Readings

Brom, John L.: Mit schwarzem Blut geschrieben. Die Kongo-Tragödie, München 1961.
Cabanes, Bernard: Du Congo Belge au Katanga, Paris 1963.
Chomé, Jules: La crise congolaise. De l'indépendence à l'intervention militaire belge (30 juin – 9 juillet), Bruxelles 1960.
Ganshof van der Meersch, Walter Jean: Fin de la souveraineté belge au Congo. Documents et réflexions, Bruxelles 1963.
Gendebien, Paul Henry: L'Intervention des Nations Unies au Congo, 1960–1964, Paris 1967.
Grünebaum, Kurt: Kongo im Umbruch, Bruxelles 1960.
Hoskyns, Catherine: The Congo. A chronology of events, January 1960 – December 1961, London 1962.
Leclercq, Claude: L'ONU et l'affaire du Congo, Paris 1964.
Lemarchand, René: Political awakening in the Belgian Congo, Berkeley, Calif., 1964.
Lumumba, Patrice: Congo – my country, New York 1962.
Merriam, Alan Parkhurst: Congo, background of a conflict, Evanston, Ill., 1961.
Ribeaud, Paul: Adieu Congo, Paris 1961.
Trinquier, Roger et al.: Notre guerre au Katanga, Paris 1963.
Verhaegen, Benoit: Congo 1961, Bruxelles 1962.
Verhaegen, Benoit: Rebellions au Congo, Bruxelles 1966.
Wauters, Arthur et al.: Le monde communiste et la crise du Congo belge, Bruxelles 1961.

1961

Walter Lippmann

New York Herald-Tribune

CHAPTER 34

REPORTS ABOUT THE SOVIET UNION IN 1961

Some Important Political Questions and How They Are Viewed in Communism

    Introductory Notes
34.1 Khrushchev Views Disarmament and Denies Neutrality
34.2 The Inevitable Run of History and Its Social Changes
34.3 The German Question and Three Ways of Answering It
34.4 Communist Philosophy and the Only Real Alternative
34.5 Two Important Talks and a New Political Philosophy
    Related Readings

Introductory Notes

In 1962, it was the turn of the Soviet Union again to provide the prize-winning subject in International Reporting. This time the honor was bestowed on the American top columnist Walter Lippmann "for his 1961 interview with Soviet Premier Khrushchev, as illustrative of Mr. Lippmann's long and distinguished contribution to American journalism." This award did indeed go to one of the most distinguished U.S. journalists though he could hardly be characterized as a foreign correspondent; at best he was an occasional or special correspondent for his newspaper on outstanding political occasions and interviewer of top politicians.

Walter Lippmann was born on September 23, 1889, in New York City. In 1896, Walter Lippmann enrolled in Dr. Julius Sachs' School for Boys, a private school on New York's West Side. Here during the next ten years he wrote pieces for student publications, distinguished himself in debating, and won a number of prizes for academic excellence. At Harvard University, which he entered in 1906, he also achieved a brilliant scholastic record and was elected to Phi Beta Kappa. He completed the requirements for his B.A. degree in three years, but graduated with his class in 1910. Briefly, while still at Harvard in 1910, Lippmann worked as a reporter for the Boston Common, *a weekly devoted to social reform. Then for about a year he wrote articles for* Everybody's Magazine *on corruption in big business, politics, and government. In the summer of 1912, Lippmann went to Maine to set down some ideas in book form, 'A Preface to Politics', which came out in 1913. Another book was published in 1914. From 1917 on Lippmann served as an assistant to the Secretary of War and later as secretary of a research organization. Upon his return to New York in March, 1919, Lippmann resumed his work on the* New Republic, *but soon left the magazine to write his famous book on 'Public Opinion', which came out in 1922. From 1921 on he belonged to the staff of the New York Pulitzer paper* The World *where, from 1923–29, he was in charge of the editorial page. From 1929 until the* World *ceased publication in February, 1931, he held the title of editor. From September 1931 on he worked as columnist for the* New York Herald-Tribune, *becoming an outstanding interpreter of world affairs. On two occasions, 1958 and 1961, Lippmann discussed with Khrushchev in Russia some crucial aspects of East-West relations.*

The following texts by Walter Lippmann, copyright 1961, are reprinted by kind permission of the International Herald-Tribune, *New York, N.Y.*

34.1 Khrushchev Views Disarmament and Denies Neutrality

[*Source: Walter Lippmann: Khrushchev to Lippmann – face to face*, in: New York Herald-Tribune *(New York, N.Y.), Vol. CXXI/No. 41,774, April 17, 1961, p. 1, cols. 1–8; p. 2, cols. 3–6.*]

On this, our second visit, my wife and I were taken on a long journey by plane and auto to Mr. Khrushchev's country place in Sochi on the Black Sea. Before we left Moscow, accompanied by two interpreters and an official of the Press Department, there was much mystery about all the details of the coming visit, such as when and where we were to see the great man. In fact, as it turned out, he had no other appointments after half past eleven in the morning, when he met us in the pinewoods near the entrance of his place. Eight hours later, a bit worn by much talk and two large meals, we insisted on leaving in order to go to bed.

I would not like to leave the impression that all eight hours were devoted to great affairs of the world. Perhaps, all told, three and a half hours were spent in serious talk. The rest of the time went into the two prolonged meals at which Mr. Khrushchev, who is on what appears to be a non-fattening diet, broke the rules, saying joyously that the doctor had gone to Moscow for a day or two. The talk was largely banter between Mr. Khrushchev and Mikoyan (First Deputy Premier), who joined us for lunch, and the banter turned chiefly on Armenian food and Armenian wine and Armenian customs, which include the compulsion to drink all glasses to the end at each toast. Though we all drank a bit more than we wanted, Mikoyan chose to regard us as American ascetics who only sipped their wine. Finally Mr. Khrushchev took pity on us by providing a bowl into which we could pour the wine as fast as Mikoyan filled our glasses.

Between this heroic eating and drinking we walked around the place, which is large, met Mr. Khrushchev's grandson and Mikoyan's granddaughter, inspected the new and very gadgety swimming pool and, believe it or not, played badminton with Mr. Khrushchev.

In the serious talks, I might say that my wife made fairly full notes, I made a few jottings, but there was no transcript and the translation was done very ably by Mr. Victor M. Sukhodrev, who is an official in the Foreign Ministry. It was understood that I was free to write what I liked when I had left Russia and to quote Mr. Khrushchev or not to quote him as seemed desirable. I shall set down my own understanding and interpretation of the most important and interesting points that he made.

For an opening I reminded him that we had last seen him in October, 1958, nearly a year before his visit to the United States. Much has happened in these two and a half years and would he tell me what seemed to him the most important events for good or evil? After a moment or two of hesitation, he replied that during this period the two main forces in the world – the Capitalist, and the Socialist – have concluded that it was useless to "test" one another by military means. I took him to mean by "test" the backing of their political aims by the threat of war.

In contrast with 1958 when he professed to believe that the United States and Germany might attack him, he spoke with confidence that, because of the growing strength of the

Communist orbit, the threat of war from our side was dying down. As a result, the United States was abandoning the "Dulles doctrine" that the neutrality of small states is "immoral." He himself welcomed President Kennedy's proposals for a neutral Laos.

You think then, I asked him, that there has been a change in United States policy? To this he replied that while there were some signs of a change, as for example in Laos, it was not a "radical" change, as could be seen in the United States attitude towards disarmament. What, I asked him, is wrong with the United States attitude? We cannot see, he replied, that any change is imminent when the subject of disarmament is put in the hands of such a believer in armaments as Mr. McCloy. We think well of Mr. McCloy and during his time in Germany we had good relations with him. But asking him to deal with disarmament is a case of asking the goat to look after the cabbage patch. I interjected the remark that the final decisions would be made by the President. But Mr. Khrushchev insisted that the forces behind the President would determine his policy. These forces behind the Kennedy administration he summed up in the one word "Rockefeller." The view that he is running the Kennedy administration will be news to Gov. Rockefeller. I should add that Mr. Khrushchev considers me a Republican, which will be news to Mr. Nixon.

Then we got onto the subject of nuclear testing. He said that the Western powers were not ready to conclude an agreement, and that this was shown, among other things, by the demand for twenty-one or perhaps nineteen inspections a year. He had been led personally to believe that the West would be satisfied with about three "symbolic" inspections. Nineteen inspections, our present demand, were nothing but a demand for the right to conduct complete reconnaissance of the Soviet Union.

I asked him about his attitude towards underground testing. He replied that the U.S.S.R. has never done any underground testing and never will. I asked why? Because, he said, we do not see any value in small, tactical atomic weapons. If it comes to war, we shall use only the biggest weapons. The smaller ones are very expensive and they can decide nothing. The fact that they are expensive doesn't bother you because you don't care what you spend and what is more many of your generals are connected with big business. But in the U.S.S.R. we have to economize, and tactical weapons are a waste. I report this without having the technical expertise to comment on it.

Then he went on to say that the second reason why he had no great hopes of an agreement was that the French are now testing and are unlikely to sign the agreement. It is obvious, he said, that if the French are not in the agreement, they will do the testing for the Americans. To which I said, and the Chinese will do the testing for you. He paused and then said that this was a fair remark. But, he added, while China is moving in the direction where she will be able to make tests, she is not yet able to make them. When the time comes that she can, there will be a new problem. We would like all states to sign a nuclear agreement.

Finally, he came to his third reason why an agreement may not be possible. It turns on the problem of the administrator of the agreement. Here, he was vehement and unqualified. He would never accept a single neutral administrator. Why? Because, he said, while there are neutral countries, there are no neutral men. You would not accept a Communist administrator and I cannot accept a non-Communist administrator. I will never entrust the security of the Soviet Union to any foreigner. We cannot have another Hammarskjold, no matter where he comes from among the neutral countries.

I found this enlightening. It was plain to me that here is a new dogma, that there are no neutral men. After all the Soviet Union had accepted Trygve Lie and Hammarskjold. The Soviet Government has now come to the conclusion that there can be no such thing as an impartial civil servant in this deeply divided world, and that the kind of political celibacy which the British theory of the civil service calls for is in international affairs a fiction. This new dogma has long consequences. It means that there can be international cooperation only if, in the administration as well as in the policy-making, the Soviet Union has a veto.

Our talk went on to Cuba, Iran, revolutionary movements in general and finally to Germany. I shall report on these topics in subsequent articles.

34.2 The Inevitable Run of History and Its Social Changes

[Source: Walter Lippmann: Soviet will 'oppose' us on Cuba – but how?, in: New York Herald-Tribune *(New York, N.Y.)*, Vol. CXXI/No. 41,775, April 18, 1961, p. 1, cols. 3–6; p. 27, cols. 1–4.]

In this article I shall put together those parts of the talk which dealt with the revolutionary movements among small nations. Mr. Khrushchev spoke specifically of three of them – Laos, Cuba and Iran. But for him these three are merely examples of what he regards as a worldwide and historic revolutionary movement – akin to the change from feudalism to capitalism – which is surely destined to bring the old colonial countries into the Communist orbit. I could detect no doubt or reservation in his mind that this will surely happen, that there is no alternative, that while he will help this manifest destiny and while we will oppose it, the destiny would be realized no matter what either of us did.

Speaking of Iran, which he did without my raising the subject, he said that Iran had a very weak Communist party but that nevertheless the misery of the masses and the corruption of the government was surely producing a revolution. "You will assert," he said, "that the Shah has been overthrown by the Communists, and we shall be very glad to have it thought in the world that all the progressive people in Iran recognize that we are the leaders of the progress of mankind."

Judging by the general tenor of what he said about Iran, it would be fair to conclude that he is not contemplating military intervention and occupation – "Iran is a poor country which is of no use to the Soviet Union" – but that he will do all he can by propaganda and indirect intervention to bring down the Shah. In his mind, Iran is the most immediate example of the inevitable movement of history in which he believes so completely. He would not admit that we can divert this historic movement by championing liberal democratic reforms. Nothing that any of us can say can change his mind, which is that of a true believer, except a demonstration in some country that we can promote deep democratic reforms.

His attitude towards Cuba is based on this same dogma. Castro's revolution is inevitable and pre-determined. It was not made by the Soviet Union but by the history of Cuba, and the

Soviet Union is involved because Castro appealed for economic help when the United States tried to strangle the revolution with an embargo. He said flatly, but not, I thought, with much passion, that we were preparing a landing in Cuba, a landing not with American troops but with Cubans armed and supported by the United States. He said that if this happened, the Soviet Union would "oppose" the United States.

I hope I was not misled in understanding him to mean that he would oppose us by propaganda and diplomacy, and that he did not have in mind military intervention. I would in fact go a bit further, based not on what he said but on the general tone of his remarks, that in his book it is normal for a great power to undermine an unfriendly government within its own sphere of interest. He has been doing this himself in Laos and Iran and his feeling about the American support of subversion in Cuba is altogether different in quality from his feeling about the encouragement of resistance in the satellite states of Europe. Mr. Khrushchev thinks much more like Richelieu and Metternich than like Woodrow Wilson. I had an over-all impression that his primary interest is not in the cold war about the small and underdeveloped countries. The support of the revolutionary movement among these countries is for him an interesting, hopeful, agreeable opportunity but it is not a vital interest in the sense that he would go to war about it. He is quite sure that he will win this cold war without military force because he is on the side of history, and because he has the military power to deter us from a serious military intervention.

His primary concern is with the strong countries, especially with the United States, Germany, and China. I could not ask him direct questions about China. But there is no doubt that in his calculations of world power, China is a major factor. I felt that he thought of China as a problem of the future, and that may be one of the reasons why for him the immediate and passionate questions have to do with Germany and disarmament. In my next article, I shall deal with what he had to say about Germany, which he discussed at some length.

For the present I should add a few miscellaneous impressions. During our walk after lunch, Mikoyan, (Frist Deputy Premier) being with us then, I tried to find out what they thought of President Kennedy's purpose to bring the American economy not only out of the current recession but out of its chronic sluggishness. For quite evidently, much of his buoyant confidence in the historic destiny of the Soviet Union is based on the undoubted material progress of Soviet industry as compared with our slow rate of growth. I had put the question to Mikoyan, assuming that he was the economic expert, but he deferred at once to Mr. Khrushchev. To Mr. Khrushchev it was certain that President Kennedy cannot succeed in accelerating American economic growth. He had, he told me, explained that to Mrs. Roosevelt when he was in New York during the American election. Why can't President Kennedy succeed? Because, he said, of "Rockefeller," and then added "du-Pont." They will not let him. This was, it appears, one of those truths that cannot be doubted by any sane man.

None of this, however, was said with any personal animus against President Kennedy. Rather it was said as one might speak of the seasons and the tides and about mortality, about natural events which man does not control. While he has no confidence in the New Frontier, he has obvious respect for the President personally, though he confessed he could hardly understand how any man who had not been in a big government for a long time could suddenly become the head of it. Moreover, as I shall report tomorrow in talking about the German question, it is clear, I think, that he looks forward to another round of international negotiations before he precipitates a crisis over Berlin.

34.3 The German Question and Three Ways of Answering It

[*Source: Walter Lippmann: A sobering up, in:* New York Herald-Tribune *(New York, N.Y.), Vol. CXXI/No. 41,776, April 19, 1961, p. 1, cols. 4–5; p. 9, cols. 1–4.*]

It was clear to me at the end of a long talk that in Mr. Khrushchev's mind the future of Germany is the key question. I sought first to understand why he thinks the German problem is so urgent, and so I asked him whether, since agreement was so far off, a standstill of five or ten years might not be desirable. He said this was impossible. Why? Because there must be a German solution before "Hitler's generals with their twelve NATO divisions" get atomic weapons from France and the United States. Before this happens there must be a peace treaty defining the frontiers of Poland and Czechoslovakia and stabilizing the existence of the East German State. Otherwise, West Germany will drag NATO into a war for the unification of Germany and the restoration of the old eastern frontier.

His feeling of urgency, then, springs from two causes: his need to consolidate the Communist East German state, the German Democratic Republic – known for short as the GDR – and second, his need to do this before West Germany is rearmed. He said several times that he would soon bring the German question to a head. Quite evidently, the possibility of nuclear arms for West Germany is not immediate. Bonn does not now have the weapons and although the possibility of it is real enough, the threat is not so urgent as to be a matter of a few months. The more immediately urgent consideration is, no doubt, the need to stabilize the East German regime, particularly in view of the flow of refugees.

My general impression was that he was firmly resolved, perhaps irretrievably committed, to a showdown on the German question. But it was evident also that he dreaded the tension – he referred to this several times – and is still looking for a negotiation which will work out a postponement and an accommodation. In talks it transpired that he is thinking of the problem as having three phases.

The first is what he considers the real and also the eventual solution. He has no hope, however, that the West will now accept it. His thesis is as follows: The two Germanies cannot be reunited. The West will not agree to a unified Communist Germany and the Soviet Union will not agree to the absorption and destruction of the GDR by West Germany. There are in fact two Germanies. The way to proceed is, then, to "codify" the *status quo* in the form of peace treaties with what he called the three elements of Germany. These three elements are West Germany, East Germany, and West Berlin. This codification would require *de facto* but not diplomatic recognition of the GDR. It would fix by international statute the position of West Berlin as "a free city," with its rights of access and its internal liberty guaranteed by the presence of "symbolic contingents" of French, British, American and Russian troops, by neutral troops under the aegis of the United Nations, and by the signatures of the two Germanies and the four occupying powers.

As I said above, Mr. Khrushchev does not expect at this time to reach this solution. He has, therefore, a second position which he called a "fallback" position. This is essentially that of the Soviets at the last Geneva conference of the foreign ministers. It would call for a

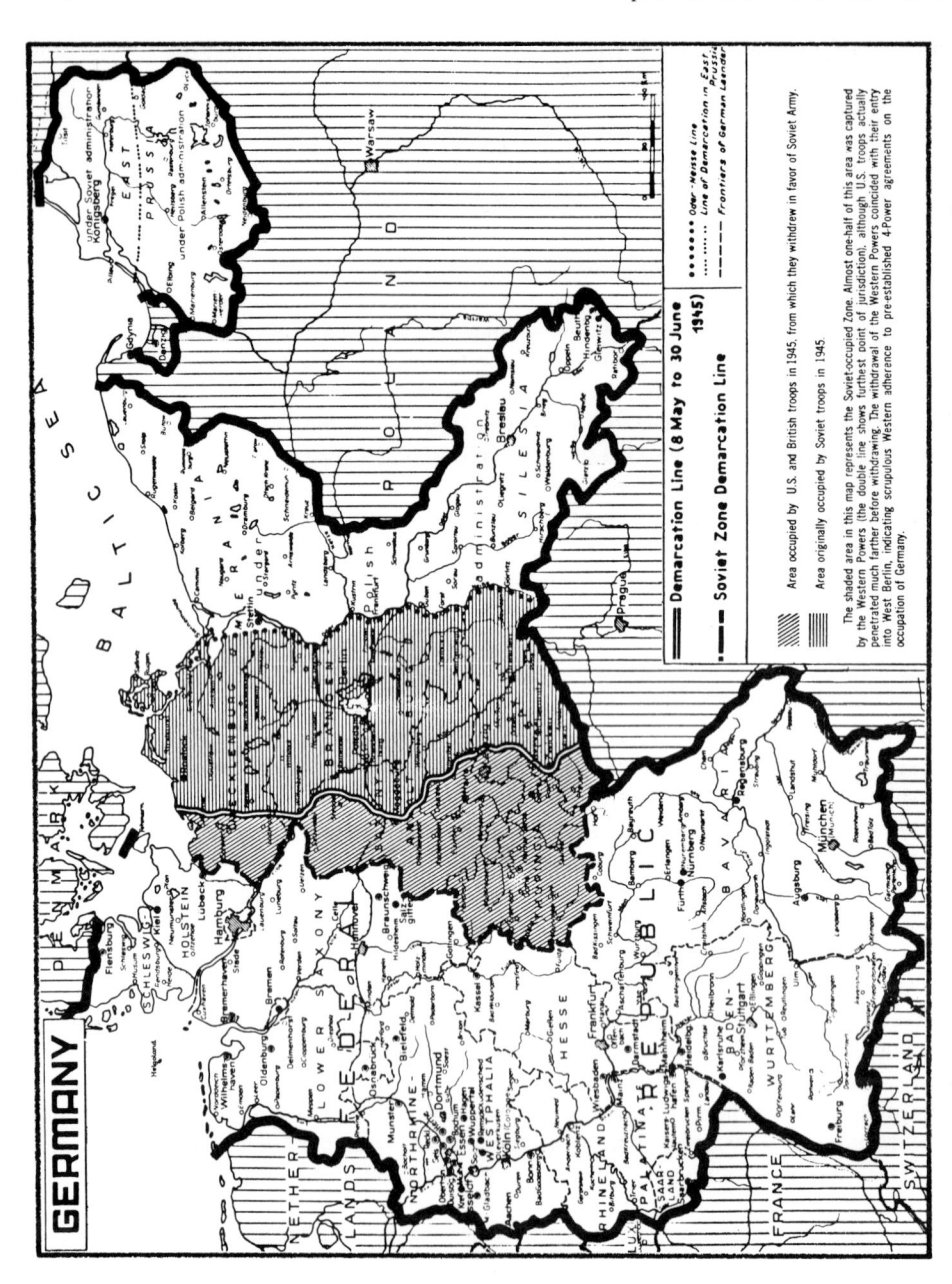

[*Source:* Jean Edward Smith: The Defense of Berlin, Baltimore, Md., 1963, opposite p. 275.]

temporary agreement. In the Russian view but not in our view this temporary agreement would have a short and fixed time limit of perhaps two to three years. During this time the two German states would be invited to negotiate on a form of unification – perhaps, though he did not say so specifically in this talk, a kind of loose confederation. At the end of the fixed period of time, if a new agreement about West Berlin along the lines I have outlined previously was reached, it would be embodied in a treaty. If no agreement was reached, the legal rights of occupation would lapse. This German solution was, as we know, refused by the West. But if there is to be another round of negotiation, variants on it are likely to be the substance of the bargaining.

If this fails, Mr. Khrushchev's third position is that he will sign a separate peace treaty with East Germany. Then the GDR will in the Soviet view be sovereign over the rights of access to West Berlin. If the Western powers refuse to do business with the GDR and use force to enter West Berlin, then the Soviet government will use the Red Army to blockade West Berlin. Though it would be foolish to undervalue his determination, the threat is not quite so fierce as it sounds. For he most certainly does not want a military showdown, and "doing business" with the GDR is a flexible and not a rigid conception.

I have confined myself strictly to reporting my understanding of the Soviet policy on Germany. If I may venture an opinion of my own, I would make these points. First, Mr. Khrushchev will not precipitate a crisis until he has had a chance to talk face to face with President Kennedy. Second, he will surely sign a separate peace treaty if he cannot negotiate a temporary accommodation, which is described under his "second position." Third, the crucial points which will determine whether the German question is resolved by negotiation or goes to a showdown are whether the prospect of nuclear arms for Germany increases or diminishes, and whether or not we say that the freedom of West Berlin, to which we are pledged, can be maintained only by a refusal to negotiate about this future.

I have been asked many times since we left the Soviet Union to come to London whether I found the whole interview encouraging or depressing. I found it sobering. On the one hand, the evidence was convincing that the U.S.S.R. is not contemplating war and is genuinely concerned to prevent any crisis, be it in Laos, in Cuba, or in Germany, from becoming uncontrollable. On the other hand, there is no doubt that the Soviet Government has a relentless determination to foster the revolutionary movement in the underdeveloped countries. This relentless determination springs from an unqualified faith in the predestined acceptance of Communism by the underdeveloped countries. The Soviet Government has great confidence in its own military forces. But it regards them not as an instrument of world conquest, but as the guardian against American interference with the predestined world revolution. I was sobered by all this because I do not think there is any bluff in it.

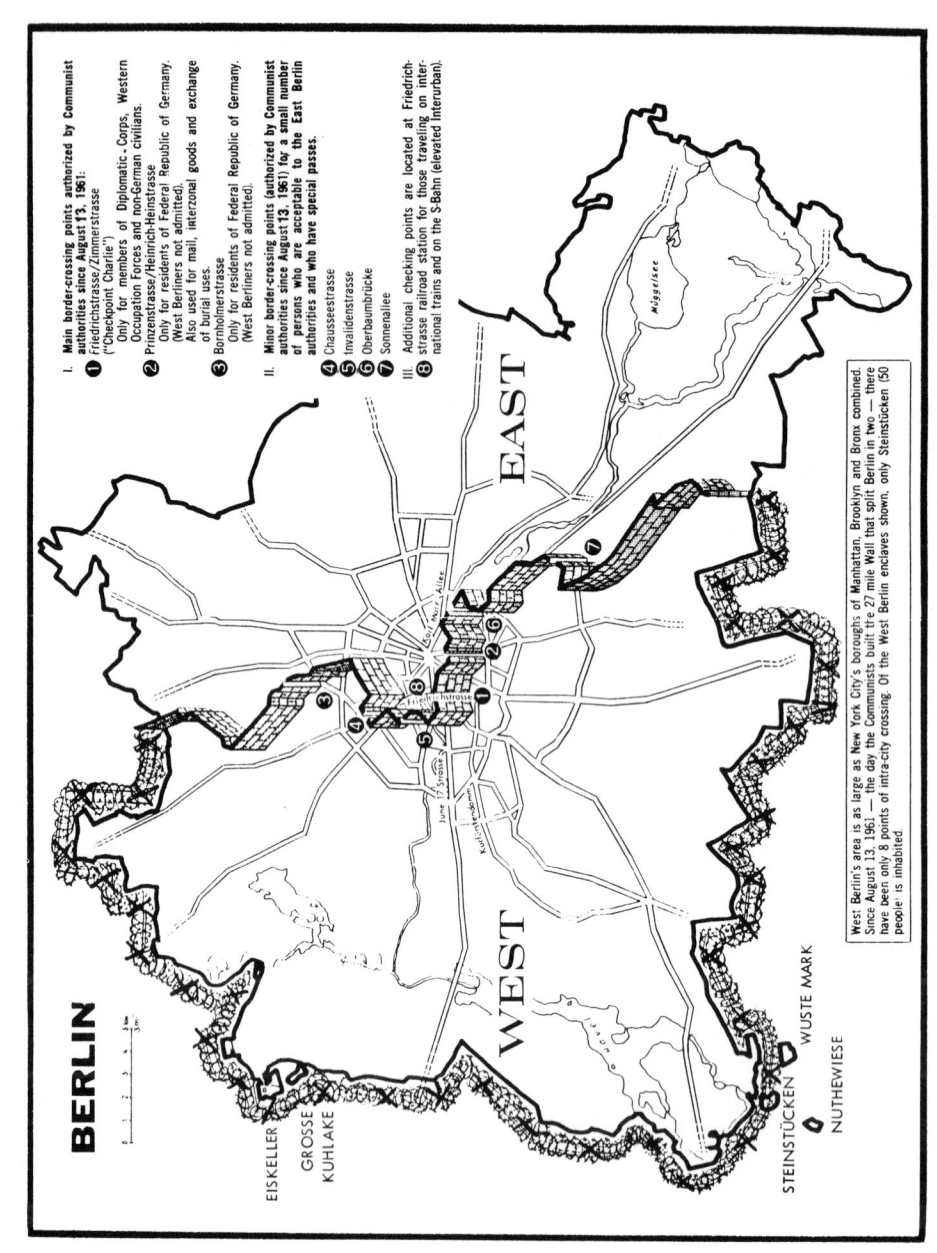

[Source: Jean Edward Smith: The Defense of Berlin, Baltimore, Md., 1963, opposite p. 274.]

34.4 Communist Philosophy and the Only Real Alternative

[*Source: Walter Lippmann: 'To ourselves be true', in:* New York Herald-Tribune *(New York, N.Y.), Vol. CXXI/No. 41,796, May 9, 1961, p. 26, cols. 4–6.*]

We have been forced to ask ourselves recently how a free and open society can compete with a totalitarian state. This is a crucial question. Can our Western society survive and flourish if it remains true to its own faith and principles? Or must it abandon them in order to fight fire with fire?

There are those who belive that in Cuba the attempt to fight fire with fire would have succeeded if only the President had been more ruthless and had had no scruples about using American forces. I think they are wrong. I think that success for the Cuban adventure was impossible. In a free society like ours a policy is bound to fail which deliberately violates our pledges and our principles, our treaties and our laws. It is not possible for a free and open society to organize successfully a spectacular conspiracy. The United States, like every other government, must employ secret agents. But the United States cannot successfully conduct large secret conspiracies. It is impossible to keep them secret. It is impossible for everybody concerned, beginning with the President himself, to be sufficiently ruthless and unscrupulous. The American conscience is a reality. It will make hesitant and ineffectual, even if it does not prevent, an un-American policy. The ultimate reason why the Cuban affair was incompetent is that it was out of character, like a cow that tried to fly or a fish that tried to walk.

It follows that in the great struggle with Communism, we must find our strength by developing and applying our own principles, not in abandoning them. Before anyone tells me that this is sissy, I should like to say why I believe it, especially after listening carefully and at some length to Mr. Khrushchev. I am very certain that we shall have the answer to Mr. Khrushchev if, but only if, we stop being fascinated by the cloak and dagger business and, being true to ourselves, take our own principles seriously.

Mr. K. is a true believer that Communism is destined to supplant capitalism as capitalism supplanted feudalism. For him this is an absolute dogma, and he will tell you that while he intends to do what he can to assist the inevitable, knowing that we will do what we can to oppose the inevitable, what he does and what we do will not be decisive. Destiny will be realized no matter what men do. The dogma of inevitability not only gives him the self-assurance of a man who has no doubts but is a most powerful ingredient of the Communist propaganda. What do we say to him, we who believe in a certain freedom of the human will and in the capacity of men to affect the course of history by their discoveries, their wisdom and their courage?

We can say that in Mr. K.'s dogma there is an unexamined premise. It is that the capitalist society is static, that it is and always will be what it was when Marx described it a hundred years ago, that – to use Mr. K.'s own lingo – there is no difference between Governor Rockefeller and his grandfather. Because a capitalist society cannot change, in its dealings with the underdeveloped countries it can only dominate and exploit. It cannot emancipate

'Izvestia' Cartoon From 1961 Attacking NATO

[*Source*: Michael M. Milenkovitch: The View from Red Square. A Critique of Cartoons from 'Pravda' and 'Izvestia', 1947–1964, New York–Buenos Aires 1966, p. 83.]

and help. If it could emancipate and help, the inevitability of Communism would evaporate.

I venture to argue from this analysis that the reason we are on the defensive in so many places is that for some ten years we have been doing exactly what Mr. K. expects us to do. We have used money and arms in a long losing attempt to stabilize native governments which, in the name of anti-Communism, are opposed to all important social change. This has been exactly what Mr. K.'s dogma calls for – that Communism should be the only alternative to the *status quo* with its immemorial poverty and privilege.

We cannot compete with Communism in Asia, Africa, or Latin America if we go on doing what we have done so often and so widely – which is to place the weak countries in a dilemma where they must stand still with us and our client rulers or start moving with the Communists. This dilemma cannot be dissolved unless it is our central and persistent and unswerving policy to offer these unhappy countries a third option, which is economic development and social improvement without the totalitarian discipline of Communism. For the only real alternative to Communism is a liberal and progressive society.

34.5 Two Important Talks and a New Political Philosophy

[*Source: Walter Lippmann: Before Paris and Vienna, in:* New York Herald-Tribune *(New York, N.Y.), Vol. CXXI/No. 41,812, May 25, 1961, p. 24, cols. 4–6.*]

The run of bad news from Cuba, Laos, Alabama is, of course, a depressing prelude to the President's trip abroad. But we must not exaggerate. While the reverses we have suffered have hurt us with our allies and friends, I do not think they will have any substantial effect, one way or the other, on the basic problems which the President will be dealing with both in Paris and in Vienna.

In Paris, the problem will be how the Western Alliance is to be managed. In Vienna, the problem will be how the relations between the two great constellations are to be controlled. The two men with whom the President will be talking are realists who calculate their policy primarily in terms of national power. There are almost no American public men who are realists in the same degree. At least they do not talk out loud about it. Gen. de Gaulle and Mr. Khrushchev believe in their own calculations of what the various powers can do, and in their own thinking they are very little impressed by (anything else), indeed they have a very high degree of immunity to public relations and "images" and that sort of thing. Mr. Khrushchev is, of course, a great propagandist. But his policy is based on a cold calculation of power.

The language of the Paris and Vienna talks will have to be the language of power politics – which deals with what nations will do in relation to what they can do when their truly vital interests are involved.

There is, I realize, a certain tactlessness in speaking of what is common to the Paris and

Vienna meetings. Indeed, I was one of those who thought that it would be more tactful if the President did not go straight from his meeting with Gen. de Gaulle to a meeting with Mr. Khrushchev. But now that the arrangements have been set – with the blessing, so I hear, of Gen. de Gaulle himself – it is useful to realize not only that the President will be talking with two realists but that their realistic calculations arise from the same factual base. This is the fact that American military supremacy, which lasted from 1945 until shortly after 1955, has been replaced by a balance of power. This is the central event of our time, and it affects profoundly and pervasively all international relations.

When the President meets Gen. de Gaulle, he will find a man who, with the insight of genius, is acutely aware of the change in the world balance of power. This awareness is the root of his disbelief in the validity of the NATO structure and strategy. This is the root of his lack of confidence, which must not be ignored, in the United States as the protector of Europe and the leader of the world. This lack of confidence is the root of his demand for intimate and continual consultation on world affairs. This, too, is the root of his insistence on a policy which may be impractical, that France have an independent nuclear force.

It would be vain to suppose that anyone can restore the American paramountcy built upon the nuclear monopoly of the postwar days. The United Nations, NATO, CENTO, SEATO – the grand political structure built upon the old paramountcy is shaken. It is this shaking which constitutes a large part of the subject matter of our diplomacy. In Mr. Khrushchev the President will meet a man who is deeply conscious of, whose policy is governed by, the new fact that there is a balance of power. Unless I am much mistaken, Mr. Khrushchev's confidence in Soviet power is accompanied by a very healthy respect for American power.

I do not share the views of those who are afraid that our reverses in Cuba and Laos have caused him to underrate American power or American determination. He knows perfectly well that the United States could taken Havana in an afternoon, and that what restrains us is not fear of Soviet missiles but a recognition of the political disaster we would precipitate throughout the hemisphere and the free world. As for Laos, he has had, of course, the certainly that we could not fight a Korean war in Indo-China. We could not fight it because in 1961 we do not have as we had in 1950 a monopoly of nuclear weapons which could in the least resort be decisive.

As I understand it, the new Soviet dogma – that all international dealing must be tripartite and by unanimous consent – rests ultimately on the same fact, that there is a balance of power. When there is a balance of power between two states, each state has a veto. Nothing can be done unless they agree. Mr. Khrushchev carries this principle to an extreme point. Thus there might be agreement to abide by the judgment of a third party. That, in effect, is what we want. Mr. Khrushchev is more vehement and more irreconcilable than his own principle requires. In any event the controlling fact in dealing with Mr. Khrushchev is his insistence upon a full recognition, with all its consequences spelled out, of the new balance of power.

Related Readings

Alexandrov, Victor: Das Leben des Nikita Chruschtschow, München 1958.
Brumberg, Abraham (Ed.): Russia under Khrushchev – an anthology from 'Problems of Communism', London 1962.
Crankshaw, Edward: Khrushchev – a career, New York 1966.
Frankland, Mark: Khrushchev, Harmondsworth, Middlesex, 1966.
Hearst, William Randolph et al.: Khrushchev and Russian challenge, New York 1961.
Kellen, Konrad: Khrushchev – a political portrait, New York – London 1961.
Khrushchev, Nikita Sergeevich: Khrushchev remembers, Boston, Mass., 1970.
Linden, Carl Arne: Khrushchev and the Soviet leadership, 1957–1964, 3rd printing, Baltimore, Md. – London 1970.
MacGregor-Hastie, Roy: The life and times of Nikita Krushchev, London 1959.
Pálóczi Horváth, György: Khrushchev – the making of a dictator, Boston, Mass., 1960.
Pistrak, Lazar: The grand tacticians. Khrushchev's rise to power, New York – London 1961.
Ronchey, Alberto: Russia in the thaw, New York 1964.
Schapiro, Leonard Bertram (Ed.): The U.S.S.R. and the future. An analysis of the new program of the C.P.S.U., New York – London 1963.
Sobel, Lester A. (Ed.): Russia's rulers – the Khrushchev period, New York 1962.
Swearer, Howard R./Rush, Myron: The politics of succession in the U.S.S.R. Materials on Khrushchev's rise to leadership, Boston, Mass., 1964.
Werth, Alexander: Russia under Khrushchev, New York 1962.

1962

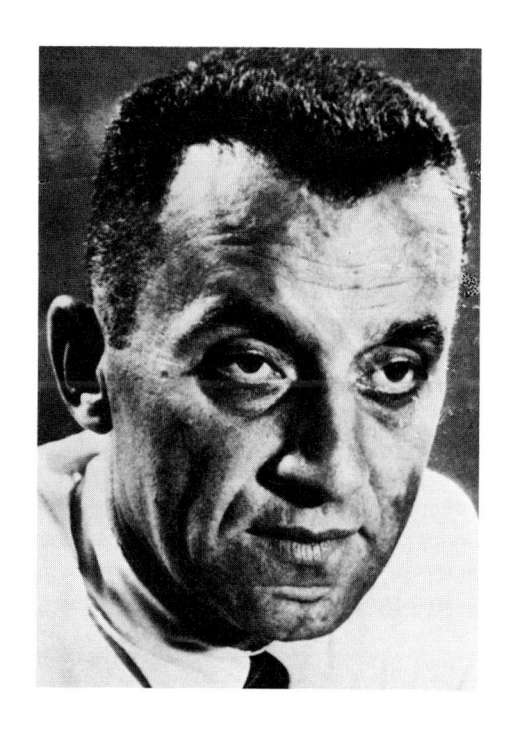

Harold V. Hendrix

The Miami News

CHAPTER 35

REPORTS ABOUT CUBA IN 1962

The Escalation of a Global Crisis and How It Was Managed in Washington

   Introductory Notes
35.1 Soviet Bases in Cuba and America's First Reactions
35.2 The Cuban Challenge and Reactions in America
35.3 Russia's Installment Effort and Her Technical Problems
35.4 An Exhibition of Power and Reasons for an Invasion
35.5 Early Intelligence and How It Was Handled
   Related Readings

Introductory Notes

Walter Lippmann, having received the preceding year's Pulitzer Prize for International Reporting for his comprehensive interview with Nikita S. Khrushchev, the 1963 subject, too, dealt – at least indirectly – with the Soviet Premier and Communist party leader. The Advisory Board on the Pulitzer Prizes bestowed the internationally oriented award on Harold V. Hendrix of the Miami News *"for his persistent reporting which revealed, at an early stage, that the Soviet Union was installing missile launching pads in Cuba and sending in large numbers of MIG-21 aircraft" in 1962.*

Harold Victor Hendrix was born on February 14, 1922, in Kansas City, Missouri. In 1941, he began his studies at the Rockhurst College before he went to the Kansas City Star *in 1944. He stayed with this newspaper until 1957, treating Latin-American questions as a columnist from 1947 on. When he changed to the* Miami News *afterwards, Hendrix covered this special political field intensively. He took advantage of his membership in the leading journalistic organization for North- and South-America, the Inter-American Press Association, to the board of directors of which he belonged for a while. His various connections rendered it possible for Hal Hendrix to find out from Miami in the second half of 1962 that Cuba was shipping military weapons to other Latin American states; some months later he was the first American journalist to report that Soviet jets, MIG 21s, had arrived in Cuba. This was at first denied by the U.S. government. But "events following his reports," the accompanying letter of the* Miami News *for Hal Hendrix's Pulitzer Prize nomination ran, "testified to an unusual accuracy in a most difficult area of getting the story right, in which the difficulty is made large not only because of the reluctance of usual information sources to speak, but also because of the gossip and rumor which rather naturally is manufactured by the emotional and frustrated sources among the Cuban exiles and among persons inside Cuba from whom certain information was gathered." For this impressive scoop Hendrix was awarded the 1963 Pulitzer Prize for International Reporting.*

The following texts by Harold Victor Hendrix, copyright 1962, are reprinted by kind permission of The Miami News, *Miami, Florida.*

35.1 Soviet Bases in Cuba and America's First Reactions

[*Source: Harold V. Hendrix: The Cuba Story – Soviets launch work on six missile bases, in:* The Miami News *(Miami, Fla.)*, 67th Year/No. 134, October 7, 1962, p. 1 A, cols. 5–8; p. 12 A, cols. 1–3.]

Construction has begun in Communist Cuba on at least a half dozen launching sites for intermediate range tactical missiles, United States intelligence authorities have advised the White House. Although official U.S. spokesmen have declined to disclose the intelligence reports, The Miami News has learned that experts have advised President Kennedy that the ground-to-ground missiles can be operational from inland Cuba within six months.

From the type of construction under way it has been determined that the launching pads will have the capability of hurling rockets that could penetrate deeply into the United States in one direction and reach the Panama Canal Zone in the opposite direction. Official observers do not believe that the Soviet Union has yet delivered the intermediate range-type missiles to Cuba. But neither do they now doubt that delivery plans have been made. "The United States has a 'grace period' of about six months insofar as these new missiles are concerned," an official observer commented yesterday. After that, once the installations are complete and the missiles emplaced, any time there is a flare-up in tensions anywhere in the world between this country and the Soviet Union, the Communists in Cuba can rattle the offensive rockets in the Caribbean."

Officials have reported that U.S. plans for a crackdown on free world shipping to Communist Cuba could slow down the launching site construction, but there is no guarantee that the Soviets will not divert their own vessels to this high-priority project. Washington also has been alerted to the fact that Communist Cuba's north coast now is solidly banked with "defensive" short-range surface-to-air missiles, capable of downing an aircraft in a 25-mile range. Officially, the State Department has announced that at least 15 to these SAM bases have been completed – adding that the total may reach 25 or more.

Behind the coastal missile emplacements, now manned jointly by Cuban military and Soviet "technicians," are an undisclosed number of ground-to-ground missile bases already operational. These are reported to have a range of about 35 miles, designed for firing on ships at sea and strategic ground installations. According to reports from Cuba, some of these shortrange "defensive" missiles now are installed within easy reach of the U.S. Naval base at Guantanamo Bay.

Meanwhile, reports from Moscow and Havana point out that shipments of military materials and personnel still are continuing to pour unchecked into Communist Cuba. The State Department has acknowledged that there are now about 4,500 Soviet "military specialists" in Communist Cuba. Outside the department, observers believe the number is closer to 10,000. Since July, according to late State Department announcements, more than 85 Soviet shiploads have arrived in Cuba ports. Red Star, the Soviet military publication, notes that ships "are on the seas daily bound for Cuba with support for our Cuban friends."

The size of Communist Cuba's air force also continues to swell, as intelligence reports

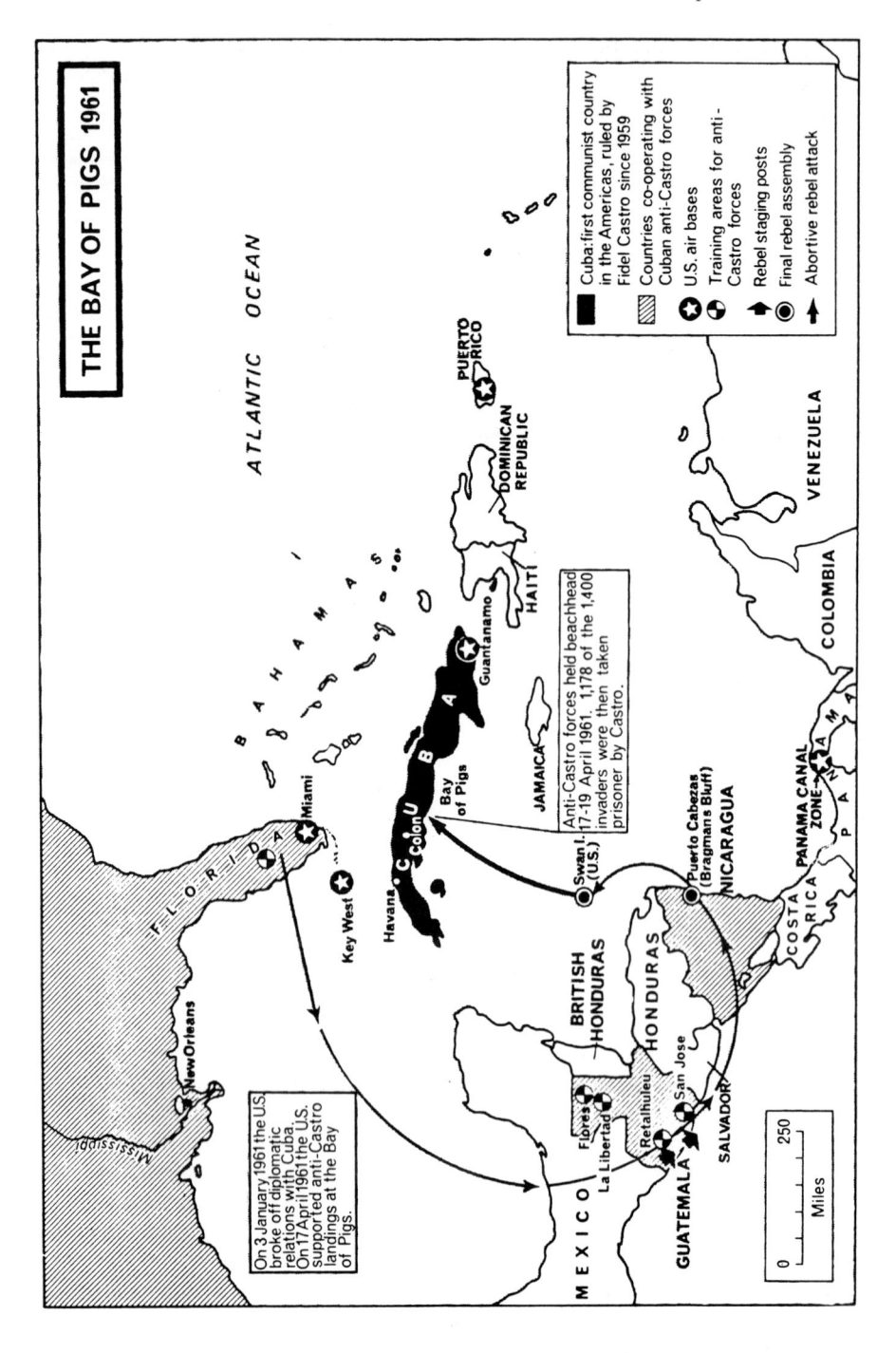

[*Source:* Martin Gilbert: American History Atlas, London 1968, p. 101.]

disclose stepped-up Russian supply lines. As first reported by The Miami News last month, the Soviets have supplied the Castro regime with at least six supersonic Mig-21 jet fighters. Intelligence sources have reported that there is evidence that at least 25 or 30 more of these most modern Soviet jet fighters will be operational in Cuba soon. Each carries heat-sensing air-to-air missiles and has a maximum speed of 1,685 miles per hour. The Mig-21s are the "frosting on the cake" for Castro's air force. The backbone of the Cuban air strength, according to published Defense Department figures in the Congressional Record, is about 100 Mig-15, Mig-17 and Mig-19 jet fighters.

On the sea, the Communists have delivered to Castro at least 16 "Komar" class guided missile patrol boats, each carrying two rockets which fire 11 to 17 miles. It has been reported by Western intelligence that the Soviets have earmarked at least two destroyers and two East German submarines for Cuba. Meanwhile, U.S. Under Secretary of State George Ball last week told a special House committee investigating Cuban arms traffic from the Soviet bloc that United States policy on Cuba "still is based on the assessment that Cuba is not a military threat."

35.2 The Cuban Challenge and Reactions in America

[*Source:* Harold V. Hendrix: Inevitable began in January 1959, *in:* The Miami News *(Miami, Fla.), 67th Year/No. 150, October 23, 1962, p. 1 A, col. 3; p. 11 A, cols. 2–4.*]

The showdown between the United States and Communist Cuba, although long in coming, was inevitable. In retrospect, it began only a few days after Fidel Castro came to power Jan. 1, 1959. Shortly after the bearded revolutionary leader came down from the hills of Cuba's Sierra Maestra mountains when President Fulgencio Batista fled from Havana on New Year's Eve, Castro declared that 200,000 gringos would die if the U.S. Marines ever set foot on Cuban soil.

Since that angry declaration in the lobby of the Havana Hilton Hotel early in January 1959, Castro has been screeching about invasions from the U.S. and working overtime to destroy the U.S. image in Cuba and throughout Latin America. Now the United States has moved to liberate Cuba from Castro and his Communist allies – and mend its shuttered image in Latin America. In launching that decisive last night against Communist Cuba, President Kennedy also has served notice on the world, that the U.S. has drawn a new line on the advance of international communism.

"The line is being drawn on the Cuban problems rather than in Berlin or the Far East, because there is more room to move in the Caribbean," commented a U.S. official to the Cuban arena. The most frightening of the apprehensions raised by President Kennedy's address to the nation on the Cuban crisis is that a bearded madman in Havana now has in his hands the dread power to fire missiles or bombs into the U.S. mainland and possibly spark World War III. President Kennedy declared that it shall be the policy of the United States to regard any nuclear attack launched from Cuba against any nation in the Western Hemisphere

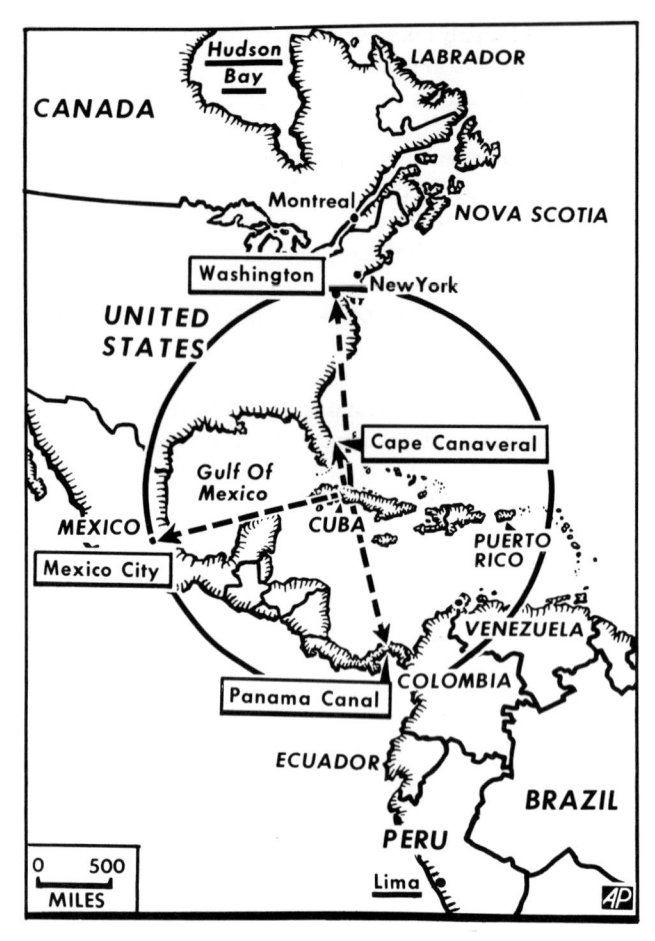

Radius of Cuban Missile Coverage
(Arrows Point To Places Within Range)

[*Source:* AP Chart, printed in: The Miami News (Miami, Fla.), 67th Year/No. 150, October 23, 1962, p. 1A, cols. 4–5.]

as an attack by the Soviet Union on the U.S. – requiring full retaliatory response from Russia.

Since the Soviets are cognizant of Castro's history of irrational and unstable behavior, it may be that they would not risk placing any pushbuttons near his itchy trigger finger. Still, it could be difficult even for the Russians in Communist Cuba to keep Castro and his fanatic henchmen away from the pushbuttons. It would still be more difficult to keep them from a capricious attack against the U.S. – if the Castro regime figures it can penetrate U.S. defense. These grim possibilities are certain now to be on the minds of Latin America's heads of state – and they will be a factor in any action taken by the Organization of American States.

OAS action to back up President Kennedy's collision with the Castro-Communist combine is expected to develop quickly, although it may not be unanimous. Brazil is likely to maneuver to throw some kind of roadblock up before the OAS action. Such a move could lead to far-reaching repercussions inasmuch as President Kennedy is still planning to visit Brazil Nov. 12. Mexico, who with Brazil has led the "hands off Cuba" fight in Latin America, has shown signs of changing its posture in light of disclosures of Castro's offensive firepower.

In his speech, President Kennedy astutely pointed out that Mexico City could easily be a target for one of Castro's intermediate range ballistic missiles. Mexico's President Adolpho Lopez Mateos, now touring the Far East, declared today in Manila that Mexico would stand by the OAS in meeting the new situation in communist Cuba. "Mexico signed the Rio de Janeiro pact and in that document it was contemplated the possibility of a country being a victim of an aggressor," President Lopez Mateos said. "In case such an event took place, Mexico would duly fulfill her duties contained in that pact."

In Central America, the U.S. will find solid support of its new tough and determined policy. This means six voices at the OAS Council table – Guatemala, El Salvador, Honduras, Nicaragua, Costa Rica and Panama. On the huge South American continent, Brazil is likely to abstain rather than fully reverse its pro-Cuba and leftist position. Chile and Ecuador, both with a high incidence of Communist activity and facing threats of strikes, may join Brazil. All the other countries – Colombia, Venezuela, Peru, Bolivia, Argentina, Uruguay and Paraguay, are expected to line up behind the U.S. program to rid the hemisphere of the Castro regime.

35.3 Russia's Installment Effort and Her Technical Problems

[*Source: Harold V. Hendrix: Hunting basis in Africa, Brazil, in: The Miami News (Miami, Fla.), 67th Year/No. 153, October 26, 1962, p. 1 A, col. 3; p. 6 A, col. 6.*]

Temporarily thwarted by the United States' naval blockade around Communist Cuba, the Soviet Union is pressuring desperately for aircraft landing rights in Africa and South America to service an armaments airlift to Havana, The News learned today.

Authoritative sources in Washington disclosed that Soviet representatives are concentrating heavy pressure on Brazil to give them transit rights for medium-range transport planes en route to Communist Cuba. The squeeze is being applied on Brazilian diplomats in Washington and by the Russian envoys assigned to the Soviet embassy in Brazil.

Although Washington sources did not link the Russian pressure on Brazil with President Kennedy's plans to visit there next month, it was reported that the White House has been in touch with the Brazilian government about the projected trip. The expectation now is that the trip, slated to begin Nov. 12 will be canceled. Press Secretary Pierre Salinger said today he probably would have something definite to say on the plans before the day is over. Reports from Brazil say the trip already has been canceled.

On the African side of the proposed airlift route, overtures are known to have been made to the government of Algerian Premier Ahmed Ben Bella, who just returned from a visit to Communist Cuba – and the United States. It has been learned that the Russians attempted to obtain transit landing rights at Dakar, but the government of Senegal rejected the proposal.

Soviet affairs specialists interpret the intense airlift pressuring as another indication that the Russians are determined to continue their military buildup in Communist Cuba. It is pointed out that medium-range rockets could be landed in Cuba by the Russian Ilyusyin 11-18 turbo-prop airliners modified for such a mission.

The African and South American transit stops are needed for such an operation because of the limited flying range of the Ilyusyin. It is not believed that Russia has sufficient long-range air transports to sustain a nonstop airlift service between the Soviet Union or any of its East European satellites and Communist Cuba.

Meanwhile, it was learned that the U.S. intelligence forces have information of additional Soviet supplied firepower in Cuba beyond that which the Defense Department has made public earlier this week. Unofficially, the White House and Defense Department have been alerted to "hard" information that nuclear warheads of the 1-megaton class now are in Cuba under tight control of Soviet military personnel.

It also has been determined that the medium-range missiles already delivered to Communist Cuba include the T-2, T-4 and T-5 models that have been observed at Soviet military displays. All are capable of delivering atomic warheads. The T-2 is propelled by liquid fuel and has an operational range of 1,500 to 1,800 miles, with an inertial or self-contained guidance system. It is about 100 feet long and weighs about 60 tons. The T-2 model has appeared in a number of the serial photographs obtained by the United States in flights over Cuba – some at an altitude as low as 500 feet.

Shipments of the T-4 and T-5 models are known to have been aboard some of the Soviet vessels that have turned back before encountering the U.S. Atlantic fleet. Photographs of the missiles on the deck of at least one Czechoslovakian ship have been obtained.

35.4 An Exhibition of Power and Reasons for an Invasion

[*Source: Harold V. Hendrix: U.S. military action inevitable, in:* The Miami News *(Miami, Fla.), 67th Year/No. 155, October 28, 1962, p. 8 A, cols. 1–5.*]

In spite of the wordy correspondence racing back and forth between Moscow and Washington over the explosive Cuban situation, direct military action by the United States is inevitable – and likely to be launched soon with lightning swiftness.

```
OUTGOING TELEGRAM  Department of State                3688

                                UNCLASSIFIED
55-L                            Classification        Oct 27  8 05 PM '62

SS      ACTION:  Amembassy MOSCOW 1015 NIACT
```

Following message from President to Khrushchev should be delivered as soon as possible to highest available Soviet official. Text has been handed Soviet Embassy in Washington and has been released to press:

QUOTE

Dear Mr. Chairman:

I have read your letter of October 26 with great care and welcomed the statement of your desire to seek a prompt solution to the problem. The first thing that needs to be done, however, is for work to cease on bases offensive missile bases in Cuba and for all weapons systems in Cuba capable of offensive use to be rendered inoperable, under effective United Nations arrangements.

Assuming this is done promptly, I have given my representatives in New York instructions that will permit them to work out this week and -- in cooperation with the Acting Secretary

Drafted by: S/S - Mr. Brubeck
Telegraphic transmission and classification approved by: S/S - Mr. Brubeck

UNCLASSIFIED
Classification

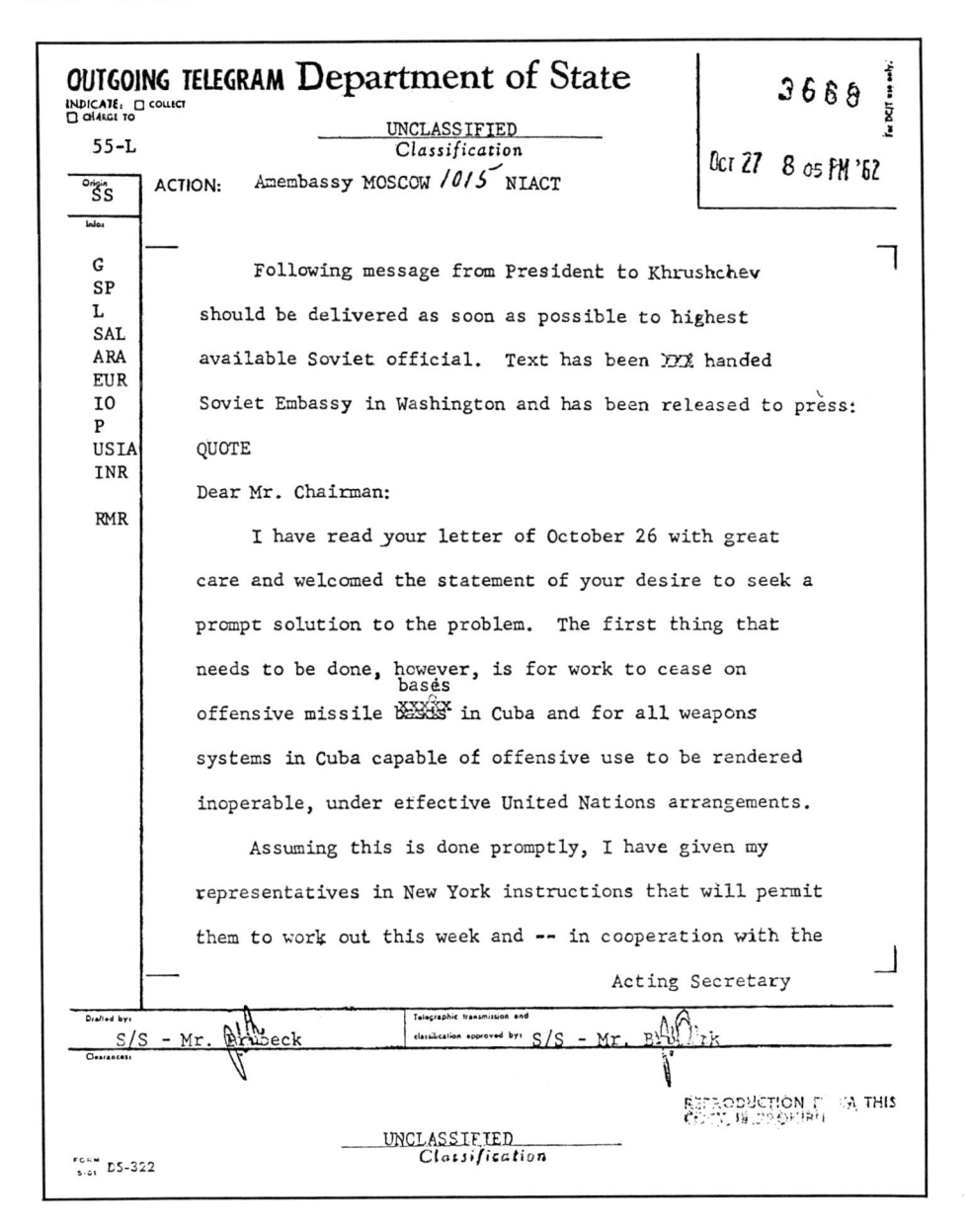

Without saying so directly, President Kennedy has in effect given the Castro-Khrushchev axis a 48-hour ultimatum to start dismantling the Soviet missile bases in Communist Cuba or face destruction of them by U.S. force. That was couched carefully in his letter last night to Premier Khrushchev dealing with possible negotiations on the Cuban problem. He commented: "There is no reason why we should not be able to complete these arrangements and announce them to the world within a couple of days."

> Page 2 of telegram to Amembassy MOSCOW   NIACT
>
> UNCLASSIFIED
>
> Acting Secretary General and your representative -- an arrangement for a permanent solution to the Cuban problem along the lines suggested in your letter of October 26. As I read your letter, the key elements of your proposals -- which seem generally acceptable as I understand them -- are as follows:
>
> 1. You would agree to remove these weapons systems from Cuba under appropriate United Nations observation and supervision; and undertake, with suitable safeguards, to halt the further introduction of such weapons systems into Cuba.
>
> 2. We, on our part, would agree -- upon the establishment of adequate arrangements through the United Nations to ensure the carrying out and continuation of these commitments -- (a) to remove promptly the quarantine measures now in effect and (b) to give assurances against an invasion of Cuba and I am confident that other nations of the Western Hemisphere would be prepared to do likewise.
>
> If you will give your representative similar instructions, there is no reason why we should not be able to complete
>
> these

A possible deterrent of significant proportions to quick U.S. direct action is the proposed visit to Havana by Acting U.N. Secretary, General U Thant. Castro late yesterday extended an invitation to the U.N. leader to discuss with him the question of the negotiation proposals sailing between President Kennedy and Premier Khrushchev. The U.N. chieftain said he would announce his decision today.

Apart from the Castro-Thant matter, President Kennedy and his strategy advisers are known to have concluded that last week's strong support from the Organization of American States is clear authority to use force in dismantling the bases – and ultimately destroying the Communist threat to the Western Hemisphere. The U.S. conclusion was quickly backed up by OAS Secretary General Jose A. Mora, who declared that any measures taken by the

> Page 3 of telegram to Amembassy MOSCOW
>
> UNCLASSIFIED
>
> these arrangements and announce them to the world within a couple of days. The effect of such a settlement on easing world tensions would enable us to work toward a more general arrangement regarding "other armaments", as proposed in your second letter which you made public. I would like to say again that the United States is very much interested in reducing tensions and halting the arms race; and if your letter signifies that you are prepared to discuss a detente affecting NATO and the Warsaw Pact, we are quite prepared to consider with our allies any useful proposals.
>
> But the first ingredient, let me emphasize, is the cessation of work on missile sites in Cuba and measures to render such weapons inoperable, under effective inter-national guarantees. The continuation of this threat, or a prolonging of this discussion concerning Cuba by linking these problems to the broader questions of European and world security, would surely lead to an intensification of the Cuban crisis and a grave risk to the peace of the world. For this reason I hope we can quickly agree along the lines outlined in this letter and in your letter of October 26.
>
> /S/ John F. Kennedy
>
> END

[*Source:* Archive, John F. Kennedy Library, Boston, Mass.]

United States to dismantle the bases would be "multilateral measures with multilateral support."

The national and hemispheric impetus to take decisive action is not likely to be slowed down by Khrushchev's letter writing, inasmuch as the United States has demonstrated during the week the Kremlin's penchant for false words, statements and pledges with respect to Cuba and other Cold War trouble spots. The buildup of U.S. military force in the United

States and throughout the Caribbean which began last Monday continued through last night, and Pentagon strategists were working into the morning. Basic blueprints for an invasion of Cuba, an air strike on the missile launching sites and for numerous other operations in the stack of the Pentagon's "contingency plans" were reported to be under constant review by the Joint Chiefs of Staff and their aides.

Meanwhile, in the Caribbean the close surveillance of Russian and Soviet-chartered ships was continuing without interruption. Observers reported that the string of vessels stretched out across the Atlantic and Caribbean was continuing to inch toward Cuba. So far, according to surveillance reports, at least 17 ships, all presumably loaded with weapons, have turned around before encountering the blockade ring around Cuba.

The Defense Department last night added to the already potent potential strike force of the United States by calling 24 troop carrier squadrons to immediate active duty. The units are used to transport paratroopers and other combat forces. When asked if the callup implied that a Cuban invasion was imminent, Assistant Secretary of Defense Arthur Sylvester declined to reply. Observers in the capital last night carefully pointed out that realistically there was little likelihood of the problem of Cuba being resolved by correspondence or negotiation at this stage.

It also was emphasized that even if Castro or Khrushchev would agree to "de-fusing" and removal of the nuclear missiles aimed at the United States, more than 250 million dollars worth of Soviet non-nuclear armaments still would be in Cuba and that an invasion threat to the Western Hemisphere by Soviet international communism still would exist. The United States has publicly announced that its policy with respect to Cuba is "to get rid of the Castro regime and remove the Communists from Cuba." Vice President Johnson, for example, has traveled across the United States with that message, and it has been echoed by dozens of other high officials from Washington in recent weeks.

35.5 Early Intelligence and How It Was Handled

[*Source: Harold V. Hendrix: Delayed action on Cuba, in:* The Miami News *(Miami, Fla.), 67th Year/No. 158, October 31, 1962, p. 12 A, cols. 3–5.*]

Now that the tensions over Communist Cuba have eased in Washington, a number of nagging questions are being asked from a number of directions. Two puzzlers are foremost: How could the United States have let the situation reach the point it did in Communist Cuba, and why did the Kennedy Administration deliberately mislead the American public by prolonged withholding and denying of intelligence reports on Soviet activities in Communist Cuba?

Indecision, which has become the hallmark of both the Eisenhower and Kennedy Administrations with respect to Fidel Castro and Communist Cuba, played a tragic role in connection with the first question. There is no pin-point answer to the second, other than the continuing struggle inside the New Frontier between the "hard action" and "soft action"

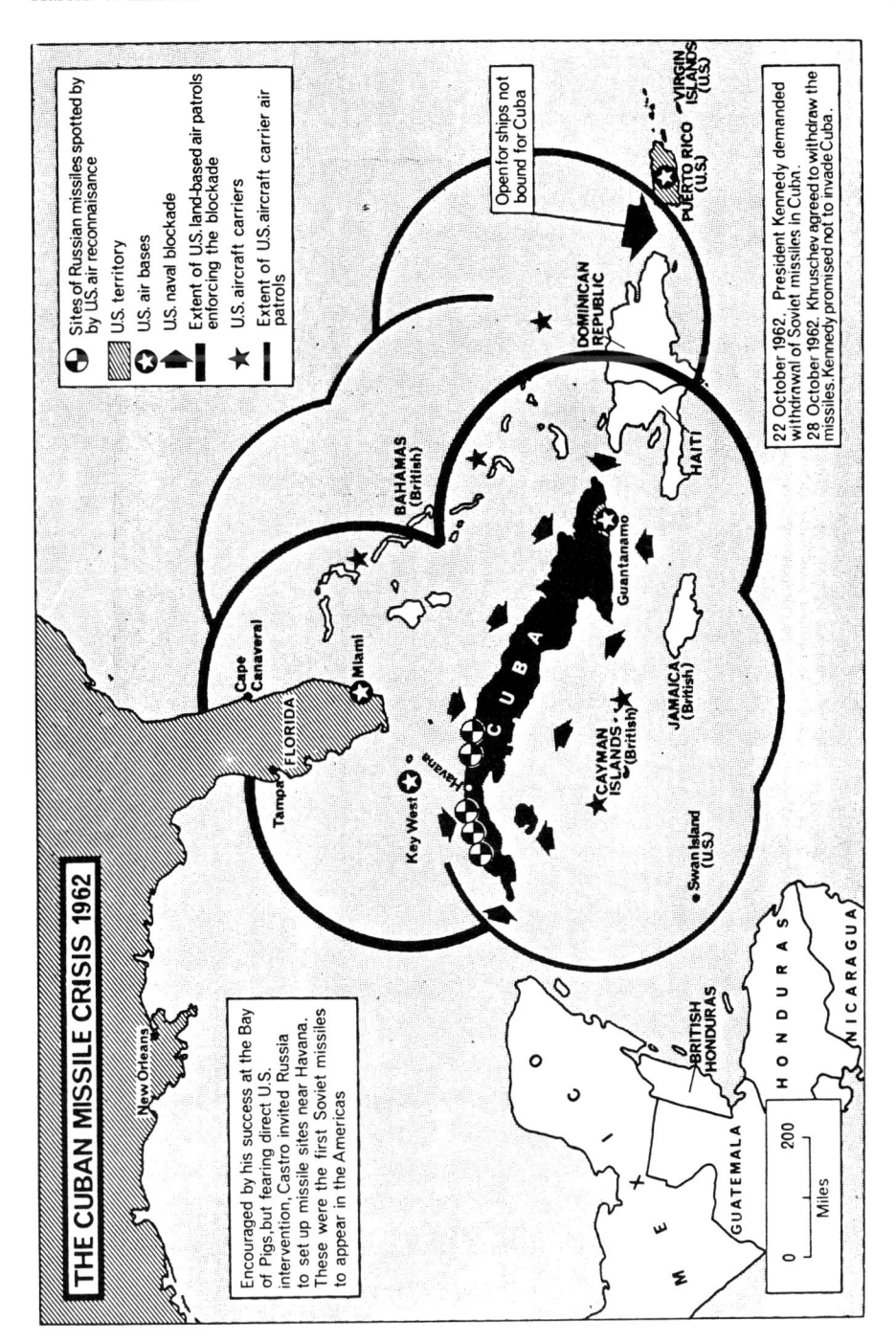

[Source: Martin Gilbert: American History Atlas, London 1968, p. 102.]

advisers on Communist Cuba. This much in the controversy is certain. The State Department and the White House had accurate intelligence several weeks before President Kennedy finally broke the news in his Oct. 22 television address to the nation.

The location of the kink, or where the data was bottled up likely never will be admitted. As late as three days before the President's speech, Under Secretary of State George W. Ball declared Communist Cuba posed no military threat to the United States. But, immediately after the President's address, the Cuban crisis and threat to the United States was being described as the most serious and grave crisis faced by the United States and the world since the explosion of World War II.

Three days before the crisis exploded into global size, the Kennedy Administration was insisting that all the Soviet weapons in Communist Cuba were "defensive." Officials scoffed at month-old reports of IRBM missiles in Cuba. It was repeated often in the previous weeks that possibly as many as 15 surface-to-air missile sites (SAMs) with a slant range of 25 miles had been installed in Cuba. Last week it was announced there were as many as 30. The State Department and White House before last week insisted that Castro had only about 60 older model MIG jet fighters in his air force, and "at least one" advanced jet interceptor (MIG-21) that was operational.

But again when the crisis became global, Castro was admitted to have more than 100 operational Soviet supplied jet fighters and at least 39 operational supersonic MIG-21s – plus a number of medium range jet bombers capable of carrying nuclear bombs and striking the United States. Obviously, this jet fighter muscle did not sprout overnight in Communist Cuba. "Hard" intelligence reports placed the planes in Cuba long before last week. Pictures of the Cuban MIG-21s even appeared in this newspaper . . . Who was asleep and why?

Related Readings

Abel, Elie: The Missile Crisis, Philadelphia 1966.
Allison, Graham T.: Conceptual models and the Cuban Missile Crisis, Santa Monica, Calif., 1968.
Allison, Graham T.: Essence of decision. Explaining the Cuban Missile Crisis, Boston, Mass., 1971.
Dinerstein, Herbert Samuel: The making of a missile crisis, Baltimore – London 1976.
Divine, Robert Alexander (Ed.): The Cuban Missile Crisis, Chicago 1971.
Hilsman, Roger: To move a nation. The politics of foreign policy in the administration of John F. Kennedy, Garden City, N.Y., 1967.
Jackson, D. Bruce: Castro, the Kremlin and communism in Latin America, Baltimore, Md., 1969.
Kennedy, Robert Francis: Thirteen days – a memoir of the Cuban Missile Crisis, New York 1969.
Kolkowicz, Roman: Conflicts in Soviet party-military relations 1962–1963, Santa Monica, Calif., 1963.
Larson, David Lbyd (Ed.): The "Cuban Crisis" of 1962. Selected documents and chronology, Boston, Mass., 1963.
Lazo, Mario: Dagger in the heart. American policy failures in Cuba, 2nd ed., New York 1970.
Mallin, Jay: Fortress Cuba. Russia's American base, Chicago 1965.
Pachter, Henry Macimilian: Collision course – the Cuban Missile Crisis and coexistence, New York 1963.
Phillips, Ruby Hart: The Cuban dilemma, New York 1963.
Plank, John (Ed.): Cuba and the United States – long range perspectives, Washington, D.C., 1967.

Scheer, Robert/Zeitlin, Maurice: Cuba – an American tragedy, rev. ed., Harmondsworth, Middlesex, 1964.
Semidei, Manuela: Les États-Unis et la révolution cubaine, 1959–1964, Paris 1968.
Thomas, Hugh: Cuba. The pursuit of freedom, New York 1971.
Trivers, Howard: Three crisis in American foreign affairs and a continuing revolution, Carbondale, Ill., 1972.

INDEX

Abbott, Douglas, 107
Abel, Elie, VI, XLVII, 207, 208, 209, 211, 213, 214, 215
Abreu, Gerado, 226
Acheson, Dean G., 96, 99
Ackerman, Carl W., XXX, XXXVI, 104
Adams, Clarence H., 107
Agramonte, Roberto, 229, 235
Akhmatova, Anna, 39
Alexander (II), Czar of Russia, 141
Alexei, Russian Patriarch, 30, 31
Allilueva, Svtlana, 172, 185, 196
Allison, Kathleen A., V
Antonov, Alexei I., 160
Ashmore, Harry S., LVIII
Astor, John Jacob, 121
Atkinson, J. Brooks, XXIV, LVII, 3, 4, 5, 6, 8, 12, 17, 38
Attlee, Clement R., 163

Bagdikian, Ben H., XLII
Bagirov, Mir D. A., 72, 73
Baker, Ralph, 121
Baker, Richard T., XXXVI
Ball, George W., 287, 296
Barber, William C., LII, 254
Barletta, Amadeo, 234
Batista y Zaldivar, Fulgencio, IL, L, 219, 220, 221, 222, 223, 225, 226, 227, 228, 229, 230, 232, 233, 234, 235, 236, 237, 238
Bauer, Richard F., V
Beech, Keyes, XXX, XXXII, LVIII, 78, 84
Ben Bella, Mohammed, 290
Benidickson, William M., 114
Beria, Lavrenty P., 24, 69, 137, 140, 148, 149, 150, 151, 152, 153, 154, 155, 156, 157, 158, 159, 160, 161, 162, 163, 195
Berlioz, Hector, 36
Bernett, Stanley P., LVIII
Bertelson, Arthur R., LIX
Bevan, Aneurin, 163
Bevin, Ernest, 5
Bigart, Homer W., XXX, XXXII, LVIII, 78
Binder, Carroll, XXV, XXVIII, LVII
Bingham, Barry, XLIV, LXI
Bisbe, Manuel, 235

Blanco, Marino Lopez, 230
Bogolyubov, Party Secretary, 72
Bohlen, Charles E., 161, 183
Bolshakov, Ivan G., 34
Borlenghi, Angel, 225
Bosch, Jean van den, 255, 257
Bradley, Omar N., 96, 126, 130, 161
Brailsford, Henry N., 47
Bravo, Leopoldo, 146
Brito, Alfredo Gonzales, 227
Britto, Milton, 134
Brkic, Hasan, 211, 214
Budenny, Semyon M., 159, 161
Bulganin, Nikolai A., XXXIX, 143, 148, 151, 159, 160, 161, 163, 172, 182, 183, 186, 187, 188, 189, 191
Byrnes, James F., 3, 5, 6

Cabrera, Ruperto, 230
Calderón de la Barca, Pedro, 37
Canizares, Jose M. Salas, 233
Canizares, Rafael Salas, 227
Canham, Erwin D., LVII, LXI
Canney, John, 79
Capone, Al(fonso), 75
Carbó, Sergio, 234
Carroll, Frank J., VI
Carter, Hodding, XLIV
Castro, Fidel, XLVII, IL, L, LVI, 222, 223, 225, 227, 228, 234, 235, 236, 237, 238, 271, 272, 287, 288, 289, 291, 292, 294, 296
Catledge, Turner, XLIV, XLVII, LXI, 208
Chand, Gyan, 58
Chandler, Norman, XLIV, LXI
Charkviani, Party Secretary, 72
Cherry, James W., 127
Chevrier, Lionel, 113, 114
Chiang Kai-shek, 96, 173, 174, 175
Chilton, William E. (III), VI
Choate, Robert, XLIV
Chomon, Faure, 223, 235
Chou En-lai, 168, 169
Christopher, Robert C., V
Chuikov, Vasily I., 159
Churchill, Winston S., 6, 12, 22, 92, 178, 179
Chutkikh, Alexander, 74

Clifford, Donald J., VI
Coan, Don, 127
Coleman, Vernon, 132, 133, 134
Conn, Jack, 128
Connally, John, 98
Conniff, Frank, XXXIX, XL, XLVI, LVIII, 172, 177, 181, 187, 191
Consuegra, Julia Elisa, 233
Cooper, Kent, XXVIII
Cowles, Gardiner, XLIV
Cowles, William H. (III), VI
Cowley, Fermin, 227, 228
Creager, Marvin H., LVII
Crosby, Bing, 34
Cuervo, Pelayo, 235
Cusido, Eugenio, 228

Dabney, Virginius, LVIII
Dalmia, Seth Ram Krishna, 55, 56
Daniels, Charles L., 83
Day, Price, XXV, LVIII, 41, 42, 43, 47, 50, 54, 57
Dayal, Rajeshwar, 263
Deck, Arthur C., LIX
Dedek, Johannes, VI
Demon, Emmett, LIX
Derthick, Everest P., LII, LIX
Detwiler, L. Edgar, 255
Dickhut, Ingrid, VI
Dioni, Gason, 257
Doares, Wade A., V
Doherty, D'Arcy M., 108
DuBois, Jules, LII
Dulles, John F., 178, 179
Dunham, Howard, 135, 136
Durbin, Deanna, 34
Dzerzhinsky, Felix, 66

Eden, Anthony, 174
Ehrenburg, Ilya, 38
Eisenhower, Dwight D., XXXIV, 93, 130, 161, 162, 177, 187, 198, 199, 234, 294
Eisenstein, Sergei, 35
Elliot, Osborn, V
Engels, Friedrich, 72

Fadeyev, Alexander, 37
Faubus, Orval E., 234
Fauntleroy, Lord, 166
Ferguson, Homer, 98
Ferguson, John D., XLIV
Firyubin, Nikolai P., 215, 217
Fischer, Erika J., VI
Fleet, James A. von, 96
Franco Bahamonde, Francisco, IL, 7

Frankel, Max, XLVII, 208
Frewer, Frank, VI
Fryer, Peter, 203
Furtseva, Yekaterina A., 217

Gage, Charles, 133
Gandhi, Mahatma, 43, 47, 48, 49, 50, 55, 56, 59
Garcia, Pilar, 227
Gaulle, Charles de, 279, 280
Gerald, Bill, 128
Geroe, Ernoe, 195
Gillen, John S., LIX
Gilmore, Eddy, XXIV, XXVIII, XXXIX, LVII, 4
Goebbels, P. Joseph, XXII
Goldberg, Rube, XXV
Goldberg, Seymour, 128
Gomulka, Wladyslaw, 239, 241, 243, 244
Gordon, George N., XXI
Gorky, Maxim, 68, 166
Gorshenin, Konstantin P., 66, 67
Govorov, Leonid A., 160
Grau San Martin, Ramón, 230, 233, 234
Grechko, Andrei, 159, 160
Greeley, Horace, 24, 117
Gromyko, Andrei A., 251
Gruson, Sidney L., XLVII, 208
Gumilev, Nikolai, 39

Hammarskjold, Dag, 258, 260, 271
Hancock, Richard, VI
Harris, Earl, 134
Harris, Walter E., 117
Harun al-Rashid, Calif, 144
Harwell, Coleman A., LVIII
Hathway, Alan, LII, LIX
Haynes, William P., 131
Hays, Howard H., LIX
Hayter, Lady, 166
Hayter, William, 168, 173, 174, 183
Hearst, Randolph, 187
Hearst, William R. Jr., XXXIX, XL, XLVI, LVIII, 172, 173, 175, 177, 178, 179, 180, 181, 183, 185, 186, 187, 188, 189, 191
Hearst, William R. Sen., XL
Heinzerling, Larry E., VI
Heinzerling, Lynn L., LII, LV, LIX, 253, 254, 255, 256, 258, 260, 264
Hellman, Lillian, 37
Hendrix, Harold V., LVI, LIX, LX, 283, 284, 285, 287, 289, 290, 294
Herbert, John R., XLIV, XLVI, XLVII, LIX
Hespe, Barbara, VI
Hevia, Carlos, 229

Index

Higgins, Marguerite, XXX, XXXI, XXXII, LVIII, 77, 78, 79, 80, 83, 85, 86
Hightower, John M., XXXII, LVIII, 91, 92, 93, 95, 97, 98, 101
Hills, Lee, XL
Himmler, Heinrich, 221
Hitler, Adolf, 14, 22, 24, 25, 31, 245, 273
Hoffmann, Aichard, VI
Hohenberg, John, XXIV, XXV, XXVIII, XXX, XXXII, XXXVI, XXXIX, XL, XLII, XLIV, LII, LIII, LV, LX, LXI, LXIII
Holmes, George R., 172
Hood, Robin, 236
Horn, Carl von, 263
Hornedo, Alfredo, 234
Hough, John T., VI
Hoxha, Enver, 214
Ileo, Joseph, 262
Ivan the Terrible, Czar of Russia, 35, 146, 150

Jackson, Andy, 201
Janssens, Emile, 255
Jinnah, Mahomed A., 50, 51, 53, 54, 55
Johnson, Earl J., LIII
Johnson, Lyndon B., 294
Jones, Jenkin L., LVIII, LIX
Jones, John, 109
Jones, Russell, XLII, LIX, 193, 194, 195, 197, 198, 201, 203, 240
Jones, William P., 131, 132
Jorden, William J., XLVII, 208
Joxe, Louis, 183
Joy, Charles T., 88, 99

Kadar, Janos, 197
Kaganovich, Lazar M., 27, 143, 150, 151, 163, 168, 169, 183, 209
Kalonji, Albert, 258, 263
Kardelj, Edvard, 209, 214, 215
Kasavubu, Joseph, 257, 261, 262, 263, 264
Keller-Hüschemenger, Brigitte, VI
Kennan, George F., 149
Kennedy, John F., LVI, 270, 272, 275, 287, 289, 291, 292, 294, 296
Kenney, George C., 88
Kerney, James Jr., XXVIII, LVIII
Khan, Liaquat Ali, 50, 53
Khrushchev, Nikita S., XXXIX, XLVII, LII, LIII, LV, LX, 72, 73, 140, 143, 148, 149, 150, 151, 152, 159, 160, 161, 163, 164, 166, 168, 169, 172, 177, 178, 179, 180, 181, 182, 183, 184, 187, 191, 204, 209, 211, 213, 214, 215, 217, 244, 248, 267, 268, 269, 270, 271, 272, 273, 275, 277, 279, 280, 284, 291, 292, 293, 294

Kirk, Grayson, XLIV, LXI
Kitchlu, Dr., 146
Klein, David, VI
Klensch, Charles H., 185
Knight, John S., XLIV
Konev, Ivan S., 159
Kraslow, David, VI
Krock, Arthur, XXVIII, XXXVI, L
Kruglov, Sergei N., 163
Kuusinen, Otto V., 215
Kuzen, Robin, V
Kuznetsov, Alexander, 69
Kuznetsov, Nikolai G., 169

Laberge, Father, 31
Lamond, Tom, 134
Langenberger, Barbara, VI
Lansky, Meyer, 233
Laurent, Julio, 226, 227
Laurier, Wilfrid, 105
Layzell, Natalie, VI
Lenin, Vladimir I., 16, 17, 24, 25, 29, 63, 66, 68, 69, 139, 140, 155, 156, 179, 180, 191
Lennox, Oswald E., 107, 108, 109, 110
Leonard, Richard H., VI
Lepeshinskaya, Olga, 166
Lerond, Jack N., 85
Lie, Trygve, 271
Lincoln, Abraham, 188
Lindsay, Edward, LVIII
Lippmann, Walter, LIII, LV, LIX, 267, 268, 269, 271, 273, 277, 279, 284
Litvinov, Maxim, 27
Livingston, Joseph A., XLII
Lopez Mateos, Adolpho, 289
Loridan, Walter, 260
Love, Edward, 134
Lucas, Jim G., XXI, XXXIV, LVIII, 125, 126, 127, 128, 131, 132, 135, 138
Lumumba, Patrice, 253, 255, 256, 257, 258, 260, 261, 262, 263, 264
Lundula, Victor, 262
Lysenko, Trofim D., 144, 145

MacArthur, Douglas, XXXII, 86, 87, 88, 91, 92, 93, 95, 96
MacCormac, John, XLVII, 208
MacDonald, Kenneth, LXI
Machado, Gerardo, 232, 236
Macmillan, Harold, 251
Mahomed, Ghulam, 53, 54
Maidenburg, Ben, LIX
Maisky, Ivan, 27
Malenkov, Georgi M., 69, 70, 140, 143, 148, 149, 150, 151, 152, 156, 160, 161, 163, 164,

165, 166, 168, 171, 179, 180, 182, 183, 184, 186, 187, 191, 209
Maleter, Pal, 196
Maloney, James, VI
Mao Tse-tung, XLVII
Maro, Alberto Salas, 233
Marshall, George C., 92, 96
Martin, David T., 95, 96
Martin, Joseph G., IL, L, LV, LIX, 219, 220, 221, 225, 228, 232, 235
Martinez, Irindido, 233
Marx, Karl H., 14, 17, 29, 37, 38, 148, 179, 277
Masaryk, Jan, 172
Masferrer, Rolando, 233
Mathews, Herbert L., XLVII
Matrosov, Alexander, 75
Matthews, Burrows, LVIII
Maugham, W. Somerset, 37
Maxwell, William D., LXI
Mayakovsky, Vladimir, 34
McClatchy, Charles M., V
McCloy, John J., 270
McCormick, Anne O'Hare, 78
McFarland, Ernest W., 98
McGann, Martin F., VI
McGill, Ralph, LIX, LXI
McKelway, Benjamin M., XLIV
Mekhlis, Lev Z., 151
Melinkov, Leonid G., 160
Menon, Krishna P. R., 49, 146
Metcalfe, John H., VI
Metternich, Clemens W. N. L., 272
Micunovic, Veljko, 215
Mikoyan, Anastas I., 143, 149, 150, 151, 161, 163, 169, 183, 184, 214, 215, 269, 272
Milanes, Esther, 227
Miller, Paul, XLIV, LXI
Millersward, S. M., 263
Mindszenty, Josef, 197, 198, 203
Minot, George E., LII, LIX
Mix, Howard, 135, 136
Mobutu, Joseph, 261, 264
Molnar, Ferenc, 37
Molotov, Vyacheslav M., XXXIX, 33, 69, 141, 143, 148, 150, 151, 152, 156, 161, 163, 164, 166, 169, 171, 172, 173, 174, 175, 177, 178, 182, 183, 184, 187, 188, 201, 209
Montgomery, Harry, LIX
Montgomery, Viscount, 162
Mora, José A., 292
Morales, Andres D., 233
Morin, Relman, XXX, XXXII, LVIII, 78
Mountbatten, Louis F., 48, 53
Muccio, John G., 88
Muirhead, John, VI

Mujal, Eusebio, 222
Murray, Ray, 88
Mussolini, Benito, 22, 234
Muzungo, Charles, 262

Nagy, Imre, 196
Nam Il, General, 98
Nehru, Jawaharlal, 41, 43, 47, 48, 49, 50, 56, 59, 183
Nehru, Motilal Pandit, 48
Nicholas (I), Czar of Russia, 141
Nicholas (II), Czar of Russia, 180
Nilin, Pavel, 35
Nixon, Richard M., 270
Nkrumah, Kwame, 255, 257
Nobel, Alfred, 144
Noland, Stephen C., LVII, LVIII
Northcutt, Stanley, 134
Nowak, Zenon, 244, 245
Noyes, Newbold Jr., LXI

O'Connell, John J., VI
O'Farril, Ramon, 226
Oppenberg, Dietrich, VI
O'Rourke, John T., LIX
Orr, Frank F., LIX
Ortega Sierra, Luis, 233

Padgett, Edmond J., 134
Padgett, Richard, 132
Palgunov, Nikolai, 151
Palinkas, Josef, 198
Palma, Albert E. de, 109
Park, Clara, 234
Partridge, Eric, 88
Patel, Vallabhbhai, 43, 47
Patterson, Donald H., VI
Pen Teh-huai, General, 98
Peron, Juan D., 225, 234
Perrault, Rene B., 116
Pervukhin, Mikhail G., 169
Peter the Great, Czar of Russia, 146
Pickford, Richard, 134
Plenn, Abel, 7
Poa, Lee Sung, 85
Polk, James, 121
Ponomarev, Nikolai, 215
Pont, Samuel F. du, 272
Porter, C. Vaughn, VI
Poskrebyshev, Alexander N., 151
Prescott, John S., VI
Preston, Cheryl, VI
Pretsch, Hans-Joachim, VI
Prio Socorrás, Carlos, 226, 229, 233, 234, 236
Prokofiev, Sergei S., 36, 37

Index

Pujol, Alonso, 229
Pulitzer, Joseph, V, XXI, XXII, XXIII, XXIV, XXV, XXVIII, XXX, XXXII, XXXIV, XXXVI, XXXVII, XXXIX, XL, XLI, XLII, XLIV, XLV, XLVI, XLVII, IL, L, LI, LII, LIII, LV, LVI, LVII, LX, LXV, LXVI, 4, 22, 42, 62, 78, 92, 104, 126, 138, 144, 172, 194, 208, 220, 240, 254, 268, 284
Pulitzer, Joseph (IV), XLV
Pulitzer, Joseph Jr., XXXVI, XL, XLIV, XLV, LXI
Pulitzer, Joseph Sen., XL
Pulitzer, Ralph, LV
Puller, Lewis B., 86, 88
Pulliam, Eugene S., LIX
Puzanov, Alexander M., 184
Pyle, Ernest T., XXI

Randall, Edwin, 132
Rankovic, Alexander, 209, 214, 215
Rapacki, Adam, 251
Reston, James, XLVII, 208
Reuter, Paul J., 62
Rhee, Syngman, 86, 88
Richelieu, Armand Jean du Plessis de, 272
Richert, Earl H., VI
Rico, Blanco, 233
Ridgway, Matthew B., 96, 97, 99, 101, 102
Robespierre, Maximilien de, 168
Rockefeller, Nelson A., 270, 272, 277
Roessler, Dietrich, VI
Rogers, John, 108, 109, 110
Rojas, Juan, 230
Rokossovsky, Konstantin K., 159
Rom, Rene, 262
Romanov, Russian Dynasty, 29
Roosevelt, Anna E., 272
Roosevelt, Franklin D., 22, 92
Rosenthal, Abraham M., XLVII, LI, LII, LIX, 239, 240, 241, 243, 245, 247, 250
Rozner, Eddie, 37
Rusk, Dean, 96
Russell, Bruce, XXV
Russell, Sam, 203
Ryumin, M. D., 157

Saburov, Maxim Z., 169
Sachs, Julius, 268
Saiz, Luis, 228
Saiz, Sergio, 228
Salazar, Antonio de Oliveira, IL
Salinger, Pierre, 289
Salisbury, Harrison E., XXXVII, XXXIX, XLVII, LII, LIII, LVIII, 137, 138, 139, 146, 152, 158, 163, 208

Sanchez, Calixto, 228
Santora, Philip J., IL, L, LV, LIX, 219, 220, 221, 225, 228, 232, 235
Schoenstein, Paul, LIX
Seltzer, Louis B., XLIV, LXI
Sergei, Russian Patriarch, 30
Sergeyev-Zensky, Sergei N., 38, 39
Serov, Ivan A., 163
Shakespeare, William, 37
Shapiro, Henry, XXXIX
Shaughnessy, Thomas G., 122
Shaw, George B., 4, 23, 37
Shepilov, Dimitri I., 209
Sheridan, Richard B., 37
Shevchenko, Taras, 36
Short, Joseph, 96
Shostakovich, Dimitri, 36, 37
Shostakovich, Galina, 37
Shostakovich, Maxim, 37
Shostakovich, Nina, 37
Shtemenko, Sergei M., 158
Siena, Joe, 127
Sierra, Jose, 234
Simmons, Walter, 133
Simonov, Konstantin, 38
Sinatra, Frank, 34
Singh, Raja Maharaj, 43
Slaskich, Ulica P., 245
Smith, George, 117
Smith, J. Kingsbury, XXXIV, XL, XLVI, LVIII, 171, 172, 173, 177, 182, 185, 186, 188, 191
Smith, Pat, 127
Smith, Walter Bedell, 162
Sneed, Hubert, 134
Sok, Wang Han, 84
Sokolovsky, Vasily D., 158, 159, 160
Sosa, Jose, 227
Sparks, Fred, XXX, XXXII, LVIII, 78
Spencer, Foster L., VI
Stakhanov, Alexei, 75
Stalin, Joseph V., XXXVII, XXXIX, 11, 12, 16, 17, 23, 24, 28, 29, 30, 31, 33, 34, 35, 37, 39, 61, 63, 65, 66, 67, 68, 69, 70, 73, 74, 84, 137, 139, 140, 141, 142, 143, 144, 146, 147, 148, 151, 152, 153, 154, 155, 156, 157, 158, 159, 161, 164, 165, 166, 168, 169, 171, 172, 182, 185, 187, 191, 244
Stalin, Vassily, 185
Stassen, Harold E., 33
Stern, Mort, LIX
Steven, William P., LIX
Stevens, Edmund W., XXV, LVIII, 61, 62, 63, 66, 68, 70, 73, 126
Stevenson, H. L., VI

Stil, Andre, 204
Stiles, Robert, 134
St. Laurent, Louis, 115, 116
Stouffer, Wilbur C., LVIII
Stowe, Leland, XXI
Stravinsky, Igor, 36
Struble, Arthur D., 88
Sukhodrev, Victor M., 269
Sulzberger, Arthur H., V
Sulzberger, Cyrus L., XXV
Summerskill, Edith, 166
Sung, Kim Il, 84, 98
Suvorov, Alexander V., 158
Swope, Herbert B., XLII, XLVII, XLVIII, LIX
Sylvester, Arthur, 294

Tabernilla, Francisco, 222, 230
Tabernilla, Francisco Jr., 222
Taylor, Glen H., 7
Thant, U, 292
Thomas, Li, 85
Thompson, Ronald E., VI
Tikhonov, Nikolai A. S., 39
Tito, Josip B., 69, 70, 209, 211, 213, 214, 215, 217
Trotsky, Leo, 69
Trujillo, Rafael, 236
Truman, Harry S., XXXII, 92, 95, 96, 174
Tshombe, Moise, 258, 260
Tunon, Jorge G., 228, 229, 230, 235
Turcsanyi, Egon, 197
Tuttle, Winslow B., 131, 132

Uglade Carrillo, Manuel, 227
Underwood, Horace G., 79
Urrutia, Manuelo, L, 238
Utesow, Leonid O., 151

Vasconcelos, Ramon, 233
Vasilevsky, Alexander M., 158, 159, 160, 161
Vega Carpio, Felix Lope de, 37
Ventura Nobo, Esteban, 225, 226, 227, 232
Viloboy, Jose Lopez, 234

Vishinsky, Andrei Y., 67, 68
Vlahovic, Veljko, 215
Volkov, Alexander P., 182, 184
Voroshilov, Klimentiy E., 148, 151, 159, 161, 183, 213
Voznesensky, Nikolai, 69, 148, 149

Wagner, Benno, VI
Walker, Walton H., 88
Walles, Thomas P., 198
Walters, Basil L., XL
Ward, Paul W., XXV, LVIII, 21, 22, 23, 25, 29, 33, 36
Warman, Manny, V
Wechsler, James A., LIX
Wehrwein, Austin C., XXXIV, L, LVIII, 103, 104, 105, 107, 111, 114, 118
Wellington, Charles G., LVIII
Wells, Toni, VI
Westover, George, 82, 83
Whitehead, Don, XXX, XXXII, XXXIV, LVIII, 78
Whitney, Thomas, XXXIX
William, Cecil, 131, 132
Williams, Eddie, 127
Wilson, Woodrow, 272
Winship, Lawrence L., LVIII
Winterton, Paul, 11
Wolff, Miles H., LVIII
Woltmann, Frederick, XXV
Wyszynski, Stefan, 247

Yagado, Genrikh G., 67
Yegolin, Alexander M., 39
Yusupov, Usman Y., 72

Zaslavski, David I., 8
Zhdanov, Andrei A., 40, 68, 69, 70
Zhikov, Todor, 214
Zhukov, Georgi, XXXIX, 158, 159, 160, 161, 162, 163, 169, 172, 183, 187
Zoshchenko, Mikhail, 39
Zullo, Rocco, 83

The Soviet Polity in the Modern Era

Edited by *Erik P. Hoffmann* and *Robbin F. Laird*

1984. 15,5 x 23,5 cm. XVI, 942 pages.
Cloth DM 168,–; approx. US $ 56.00   ISBN 3 11 010295 1
Cloth US $ 49.95 (USA and Canada only) ISBN 0-202-24164-5
Paperback DM 84,–; approx. US $ 28.00   ISBN 3 11 010294 3
Paperback US $ 24.95 (USA and Canada only) ISBN 0-202-24165-3

This anthology is a comprehensive, integrated, and stimulating collection of major Western writings on the most important elements of contemporary Soviet politics and society. The book concentrates on the domestic politics of the USSR, taking a view of the Soviet polity that is far-ranging. The editors believe it is crucial to understand the historical legacies that affect the structure and functioning of the Soviet political system. The book is designed to portray the policy-making and administrative processes and the substance of national policies, the economic and social contexts within which political power is exercised, and the ways in which the Soviet polity influences and is influenced by socioeconomic and scientific-technical developments at home and abroad.

The contributors are distinguished journalists, government officials, and scholars specializing in politics, economics, sociology, and history. All are Westerners or former Soviet citizens currently living in the West.

The Conduct of Soviet Foreign Policy

Edited by *Erik P. Hoffmann* and *Frederic J. Fleron, Jr.*

Second edition.
1980. 15,0 x 23,5 cm. X, 761 pages.
Cloth DM 150,–; approx. US $ 50.00   ISBN 3 10 700016 8
Cloth US $ 49,95 (USA and Canada only) ISBN 0-202-24155-6
Paperback DM 66,–; approx. US $ 22.00   ISBN 3 10 700016 5
Paperback US $ 18,95 (USA and Canada only) ISBN 0-202-24156-4

The editors present contrasting traditional and revisionist viewpoints, making the book a forum of controversy and discussion by including articles by Brzezinski, Pipes, Schulman, and Gati, as well as three new unpublished chapters written specifically for this volume by Laird, Hoffmann and Maxwell, to complement well-known contributions by Zimmerman, Dallin, and Ulam. Their introductory essays to each section provide a focus for classroom or scholarly debate. Professors Hoffmann and Fleron provide a provocative and extended survey of perhaps the most important single issue confronting U.S. foreign policy today.

Aldine Publishing Company
a division of Walter de Gruyter
Genthiner Strasse 13, D-1000 Berlin 30
200 Saw Mill River Road, Hawthorne, NY 10532, USA

Political Management
Redefining the Public Sphere
By *H. T. Wilson*
1984. 15,5 x 23 cm. X, 316 pages. Cloth DM 98,-
(de Gruyter Studies in Organization, Vol. 2)

Limits to Bureaucratic Growth
By *Marshall W. Meyer*
in Association with William Stevenson and Stephen Webster
1985. 15,5 x 23 cm. X, 259 pages. Cloth DM 88,-
(de Gruyter Studies in Organization, Vol. 3)

Management Under Differing Value Systems
Political, Social and Economical Perspectives in a Changing World
Edited by *Günter Dlugos* and *Klaus Weiermair*
1981. 17 x 24 cm. XIV, 868 pages. Cloth DM 148,-   ISBN 3 11 008553 4

Studies in Decision Making
Social Psychological and Socio-Economic Analyses
Edited by *Martin Irle* in collaboration with *Lawrence B. Katz*
1982. 17 x 24 cm. XVI, 917 pages. Cloth DM 176,-   ISBN 3 11 008087 7

An Encyclopedic Dictionary of Marxism, Socialism and Communism
By *Jozef Wilczynski*
1981. 15,5 x 23 cm. 660 pages. Cloth DM 118,-   ISBN 3 11 008588 7
Distribution rights for USA, Canada, Europe except Great Britain and the Republic of Eire

Standard Dictionary of Advertising, Mass Media and Marketing
English-German
By *Wolfgang J. Koschnick*
1983. 13 x 21 cm. X, 466 pages. Cloth DM 68,-   ISBN 3 11 008782 0

Management Dictionary
By *Werner Sommer* and *Hanns-Martin Schoenfeld*
English-German: 1979. 12,2 x 18,8 cm. 621 pages. Cloth DM 58,-   ISBN 3 11 007708 6
German-English: 1978. 12,2 x 18,8 cm. 542 pages. Cloth DM 58,-. ISBN 3 11 004863 9

Prices are subject to change without notice

WALTER DE GRUYTER · BERLIN · NEW YORK

D 445 .O88 1984 v.2 c.1